SEX OFFENDERS

SEX OFFENDERS

CRIMES AND PROCESSING IN THE CRIMINAL JUSTICE SYSTEM

Second Edition

SEAN MADDAN ▪ LYNN PAZZANI

ASPEN
PUBLISHING

To contact Customer Service, e-mail customer.service@aspenpublishing.com, call 1-800-950-5259, or mail correspondence to:

Aspen Publishing
Attn: Order Department
PO Box 990
Frederick, MD 21705

Printed in the United States of America.

Cover credit: rolffimages/stock.adobe.com

3 4 5 6 7 8 9 0

ISBN 978-1-5438-1759-1

Library of Congress Cataloging-in-Publication Data application is in process.

About Aspen Publishing

Aspen Publishing is a leading provider of educational content and digital learning solutions to law schools in the United States and around the world. Aspen provides best-in-class solutions for legal education through authoritative textbooks, written by renowned authors, and breakthrough products such as Connected eBooks, Connected Quizzing, and PracticePerfect.

The Aspen Casebook Series (famously known among law faculty and students as the "red and black" casebooks) encompasses hundreds of highly regarded textbooks in more than eighty disciplines, from large enrollment courses, such as Torts and Contracts to emerging electives such as Sustainability and the Law of Policing. Study aids such as the *Examples & Explanations* and the *Emanuel Law Outlines* series, both highly popular collections, help law students master complex subject matter.

Major products, programs, and initiatives include:

- **Connected eBooks** are enhanced digital textbooks and study aids that come with a suite of online content and learning tools designed to maximize student success. Designed in collaboration with hundreds of faculty and students, the Connected eBook is a significant leap forward in the legal education learning tools available to students.
- **Connected Quizzing** is an easy-to-use formative assessment tool that tests law students' understanding and provides timely feedback to improve learning outcomes. Delivered through CasebookConnect.com, the learning platform already used by students to access their Aspen casebooks, Connected Quizzing is simple to implement and integrates seamlessly with law school course curricula.
- **PracticePerfect** is a visually engaging, interactive study aid to explain commonly encountered legal doctrines through easy-to-understand animated videos, illustrative examples, and numerous practice questions. Developed by a team of experts, PracticePerfect is the ideal study companion for today's law students.
- The **Aspen Learning Library** enables law schools to provide their students with access to the most popular study aids on the market across all of their courses. Available through an annual subscription, the online library consists of study aids in e-book, audio, and video formats with full text search, note-taking, and highlighting capabilities.
- Aspen's **Digital Bookshelf** is an institutional-level online education bookshelf, consolidating everything students and professors need to ensure success. This program ensures that every student has access to affordable course materials from day one.
- **Leading Edge** is a community centered on thinking differently about legal education and putting those thoughts into actionable strategies. At the core of the program is the Leading Edge Conference, an annual gathering of legal education thought leaders looking to pool ideas and identify promising directions of exploration.

BRIEF CONTENTS

CONTENTS

4 RAPE 73

PREFACE

Much misinformation and many myths surround sex offenders and their crimes. This book provides a full accounting of what we know about sex offenders and sex offenses.

These are difficult subjects to study. The crimes and the individuals who perpetrate them are generally horrific to consider. Although the acts are heinous and the offenders themselves are deplorable, sex offenders and their offenses are subjects of morbid curiosity. Despite being widely publicized and loudly condemned, however, sex crimes and sex offenders are seldom accurately understood. To some extent, sex offending behaviors are specialized. While research has taught us a great deal, our use of the term "sex offender" as an umbrella for many types of individuals and a variety of different behaviors can interfere with effective study of sex offender behaviors, for instance, discerning the differences between sex offenders whose victims are children and those who target adults.

This book explores all the facets of sex offenders and their crimes. From the nature of sex crimes to sexual deviance to an emphasis on the crimes of rape and sexual offenses against children, this book explores all topics traditionally found in textbooks on sex offenses and offenders. In addition to these topic areas, however, this book also explores the societal response to sex offenders and sex offenses through the criminal justice system. Topics to which we pay special attention here are the interaction between sex offenders and law enforcement and investigation; the courts; and the corrections and treatments to which sex offenders are subjected. This book emphasizes punishment, corrections, and post-punishment treatment of sex offenders. The chapters on those issues evaluate all relevant topics, including sex offenders in prison, historical punishments imposed on sex offenders, sex offender recidivism, sex offender registration and notification policies (SORN), residence restrictions, civil commitments, and the treatment of sex offenders. In total, five chapters are devoted to these critical sex offender topics. Victims of sex offenders and the impact sex offenses have on their lives are also treated in depth. Finally, this book examines possible directions for future policies on sex offenders and offenses, and other topics society and the criminal justice system must address to better deal with the threat of sex offenders.

Chapters are written in a manner accessible to all audiences, and each contains a number of features that will help readers to understand, absorb, and retain the information. Chapters begin with lists of objectives to prepare readers to recognize and focus on key points and themes. In addition, each chapter contains a narrative on the topic at hand, drawn from the real world, to illustrate and provide practical perspective on the complexity and impact of the sex offense under discussion for society, perpetrator, and victim. Throughout the text, contemporary research findings and statistics provide an accurate accounting of sex offenders, helping to dispel some of the myths and misinformation that often arise in relation to sex offenders and their crimes. The chapters conclude with several items, including lists of key terms (defined in a glossary at the end of the text), exercises, and essay questions, to offer review opportunities and to aid in knowledge retention.

Building on the features of the first edition, this new edition updates the research and literature in the areas of sex offenses, sex offenders, and the criminal justice response. Throughout this edition, there are updated stories that precede the chapter to highlight actual instances of sex crimes and/or criminal justice responses to sex crimes.

Most important, this second edition incorporates an exploration of a type of behavior analogous to sex crimes that has recently received attention through the #MeToo movement: sexual harassment, especially in the workplace. We have added new material throughout the book to illustrate the similarities in behavior between sex crimes and sexual harassment, and we examine why sexual harassment is not handled through the criminal justice system as a criminal offense. The importance of the #MeToo movement to victims of sexual harassment and assault is also examined. As with other textbooks, a host of ancillary materials has been prepared for the use of instructors. The test bank includes sample examinations for all fourteen chapters in the book. PowerPoint presentations make prepping for classes easier. The accompanying teacher's manual enhances discussions found within each chapter. Finally, course outlines are available for quick snapshots of the information contained in the chapters.

ACKNOWLEDGMENTS

Numerous individuals are always instrumental in the completion of a book. We would like to thank those individuals whose efforts have helped to make this a better book. For the first edition, Elizabeth Barron, reference librarian at the University of Tampa, was instrumental in helping us to collect academic research to bolster our arguments about sex offenders and sex offender policy. In addition, Alexandria Jefferson, Michael Payne, Briana Evans, Ellen Tietjen, and Meschach Bollers provided research assistance and help with compiling supplemental materials. We are grateful for the research resources at our universities that allowed us to update the book. Special thanks goes to Nicholas Lasoff and all the fine folks at Aspen Publishing. Your diligence helped greatly in completing this book.

Finally, we would like to thank the anonymous readers who provided thoughtful comments assessing our original manuscript. Your reviews helped to produce a much better book.

SEX OFFENDERS

1

THE NATURE OF SEX CRIMES IN THE UNITED STATES

Chapter Objectives

After reading this chapter, students will be able to:

- Understand the broad nature of the terms sex offender and sex offense.
- Identify the primary sources of sex offense information in the United States.
- Demonstrate the problems associated with official sources of sex offender and sex offense information.
- Evaluate the characteristics of sex offenders in the United States.
- Examine the various social/physical arenas where sex offending occurs.

INTRODUCTION

The terms sex offender and sex offense conjure images of revulsion and loathing to the vast majority of individuals in society. The actions of sex offenders are viewed as despicable and disgusting behaviors that are unacceptable. Despite the inherent revulsion about sex offenders and their actions, Stinson, Sales, and Becker (2008) argued that society has a "fascination with sex offenders and need to understand that behavior" (p. 3). Since the early twentieth century, society has grappled with the threat of sex fiends, sexual psychopaths, sexual predators, and sexually violent predators. Social norms and criminal codes define acceptable sex behaviors very differently. The policy decisions associated with sex offending are largely attributable to a mixture of knowledge, belief, and stereotype about sex offenders and their behaviors.

While most people use the terms sex offender and sex offense loosely, it should be noted that the concepts of sex offender and sex offense are umbrella terms that indicate a wide range of individuals and behaviors. For instance:

In 2014, two female English teachers at Destrehan High School in Destrehan, Louisiana, were arrested for having three-way sexual relations with a 16-year-old male student at the school after a football game. After the game was over, Shelly Dufresne, White, age 32, and married mother of three, and Rachel Respess, White and age 24, took the student back to Respess' apartment, where the sexual encounter occurred. The encounter occurred four days before the student's 17th birthday, which is the age of consent in the state of Louisiana. It is alleged that Dufresne had sex with the student approximately 40 times, and when Respess found out, she offered the use of her apartment and eventually became sexually involved as well. Dufresne and Respess had both been the student's English teacher in different years. The incident came to light when students began talking about the student bragging about the encounter with his teachers and sharing video of the incident; the rumors resulted in the arrest of Dufresne and Respess. This case dealt with the notion of **statutory rape** *(a sexual status offense between an adult and minor as enumerated in a criminal statute). Dufresne, the daughter of a local judge, did enter a guilty plea to the charge of obscenity, which resulted in a 90-day sentence to a mental health treatment facility and deferred prison term; she was later found not guilty of any sex offense. Charges against Respess were dropped after Dufresne's acquittal.*

■■■

Dr. Nikita Levy worked at Johns Hopkins University as a gynecologist for approximately 25 years. During that time, Levy, Black and age 54, photographed and video recorded naked images of female patients from an East Baltimore clinic affiliated with Johns Hopkins. A tip to the police began an investigation into Levy's activities. Soon after Johns Hopkins was notified, Levy was fired. After an initial search of his home that he shared with his wife, Levy was arrested and then released pending the outcome of the investigation. Before law enforcement could finish its investigation, Levy committed suicide by wrapping a bag filled with helium around his head. Levy left a confession about the almost 8,000 victims he had photographed and videoed. While Levy was never convicted, Johns Hopkins University paid out $190 million in settlements to the victims.

■■■

Spring break in Florida is a time of excessive partying, drinking, and drug-taking by many college students in March every year. Over 100,000 spring breakers descend on the state of Florida alone. In Panama City Beach in March of 2015, a video went viral showing an alleged gang rape of a female who was clearly incapacitated. The offenders either assisted or digitally penetrated the victim's vagina. The video indicated there were four offenders. What makes the sex offense even more outrageous is that it occurred in the middle of the day, on the beach, while hundreds of people either watched or ignored the victimization. To date, three of the four offenders (George Kennedy, Jr., age 21, Delonte Martistee, age 22, and Ryan Calhoun, age 23) have been arrested for the crime; evidence emerged that Kennedy was the victim's boyfriend. Martistee and Calhoun were both convicted of rape and each was sentenced to 10 years in prison.

■■■

Jerry Sandusky was a former football defensive coach at Penn State University (PSU). Sandusky and his wife, Dottie, adopted six children and were foster parents to many more. Sandusky was always surrounded by children. He was known to be a "hugger," a "grabber," and a "cutup." In 1977, he and his wife began the Second Mile, a nonprofit organization devoted to troubled and disadvantaged children. The organization would help thousands of children through its annual operating budget in the millions of dollars. What no one knew was that, through the Second Mile, Sandusky was **grooming** *(sex offenders inserting themselves into a new environment around a new target before sexually molesting victims) the troubled children for later sexual victimization.*

Sandusky was successful in his role as a sex offender until things came to a partial head in 1998. In May of that year, Sandusky brought a Second Mile boy to the PSU athletic facility. Sandusky made advances on the boy by wrestling with him, kissing him on the top of the head, saying that he loved the boy, and asked the boy if he wanted to take a shower. According to the Freeh Report conducted by a former head of the Federal Bureau of Investigation (FBI):

1

> *While in the shower, Sandusky wrapped his hands around the boy's chest and said, "I'm gonna squeeze your guts out." The boy then washed his body and hair. Sandusky lifted the boy to "get the soap out of" the boy's hair, bringing the boy's feet "up pretty high" near Sandusky's waist. The boy's back was touching Sandusky's chest and his feet touched Sandusky's thighs. The boy felt "weird" and "uncomfortable" during this time in the shower (Freeh, Sporkin, & Sullivan, LLP, 2012).*

After the incident, the mother of the boy alerted the University Police Department. The police conducted a sting with the mother hosting Sandusky at her house. Even though Sandusky uttered that "I wish I were dead," no evidence emerged of sexual abuse towards her son. The situation was concluded with no charges.

Being informed he would not be the next football coach at PSU, Sandusky retired the next year in 1999. In retirement, he was given an emeritus position, which allowed him access to PSU facilities. In 2001, an assistant coach, Mike McQueary, witnessed Sandusky in the shower with another child. At the time, McQueary saw no sexual behavior, but he did hear sexual sounds; during a later trial he would say he saw Sandusky raping the boy. After witnessing the event, McQueary reported the behavior to Coach Joe Paterno, a legend in college football at that time as one of the most winningest coaches in history. Paterno reported the incident to the athletic director, Tim Curly; Curly then reported to the vice-president, Gary Schultz, and the president, Graham Spanier. At the time, the men largely concluded that it was "horsing around" and "Jerry being Jerry." Sandusky was banned from PSU facilities at that point, effectively ending his ties with PSU. No one notified law enforcement personnel.

The case against Sandusky faded into the background until 2011 when former Pennsylvania Attorney General Thomas Corbett was elected governor. Corbett believed that the case had not been investigated fully by PSU personnel. Prior to his election to governor, he had been investigating Sandusky for over two years (since 2008). When Corbett became governor, he now had inside access to PSU since the sitting governor is a member of the PSU Board of Trustees. In particular, Corbett blamed the lack of investigation on Joe Paterno, the legendary coach who had amassed much power at PSU, and Graham Spanier, who fought many of the governor's initiatives to slash funding to higher education. In December of 2010, grand jury subpoenas were issued for Paterno and other PSU administrators involved in the case. On November 4, 2011, Sandusky was charged with sexually abusing eight boys, before their 13th birthdays, from 1994 to 2009. It was reported that there were likely more victims. Curley and Schultz were charged with perjury.

In the aftermath of Sandusky's crimes, there was great fallout in Pennsylvania. Paterno was fired and died of cancer a few months later. The PSU football team was almost given the "death penalty" for failing to supervise the football program; inevitably PSU was stripped of victories, placed on probation, had scholarships reduced, and was banned from bowl games for several years. This NCAA sentence was later reduced. The PSU president, Graham Spanier, was forced to resign and was charged with child endangerment. Curley and Schultz were also fired and in addition to their charges of perjury, charges of child endangerment, conspiracy, and obstruction of justice were added. Spanier, Curley, and Shultz were all convicted of misdemeanor child endangerment. Most importantly, Sandusky was convicted of 45 of 48 counts of child sexual abuse. He was sentenced to 60 years in prison with eligibility of parole in 30 years; at that time, Sandusky will be 98 years old.

■■■

On August 11, 2012, several house parties took place in Steubenville, Ohio, that included students from several high schools in the area. Alcohol of all sorts was in ready supply. They were typical end-of-summer parties. During one party, however, an incapacitated, 16-year-old girl from Weirton, West Virginia, was repeatedly sexually assaulted by students. She was moved to other parties where she was undressed, photographed, and vaginally penetrated (rape); there were further suggestions that the victim had been urinated on. While some partygoers tried to end the abuse, these individuals were in the minority. By 10:00 P.M. or 10:30 P.M., the victim was visibly drunk. Yet, she still traveled with a football player to other parties in the area. Witnesses testified that the victim needed help walking; other witnesses explained how the alleged offenders carried the victim to the car as she slept. The victim testified that she had no memory of the incident, other than for small intervals of time. The victim woke up naked in a basement living room with three individuals the following morning. The incident may well never have come to light except that many partygoers recorded the incident on cell phones or commented on various social media sites about what had occurred. One party attendee noted the song of the night was "Rape Me" by Nirvana.

The victim's parents reported the crime on August 14, 2012, after being alerted to many pictures, videos, and social media posts about the night from friends and family members. They brought a flash drive with all the records to the police; a rape kit was inconclusive due to the time that had passed since the sexual assault (the victim had taken a shower, and toxicology would not be able to determine if she had been drugged). Prosecutors said the offenders treated the victim like a toy; she was in no position to give consent. They flashed the victim's breasts and digitally penetrated the victim's vagina on multiple occasions.

On August 22, 2012, police arrested Ma'lik Richmond, age 16, and Trent Mays, age 16, from neighboring city Bloomingdale, Ohio, for rape. Neither Mays nor Richmond had a criminal history. Both individuals were players on Steubenville's highly successful football program. The football team in Steubenville is legendary. Since 1900, it has won nine state championships and was undefeated in back-to-back seasons in 2005 and 2006. The football players in Steubenville were given wide latitude in any misbehavior; this was not the first time the Steubenville High School football team had faced sexual assault allegations. The Steubenville chief-of-police pleaded for witnesses to come forward, and several juvenile justice system personnel had to recuse themselves from the case due to their links to the football program.

The town was split on the case. Due to the fact that the perpetrators of the crime were football players on the very successful football team, many in the Steubenville community and the criminal justice system were at odds. Some in the community argued the victim deserved what had happened to her; this group believed the victim lied to cover up a night of drunken revelry that got out of control. Others in the community sided with the victim, arguing that football players were worshipped as heroes in the town; this group believed that football players were allowed to get away with behaviors that other individuals would not due to their successes on the field. In either case, Mays and Richmond were suspended from the football team.

On March 17, 2013, Richmond and Mays were adjudicated delinquent of rape in juvenile court. Through mandatory minimum sentencing, Richmond received one year in juvenile detention for penetrating the unconscious victim and Mays received two years for penetration and disseminating child pornography as the victim was a minor. Upon release, both Mays and Richmond were registered as sex offenders. In the wake of this sexual assault, several school officials (the superintendent and the IT director among them) were charged with offenses like obstructing justice, tampering with evidence, false statements, and failure to report possible child abuse.

■■■

Bill Cosby, celebrity comedian, actor, and once considered "America's Dad" for his work on The Cosby Show in the 1980s, was convicted for drugging and sexually assaulting Andrea Constand. Constand was director of operations for Temple University's women's basketball team; Cosby was an alumnus of Temple and was a leading face and key fundraiser for the university. Their paths crossed during this time period and Cosby initiated contact with Constand at her Temple office, where he wanted to discuss a business-related matter. Over a 14-month period, Cosby pursued a relationship with Constand, while Constand sought a mentoring relationship. In 2004, Constand met Cosby for career advice when she entered his Pennsylvania home; during this visit, Constand was drugged and sexually assaulted. Following Constand's report of the event, then Montgomery District Attorney Bruce Castor did not press charges. Subsequently, Cosby was forced to testify in a civil case. The deal he received for his testimony included immunity from future prosecution for any evidence provided. Despite this deal, in 2018, Cosby was tried by a new prosecutor for the sexual assault of Constand; at the end of the case, Cosby was found guilty and sentenced to serve three to ten years in prison. The conviction was one of the first in the #MeToo movement, where women came forward about experiences in the workplace with unwanted sexual advances and sexual harassment.

In 2021, after almost three years in prison, Cosby's case was overturned by the Pennsylvania Supreme Court, who ordered his release from prison. They found that the civil deposition Cosby delivered could not be used in a criminal trial according to the deal he had made. Cosby was found guilty by a jury of his peers and was set free on a procedural technicality. While Cosby could be tried again, prosecutors would have to utilize different evidence; his civil suit depositions would necessarily be suppressed from any future proceedings. Two hours after the ruling, Cosby was released from prison.

■■■

There are numerous other examples of sex offenders that we could have selected; some mundane, some more sensational, and some more salacious. What is clear from the preceding instances is that the actions of sex offenders, and sex offenders themselves, are very heterogeneous. Sex offenses span a variety of behaviors and come in all sexes, ages, races, and social statuses. For the purposes of this text, a **sex offense** is "an offense involving unlawful sexual conduct, such as [rape], prostitution, indecent exposure, incest, pederasty, and bestiality" (Garner, 2000, p. 887). You will notice that this definition includes actions that are visual or include physical contact. A **sex offender** is any individual who commits a sex offense.

Due to the varied nature of sex offenses/offenders, it is important to have an adequate understanding of this topic if criminal justice policies are going to be effective in combatting this menace. This book explores the threat of sex offenders in the United States and how the criminal justice system has evolved, mostly over the twentieth century, to combat this threat through new laws, law enforcement techniques, sentencing practices, correctional policies, and treatment decisions. Chapter 1 begins the discussion of sex offenders by focusing on the nature of sex crimes in the United States. The next section examines what we know about sex offenders and sex offending through an exploration of official data sources.

THE NATURE OF SEX CRIMES IN THE UNITED STATES

To begin the discussion of the nature of sex offenses, official data sources need to be evaluated. **Official data sources** are records collected by organizations, usually governmental, in the course of day-to-day operations. For the purposes of this text, there are two primary groups of individuals we can talk to in an effort to gauge the extent of sex offending: law enforcement and victims. Law enforcement agencies are the point agency when a victim reports a crime. Fortunately, all law enforcement agencies keep track of reported crimes. These data are collected annually by the FBI into the **Uniform Crime Report (UCR)**. Information about victims can be obtained via another avenue: the **National Crime Victimization Survey (NCVS)**. The NCVS is an annual self-report data collection that is completed by the U.S. Census Bureau. The data collected by the UCR and the NCVS show differences in the reporting of sex crimes. The following sections will explore these two sources of data, the incidence of sex offending according to both, and the problems inherent with these official sources of data on sex offending. This section will also examine a data source that is specific to offenses committed against children, the **National Child Abuse and Neglect Data System (NCANDS)**. Finally, this section presents a brief summary of empirical research that attempts to outline the nature of sex crimes.

UCR

The primary method of determining the amount of crime in the United States is the UCR collected by the FBI. This information is collected by local and state law enforcement agencies as a part of normal operations; the UCR data collection effort spans 17,000 law enforcement agencies serving the vast majority of the U.S. population. The data collected by law enforcement agencies across the country on crime is then transmitted to the FBI, where it is coalesced and crime rates across the United States are tallied. The data collected by the FBI include information on crime reports and criminal arrests and are organized by city, county, standard metropolitan statistical area, and region.

The data in the UCR is presented in summary form. As such, crimes are broken into Type I and Type II offenses. **Type I offenses**, also known as **index crimes**, include incident reports/citizen complaints about murder and non-negligent manslaughter, forcible rape, robbery, aggravated assault, burglary, larceny, motor vehicle theft, and arson. Originally, there were only seven index crimes; the eighth crime, arson, was added in 1979. **Type II offenses** are any other offenses not outlined as index crimes. Type II offenses only provide information on arrests, not on reports. This is an important distinction between the two UCR offense types. In addition to crime counts and rates, the UCR does collect other information in a limited capacity. Age, race, and gender information are collected for offenders who have been arrested for either a Type I or Type II offense.

There are largely two measures of sex crimes in the UCR: rape and sex offenses other than rape or prostitution. Rape is a Type I offense that collects information on rapes that are reported to the police. The FBI defines forcible rape as "the carnal knowledge of a female forcibly and against her will" (2015). This is now known as the legacy definition. In 2013, the term "forcible" was dropped from the UCR and the definition of rape was changed to "penetration, no matter how slight, of the vagina or anus with any body part or object, or oral penetration by a sex organ of another person, without consent of the victim. Attempts or assaults to commit rape are also included; however, statutory rape and incest are excluded" (FBI, 2015).

Sex offenses other than rape and prostitution are Type II offenses. Rather than rely on reports, these offenses are measured when an arrest occurs. These crimes include "offenses against chastity, common decency, morals, and the like. Incest, indecent exposure, and statutory rape are included. Attempts are included" (FBI, 2015).

Since rape is the best metric of sex offenses in the UCR, Table 1.1 provides the breakdowns on rape incidents and rates (both legacy and revised definitions) from

TABLE 1.1 RAPE (LEGACY AND REVISED DEFINITION) COUNT AND RATES, 1995–2019

Year	Population[1]	Violent crime[2]	Violent crime rate	Rape (revised definition)[3]	Rape (revised definition) rate[4]	Rape (legacy definition)[5]	Rape (legacy definition) rate[6]
1995	262,803,276	1,798,792	684.5			97,470	37.1
1996	265,228,572	1,688,540	636.6			96,252	36.3
1997	267,783,607	1,636,096	611.0			96,153	35.9
1998	270,248,003	1,533,887	567.6			93,144	34.5
1999	272,690,813	1,426,044	523.0			89,411	32.8
2000	281,421,906	1,425,486	506.5			90,178	32.0
2001[5]	285,317,559	1,439,480	504.5			90,863	31.8
2002	287,973,924	1,423,677	494.4			95,235	33.1
2003	290,788,976	1,383,676	475.8			93,883	32.3
2004	293,656,842	1,360,088	463.2			95,089	32.4
2005	296,507,061	1,390,745	469.0			94,347	31.8
2006	299,398,484	1,435,123	479.3			94,472	31.6
2007	301,621,157	1,422,970	471.8			92,160	30.6
2008	304,059,724	1,394,461	458.6			90,750	29.8
2009	307,006,550	1,325,896	431.9			89,241	29.1
2010	309,330,219	1,251,248	404.5			85,593	27.7
2011	311,587,816	1,206,005	387.1			84,175	27.0
2012	313,873,685	1,217,057	387.8			85,141	27.1
2013	316,497,531	1,168,298	369.1	113,695	35.9	82,109	25.9
2014	318,857,056	1,165,383	365.5	116,645	36.6	84,041	26.4
2015	320,896,618	1,199,310	373.7	126,134	39.3	91,261	28.4
2016	323,405,935	1,250,162	386.6	132,414	40.9	96,970	30.0
2017	325,147,121	1,247,917	383.8	135,666	41.7	99,708	30.7
2018	326,687,501	1,209,997	370.4	143,765	44.0	101,363	31.0
2019	328,239,523	1,203,808	366.7	139,815	42.6	98,213	29.9

Source: FBI, UCR, 2020.

[1] Populations are U.S. Census Bureau provisional estimates as of July 1 for each year except 2000 and 2010, which are decennial census counts.
[2] The violent crime figures include the offenses of murder, rape (legacy definition), robbery, and aggravated assault.
[3] The figures shown in this column for the offense of rape were estimated using the revised UCR definition of rape. See data declaration for further explanation.
[4] The figures shown in this column for the offense of rape were estimated using the legacy UCR definition of rape. See data declaration for further explanation.
[5] The murder and nonnegligent homicides that occurred as a result of the events of September 11, 2001, are not included in this table.
[6] The crime figures have been adjusted.

1995 to 2019. Table 1.1 indicates that the rate of reporting rape has decreased for most of this reporting period, the incidence of rape increased from 2014 to 2019 for both the legacy and revised definition of rape in the UCR.

Table 1.2 displays the incidence of arrests for sex crimes other than rape and prostitution from 2005 to 2019. Table 1.2 indicates that the total arrests for sex offenses

TABLE 1.2 SEX OFFENSES OTHER THAN RAPE AND PROSTITUTION, 2005–2019

Year	Sex Offenses Other than Rape
2005	91,625
2006	87,252
2007	83,975
2008	79,914
2009	77,326
2010	79,628
2011	69,225
2012	68,355
2013	57,925
2014	55,456
2015	51,388
2016	51,063
2017	48,525
2018	46,937
2019	40,796

other than rape and prostitution have also decreased between 2005 and 2019. This suggests that, overall, sex offending in relation to sex offenses other than rape is decreasing in the United States and has been doing so for some time.

Tables 1.1 and 1.2 indicate that the total number and rates of rape have decreased since 1995; the incidence of rape has increased (legacy and revised definitions) since 2015. The total number of arrests for sex offenses other than rape and prostitution have decreased since 2005. The incidence of rape reports is in line with total violent crime, as well as most other forms of crime, in the United States, both Type I and Type II offenses. While this data indicates mixed offending levels, two things are in need of consideration. First, there are still over 100,000 or 80,000 reported rapes perpetrated each year (revised and legacy definitions). Second, there are some issues with the UCR that limit the validity of the numbers above.

Despite the important information that is provided in the UCR, it should be noted that there are several key problems with this official data source. First, the UCR is especially subject to disclosure issues; this is known as the dark figure of crime. In the UCR, a crime is only recorded if someone reports the crime to the police. While many crimes go unreported, and thus unrecorded, this is especially a problem in crimes revolving around sex offenses. La Fond (2005) indicated that only a third of all sex offenses are reported to law enforcement officials. The primary reasons for victims not reporting sex crimes to the police include stigma, feelings of guilt, and a desire to forget the incident occurred. Victims may fear reprisal from the offender; as we will find throughout this book, it is very typical for the offender and the victim to know each other well. Potential reprisals can hamper a victim from reporting a sex offense. Victims may also fear mistreatment by law enforcement personnel. A victim of a sex crime will be questioned vigorously by law enforcement personnel in addition to any rape kits that are taken in the course of the investigation; the latter is very invasive to an individual who has just been sexually assaulted. A victim can view the extensive questioning as doubt by law enforcement of the victim's story. Whatever the rationale, it is clear that many victims of sex crimes do not report the incident to the police.

Second, the UCR is subject to the hierarchy rule. The **hierarchy rule** dictates that only one crime, the most serious crime, is recorded for each criminal event. So, if an offender raped and murdered a victim, only the murder would show up in the UCR numbers for a given year; the rape would not be recorded. This would necessarily decrease the number of rapes for a given year even though a rape had occurred. The hierarchy rule is a problem for UCR crime reporting.

Third, the UCR being comprised of Type I and Type II offenses sets up a scenario of trying to compare apples and oranges. Reports of crimes (Type I offenses) and arrests for crime (Type II offenses) are fundamentally different numbers. As such, it is possible for the numbers under each area to be similar, decreasing while the other is increasing, and vice versa. This is especially true for sex crimes that can take a great deal of time to investigate before an arrest occurs (for either rape or sex offenses other than rape and prostitution). A report of a crime does not necessarily yield a criminal arrest. This can be due to a myriad of factors, but it makes comparison of Type I and Type II offenses problematic.

The final problem with the UCR is that it is subject to agency prioritization. If an agency is focused on one type of crime or other, the agency is necessarily going to find more of that crime type. If the emphasis of an agency is on gang crime, more resources will be placed toward combatting this type of crime. In this singular effort, the number of gang crimes will necessarily increase in that area as opposed to another area that is maybe focusing on drug crimes. Thus, the overall numbers reported in the UCR mask individual law enforcement agencies' foci of crime control efforts in given areas.

It is clear that the UCR has some very real problems in helping us to paint a picture of sex crimes in the United States. An alternate official data source is the NCVS, which we will discuss next.

NCVS

In the UCR, the criminal definitions used and the data collected are framed by the individuals who collected this information: police organizations (Cantor and Lynch, 2000). Because police organizations collect the UCR, the data inherently has problems, as listed above. Victimization surveys overcome problems with the UCR in several manners. First, victimization surveys can gather not only crimes reported to the police, but crimes not reported to the police (Biderman and Reiss, 1967). Secondly, victimization surveys allow for more information to be collected on individuals who have criminal experiences/victimizations, especially in terms of the social context of crime. Finally, victimization surveys collect information on both people who have been victimized and those who have not; this allows for a control group across which to compare findings among the victimized (comparison) group.

The NCVS was a result of the victims' rights movement of the 1970s. The data collected from the NCVS is used primarily to examine crime in terms of the UCR's index crimes (Type I offenses) and to explore changes in patterns of victimization, including contextual information about the criminal event, over time. The interviewer uses both a screening interview and an incident form. Thus, through the assessment of the victim in the oral part of the interview, the interviewer can determine if more information is warranted on a crime, which would be collected by the use of the incident form.

The NCVS utilizes a complex, longitudinal research design; no other victim survey in the world has the same design as the NCVS (Cantor and Lynch, 2000). Primarily an interviewing technique, the NCVS utilizes a "rotating panel design." This design allows persons in a sample of households to be interviewed at six-month intervals over a three-and-a-half-year period. All members of the household who are above the age of 12 are asked about victimizations they have experienced over the last six months. The questionnaire includes information about the details surrounding a criminal event that the respondent experienced. Since it is a continuing rotating panel design, a new sample is drawn every three and a half years.

From 1993 to 2019, the NCVS has shown that the incidence of crime and crime rates have been decreasing precipitously until 2010. While this crime drop has flatlined since 2010, the overall trend line has been in a downward trajectory. In 2019, there were 1.2 million violent victimizations, with little change when compared to 2018. Between 1993 and 2019, the overall violent victimization rate, excluding simple assault, decreased from 29.1. to 7.3 per 1,000 individuals (75 percent drop). The rate of property crime has also declined over the same period. In 2019, the rate of property crime declined by 6 percent (101.4 per 1,000 individuals) over 2018 victimization levels.

The NCVS's primary measure of sex crimes is rape/sexual assault. According to the Bureau of Justice Statistics (BJS) (Truman and Langton, 2015), rape is

> the unlawful penetration of a person against the will of the victim, with use or threatened force or attempting such an act. Rape includes psychological coercion and physical force, and forced sexual intercourse means vaginal, anal, or oral penetration by the offender (p. 13).

Rape also includes penetration of any of these orifices with a foreign object and accounts for either male or female victims. The BJS (Truman and Langton, 2015) defines sexual assault "across a wide range of victimizations, separate from rape and attempted rape. These crimes include attacks or attempted attacks generally involving unwanted sexual contact between a victim and offender" (p. 13). This may include force or not; grabbing and fondling are included in the definition of sexual assault. Both rape and sexual assault are combined into one measure in the NCVS. In relation to rape/sexual assault, Table 1.3 provides the NCVS counts and rates in 2015, 2017, and 2019.

TABLE 1.3 VIOLENT CRIME AND RAPE/SEXUAL ASSAULT IN THE NCVS, 2015–2019

	2015	2017	2019
Violent Crime	5,006,620	5,612,670	5,813,410
Rate per 1,000	18.6	20.6	21.0
Number of Victims	2,650,670	3,106,340	3,054,250
Rape/Sexual Assault	431,840	393,980	459,310
Rate per 1,000	1.6	1.4	1.7
Number of Victims	204,000	208,960	212,230

Source: Morgan and Truman (2020).

As can be seen, the overall incidence, rates, and number of victims of all violent crimes increased from 2015 to 2019. Rape/sexual assault also experienced an increase over the same period according to the NCVS. While the overall number is low, recent sex offending in the NCVS hovers around 400,000 incidents each year with a total of around 200,000 victims. While the overall violent crime rate was similar to the data found in the UCR, the data in relation to sex crimes is also similar with both the NCVS and UCR indicating increases in serious sex crimes; the UCR continues to show decrease for non-rape sex crimes predicated on arrests.

How can we account for the minor differences in these two data collections? While the data rest on different data collection techniques, the differences can be attributed to the limitations of each data source. The NCVS has several limitations that impact the final reporting of crime. While established in the field as a viable alternative for measuring the incidence of criminal events, the NCVS still suffers from several problems and controversies. First, it is a very expensive means of measuring crime. It is both costly to hire the manpower for interviews and timely to conduct in its nature. Second, if the earlier data was bad (due to definitional constraints), can it be used at all as a reference for more recent data? The answer to this should be no, but researchers still do so on occasion. Finally, sexual assaults have increased at least two-fold in the presence of using computer-aided questioning software. Does this invalidate some of the earlier findings of older NCVS data collections? These are all problems that exist in the compilation of the NCVS.

Maybe the most important problem with the NCVS in relation to sex crimes deals with unreported crimes. From a press release from the BJS in 2012, there are 3.4 million violent victimizations per year that go unreported. From an internal study conducted between 1994 and 2010, the BJS determined that "an estimated 211,000 rapes and sexual assaults went unreported to police each year between 2006 and 2010. Although serious crime was generally less likely to go unreported to the police than simple assault, a higher percentage of rape or sexual assault (65 percent) than simple assault (50 percent) victimizations went unreported over the five-year period." In 2014, 46 percent of all violent victimizations were reported to the police; this means that over half were not reported to the police (Truman and Langton, 2015). The non-reporting problem is exacerbated when we look at just rape or sexual assaults. Only 34 percent of rapes and sexual assaults were reported to the police in 2014; this suggests that 66 percent of rapes and sexual assaults go unreported to law enforcement. As early as 1985, Koss referred to this under-disclosure problem as the "hidden epidemic" of rape.

NCANDS

While the NCVS only collects data about sexual assaults committed against those age 12 and older, the NCANDS focuses specifically on the abuse of children, those under the age of 18. NCANDS began in 1988 and serves as a national collection of data about child abuse and neglect collected by each of the states. These data include reports about the sexual abuse of children (U.S. Department of Health and Human Services, 2016). Data are collected from each states' child protective services (CPS) agencies, based on referrals regarding abuse or neglect that they receive. Referrals are received from sources such as medical professionals, teachers, and relatives of children who are perceived to be at risk of maltreatment or are being maltreated. All referrals are recorded by the state CPS agencies and reported to NCANDS. Referrals are either "screened in," meaning that the referral receives a response or investigation from CPS, or "screened out," meaning that the referral does not meet the agency's criteria for an investigation. From the data reported for 2019, agencies screened in an average of 54.5 percent of referrals (U.S. Department of Health and Human Service, 2021); this was down 6 percent from 2014 (60.7 percent).

A screened in referral is called a report; reports receive an investigation. Data are then collected on all reports and the children that are subjects of a report, as well as the type of services received and other details about that service, such as the response time between receiving information and beginning an investigation. Of all the victims of maltreatment that were recorded in the NCANDS for 2019, 7.2 percent were sexually abused (U.S. Department of Health and Human Services, 2016). This data source shows a 62 percent decrease in the rate of substantiated sexual abuse cases between 1990 and 2010 (Finkelhor and Jones, 2012); this was a 1 percent decrease since 2014.

The fact that the NCANDS is based on reports to CPS agencies is both a strength and a weakness for that data source. As a strength, this data source indicates the number of cases of abuse that are substantiated, which means that a professional agency has investigated and believes that the maltreatment did occur. There are not likely to be many false reports of maltreatment, or in this case of child sexual abuse, in these data. However, as was an issue for the UCR, not all cases of maltreatment are reported, either to the police or the CPS agencies. There will be a number of true cases of child sexual abuse that are not present in this data source due to the fact that no one ever reported them to CPS.

Empirical Research

While the UCR and the NCVS are the primary sources of information about sex crimes and sex offenders, there are other avenues in which we can learn about sex crimes. **Empirical studies** are research conducted by individual researchers, mostly affiliated with universities. This research is generally not conducted on a regular basis and focuses on very few subjects in a sample or specific population. In general, Terry (2013) concluded that empirical studies tend to indicate one in six women have been raped, 17 to 22 percent of women have been sexually assaulted, 2 to 8 percent of males have been sexually assaulted, most victims know the offender, and the prevalence of childhood sexual abuse is 13 percent for males and 30 to 40 percent for females. These limited findings provide an indication of how pervasive sex crimes are in society and how much information official statistics are missing. There is not enough room to discuss the many studies on sex offenders in Chapter 1. Suffice it to say, the majority of studies that inform our understanding of sex offending have their own limitations. When appropriate, key studies will be discussed throughout this book in relation to the various areas of sex offending we will examine.

No matter the source of data (NCVS, UCR, NCANDS, or empirical studies), there are problems inherent with data and research on sex offenders. Despite the limitations with official sources of data, criminologists and criminal justice personnel must do the best they can with the available statistics. These limitations make it difficult to determine the actual levels of sex offending. The next section examines the various characteristics of sex offenders in the United States.

CHARACTERISTICS OF SEX OFFENDERS

A great misunderstanding about sex offenders persists among academics, criminal justice system personnel, and the public. Throughout the twentieth century, many stereotypes about sex offenders were created and maintained. For instance, one of the most pervasive beliefs about sex offenders is that they are likely to reoffend regularly. When a criminal commits a crime after committing a previous crime, this is known as **recidivism**. Recidivism takes two forms: general and specific. General recidivism implies that the new crime is unrelated to the old crime; for instance, a person who commits theft after having committed an assault. These two crimes are not necessarily related. Specific recidivism implies that the older crime and the recently committed crime are connected. For instance, if a person committed a murder and had a previous history of aggravated assaults, this would be specific recidivism. Sex offenders are commonly believed to be specific recidivists. According to research and official data sources, this belief is not actually the case, but it serves as one of the key examples of misinformation about sex offenders. The typical sex offender is not necessarily a dirty old man trolling for children to sexually assault; likewise, sex offenders are not typically lying in wait behind a bush, waiting for a female victim to come along. As seen in the introduction of this chapter, sex offenders do not all look and behave the same.

What we know about the characteristics of sex offenders is linked to where the information comes from. There are two primary sources that provide information about the characteristics of sex offenders: psychology and criminology/sociology. The psychological literature and research tend to suggest that sex offenders are a very heterogeneous group. Individuals who are sex offenders are diverse in terms of age, gender, socioeconomic status, and intellectual functioning. Part of the reason for this is the term "sex offender." Sex offense is an umbrella term for many types of behaviors.

The criminology literature, in comparison to psychological studies, is much more concrete on the characteristics of sex offenders. Since a great deal of data on sex offenders comes from official data sources, criminologists can talk about offenders who have been arrested and processed through the criminal justice system. According to the UCR, arrested sex offenders tend to be White (66 percent), male (over 96 percent), and over the age of 18 (90 percent). In addition, there is no relationship between sex offenders and the race, ethnicity, and age of victims (Terry, 2013). Sex offenders tend to know, or at least have a passing acquaintance with, their victims. Finally, La Fond (2005) noted that almost two-thirds of victims of sex crimes are minors and the vast majority of the victims of sex offenses are females.

While sex offenders are a heterogeneous group of individuals, the vast majority of research and official statistics necessarily focuses on adult, male offenders. Sex offenders with these characteristics form the backdrop of most of the research utilized in chapters throughout this book. The remainder of this section will examine two under-evaluated groups of sex offenders: female and juvenile sex offenders. It will also examine sex offenders who commit their offenses in groups.

Female Sex Offenders

Terry (2013) suggested that relatively little is known about **female sex offenders**. As illustrated earlier in Chapter 1, females are responsible for many sex offenses. Despite the fact that females account for many sex crimes every single year, Gannon and Cortoni (2010) indicated an overall lack of emphasis on female sex offenders in research. Rather, the bulk of research on sex offenders focuses on male sex offenders.

The limited research on female sex offenders does indicate some consistency in findings. First, female sex offenders do not commit sex crimes at rates comparable to male sex offenders. Reports of female sex offending are almost nonexistent in relation to male sex offending (Peter, 2009). Research also indicates that females are responsible for 20 percent of all sex crimes (Cortoni et al., 2009). Additionally, the incidence of female sex offending has been increasing over the last decade (Cortoni et al., 2009). Saradjian (2010) argued that women who sexually abuse children are much more prevalent than has been previously thought.

Second, female sex offenders tend to have child, adolescent, and/or teenage victims. Saradjian (2010) indicated that female sex offenders tend to offend against male victims. Male victims of female sex offenders are often viewed by society to be "lucky." Many view this type of crime as less damaging to victims. Unfortunately, victims of female sex offenders tend to experience traumatic sexualization (sexual identity problems, aversive feelings about sex, overvaluing of sex, and confusion about sex), stigmatization, a feeling of betrayal, powerlessness, and identity issues (Saradjian, 2010, p. 21).

There are many limitations to the research on female sex offenders. Studies on female sex offenders should be viewed with great caution as this area of study is still in its early development. The research on female sex offenders offers conflicting results often predicated on small samples. Studies of female sex offenders also suffer methodological issues (small sample sizes which lead to generalizability issues).

It should be noted that all crime, not just sex offenses, is underreported for female offenders. Thus, any estimate of female sex crimes will be an underestimate. Not only is this type of crime underreported, but these acts are not aggressively pursued by welfare or criminal justice agencies (Saradjian, 2010). Due to the lack of focus on female sex offenders, Gannon and Cortoni (2010) argued that research must focus on how female sex offenders are similar or vary in relation to their male counterparts; additionally, the research has to evaluate the differences between different types of female sex offenders.

Juvenile Sex Offenders

While the general stereotype of sex offenders is of older, White males, juvenile sex offenders are much more prevalent than previously thought. **Juvenile sex offenders** are sex offenders who are minors in the eyes of the law, generally below the age of 18. Some studies indicate that between 15 percent and 20 percent of all sex offenses are perpetrated by juvenile sex offenders (Furby, Weinrott, and Blackshaw, 1989). Just like female sex offenders, there is a lack of empirical emphasis given to the study of juvenile sex offenders. It is clear that juveniles commit a large portion of overall sex offenses (Terry, 2013).

Zolondek et al. (2002) indicated that juvenile sex offenders are a heterogeneous group where there are few similarities across demographic characteristics, use of force, and paraphilias than other sex offenders; according to Terry (2013), juvenile sex offenders vary in age, maturity, understanding of sexuality, and development (p. 118). Juvenile sex offenders are most likely to commit their crimes between the ages of 14 and 15, and molestation of children is the most frequently occurring juvenile sex crime (Zolondek et al., 2002). More than 25 percent of juvenile sex offenders in Zolondek et al.'s (2002) research had never been blamed for the sex offense.

Some studies have found correlates of juvenile sex offending. Terry (2013) argued that juvenile sex offenders tend to experience a great deal of family dysfunction (especially violent childhoods), lack of attachments, physical abuse/neglect, and substance abuse (p. 127). Research indicates that juvenile sex offenders do not engage exclusively in sex offending; rather, these offenders tend to be generalists (Terry, 2013). In fact, most juvenile sex offenders commit more non-sex offenses than sex offenses. Weinrott (1996) argued that sexual recidivism amongst juvenile sex offenders was exceptionally low in five- to ten-year follow-up periods, while recidivism in relation to non-sex crimes was more prevalent. Research does not indicate any relationship between juvenile sex offending and alcohol, drugs, and other delinquency (Zolondek et al., 2002).

Studies have shown consistency between juvenile sex offenders and their victims. Most juvenile sex offenders are male and are fewer than five years older than the victim. Generally, juvenile sex offenders are well acquainted with their victims; in fact, many victims are younger siblings or the children of close family friends (Zolondek et al., 2002). Juvenile sex offenders tend to victimize either males or females, but generally not both. Juvenile sex offenders prefer to utilize verbal coercion over aggression or violence (Zolondek et al., 2002).

Some sex offenders are **female juvenile sex offenders**. Female juvenile sex offenders are a very small proportion of all sex offenders in general and juvenile sex offenders in particular. Frey (2010) suggested that 20 percent of all female sex offenses were perpetrated by female juvenile sex offenders. This was a decreasing trend from 1998 to 2007.

Frey (2010) argued that female juvenile sex offenders tend to be punished more harshly than males. Female juvenile sex offenders tend to have backgrounds of extreme family dysfunction (neglect and incest) and childhood maltreatment (Frey, 2010). Just like other sex offenders, female juvenile sex offenders oftentimes know their victim. Female juvenile sex offenders target male victims, generally only one victim, the age of first offense was around ten years old, and fondling was the most frequently occurring crime (Frey, 2010).

Jones (2003) indicated that the study of juvenile sex offenders has "severe methodological problems" (p. 204). This has made it difficult to make confident conclusions about the etiology of juvenile sex offenders and their behaviors. There is also a profound lack of research on female juvenile sex offenders. The available research suffers from methodological and statistical problems; these problems include small sample sizes and limited generalizability. As of today, a huge gap in knowledge remains concerning juvenile sex offenders (male and female). It is clear that juvenile sex offending is more prevalent than what is thought, but more research is necessary to fully understand this group of offenders.

Group Versus Individual Offenders

While most sex offenses include one offender and one victim, some offenses involve multiple offenders. A common term used to describe multiple offender sexual offenses is "gang rape." It is difficult to determine the percentage of rapes that are gang rapes due to issues with underreporting as well as the different types of samples used to study rape. Using a student sample, it was estimated that approximately 2 percent of women have been raped by two or more offenders in the same incident (that is not 2 percent of all rapes, but 2 percent of respondents), whereas a police sample indicated that 26 percent of all rapes involved multiple offenders (O'Sullivan, 1991). Gang rape is often studied in the context of the college campus, as it is believed that groups such as all-male fraternities and athletic teams have characteristics that can lead to gang rape (Schwartz and DeKeseredy, 1997). Gang rape is also studied in the context of comparing multiple offender sexual assaults with those committed by single offenders.

Fraternities are very masculine environments; they have become so by design. When fraternity members discuss the types of men they want to join their fraternity, they mention athletic guys who play sports, who enjoy drinking, who study in a male dominated field, who have a stereotypically handsome appearance, and who can relate to women (Martin and Hummer, 1989). Women are considered bait to fraternity members, to help them attract the right kind of pledges, and they are used as servers during fraternity parties and as sexual prey. The kinds of views of masculinity and femininity that are present in fraternities can lead to coercive sexual encounters and even gang rape (Martin and Hummer, 1989). Some believe that membership in a privileged group, such as a fraternity, may reduce thoughts in a perpetrator about the morality of his behavior as the group's consensus becomes more important (O'Sullivan, 1991).

In examining the differences between rapes with one perpetrator and those with more than one perpetrator, both victim and offenders in gang rapes are on average slightly younger than victims and offenders in single offender rapes. Both victims and offenders in gang rapes are slightly less likely to be employed than those in single offender rapes (Ullman, 1999). Gang rapes are more likely to take place in a bar or at a party than individual offender rapes, are more likely to involve a stranger perpetrator, and are more likely to involve a weapon. The victim in a gang rape is more likely to employ all types of resistance strategies, and these rapes are more likely to involve oral and anal penetration than rapes with a single offender. Gang rapes are more likely to be reported to the police and to involve physical injury (Ullman, 2007). The post-rape outcome for victims of gang rapes tends to be worse than for victims of an individual offender. These victims are more likely to have a subsequent suicide attempt and are more likely to suffer from post-traumatic stress disorder and a drinking or drug problem. They are also more likely to seek counseling than victims of single offender rapes (Ullman, 2007).

TYPES OF SEX OFFENSES

As noted above, the stereotypes of sex offenders are dirty, old men preying upon children and depraved individuals lurking in the shadows waiting to sexually violate unsuspecting women in the general vicinity. What is lost in the stereotype is the location of the sex crime: the public setting. As with the nature of sex crimes and characteristics of sex offenders, there is great heterogeneity in where sex crimes occur. From the home to public settings to the business setting, sex offenses can occur anywhere. This section examines the various physical and social arenas where sex offenses can occur. These areas include date rape, home, colleges, military, prisons, human trafficking, and the Internet.

Date Rape

As noted above, the myth of sex crimes, and rape in particular, is that they are violent crimes perpetrated by strangers. What we have seen in Chapter 1 is that most sex crimes are perpetrated by offenders who know their victims. Thus, we have to consider contexts associated with sex crimes that link the victim and the offender. One of the most prevalent arenas where this occurs is in relation to date rape. Garner (2000) defined **date rape** as "a rape committed by a person who is escorting the victim on a social occasion. Loosely, date rape is also sometimes used in reference to what is more accurately called acquaintance rape or relationship rape" (p. 1,014).

Often in the date rape scenario, victims do not see their experience as a rape because it does not match the myth of rape, including violence and resistance. Alternatively, offenders often do not see their behavior as a sex offense due to larger cultural beliefs about courtship. Law enforcement also succumbs to these cultural beliefs about rape, usually being more skeptical of date rape than sex offenses more consistent with the rape myth. The result of law enforcement's, victims,' and the offender's understanding of the situation is a lack of reporting. Research has typically shown that date rape is widely pervasive and rarely reported to the authorities. While a great deal of research has been conducted in the area of date rape, official statistics on the incidence of date rape are elusive. What is clear is that we have no way to determine what the full, or even partial, scope of date rape actually is.

Incest

One of the most prevalent places where sex crimes occur is in the home. According to Garner (2000), **incest** is "sexual relations between family members or close relatives, including children related by adoption" (p. 610). The crime of incest is a felony under statutory law. Incest is an important crime to consider as research indicates that 46 percent of children who are raped are the victims of family members (Holmes and Holmes, 2009b, p. 96). As noted previously:

> The majority of American rape victims (61 percent) are raped before the age of 18; furthermore, an astounding 29 percent of all forcible rapes occurred with a victim who was less than 11-years-old. Eleven percent of rape victims are raped by their fathers or stepfathers, and another 16 percent are raped by a relative (Holmes and Holmes, 2009b, p. 96).

These facts are at great odds with the general belief that sex offenders are strangers waiting to ensnare children with promises of candy.

Incest is a problem for the criminal justice system because it is a very underreported crime, even with respect to other sex crimes. Victims, especially child victims, have multiple reasons for not reporting incest offenses. The reasons for children not reporting incest revolve around the notion of fear. This can be a fear of retaliation, a fear that adults will not believe their accusations, or a fear of the relative being removed from the home. As such, incest is one of the least reported sex crimes likely masking a much higher incidence of occurrence.

Rape on College Campuses

Another area where sex crimes occur on a frequent basis is in the university setting. The White House declared college sex crimes as an epidemic since one in five women are sexually assaulted on campus (White House Task Force to Protect Students from Sexual Assault, 2014). As with other sex crimes, this crime is often perpetrated by an acquaintance and often goes unreported. For instance, the University of Oregon reported that around 10 percent of its students had been raped while attending the school even though many of these cases were never reported to the authorities (van der Voo, 2014).

Reports of rape on a college campus are unique in that many of these cases yield not only a criminal complaint but also a school investigation. The reason for the school investigation is linked to Title IX (education amendments of 1972), which protects students' rights to equal education. This right also includes the adequate handling of any sexually violent claims. If a school violates this right, an institution can receive financial sanctions; in the most egregious cases a university can be stripped of its federal funding. As of 2014, the U.S. Department of Education was investigating at least

55 universities for their mistreatment of sexual assault under Title IX; this number of investigations has quadrupled since 2014. Schools under investigation for violations of Title IX often lose student enrollments.

A student accusation of sexual assault does not necessarily mean that the accusation is true. School officials have to determine the merits of the student's complaint with respect to the accused's version of the event; both sides are providing two different interpretations of the event. When a claim is reported, this often begins a school adjudication process, which many victims are leery of. These non-criminal justice university processes can include harsh questioning of the victim (prior sexual history for example) conducted by university staff or other students; both of these groups are often untrained to deal with such complaints. As well, in many of the older disciplinary processes, the offender and victim were allowed to question each other during the hearing. The disciplinary hearing can result in reprimand, suspension, or expulsion from a university.

University processes pertaining to sexual crimes have been in the public's focus for some time. Many question why these cases are not left simply to law enforcement. The primary reason why there are school investigations is because the victim should not have to potentially run into their offender in a class or somewhere else on campus. Other individuals question whether a university is qualified to deal with instances of sexual violence. This question is less easy to answer.

First, most universities have some form of law enforcement under the campus umbrella. Reaves (2015) examined the makeup of law enforcement on university campuses in the United States. He found that nine in ten public campuses and four in ten private university campuses utilized sworn police officers as their campus security; the remainder were more akin to private security with law enforcement training. The vast majority of campus law enforcement officers have arrest powers (86 percent) and patrol jurisdiction (81 percent) beyond campus borders. Larger universities (5,000 or more students) tend to have law enforcement agencies complete with personnel to deal with rape prevention (86 percent of campuses). Public university law enforcement personnel were more likely to have met with groups seeking to prevent sexual violence (76 percent); this percentage was less for private schools (58 percent). In relation to law enforcement, universities tend to have the ability to potentially deal with sex crimes.

Second, in relation to sex offense complaint processes within the university, it is much more arguable that universities do not have the ability to adequately deal with sex crimes. The recent emphasis on university sexual victimization by the White House, the media, and the general public has begun to bring about change in university investigations of sexual victimizations. Universities need to effectively respond to reports of sex crimes and must have a formalized plan on how they will deal with sexual victimization. This plan includes providing someone the victim can talk to in confidence; a comprehensive sexual misconduct policy; training for school officials; better disciplinary systems; and building partnerships within the community like emergency services, rape crisis centers, and therapy providers (White House Task Force to Protect Students from Sexual Assault, 2014). In addition, schools must provide greater transparency in reporting sexual victimizations of students and improved enforcement of Title IX. Many schools are beginning to utilize a single, well-trained investigator to deal with sex crimes on campus.

University statistics on rape are often difficult to find. This is largely due to the fact that universities do not have a vested interest in displaying these statistics. No one wants their son or daughter going to the "rape school." As such, university statistics on sex crimes are not overly prevalent; this is one of the reasons the White House called for more transparency in reports of sexual victimization on college campuses. Using information from the NCVS, Sinozich and Langton (2014) examined rape and sexual assault among college-age females from 1995 to 2013. They found that the rate of rape/sexual assault for non-students (7.5 per 1,000) was 1.2 times higher than for students (6.1 per 1,000). As with other sex crimes, both students and non-students knew their victims in over 80 percent of cases. The majority of both student and non-student victims were unlikely to report their experience; both groups largely considered the sex offense not important enough to report. Most problematic, student rape victims were much less likely to report than non-student victims; for those who did not report, the most consistent rationale was stating it was a personal matter (Sinozich and Langton, 2014). After the sexual victimization, both student and non-student victims tended not to pursue assistance from a victim services agency. The Bureau of Justice Statistics has not replicated this study to date.

In response to concerns about campus sexual assault, many universities are establishing an affirmative consent standard, or "yes means yes" rather than the "no means no" slogan that has been used by those trying to stop sexual assault for years. California has been a leader in this effort, in 2014 passing legislation making "yes means yes" the standard for consenting to sexual activity on college campuses in the state (de Leon and Jackson, 2015). Effectively, this means that "affirmative, conscious, and voluntary agreement to engage in sexual activity—throughout the encounter" (de Leon and Jackson, 2015) is required for a sexual encounter *not* to be rape. The law also specifies that someone who is incapacitated by drugs or alcohol cannot give consent to sexual activity. The previous "no means no" standard puts the burden on the victim of a sexual assault to indicate to the offender that they do not consent to sexual activity, whereas "yes means yes" means both parties must have a mutual understanding of what actions they have both agreed to engage in.

1

Rape in the Military

While not a new setting for sex offenses, sexual victimization in the military has received a great deal of focus over the last decade. According to the Department of Defense (2014), sexual assault is a "significant challenge facing the United States Military" (p. 4). What makes sex crimes amongst military personnel so tenuous is the way in which these cases are handled. Sex crimes in the military are not handled through the criminal justice system. Rather, the military handles sex crimes through the chain of command and military tribunals. Due to this power dynamic, the way in which the military handles sex crimes has changed over the last several years.

Instead of reporting to the next soldier in the command chain, who may well have been responsible for the victimization, a soldier can now choose one of two reporting strategies: Restricted and unrestricted reporting. Restricted reporting is confidential and limited only to specific parties: medical, mental health, and other advocacy services. Restricted reporting avoids formal investigations and the legal process.

Unrestricted reporting will initiate a formal, independent investigation conducted outside the chain of command. It is believed these new methods of reporting are having a positive impact on the reporting of sex crimes in the military. The Department of Defense (2014) reported that changes in policy were allowing for more reporting of sexual assaults by military personnel. From 2012 to 2014, reporting of sexual assault increased by 58 percent; to 2019, the number of reports has leveled off (Department of Defense, 2020).

Black and Merrick (2013) found that the incidence of sexual victimization among military personnel was similar to the incidence of sexual victimization in the U.S. population. Morral and Gore (2014) estimated that around 20,000 active-duty military personnel (1 percent) were sexually assaulted in the past year, out of 1,317,561 soldiers. Among these incidents, 43 percent of sexual assaults against women and 35 percent of sexual assaults against men were considered to be penetrative sexual assaults. Morral and Gore (2014) argued that instances of sexual assault in the military were on the decline; this may be due to the emphasis on crimes in this setting over the last several years. While there has been more reporting of sex crimes in the military over the last several years, the Department of Defense (2020) indicated that the reports of unwanted sexual contact increased from 2019 to 2020 by 1 percent; this increase occurred for both male and female victims.

Rape in Prisons and Correctional Facilities

Even criminals who have been sentenced to correctional facilities are not immune from sexual victimization. The public believes that **prison rape**, or rape in correctional settings, is very prevalent. The idea of prison rape is so ingrained in the cultural zeitgeist, movies and television shows shot within correctional settings often display acts of sex crimes against inmates; at a minimum most movies and television shows staged in prison allude to sex crimes even if it is not shown directly. The idea of prison rape in film is so pervasive that academic work has even looked at images of male rape in prison movies (Eigenberg and Baro, 2003). Additionally, the idea of prison rape is a punchline in many jokes and a trope used by comedians. But how prevalent is sexual victimization in correctional facilities?

Without empirical data, Weiss and Friar (1974) indicated that male prison rape was a rampant phenomenon. This claim has not been supported by the majority of the research conducted since. For instance, Kreinert and Fleisher's (2005) interviews of 533 inmates across the United States indicated that a majority of inmates had never been sexually assaulted, did not ever witness a sexual assault, or have firsthand knowledge of prison rape. Despite this fact, the vast majority of inmates believed prison rape was prevalent throughout their respective prisons. One inmate, when confronted about the fact that he had never seen a rape, known a victim, or an offender, was asked how he could suggest that 70 percent of inmates were raped. The inmate responded, "Hey, rape got to be happening somewhere" (Kreinert and Fleisher, 2005, p. 5). Kreinert and Fleisher (2005) concluded that "prison rape has its own logic that creates its own reality" (p. 5).

It is clear that rape and the fear of rape are a "defining characteristic of the prison experience" (Eigenberg and Baro, 2003, p. 57). Prison rape undoubtedly occurs; we simply do not know the extent of prison rape. In 2003, Congress passed the Prison Rape Elimination Act (PREA). PREA was designed to decrease the incidence of sexual assaults in prison, jails, and juvenile correctional facilities. The fundamental belief of legislators was that rape in prison is unacceptable, even if the public could care less about the victims due to the fact that they are criminals. Judges sentence criminals to be punished, not to be raped. Those in prison who have been raped have little recourse; there are no rape crisis hotlines or counselors, inmates are rarely believed over correctional officers, and correctional officers can extend prison sentences by writing false reports for violations of prison rules. Those who support PREA believe that addressing sexual assault in prison will decrease the likelihood that an inmate will engage in violent crime upon release from prison.

One of the key features of PREA is an emphasis on collecting data about the incidence of sex crimes in prison. According to PREA, sexual assault in prison takes on three dimensions: the rape of inmates by other inmates, the rape of inmates by correctional officers (usually consensual encounters, but still a sex offense due to the power dynamic), and the rape of correctional officers by inmates. Beck, Rantala, and Rexroat (2014) indicated that correctional administrators from prisons and jails reported 8,763 allegations of sexual victimization in 2011; this figure has been increasing since 2005. In 2018, reports of sexual victimization in adult prisons had increased to 18,884 allegations; this was three and a half times as many reports as in 2012 (Maruschak and Buehler, 2021). Only 9 percent (1,673) of the allegations in 2018 were substantiated. Most reports of sexual victimizations involved staff on inmate; the remainder of sex crimes involved an inmate on inmate event. Beck et al. (2014) illustrated in inmate-on-inmate encounters that around 44 percent of victimizations included force or the threat of force, 18 percent of victimizations resulted in physical injury, and 7 percent of victimization resulted in major physical injury. While males were the predominant victim (females only account for 7 percent of all state and federal correctional institution populations), females were sexually victimized by other inmates in 22 percent of reported sexual victimizations and victimized by correctional staff in 33 percent of all reported cases. What is most interesting is that female correctional staff were responsible for more than a quarter of all staff-on-inmate sexual victimizations. Correctional staff rarely used threats of physical force or abuse of power (only 20 percent of all cases). The most likely outcome for correctional officers who sexually victimized inmates was job termination (85 percent of cases) and arrest and prosecution (56 percent of cases).

Human Trafficking and Sex Offenses

Human trafficking has received a great deal of attention over the last 20 years. Based on this attention, criminal justice agencies across the world have had to respond to this growing form of crime. **Human trafficking** is the illegal movement of individuals for the purposes of either commercial sexual exploitation (prostitution) or forced labor. Both of these infringe on an individual's rights against slavery. The acts involved with human trafficking are tantamount to kidnapping, even if the victim goes along willingly at first, and enslavement. Human trafficking is linked to poverty, migration patterns, political unrest, and societal beliefs about gender. We are most concerned here with the forcing of individuals into prostitution and sexual exploitation. Every sexual encounter of the victim with a john (client of a prostitute) is a count of rape.

Due to the relative "newness" of human trafficking, the FBI did not start collecting data on human trafficking in the UCR until 2013. The FBI (2015a) collects information on human trafficking in relation to commercial sex acts and involuntary solitude. The FBI (2020) defined human trafficking/commercial sex acts as "inducing a person by force, fraud, or coercion to participate in sex acts, or in which the person induced to perform such act(s) has not attained the age of 18 years of age" (p. 1). Across 27 states in 2014, the FBI reported that there were 295 incidents of commercial sex acts of human trafficking in the United States. Offenders who were arrested for these crimes were mostly male, White, and over the age of 18. As of 2019, most states are reporting human trafficking data to the FBI (2020). In 2019, there were 1,883 incidents of human trafficking, 1,607 of these incidents were commercial sex acts. There has been a steady increase in these offenses since 2014. Unfortunately, this information does not tell us much. The study of human trafficking is still in the early stages. Only time will help us to better understand and combat this crime in the future.

Revenge Porn

One of the most recently emerging forms of sex crime that has surfaced is predicated on advancements in technology of the Internet and cell phones, especially in relation to the cameras on cell phones. Sharing nude pictures has become common in relationships. When relationships end, this may result in hurt feelings, and the nude pictures, generally of the female partner, are an avenue to gain some level of retribution by disseminating the pictures to others across the Internet. **Revenge porn** is the "distribution of sexually explicit images of an individual where at least one of the individuals depicted did not consent to the dissemination" (Bloom, 2014, p. 237). Revenge porn is named after ex-boyfriends or ex-husbands, generally scorned, who post pictures of their former girlfriends/wives online for retribution through humiliation. The vast majority of cases involve females as the victims of this behavior; victims are generally also threatened and intimidated by third parties and their ex-partners. Bloom (2014) indicated that revenge porn can cause problems for the victims in their work lives and can lead to either suicide or attempts at suicide.

Because revenge porn is such a new phenomenon, there are multiple issues for the criminal justice system, victims, and researchers trying to address the relatively new crime type. First, in many places revenge porn is not necessarily a crime. Because the victim gave the pictures to their ex voluntarily, it is difficult for statutes to deal with the dissemination of the images. Second, law enforcement officers do not know how to deal with revenge porn. Many victims have reported that police officers "snickered" or looked amused when they reported the revenge porn. Oftentimes, law enforcement will note there is nothing they can do until a "crime" has occurred.

As of 2019, 41 states and the District of Columbia have revenge porn criminal statutes; no federal criminal statute exists for revenge porn. For the most part, revenge porn is not a criminal offense. Revenge porn is generally defined under the banner of cyberstalking, cyber harassment, blackmail, voyeurism, violation of privacy, or hacking. Victims of revenge porn in most states largely have two other legal options to revenge porn: copyright law or civil lawsuit. Either option takes a great deal of money and time; neither of these legal avenues is a guarantee of satisfaction to the victim due to the fact that once an image has been posted on the Internet, it is very difficult to remove.

Currently, the study of revenge porn is still in its developmental phase, especially since many of the criminal laws are new. It will be years before we fully understand the nature of revenge porn. The media reports that 50 percent of surveyed respondents reported sending intimate pictures to significant others; 10 percent noted that they had been threatened with the posting of intimate pictures online and the majority of these threats resulted in dissemination of the images (Bloom, 2014, p. 238).

THEORIES OF SEX OFFENDING

Why do sex offenders engage in sex crimes? As we have seen, this is not a simple question due to the fact that sex offenders are a heterogeneous group, sex offenses take on a myriad of behaviors, and there are many rationales for why sex offenders do what they do. Criminological theories of sociological background are largely ill-equipped to deal with sex offending behaviors. The only criminological theories capable of explaining sex crimes at some level are rational choice, biological, social learning, and routine activities.

Holmes and Holmes (2009b) suggested the use of a variety of theoretical paradigms to aid in explaining sex offending behavior. Psychodynamic theories offer psychological rationales for engaging in sex offenses and sexual deviance; these theories evaluate the impact of family-based explanations for explaining sex offending. Biological theories examine abnormal biological processes; an imbalance of hormone levels is an example of a correlate of some sex crimes. Feminist theories suggest sex offenses are a function of maintaining male supremacy within a society; this means sex offenses originate culturally, not individually. Social bond theories, including attachment, examine the lack of attachments/relationships in early childhood through teenage years and how this leads to sex offending; those with poor attachments are more likely to engage in sex crimes. Psychosocial theories posit an interaction between psychological and sociological factors in explaining the incidence of sex crimes. Sociobiological theories examine how the mix of an individual's biology and social environment leads to sex offending. Finally, integrated theories attempt to combine the above theories due to the fact that singular theories do not explain all forms of sex offending. These types of theories hold the most promise for explaining sex offending.

Most of the theoretical work on sex offenders has largely been applied to male sex offenders. Little work has been completed on theories of female sex offending. Harris (2010) outlined several theories to account for female sex offenders. The easiest manner of filling a void in theory for sex offenders is to simply utilize the male-oriented theories outlined above. Harris (2010) also indicated that female sex offending theories should emphasize childhood victimization, coercion by a co-offender, cognitive distortions (techniques of neutralization), background factors (family environment, abusive experiences, and lifestyle outcomes), and vulnerability.

Theoretical development on the etiology of sex offending is a work in progress. In general, there have been some commonalities amongst this line of inquiry. Terry (2013) indicated that most theories suggest a relationship between sex offending and "poor social skills, low self-esteem, misperception of social cues, and rationalization of behavior" (p. 69). Like other research on sex offenders, further theoretical development is needed to aid in our understanding of sex offenders and sex crimes.

CONCLUSION

Chapter 1 evaluated the nature of sex crimes in the United States. In particular, we examined official data sources (UCR and NCVS) that give us a picture of sex crimes in the United States, the characteristics of sex offenders, various environments where sex crimes occur, and theories attempting to explain sex offending. From this introductory chapter, it is readily apparent that there are many problems present in our search to fully understand sex offenders and their behaviors. As a concluding remark, Stinson et al. (2008) noted "we still know relatively little about what drives these individuals to commit such unusual sexual acts" (p. 4).

In this book, we summarize the current state of research on sex offenders. This book is designed to examine sex offenders and sex crimes in a comprehensive fashion. This book presents the etiology of sex offending and how the criminal justice system in America deals with the threat of sex offenders. The next section provides an overview of the chapters contained in this book.

SCOPE OF THIS BOOK

Most textbooks on sex offenders tend to focus on either the etiology of sex crimes or acts of sexual deviance that may or may not be considered criminal behavior; generally, both are not emphasized in the same book. This textbook focuses on the etiology of sex crimes, but also provides a discussion of sexual deviance. In addition, this book evaluates the treatment of sex offenders within the criminal justice system. Not only are these criminals considered to be heinous by the vast majority of society members, but these types of offenders pose unique challenges for the criminal justice system. As such, exploring sex offenders within a criminal justice context adds an important dimension to the discussion of sex crimes. This book is separated into 14 chapters. This first chapter has provided you with an overall examination of the incidence and nature of sex crimes in the United States.

The next four chapters evaluate the behaviors associated with sex crimes. Chapter 2 provides a discussion of criminal laws that determine which behaviors are criminal and which are not. Criminal law explicitly determines which actions are criminalized sex acts, the intent behind those actions, and the punishments associated with the violation of these crimes. Not all sex behavior that is out of the norm is considered to be a crime. Sexual deviance examines the gray area of some types of sexual behavior. Sometimes sexually deviant acts are criminal, while other sexually deviant acts are not. It is important to distinguish between behaviors that are sex crimes and behaviors that are merely sexually deviant. Chapter 3 evaluates sexual deviance. After we distinguish between sexual behavior that is criminal and deviant, we then discuss the two predominant forms of sex crimes: rape and sex offenses against children. Chapter 4 focuses on the crime of rape and Chapter 5 examines sex offenses against children; Chapters 4 and 5 both provide full explorations of these primary forms of sex offenses.

As already illustrated, sex offenders are a unique group of offenders. Nowhere is this more apparent than the impact of sex crimes on victims. Chapter 6 evaluates victim experiences with sex crimes. In particular, Chapter 6 emphasizes the nature and incidence of sex offense victimization, theories of victimization, and the many impacts sex offenses have on victims, both physical and psychological. In addition, Chapter 6 evaluates societal responses to the victims of sex offenses.

The remainder of the chapters focus on the treatment of sex offenders within the criminal justice system. Chapter 7 explores the issues that law enforcement has with investigating sex offenses. Issues for police officers range from a lack of reporting to determining the merits of a case before sending it to prosecutors. As you will see, sex crimes are different from most other forms of crime as police officer decisions will determine whether a case is founded or unfounded. Once the case has been founded by the police, the case is then sent to the prosecutor. Chapter 8 examines the court processing of sex offenders. Because sex offenders have all of the rights that other criminals have, sex offenders can pose a unique challenge for judicial processing. Chapter 8 evaluates the challenges posed by sex offenders to the courts. Once a sex offender has been convicted of a crime, the correctional system will handle the punishment. Chapter 9 examines the punishments sex offenders may receive if they are convicted of a sex crime. Chapter 9 focuses on the use of incarceration for sex offenders, but also examines the use of castration for sex offenders and the now abandoned use of capital punishment to deal with sex offenders.

The most important misperception about sex offenders is that they are likely to reoffend; in essence sex offenders do nothing but commit sex crimes and criminal justice system efforts do not have an impact on sex crimes. The idea of sex offender recidivism is the topic of Chapter 10. Chapter 10 explores the nature of sex offender recidivism in relation to other types of crime and illustrates why societal perceptions of sex offender recidivism are likely wrong. Misperceptions about sex offender recidivism impact the policies that are utilized against sex offenders. Chapter 11 examines the registration of sex offenders and community notification about sex offenders' whereabouts. Chapter 12 explores two policies aimed at sex offenders: residence restrictions and civil commitments. Residence restrictions limit where sex offenders can live in a community, and civil commitments are used to "incarcerate" sex offenders after their prison sentence is ended. The policies we evaluate in Chapters 11 and 12 are exclusive to sex offenders; no other criminal types get this treatment. Chapter 13 focuses on the treatment of sex offenders and whether sex offenders can actually be "cured."

Chapter 14 examines the future of sex crimes, society, and the criminal justice system. Chapter 14 provides conclusions and suggestions on how sex offenders should be handled by the criminal justice system. For the most part, the study and treatment of sex offenders are greatly hampered by poor conceptualization. Society, the criminal justice system, and academics largely use the term sex offender as a sweeping generalization that covers a wide range of behaviors; this is a mistake as will be seen across the chapters in this book. Likewise, Chapter 14 evaluates where future research, treatment, and other policies should go to help us better understand and contain the threat of sex offenders.

As with Chapter 1, examples of sex offenders and sex crimes reported in the press will serve as an introduction to our chapter discussions. Generally, these chapters will include at least one example of a sex offense or offender that is related to a given chapter topic. These examples tend to be exceptional as typical sex offense cases do not get much media attention. The types of cases for which enough information is available to provide an example receive a great deal of media attention precisely because they are not typical. They are cases that involve high-profile victims or offenders, or unusual circumstances. Each of these cases will provide elements that are useful to understanding the type of sex offense in general, but they are also useful in pointing out differences between these cases and a typical sex offense.

KEY TERMS

date rape
empirical studies
female juvenile sex offenders
female sex offenders
grooming
hierarchy rule
human trafficking
incest
index crimes
juvenile sex offenders
NCANDS
NCVS
official data sources
prison rape
recidivism
revenge porn
sex offender
sex offense
statutory rape
Type I offenses
Type II offenses
UCR

EXERCISES

1. Examine the various sources of information on sex crimes in the United States. How do each of these sources differ? What do the statistics say about sex crime in the United States?
2. Discuss the problems associated with both the UCR and the NCVS. Based on these problems, how valid are the data about sex crimes?
3. Discuss the characteristics of sex offenders who have been arrested and processed through the criminal justice system. Should we be concerned with female and juvenile sex offenders? Support your answer.
4. Select one of the various areas sex crimes occur that are inconsistent with the general myth that sex offenders are strangers and prey on women or children.

What were your thoughts before you read Chapter 1? Are your views on sex crimes changed?

5. Outline the various theoretical paradigms to account for sex offending. Describe each.

ESSAY QUESTION

Find the statistics for sex offenses in the state and city in which you currently reside. These data might be found at a state crime information center, the state police, or department of public safety. How do these statistics relate to the federal level statistics discussed in Chapter 1? How do your state sex crime statistics compare to your city crime statistics?

2

SEX CRIMES AND THE LAW

Chapter Objectives

After reading this chapter, students will be able to:

- Identify the earliest legal forms of sex offenses.
- Evaluate key legal concepts.
- Understand the nature of criminal law.
- Evaluate the various types of codified sex crimes.
- Differentiate between rape, sexual assault, and sexual battery.
- Examine the etiology of sexual harassment law.

INTRODUCTION

When the term sex crime is uttered, most individuals have a pretty clear idea of what these types of behaviors entail. If one begins to examine the nature of sex crimes, it quickly becomes apparent that there is a very subjective nature to the sex behaviors that become criminalized under the law, especially if sex crimes are evaluated across time. The earliest recorded set of legal statutes is the Code of Hammurabi. Hammurabi was the king of Babylon, the world's first metropolis, from 1795–1750 B.C. Hammurabi publicly provided his people with an entire body of laws to identify acceptable and unacceptable behaviors (Horne, 1915). These laws were inscribed on an eight-foot tall, black stone monument that was in clear public view (Horne, 1915).

The Code of Hammurabi outlined many types of behavior that were unacceptable in Babylon. The Code also identified several sex crimes. The sex offenses, and their punishments, were:

> **[127] If any one "point the finger" (slander) at a sister of a god or the wife of any one, and cannot prove it, this man shall be taken before the judges and his brow shall be marked (by cutting the skin, or perhaps hair).**
>
> **[128] If a man take a woman to wife, but have no intercourse with her, this woman is no wife to him.**
>
> **[129] If a man's wife be surprised (in flagrante delicto) with another man, both shall be tied and thrown into the water, but the husband may pardon his wife and the king his slaves.**
>
> **[130] If a man violate the wife (betrothed or child-wife) of another man, who has never known a man, and still lives in her father's house, and sleep with her and be surprised, this man shall be put to death, but the wife is blameless.**
>
> **[131] If a man bring a charge against one's wife, but she is not surprised with another man, she must take an oath and then may return to her house.**
>
> **[132] If the "finger is pointed" at a man's wife about another man, but she is not caught sleeping with the other man, she shall jump into the river for her husband.**
>
> **[154] If a man be guilty of incest with his daughter, he shall be driven from the place (exiled).**
>
> **[155] If a man betroth a girl to his son, and his son have intercourse with her, but he (the father) afterward defile her, and be surprised, then he shall be bound and cast into the water (drowned).**
>
> **[156] If a man betroth a girl to his son, but his son has not known her, and if then he defile her, he shall pay her half a gold mina, and compensate her for all that she brought out of her father's house. She may marry the man of her heart.**
>
> **[157] If any one be guilty of incest with his mother after his father, both shall be burned.**
>
> **[158] If any one be surprised after his father with his chief wife, who has borne children, he shall be driven out of his father's house.**

Most of the crimes examined in the Code of Hammurabi are largely crimes against societal norms. These crimes include slander, failing to have sex with one's wife, incest, adultery, and false charges of adultery. The punishments for these crimes range from corporal punishment (physical violence) to death. Note that there is no mention of rape, sexual assault, or sex offenses against children, with the exception of incest.

Sex crimes can also be found in the Bible. The Bible identifies adultery and coveting thy neighbor's wife in the Ten Commandments as offenses. Additionally, other areas of the Old Testament list adultery, bestiality, homosexuality, incest, lying about virginity, marrying both a woman and her daughter, masturbation, prostitution, rape, and sexual intercourse with a father's wife as unacceptable behaviors. Again, most of these "sexual crimes" listed in the Bible tend to be violations of social norms and are likely to result in execution or physical violence. "Sex crimes" in the Bible, for the most part, are not what we typically think of as sex crimes today. Generally, the "offense" was more of a violation of religious or societal norms. While social taboos have historically informed the creation of criminal laws, this merging of informal and formal laws leads to subjectivity in legal statutes. For instance, Jenkins (2004) noted that many acts have been considered illegal throughout time: abortion, anal sex (sodomy), bestiality, certain sexual positions/techniques, contraception, homosexuality, interracial relationships, masturbation, oral sex, and sex between those who are not married. Most of these behaviors are no longer considered to be criminal in the United States and most other places.

Before we can discuss how sex offenders are treated by the criminal justice system, we must first examine what behaviors constitute sex crimes. Chapter 2 evaluates the various sex crimes across the United States. In particular, we provide examples of criminal statutes that criminalize various forms of sexual behavior and explain those behaviors by examining the key elements of sex offenses outlined by the various criminal codes. The punishments associated with these sex crimes are also evaluated here. The next section of Chapter 2 provides a review of law and the criminal law in the United States.

THE NATURE OF CRIMINAL LAW

Law is a set of formalized rules that delineate acceptable and unacceptable behaviors for a population. There are many forms of law; criminal, civil (tort), administrative, military, and maritime are just some of the many legal areas. Criminal law is only one facet of the law. While there may be victims associated with a crime, the state is the plaintiff. Inherently, **criminal law** involves public wrongs where the state initiates the action (via a prosecutor), the potential punishment is loss of liberty or life, a unanimous verdict is required, and the proof must be beyond a reasonable doubt. The burden of proof in proving a crime rests with the prosecution/state. The very foundation of law is to deter individuals from engaging in unacceptable behaviors.

Under criminal law, certain behaviors that are detrimental to a society are defined as criminal; a behavior cannot be a crime without a criminal law. The goals of criminal law are allowing for individuals to peacefully coexist with each another, defining problematic behaviors, outlining the method of determining guilt, and identifying the method of punishment. Criminal law indicates specific unacceptable behaviors and prescribes the appropriate punishments for a given act. In reality, it is the punishment that separates criminal law from all other forms of law. Under criminal law, the punishment can include the loss of liberty (by being sent to either prison or jail) or loss of life (execution). All other forms of law provide primarily for monetary punishments for misbehavior. The punishment of sex offenses will be discussed more in depth in later chapters.

The two underlying concepts of the criminal law are *actus reus* and *mens rea*. For an action to be a crime, both must be present during the commission of the crime. ***Actus reus*** refers to the criminal act (or omission). For an action to be criminal, an individual has to act in a criminal fashion. A murderer must in fact murder someone. While this will undoubtedly seem like common sense, it is one of the technicalities that criminal law must address if a person is to be held accountable for their criminal acts. All actions that are criminal are outlined in statutory schemes. Additionally, failing to act (**omission**) can make an individual just as guilty as if they had committed the act themselves. If an individual is aware of a crime that is going to occur, but does not warn the authorities or potential victims, they will be held accountable for their lack of action by the criminal justice system.

Individual actions can be nuanced. For instance, is murder always wrong? The answer to this question is no. The taking of another's life is largely acceptable under certain situations. For example, if one is trying to protect themselves or another individual, they might have to take someone else's life; this concept is known as self-defense and is an affirmative defense in a court of law. Thus, just engaging in an action that is criminal is not enough to convict an individual under the criminal law. The criminal law has to evaluate the *mens rea* of an individual. ***Mens rea*** refers to the criminal mindset or intent of the individual. It is not enough that a person killed someone else, the person had to have the intention to kill the other person to be charged with murder. This can mean the difference between capital murder, first degree murder, second degree murder, or some level of manslaughter as the criminal charge. *Mens rea* is established through terms like purposively, knowingly, recklessly (indifference), or negligently (failure to perform a duty owed by the person charged) engaging in a particular behavior.

Criminal laws can be evaluated across two typologies. First, crimes can be considered to be either *male en se* or *mala prohibita*. ***Mala en se*** crimes are behaviors that are largely considered to be wrong in and of themselves; these types of crimes have a certain moral authority that comes from a society. Crimes like murder and theft are looked down upon by the vast majority of society members and would constitute examples of *mala en se* crimes. Alternatively, ***mala prohibita*** crimes are behaviors that are only considered to be bad because of the existence of a law against such behaviors. For instance, marijuana use is largely met with indifference by most members of society, however, it is still a criminalized behavior under the federal and most state criminal codes. The fact that marijuana is becoming legalized in many states illustrates the dynamic quality of *mala prohibita* crimes. Other examples of *mala prohibita* laws include gambling, prostitution, public intoxication, carrying concealed weapons, and tax evasion.

The second way we can classify criminal laws is by how serious the offense is considered to be. The criminal law can be dichotomized as felonies or misdemeanors. Felonies are more serious crimes and misdemeanors are less serious crimes. How we distinguish between the seriousness of crimes is how these behaviors are punished under the law. For the most part, **felonies** are crimes that are punishable by more than one year of imprisonment, most likely time served in a prison facility. **Misdemeanors** are crimes that are punishable by less than one year of imprisonment, time served in a jail. These are not the only punishments for those who have been convicted of felonies and misdemeanors will receive; this is just the acceptable way to differentiate the two types of crimes.

The primary forms of criminal law are statutes (codes) and cases. Statutory law is largely a function of legislative bodies but can be influenced by the executive at either the federal or state levels. The judiciary determines case law. Criminal law, both statutory and case, is a balance between the two models of crime control (protection of society) and due process (individual rights). **Crime control** deals with protecting society from criminals, whereas **due process** attempts to protect the accused's rights to ensure fairness in the case. Nowhere is this balance between crime control and due process more contentious than for individuals accused of sex crimes. Generally, these individuals have committed abhorrent offenses, yet even with the need to protect society, these individuals are innocent until proven guilty. Sex offenders, like other criminals, are afforded the same due process rights as every other type of criminal. The next section focuses on sex behaviors that have been criminalized across the Unites States.

SEX OFFENSES IN THE CRIMINAL LAW

Sex offenses represent only a fraction of the entirety of criminal law. For our purposes, a **sexual offense** is any "offense involving unlawful sexual conduct, such as prostitution, indecent exposure, incest, pederasty, and bestiality" (Garner, 2000, p. 887). As will be seen below, sexual offenses are generally violent offenses.

This section provides examples of statutory laws pertaining to sex offenses. This discussion includes verbatim laws from actual statutes and evaluates the elements of the sex offenses. To give a broad picture of the types of sex offenses, we use examples across the many state and the federal criminal codes. We omit the crimes of kidnapping, false imprisonment, stalking, and exposing another person to HIV; under current criminal justice policies, these crimes are often conflated with sex offenses. These will be discussed later in relation to current sex offender policies. We begin our discussion of sex offenses in the law with an analysis of the crime of rape, the most recognized sex offense.

Rape

Rape is the most recognizable sex offense; most other sex offenses are largely variants on the act of rape. According to Garner (2000), **rape**, in general, is defined as:

> 1. At common law, unlawful sexual intercourse committed by a man with a woman not his wife through force and against her will. Under common law, slight penetration of the vagina is required to be rape and a husband could not rape his wife; 2. Unlawful sexual activity with a person (usually a female) without consent and use by force or threat of injury. Under this conception, marital status does not matter and neither does gender when it comes to defining rape (p. 1,014).

Garner also categorized the act of rape by acquaintances, dates, spouses (marital rape), and age (statutory rape). These various types of rape are discussed more in Chapter 4 when we fully explore the topic of rape in the United States.

One example of the crime of rape comes from the Arkansas Criminal Code (2010; §5-14-103). In Arkansas:

> **(a) A person commits rape if he or she engages in sexual intercourse or deviate sexual activity with another person:**
>
> **(1) By forcible compulsion;**

> **(2) Who is incapable of consent because he or she is:**
> **(A) Physically helpless;**
> **(B) Mentally defective; or**
> **(C) Mentally incapacitated;**
> **(3) (A) Who is less than fourteen (14) years of age.**
> **(B) It is an affirmative defense to a prosecution under subdivision (a)(3)(A) of this section that the actor was not more than three (3) years older than the victim; or**
> **(4) (A) Who is a minor and the actor is the victim's:**
> **(i) Guardian;**
> **(ii) Uncle, aunt, grandparent, step-grandparent, or grandparent by adoption;**
> **(iii) Brother or sister of the whole or half blood or by adoption; or**
> **(iv) Nephew, niece, or first cousin.**
> **(A) It is an affirmative defense to a prosecution under subdivision (a)(4)(A) of this section that the actor was not more than three (3) years older than the victim.**
> **(b) It is no defense to a prosecution under subdivisions (a)(3) or (4) of this section that the victim consented to the conduct.**
> **(c)(1) Rape is a Class Y felony.**
> **(2) Any person who pleads guilty or nolo contendere to or is found guilty of rape involving a victim who is less than fourteen (14) years of age shall be sentenced to a minimum term of imprisonment of twenty-five (25) years.**
> **(d)(1) A court may issue a permanent no contact order when:**
> **(A) A defendant pleads guilty or nolo contendere; or**
> **(B) All of the defendant's appeals have been exhausted and the defendant remains convicted.**
> **(1) If a judicial officer has reason to believe that mental disease or defect of the defendant will or has become an issue in the case, the judicial officer shall enter such orders as are consistent with 5-2-305.**

The key elements of rape in Arkansas include sexual intercourse, deviate sexual intercourse, the use of force, victims incapable of consent (mentally handicapped or minors), the relationship between the victim and the offender, and the inclusion of a three-year age gap for sexual relations. Sexual intercourse or deviate sexual intercourse include oral, anal, or vaginal penetration; these terms are fully defined in another area of the Arkansas Criminal Code. The age gap of three years is to distinguish between legitimate relationships between teenagers where one of the individuals is a little older than the other. This is known as a Romeo and Juliet clause in the law to avoid improper prosecutions of legitimate relationships. An individual does not have to be guilty of every action denoted in the above statute, just one of the subcategories. While the punishment range in Arkansas for Class Y Felonies is listed elsewhere, the statute does indicate that those offenders who are found guilty of raping a victim under the age of 14 will get no less than 25 years in prison.

Some states do not use the term rape when charging individuals. Rather, terms like sexual assault, sexual battery, and sexual abuse can be used interchangeably with rape. In *Black's Law Dictionary*, Garner (2000) defined **sexual assault** as:

> 1. Sexual intercourse with another person who does not consent. In some states, the terms sexual assault has replaced the crime of rape; 2. Offensive sexual contact with another person, exclusive of rape. Examples of this include if the victim is mentally handicapped or if the offender has drugged the victim (p. 88).

Even in Garner's definition, he notes the close linkage between rape and sexual assault. This generic definition of sexual assault does denote "offensive sexual contact" which can include behaviors like groping.

In the Nebraska Criminal Code (28-319), a person commits sexual assault in the first degree if:

> **(1) Any person who subjects another person to sexual penetration (a) without the consent of the victim, (b) who knew or should have known that the victim was mentally or physically incapable of resisting or appraising the nature of his or her conduct, or (c) when the actor is nineteen years of age or older and the victim is at least twelve but less than sixteen years of age is guilty of sexual assault in the first degree.**
>
> **(2) Sexual assault in the first degree is a Class II felony. The sentencing judge shall consider whether the actor caused serious personal injury to the victim in reaching a decision on the sentence.**
>
> **(3) Any person who is found guilty of sexual assault in the first degree for a second time when the first conviction was pursuant to this section or any other state or federal law with essentially the same elements as this section shall be sentenced to a mandatory minimum term of twenty-five years in prison.**

For first degree sexual assault in Nebraska, the offense description is similar to the description of rape in Arkansas. The elements of sexual assault in Nebraska are sexual penetration, lack of consent, and victims incapable of consent. In addition, Nebraska stipulates a six-year gap in age between the victim and the offenders (a so-called Romeo and Juliet clause) and denotes a minimum 25-year prison sentence for those twice convicted of sexual assault.

In the Nebraska Criminal Code (28-320), a person commits sexual assault in the second or third degree if:

> **(1) Any person who subjects another person to sexual contact (a) without consent of the victim, or (b) who knew or should have known that the victim was physically or mentally incapable of resisting or appraising the nature of his or her conduct is guilty of sexual assault in either the second degree or third degree.**
>
> **(2) Sexual assault shall be in the second degree and is a Class III felony if the actor shall have caused serious personal injury to the victim.**
>
> **(3) Sexual assault shall be in the third degree and is a Class I misdemeanor if the actor shall not have caused serious personal injury to the victim.**

Second or third degree sexual assault in Nebraska is a function of the amount of injury a victim sustained during the sexual assault and knowledge of if the victim was mentally capable of resisting/consenting to the sexual assault.

Similar to sexual assault, sexual battery involves forced penetration of a victim. Garner (2000) noted that **sexual battery** is the "forced penetration or contact with another's sexual organs or the organs of the sexual perpetrator" (p. 119). This crime is also often used interchangeably with rape.

An example of sexual battery comes from the state of Florida. In Florida (794.011), sexual battery is noted as:

> **794.011 Sexual battery.—**
>
> **(1) As used in this chapter:**
>
> **(a) "Consent" means intelligent, knowing, and voluntary consent and does not include coerced submission. "Consent" shall not be deemed or**

2

construed to mean the failure by the alleged victim to offer physical resistance to the offender.

(b) "Mentally defective" means a mental disease or defect which renders a person temporarily or permanently incapable of appraising the nature of his or her conduct.

(c) "Mentally incapacitated" means temporarily incapable of appraising or controlling a person's own conduct due to the influence of a narcotic, anesthetic, or intoxicating substance administered without his or her consent or due to any other act committed upon that person without his or her consent.

(d) "Offender" means a person accused of a sexual offense in violation of a provision of this chapter.

(e) "Physically helpless" means unconscious, asleep, or for any other reason physically unable to communicate unwillingness to an act.

(f) "Retaliation" includes, but is not limited to, threats of future physical punishment, kidnapping, false imprisonment or forcible confinement, or extortion.

(g) "Serious personal injury" means great bodily harm or pain, permanent disability, or permanent disfigurement.

(h) "Sexual battery" means oral, anal, or vaginal penetration by, or union with, the sexual organ of another or the anal or vaginal penetration of another by any other object; however, sexual battery does not include an act done for a bona fide medical purpose.

(i) "Victim" means a person who has been the object of a sexual offense.

(j) "Physically incapacitated" means bodily impaired or handicapped and substantially limited in ability to resist or flee.

(2)(a) A person 18 years of age or older who commits sexual battery upon, or in an attempt to commit sexual battery injures the sexual organs of, a person less than 12 years of age commits a capital felony, punishable as provided in ss. 775.082 and 921.141.

(b) A person less than 18 years of age who commits sexual battery upon, or in an attempt to commit sexual battery injures the sexual organs of, a person less than 12 years of age commits a life felony, punishable as provided in s. 775.082, s. 775.083, s. 775.084, or s. 794.0115.

(3) A person who commits sexual battery upon a person 12 years of age or older, without that person's consent, and in the process thereof uses or threatens to use a deadly weapon or uses actual physical force likely to cause serious personal injury commits a life felony, punishable as provided in s. 775.082, s. 775.083, s. 775.084, or s. 794.0115.

(4)(a) A person 18 years of age or older who commits sexual battery upon a person 12 years of age or older but younger than 18 years of age without that person's consent, under any of the circumstances listed in paragraph (e), commits a felony of the first degree, punishable by a term of years not exceeding life or as provided in s. 775.082, s. 775.083, s. 775.084, or s. 794.0115.

(b) A person 18 years of age or older who commits sexual battery upon a person 18 years of age or older without that person's consent, under any of the circumstances listed in paragraph (e), commits a felony of the first degree, punishable as provided in s. 775.082, s. 775.083, s. 775.084, or s. 794.0115.

(c) A person younger than 18 years of age who commits sexual battery upon a person 12 years of age or older without that person's consent, under any of the circumstances listed in paragraph (e), commits a felony of the first degree, punishable as provided in s. 775.082, s. 775.083, s. 775.084, or s. 794.0115.

(d) A person commits a felony of the first degree, punishable by a term of years not exceeding life or as provided in s. 775.082, s. 775.083, s. 775.084, or s. 794.0115 if the person commits sexual battery upon a person 12 years of age or older without that person's consent, under any of the circumstances listed in paragraph

(e), and such person was previously convicted of a violation of:

1. Section 787.01(2) or s. 787.02(2) when the violation involved a victim who was a minor and, in the course of committing that violation, the defendant committed against the minor a sexual battery under this chapter or a lewd act under s. 800.04 or s. 847.0135(5);

2. Section 787.01(3)(a)2. or 3.;

3. Section 787.02(3)(a)2. or 3.;

4. Section 800.04;

5. Section 825.1025;

6. Section 847.0135(5); or

7. This chapter, excluding subsection (10) of this section.

(e) The following circumstances apply to paragraphs (a)-(d):

1. The victim is physically helpless to resist.

2. The offender coerces the victim to submit by threatening to use force or violence likely to cause serious personal injury on the victim, and the victim reasonably believes that the offender has the present ability to execute the threat.

3. The offender coerces the victim to submit by threatening to retaliate against the victim, or any other person, and the victim reasonably believes that the offender has the ability to execute the threat in the future.

4. The offender, without the prior knowledge or consent of the victim, administers or has knowledge of someone else administering to the victim any narcotic, anesthetic, or other intoxicating substance that mentally or physically incapacitates the victim.

5. The victim is mentally defective, and the offender has reason to believe this or has actual knowledge of this fact.

6. The victim is physically incapacitated.

7. The offender is a law enforcement officer, correctional officer, or correctional probation officer as defined in s. 943.10(1), (2), (3), (6), (7), (8), or (9), who is certified under s. 943.1395 or is an elected official exempt from such certification by virtue of s. 943.253, or any other person in a position of control or authority in a probation, community control, controlled release, detention, custodial, or similar setting, and such officer, official, or person is acting in such a manner as to lead the victim to reasonably believe that the offender is in a position of control or authority as an agent or employee of government.

(5)(a) A person 18 years of age or older who commits sexual battery upon a person 12 years of age or older but younger than 18 years of age, without that person's consent, and in the process does not use physical force and violence likely to cause serious personal injury commits a felony of the first degree, punishable as provided in s. 775.082, s. 775.083, s. 775.084, or s. 794.0115.

(b) A person 18 years of age or older who commits sexual battery upon a person 18 years of age or older, without that person's consent, and in the process does not use physical force and violence likely to cause serious personal injury commits a felony of the second degree, punishable as provided in s. 775.082, s. 775.083, s. 775.084, or s. 794.0115.

(c) A person younger than 18 years of age who commits sexual battery upon a person 12 years of age or older, without that person's consent, and in the process does not use physical force and violence likely to cause serious personal injury commits a felony of the second degree, punishable as provided in s. 775.082, s. 775.083, s. 775.084, or s. 794.0115.

(d) A person commits a felony of the first degree, punishable as 775.082, s. 775.083, s. 775.084, or s. 794.0115 if the person commits sexual battery upon a person 12 years of age or older, without that person's consent, and in the process does not use physical force and violence likely to cause serious personal injury and the person was previously convicted of a violation of:

1. Section 787.01(2) or s. 787.02(2) when the violation involved a victim who was a minor and, in the course of committing that violation, the defendant committed against the minor a sexual battery under this chapter or a lewd act under s. 800.04 or s. 847.0135(5);
2. Section 787.01(3)(a)2. or 3.;
3. Section 787.02(3)(a)2. or 3.;
4. Section 800.04;
5. Section 825.1025;
6. Section 847.0135(5); or
7. This chapter, excluding subsection (10) of this section.

(6)(a) The offenses described in paragraphs (5)(a)-(c) are included in any sexual battery offense charged under subsection (3).

(b) The offense described in paragraph (5)(a) is included in an offense charged under paragraph (4)(a).

(c) The offense described in paragraph (5)(b) is included in an offense charged under paragraph (4)(b).

(d) The offense described in paragraph (5)(c) is included in an offense charged under paragraph (4)(c).

(e) The offense described in paragraph (5)(d) is included in an offense charged under paragraph (4)(d).

(7) A person who is convicted of committing a sexual battery on or after October 1, 1992, is not eligible for basic gain-time under s. 944.275. This subsection may be cited as the "Junny Rios-Martinez, Jr. Act of 1992."

(8) Without regard to the willingness or consent of the victim, which is not a defense to prosecution under this subsection, a person who is in a position of familial or custodial authority to a person less than 18 years of age and who:

(a) Solicits that person to engage in any act which would constitute sexual battery under paragraph (1)(h) commits a felony of the third degree, punishable as provided in s. 775.082, s. 775.083, or s. 775.084.

(b) Engages in any act with that person while the person is 12 years of age or older but younger than 18 years of age which constitutes sexual battery under paragraph (1)(h) commits a felony of the first degree, punishable by a term of years not exceeding life or as provided in s. 775.082, s. 775.083, or s. 775.084.

(c) Engages in any act with that person while the person is less than 12 years of age which constitutes sexual battery under paragraph (1)(h), or in an attempt to commit sexual battery injures the sexual organs of such person commits a capital or life felony, punishable pursuant to subsection (2).

(9) For prosecution under paragraph (4)(a), paragraph (4)(b), paragraph (4)(c), or paragraph (4)(d) which involves an offense committed under any of the circumstances listed in subparagraph (4)(e)7., acquiescence to a person reasonably believed by the victim to be in a position of authority or control does not constitute consent, and it is not a defense that the perpetrator was not actually in a position of control or authority if the circumstances were such as to lead the victim to reasonably believe that the person was in such a position.

(10) A person who falsely accuses a person listed in subparagraph (4)(e)7. or other person in a position of control or authority as an agent or employee of government of violating paragraph (4)(a), paragraph (4)(b), paragraph (4)(c), or paragraph (4)(d) commits a felony of the third degree, punishable as provided in s. 775.082, s. 775.083, or s. 775.084.

It should be noted that the Florida Statute for sexual battery is more comprehensive than the statutes in Arkansas (rape) and Nebraska (sexual assault). Unlike the previous examples, the Florida Statute defines key terms within the statute itself. The key elements of sexual battery in Florida include lack of consent, penetration (oral, anal, or vaginal), the use of a sexual organ or other object for sexual penetration, and an age-gap between the victim and the offender (Romeo and Juliet clause).

Sexual Assault on a Child

Rape is something that can occur to any individual. Most legislative bodies have moved to regard rape on minors as a separate and more heinous offense due to the victim's immaturity or inability to protect him/herself. In previous eras, even in the United States, it was common for individuals to be married by the age of 12. This began to change in the late nineteenth century through the Child Savers Movement. During this movement, children began to gain a newfound status. Up to this point, children who committed a crime or were victimized were treated like adults. The Child Savers Movement resulted in greater protections for minors and specialized punishments for juvenile offenders; this movement resulted in the creation of the juvenile justice system in the United States.

The first suggestion that child sexual abuse is the most pervasive form of sex offense occurred in 1894 (Logue, 2012b). In the late 1800s, almost half of the states raised the age of consent from the lower teens to between 16 and 18 years of age. This resulted in the creation of statutory rape, child molestation and child sex abuse laws. Garner (2000) indicated that **child abuse** was the "act or series of acts of physically or emotionally injuring a child. Child abuse may be intentional (as with sexual molestation)" (p. 8). Garner (2000) defined **child molestation** as "any indecent or sexual activity on, involving, or surrounding a child, usually under the age of 14" (p. 817). Two other forms of child sex abuse are sexual abuse and pederasty. **Sexual abuse** (also known as **carnal abuse** and **child cruelty**) is defined by Garner (2000) as "An illegal sex act, especially one performed against a minor by an adult" (p. 8). In some states, the term sexual abuse has also replaced the concept of rape. **Pederasty** is "anal intercourse between a man and a boy" (Garner, 2000, p. 924).

As noted above, many states use sex offense terms interchangeably to criminalize certain forms of behavior. Like the crime of rape, states use many different terms to criminalize child sexual abuse. Primarily, these include sexual assault on a minor, unlawful sexual conduct with a minor, and sexual misconduct with a minor. An example of child sexual assault is provided by the Wisconsin Criminal Code. In Wisconsin, sexual assault pertains to only minors (in the above example, sexual assault was a synonym for rape).

> **(1) First degree sexual assault.**
>
> **(a) Whoever has sexual contact or sexual intercourse with a person who has not attained the age of 13 years and causes great bodily harm to the person is guilty of a Class A felony.**
>
> **(b) Whoever has sexual intercourse with a person who has not attained the age of 12 years is guilty of a Class B felony.**

> **(c) Whoever has sexual intercourse with a person who has not attained the age of 16 years by use or threat of force or violence is guilty of a Class B felony.**
>
> **(d) Whoever has sexual contact with a person who has not attained the age of 16 years by use or threat of force or violence is guilty of a Class B felony if the actor is at least 18 years of age when the sexual contact occurs.**
>
> **(e) Whoever has sexual contact or sexual intercourse with a person who has not attained the age of 13 years is guilty of a Class B felony.**
>
> **(2) SECOND DEGREE SEXUAL ASSAULT. Whoever has sexual contact or sexual intercourse with a person who has not attained the age of 16 years is guilty of a Class C felony.**
>
> **(3) FAILURE TO ACT. A person responsible for the welfare of a child who has not attained the age of 16 years is guilty of a Class F felony if that person has knowledge that another person intends to have, is having or has had sexual intercourse or sexual contact with the child, is physically and emotionally capable of taking action which will prevent the intercourse or contact from taking place or being repeated, fails to take that action and the failure to act exposes the child to an unreasonable risk that intercourse or contact may occur between the child and the other person or facilitates the intercourse or contact that does occur between the child and the other person.**

Sexual assault in Wisconsin revolves around victims who are under the age of 13. The elements of child sexual abuse in Wisconsin include sexual contact, sexual intercourse, great bodily harm, and includes multiple caveats for various ages. Most importantly, this statute includes a discussion of those who fail to act to protect victims from sexual assault.

Another example of child sexual assault can be found in the Ohio Criminal Code; in Ohio, the crime is referred to as unlawful **sexual misconduct** with a minor.

> **2907.04 Unlawful sexual conduct with minor.**
>
> **(A) No person who is eighteen years of age or older shall engage in sexual conduct with another, who is not the spouse of the offender, when the offender knows the other person is thirteen years of age or older but less than sixteen years of age, or the offender is reckless in that regard.**
>
> **(B) Whoever violates this section is guilty of unlawful sexual conduct with a minor.**
>
> **(1) Except as otherwise provided in divisions (B)(2), (3), and (4) of this section, unlawful sexual conduct with a minor is a felony of the fourth degree.**
>
> **(2) Except as otherwise provided in division (B)(4) of this section, if the offender is less than four years older than the other person, unlawful sexual conduct with a minor is a misdemeanor of the first degree.**
>
> **(3) Except as otherwise provided in division (B)(4) of this section, if the offender is ten or more years older than the other person, unlawful sexual conduct with a minor is a felony of the third degree.**
>
> **(4) If the offender previously has been convicted of or pleaded guilty to a violation of section 2907.02, 2907.03, or 2907.04 of the Revised Code or a violation of former section 2907.12 of the Revised Code, unlawful sexual conduct with a minor is a felony of the second degree.**

The key element of this crime is that no individual who is 18 or older shall engage in sexual relations with another person when the offender is cognizant that the other person is 13 but less than 16. This statute contains a Romeo and Juliet provision (four years older). Age difference also matters in terms of the degree of the felony.

Another term used synonymously with child sexual abuse is sexual misconduct with a minor. The example below comes from the state of Washington.

RCW 9A.44.093—Washington State

Sexual misconduct with a minor in the first degree.

(1) A person is guilty of sexual misconduct with a minor in the first degree when: (a) The person has, or knowingly causes another person under the age of eighteen to have, sexual intercourse with another person who is at least sixteen years old but less than eighteen years old and not married to the perpetrator, if the perpetrator is at least sixty months older than the victim, is in a significant relationship to the victim, and abuses a supervisory position within that relationship in order to engage in or cause another person under the age of eighteen to engage in sexual intercourse with the victim; (b) the person is a school employee who has, or knowingly causes another person under the age of eighteen to have, sexual intercourse with an enrolled student of the school who is at least sixteen years old and not more than twenty-one years old and not married to the employee, if the employee is at least sixty months older than the student; or (c) the person is a foster parent who has, or knowingly causes another person under the age of eighteen to have, sexual intercourse with his or her foster child who is at least sixteen.

(2) Sexual misconduct with a minor in the first degree is a class C felony.

(3) For the purposes of this section:

(a) "Enrolled student" means any student enrolled at or attending a program hosted or sponsored by a common school as defined in RCW 28A.150.020, or a student enrolled at or attending a program hosted or sponsored by a private school under chapter 28A.195 RCW, or any person who receives home-based instruction under chapter 28A.200 RCW.

(b) "School employee" means an employee of a common school defined in RCW 28A.150.020, or a grade kindergarten through twelve employee of a private school under chapter 28A.195 RCW, who is not enrolled as a student of the common school or private school.

2

RCW 9A.44.096

Sexual misconduct with a minor in the second degree.

(1) A person is guilty of sexual misconduct with a minor in the second degree when: (a) The person has, or knowingly causes another person under the age of eighteen to have, sexual contact with another person who is at least sixteen years old but less than eighteen years old and not married to the perpetrator, if the perpetrator is at least sixty months older than the victim, is in a significant relationship to the victim, and abuses a supervisory position within that relationship in order to engage in or cause another person under the age of eighteen to engage in sexual contact with the victim; (b) the person is a school employee who has, or knowingly causes another person under the age of eighteen to have, sexual contact with an enrolled student of the school who is at least sixteen years old and not more than twenty-one years old and not married to the employee, if the employee is at least sixty months older than the student; or (c) the person is a foster parent who has, or knowingly causes another person under the age of eighteen to have, sexual contact with his or her foster child who is at least sixteen.

(2) Sexual misconduct with a minor in the second degree is a gross misdemeanor.

(3) For the purposes of this section:

(a) "Enrolled student" means any student enrolled at or attending a program hosted or sponsored by a common school as defined in RCW 28A.150.020, or a student enrolled at or attending a program hosted or sponsored by a private school under chapter 28A.195 RCW, or any person who receives home-based instruction under chapter 28A.200 RCW.

(b) "School employee" means an employee of a common school defined in RCW 28A.150.020, or a grade kindergarten through twelve employee of a private

school under chapter 28A.195 RCW, who is not enrolled as a student of the common school or private school.

[2009 c 324 §2; 2005 c 262 §3; 2001 2nd sp.s. c 12 §358; 1994 c 271 §307; 1988 c 145 §9.]

In Washington, victims of sexual misconduct with a minor are under the age of 18. The key element of the offense is sexual contact with an individual under the age of 18. The law includes caveats for foster parents, school employees, and relationships where there is a differential power dynamic at play; for instance, a grade school teacher and student sexual relationship or an employer-employee sexual relationship. In this scenario, victims may feel compelled to engage in the relationship for gain or maintain favor/benefit from the offender. Finally, the law also includes a Romeo and Juliet clause of five years.

Sexual Exploitation of a Child

At the end of the twentieth century, one of the more heinous sex offenses involved the creation and dissemination of child pornography, sometimes referred to as **child porn** or **kiddie porn**. It was 1977 when the Sexual Exploitation of Children Act made child pornography illegal. According to Garner (2000), **child pornography** is "material depicting a person under the age of 18 engaged in sexual activity. It is not protected under the First Amendment" (p. 947). Examples of child pornography include magazines, books, pictures, and images obtained over the Internet. Holmes and Holmes (2002b) argued that the purpose of child pornography was the sexual gratification of the viewer.

While there are statutes against child pornography at both the state and federal levels, it is the federal government that deals with most of these cases. The U.S. Code defines crimes associated with child pornography:

Child pornography

(a) Any person who employs, uses, persuades, induces, entices, or coerces any minor to engage in, or who has a minor assist any other person to engage in, or who transports any minor in or affecting interstate or foreign commerce, or in any Territory or Possession of the United States, with the intent that such minor engage in, any sexually explicit conduct for the purpose of producing any visual depiction of such conduct or for the purpose of transmitting a live visual depiction of such conduct, shall be punished as provided under subsection (e), if such person knows or has reason to know that such visual depiction will be transported or transmitted using any means or facility of interstate or foreign commerce or in or affecting interstate or foreign commerce or mailed, if that visual depiction was produced or transmitted using materials that have been mailed, shipped, or transported in or affecting interstate or foreign commerce by any means, including by computer, or if such visual depiction has actually been transported or transmitted using any means or facility of interstate or foreign commerce or in or affecting interstate or foreign commerce or mailed.

(b) Any parent, legal guardian, or person having custody or control of a minor who knowingly permits such minor to engage in, or to assist any other person to engage in, sexually explicit conduct for the purpose of producing any visual depiction of such conduct or for the purpose of transmitting a live visual depiction of such conduct shall be punished as provided under subsection (e) of this section, if such parent, legal guardian, or person knows or has reason to know that such visual depiction will

be transported or transmitted using any means or facility of interstate or foreign commerce or in or affecting interstate or foreign commerce or mailed, if that visual depiction was produced or transmitted using materials that have been mailed, shipped, or transported in or affecting interstate or foreign commerce by any means, including by computer, or if such visual depiction has actually been transported or transmitted using any means or facility of interstate or foreign commerce or in or affecting interstate or foreign commerce or mailed.

(c)

(1) Any person who, in a circumstance described in paragraph (2), employs, uses, persuades, induces, entices, or coerces any minor to engage in, or who has a minor assist any other person to engage in, any sexually explicit conduct outside of the United States, its territories or possessions, for the purpose of producing any visual depiction of such conduct, shall be punished as provided under subsection (e).

(2) The circumstance referred to in paragraph (1) is that—

(A) the person intends such visual depiction to be transported to the United States, its territories or possessions, by any means, including by using any means or facility of interstate or foreign commerce or mail; or

(B) the person transports such visual depiction to the United States, its territories or possessions, by any means, including by using any means or facility of interstate or foreign commerce or mail.

(d)

(1) Any person who, in a circumstance described in paragraph (2), knowingly makes, prints, or publishes, or causes to be made, printed, or published, any notice or advertisement seeking or offering—

(A) to receive, exchange, buy, produce, display, distribute, or reproduce, any visual depiction, if the production of such visual depiction involves the use of a minor engaging in sexually explicit conduct and such visual depiction is of such conduct; or

(B) participation in any act of sexually explicit conduct by or with any minor for the purpose of producing a visual depiction of such conduct;

shall be punished as provided under subsection (e).

(2) The circumstance referred to in paragraph (1) is that—

(A) such person knows or has reason to know that such notice or advertisement will be transported using any means or facility of interstate or foreign commerce or in or affecting interstate or foreign commerce by any means including by computer or mailed; or

(B) such notice or advertisement is transported using any means or facility of interstate or foreign commerce or in or affecting interstate or foreign commerce by any means including by computer or mailed.

(e) Any individual who violates, or attempts or conspires to violate, this section shall be fined under this title and imprisoned not less than 15 years nor more than 30 years, but if such person has one prior conviction under this chapter, section 1591, chapter 71, section 1591, chapter 71, chapter 109A, or chapter 117, or under section 920 of title 10 (article 120 of the Uniform Code of Military Justice), or under the laws of any State relating to aggravated sexual abuse, sexual abuse, abusive sexual contact involving a minor or ward, or sex trafficking of children, or the production, possession, receipt, mailing, sale, distribution, shipment, or transportation of child pornography, such person shall be fined under this title and imprisoned for not less than 25 years nor more than 50 years, but if such person has 2 or more prior convictions under this chapter, chapter 71, chapter 109A, or chapter 117, or under section 920 of title 10 (article 120 of the Uniform Code of Military Justice), or under the laws of any State relating to the sexual exploitation of children, such person shall be fined under this title and imprisoned not less than 35 years nor more than life. Any organization that violates, or attempts or conspires to violate, this section shall be fined under this title. Whoever, in the course of

> **an offense under this section, engages in conduct that results in the death of a person, shall be punished by death or imprisoned for not less than 30 years or for life.**

The key elements of the federal statute for child pornography include foreign or interstate commerce (to address shipping or the use of the Internet to disseminate illicit materials), minors, sexually explicit conduct, the role of parents/guardians, and the use of computers. Most importantly, the statute calls for fines and a 15- to 30-year prison sentence for first time offenders. For those with a prior criminal conviction for child pornography, the prison sentence will be between 25 and 50 years. If the offender has two or more prior convictions for child pornography, the prison sentence will be between 35 years and life.

Incest

Another form of sexual offense that tends to include children is incest. Garner (2000) defined **incest** as "sexual relations between family member or close relatives, including children related by adoption. This offense was not a crime under English common law" (p. 610). As noted above, historically, incest was policed by religious institutions (like the church). One example of incest comes from the Alabama Criminal Code.

> **Section 13A-13-3**
>
> **Incest.**
>
> **(a) A person commits incest if he marries or engages in sexual intercourse with a person he knows to be, either legitimately or illegitimately:**
>
> **(1) His ancestor or descendant by blood or adoption; or**
>
> **(2) His brother or sister of the whole or half-blood or by adoption; or**
>
> **(3) His stepchild or stepparent, while the marriage creating the relationship exists; or**
>
> **(4) His aunt, uncle, nephew or niece of the whole or half-blood.**
>
> **(b) A person shall not be convicted of incest or of an attempt to commit incest upon the uncorroborated testimony of the person with whom the offense is alleged to have been committed.**
>
> **(c) Incest is a Class C felony.**
>
> **(Acts 1977, No. 607, p. 812, §7010.)**

Incest in Alabama pertains to sexual relations between the offender and ancestors, sibling (full, half-blood, or adoption), stepchildren/parent, and aunts/uncles/nephews/nieces. The offense requires corroboration and cannot be based simply on one party's word.

Prostitution

Another form of sex offense outlined in criminal codes is prostitution. **Prostitution** is defined as the "act or practice of engaging in sexual activity for money or its equivalent; commercialized sex" (Garner, 2000, p. 992). Many do not consider prostitution to be a sex crime. Rather, it is more of an economic crime in the sense that services are paid for and then rendered. Throughout history, prostitution has been legal. Since sexual behavior is associated with this crime, we include here an example from the Vermont Criminal Code.

> **§ 2632. Prohibited acts**
> **(a) A person shall not:**
> **(1) Occupy a place, structure, building or conveyance for the purpose of prostitution, lewdness or assignation;**
> **(2) Knowingly permit a place, structure, building or conveyance owned by the person or under the person's control to be used for the purpose of prostitution, lewdness or assignation;**
> **(3) Receive or offer, or agree to receive, a person into a place, structure, building or conveyance for the purpose of prostitution, lewdness or assignation;**
> **(4) Permit a person to remain in a place, structure, building or conveyance for the purpose of prostitution, lewdness or assignation;**
> **(5) Direct, take or transport or offer or agree to take or transport a person to a place, structure, building or conveyance or to any other person knowingly, or with reasonable cause to know that the purpose of such directing, taking or transporting is prostitution, lewdness or assignation;**
> **(6) Procure or solicit or offer to procure or solicit a person for the purpose of prostitution, lewdness or assignation;**
> **(7) Reside in, enter or remain in a place, structure or building or enter or remain in a conveyance for the purpose of prostitution, lewdness or assignation;**
> **(8) Engage in prostitution, lewdness or assignation; or**
> **(9) Aid or abet prostitution, lewdness or assignation, by any means whatsoever.**
> **(b) A person who violates a provision of subsection (a) of this section shall be fined not more than $100.00 or may be imprisoned not more than one year. For a second offense such person shall be imprisoned for not more than three years. (Amended 2001, No. 49, §14, eff. June 12, 2001.)**

The key elements of prostitution allow the prosecution of those who perpetrate street prostitution, brothel prostitution, escort services, and massage parlors. The law does not distinguish between the **"johns"** (patrons of prostitutes) and the prostitutes themselves. The punishment in Vermont for prostitution is no more than a $100 fine and no more than one year of confinement.

Indecent Exposure

Several forms of sex offense require no physical contact between the victim and the offender. The first of these is indecent exposure. **Indecent exposure** is defined as an "offensive display of one's body in public, especially of the genitals (also known as exposure of person)" (Garner, 2000, p. 616). In the Idaho Criminal Code, indecent exposure is criminalized as:

> **Every person who willfully and lewdly, either:**
> **(1) Exposes his or her genitals, in any public place, or in any place where there is present another person or persons who are offended or annoyed thereby; or,**
> **(2) Procures, counsels, or assists any person so to expose his or her genitals, where there is present another person or persons who are offended or annoyed thereby is guilty of a misdemeanor.**
> **Any person who pleads guilty to or is found guilty of a violation of subsection (1) or (2) of this section or a similar statute in another state or any local jurisdiction**

for a second time within five (5) years, notwithstanding the form of the judgment(s) or withheld judgment(s), is guilty of a felony and shall be imprisoned in the state prison for a period not to exceed ten (10) years.

The elements of indecent exposure entail exposing a sexual organ to people who are "offended" or "annoyed." In addition to the individual exposing him/herself, this statute also includes those who procure, counsel, and assist an individual in exposing themselves. In relation to punishment, the first conviction of this crime is only a misdemeanor. All additional convictions are treated as felonies with prison terms increasing in five-year increments. In many states, the crime is more severe if a minor witnesses the indecent exposure.

Voyeurism

A sex crime similar to indecent exposure is voyeurism. As with indecent exposure, voyeurism does not entail direct or physical contact between the victim and the offender. **Voyeurism** is the act of observing another person in the act of undressing or some kind of sexual act. In the Louisiana Criminal Code, the crime of voyeurism is outlined as:

A. Voyeurism is the viewing, observing, spying upon, or invading the privacy of a person by looking through the doors, windows, or other openings of a private residence without the consent of the victim who has a reasonable expectation of privacy for the purpose of arousing or gratifying the sexual desires of the offender.

B. (1) Whoever commits the crime of voyeurism, upon a first conviction, shall be fined not more than five hundred dollars, imprisoned for not more than six months, or both.

(2) Upon a second or subsequent conviction, the offender shall be fined not more than one thousand dollars, imprisoned with or without hard labor for not more than one year, or both.

The State of Louisiana defines voyeurism as observing or invading the privacy of another in a residence with the intent of sexual gratification. The penalty for the first offense is a fine of $500 or less and/or six months or less in jail. As with the act of indecent exposure, the first crime is treated as a misdemeanor; subsequent convictions are treated as felonies. The penalty for a subsequent offense is a fine of $1,000 or less and/or imprisonment of one year or less.

Bestiality

One of the most disturbing sex crimes revolves around sexual relations with animals. **Bestiality** is the act of having sexual intercourse with an animal. An example of a criminal law against bestiality comes from the South Dakota Criminal Code.

§22-22-42 Bestiality — Acts constituting — Commission a felony.

22-22-42. Bestiality — Acts constituting — Commission a felony. No person, for the purpose of that person's sexual gratification, may:

(1) Engage in a sexual act with an animal; or

(2) Coerce any other person to engage in a sexual act with an animal; or

(3) Use any part of the person's body or an object to sexually stimulate an animal; or

(4) Videotape a person engaging in a sexual act with an animal; or
(5) Kill or physically abuse an animal.

Any person who violates any provision of this section is guilty of the crime of bestiality. Bestiality is a Class 6 felony. However, if the person has been previously convicted of a sex crime pursuant to § 22-24B-1, any subsequent violation of this section is a Class 5 felony.

Source: SL 2003, ch 127, §1; SL 2005, ch 120, §406.

The elements of bestiality include sexual acts with animals, coercion of others to engage in sexual acts with animals, videotaping acts of bestiality, and killing or physically abusing an animal for the purpose of sexual gratification. The crime of bestiality in South Dakota is a felony.

Sexual Relations with a Corpse

Another of the more disturbing sex offenses denoted in criminal law is sexual acts with dead bodies. **Necrophilia** is an attraction to dead bodies that may result in sexual intercourse with that dead body. An example of a necrophilic act is found in the Nevada Criminal Code under sexual penetration of a dead body.

2

1. A person who commits a sexual penetration on the dead body of a human being is guilty of a category A felony and shall be punished by imprisonment in the state prison for life with the possibility of parole, with eligibility for parole beginning when a minimum of 5 years has been served, and shall be further punished by a fine of not more than $20,000.

2. For the purposes of this section, "sexual penetration" means cunnilingus, fellatio or any intrusion, however slight, of any part of a person's body or any object manipulated or inserted by a person into the genital or anal openings of the body of another, including, without limitation, sexual intercourse in what would be its ordinary meaning if practiced upon the living.

The elements of sexual penetration of a dead body in Nevada are sexual penetration, dead body, and human being. To be convicted of sexual penetration of a dead body the offender must sexually penetrate a human corpse. The punishment for sexual penetration of a dead body in Nevada is a minimum of five years in prison with a potential fine of not more than $20,000.

Sexual Harassment

The #MeToo and Time's Up movements have brought the concept of sexual harassment to the forefront of consideration for sex offenses and associated behaviors. While not a criminal act, sexual harassment is correlated with sex offending in part due to recent high-profile cases. The most prominent cases involved Harvey Weinstein and Bill Cosby. In both instances, the sexual harassment led directly to sexual offending. Unwanted touching, physical intimidation, and extreme forms of coercion will be handled by the criminal law, generally as some form of sexual assault; in these instances, victims should contact the police. Even though sexual harassment is not a crime, the close association with sexual offending leads to its discussion here. Garner (2000) defines sexual harassment as a "type of employment discrimination consisting in verbal or physical abuse of a sexual nature" (p. 117). There are two forms of sexual harassment: hostile work environment and quid pro quo. In hostile work environment sexual harassment, "an employee is subject to unwelcome verbal or sexual behavior that is either severe or pervasive" (Garner, 2000, p. 117). Garner provides the example of an employee who sends pornographic emails to a colleague at the company who finds such content offensive. According to Garner (2000), quid pro quo sexual harassment occurs when "the satisfaction of a sexual demand is used as the basis of an employment decision" (p. 117). Garner (2000) provides the example of an employer/boss/manager firing or demoting an employee/subordinate for refusing to go out on a date with the employer/boss/manager. Neither form of sexual harassment is a crime.

The primary law that protects individuals from sexual harassment is Title VII of the Civil Rights Act of 1964. Since Title VII is too large to reprint here, we will outline the key parts of the law. The most common forms of discrimination under Title VII are: disparate treatment, disparate impact, mixed motive discrimination, retaliation, and creation of a hostile work environment. Title VII prohibits sexual discrimination specifically; this includes sexual harassment (it should be noted that the term "sexual harassment" is not mentioned in the law itself). Title VII also outlaws retaliation against employees who have filed a Title VII claim. An employee who makes a sexual harassment claim becomes a member of a protected group as the direct result of an adverse employment practice/decision.

Title VII claims need to be followed up with an official complaint to the Equal Employment Opportunity Commission (EEOC) or equivalent state agency. This must occur before any cases can be brought in court. Under the EEOC, claims can be made for: sexual advances; requests for sexual favors; any verbal conduct of a sexual nature; any physical conduct of a sexual nature; written/verbal sexual conduct; and vulgar, crude, and/or sexist language. According to the EEOC, harassers or victims can be male or female. The harasser can be the victim's supervisor, an agent of the employer, a supervisor in a different department/area, a co-worker, and/or a non-employee (a vendor or customer for instance). A victim does not have to be the individual harassed; the victim is simply anyone affected by the conduct in question. A claim of sexual harassment does not require the victim to be terminated from employment or to have sustained some economic injury. Under the EEOC, the harasser's conduct only has to be unwelcome. In most instances, claims to the EEOC must be made within six months from the last discriminatory incident or adverse action.

Sexual harassment is notoriously difficult to prove in courts. The key evidence in these cases tends to be the accounts of the accuser and the accused. As well, accusers are required to provide employers with the opportunity to address and/or cure the problem. In cases where the employer is on notice, or should have had notice, that an employee was engaging in potential sexual harassment, the victim does not have to provide notice. Despite the difficulties in court, a sexual harassment claim under Title VII does have practical consequences. First, the anti-retaliation feature of Title VII can protect employees under federal and state (see next paragraph) laws. Retaliation will serve as new claims should they occur. Second, any claims are part of the public record. Thus, all claims made against an individual will follow that individual no matter the outcome of the case.

While Title VII is the primary mechanism for dealing with sexual harassment, many states have laws that can be used against sexual harassment specifically or to protect employees generally. According to Bloomberg Law, most states either have a specific law against sexual discrimination/harassment in the workplace or are covered under preexisting fair employment laws. Several states are now working on legislation to prohibit the use of non-disclosure agreements (NDAs) in cases involving sexual harassment; this legislation would also mandate training on sexual harassment in workplaces. With the recent emphasis on high profile sexual harassment cases, these types of laws will continue to evolve over the next decade

CONCLUSION

Chapter 2 has examined sex crimes within the context of the criminal law. Today, most behaviors that are considered to be sex offenses have been identified across the various legal codes, both federal and state. In general, most new laws that go into effect in relation to sex offenses further clarify the *mens rea* associated with sex crimes. For instance, in California in September of 2014, the legislature passed the "yes means yes" law. The standard for convicting a criminal of rape had been if the victim said no at any point during the sexual intercourse. This standard has resulted in ambiguity in prosecuting sex offenders. In California, the new standard requires ongoing affirmative consent from both (or more) parties engaging in a sexual act. The affirmative consent can be withdrawn at any point during sexual intercourse. This law also noted that affirmative consent cannot be given if one party is intoxicated (alcohol or drugs) or asleep/incapacitated.

As was seen at the beginning of Chapter 2, actions and behaviors that are considered to be sex offenses have a temporal quality to them. All sexual behaviors have a subjective quality. Whether the behavior is acceptable or unacceptable is linked to social norms. If the behavior varies enough from societal norms, the behavior will likely be criminalized. If not, the behavior may be treated as some form of deviance. Deviance is handled more by social institutions. Sexually deviant acts are those behaviors that occur at the crossroads between sex crimes and culturally accepted norms.

Chapter 3 examines behaviors that are sexually deviant. These actions can be criminal or simple norm violations. Even if these behaviors are crimes, they are much more likely to go unreported to the criminal justice system than the crimes outlined in Chapter 2.

KEY TERMS

actus reus
bestiality
carnal abuse
child abuse
child cruelty
child molestation
child porn
child pornography
crime control

criminal law
due process
felonies
incest
indecent exposure
johns
kiddie porn
law
mala en se
mala prohibita
mens rea
misdemeanors
necrophilia
omission
pederasty
prostitution
rape
sexual abuse
sexual assault
sexual battery
sexual misconduct
sexual offense
voyeurism

EXERCISES

1. Explain the relationship between rape, sexual assault, and sexual battery. In the state in which you reside, which term is used in the statutory code?
2. Discuss the goals of law. How do laws about sex crimes meet these goals?
3. Identify and explain the sex offenses where there is no physical contact between the victim and the offender.
4. Explain the relationship between felonies and misdemeanors. What is the importance of the differences between the two types of crime?
5. Discuss the legal topic of sexual harassment. Should it be included within the framework of criminal law? Why or why not?

ESSAY QUESTIONS

1. For the state in which you reside, collect all the sex crimes codified by law. Discuss the *actus reus*, the *mens rea*, the elements of the offense, and any punishments denoted in the statutes.
2. Select either child pornography, prostitution, or voyeurism, and respond to the following questions. Is the crime you selected *male en se* or *mala prohibita*? Why do you think so? What type of penalty do you think would be appropriate for this crime, and why?
3. How are the sex-related offenses listed in the Code of Hammurabi similar to and different from the sex offenses discussed in Chapter 2? What offenses are in the Code of Hammurabi that are not discussed as crimes today? What offenses are crimes today that were not listed in the Code of Hammurabi?

3

SEXUAL DEVIANCE

Chapter Objectives

After reading this chapter, students will be able to:

- Understand the concept of deviance.
- Identify the different forms of sexual deviance.
- Explain the etiology of the various forms of sexual deviance.
- Evaluate the research findings on sexual deviance.
- Explain the term paraphilia.

INTRODUCTION

In Chapter 2, we explored sexual behavior that was classified as criminal (sex offenses). It is criminal law that defines certain behaviors to be criminal and other behaviors to be not criminal. In the end, criminal law is rule-breaking behavior at its core. Criminal activities are a specialized form of rule-breaking due to the fact that the sanctions associated with criminal acts can be extensive. At the top end, someone who has been convicted of a criminal act can lose his/her life (execution) or his/her liberty (prison or jail time). Criminal law does not encompass the full range of rules that are applied to humans. We encounter many other types of rules on a daily basis. These can include rules associated with jobs, school, religion, or other informal groups. Across the various groups, instituted policies and **norms** tend to regulate individual interactions. Sanctions for breaking rules in any of these groups is nothing as intensive as sanctions in the criminal justice system, yet can sometimes have a greater impact. Take the following example.

Beginning in 2020, U.S. Representative Matt Gaetz (R-Florida) came under investigation for a relationship with an underage woman (17 years old) and whether his involvement with another young woman violated federal sex trafficking and prostitution laws. This investigation stemmed from the investigation of another Florida politician. Congressman Gaetz has denied the allegations. While these acts are still under investigation, other aspects of the story pertain directly to sexual deviance.

When politicians find themselves in political crises, it is common for other politicians from their respective political parties to come to their defense. One of the few times this does not occur is in instances involving criminality, generally, and sex offenses, specifically. For Gaetz, a few of his Republican colleagues came to his defense; the vast majority of his colleagues remained silent, almost ostracizing him. One of the reasons for this was widely reported to be linked to Gaetz's behavior. Allegedly, Gaetz had a history of showing fellow lawmakers photos/videos of naked women with whom he claimed to have had sexual relationships. One such video showed a nude woman gyrating with a hula hoop. Gaetz even shared these images on the floor of the House of Representatives. While some have suggested the lack of support for Gaetz stemmed from his image as a firebrand, it has been reported that the showing of the sexted images was likely the real reason. Gaetz's actions were viewed as deviant to most of his colleagues.

An action that violates societal or group norms is considered deviant. A deviant act, sometimes referred to as a faux pas, is an act that is not congruent with a situation or in a particular group setting. Like criminality, **deviance** is rule-breaking behavior, but sanctions for deviant acts tend to be more informal. While no loss of liberty or life are associated with responses to deviance, the sanctions can still have dramatic effects on individuals.

Deviance, especially in the realm of sexual behavior, often overlaps with criminality (see the case of Matt Gaetz, above). Chapter 3 evaluates other forms of sexual behavior that may be sex offenses, deviant, or some combination of the two. What is important about these particular actions is that the behavior is largely punished through informal mechanisms. In particular, Chapter 3 discusses the history and nature of the study of the sociology of deviance. We then evaluate the primary forms of sexual deviance and research on each category of sexual deviance.

DEVIANCE

The study of criminology is largely based on the study of deviance. In fact, most criminological theories attempt to explain deviance in addition to criminality (Higgins and Butler, 1982). Best (2004) noted the term deviance did not emerge until after World War II, stemming from the attempt to merge statistical analysis and sociological theory. Before World War II, many terms for deviance were employed to explain rule-breaking behavior: anomie, degeneracy, psychopathology, social problems, and even criminology (Best, 2004). Many statistics attempt to evaluate the mean, or average. What is crucial in statistical analyses is how individuals differ from the mean. Individuals who differ from the mean can be said to deviate from the average. In fact, one of the key statistics used in statistical analyses is termed standard deviation. It was only a matter of time before this term would be used to examine societal norms and values by sociologists and criminologists.

Erikson (1986) noted the lack of behavioral boundaries for the study of deviance. As such, definitions of deviance differ dramatically. This has led to many definitions of deviance across the field of sociology/criminology. Clinard (1968) defined deviance as

> A violation of certain types of group norms; a deviant act is a behavior which is proscribed in a certain way... Only those deviations in which behavior is in a disapproved direction and of sufficient degree to exceed the tolerance limit of the community constitute deviant behavior (p. 28).

Dinitz, Dynes, and Clark (1969) defined deviance as "the departure of certain types of behavior from the norms of a particular society at a particular time" (p. 4). Matza (1969) defined deviance as "to stray (deviate) as from a path or standard" (p. 10). Higgins and Butler (1982) defined deviance as "behavior, ideas, or attributes of an individual(s) which some, though not necessarily all, people in a society find wrong, bad, crazy, disgusting, strange, immoral—in other words offensive" (p. 2). Tittle and Paternoster (2000) stated that deviance indicated behaviors that are socially disapproved. What is common across definitions of deviance is that they indicate norm or rule violations. According to Liska (1987), these "definitions shift attention from deviance as a pattern of behavior to deviance as a social definition or label which some people used to describe the behavior of others" (p. 2).

3

While there are commonalities across definitions of deviance, Liska (1987) noted that "the commonality underlying deviant behaviors is difficult to identify" (p. 1). Liska (1987) indicated that the study of norm violations "refers to the study of behavior which violates social rules and of the individuals who violate them" (p. 2); this can include violation of all rules of social behavior including both socially harmful behavior and "relatively innocuous behavior." Behaviors can range from homicide to nose picking. In addition, rule violations are evaluated in relation to most members of society and rule violation by small groups of individuals/organizations (Liska, 1987). Norms, then, are only a reference point; normative change is not the focus of the study of deviance. Liska (1987) argued that deviance as a social definition should be evaluated by two questions: (1) What is labeled deviance? and (2) Who is labeled deviant?

Erikson (1986) argued that deviants violate rules of conduct that are highly respected by the rest of the public. As the community comes together in solidarity to admonish and/or punish the deviant, the group necessarily forms a tighter bond of solidarity. Erikson (1986) suggested that deviance "is not a property inherent in any particular kind of behavior; it is a property conferred upon that behavior by the people who come into direct or indirect contact with it" (p. 6). Thus, learning about the individual deviant is meaningless; what is more important is to observe the standards/norms of the group responding to the deviant behavior.

Societies "create" crime by passing laws (Vold, Bernard, and Snipes, 2002). Laws are merely a society's reaction to behavior that is viewed as problematic. Societal responses include the minimization/elimination of troublesome behaviors via sanctions. Vold et al. (2002) argued that "campaigns to define and suppress deviance are always launched in the name of benefitting the whole of society, but they are often promoted and supported by those who benefit directly" (p. 220). Thus, deviant behavior is but one aspect of deviance; the overall reaction to the behavior is just as important.

Deviance is largely regulated by morals, norms, and values, but the determination of deviance through morals, norms, and values is subjective. Violation of these norms usually results in informal sanctions. Informal sanctions take on a myriad of forms. These types of sanctions can include staring, cursing, and loss of friends (among many types of reaction). Alternatively, criminality is regulated solely through the development, implementation, and maintenance of laws, especially criminal laws. Violation of criminal laws is more objective; those who violate the criminal law will be subject to formal sanctions that are established in the law. The primary forms of formal sanctions occur via institutional and community corrections (prison, probation, treatment, etc.).

For Tittle and Paternoster (2000), criminal behavior is a special form of conduct; it can encompass acts that are deviant or not deviant. They explored marijuana use in their work. Marijuana possession or distribution is against the law; however, most individuals in society do not view marijuana use negatively. Marijuana use can be treated formally (arrest, conviction, and punishment), informally (the drugs can be seized by police who then let the offender go), or some combination of both (drugs seized by the police but the offender is given a ticket for some lesser crime). Deviant behavior can be routine or it can be dramatic/exotic. Deviant behavior may be criminal or it may not. Likewise, criminal behavior is not always deviant. The two terms should never be treated as synonymous.

Lemert (1967) argued that deviance could be categorized as primary and secondary deviance. **Primary deviance** is the first deviant act that violates norms in which the individual does not consider him/herself to be a deviant. Prior to being caught in the act of deviance, any deviant act is inconsistent and infrequent (Kubrin, Stuckey, and Krohn, 2009). When an individual is caught, that individual is often labeled as deviant. Allegedly, this societal reaction to deviance begins to affect the individual's self-conception. A person who has been labeled by formal or informal sanctions may be pushed into behavior that is consistent with the label. Thus, the individual's deviant behavior changes in form and function: sporadic deviance can stabilize into more regular deviant behavior (Kubrin et al., 2009, p. 202). **Secondary deviance** is any deviant behavior that results from the imposition of a label. This behavior would likely not have occurred without the presence of the societal reaction via the label.

Tittle and Paternoster (2000) further classified the key forms of deviance with respect to middle-class values. They listed apostasy (betrayal of nation), intrusion (crime—rape, voyeurism, and record spying), indiscretion (prostitution, homosexual behavior, incest, bestiality, adultery, and swinging), bizarreness (mentally ill behavior), irresponsibility (violation of trust), alienation (unemployment and hermitry), hedonism (atheism and alcoholism), deceitfulness (selfishness), disruption (quarreling and boisterousness), and uncouthness (rudeness and private behavior in public places—nose picking, for instance).

Downes and Rock (1998) noted that the sociology of deviance is a collection of the key criminological theories (social disorganization, anomie/strain, subculture, labeling, control, and radical theories). They also indicated that deviance is ambiguous. "People are frequently undecided whether a particular episode is deviant or what true deviance is" (Downes and Rock, 1998, p. 4). Wilkins (1965) illustrated the subjective nature of deviance. Wilkins (1965) noted that due to the subjectivity associated with norms and conformity, "there are no absolute standards" when dealing with the concept of deviance. At some point, "some form of society or another has defined almost all forms of behavior that we now call 'criminal' as desirable for the functioning of that form of society" (p. 46). In addition, across various societies in existence today, criminal and deviant behavior are defined and treated in different ways. Legal definitions and cultural definitions of deviance determine the formality of sanctions associated with various forms of deviance. In the end, a "society in which a large proportion of the population regularly practice a given form of behavior will tend to permit the behavior and not define it as deviant" (Wilkins, 1965, p. 49).

Higgins and Butler (1982) suggested that all members of society engage in deviance to some degree or another. Because of this fact, they suggest that deviance is in fact integral to a functioning society. Nowhere is there a finer distinction in human behavior than in the area of sexual behavior. Many forms of sexual behavior do not rise to the level of criminal offending, but are definitely considered to be deviant.

Holmes and Holmes (2009b) addressed the idea of what normal sex is. Different people have different ideas about what is normal when it comes to sexual behaviors. Even a single individual's ideas about sexual behavior can change across different stages of the life course. Holmes and Holmes (2009b) used four criteria to determine the normalcy of sexual behavior. The first was the statistical standard; if more than 50 percent of the population practiced a certain sexual behavior, it can be considered normal. The second is the cultural standard; the concept of deviance is a function of the needs of society (friends, family, and educational or religious institutions). The third standard is religious normalcy, which varies depending on the importance of religion in a person's life. Religion dictates normal sexual behavior in this area. The fourth standard is arguably the most important: the subjective standard. The subjective standard works off all the former ways of establishing normal sexual behavior. Under this category, individuals need to know that what they are doing is in fact normal. All of these categories suffer from subjectivity. Sexual norms are not static, but change in time (Holmes and Holmes, 2009b). For instance, it was once common for females of the age of 12 to be married; in the classic play *Romeo and Juliet* by Shakespeare, Juliet was merely 13 years old, an age too young by modern standards in most industrialized countries. The next section examines the various forms of sexual deviance.

SEXUAL DEVIANCE

Sexual deviance is a specialized form of deviance that pertains to deviance associated with sexual behavior. Wiederman (2003) noted that whenever sexuality is involved, "issues of value judgment and what is acceptable versus unacceptable comes into play" (p. 321). Even though it is a subcategory of deviant behavior, sexual deviance is a large field of study. There are entire books dedicated to the subject. The primary question addressed in these sources is how we determine what sexual behaviors are deviant and which forms of sexual behavior are not deviant. The manner in which social scientists identify sexual behaviors to be deviant is through the use of the *Diagnostic and*

Statistical Manual of Mental Disorders (*DSM-5*) (now in its fifth edition). The *DSM-5* is compiled by the American Psychiatric Association, which addresses the full gamut of mental illnesses from eating disorders to depression to schizophrenia. The *DSM-5* indicates when behavior becomes so severe that it must be classified as a disorder.

Most importantly for our discussion, the *DSM-5* also evaluates sexual deviance or what it terms paraphilic disorders. Stekel (1924) first coined the term **paraphilia**, which translates as "loving something outside of the norm or love of the perverse" (Wiederman, 2003, p. 315). Today, paraphilia indicates "any intense and persistent sexual interest other than sexual interest in genital stimulation or preparatory fondling with phenotypically normal, physically mature, consenting human partners" (American Psychiatric Association, 2013, p. 1). Paraphilias can focus on erotic activities (spanking, for example) or on the erotic targets of individuals (interest in children, corpses, or animals). A paraphilic disorder can cause distress to an individual or can mean personal harm to others. Just because a person engages in a paraphilic act does not mean that the individual suffers from a paraphilic disorder.

The nine paraphilic disorders denoted by the *DSM-5* are exhibitionism, fetishism, frotteurism, pedophilia, sexual sadism, sexual masochism, transvestic fetishism, voyeurism, and paraphilias not otherwise specified. These disorders are not a complete list of paraphilic disorders because of the "or anything else" nature of paraphilias not otherwise specified. Overall, these disorders can be aggregated into two groups: (1) anomalous activity preferences (courtship disorders—voyeuristic, exhibitionistic, and frotteuristic disorders, and disorders involving pain and suffering—sexual masochism and sexual sadism disorders); and (2) anomalous target preferences (pedophilic, fetishistic, and transvestic disorders [American Psychiatric Association, 2013]). According to the *DSM-5*, it is common for individuals to suffer from two or more paraphilias. While there have been some changes to the *DSM-5*, mostly in relation to drug addiction, there have been no changes in definitions or substance of the sexual paraphilias. In all likelihood, any changes to these would not be introduced until the production of the *DSM-6*.

Before discussing the sexual paraphilias, a few more bits of information about paraphilias is warranted. First, paraphilias are largely male-oriented; but individuals from all races and socioeconomic statuses can suffer from paraphilic disorders (Wiederman, 2003). Second, most paraphiliacs do not become violent (Terry, 2013). Third, paraphilic acts rarely come to the attention of authorities due to the private nature of the acts, the involvement of strangers, the quick nature of the act, or victims not realizing they have been victimized (Terry, 2013). Finally, paraphilias must be distinguished between criminal offenses as language for both are commonly used interchangeably; to do so is erroneous. Terry (2013) illustrated this with the pedophilia disorder. A person cannot be convicted of pedophilia but can be diagnosed with pedophilia. Overall, De Block and Adriaens (2013) give an excellent overview of the history and evolution of paraphilia.

Exhibitionism

According to the American Psychiatric Association (2013), exhibitionism is one of the most oft-treated paraphilias. **Exhibitionism** is the "exposure of genitals to a stranger"

(Terry, 2013, p. 46). The subtypes of exhibitionism are linked to the age and/or physical maturity of the victim (American Psychiatric Association, 2013). Victims can be non-consenting adults, children, or both. According to the *DSM-5*, exhibitionism becomes a disorder when recurrent genital exposure to unsuspecting others on at least three victims on separate occasions occurs.

Murphy and Page (2008) argued that the extent of exhibition is unknown. Murphy and Page (2008) placed the incidence of exhibitionism in males between 2 percent and 4 percent of the entire population; they estimated that the incidence of exhibitionism among females to be "much lower." The onset of exhibitionism occurs during adolescence, usually later than the onset of normative sexual interests (Murphy and Page, 2008). Little is known about the persistence of exhibitionism over time (Murphy and Page, 2008).

Marsh et al. (2010) examined voluntary admittances to psychiatric facilities to examine the prevalence of paraphilias (N=112). Very few (13.4 percent) subjects had at least one diagnosable paraphilia. In particular, voyeurism (8 percent), exhibitionism (5.4 percent), and sexual masochism (2.7 percent) were the most frequently occurring disorders. Patients with paraphilias were more likely to have attempted suicide, been sexually abused, and had more hospitalizations. Marsh et al. (2010) concluded that paraphilias seemed to be more common than previously thought.

Piemont (2007) noted the "compulsion to sexually expose oneself appears to be commonly motivated by fears of psychic emptiness and interpersonal powerlessness" (p. 92). Piemont (2007) linked exhibitionism to early sexual and emotional trauma. For Piemont (2007), "Unconscious wishes to be seen, to have an effect, and to experience evidence of one's own existence through reactions of an external object are gratified in the commission of this perverse act" (p. 93). Swindell et al. (2011) found a link between sharing a tub with a female, allowing a female partner to look at his genitals, and being allowed to be nude in the mother's presence and future exhibitionism. All of these were positive conditioning experiences associated with arousal and pleasure. In addition, the *DSM-5*, also links exhibitionistic disorder to antisocial history, antisocial personality disorder, alcohol misuse, pedophilic sexual preference, sexual impulsivity, hypersexuality, psychological impairment, and subjective distress (loneliness, sexual frustration, shame, etc.).

It has been suggested that psychopathology is greater among exhibitionists with more extensive histories of exhibitionism (Forgac, Cassel, and Michaels, 1984). This fact could suggest a link to criminality. Forgac et al. (1984) evaluated this hypothesis. The analysis indicated that there is no relationship between increasing exhibitionistic events and an increase in psychopathology. In addition, no link was found between the overall number of exhibitionistic offenses and other forms of criminality.

Several points are clear from the review of the literature on exhibitionism. First, exhibitionism is rare among females (Morin and Levenson, 2008). The study of exhibitionism focuses on males, and the available studies either ignore female subjects or find no females who report exhibitionistic behaviors. Second, even among males, there is very little research on exhibitionism, and the available research suffers from moderate to severe limitations that decrease the ability of the empirical work to generalize to larger populations (Langstrom, 2010). Finally, great overlap exists between exhibitionism and other paraphilias (Langstrom, 2010).

Fetishism

Kafka (2010a) noted that the terms **"fetish"** and **"fetishism"** are used "to specifically describe an intense eroticization of either non-living and/or specific body parts that were symbolically associated with a person" (p. 357). Terry (2013) argued that fetishism "involved sexual fantasies and urges involving inanimate objects" (p. 47); in addition, the emphasis may be on actions or body parts (partialism). The object, behavior, or body part is key for sexual arousal in the individual with a fetish (Terry, 2013). Fetishism becomes a disorder when, over a period of six months, an individual experiences intense and recurrent "sexual arousal from either the use of non-living objects or a highly specific focus on non-genital body part(s), as manifested by fantasies, urges, or behaviors . . . Fetish objects are not limited to articles of clothing . . . or devices" (American Psychiatric Association, 2013, p. 16).

There are many different fetishes, and an individual can have many types of fetish at the same time. Wiederman (2003) suggested that any object has the potential of serving as a fetish; examples include hairbrushes, artificial limbs, safety pins, snails, cockroaches, whips, roses, and eyeglasses (p. 317). The most common fetishes are clothing, especially lingerie and shoes (Terry, 2013). In addition, most people, at one time or another, have had some fetish or another. "Fetishistic disorder can be a multisensory experience, including holding, tasting, rubbing, inserting, or smelling the fetishistic object while masturbating" (American Psychiatric Association, 2013, p. 16).

Partialism is another form of fetishism in which the individual arousal focuses on a particular body part—feet for example. Examples of fetishes and partialisms include abasiophilia (individuals with limited/no mobility), acrotomophilia (amputees), agalmatophilia (statues/dolls/mannequins/etc.), albutophilia (water), altocalciphilia (high-heeled shoes), alvinolagnia (stomach), coprophilia (feces), crurofact (legs), plushophilia (stuffed animals/dolls), oculophilia (eyes), symphorophilia (watching/staging accidents), urophilia (urine), and vorarephilia (being consumed by another).

While the research is limited on fetishism, there are several conclusions we can draw from this line of inquiry. First, fetishes are largely the domain of males (American Psychiatric Association, 2013). Second, Kafka (2010a) also indicated that fetishism is either uncommon and/or underreported. Third, the American Psychiatric Association (2013) reports that fetishistic disorder causes sexual dysfunction in relationships and can push the individual toward solitary sexual activity. Fourth, Coskun and Ozturk (2013) argued that the onset of fetishism in adolescence is only an assumption due to the limited nature of empirical studies. Fetishes can develop prior to adolescence; after development, the fetishistic disorder is continuous but fluctuates in intensity/frequency over time (American Psychiatric Association, 2013). Finally, fetishes can either be harmless or lead to dangerous or criminal behavior (Terry, 2013).

Frotteurism

Frotteurism may be the least understood of all the paraphilias. The American Psychiatric Association (2013) defines **frotteurism** as "intense sexual arousal from touching or rubbing against a non-consenting person, as manifested by fantasies, urges, or behaviors" (p. 7). The frotteur may touch his genitals to an unsuspecting individual or brush against another persons' genitals or breasts (Terry, 2013). In some cases, frotteurists achieve orgasm during the act.

Guterman et al. (2011) argued that frotteurism is "rampant" on public transportation; many cities in the world (Mexico City, Rio di Janeiro, and Tokyo, for example) have implemented women-only cars to deal with the issue. Guterman et al. (2011) indicated that in the majority of cases, individuals with frotteurism "go to crowded public spaces (e.g., shopping malls, subways, elevators), seek out unsuspecting targets, usually females, and rub their body parts such as their hands or genitals against the breasts, legs, and buttocks of the victim" (p. 59). While these actions are generally considered to be criminal, groping cases are oftentimes not reported to the police; this is due to victims being unaware of the activity in many incidents (Guterman et al., 2011). In the cases where there is a report, the frotteurist will oftentimes deny engaging in the act. This makes prosecution of any criminal behavior difficult.

Research on frotteurism is rare. Kafka (2010) concluded that 10 to 14 percent of adult males receiving outpatient treatment meet the diagnosis for frotteuristic disorder. Antisocial behaviors and hypersexuality are risk factors for frotteurism.

Langstrom (2010) hypothesized that frotteurism may occur in as many as 30 percent of all males. Alternatively, Krueger and Kaplan (2008) noted that frotteurism in females was rare. Guterman, Martin, and Rudes (2011) noted that, overall, frotteurism is a rare phenomenon.

The onset of frotteurism occurs in late adolescence or emerging adulthood (American Psychiatric Association, 2013). Children may also touch or rub without a diagnosis of frotteuristic disorder. Indeed, there is no minimum age requirement for diagnosis of frotteuristic disorder, but it can be difficult to discern from normal developmental behaviors. The *DSM-5* (2013) notes that the persistence of frotteurism is unclear in individuals.

Pedophilia

Probably the best-known paraphilia is pedophilia; this is interesting as it is one of the more recent paraphilias and least understood by the public. The term pedophile was only added to the *DSM* in 1987. The term pedophilia is oftentimes used synonymously with the term child molester by the public. It is incorrect to link child molesters to the disorder of pedophilia. Not all pedophiles are child sex offenders. Many pedophiles may be attracted to children, but never engage in the behavior.

Wiederman (2003) wrote that **pedophilia** "involves sexual interest in prepubescent children, usually age 13 years or younger" (p. 318). It is not uncommon for individuals who molest children to have no sexual attraction to children. Wiederman (2003) suggested this fact can make it extremely difficult to study pedophiles. Pedophilia becomes a disorder when, over a period of six months:

> there are recurrent and intense sexually arousing fantasies, sexual urges, or behaviors involving sexual activity with a prepubescent child or children (generally age 13 or younger), the individual acted on these urges or was caused distress by the urges, and is at least 16 years old and at least 5 years older than the child/children" (American Psychiatric Association, 2013, p. 13).

Marshall (1997) indicated that many men who sexually molested a child did not experience recurrent fantasies or urges. The American Psychiatric Association (2013) reported that pedophilia is linked to antisocial behavior, alcohol/substance abuse, obsessive-compulsive disorder, and sexual victimization as a child (Hall and Hall, 2007).

According to Litton (2006), pedophiles will often approach victims seeking friendship; these individuals may work in schools or other jobs where children are plentiful. Litton (2006) indicated that pedophiles will not typically force sex on younger victims, but will generally opt for oral sex (fellatio or cunnilingus); sexual intercourse is more likely when the victim is older. It is rare for a pedophile to do anything other than sexually violate the victim (assault or murder for instance).

According to the American Psychiatric Association (2013), the prevalence of pedophilia is unknown. Some have attempted to evaluate pedophilia by using official reports of child molestation; regardless of metric, the odds are great that pedophilia is very pervasive (Marshall, 1997). It is likely lesser in females than in males; however, Litton (2006) noted that most pedophiles do not fit the "dirty-old-man" stereotype that is prevalent in society. While the onset occurs during puberty, pedophilia is a lifelong condition (American Psychiatric Association, 2013). It is difficult to diagnose pedophilia due to its co-occurrence with adolescent development (American Psychiatric Association, 2013). The American Psychiatric Association (2013) notes that pedophilia is one of the most oft-treated paraphilias. Many of these individuals have families with children (Murray, 2000).

Pedophilia involves the "sexual attraction to prepubescent children, and, if these desires are acted upon, could cause significant harm" (Terry, 2013, p. 48). Many of the children that attract individuals are not prepubescent. Thus, the term pedophile does not cover the wide range of victims. Two terms have emerged to cover attraction to minors older than the age of 13: **ephebophilia** and **hebophilia**. Both are largely defined as the same thing. According to Franklin (2010), hebophilia describes sexual attraction to adolescents. Franklin (2010) noted that the term hebophilia (and ephebophilia) is relatively new.

Of all the sexual paraphilias outlined in the *DSM-5*, pedophilia is currently the most researched, even though the subjects are elusive to identify. Studies have examined the etiology of pedophilia (Marshall, 1997; Seto, 2018). This line of research has studied the interaction between the biological, psychological, and social causes of pedophilia. Research has also evaluated the therapists' experiences with pedophiles (Bach and Demuth, 2018) and public perceptions of pedophiles (Richards, 2018). The most important research for the *DSM-5* in relation to pedophilia was conducted by Seto and colleagues (2016). Their evaluation of the reliability and validity of the *DSM-5*'s diagnostic criteria was the only such study since evaluations of the *DSM-IV*. Their work, which established both the reliability and validity of the current *DSM*, will be useful as it evolves in future editions. Other research has indicated the impact of technology on pedophilia. It is clear that technology has helped pedophiles in their pursuits. Durkin (2002) argued that the Internet has made the lives of pedophiles easier. Pedophiles use the Internet to exchange child pornography, locate potential victims, engage in inappropriate communications with children, and correspond with other pedophiles for support and encouragement (Durkin, 2002).

Sexual Sadism

The term sadism is derived from the Comte Donatien-Alphonse-Francois, marquis de Sade, "whose life and writings were filled with incidents and images of sexual cruelty" (Weinberg, 2006, p. 18). Nitschke et al. (2012) noted that sadism is not a recently evolved behavior; they illustrated that the *Kamasutra* discussed many sadistic techniques, and sadomasochistic clubs existed as early as the eighteenth century. Von Krafft-Ebing (1965) was the first to discuss sexual sadism as a psychological disorder that revolved around the infliction of humiliation, pain, and/or suffering.

Sexual sadism occurs when the individual takes excitement/gratification from the psychological or physical suffering of another person. Warren and Hazelwood (2002) wrote that the fantasy of sexual sadists

> involves a variety of verbal, physical, and sexual behaviors involving the domination, control, and suffering of partners. Such fantasized behaviors may include the scripting of a partner to verbally demean or degrade herself, inflicting physical pain through the use of implements or devices, and forcing the partner to engage in sexual acts alien to her experience (p. 76).

Sadism becomes a disorder when, over a six-month period, the individual experiences "recurrent and intense sexual arousal from the physical or psychological suffering of another person, as manifested by fantasies, urges, or behaviors and the individual has acted on these urges with a non-consenting person or cause clinical distress" (American Psychiatric Association, 2013, p. 11). Sadists are noticed by the police only when their acts become so extreme that the violence is reported by a victim.

The onset of sadism occurs across the teenage years for both males and females (American Psychiatric Association, 2013). Fedoroff (2008) noted that the true prevalence of sexual sadism is unknown; current research makes any generalizations difficult. Sadists tend to increase in severity over time (Terry, 2013). Sadism has also been associated with individuals who watch sadistic pornography. Research in this area is predominated by male subjects, but the information is very limited. Pflugradt and Allen's (2012) research indicated that male and female sadists only differed in two respects: female sadists tended to have a co-offender, as the two operate as a "pseudo-family unit," and female sadists tend to have a pre-existing relationship with their "victim(s)."

Warren and Hazelwood (2002) examined sexual sadism among wives and girlfriends of sexually sadistic males; overall, they found the relationships to be complex. The subjects reported early experiences with physical abuse and/or incest. The subjects had managed to attain normative lifestyles (including sexual behaviors) before meeting their sexually sadist significant other. What was clear across all subjects was that the lives of the subjects changed drastically after meeting their sadist husbands/boyfriends. Warren and Hazelwood's (2002) research found that many of the subject's significant others perpetrated higher levels of incest than the general population.

Another line of research links sadism to more dangerous sexual behaviors. **Hypoxia** is the deprivation of oxygen (Terry, 2013). **Autoerotic asphyxiation** is the constriction of oxygen during masturbation or sexual intercourse where a strangulation device of some sort is used (belt, bag, chemicals, choking, etc.); both males and females participate in this behavior (Terry, 2013). Research has linked sadism and autoerotic asphyxiation.

Some studies have attempted to link sadism with sex crimes. Robertson and Knight (2014) evaluated the link between sexual sadism, violence, and sexual crimes. In their study, sadism and psychopathy were linked to non-sexual violence, sexual violence, increased instances of violence, and elevated severity of violence; alternatively, there was only a minor relationship between sadism and psychopathy (Robertson and Knight, 2014). These results would suggest a link between sadism and criminality. Among civilly committed sex offenders in the United States, less than 10 percent have been diagnosed with sexual sadism disorder (American Psychiatric Association, 2013). According to Krueger (2010b), 37 to 75 percent of those who have perpetrated a sexually motivated homicide are diagnosed with sexual sadism disorder.

Many issues are associated with the paraphilia of sadism. Nitschke et al. (2012) argued that the reliance on patients to divulge violent sexual fantasies or actions was one of the biggest limitations with sadism research. This is potentially a problem for public safety and an individual's future behavior via stigmatization (Nitschke et al., 2012). There are also relatively few studies in this area; most of the existing studies overly rely on convenience samples (Krueger, 2010b). Another key issue surrounds the diagnosis of sadism. Nitschke et al. (2012) identified the poor interrater reliability associated with the diagnosis of sexual sadism. In other words, different psychiatrists will differentially diagnose similar patients. Finally, Fedoroff (2008) argued that sexual acts revolving around domination should be distinguished between consensual and non-consensual partners as motivations are mixed.

Sadism is often linked with masochism due to the similarity of the behaviors. Many individuals are diagnosed with both disorders; this combined disorder is sadomasochism. Weinberg (2006) noted that **sadomasochism** is about "dominance and submission and not necessarily about pain" (p. 33). Outside the sexual area, this does not apply. In masochism, the target of demeaning psychological and/or physical humiliation/pain is the self rather than others. The next section explores this topic further.

Sexual Masochism

The term "masochism" was derived from the writer Leopold Ritter von Sacher Masoch, whose novels dealt with personal pain and humiliation (Weinberg, 2006). Von Krafft-Ebing (1965) suggested sexual masochism as

> a peculiar perversion of the psychical sexual life in which the individual affected, in sexual feeling and thought, is controlled by the idea of being completely and unconditionally subject to the will of a person of the opposite sex; of being treated by this person as a master, humiliated and abused (p. 86).

The *DSM-5* (2013) defines **sexual masochism** as "intense sexual arousal from the act of being humiliated, beaten, bound, or otherwise made to suffer, as manifested by fantasies, urges, or behaviors" (p. 9).

The prevalence of sexual masochism is unknown (American Psychiatric Association, 2013). It has been estimated that less than 3 percent of the population in Australia had been involved in sexual masochistic/sadistic acts in the preceding year (American Psychiatric Association, 2013). The age of onset for sexual masochism is generally in the late teens, although it can occur in early puberty or even childhood (Freund et al., 1995). Very little is known about the persistence of sexual masochism. Sexual masochists tend toward pornography depicting sexual masochism (American Psychiatric Association, 2013).

As with sadism, the *DSM-5* (2013) also linked sexual masochism to asphyxiaphilia since some forms of sexual masochism relate to "the practice of achieving sexual arousal related to restriction of breathing" (p. 9). Sexual masochists have a risk of accidental death via asphyxiation and autoerotic activities (Hucker, 2011; Cairnes and Ranier, 1981). Even with the link between sexual masochism and hypoxia, Krueger (2010a) indicated that sexual masochism rarely results in severe harm or death to participants of such sexual behavior.

Krueger (2010a) outlined the primary criticisms of the inclusion of masochism in the *DSM-5*: they are not mental disorders, are unspecific, and unnecessary. In addition, there are very few studies on sexual masochism. Indeed, Krueger (2010a) noted there were fewer studies on masochism than on sadism. Finally, Krueger (2010a) argued that the incidence of masochism might actually be higher than previously believed due to the association between sadism and masochism and the inability of the *DSM-5* to distinguish between all similar forms of behavior.

Transvestic Fetishism

Transvestic fetishism "involves men who keep a collection of women's clothing and intermittently use it to cross-dress" (Terry, 2013, p. 47). There are a variety of motivations for cross-dressing; these can include gender identity issues (not sexually motivated in this case), attention, aesthetic appeal, and dramatic effect (Wiederman, 2003). Blanchard (2010) noted the four key elements of transvestic fetishism disorder: cross-dressing, association with sexual arousal, biological male, and a heterosexual orientation. Langstrom and Zucker (2005) denoted two types of cross-dressers: nuclear (periodic) transvestites, who are typically satisfied with cross-dressing only, and marginal transvestites, who desire further feminization via hormone therapy or surgery.

Transvestic fetishism disorder occurs when, over a period of six months, the individual experiences recurrent and intense "sexual arousal from cross-dressing, as manifested by fantasies, urges, or behaviors. These cause clinically significant distress in social, occupational, or other important areas of functioning" (American Psychiatric Association, 2013, p. 18).

Overall, little is known about the etiology of transvestic fetishism. Its prevalence is unknown and it may begin in childhood. The act can be for peace of mind or it can be accompanied by autogynephilia, or a male's sexual arousal by thoughts/images of the self as a female (American Psychiatric Association, 2013). Transvestic fetishism can be continuous or episodic; it is not uncommon for those with transvestic fetishism disorder to quit cross-dressing upon falling in love, but this will only be temporary (American Psychiatric Association, 2013). The severity of the disorder is thought to be greatest in adulthood. In many individuals, the excitement of cross-dressing dissipates over time.

Some facts about transvestic fetishism have been ascertained. The majority of those with transvestic fetishist disorder are heterosexuals (American Psychiatric Association, 2013; Terry, 2013). Wiederman (2003) noted both men and women, straight or gay, can experience transvestic fetishism, but generally it is only diagnosed for males. Like sexual masochism and sadism, Langstrom and Zucker (2005) noted that transvestic fetishism is linked to risky sexual acts, like autoerotic asphyxia.

As with other paraphilias, there is not a lot of research on transvestic fetishism. Langstrom and Zucker (2005) evaluated the incidence of transvestic fetishism in the population. Evaluating 5,250 subjects in Sweden, Langstrom and Zucker (2005) found that only 3 percent of males reported sexual arousal from cross-dressing. Unlike previous studies, this one also found women who gained sexual arousal from cross-dressing; unfortunately, these individuals were rare and higher order statistical analyses could not be performed on this group. Most importantly, Langstrom and Zucker (2005) found a link between cross-dressing and childhood sexual abuse. In addition, none of the subjects reported that other men were the focus of their sexual attraction. Langstrom and Zucker (2005) found that over 50 percent of their subjects did not consider cross-dressing to be an acceptable practice.

Zucker et al. (2012) studied adolescent involvement with transvestic fetishism. Zucker et al. (2012) found that adolescents with transvestic fetishism also had high rates of "general behavior problems and poor peer relations" (p. 151). As with adults, adolescents diagnosed with transvestic fetishism were predominantly heterosexual in their sexual orientation.

Blanchard (2010) concluded that transvestic fetishism should be separated into two categories of transvestism and fetishism. The rationale for this was due to research findings that transvestites who reported fetishism were less likely to maintain perpetual female identities, whereas those who reported autogynephilia were four times as likely to have unwavering female identities (Blanchard, 2010). To date, and as of the current version of the *DSM*, this split has not occurred.

Voyeurism

Voyeuristic acts are the most common form of sexual deviance. Unfortunately, less has been written on voyeurism than about any other form of sexual deviance (Davis, 2002; Rye and Meaney, 2007). Yalom (1960) defined **voyeurism** as an "exaggerated desire to see by stealth, a member of the opposite sex (generally) in some stage of undress, redress, in a sexual act or the act of excretion . . . a wanton desire which is so intense that it surpasses the sexual act" (p. 22); voyeurism is often a result of obsession and compulsion. According to the *DSM-5*, voyeurism involves individuals who gain "sexual arousal from observing an unsuspecting person who is naked, disrobing, or engaged in sexual activity" (American Psychiatric Association, 2013, p. 2). Fenichel (1945) and von Krafftt-Ebing (1965) likened voyeurism to sexual immaturity indicating an "arrested psycho-sexual development."

Davis (2002) noted that voyeurism was actually a catch-all term for peeping-Tomism, inspectionalism, and scoptophilia (watching sexual acts). The *DSM-5* identifies two types of voyeurs, non-disclosing and recurrent. Non-disclosing voyeurs are those who have repeatedly spied on others in separate occasions, but do not attribute the behavior to fantasies or urges and may claim the activity was accidental and/or nonsexual. Recurrent voyeurs have perpetrated voyeurism on at least three different victims on separate occasions. In either case, Yalom (1960) argued that part of the sexual appeal of voyeurism lay in the potential of being caught.

According to Lavin (2008), the total prevalence of voyeuristic disorder is unknown. Langstrom and Seto's (2006) research indicated that voyeuristic disorder occurs in

12 percent of all males and 4 percent of all females, but voyeurism is clearly uncommon in females. Voyeurism begins during adolescence, but the minimum age of diagnosis is 18 due to disentangling normal adolescent sexual activity/curiosity. Davis (2002) noted that voyeurs tend to offend in a close proximity to their residence; they have a particular pattern and commence at a particular time. The latter could be more attributable to the activities of the victim more than the voyeur.

There are many correlates to voyeuristic acts. Langstrom and Seto (2006) linked voyeurism to childhood sexual abuse, substance misuse, sexual preoccupation, and hypersexuality. Davis (2002) indicated that voyeurs were typically male, the intended victim was female, peeping began with a mother/caregiver, had inadequate sexual experiences, reported masturbating while watching in 60 percent of cases, have a very low marriage rate, are single children or had no older siblings, and rarely had female friends growing up.

Langstrom and Seto (2006) examined the incidence of voyeurism in a nationally representative sample of Sweden in 1996. Of those interviewed (ages 18 to 60), 7.7 percent of the population indicated becoming sexually aroused by spying on others having sex. Voyeurism was related to being male, the existence of more psychological problems, dissatisfaction with life, and greater sexual interest and activity in general (more sexual partners, greater arousability, greater frequency of masturbation, and greater frequency of use of pornography). Most importantly, Langstrom and Seto (2006) indicated that those subjects who reported engaging in voyeurism reported other atypical sexual behavior.

3

Generally, the act of watching produces the sexual gratification and the voyeur will not seek out real sexual activity with the victim, but this is not always the case (Davis, 2002). Davis (2002) argued that voyeurism is a common precursor to sexual offending; Terry (2013) also suggested that voyeurism is a gateway behavior that can lead to rape. Davis (2002) argued that 75 percent of serial rapists and 43 percent of non-serial rapists had a history of voyeurism. Research indicates that serial rapists and sexual murderers have a prior history of voyeuristic behavior; however, not all serial rapists or sexual murderers are voyeurs (Davis, 2002). Clearly, voyeurism should be considered a red flag for other sexually deviant offenses (Davis, 2002).

Despite limited research, we do know key facts about voyeurs. First, due to the association between voyeurism and masturbation, voyeurs are most likely to be arrested for either indecent exposure or public indecency (Davis, 2002). Second, Davis (2002) noted that serial or repetitive voyeurism is related to violent behavior. Third, Posner (1992) argued voyeurism is linked to privacy invasion, which causes emotional distress in victims. Fourth, voyeurs seldom seek out mental health services; rather, most voyeurs who get mental health care tend to be ordered to do so by the criminal justice system (Davis, 2002). Despite our current level of knowledge, Rye and Meaney (2007) concluded "we know very little about the psychological and social motives for engaging in non-clinical voyeuristic activity" (p. 48).

Paraphilia Not Otherwise Specified

The *DSM-5* (2013) denotes eight explicit paraphilias. Many paraphilias are relatively uncommon. These types of paraphilias are captured in the category of **paraphilias not otherwise specified (NOS)**. Table 3.1 lists these paraphilias and their explanation.

TABLE 3.1 PARAPHILIAS NOT OTHERWISE SPECIFIED

Paraphilia NOS Category	Erotic Focus
Abasiophilia	Lamed or crippled partner
Acrotomophilia	Amputation in partner
Adolscentilism	Impersonating/being treated like adolescent
Andromimetophilia	Andromimetic partner
Apotemnophilia	Own amputation
Autagonistophilia	Being observed/on stage
Autogynophilia	Image of self as woman
Chrematistophilia	Being forced to pay
Copraphilia	Feces
Formicophilia	Small creatures
Gerontophilia	Elderly partner
Gynamimetophilia	Gynomimetic partner
Gynandromorphophilia	Cross-dressed feminized male
Hybristophilia	Partner committed crime or outrageous act
Hypoxyphilia	Reduced oxygen intake
Infantilism	Impersonating/being treated like infant
Kleptophilia	Stealing
Klismaphilia	Enemas
Mixoscopia	Viewing couple having intercourse
Mysophilia	Filth
Morphophilia	One or more body parts on partner
Narratophilia	Obscene language with sexual partner
Necrophilia	Corpses
Olfactophilia	Odors
Partialism	Focus on body part
Pictophilia	Pornographic pictures or videos
Saliromania	Soiling/damaging clothing/body
Scoptophilia	Viewing sexual activity
Somnophilia	Sleeping partner
Stigmatophilia	Partner has tattoo, piercing, or scarified
Symphorophilia	Stage-managed disaster
Telephone Scatophilia	Telephone obscenities to victim
Triolism	Observing partner having sex
Urethral Manipulation	Insertion of objects
Urophilia	Urine
Vampirism	Blood
Vomerophilia	Vomiting
Zoophilia	Animals

Source: Adapted from Milner and Dopke (1997) and other sources.

To be a disorder, all of the above paraphilias must be present for six months and must cause distress for the individual. These paraphilias not otherwise specified are linked to the previous paraphilias. It is common for paraphilias to overlap. For instance, several of the paraphilias listed in Table 3.1 were discussed in passing when we talked about fetishes earlier in Chapter 3.

CONCLUSION

Chapter 3 examined behaviors that are sexually deviant. While these behaviors are deviant, they are only sometimes criminal under law. Generally, the various behaviors associated with sexual deviance are actions that are just slightly less serious than sex crimes. In the study of sex crimes, it is important to be able to distinguish between actions that are crimes and actions that simply run afoul of societal norms.

Terry (2013) indicated that paraphilias are sexual disorders that can result in sexual fantasies and urges in relation to behaviors, individuals, and/or objects. For Terry (2013), paraphilias can be a gateway to criminal offending. The topic of sexual deviance is valuable to our discussion due to its potential link to sex crimes. Holmes and Holmes (2009b) argued that "many rapists, lust murderers, and sexually motivated serial killers have histories of sexual behavior that reflect patterns that in the past have been considered only nuisances" (p. 63). As seen in Chapter 3, there is research that links many of the paraphilias outlined in the *DSM-5* to individuals who perpetrate the most serious sex crimes. This can also be seen in the current link between sexual harassment and sexual offenses discussed in the preceding and subsequent chapters. Any definitive conclusions about the correlations between sexual deviance and sex crimes should be cautious due to a couple of points.

The first two impediments to making conclusions about the link between sexual deviance and sex crimes revolve around research efforts. First, to say that research across all the paraphilias is lacking is an understatement (Wiederman, 2003). The *DSM-5*, which outlines when sexual deviance can be determined to be a disorder, indicates a lack of research across all of the paraphilias. This lack of research puts into question most of the facts we have ascertained about sexual deviance as outlined by the American Psychiatric Association. More research is clearly necessary in this area. A second issue that limits our knowledge of sexual deviance is in relation to the samples/populations used to conduct the extant research. As we will see in later chapters, the study of sex offenders is only as good as the victims who report the sex crimes. Many are unwilling to do so. This is true in the area of sexual deviance as well. Most studies are based on clinical studies where the patients suffering from a paraphilic disorder must acknowledge that they experience particular urges. Many self-reported studies are limited due to subjects who fail to report what they have done or not done. This is true for psychiatric patients who may or may not report that they are experiencing symptoms of paraphilic disorders. This too decreases the ability of studies to evaluate the etiology of sexual deviance.

The third problem associated with the study of sexual deviance focuses on the inherently subjective nature of all disorders outlined in the *DSM-5*. Historically there have been behaviors that have been considered to be disorders in previous versions of the *DSM* that have been later deleted for one reason or another. In relation to sexual deviance, the most studied paraphilic disorder in the history of the *DSM* was homosexuality (De Block and Adriaens, 2013). As you can tell from the discussion in Chapter 3, homosexuality was not listed as a paraphilia. In fact, homosexuality was dropped from the DSM in 1973. As such, behaviors that are considered a disorder today may not be so tomorrow. What is considered a disorder is a dynamic decision, which allows for subjectivity in the determination of what behaviors are paraphilic.

Shindel and Moser (2011) noted that diagnosing paraphilias as disorders has come under scrutiny in recent years. Shindel and Moser (2011) argued that the criteria to diagnose such behavior as disorders is not clearly outlined, is unsupported by empirical research (of which there are few studies anyway), and the criteria often are applicable to those who do not have such disorders. Shindel and Moser (2011) concluded that the *DSM-5* criteria are tautological in their application. This is an important limitation built into the *DSM* and the study of sexual deviance.

Finally, the history of psychiatry and sexual abnormality has been largely atheoretical, focusing rather on the symptoms and diagnoses (De Block and Adriaens, 2013). Theory is greatly needed in this area. Part of the problem in the study of sexual deviance has been the separation of sexual deviance and mental disorders. Because the two have been inseparable, the emphasis has been placed on the various symptoms associated with sexual deviance, while ignoring the theory about why those symptoms should be indicative of sexual deviance. Theoretical development is greatly needed in the study of sexual deviance.

This ends the discussion of behaviors that, while deviant, often do not rise to the level of sex crimes. The next chapters will begin a more extensive discussion of specific sex behaviors that are in fact crimes. The next two chapters will evaluate the crimes of rape and sex offenses against children.

KEY TERMS

autoerotic asphyxiation
deviance
ephebophilia
exhibitionism
fetishism
frotteurism
hebophilia
hypoxia
norms
paraphilia
paraphilia NOS
partialism
pedophilia
primary deviance
sadomasochism
secondary deviance
sexual deviance
sexual masochism
sexual sadism
transvestic fetishism
voyeurism

EXERCISES

1. Explain the concept of deviance. How does deviant behavior differ from criminal behavior?
2. Explore the differences between primary and secondary deviance.
3. Choose a paraphilia and explain it. When does it rise to the level of a disorder?
4. Explain how pedophilia differs from sex offenses against children. What does the research reveal about this type of paraphilia?
5. What are the limitations associated with paraphilias?

ESSAY QUESTIONS

1. Select a paraphilia. Find a peer-reviewed research article that explores the particular paraphilia you chose. Discuss the findings of the research and the limitations associated with those findings.
2. Find a media story that focuses on one of the paraphilias discussed in Chapter 3. Describe the incident and sexual deviant. Was the deviant treated as a criminal?
3. As noted in Chapter 3, homosexuality was once considered a paraphilia. Explain why this fact is a problem in the study of all paraphilias and sexual deviance.

4

RAPE

Chapter Objectives

After reading this chapter, students will be able to:

- Understand different sources of data about rape.
- Understand how rape rates have changed over time.
- Explain the different typologies of rapists.
- Explain the common characteristics of a rape incident.
- Discuss theories explaining why rape occurs.
- Understand rape myths and the stereotypical conception of rape.

INTRODUCTION

Chapter 3 explored sexual deviance, acts that sometimes fall in the gray area between criminal and off-putting. Chapter 4 specifically examines acts that are patently criminal under the law: **rape**. In particular we focus on adult male rapists, the typologies of these offenders, the theories associated with rape, and some of the circumstances and cultural perceptions surrounding rape. Here is an example of a well-known individual who has been convicted of rape.

> *Former heavyweight champion boxer Mike Tyson was convicted in 1992 (at the age of 25) of raping an 18-year-old female in Indiana. Unlike the stereotype of the masked man stalking a stranger with a weapon and raping her (Estrich, 1987), Tyson and his victim were acquainted; the victim voluntarily went to his hotel room, a situation that for some would be considered victim-precipitated rape (Amir, 1967) and for much of the general public would be evidence that the victim intended to have consensual sex with Tyson (Burt, 1980).*

At the time, the fact that Tyson was convicted was noteworthy because of the acquaintance between the victim and offender and because the victim did not suffer serious physical injury. The judge in the case, Judge Patricia Gifford, who denied Tyson's request for bail while he appealed his conviction, argued that "rape is rape" and that the law "never mentions whether a defendant or a victim are acquainted" (Shipp, 1992). Tyson later appealed his conviction with the help of famed defense lawyer Alan Dershowitz, but he was unsuccessful. He ended up serving three years of a ten-year sentence with four years suspended and three more reduced for good behavior (Stern, 2013). To this day, Tyson still denies the event was a rape and insists the sex was consensual, claiming that he was convicted due to his status and stereotypes associated with his race (Stern, 2013).

Tyson's history includes psychological disorders and numerous aggressive incidents, both before and after the rape conviction. Most notably, in 1997 Tyson bit off a piece of Evander Holyfield's ear during a boxing match for the heavyweight championship of the world, perhaps because he was frustrated at the prospect of losing the match. He consequently lost his license to box in Nevada and subsequently applied for a new license in New Jersey a year later. Due to an emotional outburst during the application hearing, however, Tyson withdrew his application to box in New Jersey and sought instead to have his Nevada license reinstated. This led to a comprehensive psychological evaluation by a team of experts who found Tyson suffered from depression, was irritable and angry, and attributed his problems to others (Ewing and McCann, 2006). As we will see in Chapter 4, such characteristics are not unusual in those who commit rape.

Chapter 4 provides an overview of the topic of rape. We take a more detailed look at the rape statistics examined in Chapter 1, the problems inherent in those data, and issues associated with the underreporting of rape. Various theories underlying the act of rape are evaluated, typologies of rapists are described, and the primary myths associated with rape are considered. Finally, Chapter 4 concludes with an examination of the victim/offender relationship, alcohol and substance use, and other characteristics and correlates of rape.

RAPE STATISTICS

As discussed in Chapter 1, two official sources of data are available on how much rape occurs in the United States. The first is the **Uniform Crime Reports (UCR)**, which relies upon rapes reported to the police to develop a rape rate. The other is the **National Crime Victimization Survey (NCVS)**, which develops a rape rate based on rapes reported to trained survey workers in a victimization study. As will be discussed later, rape is a considerably underreported crime, meaning that the two sources of data will have divergent rates of rape, although both are still useful in evaluating the prevalence of rape.

According to the UCR, for 2012, 27.1 rapes per 100,000 people occurred in the United States. This rate should be evaluated with caution as the denominator is all people, rather than just women, who, at the time these data were collected, were the only people who could be raped according to the UCR's definition of forcible rape. The definition of rape used for these data is "the carnal knowledge of a female forcibly and against her will" (UCR Offense Definitions, 2014, para. 3). This definition has generally been interpreted to mean penile penetration of the vagina only, and so excludes many forms of sexual assault that some would consider rape. It also excludes sexual assaults committed against men. In 2013, the definition of forcible rape changed to "penetration, no matter how slight, of the vagina or anus with any body part or object, or oral penetration by a sex organ of another person, without the consent of the victim" (UCR Offense Definitions, 2014, para. 3). This specifically includes a greater number of sexual offenses and offenses committed against men. Using this new definition, the UCR found a rate of 35.9 rapes per 100,000 population in 2013 and 36.6 in 2014. This increase in the rape rate reported by the UCR is not due to great increases in sexually assaultive behavior, but due to the more inclusive definition counting more incidents already occurring as forcible rapes. In fact, the UCR still reports rape rates using the "legacy definition" in addition to the revised definition, and the legacy definition rates continue to be lower than the revised definition rates. See Table 4.1 for comparison. Regardless of the definition used, rape rates have been trending upwards in recent years. In 2019, the latest year for which complete information is available, the legacy definition rape rate was 29.9 per 100,000 and the revised definition rate was 43.6 per 100,000.

Figure 4.1 shows how rates of forcible rape have changed over time, according to the UCR data using the legacy definition of rape and, in recent years, the revised definition. The steep increase in the rape rate between the early 1960s and the 1980s is likely reflective both of the general increase in violent crime as recorded by the UCR during this time period (Blumstein, 2006) and due to an increase in the reporting of rape cases to the police, perhaps as awareness and victim support improved (Baumer and Lauritsen, 2010). As stated above, these data are only forcible rapes reported to the police, and rapes reported to the police tend to differ from non-reported rapes in terms of the victim-offender relationship and the perceived severity of the incident, based on injury, weapon use, and degree of resistance (Bachman, 1998; DuMont et al., 2003). Thus, these crimes are going to be more similar to the stereotype of the "real rape" discussed on page 83, than to the more frequently occurring acquaintance rape.

4

TABLE 4.1 UCR RAPE RATES PER 100,000 USING LEGACY AND REVISED DEFINITION OF RAPE

Year	Legacy Definition	Revised Definition
2011	27.0	NA
2012	27.1	NA
2013	25.9	35.9
2014	26.6	37.0
2015	28.4	39.3
2016	30.0	40.9
2017	30.7	41.7
2018	30.9	42.6
2019	29.9	43.6

Source: UCR, FBI.
https://ucr.fbi.gov/crime-in-the-u.s/2019/crime-in-the-u.s.-2019/tables/table-1

FIGURE 4.1. UCR RAPE RATES PER 100,000 POPULATION, 1960–2019

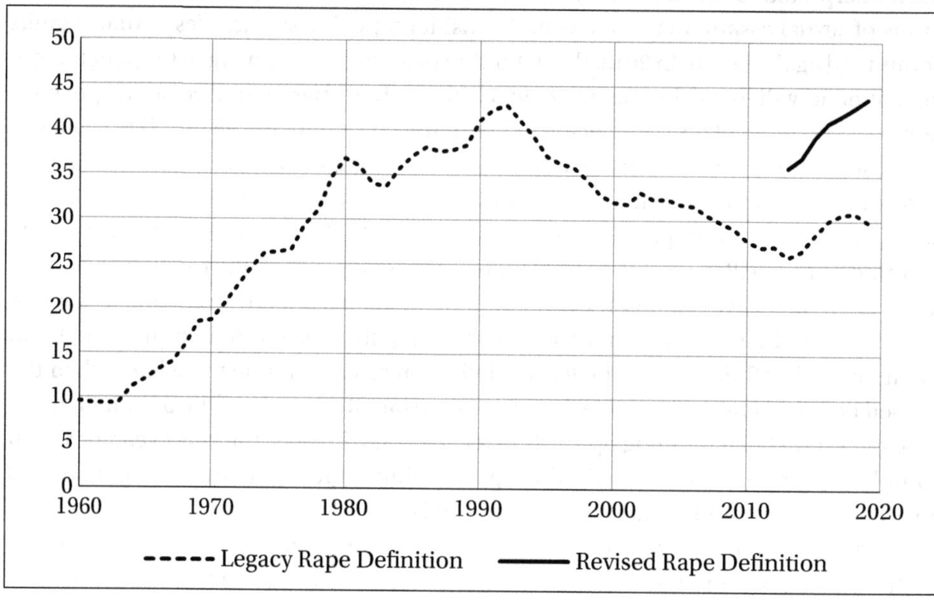

Source: FBI.

The NCVS gathers data and reports rape rates in a different way from the UCR. The NCVS is based on victim responses to a nationally representative survey. It reports rapes per 1,000 females age 12 and over. Because the NCVS does not base rape rates on those incidents reported to the police, the rates are higher, although this method of data collection is still not going to account for all unreported rapes, as victims may not disclose a rape to the individual administering the survey, or the household member being interviewed may not know about the rape of another member of the household. In 2019, the NCVS reports 1.7 completed rapes per 1,000 females age 12 and over (170 per 100,000 females age 12 and over; remember the UCR uses total population). Similar to the UCR, in Figure 4.2 the NCVS shows a trend of rape decreasing beginning in the 1990s, again similar to the trend for overall violent crime (Blumstein, 2006). Recent years show a possible trend towards increasing rape rates.

As with the UCR redesign in 2013, the NCVS was also redesigned, with new questionnaires being used beginning in 1992 to capture incidents of rape and sexual assault that previously went unreported. The older version of the survey asked yes or no questions regarding rape and sexual assault, whereas the redesigned survey defines rape for the respondent as

> forced sexual intercourse and includes both psychological coercion as well as physical force. Forced sexual intercourse means vaginal, anal, or oral penetration by the offender(s). This category also includes incidents where the penetration is from a foreign object such as a bottle (Bachman and Saltzman, 1995, p. 6).

Prior to this redesign, the survey (at the time known as the National Crime Survey) did not specifically ask about rape, but asked if "anyone tr[ied] to attack you in some other way" after asking if anyone stole something from them, beat them up, used

FIGURE 4.2. NCVS RAPE/SEXUAL ASSAULT RATES PER 1,000 FEMALES AGE 12 AND OLDER, 1995–2019

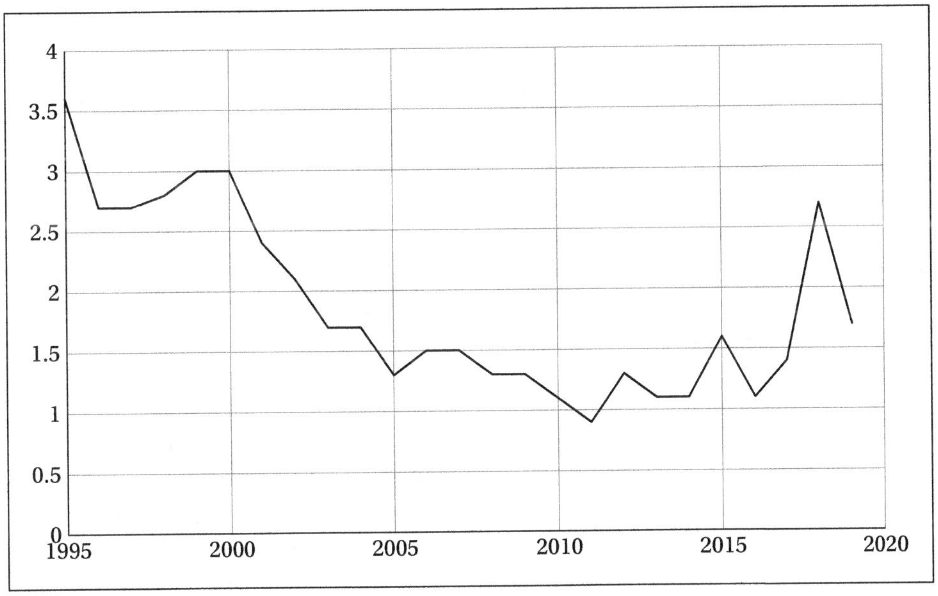

Source: Planty, et al. (2016), Truman & Langston (2015), Morgan & Truman (2020).

4

a weapon against them, or robbed them. The intent was that this question would illicit respondents to disclose if they had been raped (Eigenberg, 1990, p. 657).

In addition to data sources that report a yearly rate of rape, multiple studies have attempted to estimate a lifetime prevalence of rape. One of the longest standing and most well-known surveys used to estimate the prevalence of rape is the **Sexual Experiences Survey (SES)**, which is a 12-question survey (13 for women, as the female survey includes the question "have you ever been raped?") designed to estimate the frequency with which force and coercion are used in sexual encounters and is given to both men and women (Koss and Oros, 1982). In the first report using the Sexual Experiences Survey, 6 percent of college women indicated that they had been raped, although over 30 percent indicated some degree of unwanted or forced sexual activity and 23 percent of college men reported engaging in a degree of sexual aggression (Koss and Oros, 1982). In a 1987 redesign of the Sexual Experiences Survey, which included ten questions and did not ask specifically if the respondent had been raped, 44 percent of college women reported some degree of unwanted sexual activity and 19 percent of men indicated that they had engaged in a degree of sexual coercion (Koss, Gidycz, and Wisniewski, 1987). In a more recent study using the Sexual Experiences Survey and a community sample of women, 17.2 percent responded "yes" to questions indicating that they had been raped (Testa et al., 2004). One consistent finding using survey instruments such as the SES, is that often respondents will indicate that they have had an experience that meets the legal definition of rape, but that they do not personally label the experience rape, a situation known as **unacknowledged rape** (Koss, 2011). In Marsil and McNamara's (2016) study of college students, 11.1 percent of female students indicated an experience that met the definition of rape, but only 3.6 percent self-identified as rape victims during the time they were enrolled in the study. They also report that 5.2 percent of men had an experience that met the definition of rape, but only 1.4 percent self-identified as rape victims (Marsil and McNamara, 2016).

Another widely cited and methodologically sound source of data on the prevalence of rape is the **National Violence Against Women Survey (NVAWS)**, conducted in 1995 and 1996. This is a nationally representative survey funded by the National Institute of Justice, Office of Justice Programs, U.S. Department of Justice, and Centers for Disease Control and Prevention (CDC), in which 8,000 women were surveyed by telephone and asked about their experience with various types of violence. In this survey, 14.8 percent of the female respondents indicated that they were the victim of a completed rape, and an additional 2.8 percent were the victim of only an attempted rape. When looking only at rapes that had occurred in the previous year, the NVAWS study estimated a rape rate four times greater than the NCVS rate in 1995. A possible explanation for this difference is the more explicit language used by the NVAWS compared to the NCVS and the increased number of questions designed to illicit positive rape responses (Tjaden and Thoennes, 2006).

While the NVAWS was conducted one time, the CDC now conducts an ongoing study called the **National Intimate Partner and Sexual Violence Survey (NISVS)**. This study is conducted over the telephone using a nationally representative sample of adult men and women. The survey asks respondents about lifetime prevalence and the past 12 months, and measures a number of types of violence, including rape and other unwanted sexual activity (Smith et al., 2017). In 2015, the most recent year for which data are available, the NISVS found that 1.2 percent of women had experienced an attempted or completed rape in the previous 12 months, and 21.3 percent had experienced the same at some point in their lifetime (Smith et al., 2018). Among men, 0.7 percent had been made to penetrate (including attempts) someone in the previous 12 months, and 7.1 percent had experienced the same at some point in their lifetime. The survey also found that 2.6 percent of men had been the victim of an attempted or completed rape in their lifetime (Smith et al., 2018). The NISVS is a valuable tool in that it is nationally representative and measures both lifetime prevalence and prior year rates. Many self-report victimization surveys use convenience samples (such as college students) which do not allow for the same degree of generalization.

Responses on surveys about sexual violence depend upon the type of question(s) used to illicit the response, and the population studied. Behaviorally specific wording of questions has been shown to illicit higher rates of rape (Fisher, 2009). Behaviorally specific questions are those where rape is specifically described in terms of body parts and actions and force or coercion. These questions are less ambiguous than direct questions about rape and respondents are less likely to overlook an experience or to believe their experience does not fit the definition of rape. Koss (1993) reviewed previous literature where the scope of rape had been measured and found lifetime rape rates ranging from 5 to 12.7 percent for adolescent girls, 13 to 27 percent for college women, and 5.9 to 24 percent for adult women.

THEORIES EXPLAINING RAPE

Criminological theories, such as social learning theory or routine activities theory, can be applied specifically to the crime of rape to explain the behavior. In addition, there are theories that are specific to rape: evolutionary, feminist, and male peer-support. These specific theories are discussed below.

Evolutionary Theory

Evolutionary theory is based on the difference in the amount of time and effort that men and women must put forth in reproduction, which suggests that men and women have different sexual motivations. Women, who gestate, nurse, and become the primary caregiver of offspring, are motivated to minimize their sexual contact and limit reproduction except with men who demonstrate a likelihood of remaining with her after conception. Conversely, men have a relatively low investment in reproduction and thus it is in their interest to mate with as many female partners as possible. Additionally, men are less able to be certain about whether they are the biological father of a particular child, so to be sure they reproduce they must mate with multiple females. An adaptation to the biological desire to reproduce and the low investment in reproducing can be forced copulation or rape (Ellis, 1989).

In 2000, Thornhill and Palmer wrote a somewhat controversial book called *A Natural History of Rape*, which examined the evolutionary basis of rape. In it, they examined "whether human rape is a product of adaptations designed specifically to increase a male's reproductive success or whether it is a by-product of adaptations designed for attaining sexual access to consenting partners" (Thornhill and Palmer, 2000, pg. 60-61). The authors reject an aspect of feminist theory (see below) stating that rape is an expression of power and control, and instead believe that the motives behind rape are sexual (Ward and Siegert, 2002). While Ward and Siegert (2002) note that all serious attempts to explain rape should be considered, and that the explanation proposed by Thornhill and Palmer may account for some of the motivation behind rape, it does not serve as an exclusive argument. They state that Thornhill and Palmer have not proved that their explanation of rape is superior to social science explanations (Ward and Siegert, 2002).

Feminist Theory

Feminist theory explains that rape is a result of patriarchy, an established system whereby men dominate the economic, political, and social arenas. Women's exclusion from politics prevents them from taking action to control, prevent, and punish rape. Rape is part of a cyclical social process. The inequality in society increases the tendency for men to disregard women to the extent that raping them is acceptable, and the fear of rape restricts women's full participation in society and maintains the social inequality that is at the root of rape. Feminists tend not to consider rape a result of the need for sexual gratification, but a result of the male need to exert power and control over women (Ellis, 1989).

Although feminists may think of rape as universal (Brownmiller, 1975), at least in Western society, anthropological research indicates that there are tribal societies that are relatively rape-free, and these societies differ from those that are rape-prone in a number of ways that feminists would find relevant. Rape-free societies differ from rape-prone societies in that women are not excluded from decision making, there is less acceptance of interpersonal violence, and men and women are responsible for the same types of tasks (lack of sexual separation). In these societies, there is mutual respect for both sexes and rape is rare or non-existent (Sanday, 1981).

Male Peer Support Theory

The work behind the **male peer support theory** first began in the 1980s; the theory was later refined by Walter DeKeseredy and Martin Schwartz in 1987. This theory sought to explain the abuse of women, not rape specifically, although the work on this theory deals extensively with rape and sexual assault. The theory suggests that when individual males sought the support of their all-male peer groups, generally in response to relationship stress, these peer groups would respond with advice that was supportive of violence against women. Indeed, the ideology of such peer groups is that "woman abuse is acceptable or preferred behavior under certain conditions" (DeKeseredy and Schwartz, 2013, p. 50). These conditions might include situations where a woman challenges a man's authority or dominance, and it is these types of situations where men often seek support from their peer groups (DeKeseredy and Schwartz, 2013).

DeKeseredy and Schwartz (2013) maintain that violence against women is common, and considered so acceptable in North American culture that institutions such as colleges and sports teams will seek to cover up acts of violence committed by their students or athletes and blame the victim for her own abuse. The norm of violence being acceptable and women being at fault for their victimization means that when men are bonded to society in a normal way they receive messages in support of woman abuse. In fact, they argued that "it is men who do not engage in woman abuse, who are the deviants, and whose bond to the dominant patriarchal social order is weak or broken" (DeKeseredy and Schwartz, 2013, p. 73). This support for woman abuse is found in college environments, poor urban communities, public housing, and rural areas alike (DeKeseredy and Schwartz, 2013).

The theory has recently been expanded in scope to include the influence of women's messages about sexual aggression, the messages within the LGBTQ community, and the influence of technology, such as social media, on how the messages in support of violence against women are delivered (Schwartz, 2021). Research using a college student sample has shown that members of the LGBTQ community were more likely to be associated with peers who are abusive, are more likely to receive pro-abuse messages, and were more likely to report having been sexually assaulted than heterosexual respondents. However, peer support for abuse was associated with the likelihood of sexual assault and stalking in both the LGBTQ and heterosexual groups (DeKeseredy et al., 2017). The pro-abuse messages that people encounter are now more available than ever as they appear on social media platforms, such as incidents where users post comments minimizing violence against women or blaming the victim of that violence (Schwartz, 2021).

RAPE TYPOLOGIES

Not all rapes happen in the same manner, and not all rapists act with the same motivations. Several researchers have sought to classify rape and rapists into different categories, allowing for a better understanding of specific incidents and individuals. This section describes prominent typologies, **Groth's typology**, **Holmes and Holmes' typology**, **Shotland's typology**, and Estrich's **"real rape"** typology, and each category within them, along with the strengths and weaknesses of each typology.

Groth's Typology

In 1979, Nicholas Groth published a book with Jean Birnbaum called *Men Who Rape: The Psychology of the Offender*, in which they discussed rape as being a symptom of psychological problems in the offender. The offender commits rape not as a result of sexual desire, but as a result of non-sexual needs. They divide rapes into three categories: anger rape, power rape, and sadistic rape (Groth, 1979).

Anger Rape

In sexual assaults classified as anger rapes, the rape is a means for the offender to vent feelings of rage, and he uses a sexual attack, rather than a purely physical one, because rape is a way to harm a woman more than would be the case with a physical attack. In fact, during anger rapes, the offender will often force the victim to engage in acts that may be regarded as especially degrading as a means of increasing the harm done to her. This type of attack also displays anger in the use of physical force, including more force than would be necessary to ensure compliance, and the use of abusive language.

The motives behind an anger rape are not sexual, but rather are related to feelings of mental distress, which are often associated with an upsetting circumstance involving a woman in the offender's life. The offender may act out against a different woman by attacking and raping her, using her as a substitute for the woman in his life who is the real target of his anger. He may also attack that woman directly. Anger rape offenders often have had trouble in their personal lives, including trouble maintaining relationships; they rape on infrequent and sporadic occasions; and because the rape does actually serve to reduce their anger, it may take another incident before the anger reaches a point where they feel the need to attack again (Groth, 1979).

Power Rape

A power rape offender feels inadequate and seeks to possess a woman sexually in order to prove that he is masculine and desirable. This type of rapist does not want to cause physical injury to his victim, and only uses the degree of force necessary to gain compliance. The power rapist will often fantasize about a sexual scenario in which he overpowers a woman who comes to enjoy the sexual encounter. He may communicate with the victim both to give orders and to discuss her sexual desires. During the offense he will also seek assurance from the victim that he is sexually satisfying her.

To help assure himself that he is powerful and virile, the power rapist often wants to believe that the victim not only consented to the encounter, but that she enjoyed it. He may attempt to spend time with the victim after the assault, or set up a future meeting with her. In fact, if the victim agrees to such a meeting, this is a common method of apprehending the offender, who will refuse to believe that the victim did not enjoy the encounter and that she "cried rape" in order to protect her reputation.

While these rapists may believe that sexual gratification was the reason for committing the assault, it seems that they are using sexual conquest to control the victim. Power rapists tend not to find the attack sexually satisfying and may rape repeatedly in order to find a victim who will be satisfied by his performance and will reassure him of his masculinity (Groth, 1979).

Sadistic Rape

A sadistic rapist wishes to punish and destroy his victim, and he uses sex and physical and psychological torment as the means of doing this. Sadism comes from both sexuality and aggression and the offender is aroused by the victim's suffering. Sadistic rapes may include ritualistic acts and particularly physically tormenting acts. The sexual areas of the victim's body become targets for abuse. A sadistic rapist, in some cases, may not penetrate the victim himself, but may use other objects to do so, and will become excited by inflicting pain and indignities upon the victim. Sadistic rapists are aroused by being aggressive and feeling powerful, and for some, engaging in sexual acts is not necessary to stimulate this arousal. For others, aggression and inflicting pain are precursors to sexual acts. In some cases, the victim of a sadistic rape is also murdered.

Sadistic rapes are generally premeditated, with a victim selected based on her having a specific characteristic that the offender selects, which may represent something that he wishes to harm. These offenders take precautions against being discovered, and plan their attacks carefully. They will rape repeatedly, often increasing the violence of the rape with each attack as a means to increase excitement. These offenders, while particularly violent and often believed to be psychotic, can actually blend into society well. People who know them find them charming and are surprised when they are informed about their actions (Groth, 1979).

Limitations and Critiques of the Groth's Typology

These types were created by Groth (1979), who utilized interviews from incarcerated rapists, meaning that only those rapists whose crimes were deemed serious enough to report, charge, and convict in the 1970s were included. This means that many acquaintance and marital rapes were not represented and that they may not fit neatly into this typology. Conversely, this typology does conform to the feminist mantra that rape is not about sex, but that it is about power and control (Ellis, 1989). In this typology rape is used as a weapon because of a psychological need to express anger, demonstrate power, or become excited by aggression and harming someone. Thus, for the rapists who are represented, this typology is not inconsistent with a dominant viewpoint about the causes of rape.

Holmes and Holmes' Typology

In 1991 Stephen Holmes and Ronald Holmes published the first edition of their book *Sex Crimes: Patterns and Behavior*, in which they discussed sexual deviance and provided a typology of rapists. This book was revised for the second edition in 2002 and for the third edition in 2009. Holmes and Holmes divide rapists into four categories: power reassurance rapists, anger retaliation rapists, power assertive rapists, and, like Groth (1979), sadistic rapists.

Power Reassurance Rapist

In contrast to the categories in Groth's typology, the power reassurance rapist (also called the compensatory rapist) commits his offense for sexual reasons. Having sex with and possessing another person makes him feel powerful, where otherwise he would feel invalid. The acts he commits during the rape are an expression of his sexual fantasies, which often include the victim enjoying the encounter. This type of rapist will generally not use more force than is required to gain compliance, and he will ask the victim for reassurance that she enjoyed the rape to make him feel more powerful. He may ask the victim if he can return to her, or will choose other victims and rape repeatedly. This type of rapist may also collect trophies from the victim or her home (Holmes and Holmes, 2002b).

The power reassurance rapist's background is not particularly remarkable. He generally has low educational attainment and works in a job that is not challenging, but is a good employee. This low status and his lack of success with social relationships are associated with low self-esteem. He may live with his mother who may have dominated him or sexually abused him through seduction (Holmes and Holmes, 2002b).

Anger Retaliation Rapist

The anger retaliation rapist perceives that he has suffered some degree of unfairness relating to women. To retaliate against all women, he rapes a victim with the intention of harming her. During the rape, he will often commit acts designed to humiliate the victim, such as ejaculating on her or forcing her to perform oral sex after raping her anally. This type of attack is aggressive, and may include elements of verbal aggression such as offensive language, and may even escalate to murder. For this type of rapist, the motives behind the assault are not sexual; rather the assault occurs to express anger and to hurt the victim (Holmes and Holmes, 2002b).

Anger retaliation rapists generally do not come from healthy homes, with many suffering physical abuse as a child. These rapists often experience family separation due to divorce or as a result of being placed in foster care; most are raised by single females. A negative relationship with his caregiver results in unfavorable feelings toward all women. The anger retaliation rapist views himself as very masculine, and may be involved in sexual relationships outside of his marriage, is often involved in physically aggressive sports, and has a job with a great deal of excitement. He generally has a short temper and will rape as a result of an incident involving a significant woman in his life that angers him. His assaults are unplanned, not committed frequently (every six months to a year), and are often committed near his home (Holmes and Holmes, 2002b).

Power Assertive Rapist

The power assertive rapist, also called the exploitive rapist, believes that he is superior to women simply because of his gender, and he commits sexual assaults because his understanding of his gender role suggests that he should. He does not take care to ensure the victim's satisfaction or comfort, and will use violence to gain her compliance. He often commits multiple assaults upon his victim, although he may experience premature ejaculation. The motives for the power assertive rapist are, similar to the anger retaliation rapist and those in Groth's typology, not sexual but predatory (Holmes and Holmes, 2002b).

The power assertive rapist also comes from a troubled background. Most suffered physical abuse as children and most were raised by a single parent. He may have had several unsuccessful marriages. He tries to demonstrate a masculine image and may do so by loudly attempting to pick up women at bars. His car, manner of dress, and occupation also demonstrate masculinity. Because he believes masculinity entitles him to rape women, he does not attempt to conceal his identity and does not intend to make contact with his victim in the future. He plans his attacks and brings a weapon, and will commit offenses every 20 to 25 days (Holmes and Holmes, 2002b).

Sadistic Rapist

The sadistic rapist associates physical aggression with sexual satisfaction, and thus rapes in a violent and frightening manner as an expression of his sexual fantasies. The sadistic rapist is the most dangerous of the groups in this typology and will escalate to killing his victims if not caught. This type of rapist plans out his attacks, carefully selects his victim, takes her to a location he can control, and uses materials to immobilize or hinder the senses of his victim in order to increase her fear. He has a specific plan for each rape he commits, and may require the victim to perform certain acts or say certain words in order for him to experience arousal (Holmes and Holmes, 2002b).

Like the power assertive and anger retaliation rapists, the sadistic rapist may come from a troubled background, but there are more specific elements including potentially having a father who is a rapist or having problems with sexuality as a juvenile. As an adult, the sadistic rapist can put on a good public appearance by living in a good neighborhood, having a good job, and having successful interactions with his family. He is neat and tidy in his appearance and property, including his car (which he may use to stalk victims). Despite the image he projects, he may also be generally aggressive when he does not get what he wants, and may use recreational drugs (Homes and Holmes, 2002b).

Limitations and Critique of Holmes and Holmes' Typology

Similar to Groth's typology, this categorization of offenders may not include acquaintance and marital rapists, as the description of each type of rapists' victim selection would not fit with the typical acquaintance rape scenario. They involve stalking a stranger, a planned attack, or an attack on a woman other than a significant other as a result of a conflict with a significant female in his life. None of these categories include the possibility that the offender selects a victim close to him, and the involvement of alcohol or drugs is not discussed (with the exception that the sadist rapist may be a recreational drug user) as a factor in the assault. Holmes and Holmes (2009b) note in their third edition that while recent research has focused on acquaintance rape, stranger rape still happens, and these are more likely to escalate into sexual murders, making the study of these rapists important.

Unlike Groth's typology, the power reassurance rapist in the Holmes and Holmes' typology does commit his offenses for sexual motives. While this may not fit with the feminist perspective that rape is about power and control (Ellis, 1989), it does allow for a diversity of motives that may be useful in classifying rapists.

Shotland's Typology

R. Lance Shotland (1992) takes a different approach to categorizing rapists, as he specifically looks at what he calls "courtship rape," or rape that occurs when the offender and victim are in or are beginning a romantic relationship. This is a significant deviation from the typologies of Groth (1979) and Holmes and Holmes (2002b, 2009b), which classify rapists who are likely to be stranger rapists. Shotland's typology does not examine stranger rapes, so it does not cover all types of rapists. The exclusion of these types of rapes is no more problematic than the exclusion of acquaintance rape from the Groth (1979) and Holmes and Holmes (1991, 2002b, 2009) typologies; it could be argued that these two groups of rapists should be categorized separately.

The Shotland typology categorizes courtship rape based on the length of the relationship and the onset of sexual activity within the relationship. Much of the research leading to this typology was conducted with college students. Rapes that occur in different stages of the relationship, Shotland argues, are potentially the result of different causes, and the response of the victim within the relationship may depend on the type of relationship as well. Shotland divides courtship rape into five categories: beginning date rape, early date rape, relational date rape, and rape within sexually active couples, which is further divided into those that involve battering and those that do not (Shotland, 1992).

Beginning Date Rape

Shotland (1992) noted that previous research has indicated that college students do not typically expect to have sex with their dating partner during the first few dates, so it is unlikely that miscommunication about sexual expectations is the reason for this type of courtship rape. Indeed, men that rape their dates in the beginning of the relationship may have done so intentionally and may have taken a woman on a date in an attempt to isolate her so that he may do so. It is also possible that these men do expect (unreasonably, based on prior research showing people do not expect sex during the first few dates) that their dates will agree to sex, and if the woman does not they are willing to use force to obtain it. This type of courtship rapist is more sexually aggressive than others, and is constantly seeking new sex partners and using new methods of obtaining sex. The beginning date rapist is typically a misogynist, agrees with rape-supportive statements, has past antisocial acts, and frequently coerces women into sex (Shotland, 1992).

Early Date Rape

Early date rape occurs in the stage of a couple's relationship where they have had a few dates but have not yet established rules about sexual activity which each would expect to have respected. This type of rape is a result of miscommunication based on how men and women perceive sexual intentions differently. Previous research has shown that in identical situations where men and women are interacting, women observers will perceive less sexual intent between the parties than will men observers (Shotland, 1992). Thus, when men and women are interacting outside of a research setting, a man may interpret that the woman has conveyed a degree of sexual intent when the woman does not perceive that she has indicated any. Shotland argued that these differences in perception of sexual intent do not, per se, lead to date rape. Were it to become clear that a miscommunication had occurred, the woman could provide clarification and a typical male will stop seeking sexual activity to which the woman does not consent (Shotland, 1992).

Males who commit early date rape do not have the same characteristics as men who do not rape at all (Shotland, 1992). Early date rapists may place a higher importance on sexuality, feel the impact of sexual deprivation more intensely, and have a more difficult time with sexual impulse control than non-rapist males. During a date where an early date rape occurs, the man and woman are likely to be engaging in some form of consensual sexual activity, and the man may wish for more sexual intimacy or sexual intercourse. Should the woman refuse, the early date rapist may be caught in a cycle of anger and sexual arousal, wherein the heightened arousal from his anger is misinterpreted by him as sexual arousal and he desires more sexual activity. He may once again be frustrated by the woman's refusal, again become angry, and again interprets this arousal as sexual arousal. This cycle is called excitation-transfer. In this situation, it becomes more likely that a rape will occur (Shotland, 1992).

Relational Date Rape

When couples are in an established relationship, they know and understand each other's sexual expectations. It is not likely that a misunderstanding about sexual intent is the reason behind date rape that occurs in this stage of the relationship. In cases where relational date rape occurs, the man has less power than the woman because he is more committed to the relationship. In most relationships men have more power or share power with their partners, so he may feel disadvantaged compared to other men in similar types of relationships. He may also be frustrated that he feels the relationship is unequal and views sex as an expression of her love. He may believe in the rape myth (discussed in the next section) that women enjoy being forced to have sex, and believe that if he uses force against her resistance, she will eventually succumb and enjoy the encounter. Her resistance may arouse him through the excitation-transfer process (Shotland, 1992).

Rape within Sexually Active Couples

This category within the typology assumes that the couple already have (or had) an established sexual relationship. Shotland (1992) relied upon literature about marital rape to describe the two categories of rape within sexually active couples. He noted the relationship between rape and battery within a marriage, in that wives who are raped are likely to have also been beaten, whereas wives who are beaten are less likely to have also been raped. Thus, most rape within sexually active couples is with battery; Shotland (1992) further delineated this category by those rapes that occur with and without battery.

Men who rape within a sexual relationship but do not batter their partners are different from those who do batter. These rapists may have had a more pro-social upbringing where they learned that disputes are not settled with violence, and that hitting a woman is unacceptable (Shotland, 1992). While they would not resort to violence to obtain sex, they have internalized the rape myths that women enjoy being forced to have sex and that men are entitled to sex due to their gender, a trait they share with relational date rapists. These men also may not have to resort to violence because they tend to be physically larger than battering men who rape within sexual relationships (Shotland, 1992).

Rape within sexually active couples that does not include battering is more likely to happen in unmarried couples than married ones, due to the differences in relational dynamics (Shotland, 1992). In unmarried couples, the woman may have more independence financially, and may be more likely to leave the relationship if violence occurs. Within these relationships where the man rapes but does not batter, it is likely that the woman holds more power and that the man is conscious of the inequality. The man rapes due to his desire to take what he thinks he deserves.

Victims of rape within sexually active couples who are not battered are unique in their childhood backgrounds. These women are more likely than victims who are battered to have suffered sexual abuse as a child, yet they are unlikely to have suffered from childhood physical abuse (Shotland, 1992). This background suggests that these victims have learned to tolerate sexual abuse, but they would not tolerate physical abuse. It is also possible that, as a result of childhood sexual abuse, the woman does not like sex. This leads to sex being a contentious issue in the relationship. This does not mean that most men in a relationship where his partner is less interested in sex would rape; men who rape but do not batter in these relationships have different characteristics from the average man. That is, they desire control and believe that they deserve sex.

Men who rape within sexual relationships and also batter are violent against not only their partners, but against others as well. They rape to prove their masculinity and may do so after any disagreement to demonstrate their superiority. Men who rape and batter within their relationship believe that forcing a woman to have sex is one of the most impressive indicators of their superiority (Shotland, 1992). These men come from less desirable backgrounds than men who do not batter, in that they may have been physically and/or sexually abused themselves. Due to the prior abuse, these men may be suffering from post-traumatic stress disorder and their anger is increased during emotional arousal by that condition (Shotland, 1992).

Victims of rape and battery within a relationship are more likely than those who are not battered to have suffered physical and sexual abuse as a child and sexual abuse committed by someone else as an adult (Shotland, 1992). Their traumatic pasts make it more likely that they will tolerate physical and sexual abuse in their relationship. The rapist who also batters selects women who are more dependent than women who are not battered. They tend to be economically dependent, and also have mental illness and self-esteem problems, so they are more easily dominated.

Limitations and Critique of Shotland's Typology

It is noteworthy that Shotland (1992) categorized rape within a dating relationship when previous typologies have not included this common form of sexual violence. The categories within the typology are based on the length of the relationship, and it is possible that there are other factors that differentiate rapists in relationships. It also does not include rapists who rape people known to them, but with whom they are not in a romantic relationship.

Shotland's typology is based on the assumption that people do not expect or anticipate sexual intimacy at the beginning stages of a relationship. This is supported by research from 1981 that uses college students as subjects, so it is quite possible that standards have changed or that college students' attitudes do not generalize to the whole population. In fact, if we can use college student opinions to support assertions about sexual expectation, in more recent research, it seems that college students accept and expect many forms of casual sexual intimacy outside of relationships and that there are accepted ground rules for these interactions (Wentland and Reissing, 2011). This would indicate that the suggestion that sexual miscommunication is unlikely at the beginning of a relationship because no one expects sex may not be accurate in the present day. Perhaps these ground rules and expectations would lead to a blending of the beginning and early date rape categories.

Estrich and Real Rape

Although not a typology of rapists, Estrich's work is a typology of how society views rape; she distinguishes between real rape and simple rape. According to Estrich, people tend to accept events as real rapes if they include a number of characteristics that are stereotypically associated with rape. The victim and offender must have no previous relationship, there is a weapon with violence and/or the threat of violence, and the offender forces sex upon the victim under threat of death. The victim acts appropriately upset and immediately notifies law enforcement of the crime. These crimes are taken seriously by police officers, prosecutors, juries, medical providers, counselors, and the general public (Estrich, 1987).

Simple rape is anything that deviates from the stereotype of a real rape. These include cases where the victim and offender are dating or have had a previous sexual relationship, the victim was not beaten or threatened with violence, is not seriously injured, or has been doing something that might lead others to believe she consented or would have consented to sexual relations. Such actions might include accepting a ride from the offender, drinking with the offender, or wearing provocative clothing.

When situations of this nature occur, some may believe the incident does not constitute a rape, while others may believe that while it is technically a rape, it is not the kind of case to take seriously (Estrich, 1987).

Estrich (1987) argued that, regardless of the characteristics of the victim, the relationship between the victim and offender, and the circumstances of the crime, all rape is real rape (Estrich, 1987). Discussion of these two perceptions of rape is also a good transition to discussing rape myths, or widely held negative, but incorrect, views about rape and rape victims (Burt, 1980).

RAPE MYTHS

Rape myths, as stated above, are widely held negative beliefs about rape and rape victims. Essentially, they consist of culturally supported acceptance of rape (Burt, 1980). In addition to research on the prevalence of rape myth acceptance, there have been multiple studies relating to how rape myth acceptance is associated with other culturally held beliefs and the likelihood of prosecution in rape cases (see Burt and Albin, 1981; Spohn, Beichner, and Davis-Frenzel, 2001). There are four main categories of rape myth as they relate to women: nothing happened, no harm was done, she wanted it, and she deserved it (Burt, 1991).

Nothing Happened

The "nothing happened" myth suggests that women have multiple motivations for fabricating rape charges against men. This myth would include perceptions that either no sexual intercourse occurred at all, or that while there was sex, the act was not a rape. In this category of rape myth is the belief that women, particularly unattractive women, will fabricate stories of rape, where no sex occurred with anyone, to make themselves feel or appear desirable. They also may make up claims of rape to retaliate against an ex-lover or someone who has spurned advances. Also in this category is the belief that women will tell the police she has been raped in order to make a valid excuse for an out-of-wedlock pregnancy (Burt, 1991).

No Harm Was Done

In this group of rape myths, the perception is that sex did occur, but that it was not really a rape because the woman was not harmed. These myths apply particularly to women who have had multiple sexual partners, members of minority groups, or those stereotyped as a "bad girl." The reaction is that if a woman is not a virgin, she no longer has the right to refuse to consent to sex with anyone ever again. This group of myths deny that rape is any different from consensual sex for women if they are not sexually pure (Burt, 1991).

She Wanted It

This group of myths centers around the belief that women never really mean "no," but that they are meant to resist sexual encounters to protect their reputation or "keep things interesting," when in reality they wish to consent. Consent differentiates consensual sex from rape, and if women are always truly consenting, despite any resistance they may give, then they cannot be raped. Some people believe that resistance is to be overcome and that women find the force required to do so sexually arousing. Like the "no harm" myth, the "she wanted it" myth is particularly damaging for women with previous sexual relationships outside of marriage and for women in groups who are stereotyped to be sexually promiscuous (Burt, 1991).

She Deserved It

In this group of myths, the occurrence of forced sex is accepted, but so too is the belief that the woman did something to cause it, making the act not really rape. Women are believed to deserve rape if they wear provocative clothing, begin any form of consensual sexual activity with a man, or put themselves in situations where exposure to danger is possible, such as walking alone at night (Burt, 1991).

RAPE VICTIM/OFFENDER RELATIONSHIP

Despite the stereotypical definition of "real rape" or the fact that most rapist typologies account for only the types of rapes that are committed by strangers, most rapes are in fact committed by someone known to the victim. Using NCVS data for the years 2005–2010, only 22 percent of rapes were committed by strangers, and 78 percent were committed by non-strangers. Giving more detail to the non-stranger group, the offenders are nearly evenly split between well-known and casual acquaintances (36 percent) and intimate partners (34 percent), with only a small percentage of rapes by known offenders being committed by a relative (6 percent) (Planty et al., 2013).

Although the NCVS is a well-respected source of data about rape, it is still instructive to examine the data provided in other sources. The NVAWS, based on lifetime prevalence of rape, found that only 16.7 percent of rape victims were assaulted by strangers. A large group, 43 percent, reported being raped by a current or former intimate partner at some point in their lifetime, 27.3 percent reported being raped by an acquaintance, and 22.4 percent reported being raped by a family member other than a spouse (these percentages do not sum to 100 percent because some respondents reported multiple victimizations) (Tjaden and Thoennes, 2006).

These data indicate that rape by someone known to the victim is more common than rape committed by strangers. Thus, discussing some of the research on the correlates of acquaintance rape is useful. Muehlenhard and Linton (1987) examined the characteristics of dates during which a sexual assault occurred and recent dates where sexual assaults did not occur in a sample of college women. They found that on dates where a sexual assault occurred it was more common for the man to have initiated the date, to have paid for the date, and to have been the one who drove. They also found that heavy alcohol or drug use occurred on the dates that led to sexual assault more commonly than on the dates that did not lead to sexual assault. Finally, dates that involved "parking" or "'making out' in a car or truck" (Muehlenhard and Linton,

1987, p. 192) were more likely to lead to sexual assaults than those dates that did not involve parking.

Recent research on acquaintance rape has focused on the societal reaction to such, especially the conditions under which blame is attributed to the victim. A consistent finding is that men blame rape victims in general, and acquaintance rape victims in particular, for their assault to a greater extent than women do (Hockett et al., 2015). People who rank high in hostile sexism, that is, they hold "combative and adversarial gender role attitudes" (Angelone, Mitchell, and Grossi, 2014, p. 2,294) are more likely to have negative views of acquaintance rape victims, including attributing responsibility to the victim, believing that the victim may be lying, and that she was not traumatized by the event (Angelone, Mitchell, and Grossi, 2014). When female victims of acquaintance rape are sexually objectified, they are more likely to be blamed for their assault and the perception that they suffered as a result of the assault is decreased (Loughnan et al., 2013). It should be noted that Felson and Palmore (2018) found that rape victims in hypothetical scenarios presented to college students were not assigned any more blame than victims of other types of crimes, and indeed, were less likely to be assigned direct blame than victims of other crimes. Another factor that is shown to increase blame attributed to the victim is the victim's use of alcohol or other intoxicating substances.

4

RAPE AND SUBSTANCE USE

In most states, when a woman is incapacitated, such as would occur with a certain degree of alcohol use, she is unable to give consent to have sexual intercourse; sexual intercourse with a female in such an incapacitated state would be considered rape. The legal situation surrounding the use of alcohol and other intoxicating substances was discussed earlier in the book. Here we will examine how intoxicating substances are related to rape in a social context.

In his study of reported rapes in Philadelphia in 1958 and 1960, Amir (1971) noted that alcohol was involved in a significant minority of cases. In one-third of the cases he studied, the victim (10 percent), offender (3 percent), or both (21 percent) had been using alcohol prior to the rape, as recorded by the police report. Since then, the role that alcohol plays in rape has been widely studied, including questioning the role that alcohol may play in actually causing rape, as well as how alcohol is associated with victims' and offenders' (and research participants') perceptions of the incident (Richardson and Hammock, 1991).

Research has consistently shown that when alcohol is consumed prior to a rape occurring, individuals will place more blame on the female victim of the assault, and will assign less blame to the male perpetrator, both in the context of a rape trial, and in perceptional studies (Finch and Munro, 2007; Richardson and Campbell, 1982; Sims et al., 2007). The feminine gender role involves guarding one's purity and controlling men's sexual access, while the male gender role involves seeking sex (Warshaw and Parrot, 1991). Thus when women drink and are raped they are considered responsible, as they did not properly adhere to their gender role. When a man uses alcohol and commits a rape, he can be considered less responsible because, while adhering to his gender role, alcohol inhibited his ability to recognize signs that the woman did not want to have sex. Indeed, convicted rapists will often attribute their behavior to drunkenness as a means of justifying it (Scully and Marolla, 1984).

Alcohol is the most common intoxicating substance associated with sexual assault; in most **substance-related sexual assaults** the victim consumes the drugs or alcohol voluntarily. In their study of drug-related sexual assault (not only rape), Lawyer et al. (2010) reported that 84.4 percent of the victims who were assaulted while incapacitated consumed the substance voluntarily. All of those victims had consumed alcohol, over 40 percent had consumed marijuana (in addition to alcohol), and less than 5 percent had also taken what would often be considered a "date-rape drug" (gamma hydroxybutyric acid [GHB] or Rohypnol). Of the 15.6 percent of the victims who had not consumed the substance voluntarily, most (75 percent) were given alcohol, and nearly 60 percent were given GHB or Rohypnol (Lawyer et al., 2010). While GHB and Rohypnol are generally considered date-rape drugs, perhaps alcohol deserves to be included in that category as well.

In a study of women in their first year of college, Carey et al. (2015) found that incapacitated rape (those that involved alcohol or drugs such that that woman was unable to consent or resist) was more common than forcible rape. By the end of their first year in college, 26 percent of women in the study reported having been the victim of an incapacitated rape during their lifetime and 22 percent reported being the victim of a forcible rape (Carey et al., 2015). Keep in mind these findings are for first-year college women and may not be generalizable to the whole population of women. Victims of incapacitated rape are less likely to seek police, rape crisis, or medical help than victims of forcible rape. While there are many reasons not to seek help after a rape, the biggest difference between victims of incapacitated and forcible rape is that those who were incapacitated were less likely to acknowledge the incident as a rape (Walsh et al., 2015). This means they may not believe that they are legitimate seekers of such services.

OTHER CHARACTERISTICS OF RAPE

Using NCVS data for 2005 to 2010, the highest rates of rape occur for victims who are aged 12 to 17 (4.1 per 1,000 females of that age group) and then 18 to 34 (3.7 per 1,000). The rate drops off sharply for those who are 35 to 64 (1.5 per 1,000) and 65 or older (0.2 per 1,000). In addition to rape victims generally being in the younger age categories, they are also more likely to be divorced/separated (4.4 per 1,000 females in that category) and never married (4.1 per 1,000) compared to those who are married (0.6 per 1,000) or widowed (0.8 per 1,000). Rates of rape are also higher for victims with a household income of less than $25,000 (3.5 per 1,000 females in that category) compared to those with a household income of $25,000 to $49,999 (1.9 per 1,000) and $50,000 or more (1.8 per 1,000). Rates of rape victimization are highest for women who are American Indian/Alaska Native (4.5 per 1,000 females of that race), although this rate is based on a small sample and may not be completely accurate compared to women who are Black (2.8 per 1,000), White (2.2 per 1,000), and Hispanic/Latina (1.4 per 1,000). Finally, women in rural communities have higher rates of rape victimization (3.0 per 1,000 females in that type of area) than women in urban (2.2 per 1,000) and suburban (1.8 per 1,000) communities (Planty, 2013).

Moving from rape rates to the percentage of rapes reported in the NCVS from 2005 to 2010 that include particular characteristics, most rapes (90 percent) involve only one offender, while 10 percent involve two or more offenders. Additionally, most rapes (83 percent) do not involve a weapon, while 6 percent involve a firearm and 4 percent a knife, and in 6 percent of incidents the victim was unsure if there was a weapon present. Victims report sustaining injury in the majority of rape incidents (58 percent); however, in 65 percent of the cases where the victim was injured, she did not receive treatment, indicating that the injury was likely minor. Only 20.3 percent of rape incidents involve injury where the victim receives treatment. Finally, most victims (77 percent) do not receive assistance from any sort of victim service agency (Planty et al., 2013).

REPORTING RAPE

The low incidence of reporting rape to the police reduces the ability of the legal system to deter the crime. When a rape is unreported, the offender cannot be apprehended, and this may result in rapists and potential rapists perceiving that the likelihood of being caught is low (Bachman, 1998). As discussed earlier in Chapter 4, the rates of rape reported to the police are much lower than the rates of rape reported in the NCVS, a data source that does not rely upon police reports. This indicates that many rapes are not reported to the police. Indeed, of the rapes disclosed to the NCVS between 2005 and 2010, only 36 percent were reported to the police. In more recent years, NCVS data shows that 24.9 percent of rapes and sexual assaults were reported to the police in 2018, and 33.9 percent were reported in 2019 (Morgan and Truman, 2020). The most common reasons for reporting were to protect the victim and household from further crimes by the offender (28 percent), to stop the incident or prevent escalation (25 percent), a duty to tell police because it was a crime (21 percent), and to catch the offender and prevent him from reoffending (17 percent). For victims who did not report their assault to the police, the most common issues cited as the most important reason for not reporting were fear of reprisal (20 percent), the perception that the police would not do anything to help (13 percent), and the belief that the assault was a personal matter (13 percent) (Planty et al., 2013).

Data sources that use behaviorally specific wording in their questions generally find even lower rates of reporting rape and sexual assault to the police than the NCVS. The NVAWS found that less than 20 percent of sexual assaults are reported (Tjaden and Thoennes, 2006). Using a community sample and a college student sample, Spohn et al. (2017) also found lower rates of reporting to the police, and noted that college students are less likely to report rapes to the police than women in the community. They found that 9.1 percent of college students who were raped reported to the police, whereas 17.6 percent of women in the community reported their rapes to the police (Spohn et al., 2017).

The statistics above do not take into account the victim and incident characteristics that may also be related to the likelihood of a victim reporting a rape to the police. Spohn et al. (2017) found that an important factor associated with whether a victim reports a rape or sexual assault to the police is whether they perceive the incident to be a rape. As discussed earlier, many women will report having an experience that meets the definition of rape, but do not label it rape themselves. Using data from the 1992–1994 NCVS, Bachman (1998) determined that women who sustained physical injury in addition to the rape were more likely than those who did not sustain physical injury to report their victimization to the police. She also found that African American victims were more likely to report their victimization than victims of other races. Surprisingly, being assaulted by a stranger and the offender having a weapon were not statistically significantly related to the likelihood of reporting when other variables were held constant (Bachman, 1998). A study in Canada produced similar results. Women who sustained injury, whose rape involved the use of physical force, and the presence of indicators of adherence to the "real rape" stereotype were more likely to report their assaults to the police (DuMont, Miller, and Myhr, 2003).

CONCLUSION

As Chapter 4 shows, rape is a common and underreported crime; however, the difficulty of collecting data about rape makes it impossible to say exactly how common or how underreported. From victimization surveys we know police report data is not complete, but these surveys still do not include the assaults committed against people who prefer not to disclose them on surveys or against people who do not identify themselves as rape victims (Koss, 1985). Thus, there are more rapists and more rape incidents than these data can account for. We can also conclude that the majority of rapes do not fit the stereotype of the masked man in the bushes with a weapon and the virtuous, sober victim who notifies the police right away. Again, due to the difficulty in collecting accurate data about rape, we cannot say with certainty what percentage of rapes are committed by someone known to the victim, or what percentage of them involve the use of an intoxicating substance.

While exact information about the nature and extent of rape may not be available, it is useful to examine the characteristics of rape with the data we do have. We have evaluated some victim characteristics; rape characteristics, such as the use of a weapon and the relationship between the victim and offender; the use of substances both as they are associated with rapes occurring and as they are used specifically for the purpose of committing a rape; the likelihood of reporting a rape; and several typologies of rapists. Chapter 4 has focused on rapists who offend against adult women. In Chapter 5 we will examine the characteristics of sex offenders who offend against children.

KEY TERMS

evolutionary theory
feminist theory
Groth's typology
Holmes and Holmes' typology
male peer support theory
National Crime Victimization Survey (NCVS)
National Intimate Partner and Sexual Violence Survey (NISVS)
National Violence Against Women Survey (NVAWS)
rape
rape myths
real rape
Sexual Experiences Survey (SES)
Shotland's typology
substance-related sexual assault
Uniform Crime Reports (UCR)
unacknowledged rape

EXERCISES

1. Find a recent news story about rape. How does the situation described in the story compare to the "real rape" stereotype?
2. What are the strengths and weaknesses of each of the typologies of rapists presented in Chapter 4?
3. How is the use of alcohol and drugs associated with rape?

ESSAY QUESTIONS

1. Discuss the popular conception of rape based on the "real rape" stereotype and rape myths. How do the characteristics of rape incidents compare to this conception? What are the effects of popularly held beliefs about rape on the likelihood of a victim reporting a rape?
2. Discuss the two main methods of measuring rape (the UCR and the NCVS) and the strengths and weaknesses of each. What are the challenges associated with measuring rape? How might you design a survey or measurement system that would address some of these challenges?
3. Briefly describe each of the theories about the causes of rape discussed in Chapter 4. Which theory do you think sounds most compelling and why?
4. What information about rape from Chapter 4 surprised you? What did you think before reading Chapter 4? Has the information changed your opinion? Why or why not?

5

SEX OFFENSES AGAINST CHILDREN

Chapter Objectives

After reading this chapter, students will be able to:

- Describe the various types of sexual offenses against children.
- Understand the difficulties associated with measuring child sexual abuse.
- Identify estimates of rates of childhood sexual abuse.
- Describe several typologies categorizing sexual offenders with child victims.
- Describe the characteristics of offenders and victims of child sex offenses.
- Recognize issues relating to child pornography.
- Explain the justifications used by pedophile groups.
- Explain issues relating to statutory rape.
- Understand the justifications used by sex offenders with child victims.

INTRODUCTION

Jeffrey Epstein was a very wealthy man. He came from a middle-class background and did very well in school, skipping two grades to graduate high school at age 16. Although he attended two colleges, he never received a degree (Pak, 2020). He began his career teaching at a private school in 1974 at the age of 21, despite his lack of a college degree. Students remember him as popular and always having a group of girls around him, although no instances of impropriety were reported. He was fired two years later because his teaching was not high quality (Schuknecht, 2019). He then went to work for Bear Stearns as a junior assistant and began to climb the *ranks very quickly due to his ability to advise wealthy clients. Despite his success, he left Bear Stearns and opened his own firm, Epstein and Co., in 1981, where he managed the wealth of people with $1 billion or more (Thomas, 2002). He developed a reputation for enjoying the company of beautiful women and wealthy and famous friends. At the same time, he became romantically linked with Ghislaine Maxwell, the wealthy daughter of a media giant (Thomas, 2002).*

Epstein is also a convicted sex offender whose victims were minors. In 2005, a woman called the Palm Beach police department to report that her 14-year-old stepdaughter had engaged in sexual activity with a middle-aged man and that he had given her money (Lewis and Swaine, 2015). The teenager reported that Epstein made her take off her clothing and had her massage him as he masturbated. The Palm Beach police department began an investigation, and this launched an investigation into Epstein by the FBI, in which they gained access to his telephone calls and the trash from his mansion. They eventually identified approximately 40 potential victims of Epstein (Lewis and Swaine, 2015). The investigation found that Jeffrey Epstein's assistants lured underage girls to his house, where they would engage in forms of sexual activity for money. Some of the victims gave him massages while naked, and others had sexual intercourse with him (Lewis and Swaine, 2015).

Despite the large number of young victims, Epstein's conduct resulted in fairly limited legal sanctions. The FBI investigation did not lead to any federal charges in exchange for Epstein pleading guilty to state charges of "soliciting and procuring a person under the age of 18 for prostitution" (Swaine, 2015). He was sentenced to 18 months (Swaine, 2015), of which he served 13 in a work release facility. He also had to register as a sex offender and pay restitution (Balsamo and Tucker, 2020). Indeed, the no prosecution agreement (NPA) prompted an investigation into then U.S. attorney Alexander Acosta's conduct, but it concluded that, while he exercised poor judgement, there was no misconduct (Balsamo and Tucker, 2020). Numerous civil suits followed the conviction, many against Epstein and Maxwell jointly, as it was alleged that Maxwell assisted Epstein by recruiting underage girls and by sexually abusing them herself (Corbett, 2019).

Even more alarming than the accusations of involvement in the prostitution of minors, several years after his release from custody, Epstein was accused of involvement in sex trafficking during the same period he was engaged in the activities from which the previous conviction arose (Gajanan, 2019). An investigation suggested that Epstein had flown women and underage girls in to his homes, including one in Manhattan, for "sex parties" (Chaitin, 2019).

Epstein was arrested in July 2019 and was subsequently denied bail, despite his offer to provide bond of at least $100 million, due to the risk he posed to previous and future victims and the fact that he was a flight risk (Mangan & Breuninger, 2019). About a month later, while in custody, Epstein was found dead of what appeared to be suicide in which he hanged himself with a bedsheet. This was after a previous possible suicide attempt, which Epstein claimed was an assault by another inmate. Due to concern for his safety, the jail was meant to be monitoring him closely. On the night of the suicide, there were several irregularities in the jail that resulted in less monitoring than was called for (Sisak, Balsamo, and Leumeister, 2019). As a result of his death, the investigation into his involvement in sex trafficking shifted to *focus on possible co-conspirators, including Ghislaine Maxwell. In December 2021, Maxwell was found guilty of federal charges of "sex trafficking of a minor, transporting a minor with the intent to engage in criminal sexual activity," and three other charges (del Valle, 2021).*

The common perception of sexual offenses against children may be the image of a strange man with candy trying to lure a child into a van, planning to commit a sexual homicide. Jeffrey Epstein likely used power and wealth as a lure. In fact, there are a range of different types of sexual offenses against children, which include different types of acts, victims of different ages and genders, and offenders of different ages, genders, and relationships with the victims. The types of acts can be divided into **non-contact sexual offenses**, including exhibitionism and the consumption of child pornography, and contact sexual offenses, such as rape. The victims in these offenses can be anyone under the age of 18 and the offenders can be adults or juveniles. Particular types of sexual offenses that will be discussed in Chapter 5 include statutory rape, contact and non-contact offenses, and offenses that are aided by the Internet, including the production and consumption of child sexual exploitation material, also called child pornography. We begin our discussion with an exploration of the nature of sex offenses against children.

THE NATURE OF CHILD SEX OFFENSES

Before addressing the issues related to the accuracy of data about **child sexual abuse**, it is important to note that there are several types of statistics in this area, which will yield drastically different interpretations. The first type of study that attempts to estimate the rate of child sexual abuse is an **incidence study**, in which the number of cases reported within a one-year period would be recorded and an annual rate produced. This type of study usually relies upon cases that have been reported through official data (Martin and Silverstone, 2013). The second type of study is a **retrospective prevalence study**, in which an adult sample is asked to recall sexual abuse that took place at any point during their childhood; this type of study produces a lifetime prevalence rate. This method includes abuse that was not reported to official sources. A combination of these two approaches, a **retrospective incidence study**, would ask youths to recall sexual abuse incidents that occurred within the last year, and thus, an annual rate that is not limited to reported incidents only is produced (Martin and Silverstone, 2013).

Studies regarding rates of the **disclosure** of childhood sexual abuse have varying results that may depend on the type of sexual abuse being studied, the time period between the abuse and disclosure, and to whom the abuse was reported. A review of 11 studies of disclosure of childhood sexual assault found that between 31 percent and 87 percent of child sexual abuse victims disclosed the abuse to someone, and that between 10 percent and 18 percent reported the abuse to the authorities (London et al., 2005). The average rate of disclosure during childhood to anyone, from these studies, is approximately 33 percent (London et al., 2005). All of these studies produced overestimates of the rate of disclosure because they looked at the percentage of adults who disclosed to a researcher that they had been sexually abused as a child who also disclosed their abuse as a child. There would also be a number of adults who were sexually abused as children who did not disclose this to researchers, so their nondisclosure would not be counted in the study.

Children who are sexually abused are often told to keep the abuse a secret, told that they will not be believed, will get the offender in trouble, or that they or someone else will be harmed if they tell (Summit, 1983). They may feel helpless to stop the abuse and, when the abuser is someone within the family, may feel that telling about the abuse would destroy their family; the victim would believe it is their fault in this scenario. For these reasons, children typically do not disclose, disclose only after significant time has passed, or disclose in a way that adults do not believe. When they do disclose, they often reverse their disclosure in the face of the reaction from family members (Summit, 1983).

Children who are sexually abused may have a number of reasons to keep the abuse a secret, but some factors are positively related to quick disclosure. For instance, children are more likely to disclose sexual abuse quickly if the offender is someone outside of the child's family, rather than a family member (Goodman-Brown et al., 2003). Younger children also disclose sexual abuse more quickly, perhaps because they are less likely to feel responsible for the event or because they are not as embarrassed by discussing potentially taboo sexual topics (Goodman-Brown et al., 2003). For younger children, it is actually more common for the abuse to be discovered accidentally by an adult than for the child to disclose (Alaggia et al., 2019). For males, the main concerns about disclosing sexual abuse as they entered adolescence were a fear of being perceived as homosexual and/or a fear of being perceived as a victim (Alaggia, 2005). It is also possible that for males who are abused by a woman, norms about masculinity were responsible for them not disclosing the abuse, as they fear they will be ridiculed, or even envied (Gagnier and Collin-Vezina, 2016). For girls, barriers against telling someone about the abuse were that they felt responsible for the abuse and that they feared being blamed or not believed (Alaggia, 2005).

A recent increase in qualitative studies on disclosure of childhood sexual abuse has uncovered more information about the process of disclosure. It has been found that disclosure is not generally a one-time event, but rather an ongoing and dynamic process, where certain situations are more likely to lead to disclosure. These situations include discussions during sexual abuse prevention programs or being specifically asked about sexual abuse (Alaggia et al., 2019). Researchers have also come to understand that social-ecological factors affect how likely a victim of child sexual abuse is to disclose. For instance, dysfunctional family contexts, such as those where other child abuse or domestic violence is present, are less likely to result in disclosure. Family structures that are patriarchal or that have clearly defined stereotypical gender roles are also less likely to lead to disclosure (Alaggia et al., 2019). An unsupportive school environment, as well as cultural factors, such as sexuality being taboo, or women being devalued, may also make a child less likely to disclose sexual abuse (Alaggia et al., 2019).

Because most childhood sexual abuse is not disclosed to anyone during childhood, and disclosed incidents are not always reported to the authorities, statistics on the frequency of child sexual abuse cannot be considered accurate. As discussed below, researchers have made attempts to include as many cases of child sexual abuse as possible in their studies that report rates and prevalence, but the reader must remember these numbers are underestimates.

Sex Crimes Against Children

With the caveats about the accuracy of data on child sexual abuse in mind, most studies estimate a lifetime incidence of child sexual abuse of between 12 percent and 18 percent for girls between the ages of 2 and 17, and between 5 percent and 8 percent for boys ages 2 to 17. This is limited to "higher-impact" types of abuse, including genital touching, attempted penetration, and penetrative sexual acts, and does not include non-contact offenses (Martin and Silverstone, 2013). Given the negative consequences of child sexual abuse victimization (discussed later in Chapter 5) these figures are alarming. Studies also suggest that most child sexual abuse is not reported to police or child protective services (CPS) (Martin and Silverstone, 2013), meaning the perpetrator is never punished or treated in response to their offense.

In response to the bias produced by incidence studies and the lack of specific time period associated with prevalence studies, the U.S. government mandates that the **National Incidence Study (NIS)** of Child Abuse and Neglect be conducted periodically. Most recently, the NIS-4 was completed using data from 2005 and 2006 (Sedlak et al., 2010). This study collected data on cases of child abuse and neglect investigated by CPS as well as those reported but not investigated to CPS and those recognized by community professionals but not reported to CPS. It employs a nationally representative design, so the results can be generalized to the population of the United States (Sedlak et al., 2010). Because this study has been done during four different time periods using the same methodology, comparisons can be made. Between the 1993 study and the 2005–2006 study, the number of sexually abused children decreased by 38 percent, as physical and emotional abuse also decreased (Sedlak et al., 2010). This still leaves a rate of 2.4 per 1,000 children being sexually abused during that year-long time period. Girls were more likely to be sexually abused than boys. Lower socioeconomic status was also associated with a greater risk of sexual abuse (Sedlak et al., 2010).

The **National Survey of Children's Exposure to Violence (NatSCEV)** has been conducted three times, with the most recent data coming from 2013 to 2014, known as the NatSCEV III. This survey is nationally representative and is conducted over the telephone. The survey asks respondents about a range of types of abuse and exposure to violence, including different types of sexual abuse and assault, and can produce both lifetime prevalence and past year rates of violence. It should be noted that respondents aged 10 to 17 speak directly with the interviewer, whereas if the child is age 9 or younger, the interview is conducted with the parent or caregiver who is most familiar with the child's experiences (Finkelhor et al., 2015). This is important to remember because it is possible that the parent being interviewed is either unaware of, or actually responsible for, one or more sexual offenses against the child, and would be unable or reluctant to disclose that information.

Based on the data collected in the NatSCEV III, 5.9 percent of female children and 4.1 percent of male children experienced some form of sex offense in the year prior to the survey. For all children aged 10 to 13, 6.4 percent had been the victim of some type of sex offense in the prior year. Females aged 14 to 17 were at the highest risk, with

16.4 percent experiencing a sex offense in the year prior to the study (Finkelhor et al., 2015). Notably, 4.4 percent of females and 3.3 percent of males aged 14 to 17 were victims of an attempted or completed rape in the year prior to the survey, and 12.9 percent of female and 5.1 percent of males in that age category had experienced attempted or completed rape in their lifetime. Some sex offenses against children in the older age groups are committed by peers, with 2.8 percent of males and 2.1 percent of females aged 14 to 17 reporting a sexual assault committed by a peer in the year prior to the survey. For lifetime prevalence, 10.7 percent of females and 5.1 percent of males report being the victim of a sexual assault committed by a peer (Finkelhor et al., 2015). The NatSCEV III data show low rates of most types of sex offenses committed against younger children, but the method of data collection and low rates of disclosure should be kept in mind.

The most common scenario when an adult sexually assaults a child is for a male adult to assault a female child. This gender dyad makes up nearly 65 percent of sexual assaults with child victims. Just over 15 percent of such assaults are male adults assaulting male children, 14 percent are female adults assaulting male children, and almost 6 percent are female adults assaulting female children (Hamby, Finkelhor, and Turner, 2013). Of those cases of sexual abuse against a child that are reported to the authorities, the most common relationship is that the offender is the victim's father, stepfather, or other relative (Titcomb, Goodman-Delahunty, and De Puiseau, 2012).

It is commonly thought that sexual offenders with child victims will only abuse victims of one gender; however, a fair amount of "crossover" among sex offenders has been shown in the research. In many studies, over 20 percent of sexual abusers of children have victims of both genders (Levenson, Becker, and Morin, 2008). Of those offenders with multiple victims, offenders who have victims age six or younger are the most likely to have victims of both genders, while those who have victims age seven or older are more likely to select victims of one gender or another (Levenson, Becker, and Morin, 2008).

Characteristics of Offenders

There are many misunderstandings about the characteristics of pedophiles and child molesters. The perspective of the child molester as a "dirty old man" is not correct, as most sexual offenders with child victims are under age 35. While the common belief that pedophiles are largely males is true, there are a significant number of female pedophiles as well. It is more difficult to identify these individuals, as societal reactions to their crimes tend to be less punitive, even to the extent of people believing that victims of abuse by females are "lucky" (Holmes and Holmes, 2009b). Along with the "dirty old man" stereotype is the perspective that child molesters are strangers who hunt for children. In contrast to this belief, most offenders know their victims and use that relationship to abuse them. On average, child molesters are no less intelligent than the general public, they are not drug abusers (although about one-third of child molesters report having an alcohol problem), they do not have serious criminal records, and few are considered legally insane. Despite the commonly held belief that homosexual men are more likely to abuse children, no studies on the topic have supported that belief (Holmes and Holmes, 2009b). Child molesters do typically have multiple victims. While estimates vary, for child molesters who have been caught, studies suggest that the number of victims ranges from six to more than 200 before being apprehended (Holmes and Holmes, 2009b).

Many child molesters engage in a process called "**grooming**" prior to beginning their sexual abuse of a child. Craven et al. (2006) provide the following definition of grooming:

> A process by which a person prepares a child, significant adults and the environment for the abuse of this child. Specific goals include gaining access to the child, gaining the child's compliance and maintaining the child's secrecy to avoid disclosure. This process serves to strengthen the offender's abusive patterns, as it may be used as a means of justifying or denying their actions (Craven et al., p. 297).

Grooming the environment and significant adults is a process of gaining the trust of adults in the child's life as a way of obtaining access. Offenders may also work in positions of trust or in areas where access to children is common. To gain adults' trust, the offender may be "charming, very helpful, and have insider status" (Craven et al., 2006, p. 293). It is important to note that when family members sexually abuse children, they are automatically in a position of trust, and already have a location with access to the victim. Parent abusers may isolate the selected child from other family members and develop a special relationship with the child. Grooming the child occurs both physically and psychologically, and refers to building a relationship with the child and gradually introducing sexual topics and touch (Craven et al., 2006). The gradual introduction of sexual abuse can make it so the child does not realize anything inappropriate is happening, but abusers will also use threats and bribes to keep continued compliance and to prevent disclosure. The offender will tailor the grooming to the child's specific circumstances and, based on their response during grooming, will often make the child feel to blame for the abuse (Craven et al., 2006).

TYPES OF CHILD SEX OFFENDERS

As with sex offenders who commit their offenses against adults, researchers have found it useful to classify sex offenders who commit their offenses against children in a number of ways. This can be done based on theory; clinically, based on psychiatric symptoms; pragmatically, according to their treatment needs or recidivism risk; or statistically, based on scores on various assessments (Mandeville-Norden and Beech, 2009). These typologies tend to classify offenders within general categories, such as **pedophiles**, who have sexual responses to prepubescent children, and **hebephiles**, who have sexual responses to pubescent children. If the offender has a familial relationship with the child, this is called **incest** (Groth and Burgess, 1977). It is also possible for someone to be a **child molester** (committing a sexual offense against a child) without being a pedophile (having a sexual interest in children) (Feelgood and Hoyer, 2008). As noted in Chapter 3, pedophilia is a psychiatric classification (Bickley and Beech, 2001), while child molester is a legal classification. We also now recognize another group of offenders who have minor victims: statutory rapists. It seems that these offenders have not been considered particularly abnormal or worthy of classification (Franklin, 2010). Karpman (1954) stated, "the non-pathological offender is defined as an individual who commits normal sex acts which are considered sex offenses, e.g., statutory rape" (p. 51).

Most typologies categorize people who have committed an illegal sexual act with a child, and call them pedophiles (Feelgood and Hoyer, 2008). Typologies also primarily deal with adult offenders (Groth and Burgess, 1977), although juveniles do commit offenses against children. In the following subsections, we discuss the Cohen et al. (1969), Groth and Burgess (1977), Massachusetts Treatment Center: Child Molester (Knight, Carter, and Prentky, 1989), and Holmes and Holmes (2009b) typologies.

Cohen, Seghorn, and Calmas Typology

Cohen, Seghorn, and Calmas (1969) categorized child sex offenders based on the type of sexual assault they committed, the intentions behind the act, and the "developmental history of the offender" (p. 251). They found three types of offenders based on their clinical studies: the pedophile-fixated type, the pedophile-regressed type, and the pedophile-aggressive type. Pedophile-fixated type offenders have been unable to develop relationships with peers during any stage of his life and is only comfortable around children. He may seek employment that allows him frequent contact with children (Cohen et al., 1969). The desire of these types of offenders is to "touch, fondle, caress, suck, and smell the child" (Cohen et al., 1969, p. 251) and they will only begin sexual behavior after a period of courtship with the child. Generally, the child is known to the offender, and the offender may also spend time acquiring the trust of the child's parents (Cohen et al., 1969).

The pedophile-regressed group of offenders is similar to the pedophile-fixated group in their sexual behavior with a child, in that they do not desire penetration. This group is different in their development. These offenders typically had normal social relationships with peers and may have had some heterosexual dating experiences as an adolescent. Despite an unremarkable background, this type of offender begins to develop problems as he enters adulthood. He feels inadequate as a man, and adjusts poorly to the demands of adulthood, such as work and marriage (Cohen et al., 1969). Preceding his sexual offense against a child, this type of offender is often confronted by his sexual inadequacy or lack of masculinity, frequently as a result of a wife or girlfriend having an affair. These offenders are more impulsive in their assaultive behavior and do not seek out a familiar child with whom to have a relationship. For this group of offenders, the victim is almost always female (Cohen et al., 1969).

The third group of offenders, the pedophile-aggressive type, combines sexual and aggressive aspects. These offenders generally select boys as their victims and subject them to brutal assaults. They will often penetrate their victims orally or anally with objects or their penis. These offenders become increasingly sexually excited as aggression increases. They do not generally reach orgasm as a result of the assault, or if they do, must do so through masturbation (Cohen et al., 1969).

One criticism of the Cohen et al. (1969) typology leveled by Feelgood and Hoyer (2008) is that the label "pedophile" is often used in place of the label "child molester." For the pedophile-regressed offenders, it does not seem that they have a persistent attraction to children, but rather that they use a child as an object upon whom they can prove their masculinity after having been rejected by the object of their attraction: adult females. It seems in this particular group the label "pedophile" may be misapplied. Of course, when this typology was constructed, not nearly as much was known about paraphilias, including pedophilia.

Groth and Burgess Typology

Groth and Burgess (1977) categorized offenses against children based on the type of behavior and motivation for the offense; this resulted in two types of child sex offender: sex-pressure offenses and sex-force offenses. Sex-pressure offenses do not include much, if any, physical force to complete the assault. Offenders in these assaults will use either "enticement, in which he attempts to sexually engage the child through persuasion or cajolement, or entrapment, in which he takes advantage of having put the child in a situation where the victim feels indebted or obligated in some way to the offender" (Groth and Burgess, 1997, p. 257). This type of offender attempts to make the victim cooperate or consent to sexual contact using positive attention or bribes. If the child resists, the offender will generally stop his advances. This offender is emotionally involved with the victim and cares for him or her. The motivation appears to be a need for contact and affection, and the offender is better able to achieve that with a child than an adult. There may or may not be a prior relationship between the offender and the child victim (Groth and Burgess, 1977).

In sex-pressure offenses, the victim will sometimes report that they found the experience pleasurable, or at least not frightening. This type of offense is more about an emotional connection, and the offender is often warm and affectionate to the child. In order to keep this connection, the offender must avoid being discovered by people who would seek to stop the contact, as these types of offenses are ongoing with the same victim (Groth and Burgess, 1977). The offender can prevent the victim from telling about the abuse by telling him or her that the abuse is a secret they keep together, or may threaten the victim with harm if he or she does tell. The pressure not to tell may make the victim feel afraid. They may be afraid of punishment or harm, being abandoned if they do tell, or not being able to explain to someone else what has happened (Groth and Burgess, 1977).

The second category of offense is the sex-force offense. These are different from sex-pressure offenses in that the offender threatens or uses physical force to commit the offense. There are two types of sex-force offenses: the exploitive assault and the sadistic assault (Groth and Burgess, 1977). In the exploitive assault, the offender uses threats of violence or violence to counteract any resistance the child may employ. The offender does not intend to hurt the victim, but will do so if necessary to achieve compliance. The degree of physical force is generally only that which is necessary to commit the sexual assault. The motive for this offense is sexual relief rather than emotional engagement. Victims of the exploitive type of sex-force offense will experience fear and symptoms relating to it, and may withdraw or run away (Groth and Burgess, 1977).

The other type of sex-force offense is the sadistic assault. These offenders make up a small portion of the sex-force offenders. They gain pleasure from hurting the child, and find sexuality and aggression becoming intertwined. The offender plans out specific acts of violence and sexual abuse and fantasizes about committing these acts; thus, these offenses are premeditated (Groth and Burgess, 1977). The victim's fear and suffering are exciting to the offender in the sadistic assault. The victims of this type of assault are often badly beaten, injured, and will require medical care (Groth and Burgess, 1977).

Massachusetts Treatment Center: Child Molester, version 3 (MTC:CM3)

Knight, Carter, and Prentky (1989) studied child molesters at the Massachusetts Treatment Center who had been civilly committed as sexually dangerous predators. Their research led to the revision of a classification system and created the **Massachusetts Treatment Center: Child Molester, version 3 (MTC:CM3)** typology. They excluded several types of offenders from their classification system, such as those who only had familial victims (incest offenders) and those who had victims who were both under 16 as well as 16 and older (Knight, Carter, and Prentky, 1989). Based on these criteria for inclusion in the study, their typology may not be representative of child molesters as a whole, but rather the most severely disturbed child molesters. The typology is presented as a flow chart (see Figure 5.1), with several decisions to make about each offender to determine how to classify him (Knight et al., 1989).

FIGURE 5.1. KNIGHT, CARTER, AND PRENTKY (1989) CHILD SEX OFFENDER TYPOLOGY FLOWCHART

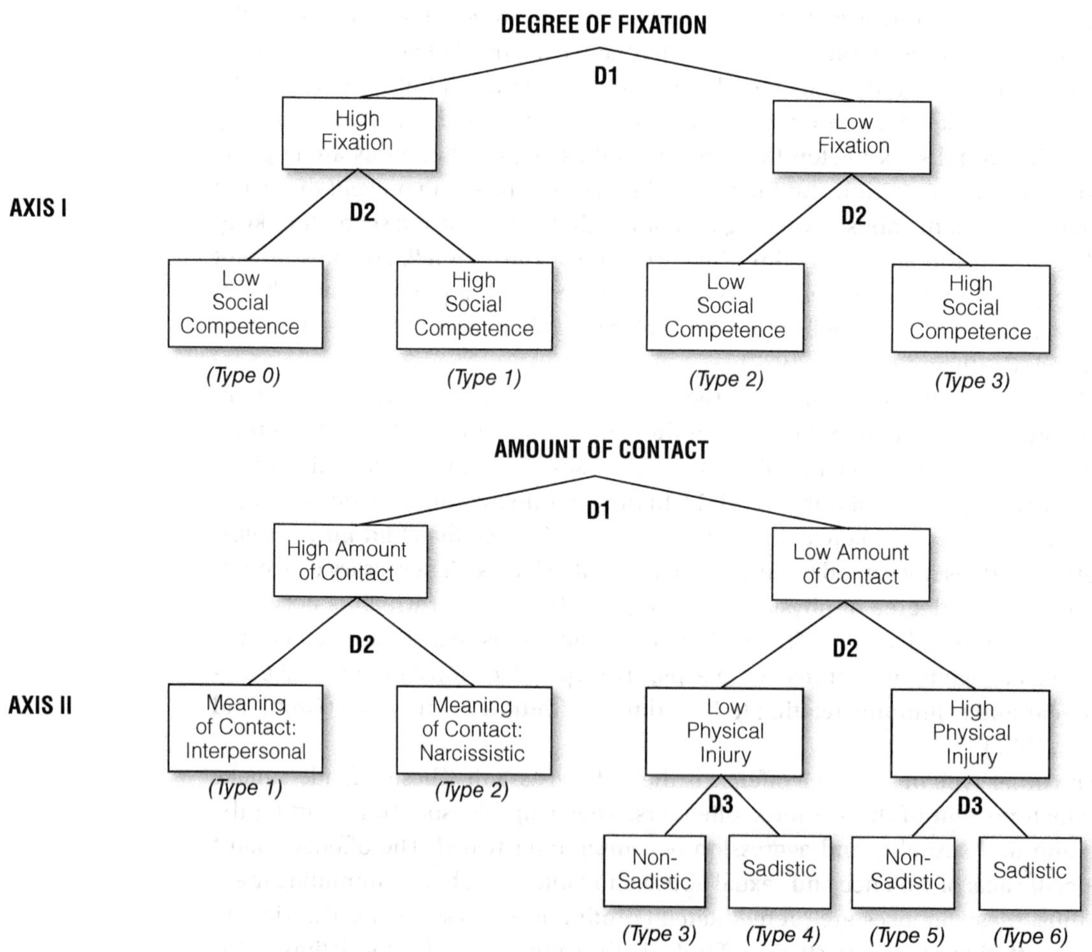

Source: Knight, R., Carter, D., and Prentky, R. (1989). A system for the classification of child molesters: Reliability and application. *Journal of Interpersonal Violence*, *4*(1), 3-23.

First, offenders are classified on Axis I of the typology, with the first decision being whether the offender has a high or low degree of fixation on children. If the offender has children as the focus of his fantasies and this has been going on at least six months, the offender is rated as "high fixation" and rated as "low fixation" otherwise (Knight et al., 1989). The second decision to make in classifying sex offenders along Axis I is regarding their degree of social competence, which will be rated as either high or low. To be considered "high social competence" the offender must have two or more of the following, lasting over an extended period of time: a single job; a sexual, cohabiting relationship with an adult; significant parenting responsibility; active membership in an adult organization, such as a sports club; or, a friendship with an adult. If the offender meets fewer than two of these criteria, he is considered "low social competence" (Knight et al., 1989). Thus, for Axis I, there are four types of child molesters: Type 0, with high fixation and low social competence; Type 1, with high fixation and high social competence; Type 2, with low fixation and low social competence; and, Type 3, with low fixation and high social competence (Knight and Prentky, 1990).

Offenders are also classified on Axis II, which classifies offenders on their type of activity with children. First, it is determined whether they have a high or low degree of contact with children. To be considered "high contact" the offender must have evidence of time spent with children, both sexual and nonsexual contact. A job that allows the offender frequent contact with children would qualify for the nonsexual contact (Knight et al., 1989). For those that are low contact, the next decision to make is the degree of physical injury inflicted on victims, whereas for those that are high contact the next decision is the meaning of the contact to the offender. It is rare for high contact offenders to act with aggression that causes physical injury, so they are not classified along those lines. For the high contact offenders, the meaning of the contact can either be interpersonal or narcissistic (Knight et al., 1989). For those where the meaning of the contact is interpersonal, the offender feels that the relationship is mutual, and that the child is gaining something from their relationship. The sexual contact is primarily fondling and not genital contact. For those where the meaning of the contact is narcissistic, the main interest in the child is sexual satisfaction; thus, sexual activity with the child often includes penetration (Knight et al., 1989).

For the low contact offenders, the next decision is whether there was "low physical injury" or "high physical injury." The offender is considered to have caused low physical injury if there were no lasting injuries to the child and the violence was minimal, such as pushing or holding the victim down. More substantial violence or lasting injuries such as bruises or cuts are considered to have caused high physical injury (Knight et al., 1989). The next decision to be made, for both the high and low physical injury groups, is whether the acts were sadistic or non-sadistic. For the low physical injury group, the decision about whether the offender is sadistic is made based on a description of his fantasies, such as whether they include descriptions of bondage or include elements such as spanking. For the high physical injury group, this decision can be based on the offenses themselves, such as whether the offender was aroused by the fear or pain experienced by the victim (Knight and Prentky, 1990). Thus, for Axis II, offenders are categorized into six groups: Type 1, which is high contact, interpersonal; Type 2, which is high contact, narcissistic; Type 3, which is low contact, low injury, non-sadistic; Type 4, which is low contact, low injury, sadistic; Type 5, which is low contact, high injury, non-sadistic; and Type 6, which is low contact, high injury, sadistic (Knight and Prentky, 1990). There has been an additional revision to the typology and flowchart (see Knight and King, 2012) not presented here.

While the MTC:CM3 has been widely studied and validated, a criticism of the typology is that the data that led to its creation, and the data used in validation studies, come from mostly White offenders (Schaaf et al., 2019). As child molesters are a more diverse group than the samples, Schaaf and colleagues (2019) undertook a validation study using an ethnically diverse sample including White, Black, and Latino child molesters. Each offender in their study was classified along Axis I and Axis II, and then the percentage of offenders who fit into each type was computed by race. While they found it possible to classify all the offenders using the MTC:CM3 with a very high degree of reliability, they did find some differences in the proportion of each racial group that fell into the Axis I types. Specifically, White child molesters were overrepresented in Type 0 (high fixation with low social competence), Black child molesters were overrepresented in Type 2 (low fixation with low social competence), and Latino child molesters were overrepresented in Type 3 (low fixation with high social competence) (Schaaf et al., 2019). They did not find a difference in how child molesters were classified on Axis II. They concluded that the MTC:CM3 was reliable enough to be used to classify child molesters from a racially diverse population (Schaaf et al., 2019).

Holmes and Holmes Typology

Holmes and Holmes (2009b) classify child molesters based on their acts with their victims, their personality, and their sexual preferences. They developed four categories of offender: the mysoped, the regressed offender, the fixated offender, and the naïve offender. The mysoped is the category of child molester that most closely fits the stereotype of these offenders. The mysoped is usually male and has the desire to physically harm his victims while molesting them. This type of offender will abduct children who are strangers to him using force or a weapon. This type of child molester is most likely to commit fatal violence, may mutilate the child's body, and may commit acts of necrophilia with it. These offenders do not have frequent contact with children, are not highly socially competent, and are most likely to have a substance abuse problem, a criminal record, and not be married (Holmes and Holmes, 2009b).

The remaining categories of offenders do not display the significant violence that the mysoped does. The regressed child offender typically has a normal social history, including relationships as an adolescent, and is married or has a long-standing partner, but some negative event in his life triggers his offending. He offends against victims due to opportunity, usually has female victims, and prefers children with whom he does not have a relationship. This type of offender is unlikely to reoffend if the situation that triggered the offending can be resolved (Holmes and Holmes, 2009b). The fixated offender paused his psychosexual development during childhood, during a point when he found children attractive. This offender has a persistent interest in children and is uncomfortable around adults. He does not wish to harm children, as he loves them, and finds them less critical of him than adults would be. He develops a relationship with his victim, and sexual activity is gradually introduced (Holmes and Holmes, 2009b). Finally, the naïve offender may have a brain disorder that prevents him from understanding that sexual contact between adults and children is not acceptable. He also would not understand the harm he has caused the child. Naïve offenders tend not to desire intercourse but, rather, wish to fondle the victim (Holmes and Holmes, 2009b).

ONLINE SEX OFFENDING

The ubiquity of the Internet has given people with a sexual interest in children a new avenue to pursue these desires. Several types of sex offending against children can be committed using the Internet. Mainly, the Internet can be used as a means of contacting children for the purposes of sex offenses, and it can be used as a means of distributing and viewing child pornography. In this section, we discuss types of sex offenders who use the Internet and focus on Child Sexual Exploitation Material (CSEM).

Chat Room Sex Offender Typology

Some sex offenders use the Internet to contact children, and they may have different motivations behind that contact. Briggs, Simon, and Simonsen (2011) classified sex offenders who contacted someone they thought was a child using social media or chat rooms. They studied offenders who were communicating with police officers posing as female teenagers and classified them into two groups: contact-driven offenders and fantasy-driven offenders (Briggs et al., 2011). The contact-driven group of offenders contacted their victims online but desired to set up an in-person meeting and have a sexual relationship with the victim. Offenders were given this classification if, during the online chat, they set up a time and place to meet the victim. They may engage in some sexual chatting, but the ultimate goal was sexual climax while meeting with the victim in person (Briggs et al., 2011). In contrast, for the fantasy-driven offender group the ultimate goal was sexual climax during the online interaction. They engaged in more online sexual behavior, such as cybersex and using a web camera to send sexual images of themselves. A few of the fantasy-driven offenders did attempt to set up meetings with the victim, but this was generally for the purposes of improving cybersex (Briggs et al., 2011).

These two offender groups differ in a number of ways. For the contact-driven offenders, many tried to set up a meeting with the victim within the first day of initiating online contact. The fantasy-driven offenders communicated with their victims for an average of nearly 33 days (Briggs et al., 2011). The contact-driven offenders were younger than the fantasy-driven offenders and were less likely to have ever been married. Contact-driven offenders were also less likely to be employed than fantasy-driven offenders. Fantasy-driven offenders were more likely to be diagnosed with a paraphilia and were more likely to have a narcissistic personality disorder than contact-driven offenders. Both types of offender used pornography compulsively, had one-night stands regularly, and had sex with prostitutes (Briggs et al., 2011).

Online Solicitation Offenders

More recently, DeHart and colleagues (2017) classified offenders who used the Internet for the sexual solicitation of minors. Using case files from convicted offenders who used the Internet to contact children, but were actually in contact with undercover police, they analyzed chat logs, emails, and social media activity to develop the following categories: cybersex only, cybersex/schedulers, schedulers, and buyers. Cybersex-only offenders had the longest interactions with victims, which could often include online contact over the course of several months. They frequently exposed themselves on camera or asked for sexually explicit pictures of the victims. Their chat logs include graphic content where they may guide a victim's masturbation and ask about sexual features of the victim. While it is common for them to discuss meeting, they do not arrange specific times or locations, and generally speak more hypothetically about meeting (DeHart et al., 2017). Cybersex/schedulers were very similar to cybersex only offenders in the content of their online conversations, but they did schedule specific locations and times to meet. It should be noted that canceling or not showing to the meeting was most common for this group, which could be because working out the details of scheduling was part of their fantasy, or because they were concerned that the meeting may be a law enforcement trap (DeHart et al., 2017).

In contrast to cybersex only and cybersex/schedulers, schedulers' chats with victims were shorter, often completed in less than a day. They typically did not share sexually explicit images or request them, and they often stated specific interests and were seeking to "hook up" with the victim. These offenders would go through the process of identifying locations and times to meet with the victim (DeHart et al., 2017). Buyers are similar to schedulers in that their interactions are shorter. They are looking to exchange money for sexual activity with the victim, which they often do by responding to personal ads. The main content of the conversation is arranging times and locations as well as agreeing upon price. While they were unlikely to send sexually explicit images of themselves, they frequently requested images, often with specific content, as proof that the minor was who they said they were (DeHart et al., 2017).

Child Sexual Exploitation Material

The term "**Child Sexual Exploitation Material (CSEM)**" can be used to describe depictions of child exploitation, including those commonly known as **child pornography**, but it also includes additional material such as audio or written descriptions of child exploitation (Merdian et al., 2020). According to Frangez et al. (2015) the distinction in terminology is important, as the term "child pornography" may be mistaken for other, legal types of pornography, and by minimizing the seriousness of the crime, the term does not convey respect to the victim. Nonetheless, much research, particularly that which is not very recent, uses the term "child pornography" when describing these depictions; but it is important to remember that there is a child victim in images known as child pornography. "CSEM" may be more of a descriptive term and "child pornography" a legal term.

Child pornography is defined in the United States Code as "any visual depiction of sexually explicit conduct involving a minor" (United States Department of Justice,

2020, para. 1) and notes that "sexually explicit" does not necessarily mean a sexual act is involved and may include sexually suggestive images. The definition of images includes digital images and electronic data that could be used to create a visible image (United States Department of Justice, 2020). In a more academic context, child pornography may be defined as "the use of underage children in various media for the purposes of sexual arousal for the viewer" (Holmes & Holmes, 2009b, p. 135). For these purposes, anyone under the age of 18 is a child, so their use in pictures and films of an erotic nature is child pornography and is criminal in the United States and many other countries. In the United States it is illegal to produce, possess, and distribute child pornography (Holmes and Holmes, 2009b).

CSEM was in existence long before the ubiquity of the Internet, but currently the Internet is the main way that child pornography is distributed. Because of the ease with which such material can be transmitted across countries, enforcement of child pornography laws has become complicated (Holmes and Holmes, 2009b). Steel et al. (2020) identified five different periods during which CSEM offenders made use of increasingly sophisticated technology. The first of these periods started in 1987, when networking capabilities were not as advanced as they are now, and these offenders would store images on floppy disks or removable storage devices, and they could use electronic bulletin board systems and email to contact each other and exchange images (Steel et al., 2020). As technology advanced, CSEM offenders made use of websites, peer-to-peer networks, the dark web, and currently the main technologies in use are mobile phones and messaging, and streaming. The increased sophistication of available technologies has also increased the degree to which offenders can take measures to avoid detection (Steel et al., 2020).

Much of the child pornography that is produced, and for which arrests are made, contains images of children being penetrated, while a substantial minority includes images of sadism, violence, and torture (Wolak et al., 2011). Child pornography is produced for the most part by sexual abusers who have access to a child with whom they have a relationship of some kind and use the material for themselves; other child pornography is produced for profit, either with a child obtained by the offender or by online predators who ask for images from adolescents or use hidden cameras (Wolak et al., 2011).

For those that produce child pornography, it is most common to have a relationship with the child in the material, such as an acquaintance of a family member, followed by 25 percent who, alarmingly to parents of tech savvy teens, met the victim online. It was rare for the offender to be a stranger or the child's pimp. Most producers of child pornography also committed separate contact sexual offenses against children (Wolak et al., 2011). The most common means of engaging the child in the production of pornography is through romance or friendship, followed by coercion or pressure and the use of alcohol or drugs. The use of violence was rare (Wolak et al., 2011). In this study, only about one-third of the offenders produced videos, with most using still images; only 25 percent of the producers of child pornography distributed the images to others (Wolak et al., 2011). Most of the offenders who produced child pornography were male, White, age 26 or older, single, employed, were not registered sex offenders, and possessed child pornography in addition to what they had produced. Most of the victims of child pornography in the Wolak et al. (2011) study were female, White, and were age 13 or older.

In addition to individuals who produce child pornography, there are many who possess child pornography but do not produce it themselves. In a study conducted for the National Center for Missing and Exploited Children, Wolak, Finkelhor, and Mitchell (2005) found that more than 99 percent of those arrested for possessing child pornography were male, most were White, age 26 or older, about equally likely to be single or married, and most were employed. The demographics of the average possessor of child pornography are very similar to the demographics of the average producer of child pornography. Of those arrested for possessing child pornography, 46 percent had access to a child in their home, through work, or through an organized activity (Wolak et al., 2005).

Contact between possessors of child pornography and children is alarming, as illustrated in a study of Canadians arrested for child pornography. Nearly 38 percent of these Canadian offenders possessing child pornography also committed a contact sexual offense against a child (Seto and Eke, 2005). Of those with a history of both child pornography and contact sexual offenses, 9.2 percent committed a contact sexual offense after their arrest and during the study period and 6.6 percent committed a **non-contact sexual offense** (Seto and Eke, 2005). Using several methods of determining if an individual arrested for possession of child pornography had also committed a contact offense, Bourke and Hernandez (2009) found that 85 percent of their subjects had also sexually abused a child. These researchers call into question the myth that possessors of child pornography are not harming anyone or simply made a few bad clicks on an Internet search. It should be noted that both the studies discussed here involved offenders who had been arrested. It is possible that there are indeed unlucky clickers who end up possessing child pornography but are not arrested due to the relative lack of severity of their crime.

In addition to the traditional conception of child pornography, where a child is depicted in an obscene manner and the images are collected by older males, a practice known as "sexting" has become a new area in enforcement of child pornography laws. Sexting refers to sending sexual images, such as nude pictures, over cell phones or other electronic devices. Research shows that this is a fairly common practice among teenagers, with 28 percent of 16-year-olds and 31 percent of 17-year-olds having sent or received a nude image or video (Mitchell et al., 2012). Among other concerns about this behavior is that youth under the age of 18 may be creating child pornography by taking such images, and they may be distributing it by sending it to a romantic partner, who then also possesses child pornography. Indeed, teens are being charged with such offenses, resulting in some becoming registered sex offenders (Moak, Walker, and Lee, 2011). While these images may meet the legal definition of child pornography, they likely were not the intended targets of laws that were created before this technology proliferated. A risk associated with sexting is that images taken and sent consensually may be forwarded to other individuals without the consent of the subject of the image. This may cause the victim to be traumatized and to experience sexual harassment. While these situations may be more appropriate for legal intervention, some laws do not take into account whether the images were sent consensually, but rather focus on the illegality of the content of the images (Krieger, 2017).

Pro-Pedophile Groups

For a suggested annual donation of $40, adult men who are sexually interested in boys, or those who are supportive of them, can support the **North American Man/Boy Love Association (NAMBLA)** and receive newsletters and publications from the organization. Established in 1978, this is the most well-known organization of its type. NAMBLA states that its goal is to "end the extreme oppression of men and boys in mutually consensual relationships" and "support the rights of youth as well as adults to choose the partners with whom they wish to share and enjoy their bodies" (www.nambla.org). They state that ageism is the problem that causes people to be opposed to these types of relationships, as children are not given the rights to make decisions about their bodies and relationships. The organization's website is clear that it does not support or encourage anyone to break the law but wishes to end the stigmatization associated with relationships with children, particularly as it is codified in age of consent laws (www.nambla.org).

NAMBLA attempts to use social science to justify its position on relationships between adults and children. The organization cites a meta-analysis published in the *Psychological Bulletin* in 1998; NAMBLA claimed that this study demonstrated that there was no connection between boys' experiences of sexual abuse and their later adjustment (www.nambla.org). The use of this study caused quite a stir in the American Psychological Association (APA), such that the APA had to send NAMBLA a "cease and desist" letter (Garrison and Kobor, 2001). NAMBLA had taken the study's results out of context in order to support its mission. The citation still appears on NAMBLA's list of recommended readings (www.nambla.org).

5

In addition to the general philosophy of accepting relationships between adults and children, the NAMBLA website provides information about the criminal justice system, stories about experiences boys have had with men, and ostensibly provides access to several publications. At the time the first edition of this book was being written, the Web links to the NAMBLA Bulletin were broken, and the sections of the website describing a "sex panic" were under construction (www.nambla.org). At the time this second edition was being written, these links were still under construction or broken, but there is now an order form that can be sent by mail to obtain publications, and some selections from the bulletin are available on the website. NAMBLA is careful about protecting itself and its members from social and legal trouble. Donations can be made anonymously, and correspondence sent from NAMBLA does not contain its name in the return address. In its Prison Program, through which members can write to inmates convicted of child sex offenses, or incarcerated "boy-lovers" (www.nambla.org), NAMBLA cautions that the mail can be read when it is inspected for contraband, and that pen pals should "avoid writing about any activities, whether real or imagined, that could be considered illegal" (www.nambla.org).

NAMBLA also appears to advocate for youth in contexts outside of supporting their ability to form consensual relationships with adults. For instance, the organization condemns the use of corporal punishment to discipline children and does not support war, which results in the death and suffering of children (www.nambla.org). This would seem to make their position more reasonable; however, it is clear that the main goal of NAMBLA is to legitimize behavior that is illegal because of the popular perspective that these types of relationships and sexual contacts are harmful to children. The organization seeks support from those involved in finding peer-reviewed research and data that support their position (www.nambla.org). NAMBLA messages and information have been found posted on other Web resources specifically for pedophiles. The Internet has made it easier for pedophiles to reach each other and for groups like NAMBLA to recruit other members (Durkin, 1997).

According to DeYoung (1989), NAMBLA uses several techniques of neutralization described by Sykes and Matza as a way of justifying their support of beliefs and actions that are considered wrong by mainstream society. The group uses denial of injury by claiming that sexual behavior with children is not harmful to them, and, despite the vast amount of social science evidence to the contrary, focuses on the positives. The group does this by including letters from boys who describe the beneficial effects of a relationship with an adult male. These benefits include things such as getting out of an abusive home situation or the boy discovering his own sexuality (DeYoung, 1989). The group also uses the technique of condemnation of the condemners. Condemnation of those who commit child sexual abuse is quite strong and NAMBLA is equally strong in its condemnation of society and the criminal justice response to child sexual abuse. The group's publications mock individual mental health providers and criminal justice professionals, sometimes by name, who work to help victims and punish offenders (DeYoung, 1989).

NAMBLA also makes an appeal to higher loyalties to justify their philosophy and behavior. They believe the more important interest is "the liberation of children from what it characterizes as the repressive bonds of society" (DeYoung, 1989, p. 120) by allowing them to explore their sexuality and giving them rights and decision-making power restricted to them by mainstream society. It also allies with the causes of mainstream organizations concerned with social welfare (DeYoung, 1989). Finally, the group uses denial of the victim, wherein the victim is perceived to have deserved the outcome. NAMBLA believes and espouses the fact that children can give consent to sexual activity with adults and that children are often the instigators of such activity. DeYoung (1989) believes that this last technique of neutralization is least likely to be successful, as, although NAMBLA does not believe in their legitimacy, there are age of consent laws that define the child as a victim.

STATUTORY RAPE

According to Oberman (1994), girls will often "consent to sex to feel liked or loved, to feel closer to someone, [or] to become popular" (p. 19), but generally not as a result of their own sexual desire. Girls begin engaging in sexual activity at a time when their self-esteem, body image, and assertiveness are all declining dramatically (Oberman, 1994). This suggests that girls are vulnerable to sexual exploitation, not that they should have the autonomy to make their own sexual decisions (Oberman, 1994). Indeed, all states have some form of **statutory rape** law, which makes it a crime to engage in sexual activity with a minor of a certain age, regardless of that individual's "consent" to the activity. Statutory rape laws originally provided that only females could be victims and only males offenders; however, feminists pushed for these laws to become non-gender-specific as a way of demonstrating that males and females both have sexual agency (Tenzer, 2019). While laws are now gender neutral, they vary decidedly by state, with some having one cutoff age, some having a minimum age for consent and including an age differential between the victim and offender, and some requiring that the offender be above a certain age for sexual activity to be considered a crime (Glosser, Gardiner, and Fishman, 2004). The laws will also vary on whether the act is a misdemeanor or felony based on the age of the victim and the offender, and will vary on the seriousness of the penalty imposed (Glosser et al., 2004).

In statutory rape cases that are reported to the police, 95 percent of victims are female, and of those offenses with female victims, 99 percent of the offenders were male (Troup-Leasure and Snyder, 2005). It seems that offenses against male victims are more likely to be known to the police when there is a greater age difference between the victim and offender compared to when there is a female victim. When the victim of a statutory rape is male, the offender is age 21 or older in 70 percent of the cases, whereas if the victim is female, the offender is age 21 or older in only 45 percent of the cases. The median age difference between male victims and female offenders is nine years, whereas the median age difference between female victims and male offenders is six years (Troup-Leasure and Snyder, 2005). In nearly all statutory rape cases known to the police, the victim and offender were either in a dating relationship or were acquaintances. Unlike forcible rapes reported to the police, statutory rapes generally do not include the use of a weapon or bodily injury to the victim. Arrest occurred in 42 percent of the statutory rape cases reported in this study; the likelihood of arrest went down as the age of the victim increased (Troup-Leasure and Snyder, 2005).

Statutory rape laws are not necessarily applied uniformly. Most incidents that would legally be considered statutory rape are not brought to the attention of the authorities, and very few of those incidents involve same-sex partners (1 percent); when an incident reported to the police involved same-sex partners, it was more likely to result in an arrest and even more so if the partners were in a romantic relationship (Chaffin, Chenoweth, and Letourneau, 2016). For male offender/female victim incidents, a romantic relationship reduced the likelihood of an arrest, in contrast to the affect a relationship had with same-sex partners. In incidents where a male was the victim and a female was the offender, the likelihood of arrest was the smallest of all the types of gender pairings (Chaffin et al., 2016). This study also found that statutory rape incidents with a White victim were more likely to result in arrest than those with a Black or Hispanic victim (Chaffin et al., 2016).

In a college student sample, 24 percent of women reported having had consensual sexual intercourse at age 13, 14, or 15 (Leitenberg and Saltzman, 2003); in other words, an experience that, depending on the jurisdiction, may have been considered statutory rape. For the majority of the sample, the male partner was two to four years older than the female. The younger the girl was when she had intercourse, the more likely the partner was to be five or more years older (31 percent of those who were age 13 and 13 percent of those who were age 15) (Leitenberg and Saltzman, 2003). While the group of women who had consensual sex as a young teen was not compared to women who had consensual sex at a later age, within the group, there were not many statistically significant differences in psychological symptoms based on how old the woman was when she first had intercourse or the age difference with the partner. Only those who were 13 when they first had intercourse had higher levels of psychological distress than the rest of the group. The degree of current sexual satisfaction did not vary statistically significantly for any of the groups (Leitenberg and Saltzman, 2003).

Because young adults are a group that is strongly impacted by statutory rape laws, it is interesting to examine their perceptions of such laws. Studies of these perceptions indicate that most young adults do not believe that relationships between teenagers and young adults should be considered criminal, although as the age gap between the victim and offender increases, they are more likely to consider a sexual relationship a crime (Oudekerk, Farr, and Reppucci, 2013) or to be critical of the sexual relationship (Koon-Magnin and Ruback, 2013). Being aware of statutory rape laws does not increase the degree to which study respondents condemn sexual activity between adolescents (Koon-Magnin and Ruback, 2013). It seems that statutory rape laws, as they are defined in many states, are not perceived as legitimate by young adults.

One of the most cited reasons for statutory rape laws is to prevent teenage pregnancy. Girls who become mothers when they are younger than the age of consent in their state with partners who are adults are clearly victims of statutory rape in the legal sense, regardless of how they define it themselves. When these girls are interviewed, they express varying opinions about statutory rape and relationships with older men. For girls who were still in a relationship with their older partner, statutory rape laws were considered unnecessary, because they did not view the relationship as deviant and had not experienced problems as a result of the relationship (Higginson, 1999). Others did not view statutory rape laws as necessary due to the age difference between them and their partner being meaningless, although some qualified that an age difference larger than the one in their relationship might be "gross" (Higginson, 1999, p. 29). Other reasons for believing that statutory rape laws were unnecessary were the perceptions that peers were also involved in relationships with older men, approval from parents and teachers, the feeling that if their boyfriends loved them, there was nothing wrong with the relationship, the thought that consensual sex should not be illegal, and that young teenagers were mature enough to consent to sexual activity (Higginson, 1999).

In contrast, other girls were angry with their older ex-partners for having pursued them, stating that there must be something wrong with an older man who would be interested in a young girl. Other girls felt that the age gap in their relationship was wrong due to the experiences they had with being abused and manipulated, and a few said they were tricked into getting pregnant by men who told them they were infertile. Some of these girls thought statutory rape laws could be useful in preventing other girls from being taken advantage of (Higginson, 1999). Other girls were aware of the deviant nature of their relationships, as evidenced by their attempts to hide their true age from their boyfriends, but excused their deviance by stating that they were not ultimately responsible for their relationships. For instance, boys their own age were too immature or would not be suitable father figures for their child. Others claimed a lack of responsibility due to the missing father figure in their own life and the need to have an older man fill that role (Higginson, 1999). Overall, those who felt responsibility for their involvement in their relationship with an older man did not feel the need for statutory rape laws, while those who felt more victimized and less responsible for being involved with an older man did believe statutory rape laws could help protect girls like themselves (Higginson, 1999).

ABUSE OF AUTHORITY

Another scenario in which an adult has sexual contact with a child, although different from a statutory rape situation, is when an adult in a child's life abuses their authority to coerce the child into being involved in the sexual contact. Child sexual abuse does not always "occur under conditions of danger, threat, and violence. Many abusers, misusing their authority or manipulating moral standards, act with the child's trust" (Finkelhor, 1987, p. 352). Anyone who is in a position of authority over a child, such as a teacher, coach, daycare staff, or clergy has that child's trust and can misuse it in order to sexually abuse that child. The focus here will be on teachers and clergy.

In 2002, a large number of victims came forward to accuse Catholic priests of having sexually abused them as children. This led to several large studies of sexual abuse within the Catholic Church (Terry and Ackerman, 2008). In the majority of cases where Catholic priests sexually abuse children, the victim is a male child, and in nearly all cases the child is known to the priest. In fact, the priest often socialized in the victim's home, although the abuse most often took place in the priest's residence (Terry and Ackerman, 2008). It is likely that the ability for the priests to have unsupervised contact with mostly male altar servers is the situation that allows the abuse to happen. Terry and Ackerman (2008) also note that the mean onset of priests committing sexual abuse is 11 years after they enter the priesthood, which is a time when many priests move into the parish residence.

A study of adult male survivors of childhood sexual abuse by clergy examined the retrospective experience of abuse as well as the way in which it affected these men as adults. Fater and Mullaney (2000) found ten themes through interviewing these survivors. They found that these survivors were often initially attracted to the priest's character and wanted to try to please him. Sexual abuse was often seen as a sign of approval. Survivors had vivid memories of the details of their assaults, including physical sensations as well as recall of their surroundings. They also perceived themselves as vulnerable as children and believed that the priest selected them specifically and on purpose (Fater and Mullaney, 2000). The survivors of this abuse often remained silent as a result of negative feelings and self-blame, as well as threats or implied threats from their abuser. They experienced terrible emotional pain as a result of the abuse, and many became suicidal. The abuse affects all areas of survivors' lives as adults, including their self-concept and their relationships. They also lost spirituality and felt anger and mistrust toward the church. Emotional recovery was difficult, but some survivors are optimistic, and their recovery sometimes led to seeking to help or protect others from suffering similar abuse (Fater and Mullaney, 2000).

Another major form of abuse of authority over children is sexual abuse committed by teachers. While the most attention has historically been placed on male teachers sexually abusing female students, other gender dyads do occur. Female teachers as sexual abusers have been gaining more attention (Knoll, 2010). College students taking part in a vignette study rated sexual contact between a male teacher and female student more negatively than sexual contact between a female teacher and male student (Fromuth and Holt, 2008). This is likely due to sex role stereotypes, where males are meant to be seeking sexual contact and females are meant to be preventing sexual access. Thus, a male student having sexual contact with a female teacher would be seen as fitting with his gender role and potentially enhance his reputation. Indeed, Fromuth and Holt (2008) found that the perception was that a male student having a sexual relationship with a female teacher would be seen as "cool" by his friends, and this effect increased as the student got older. For female students of any age (9, 12, or 15), having sexual contact with a male teacher was rated as less likely to be considered "cool" by the girl's friends.

In a large study of 8th to 11th grade students, 9.6 percent of students had experienced "contact and/or non-contact education sexual misconduct that was *unwanted*" (Shakeshaft, 2004, p. 17). Teachers who have time alone with individual students, such as music teachers or coaches, are more likely to commit acts of sexual abuse against their students than typical classroom teachers. Most studies find that a substantial majority of teachers who commit sexual abuse against their students are male—somewhere between 80 percent and 96 percent—although when students are surveyed about sexual abuse that prevalence declines dramatically. An analysis of data collected by the American Association of University Women (AAUW) showed a gender breakdown of offenders of 57 percent male and 43 percent female. As noted earlier, when female teachers have sexual contact with male students, the male students "have been socialized to believe they should be flattered or appreciative of sexual interest from a female" (Shakeshaft, 2004, p. 25) and so they may not view this as abuse or report it to an adult. The AAUW data also show that approximately 15 percent of educator sexual abuse is a male teacher offending against a male student, and approximately 13 percent is a female teacher offending against a female student.

Teachers tend to select students they can control, such that they are likely to comply with the request to engage in a sexual relationship and they are likely to remain silent about the abuse. These students often have troubled home lives or emotional problems. Children with disabilities are also susceptible to abuse by teachers (Shakeshaft, 2004). Offending teachers keep the students they are abusing from telling anyone by using intimidation, threats, and making the students feel responsible. The students often receive "attention, gifts, physical pleasure, and feelings of belonging or attractiveness" (Shakeshaft, 2004, p. 33) as a result of the abuse, so they may not view the interactions as abuse at all. If they do tell someone about the abuse, these reports are often overlooked or not believed. The next section will examine the cognitive processes that may allow teachers, as well as other sexual abusers of children, to engage in these activities.

JUSTIFICATION, RATIONALIZATION, AND COGNITIVE DISTORTIONS

Offenders who sexually abuse children have thought processes about that type of activity that may be different from the average person's thought processes. One way of describing this is with the term "**cognitive distortion**."

> Cognitive distortions are the products of conflict between external reinforcements and internal self-condemnation. Child molesters frequently maintain secrecy due to fear of discovery, but that same secrecy also prevents the molester from being confronted with negative feedback about their behavior from the child they harm, the laws against child molestation, and the negative attitudes of those around them regarding their child molestation (Abel et al., 1989 p. 138).

Cognitive distortion scales include items such as "when a young child has sex with an adult, it helps the child learn how to relate to adults in the future," "most children 13 (or younger) would enjoy having sex with an adult, and it wouldn't harm the child in the future," "I show my love and affection to a child by having sex with her (him)," "when a young child walks in front of me with no or only a few clothes on, she (he) is trying to arouse me," and "when children watch an adult masturbate, it helps the child learn about sex"(Abel et al., 1989, p. 151), that are answered using a Likert type scale to indicate degree of agreement or disagreement with the statement.

Studies using scales designed to measure cognitive distortions that are supportive of child molesting have found that child molesters rank higher on agreement with items in these scales than does the general population (Abel et al., 1989), rapists, and violent offenders (Feelgood, Cortoni, and Thompson, 2005). Hayashino, Wurtele, and Klebe (1995) found that child molesters who had victims outside of their family members ranked significantly higher on cognitive distortions than child molesters who were incestuous, and also ranked higher than rapists, incarcerated non-sex offenders, and laypersons. Incestuous child molesters did not differ significantly from any of these other groups on their level of cognitive distortion, which suggests these thought processes are more important for non-familial child sex offenders.

Five different themes explain the majority of cognitive distortions held by sexual offenders with child victims. The first is that children are sexual objects. Offenders believe that children are able to make decisions about what pleases them sexually in the same way that adults are and that these decisions are legitimate. An offender who holds cognitive distortions with this theme would believe that children initiate sex with adults and would perceive children's actions as purposely sexually provocative (Ward and Keenan, 1999). The second theme is that of entitlement, which includes beliefs that some people are better than others and they have the right to have their needs met above others. Offenders with this group of cognitive distortions will believe that others will also perceive their superiority and their right to have their sexual needs met by children. Children are perceived to be of lower status and to enjoy the sexual activity and domination the offender initiates (Ward and Keenan, 1999).

The third theme is that the world is dangerous, and there are two types of beliefs associated with this theme. First, the offender believes he has to fight back and win control over others by punishing people who would harm him. For this type of offender, sexual abuse would be considered a just punishment. Second, the offender believes that adults are unreliable and children are dependable. Thus, children can provide for and understand the offender's needs and will not reject him, as an adult might do (Ward and Keenan, 1999).

The fourth theme is uncontrollability, wherein the offender believes that human nature is shaped by early experiences or biology and these factors have caused him to be sexually attracted to children. Because he cannot control his sexual desires he must allow himself to express them, and does not view himself as responsible for his urges or behavior. The use of drugs or alcohol may also be part of this theme, where the offender believes he could not have controlled his behavior due to the influence of a substance (Ward and Keenan, 1999). The fifth theme is regarding the nature of harm. Offenders with these types of cognitive distortions believe that sexual activity will not harm a child. They also believe that there are degrees of harm, so if a sexual offense could have been more harmful, or more serious, then lesser offenses are considered more acceptable. The offender also believes that any negative response by the child would be due to society's reaction to the offense rather than the sexual activity itself (Ward and Keenan, 1999).

When child molesters are reported to the authorities, they are forced to explain their actions in ways that they believe might be considered acceptable. In a study of convicted child molesters, several types of justifications emerged. Offenders used the excuse of bathing the victim, making sure he or she was clean, or applying medication or lotion as an explanation for their behavior. Offenders that use this excuse state that any sexual contact was accidental (Fulkerson and Bruns, 2014). Offenders also excuse their behavior by blaming it on the victim sexually enticing them. The offender may mistake behavior that is not sexual for acts that indicate the child is interested in sexual activity (Fulkerson and Bruns, 2014).

Finkelhor and Araji's Four-Factor Model Explaining Pedophilia

Finkelhor and Araji (1986) use the term "pedophilia" to describe a condition in which people have a sexual interest in children, whether or not they act upon that interest. To be classified as a pedophile, these individuals do not need to have exclusive interest in children. The researchers used previous literature to develop a four-factor model of theories that explain pedophilic behavior. They state that theories have attempted to explain one of four things: "(a) why a person would find relating sexually to a child to be emotionally gratifying and congruent; (b) why a person would be capable of being sexually aroused by a child; (c) why a person would be frustrated or blocked in efforts to obtain sexual and emotional gratification from more normatively approved sources; and (d) why a person would not be deterred by the conventional social restraints and inhibitions against having sexual relationships with a child" (Finkelhor and Araji, 1986, p. 148).

The factor that goes with the first of these items is called emotional congruence; that is, convergence of "the adult's emotional needs and the child's characteristics" (Finkelhor and Araji, 1986, p. 148). Theories that evaluate this factor suggest that pedophiles have the emotional needs of a child so children fulfill these needs; that they have low self-esteem and relating to a child gives them a sense of power; that they identify with an aggressor who made them feel powerless as a child; or that they are narcissistically in love with themselves as a child and thus children who represent the adult's lost youth become love objects (Finkelhor and Araji, 1986).

Factor two explains the adult's sexual arousal to children. They note that many theories conflate explaining why a person would have their emotional needs met by a child with why a person would be sexually aroused by a child, but that these two drives do not necessarily go together, as people can have their emotional needs met in non-sexual manners. Those who do attempt to explain purely sexual arousal to children suggest that someone who is sexually aroused by children may have had early sexual experiences which conditioned them to be aroused by children when they are adults. As most children have sexual experiences with other children and do not become pedophiles, it is possible that these early experiences were traumatic (sexual abuse) and that the trauma causes that conditioning. Early sexual abuse also provides a model for an adult who finds children sexually arousing, as would pornography that features children. Another possibility is attribution error, such as would occur when the fondness one feels for a child is mistaken for sexual arousal, or when an adult suffers from sexual deprivation and mistakes emotional arousal for sexual arousal. Repeated fantasies involving children will reinforce this attribution (Finkelhor and Araji, 1986).

Factor three is called blockage, which includes explanations for why some people are unable to have their emotional and sexual needs met in an adult relationship. This factor is split into developmental blockages and situational blockages. Developmental blockages include Oedipal complexes where people have emotions regarding their mothers or "castration anxieties" that make it harder to have a relationship with an adult woman. It is also possible that a person would find relationships with adult women difficult if they were impotent in their first sexual experiences, and thus come to believe that adult sexuality is frustrating. A situational blockage is often used to explain incest, suggesting that a father would seek sexual access to his children if his wife were sexually unavailable and he was too inhibited to seek a sexual relationship from other sources or from masturbation (Finkelhor and Araji, 1986).

The fourth factor is called disinhibition, and these theories seek to explain why some adults do not have the typical inhibitions against having sexual contact with children, despite their desire. These theories suggest that pedophiles may have poor impulse control in general, or may have problems with cognition related to senility, neurological impairment, alcoholism, or psychosis, such that these inhibitions are not present as they typically would be. Inhibitions may also be reduced in the case of step-parenting or family separation compared to a situation where a father was present during his biological child's early life. A biological relationship with a child and being present for the child's early development could reduce the likelihood a father would offend against them. The patriarchal family structure where a man expects to be obeyed may also support incestuous pedophilia (Finkelhor and Araji, 1986). The culture may also implicitly condone excuses for pedophilia by blaming victims and failing to impose penalties on offenders; "[a]nything that reinforces excuses for pedophilia . . . acts to reduce inhibitions" (Finkelhor and Araji, 1986, p. 155).

Finkelhor and Araji (1986) state that a theory of pedophilia is not complete unless it addresses all four of these factors and note that many theories do not do so. In addition to the four factors that explain pedophilic behavior, Finkelhor and Araji (1986) also classify pedophiles along two different dimensions. They suggest that pedophiles be classified along a continuous scale (rather than discrete categories) according to strength of pedophilic interest and the exclusivity of their pedophilic interest. Each pedophile could be classified on each of these dimensions. This is different from the common approach of using several discrete categories into which pedophiles are placed.

IMPACT ON VICTIMS

The consequences for child victims of sexual assault are great and many. **Initial effects** of childhood sexual abuse are those that affect the victim during the time period that the abuse is ongoing and up to two years after the abuse stops (Browne and Finkelhor, 1986). There are also **long-term impacts** that will affect the victim long after the abuse has stopped, well into adulthood; these impacts may never be resolved without treatment. The initial effects of childhood sexual abuse include a great variety of psychosocial problems, such as overall disturbance, "sleep and eating disturbances, fears and phobias, depression, guilt, shame, and anger" (Brown and Finkelhor, 1986, p. 67), as well as externalizing problems, such as aggression and antisocial behavior. Not all of these symptoms are experienced by every victim of childhood sexual abuse, but some of the symptoms are experienced by most victims.

In addition to the psychological symptoms, initial effects of childhood sexual abuse may include age-inappropriate sexual behavior. Children who have been victimized may display "open masturbation, excessive sexual curiosity, and frequent exposure of the genitals" (Browne and Finkelhor, 1986, p. 68). Victims of childhood sexual abuse are more likely than others to have problems in school and to run away from home, particularly victims of sexual abuse perpetrated by a family member (Browne and Finkelhor, 1986).

The long-term effects of child sexual abuse are many and far reaching. A common issue associated with having been sexually abused as a child is suffering from depression as an adult. While not all victims of childhood sexual abuse suffer from depression, there is a greater likelihood for victims compared to control groups who have not been victimized (Brown and Finkelhor, 1986). Similarly, victims of childhood sexual abuse are more likely to have a suicide attempt or suicidal ideation, anxiety and tension, feelings of isolation, and low self-esteem compared to control groups who have not been victimized (Brown and Finkelhor, 1986). Although much of the research done on the long-term effects of child sexual abuse have been done with female samples, a comparison study found no difference in the negative psychological impacts experienced by women and the negative psychological impacts experienced by men (Briere et al., 1988).

Related to the psychological impacts of childhood sexual abuse is the increased risk of alcohol problems associated with childhood sexual abuse. As adults, women who were victims of childhood sexual abuse have more alcoholic beverages per year than women who were not victimized, although this does not specifically indicate an alcohol problem, per se. Victimized women were also more likely to be dependent on alcohol and were more likely to report problems associated with their alcohol use, such as being involved in fights, having health problems as well as legal, work, and family problems associated with their alcohol use. The association between abuse and alcohol problems was stronger for women who suffered from sexual abuse as children compared with those who suffered from physical abuse as children (Lown et al., 2011). Research has also consistently found that women who were sexually abused as children are more likely to be sexually assaulted as adults. In a review of such studies, Arata (2002) found that women who were sexually abused as children were two to three times more likely to be sexually victimized as adults, a phenomenon known as **revictimization**. For those that do experience rape as an adult, the impact of the adult rape may be greater for those who had also experienced childhood sexual assault, with that group experiencing more self-blame, using less-adaptive coping strategies, and having more dissociative symptoms (Arata, 2002). This may lead to a more difficult time recovering from the rape for the group who had also been sexually victimized as children.

Some researchers suggest that personality factors may be responsible for the connection between childhood sexual victimization and revictimization as an adult (Arata, 2002). Low assertiveness has been studied as a causal factor in adult sexual assault victimization, although it is not clear if this trait is a result of childhood sexual victimization (Arata, 2002). As discussed above, victims of childhood sexual abuse are more likely to use alcohol, which is a risk factor for adult sexual assault victimization, and a possible reason for the revictimization findings. Another possibility is that victims of childhood sexual abuse have more sexual partners as adults than people who did not experience childhood victimization, and a greater number of consensual partners is associated with a greater risk of sexual assault (Arata, 2002).

CONCLUSION

Many types of sexual offenses occur against children, and many motivations and cognitive distortions related to engaging in them. As we have seen, the effects of childhood sexual abuse on the victim are great and far reaching. While there is a great deal of overlap between child sexual exploitation material offenses and contact sexual offenses against children, other offenses, such as statutory rape, are different in their origin and potentially their impact on the victims. Offenders use many methods, including the Internet and pedophile groups, to target their victims, although a majority of victims and offenders have at least an acquaintance in common with each other and the offender typically uses coercive or relational methods of beginning the abuse, rather than violence. Victims do not typically disclose their abuse to others, and if they do, may not do so immediately, making the law enforcement response to childhood sexual abuse difficult and inconsistent.

In Chapter 6 we will go into more depth regarding the victims of all types of sex crimes. Chapter 6 explores the theories behind victimization as well as the effects of victimization, including more information on child victims. We will also examine how victims interact with law enforcement and the courts.

KEY TERMS

child sexual abuse
child molester
child pornography
Child Sexual Exploitation Material (CSEM)
cognitive distortion
disclosure
grooming
hebephile

incest
incidence study
initial effects
long-term impacts
Massachusetts Treatment Center: Child Molester, version 3 (MTC:CM3)
National Incidence Study (NIS)
National Survey on Children's Exposure to Violence (NatSCEV)
North American Man/Boy Love Association (NAMBLA)
non-contact sexual offense
pedophile
retrospective incidence study
retrospective prevalence study
revictimization
statutory rape

EXERCISES

1. Describe one initial effect and one long-term effect related to being the victim of childhood sexual abuse.
2. Describe the three ways in which rates of childhood sexual abuse are measured. What is a strength of each approach?
3. How does NAMBLA seek to justify its existence and viewpoints, given that mainstream society condemns sexual relationships between adults and children?

ESSAY QUESTIONS

1. What are some of the main barriers to effectively measuring the amount of child sexual abuse that occurs? How might these barriers also impair effective law enforcement of child sexual offenses? What could be done to help reduce these barriers and encourage disclosure from abused children?
2. Select one of the typologies of child sex offenders discussed in Chapter 5, and describe each category of offender. What is one strength and one weakness of the typology you have chosen?
3. What beliefs did you have about child sex offenders before you read Chapter 5? How is the information you read about these offenders similar to and different from what you believed? Did Chapter 5 change your views? Why or why not?
4. Compare child sexual abusers who abuse their authority in order to abuse children with one of the other types of abusers discussed in Chapter 5. How are they similar and how are they different?

6

THE VICTIMS OF SEX OFFENDERS

Chapter Objectives

After reading this chapter, students will be able to:

- Identify the degree and types of sexual victimization suffered by different groups.
- Describe theories of sexual victimization.
- Understand the impacts of sexual victimization on mental health.
- Understand the impacts of sexual victimization on physical health.
- Explain how different factors influence the impact of sexual victimization.
- Understand how society responds to victims of sexual offenses.
- Describe some strategies used to fight back against a culture supportive of sexual victimization.
- Explore how victims of sexual offenses are counseled.

INTRODUCTION

In the previous two chapters we examined rape and sex offenses against children. In this chapter we will take a closer look at the victims of sex offenses. Victims of sex offenders can suffer tremendously; this includes physical, psychological, and social forms of suffering. Their suffering can be made worse by feelings of self-blame and blame attributed to them by others. This blame can sometimes have tragic consequences.

Cherice Moralez is one example of a victim who was so damaged by sexual assault and the aftermath that she chose to take her own life. Cherice was 14 years old when her 47-year-old teacher, Stacey Rambold, raped her repeatedly in his home, office, and car in Billings, Montana, throughout 2007. Cherice's mother noticed something was wrong with her daughter when her grades declined and there were significant changes in her personality. When a friend she had confided in during a church counseling group told Cherice's mother what had happened, she contacted the police (McLaughlin, 2013). What followed demonstrates victim blaming and rape myth acceptance that are all too common in society. Cherice was bullied and harassed by her classmates for coming forward with her story. Just before her 17th birthday, in 2010, Cherice died of a self-inflicted gunshot wound to the head. This was before her teacher's case had gone to trial (McLaughlin, 2013).

As a result of Cherice's death, the prosecution entered an agreement with Rambold that if he successfully completed sex-offender treatment, all charges against him would be dropped. Rambold failed to tell his counselors about his current relationships with adult women and that he had contact with his minor nieces and nephews, both of which violated his agreement with the court. Due to this violation, Rambold's case was returned to court (Vercammen and Lah, 2013). Cherice's situation made national news in 2013 when Rambold was convicted and the judge, C. Todd Baugh, gave Rambold a meager sentence of 30 days in jail and made disparaging remarks about the victim. Baugh stated that Cherice was "older than her chronological age" and was "as much in control of the situation" as Rambold. In defending his remarks, Baugh said "I think that people have in mind that this was some violent, forcible, horrible rape . . . but it wasn't this forcible beat-up rape" (Bacon, 2013).

While Baugh technically sentenced Rambold to 15 years in prison, he suspended all but 31 days and gave him credit for one day served. Rambold's 30-day jail sentence resulted in public outcry, Internet petitions for Baugh's resignation, and eventually legal intervention. Montana law requires a minimum of a four-year sentence for the rape of a victim under the age of 16; only a maximum of two years can be suspended (Zuckerman, 2014). While Rambold did serve his 30 days, the Montana Supreme Court ruled that his sentence was too short; his case was reassigned to a new judge for resentencing (Brown, 2014). In September of 2014 Rambold was resentenced and received a 15-year prison sentence, with five years suspended (Serna, 2014). While the downplaying of her rape and the blame attributed to her are sadly not out of the ordinary, what makes Cherice's case unique is the public response leading to resentencing of the perpetrator.

While it is not certain that the rape and negative reactions from others were directly related, or completely responsible for Cherice's suicide, her family filed a wrongful death suit against Rambold and against the school district where he worked. They received a confidential settlement from Rambold (Tuttle, 2012) and a $91,000 settlement from the school district (Collins, 2013), both of which were reached before the publicity surrounding the 30-day sentence. These rulings suggest that the rape was linked to the suicide.

We will also be examining methods victims have used to take back their power and to gain solidarity with one another. Nowhere is this more apparent than in the #MeToo movement that experienced a resurgence after the allegations against film producer Harvey Weinstein.

Harvey Weinstein is a former film producer and co-founder of Miramax Films (Mason, 2004), whose decades of alleged sexually abusive actions eventually lead to his conviction for rape and sexual assault and to his incarceration (Barr, 2020). What is noteworthy about the Weinstein case is not the fact that a rich and powerful man would abuse his power to commit such acts, but rather, the courage of his victims to expose his actions and the degree of public attention the scandal put on rape and sexual assault in general (Peters and Besley, 2019).

In October 2017, The New York Times *and* The New Yorker *published reports indicating Weinstein had committed multiple acts of sexual assault, sexual harassment, and rape. Within weeks, over 80 women—actresses, Weinstein employees, and others—came forward with their stories of being abused by Weinstein. (Williams, 2017). Prominent accusers included actresses Gwyneth Paltrow, Angelina Jolie, Rose McGowan, and Ashley Judd.* The Los Angeles Times *published a list of all known accusers, which included over 100 names, and noted that others who remained anonymous were not included (Saad, 2018).*

How did Weinstein get away with this pattern of sexually abusive behavior for decades? He had power over his victims in that many did not want to miss out on career opportunities. He also silenced some victims by insisting that employees of the Weinstein Company sign contracts agreeing that they would not say anything to criticize or harm the reputation of the company's leaders or the business itself. Finally, he paid some victims to stay silent, which included an agreement that they could not talk about his behavior (Kantor and Twohey, 2017). Indeed, the better question is, how was he ever stopped?

While the media was reporting on the accusations against Weinstein and the number of accusers was quickly increasing, the use of the phrase "Me Too" or "#MeToo" on social media platforms also increased dramatically. On October 15, 2017, actress Alyssa Milano posted "If you've been sexually harassed or assaulted write 'me too' as a reply to this tweet" (Milano, 2017). Tens of thousands of people replied to that post (Milano, 2017), and hundreds of thousands of people used the hashtag on their own social media pages (Peters and Besley, 2019). The #MeToo movement is discussed later in the chapter, but solidarity and the sheer number of accusations appear to have been part of what stopped Weinstein.

Despite the number of accusations, finding charges related to crimes still within the statute of limitations and with victims willing to testify was a difficult task. Weinstein was charged in New York with rape, sexual abuse, and predatory sexual assault (McKinley, 2018). He was found guilty of rape in the third degree and criminal sex acts in the first degree, and he was acquitted on several other charges. He was sentenced to 23 years in prison (Ransom, 2020). Weinstein was later extradited to California, where he will face trial for several more counts of sexual assault (Serjeant, 2021).

Chapter 6 examines the various types of victims of sexual crimes. The focus is on adult females, adult males, and child victims of sex offenders. Chapter 6 explores how often these groups are victimized as well as the physical, emotional, and social consequences of their victimization. We will also evaluate the theoretical approaches that attempt to help us understand the etiology of victimization. Finally, we examine some ways in which victims have fought back, as well as short-term counseling and long-term treatment options for the mental health problems associated with sexual victimization.

VICTIMS

Sex offenses are more common than most people would expect, but determining just how common, who is likely to be victimized, and in what way is difficult to ascertain due to issues associated with collecting data about this sensitive subject. Not all sexual victimizations are reported to the police, so official data tend to underreport the amount of sexual violence that occurs. Even victimization surveys, where individuals are contacted to take a survey about their experience with violence, may not capture all incidents of sexual violence due to unwillingness to report their experience to survey takers. Additionally, much of this research is done with specific populations, such as college students or members of the military. Even those surveys, such as the National Crime Victimization Survey (NCVS) (discussed in previous chapters), which study a broad range of the population, often leave out victimization suffered by children. To further complicate the issue, determining what types of sexual offenses will be studied and defining what a sexual offense is can be difficult. Some sources of data count only completed rapes while others include attempted rapes. Other forms of sexual violence and assault that are not considered rape, such as unwanted touching, are sometimes included and sometimes not.

This section will explore the various types of victims. In particular, we break down victims by adults and minors. Adult victims are further disaggregated by gender. Because of the issues associated with the reporting of sex offenses, the limitations of the data used in this section will also be discussed.

Adult Women

One widely used source of data regarding the sexual victimization of adult women is the **National Violence Against Women Survey (NVAWS)**, which was undertaken from 1995 to 1996. For this survey, 8,000 men and 8,000 women were surveyed about their experience with violence and reported on the lifetime prevalence of violence including sexual assault. While the survey included only individuals aged 18 and older, the respondents answered questions about violence that had occurred throughout their life, including victimizations suffered as children (Tjaden and Thoennes, 2006). According to this survey, 17.6 percent of adult women have experienced a sexual assault at some point in their lifetime (Tjaden and Thoennes, 2006). This survey's data shows that a large portion of victims were first raped when they were young: 2.2 percent were age 4 or younger at the time of their first rape, 11.5 percent were between ages 5 and 9, 15.3 percent were between ages 10 and 14, 34.2 percent were between ages 15 and 19, 18.2 percent were between ages 20 and 24, 9.2 percent were between ages 25 and 29, 6.8 percent were between ages 30 and 39, and 2.6 percent were age 40 or older (see Figure 6.1).

For many (55.7 percent), their first assault was their only assault, but for a significant portion of respondents (44.3 percent) there were multiple sexual assaults throughout their lifetime (see Figure 6.2). The group who faced 15 or more assaults

FIGURE 6.1. AGE AT FIRST SEXUAL ASSAULT: FEMALES

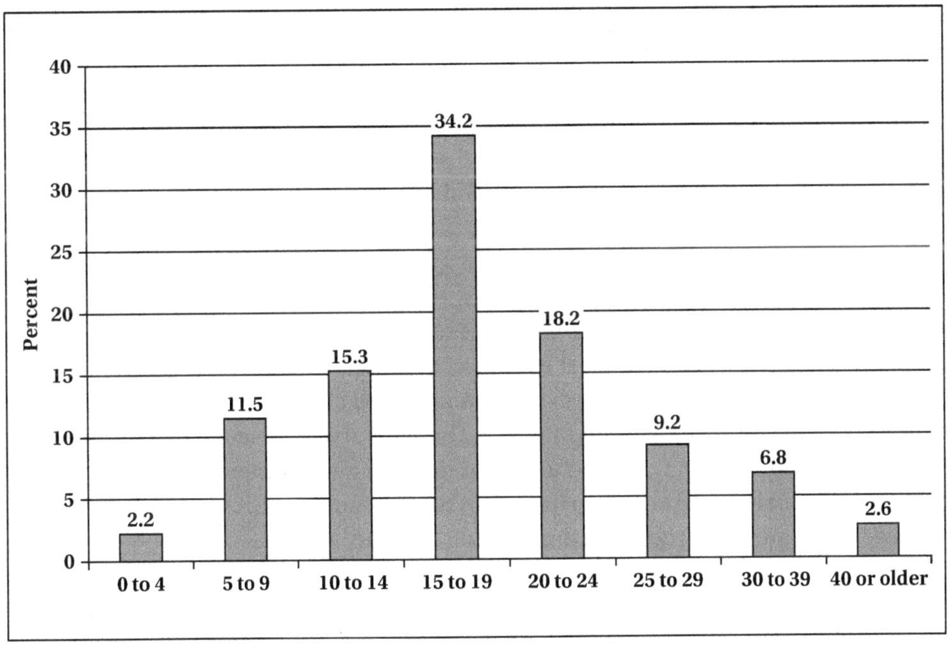

Source: Pazzani (2003).

FIGURE 6.2. NUMBER OF SEXUAL ASSAULTS DURING LIFETIME: FEMALES

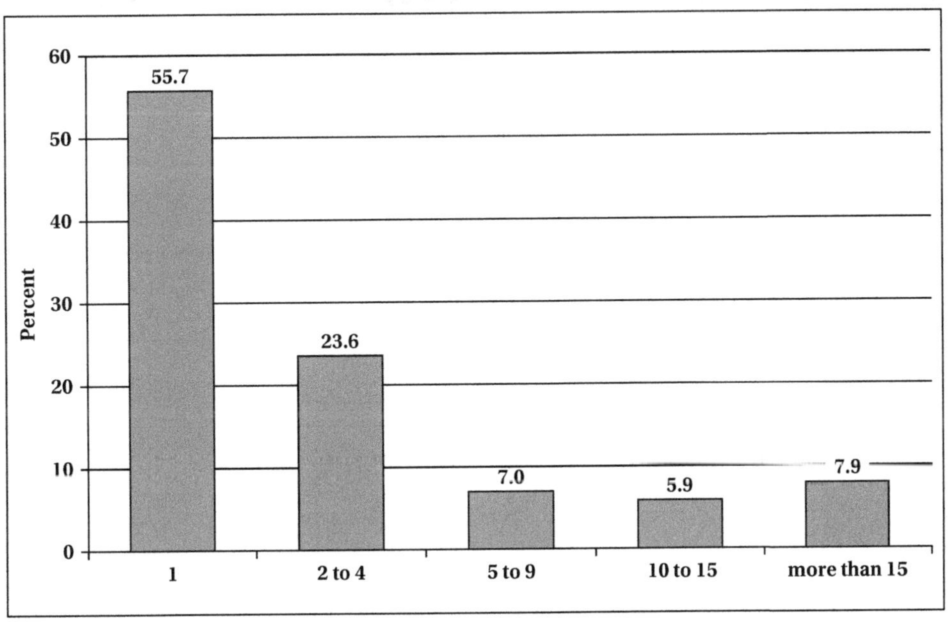

Source: Pazzani (2003).

during their lifetime may be accounted for by assailants who knew their victims well and assaulted them multiple times during their relationship (Pazzani, 2003). Most victims were assaulted by only one rapist (78.2 percent); however, there were many victims who faced multiple sexual assaults by multiple assailants. Almost 14 percent (13.5 percent) of victims were assaulted by two rapists, and 9.3 percent of victims were assaulted by three or more rapists (Tjaden and Thoennes, 2006).

It is concerning that for many women, the process of recovering from a rape (discussed later in Chapter 6) may be interrupted by repeated assaults.

Adult Men

It is a common belief that males cannot be sexually victimized. Sexual offenses against men do not get the same empirical emphasis as sexual offenses involving female victims. As such, there are few sources of data upon which to rely when evaluating the extent of male victimization of sex offenses. The same survey discussed in the previous section on adult women was used to gather data from adult men about their experiences with sexual victimization. In the NVAWS, 3 percent of men interviewed reported having been raped at some point during their lifetime. More men (83.3 percent) than women (78.2 percent) had only one sexual offender, although this difference was not statistically significant (Tjaden and Thoennes, 2006). As with the survey's results for women, the male respondents were all adults but reported on sexual assaults that occurred throughout their lifetime. Even more so than for women, sexual assaults against men tended to initiate while the victim was young (see Figure 6.3); 48 percent

FIGURE 6.3. AGE AT FIRST ASSAULT: MALES

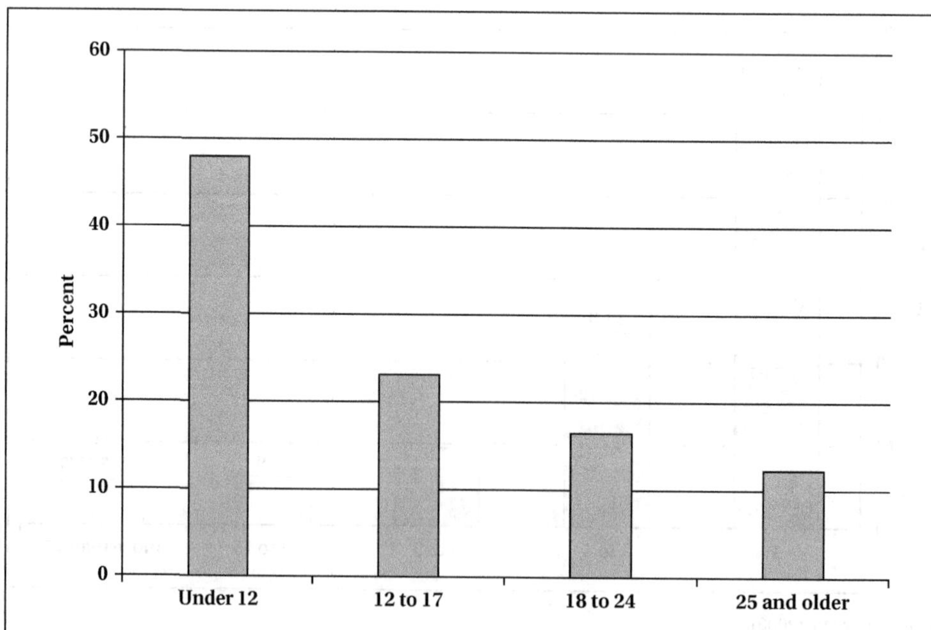

Source: Pazzani (2003).

of first sexual assaults occurred when the victims was under the age of 12, and 23 percent occurred between the ages of 12 and 17. Only 16.6 percent of first sexual assaults occurred when the victim was 18 to 24 years old, and 12.3 percent occurred when the victim was 25 years old or older (Tjaden and Thoennes, 2006).

The largest group of male rape victims are raped by acquaintances (49.3 percent), followed by strangers (22.8 percent) and relatives (22.8 percent); very few male victims of sexual assaults were raped by dates, partners, or spouses. Sex offenses committed against men are statistically significantly less likely to result in penetration than those committed against female victims (29.0 percent versus 62.2 percent) and are less likely to result in physical injury to the victim (16.1 percent versus 31.5 percent) (Tjaden and Thoennes, 2006). Males are less likely than females to report rapes that occur when they are adults to the police (12.9 percent versus 19.1 percent) (Tjaden and Thoennes, 2006). This could suggest there are many more male victims out there that simply do not report their victimizations due to the embarrassment and prevailing, yet misleading, notion that males cannot be raped.

Children

While the reporting of sexual offenses is low for adult men and women, it is especially difficult to estimate how many children are victims of sex offenders because of reporting issues. Many children do not report their abuse to their parents, who then may not have reason to contact the police. Children are often abused by family members, who, of course, are unlikely to report themselves to the police. Children are often silent about abuse because they experience fear regarding consequences for the family, the expectation that they will be punished, or they are frightened of the offender. Male children who are abused by adult males also experience concern that they will be perceived as homosexual (Hunter, 2011). Children also express concerns about not being believed, and experience self-blame related to the incident (McElvaney, Greene, and Hogan, 2014). When children do tell their parents they are being abused, the parents may choose to deal with the issue privately or not to deal with it at all. Sometimes the offender is providing financial or emotional support to the family, guardian(s), or parent(s) that the parent does not want to lose (Knott, 2014). Because of these issues, official sources of data about **child sexual abuse** victims must be understood to significantly underrepresent the amount of child sexual abuse that occurs.

The **National Incidence Study (NIS)** is one such source of official data. This study utilizes reports of child maltreatment to child protective service agencies as well as those reported by professionals in the community. This study uses two different standards to determine if a particular case can be considered child maltreatment: the harm standard and the endangerment standard. For the harm standard there must be evidence that the child was directly harmed; for the endangerment standard the report of maltreatment must be substantiated or a community professional must believe the child is endangered, but it does not require direct evidence of harm (Sedlak et al., 2010). The NIS has been conducted four times, most recently using data from 2005 and 2006, and these data indicate that 1.8 per 1,000 children experienced sexual abuse using the harm standard and 2.4 per 1,000 children experienced sexual abuse using the endangerment standard during those years. Sixty percent were sexually abused by their parent or step-parent (Sedlak et al., 2010). Again, because it is difficult to identify all instances of child sexual abuse, it should be assumed that these numbers are an underestimate of the true rates.

Despite the limitation of official sources of data, it would also be difficult to conduct victimization surveys with children due to ethical and logistical issues. As such, the most common method of studying child sexual abuse is by interviewing or surveying adults who answer questions about their childhood. While this type of data may have less underreporting, there will still be some offenses that respondents do not disclose. Most importantly, what is reported may be from years in the past; this means that it will not help determine how much child sexual abuse is occurring now and that any information given may suffer from problems with accurate recall of memories (London et al., 2005). This latter point can mean some may underreport past experiences with victimization or over-report past experiences, a phenomenon known as telescoping.

Finkelhor (1994) reviewed 19 studies where adults were asked to recall experiences of sexual abuse as a child. These studies had varying methodologies and screening questions to determine if the respondent had been sexually victimized as a child, so it is expected that they would produce different rates of childhood sexual victimization. These studies report rates of childhood sexual victimization between 7 to 38 percent for females and 1 to 16 percent for males (Finkelhor, 1994). There is some evidence that women born around World War II had higher rates of childhood sexual abuse than women who are both older and younger than them, although this could be an indicator of subject comfort in talking about these experiences with particular researchers (Finkelhor, 1994).

Using the **National Incident-Based Reporting System (NIBRS)**, a data set that utilizes police report data and provides more detailed information about each crime, Snyder (2000) studied the characteristics of sexual assaults recorded in NIBRS between 1991 and 1996 to compare child sexual assault to other sexual assaults. Of all sexual assaults in the 12 states that provided data to NIBRS, 14 percent involved victims that were age 5 or younger, 20.1 percent involved victims between the ages of 6 and 11, and 32.8 percent involved victims between the ages of 12 and 17 (Snyder, 2000). Over two-thirds of the victims of sexual assault in these data were under the age of 18, or minors. Children made up the majority of victims of forcible fondling (84 percent), while they made up less than half of the victims of forcible rape (46 percent). Child victims of sexual assault are also more likely to be male than adult victims, with 30.6 percent of victims age 5 and younger being male, 25.1 percent of those between the age of 6 and 11 were male, and 9.1 percent of those between the ages of 12 and 17 were male, compared with less than 5 percent males for all adult age categories (Snyder, 2000).

THEORIES OF VICTIMIZATION

There are many theoretical explanations for why some individuals are at a higher risk for sexual victimization than others. The feminist explanation for sexual victimization suggests that we have a patriarchal culture and rape supportive beliefs which expose all women to the risk of sexual victimization; however, research has shown that not all women share the same risk (Mustaine and Tweksbury, 2002). Thus, there must be other factors related to the risk of sexual victimization. Possible theoretical explanations include routine activities theory, lifestyle theory, and victim precipitation.

Routine Activities and Lifestyle Theory

Routine activities theory is a criminological theory that does not focus on the offender, but rather the conditions under which offenses occur. Cohen and Felson (1979) proposed that criminal events, and thus criminal victimization, are most likely to occur when three elements co-occur in time and space: a motivated offender, a suitable target, and an absence of capable guardians. People engage in activities at home, at their jobs away from home, and during other activities when they are not at home. Cohen and Felson (1979) argued that to the extent that society has shifted to focus on jobs and activities away from home, there is a greater likelihood that people will encounter motivated offenders while acting as suitable targets and not having capable guardianship.

Lifestyle theory is very similar to routine activities theory. Hindelang, Gottfredson, and Garofalo (1978) stated that it is lifestyle characteristics or behaviors that place a person at risk for criminal victimization. When a person comes into contact with potential offenders due to their lifestyle, it creates the potential for victimization to occur. Such lifestyle factors would include associating with criminals or being outside of the home at night. The routine activities/lifestyle approach has been studied extensively as it relates to sexual victimization, and Cohen and Felson (1979) also supported their theory with data that show that most rapes (and other violent crimes) occur away from home and are committed by a stranger.

6

Belknap (1987) used data from the National Crime Survey (a precursor to the NCVS, discussed in other chapters) between 1973 and 1982 to test routine activities theory as it relates to sexual victimization. She found support for the theory, with most rapes occurring when people are out of the house (at night and during the summer). Women who are in an age group most likely to be outside the home are at an increased risk, women who are married or widowed are at a reduced risk of sexual victimization, and women who engage in activities that take them outside the home, such as working, are at a greater risk than women who stay home. Although she found strong support for routine activities theory, there were some factors that did not support the theory. For instance, 39 percent of rapes took place in or near the home, and there was a greater risk of rape in dwellings with a greater number of housing units, which does not support the guardianship aspect of routine activities theory (Belknap, 1987).

It must be noted that the data used by Cohen and Felson (1979) and Belknap (1987) were from a time before intimate partner violence and acquaintance rape were well-known concepts and thus may not have been included in the victimization survey used for their analysis. Indeed, one of the least safe places for women is generally considered to be with male intimates (Koss et al., 1994), who happen to be the people Cohen and Felson (1979) would have called capable guardians. Schwartz and Pitts (1995) evaluate sexual assault from a routine activities perspective that fits in with the feminist perspective. They discuss likely offenders, who are males searching for the opportunity to sexually assault women and may do so by getting them drunk for that purpose, and suitable targets, who are women who are more likely to be sexually victimized if they go out drinking and if they know men who attempt to get women drunk to have sex with them. They also discuss that other males who could provide protection but fail to do so because of the support for rape in masculine culture indicates a lack of capable guardianship.

Not all studies seek to blend the feminist perspective with the routine activities perspective, but many other studies still find at least limited support for the routine activities approach. Franklin et al. (2012) found that, in a sample of college students, women who spent more days on campus and those who spent more days partying had an increased risk of sexual victimization. This was suggested to be due to the increased exposure to likely offenders. They also found that those women who participated in drug sales had an increased risk of sexual victimization as a result of their proximity to likely offenders.

Victim Precipitation

The following is a more historical view of the causes of rape victimization, and the critiques of this theory will be discussed below. Menachem Amir came up with the concept of **victim-precipitated** rape in 1967, working from Marvin Wolfgang's concept of victim-precipitated homicide developed for his dissertation (and a book, Wolfgang, 1958) based on a study of all homicides in Philadelphia between 1948 and 1952. Amir (1967) stated that because rape is a situation in which the offender and victim interact it is possible that the offender will interpret the victim's behavior as an invitation for sexual contact. Victims can give this signal by an act of commission, such as agreeing to take a ride from a stranger, or by an act of omission, such as failing to react forcefully enough to the offender's sexual suggestions. The important factor is not whether the victim intends to be seductive, but how the offender perceives her actions. In examining all rapes reported to the police in Philadelphia in 1958 and 1960, Amir (1967) found that 19 percent of the assaults met his definition of victim precipitation. Amir also found that victim precipitation was more likely in cases where the victim was White; there was alcohol use by the victim, offender, or both; the victim had a bad reputation; and, the rape occurred outside either the victim's or offender's residence. In victim-precipitated rapes Amir (1967) found it was more likely that the level of force was "roughness" as opposed to a brutal beating, more likely that there would be sexual humiliation during the rape, and more likely that the victim and offender would be acquainted.

While Amir (1967) found that 19 percent of forcible rapes were victim precipitated, another study using 17 cities rather than Amir's single city found a much lower percentage. Curtis (1974), using a much narrower definition of victim precipitation, found that victim precipitation was present in just 4 percent of cleared rapes and 6 percent of uncleared rapes. This was the lowest percentage of victim precipitation compared to homicide, aggravated assault, armed robbery, and unarmed robbery.

Not surprisingly, many who study sexual victimization are hostile to the idea of victim precipitation, stating that this concept is victim-blaming (Berger and Searles, 1985) and that rape is never the victim's fault. Indeed, many of the items on the rape myth acceptance scale (Burt, 1980) reflect the idea that victim precipitation is a myth. Items such as

- A woman who goes to the home or apartment of a man on their first date implies that she is willing to have sex.
- In the majority of rapes, the victim is promiscuous or has a bad reputation.
- If a girl engages in necking or petting and she lets things get out of hand, it is her own fault if her partner forces sex on her.
- Women who get raped while hitchhiking get what they deserve (Burt, 1980, p. 223).

These are specifically the types of things Amir (1967) would consider victim precipitation. In Burt's work, and the work of many others who study rape myth acceptance, these items are considered "prejudicial, stereotyped, or false beliefs about rape, rape victims, and rapists" which create "a climate hostile to rape victims" (Burt, 1980, p. 217). Despite the persistent message that these are false beliefs, they are still widely held. In a study of college students, Cowan (2000) found that participants rated the degree of victim precipitation higher in cases of date and partner rape, compared to stranger and acquaintance rape. For date and partner rape, they also did not strongly attribute the cause of the rape to male pathology or male hostility. Koss (2011) goes so far as to call Amir's study "discredited," although it is clear the idea of victim precipitation persists in society.

IMPACT ON VICTIMS

Each victim will experience a sexual offense differently and react differently, but there are some trends in the type of victim responses. Victim responses may vary based on their pre-existing support system, their mental health before the assault, the type of assault, and numerous demographic factors. In general, those who are victims of sex offenses have worse mental and physical health statuses than those who have not been victimized; individuals who are victimized will also experience a number of other social and economic consequences.

An interesting effect of the cultural views about rape (discussed later in Chapter 6) is that not all victims of sex offenses may consider themselves victims. Koss (1985) identified "unacknowledged rape victims" by noting that women would answer "no" to a direct question asking if they had ever been raped, but would describe non-consensual sexual encounters that met the legal definition of rape. Koss found that 43 percent of the women she surveyed whose experiences met the legal definition of rape did not label themselves rape victims (Koss, 1985). Later studies have come up with varying percentages of unacknowledged rape victims ranging from 48 to 73 percent (Peterson and Muehlenhard, 2004). Not labeling an unwanted sexual encounter a rape, however, does not shelter a victim from the psychological harm of victimization. Both victims who label their experience rape and those who do not label their encounters as rape have more psychological distress, lower scores in relation to well-being metrics, more alcohol use, and more sexual partners than do non-victims (McMullin and White, 2006).

Physical Health

Victims of sexual offenses may suffer physical health issues. Some physical health consequences of sexual offenses may be more obvious than others. There are immediate physical health concerns associated with a sexual offense such as treating any physical injuries the victim may have suffered; these injuries can include broken bones to minor cuts and bruises, internal injuries, and/or genital trauma. As discussed in Chapter 4, most victims of rape do not experience significant physical injury (Tark and Kleck, 2014) or receive medical treatment for injuries. For those who do experience physical injury that requires treatment, often those needs must be addressed before a forensic medical exam can be conducted.

In addition to immediate physical injuries, there is also a risk of sexually transmitted diseases (STDs) and pregnancy associated with sexual assault. Indeed, when a child is diagnosed with an STD, sexual abuse is generally suspected (Drezett, de Vasconcellos et al., 2012). In addition to the risk of STDs as a result of the sexual assault, victims are at an increased risk of contracting STDs after the assault, perhaps as a result of riskier sexual behaviors that may be associated with poor mental health outcomes related to the assault (Wingood and DiClemente, 1998).

Some victims may experience injury that disables them or requires ongoing treatment; however, most additional usage of medical services by victims of sex offenses is related to conditions that cannot be traced directly back to the assault itself. In fact, characteristics of the assault, such as suffering injury, have been found to be unrelated to the relationship between sexual assault victimization and poor health (Amstadter et al., 2011). Female victims of sexual assault make more frequent visits to their primary care providers than do women who have not been victimized. Victims of sexual assault have also been found to have more physical symptoms than non-victims, including headaches, chest pains, and fatigue; they also have greater anxiety about their overall health (Stein et al., 2004). Victims of sex offenses are also more likely to suffer from chronic pain, gastrointestinal issues, and gynecological problems (Zinzow et al., 2011).

These are conditions that would not be directly caused by the assault, and there is no evidence that experiencing a sexual assault causes a woman to require more medical services than those who have not been victimized. Nevertheless, a correlation between sexual assault and medical conditions exists. This link has been established for victims of child sexual abuse as well as victims of adult sexual assault (Irish, Kobayashi, and Delahanty, 2010). One possible explanation for this link is the relationship between mental and physical health, and the poor mental health outcomes related to being the victim of a sex offense. Not only are there physical health consequences for those who have been victims of sexual assault; poor health is also associated with other issues such as low income, experiencing **post-traumatic stress disorder (PTSD)**, experiencing a major depressive episode, and use of illicit drugs (Zinzow et al., 2011).

Mental Health

While there are varying reports of the total number of victims of sexual violence who suffer from PTSD, it is certainly a significant number of individuals. It is therefore instructive to examine the definition of PTSD. The most recent diagnostic criteria for PTSD provided by the *Diagnostic and Statistical Manual V* (*DSM-5*) requires exposure to a traumatic event and several groups of psychological and behavioral symptoms. In order to be diagnosed with PTSD, someone who has experienced a traumatic event must also suffer from intrusion symptoms, where the event is re-experienced through flashbacks or in other manners; avoidance symptoms, where the individual attempts to distance themselves from things that remind them of the traumatic event; negative changes in thought processes or moods that started or became worse after the traumatic event; changes in arousal and reactivity, such as hyper-vigilance; and finally, the symptoms must last for at least one month and cause impairment in functioning (American Psychiatric Association, 2013).

There has been some debate regarding whether victims of sex offenses committed by strangers suffer more or less serious consequences than victims of sex offenses committed by acquaintances or intimates (Katz, 1991). Those who are victimized by strangers are likely to experience greater physical violence and are more likely to be in fear for their life. Some might argue that this type of assault is more "serious" and causes more severe psychological responses. In contrast, these victims may be less likely to blame themselves (self-blame still occurs for these individuals) because the attack may be considered more random and less related to the actions of the victim. Those who are victimized by someone they know may experience psychological consequences first as a result of experiencing a loss of trust, and second due to the higher degree of self-blame experienced as they may believe the assault was related to their own judgment or actions.

Many demographic factors, assault-related variables, and the type of response by others that a victim experiences may influence the victim's likelihood of developing PTSD and the severity of the PTSD symptoms. Victims who sustained physical injury as a result of the sexual assault and those who perceived that their life was in danger have greater PTSD severity (Ullman and Filipas, 2001). The way others react to a rape victim is important as "a range of negative social reactions including victim blame, treating the victim differently, distraction, egocentric reactions, and controlling responses are related to greater PTSD symptom severity" (Ullman and Filipas, 2001, p. 385).

Related to PTSD, Burgess and Holmstrom (1974) introduced **rape trauma syndrome** to describe the impact of rape upon the survivor. They divide the response to rape into two phases: the acute or disruptive phase and the long-term process of reorganization. The acute phase can last from a few days to a few weeks. During this phase, the victim of a sexual assault will have physical and emotional symptoms of stress. During the reorganization phase, which can last a few months to years, the victim must evaluate his or her life to regain a sense of control (Burgess and Holmstrom, 1974).

Wasco (2003) argued that the PTSD framework does not capture the extent of the harm done to a victim of a sexual offense. Victims of rape experience psychological distress as a result of a loss of self-worth, feelings of objectification, and the self-blame discussed above. Wasco (2003) also argued that not all groups experience this trauma in the same way. Victims from dominant social groups (White, middle class), who are likely to believe that the world is generally a fair place and that bad things do not happen to good people, may experience a shattering of their worldview. Groups who do not experience the world as fair may not have their worldview destroyed, but they may experience distress from other sources that researchers do not fully understand (Wasco, 2003). In addition to psychological symptoms, there are social consequences. Wasco (2003) argued "some of the most significant harm of rape is manifested as disconnection from others, reduced capacity for intimacy, inability to comfort oneself, and distorted loyalty in friendships, marriages, and/or living arrangements" (p. 317).

Self-blame is one of the most common responses to sexual victimization. Victims often feel responsible for causing a sexual offense if it is at all possible to perceive that their behavior either contributed to or failed to prevent the assault. Blame can focus either on the victim's actions leading up to the assault, or the victim's negative moral character, which makes the victim deserving of the sexual assault (Janoff-Bullman, 1979). Self-blame is strongly associated with depression; those who blame themselves for the rape as a result of their characters rather than their actions are more likely to experience depression (Janoff-Bullman, 1979).

In addition to the mental health outcomes discussed above, sexual victimization is associated with substance abuse problems (Acierno et al., 2000). While we discussed the risk of becoming a victim of a sexual offense when using alcohol and other drugs in Chapter 4, it is a complex relationship. Those who are victims of sexual offenses may be heavier alcohol and drug users to begin with, but there is still evidence that sexual victimization is associated with an increase in the use of alcohol and drugs. While sexual victimization is related to a greater likelihood of problems with alcohol, it also seems that for victims who are problem drinkers, other sexual-assault-related problems, such as the occurrence and severity of PTSD, are increased (Ullman et al., 2008).

Another risk related to sexual victimization is future sexual victimization. Those who have a history of a sexual assault are at a greater risk for experiencing sexual victimization than those who do not have such a history (Tjaden and Thoennes, 2000; Gidycz et al., 1993). This could be related to the other consequences of sexual victimization, such as self-blame, substance use, and emotional problems. It could also be related to higher risk environments. Miller, Markman, and Handley (2007) found that those who experienced greater self-blame related to an assault had a higher risk of being revictimized. Another study found that those who suffered a sexual assault while incapacitated were at a greater risk for another incapacitated sexual assault, and that this risk was associated with having greater alcohol consumption and more emotional problems (Messman-Moore, Ward, and Zerubavel, 2013). It seems that the emotional consequences of sexual victimization put one at risk for future victimization and thus more emotional consequences.

SOCIETAL REACTIONS TO VICTIMS

Just as self-blame is very common in victims of sex offenses, it is common for others in society to blame victims for their sexual assault or have negative reactions to victims.

Victims who have high levels of social support from friends or family tend to be seen as less at fault for their sexual assault. This is likely because others see that the victim is considered credible (Anderson and Lyons, 2005). There are different types of sexist attitudes that are associated with victim blaming. People with a "benevolent sexism" attitude (the belief that women are pure and special, and should be protected) are prone to blaming victims of acquaintance assaults. The benevolent sexist attitude makes women the guardians of sexual purity, so in cases where there is potential for consensual sex to occur, the woman's behavior is often seen as the cause of the assault. Victims of acquaintance sexual assault are often seen to be violating gender norms, leading to the conclusion that she is not a "good woman" and does not deserve to be protected. The attribution of blame is reduced when the offender is a stranger because the potential for a woman to have acted in a way that destroys her sexual purity is lower (Abrams et al., 2003). The reduction in blame attributed to victims of stranger assault does not occur for people with hostile sexist attitudes. Individuals who are hostile sexists may assume that a woman is exaggerating a claim of sexual assault and is using her sexuality to her advantage, to gain money or attention, for instance (Yamawaki, 2007).

Women tend to attribute more blame to rape victims who are very similar to themselves, and to victims who are very dissimilar, but less blame when they are neutral about the victims (Johnson, 1995). To protect a woman's worldview that rape cannot happen to people like her, she must ascribe blame to similar victims. This allows her to believe she would be able to prevent an assault by not behaving in the same manner as the victim. Moreover, victims who are very dissimilar from an observer are seen as contributing to the assault by the very fact that their characteristics are unlike those of the type of women who cannot be raped (Johnson, 1995). Male victims tend to have even more blame ascribed to them (Rye, Greatrix, and Enright, 2006).

6

Victim blame is associated with the belief in rape myths (Burt, 1980; see Chapter 4). In Burt's (1980) study using a random sample of adults, *half* of the sample agreed with the statements "A woman who goes to the home or apartment of a man on the first date implies she is willing to have sex" and "In the majority of rapes, the victim was promiscuous or had a bad reputation" (p. 229). In addition, half of the subjects believed that more than 50 percent of rape incidents are fabricated to get back at a man or to cover up an illegitimate pregnancy. In 1980, as Burt put it, "the world [was] indeed not a safe place for rape victims" (p. 229). Rape myth acceptance is still studied in the current cultural context. Lonsway and Fitzgerald (1995) found that those who had higher levels of hostility toward women also had higher rape myth acceptance. Aosved and Long (2006) found that rape myth acceptance was correlated with other oppressive belief systems, such as sexism, racism, homophobia, ageism, classism, and religious intolerance. They also found that males had higher levels of rape myth acceptance than females.

Although most research does not measure the absolute magnitude of these beliefs, it is telling that, among college women, hours of television watched is positively associated with rape myth acceptance and the belief that most rape charges are false (Kahlor and Morrison, 2007). As a major source of cultural information and a reflection of cultural beliefs, this association indicates that rape myths are still very much a part of U.S. culture. Rape myth acceptance continues to have consequences as well, with people who have higher levels of rape myth acceptance, adversarial sex beliefs, sexual conservatism, and acceptance of interpersonal violence indicating less willingness to have close relationships with rape victims. It is striking that, regardless of their level of rape myth acceptance, only 38 percent of a student sample indicated that they would be willing to marry a rape victim (Shechory and Idisis, 2006).

VICTIMS FIGHT BACK

For decades, women have used various methods to draw attention to the culture that accepts and normalizes sexual violence against them. Rape crisis centers began to form in the early 1970s as part of a grassroots movement (Schmitt and Martin, 1999) to support women and institute change. The 1970s also saw a new emergence of activism related to sexual violence, including activities such as Take Back the Night marches, which began as a response to the suggestion that women needed to stay off the streets at night in order to be safe from violence (Wooden, 2000). Take Back the Night marches continue to be held, often on college campuses, to this day.

As technology and access to different forms of media advance, activism has taken on a different shape. One well-known response to the acceptance of sexual violence on college campuses is the documentary film, *The Hunting Ground*, released in 2015. The film highlights alarming statistics about sexual violence and features interviews with survivors of sexual violence at several highly ranked universities as they discuss the dismissive administrative response to their reports of this violence. The film also follows the journey of survivors filing a Title IX[1] lawsuit as a result of their universities' failure to protect them from sex-based discrimination (Johnston, 2017). The film is often used as a way to start discussions about sexual violence in classes and as part of awareness events. The media, in particular social media, has become an important part of activism about sexual violence.

#MeToo Movement

The **#MeToo movement** gained popularity in 2017 after actress Alyssa Milano posted a message about sexual assault and harassment on her Twitter page, but it did not begin there (Cossins, 2020). Activist Tarana Burke wanted to encourage survivors to share their stories of sexual abuse, find them help and resources, and encourage healing. She named the movement "me too" to express solidarity among those affected (Jaffe, 2018). When Milano tweeted the phrase in 2017, its use and the hashtag #MeToo started taking off almost immediately. Within 24 hours, it had been retweeted hundreds of thousands and times. Nearly half of Facebook users in the United States are friends with someone who participated in the movement by sharing a story of sexual violence or harassment (Tambe, 2018).

1. Title IX refers to Title IX of the Education Amendments Act of 1972, which "prohibits discrimination on the basis of sex in education programs and activities" (United States Department of Justice, 2012, p. 1), which includes the disruption of educational activities caused by sex-based violence or harassment (United States Department of Justice, 2012).

What effect did the popularity of the #MeToo movement have? There are two types of impacts that should be evaluated. First, how did sharing on social media as part of the #MeToo movement affect the individuals who made such posts? Second, was there any broad social change associated with the movement? In a study of those who participated in a previous online hashtag (#BeenRapedNeverReported), Mendes, Ringrose and Keller (2018) found both positive and negative impacts associated with sharing. For some who shared, they felt the responses they received were supportive and the experience seemed a way of building solidarity with others. Some also felt that sharing feminist views was a way of impacting people who did not share those views and of making social change, which they found valuable. However, a majority of the respondents in this study also noted that they experienced online harassment related to their posts, with strangers using sexist and abusive language towards them or making threats against them (Mendes, Ringrose, and Keller, 2018).

Socially, the #MeToo movement has meant many things. It has drawn attention to the magnitude of the problem of sexual assault and harassment and to the norms in which victim blame is acceptable (Cossins, 2020). The movement has also been associated with some concrete change. It led to the accusation of prominent men in media and politics, some of whom were removed from their positions or resigned (Tippett, 2018). It also drew attention to outdated policies related to sexual harassment, such as that of the United States Congress, which required a "cooling off" period of 30 days where an accuser must continue working with the person they have accused of harassment (Tippett, 2018). This policy was changed to eliminate the cooling off period and mandatory mediation for the victim (Linderman, 2018). The #MeToo movement also became associated with other movements for change including Time's Up, which was specifically about sexual harassment and violence in the workplace (Langone, 2018) and the #HowIWillChange hashtag campaign wherein men would post on social media the things they intended to do to stop sexual harassment and violence (Harlow et al., 2021).

There has also been some backlash to the #MeToo movement. Some men have expressed fears about engaging with women in a work setting as they believe that in the #MeToo era, it is more likely they will be wrongfully accused of sexual harassment or violence (Leopold, 2019). Some critics of the movement also note the possible consequences for someone publicly accused of sexual misconduct. Former president Donald Trump, for instance, tweeted these concerns with a reference to a lack of due process for those accused (Wexler, Robbennolt, and Murphy, 2019). Indeed, those accused publicly, but not convicted of any crime or found in the wrong by any court, have suffered harm to their reputations and careers (Akel, 2018). While some may argue that these consequences for a supposedly innocent person are wrong, part of the argument behind the #MeToo movement is that current legal responses to sexual violence and harassment are inadequate (Cossins, 2020).

COUNSELING VICTIMS AND RECOVERY

There are two types of counseling that victims of sexual offenses often receive: **rape crisis counseling** and professional mental health counseling. First, for those that report their assault or contact a rape crisis center, crisis counseling deals with the immediate aftermath of the assault. Rape crisis centers started in the 1970s as grassroots organizations responding to what those involved viewed as unfair treatment by medical personnel, law enforcement, and the legal system. They began as volunteer organizations with no public funding, but today most are state funded and work in conjunction with other organizations such as hospitals and police departments (Bergen and Maier, 2011). Most rape crisis centers provide a hotline for survivors to call for crisis counseling and referrals for services and offer some form of accompaniment for victims at the hospital or police station directly following a rape. They may also offer short-term counseling for rape victims at the center (Gornick, Burt, and Pittman, 1985).

In addition to shock, anger, fear, and other emotions that may cause distress, survivors of sexual offenses often face other immediate concerns that a trained rape crisis counselor can address. Victims may be concerned about the safety of their location immediately following the assault, the reactions of their significant others, their upcoming forensic medical exam, or what they should tell their children. It is the job of the rape crisis counselor not to go through a standard set of responses, but to determine what the primary concerns of the victim are and to address those. For instance, if finding appropriate shelter is the most pressing issue for the victim, it may not be possible to access other emotions; other emotional responses may be exacerbated as well.

When primary concerns are addressed, which may be separate from the emotional responses one would anticipate, the rape crisis counselor must determine what type of immediate response the victim is having. Victims that respond with anger are different from those who respond with overwhelming self-blame. Rape crisis counselors must also understand that the emotional response of the victim may be misdirected or that they may be treated in a hostile manner, not because the victim is angry at the counselor, but because he or she does not know how to process what has happened. Crisis counselors must treat these responses with understanding. They are also often present to help explain the process that the victim will be going through. Facing the unknown of medical exams and police interviews can increase fear and anxiety, and if the procedures are explained and the counselor is there to ensure that the process is not more distressing than necessary, the victim may have a better response. Indeed, while lacking a control group, Westmarland and Alderson (2013) found that victims who worked with a rape crisis center showed improvement over time in terms of empowerment and control over their lives.

While crisis counseling is important, it cannot begin to address the depth of mental health care that a victim may need. After dealing with immediate needs and the initial shock of the assault, the victim may develop symptoms of PTSD, as discussed above, and may benefit from further help in dealing with this issue. There has been some tension between rape crisis centers, which can provide at least short-term counseling assistance, and professionals in the mental health field, who rape crisis workers generally see as untrained in sexual assault issues (Woody and Beldin, 2012). Despite this tension, rape survivors are often referred to community mental health providers or independently seek treatment from these providers. Cognitive behavioral therapy has generally been considered the most successful form of treatment for people suffering from mental health conditions as a result of trauma. **Cognitive behavioral**

therapy works off of three principles: thinking can affect behavior, thought process can be altered, and behavioral change may be achieved through changes in the thought process (Dobson and Dozois, 2010). While there are many different types of cognitive behavioral therapy, these are generally based on short-term treatment and rely upon the client identifying problematic thought processes in order to modify them, which may be done through intervening in the problematic thought process with rational responses to it (Dobson and Dozois, 2010). Regardless of the type of therapy received, victims of sex offenses rely upon their long-term counselors to help them through some very distressing changes in their lives.

Unfortunately, not all people working in mental health fields are able to treat victims of sex offenses in ways that are helpful. Even counselors who want to help victims of sexual assault may believe they are helping by making the victim examine the characteristics of his or her behavior that caused the assault to help them change for the better (Pitts and Schwartz, 1993). Even mental health counselors can be influenced by the rape myth accepting culture that was discussed earlier, which can be very harmful to victims recovering from a sexual offense. As sexual assault is such a common problem, and people who have been sexually victimized are consumers of mental health services at a higher rate than non-victims, it is essential that mental health professionals be trained in the realities of sexual assault and the harm that can be done by encouraging self-blame.

While one cannot deny the devastating consequences of sexual victimization, there are some victims who use the experience to change in positive ways as well. Burt and Katz (1987) found that victims in their study improved their self-concept and had reduced passivity. Wasco (2003) also notes that there are some victims who do manage to respond in positive ways, including becoming an activist or advocate, attempting to help others, and focusing on positive coping strategies.

CONCLUSION

Victims of sexual offenses come from every demographic group, and many experience severe reactions to the trauma they have suffered. They are tremendously affected by the responses of others such as law enforcement officers, the legal system, friends and family, and mental health counselors. Victims of sexual offenses are very susceptible to engaging in self-blame related to their assault, and others in the community are also prone to blame victims for what happened to them. Compassionate responses to sexual victimization can help aid in recovery while other types of responses can increase suffering. Because of the great trauma associated with sexual victimization it is essential we take steps to reduce sexual offending and to improve services to those who have been victimized.

In Chapter 7 we begin to explore the criminal justice system's involvement with sex crimes, sex offenders, and victims. The components of the criminal justice system are law enforcement, the courts, and the correctional system. We begin the analysis of the criminal justice response to sex crimes with the impact of law enforcement on sex crimes. Chapter 7 will evaluate the criminal investigation and law enforcement approaches to sex offenses.

KEY TERMS

child sexual abuse
cognitive behavioral therapy
lifestyle theory
#MeToo movement
National Incidence Study (NIS)
National Incident-Based Reporting System (NIBRS)
National Violence Against Women Survey (NVAWS)
post-traumatic stress disorder (PTSD)
rape crisis counseling
rape trauma syndrome
routine activities theory
self-blame
victim precipitation

EXERCISES

1. Describe the symptoms of PTSD.
2. What are the characteristics of people who are most likely to engage in victim blame?
3. How does the physical health of victims of sex offenses compare to that of non-victims?

ESSAY QUESTIONS

1. Describe the reaction of many scholars of sexual violence to the theory of victim-precipitated rape. Based on what you have read about their reactions, how do you think the widespread belief in this concept impacts victims of sexual violence?
2. In what ways are a victim's mental health and physical health impacted after a sexual assault?
3. What factors are related to trouble with the accurate measurement of child sexual abuse? How might you design a study that would address at least one of these problems?
4. How might the presence of a rape crisis counselor during police interviews and forensic medical examinations of a victim of sexual assault help a victim? Can you think of any possible negative reactions to the presence of a rape crisis counselor?

7

SEX OFFENDERS AND LAW ENFORCEMENT

Chapter Objectives

After reading this chapter, students will be able to:

- Describe the initial police response to a report of sexual assault.
- Explain the content of the typical police interview of a victim of sexual assault.
- Understand how this interview and police attitudes may affect the victim.
- Understand the forensic medical examination of victims of sexual offenses.
- Discuss the use of rape kits and untested rape kits.
- Discuss several types of forensic evidence that may be used in the investigation of sex offenses.
- Explain the content and strategies of interrogating a suspect in a sexual offense.
- Understand the factors associated with false allegations of sexual assault.

INTRODUCTION

In 1982, police in Washington state came to believe they had a serial killer working near the Green River area, just outside Seattle. Six bodies had been found in a short period in and around the river. All six bodies were those of women who had been strangled. It was discovered that, in addition to their deaths, the women had in common another factor: they all worked as prostitutes. This led police to begin interviewing prostitutes in the area where the women had worked in Seattle (Bell, n.d.). In King County, where the bodies were discovered, they created the Green River Task Force, which was made up of detectives from different law enforcement agencies around the country (Maleng, 2003). They heard multiple accounts of a man in a blue and white truck soliciting prostitutes, brutally raping them, and making comments about the murders (Bell, n.d.).

Police apprehended the man who committed those rapes, but they doubted that he was also the Green River Killer because he had released, rather than killed, his victims. The investigation continued, and more women and girls who worked as prostitutes disappeared (Bell, n.d.). In one case, the boyfriend of a missing girl saw her having an argument with the driver of a truck and saw her get into the truck. He followed the truck but lost it, although he spotted it again days later and this time followed it to the home of Gary Ridgway. He called the police, who came and interviewed Ridgway. The police were satisfied by his responses that he was not involved (Bell, n.d.).

More and more women and girls, most of whom worked as prostitutes, disappeared or were discovered dead, seemingly killed in the same manner and left in the same location as others thought to have been victims of the Green River Killer. An offer of help came from an unexpected source. Convicted serial killer Ted Bundy offered to assist the FBI by giving them an insight into a killer's mind and perhaps helping discover the killer's relationship to the victims and where he might live (Bell, n.d.). In 1987, police were again led to Gary Ridgway. He had had contact with the police several times for incidents involving prostitutes, including the contact in 1983 when the boyfriend of a missing woman had followed him to his house (Bell, n.d.). Ridgway's ex-wife also told investigators that he often went to the sites where bodies had been found. Police were granted a warrant to search Ridgway's house; they took samples from him but did not have enough evidence to arrest, so they released him (Bell, n.d.). During these police contacts, Ridgway took a polygraph test, during which he denied killing women; the test indicated he was being truthful (Maleng, 2003).

At the time Ridgway had given samples, in 1988, biological evidence was sent for analysis, but with the technology that existed at the time it was not possible to get a DNA profile. With improved technology and a larger task force in 2001, semen samples from the first few victims that were found were analyzed and came back as a DNA match for Gary Ridgway. Based on this DNA match, he was arrested (Maleng, 2003). Once there was a match for one victim and one dumpsite, the taskforce went about gathering details about his background and his actions related to the murders and sexual offenses he committed. For instance, a private laboratory found a useful forensic match that linked Ridgway to two victims. They found traces of paint on the two victims' clothing that matched the paint used in Ridgway's job as a truck painter (Maleng, 2003).

Ridgway was originally charged with seven counts of aggravated first-degree murder, although there was suspicion that he was responsible for many more murders. The prosecutor intended to seek the death penalty. Ridgway's attorneys contacted the prosecutor's office informing them that if they would not seek the death penalty, Ridgway would plead guilty to those counts and an additional 40 or more murders, as well as provide information about the crimes and the locations of undiscovered bodies (Maleng, 2003). This plea was accepted, with the condition that if there were subsequent murders Ridgway failed to disclose and were later discovered, prosecutors could seek the death penalty for those (Maleng, 2003).

During the interviews that followed this agreement, Ridgway admitted to a number of other murders, although he said he killed so many women that his knowledge of specific victims' identities is poor. He did have detailed memories of where the bodies had been dumped, and other details about the murders (Maleng, 2003). Ridgway took great care not only to avoid detection, but also to mislead investigators. He would leave cigarette butts and chewing gum that were not his near the body, as well as pamphlets that might suggest he was a traveling salesman. He also went as far, in 1984, as to write a letter to a local newspaper that gave false information about the killer and his motivations. Unfortunately, an FBI expert determined that this letter was not written by the real Green River Killer, so it was not used to lead investigators to Ridgway (Maleng, 2003).

Gary Ridgway pled guilty to 48 counts of aggravated murder in the first degree, although there is speculation that he is responsible for more deaths. He is currently serving life without the possibility of parole. Ridgway's case involved more contact with the police and more investigation of forensic evidence than a typical sex offender, but this case illustrates the methods and the types of evidence that are used in investigating a sexual offense. These methods and evidence will be discussed further in Chapter 7.

OVERVIEW OF RESPONSE TO A REPORTED SEXUAL OFFENSE

When a crime is reported, a **patrol officer** responds to perform several functions, including the first and most basic investigation of the crime (Lyman, 2014). In the case of a violent crime, as patrol officers are often the first type of professional to respond, the officers must provide first aid if necessary and obtain medical help for those who may need it. When injuries have been addressed, the officers may begin collecting information that will be useful to other investigators. The first responding patrol officers must determine what has happened, and if they are responding to the crime scene, they must prevent contamination of that scene (Lyman, 2014). In the case of sexual assault, the victim's body is a significant source of evidence, and she (or he) must be instructed not to bathe, change clothes, or take any other action that might compromise the collection of evidence (Moreau, 1993).

The preliminary information an officer collects comes from the victims and witnesses to the crime. While the patrol officers may not conduct detailed interviews, they should obtain basic information such as identifying information of those answering questions and a basic description of what happened from each victim and witness. These individuals should be separated so that they do not have the opportunity to discuss their version of events, which may lead to some alteration of their stories (Lyman, 2014). The patrol officers should document any information they receive in writing, particularly details such as locations, times, and dates, and information about the victims and suspects (Lyman, 2014).

After the patrol officers have determined that the elements of a crime are present and have gathered basic information, further investigation is needed, including the collection of evidence (Lyman, 2014). In the case of sexual offenses that have occurred within a few days of the report, a specific type of evidence is usually collected, called a **rape kit**. To complete a rape kit, the victim is transported to a local hospital or other medical facility where a doctor, nurse, or a specialized **sexual assault nurse examiner (SANE)** can collect evidence and provide certain kinds of medical treatment (Zeccardi and Dickerman, 1993). The rape kit evidence can only be collected with the consent of the victim and is done at no expense to the victim, as the Violence Against Women Act mandates that states will pay for the cost of rape kits (Corrigan, 2013). More details about the rape kit are discussed later in this chapter.

A **detective** will generally become involved in a sexual offense investigation after the initial information is gathered by patrol officers and physical evidence is collected. A detective will have a victim tell his or her story and work to sort out any inconsistencies. There are often several changes in the way the story is reported before there is a version that the detective feels is accurate (Schwartz, 2010). After a detective has obtained all the facts and there is a suspect identified, he or she may hand the case over to a prosecutor; however, when these changes in the story are recorded it is less likely that a prosecutor will file charges against the suspect. Detectives also have the option to "unfound" cases that they do not believe were crimes (Schwartz, 2010).

LAW ENFORCEMENT RESPONSE TO SEXUAL OFFENSES

As noted above, when a sexual offense is reported to the police, the first responder is usually a patrol officer. That officer is responsible for assessing what has happened and determining if evidence needs to be collected. The main way these tasks are accomplished is through interviewing the victim. The victim in a sexual offense is often the only witness, as these offenses are not frequently committed out in the open. The manner in which this first contact occurs is very important to both the police, as it determines the victim's openness with the officer and the type of information gathered, and the victim, as this contact sets the stage for her (or his) recovery (Burgess and Hazelwood, 1993).

Interviewing the Victim

Interviewing the victim of a sexual offense is very different from interviewing a suspect. Victims of sexual offenses are often traumatized, have had their trust broken, are embarrassed and unwilling to disclose details of the assault, and may feel that those around them are likely to judge them. While it is important to the police to obtain accurate information as quickly as possible, being empathetic and patient with the victim may elicit this information in a more reliable manner than the more demanding tone often taken with suspects (Burgess and Hazelwood, 1993).

Several strategies can help the police officer obtain the most useful information while also allowing the victim to feel as at ease as possible. The interviewer should be empathetic and emphasize that the victim was not at fault, assure the victim of her (or his) safety at the time of the interview, and make the victim feel confident in the interviewer's experience and qualifications (Burgess and Hazelwood, 1993). The following are guidelines suggested by Burgess and Hazelwood (1993) to improve the victim's experience with the interview and obtain quality information:

1. Give the victim information about the interview process and request her feedback.
2. Give the victim as much control as possible, asking how she would like to describe the event.
3. Respond to her requests, particularly in attempts to make her more comfortable.
4. Reassure the victim if she expresses feelings of guilt, fear, or humiliation.
5. Allow for breaks or low-stress questions after asking questions that may be humiliating or have to do with sex acts.
6. Start off using professional terminology for body parts and sex acts, and then explain if they are not understood.
7. Make sure questions are worded in a way that is not judgmental or threatening.
8. Help the victim to understand that sexuality is not the main issue in the crime; rather, force and the exercising of power and control are important elements of the crime.
9. Be factual and professional, taking care to make sure the victim does not perceive the interviewer to be voyeuristic.

Burgess and Hazelwood (1993) also provide guidelines for concluding the interview in a manner that is not upsetting to the victim and increases the likelihood that she will continue to want to participate in the investigation.

1. Inform the victim of the next step in the investigation, so she does not feel that she is being discarded.
2. Give the victim a phone number she can call to be updated on the progress of the investigation.
3. Refer the victim to support services that can assist her.
4. Ask the victim if she has questions regarding the next steps in the investigation and what is expected of her.
5. Thank the victim for taking the time to be interviewed and make sure she feels confident that her assistance has helped the investigation.

Research has shown that there are differences in the way victims and police interact in cases where charges are filed and in cases where charges are not filed. There are a number of potential explanations for this, including the types of statements recorded by police in the report, or the victim's desire to cooperate. Regardless of the causal process, victims who felt "vulnerable, uncomfortable, and guarded" (Patterson, 2011, p. 1,359) with police at the beginning of the interview were less likely to be involved in a case where charges were filed than when the victim felt comfortable and safe (Patterson,

2011). In cases where no charges were filed, victims were more likely to report that police questioned their behavior or asked questions too quickly and abruptly, making it more difficult for the victim to talk to them openly. Victims with unprosecuted cases also were more likely to experience disbelief from the police, including being told that they could be charged for making a false report (Patterson, 2011). The victim's experience with law enforcement will be discussed in greater detail later in this chapter.

In addition to being empathetic and supportive, it is important that the interviewer gain as much detailed information as possible. Many reports submitted for behavioral analysis are found to be lacking important details that would help develop a profile of the rapist (Hazelwood and Burgess, 1993). More detailed interviews of the victim should be completed by a detective, after the initial interview and the collection of forensic evidence is complete. In cases where the identity of the rapist is not known, it is helpful to develop an idea of his personality and motivations for committing the sexual offense. Hazelwood and Burgess (1993) recommend getting the following types of information from victims in order to help develop this profile:

1. The way the offender approached the victim and gained control.
2. How the offender maintained control.
3. The types of physical force used and when they were used.
4. The type of resistance, if any, employed by the victim.
5. The offender's reaction to any resistance.
6. Whether the offender experienced any sexual dysfunction.
7. All types of sex acts in which the victim was forced to engaged, and the order in which they occurred.
8. Anything the offender said, and his tone.
9. Anything the offender required the victim to say.
10. If the offender's attitude changed at any point during the assault, and what happened immediately before it changed.
11. Any actions to prevent the victim from identifying the offender.
12. Whether the offender took any of the victim's personal belongings.
13. Whether the victim has any information to lead her to believe she was specifically targeted, such as contact from strangers before or after the assault.
14. How people familiar with the offender on a daily basis would describe him.

All of these types of information can help determine why an offender commits particular types of assaults, may help link the crime to other sex offenses that have been reported, and may help identify the offender (Hazelwood and Burgess, 1993).

Discretion

Despite protocol indicating that patrol officers should take reports, detectives should investigate, and then prosecutors should make charging decisions, there are a number of areas where both patrol officers and detectives can determine the future of a complaint of sexual assault before it reaches the prosecutor. For instance, as was occurring in Baltimore, Maryland, police officers can simply refuse to take a report. The *Baltimore Sun* found that 40 percent of calls to 911 reporting a sex crime in 2009 and 2010 never made it to a sex crimes detective, as the police officers who responded to the call simply did not take a report (Fenton, 2010). In addition, when reports of sex offenses were taken, 35 percent of them were "unfounded," a much higher percentage than other cities (Fenton, 2011).

A similar scandal was discovered in Philadelphia. In 1983 Philadelphia had a rate of 43 percent of all rape cases "unfounded." When questioned by the Federal Bureau of Investigation (FBI) about this high percentage of "unfounded" rapes, the sex crimes unit claimed that no legitimate rape cases had been "unfounded," stating that since they accepted all complaints, it was reasonable that such a high percentage would be false complaints. Regardless, the FBI pressured Philadelphia to get its "unfounded" rate closer to average (Fazlollah, Matza, and McCoy, 1999). In 1984, the "unfounded" rate was 16 percent, seemingly a great improvement in the way victims of sex offenses were treated. Unfortunately, the Philadelphia police department used two tactics to reduce this rate, neither of which was beneficial to victims of sex offenses. First, rape complainants were asked to take lie-detector tests, and some were arrested for filing false complaints, both discouraging people from making reports in the first place. Second, the police were classifying many reports of sexual assault as "investigation of a person," which means they did not show up as either rapes or "unfounded" rapes (Fazlollah, Matza, and McCoy, 1999).

These cities receiving media attention for systematically ignoring rape complaints, pressuring victims to recant, and "unfounding" rape complaints does not mean that they are the only cities in which sexual offenses are treated in this manner. Yung (2014) studied the rape statistics reported by 210 police departments with populations over 100,000 people between 1995 and 2012 and found that 22 percent had "irregularities" in the data that would indicate rapes were being undercounted. Many of the cities identified as those that undercount rape have also been identified as cities with large numbers of untested rape kits (discussed later in Chapter 7) in storage (Yung, 2014).

Not all types of sexual offenses and victims are dealt with in the same manner by police. There have been many studies examining how offense and victim characteristics influence the way the police treat the case. For instance, sexual offenses that are accompanied by another crime, such as a robbery, are more likely to be cleared by arrest than those where the sex offense is the only crime (Addington and Rennison, 2008). This indicates that these crimes may be taken more seriously by police and given a higher priority in investigation. Additionally, although alcohol is a factor in many sexual offenses, it seems that its use influences the way police officers perceive the case. Schuller and Stewart (2000) found that when the victim had been using alcohol, police found her less credible, and that this effect increased as the perceived degree of intoxication increased. As perception of the victim's degree of intoxication increased, officers believed she was more interested in having sex and less clear about her communication that she was not interested in sex. Interestingly, while the officers viewed the case as weaker when the victim was intoxicated, intoxication did not influence the response the officers said they would have to the assault (Schuller and Stewart, 2000). It should be noted that this study was done with police officers in Australia; outcomes with officers in the United States could be different.

Police officers are part of the society that has a generally high acceptance of rape myths; officers' beliefs in these rape myths may affect their report taking and investigation decisions. Indeed, Page (2008) found that police officers who ranked higher on rape myth acceptance were less likely to say they would pursue an investigation where the victim did not fit the "genuine victim" stereotype; that is, they were not virgins, had a relationship with the perpetrator, did not resist, or did not report the rape immediately (Page, 2008). It also seems that specialized training in how to handle sexual assault victims does not influence police officers' rape myth beliefs or the level of blame attributed to the victim (Sleath and Bull, 2012). The way a police officer perceives and responds to a victim and a sexual offense has important implications for the investigation of the sex offense, but it also has a strong impact on the victim.

Forensic Medical Examinations for Victims of Sexual Offenses

Assuming the police take a report regarding a sexual offense and the offense has occurred recently, the victim will generally be taken for a **forensic medical examination**, often called a rape kit or a sexual assault kit. The rape kit actually refers to the standardized set of evidence collection tools and receptacles that are generally packaged together and used for all forensic medical examinations of victims of sexual offenses (U.S. Department of Justice, 2013b). This kit should include blank labels so that all evidence collected can be identified, as well as standardized forms for patient consent, history, and documentation of visible injuries. There will also be materials used in the collection and preservation of the victim's clothing, any foreign materials collected from the clothing or body, and multiple swabs of the body and genitals (U.S. Department of Justice, 2013b).

Before beginning a forensic medical examination, the medical professional will take a history from the victim, which includes medical information as well as other details relevant to the collection of evidence, such as whether the victim has recently been sexually active. This particular piece of information is important because DNA could be present from earlier consensual sexual encounters, as well as from the sexual assault. Consensual encounters can also cause a small amount of genital trauma, which could be visible upon examination. DNA may be collected from any consensual partners for comparison purposes (U.S. Department of Justice, 2013b). The medical professional will also need to know about any actions taken by the victim after the assault that may affect the findings of the examination. If the victim has changed clothing, bathed, or even eaten or smoked, this could affect the findings of the examination (U.S. Department of Justice, 2013b).

After the victim is interviewed by the medical professional, the collection of evidence will begin. The first step is to collect a victim's clothing, which can later be examined for materials that may link an offender or location to the assault, as well as for damage that may show evidence of force. Clothing is collected with the victim standing over a white cloth so that any material dislodged from the clothing while it is being removed will be collected in the cloth. Each item of clothing is placed in a separate paper bag, which is labeled and sealed (U.S. Department of Justice, 2013b). The victim's body is then examined for debris as well as for dried or moist secretions, which can be swabbed and collected as evidence. The victim is also examined using an alternate light source, which will cause body fluids to fluoresce (emit light), and those areas should be swabbed as well (U.S. Department of Justice, 2013b).

The victim's fingernails are of particular interest to forensic medical examiners. If the victim scratched the offender or his clothing, evidence may be present under the fingernails. Also, fingernails may break and provide evidence of a struggle. Any damage to the fingernails is documented using photography; samples are collected from beneath the fingernails by either cutting, scraping, or swabbing the area (U.S. Department of Justice, 2013b). The victim's body is also examined for any injuries, which are documented on the forensic medical examiner's report, as well as photographed. Generally, digital photography is used, and the injuries are given perspective by including a ruler held up to the injury in the photograph (U.S. Department of Justice, 2013b).

Another potential source of evidence is the victim's pubic hair. The pubic hair is combed onto a piece of paper and the paper and comb are collected as evidence. There may be hair transferred from the perpetrator to the victim in this area, and secretions such as semen may be present in the pubic hair. Some of the victim's own head and pubic hair may also be collected as reference samples for when the evidence is later examined (U.S. Department of Justice, 2013b).

Depending on the location of penetration during the sexual assault, the medical professional will examine the mouth, anus, and/or (for women) vagina for injuries and traces of semen or other material to be submitted into evidence with the rape kit (Zeccardi and Dickerman, 1993). This is done by swabbing the external genital area for biological samples, as well as taking samples from inside the vagina and from the cervix. Any visible injuries are photographed. Often forensic medical examinations will include the use of a colposcope, which is a magnifying device that allows the medical professional to observe injuries that might be missed with the naked eye. Another technique to observe genital injuries includes the use of toluidine blue dye, which is applied to the external genitalia and then washed off, with the dye then adhering to any areas of broken skin. These areas are also photographed (U.S. Department of Justice, 2013b). All evidence is labeled and stored in a locked refrigerator so that the chain of custody is preserved and the evidence can later be examined by police analysts (Zeccardi and Dickerman, 1993).

In addition to the collection of evidence, it is a common practice to offer the victim prophylactic treatment for pregnancy (in women of child-bearing age) and sexually transmitted diseases. Hormonal treatment, often called the "morning after pill," can be offered to prevent pregnancy; antibiotics can be offered to reduce the risk of contracting diseases such as syphilis and gonorrhea (Zeccardi and Dickerman, 1993).

After evidence is collected, it may be examined in a crime laboratory associated with the police department, if it is determined that the evidence may be useful for identification of a suspect or for prosecution. In a recent study, 40 percent of rape kits collected on adolescent victims were not submitted to the crime lab for analysis, and this may be based on the perception of the legitimacy of the case (Shaw and Campbell, 2013). Although a rape kit may be collected, further interviews with the victim by detectives, rather than patrol officers, are generally carried out before this evidence is processed. Unanalyzed rape kits will be discussed in greater detail later in Chapter 7.

VICTIM EXPERIENCE WITH LAW ENFORCEMENT

Most victims of sexual offenses do not report their assault to law enforcement. The reasons for not reporting a sexual assault are many, but an important consideration is often a victim's concern that they will be treated badly by police personnel, not be believed by law enforcement, or the prediction that not much will come of reporting the assault. These concerns are more likely when the victim does not consider the crime to be very serious (Goudriaan, Lynch, and Nieuwbeerta, 2004). There are considerable mixed results in evaluating victim experiences with police; some studies have reported fairly positive experiences and others quite negative (Frazier and Haney, 1996). The accuracy of victim concerns about their interactions with the police is unclear. One study indicating poor experiences with the police discovered that victims who did report their assault to the police had worse mental and physical health outcomes compared to those who did not report their assault. This was especially true in cases where the assault was reported but the case was not prosecuted (Campbell et al., 2001).

Victims of sexual trauma need support, to be believed and reassured that they were not at fault for their attack, and sensitivity to their individual circumstances (Holzman, 1996). Unfortunately, these needs may not be concordant with the needs of police investigators for most types of crimes. In fact, normal police procedures may be a significant contributing factor in the development of post-traumatic stress disorder (Herman, 2003). The manner in which questions are asked of victims can leave them feeling blamed, as investigators are often looking for holes in the story, things that do not make sense, or an ulterior motive for reporting an assault (Bouffard, 2000).

Some evidence indicates that police may not treat all rape victims the same, with those perceived to have questionable moral characters or who were engaged in risky behavior being viewed less sympathetically by police (Campbell and Johnson, 1997; Campbell, 1998). Under the "real rape" paradigm (see Chapter 4), date rapes, rapes committed against unconscious women, cases where the victim and offender have had a past intimate relationship, and assaults against women stepping outside of their traditional role tend not to be considered serious, or even unacceptable. Research shows that police officers take cases that do not fit into the "real rape" paradigm less seriously (Jordan, 2004).

As police officer beliefs about sex offenses may impact their behavior toward victims, their beliefs, as well as victims' experiences with officers, are of interest to researchers. In a 1978 study, police officers were more likely than citizens or counselors, and about equally likely as convicted rapists, to believe that the victim's behavior causes rape. Overall, in this study, police officer attitudes were more similar to rapists' attitudes than citizens' or counselors' attitudes (Field, 1978). Another study found that police are likely to be skeptical of cases that do not adhere to the stereotypical rape formula, indicating a belief in rape myths (Lonsway, Welch, and Fitzgerald, 2001). Police culture may have changed significantly, particularly since the 1978 study, and it should be noted that a more recent study found relatively low levels of rape myth acceptance in police officers, with 93 percent of officers agreeing that "any woman can be raped." This same study also found a small subgroup of officers who wrote unsolicited hostile and sexist comments on the survey (Page, 2010). The same author, in a different study, found that police officer rape myth acceptance went down as the officer's level of education increased, and as the officer's experience handling rape investigations increased (Page, 2007). An officer's level of rape myth acceptance may indeed influence the way they perceive rape reports. In a study of officers' responses to written descriptions of rape scenarios, those with higher levels of rape myth acceptance placed more responsibility for an assault on the victim and less on the perpetrator, and they had a lower belief in the case's authenticity compared to officers with low rape myth acceptance (Hine and Murphy, 2019).

Police officer attitudes are important for predicting how an officer may respond to a sexual assault and how he or she will treat a victim, but the victim experience itself is perhaps more instructive. In one study, nearly half of victims who reported their sexual assault to the police indicated dissatisfaction with the police interview. In contrast, 90 percent of victims expressed satisfaction with the medical services they received and 90 to 100 percent were satisfied with the Sexual Assault Center services (Monroe et al., 2005). A victim's experience with being blamed and having her personal life examined and used to discredit her, often a part of their experience with law enforcement and emergency medicine, is often called the "second rape." When the medical and legal systems do not help or even believe the victim, she may feel more ashamed, may not be interested in participating in prosecution, and may have negative physical and mental health outcomes (Campbell et al., 2001). Women report shock and embarrassment when police officers treat them as if they are the problem, instead of the perpetrator, or are not sensitive to their trauma and personal needs (Jordan, 2002).

INVESTIGATION

After a victim has been interviewed by a patrol officer, undergone a forensic medical exam, and been interviewed by a detective, there are a number of different types of evidence that can be analyzed to help support a criminal charge and prosecution of the offender. Forensic evidence can help establish the identity of the offender, if unknown, or support the victim's claim that the encounter was nonconsensual. As discussed above, a victim of a recent sexual offense generally undergoes a forensic medical examination and evidence is collected in a rape kit. This process can be difficult for the victim, but not all rape kits are being analyzed or used as evidence (Corrigan, 2013).

Untested Rape Kits

Towards the end of the first decade of the 2000s, a problem with rape investigation was brought to the public's attention through media coverage. Many large cities had rape kits in storage that had not been tested, numbering in the thousands. Detroit, Michigan, for instance, had over 11,000 untested rape kits in storage; Memphis, Tennessee, had over 12,000; Dallas, Texas, had more than 4,000; and Phoenix, Arizona, had almost 3,000 untested rape kits (Alter, 2014). In Detroit, one prosecutor decided to begin having the backlog of rape kits tested, and of the first 3,231 kits she had tested, 567 came back with a DNA match, 87 of which were to serial rapists (Alter, 2014).

There are many reasons a law enforcement agency might not submit a rape kit for analysis. One important reason found by Strom and Hickman (2010) is that the police do not have a suspect for the crime. This is a particularly confusing reason not to submit forensic evidence that may contain DNA, as the possibility of finding a DNA match would help police identify a suspect (Patterson and Campbell, 2012). Strom and Hickman (2010) also found that police did not submit forensic evidence because a suspect had already been adjudicated without the need for forensic testing (so in that case testing would be a waste of resources) and when they did not expect charges would be filed. They also found that there were often problems with not expecting laboratory results in a timely fashion and not being able to fund the analysis of evidence (Strom and Hickman, 2010). These reasons for submitting or not submitting a rape kit for testing imply that the police use rape kit analysis as a way of supporting prosecution for strong cases, but not as a tool in investigating rapes or building a strong case when other evidence is not strong (Campbell and Fehler-Cabral, 2018).

In a detailed study of the reasons behind the backlog of 11,000 untested rape kits in Detroit, Campbell and Felher-Cabral (2018) interviewed law enforcement personnel and reviewed case files for a sample of the untested rape kits. They learned that police found the researchers' focus on untested kits to be frustrating, as they viewed the case, not the kit, to be the important issue. One interviewee said the untested kits were from "cases that we couldn't or wouldn't do anything about" (Campbell and Felher-Cabral, 2018, p. 87). A key reason police couldn't do something about many cases had to do with limited resources. Given the limited resources, they had to make a choice about which cases would get their attention. In cases where police doubted the victim's credibility for reasons such as suspecting her of being a prostitute, she was a teenager, or she knew her attacker, they tended not to devote resources to investigation (Campbell and Felher-Cabral, 2018). Of course, all of these situations can and do apply in reports of rapes that occurred, but police officers can hold views accepting of rape myths just as members of the public do.

In their seven-year study, Patterson and Campbell (2012) found 41.4 percent of rape kits were not submitted for analysis; whether the kit was submitted was related to some factors that may influence perception of the assault. For instance, when the victim suffered physical injury (non-genital) the rape kit was more likely to be submitted. This suggests that these cases are considered more serious and more worthy of investigation. They also found that if the victim had bathed after the assault and prior to the forensic medical examination the police were less likely to submit the rape kit for analysis. This may be due to the perception that the kit is unlikely to yield DNA evidence, although in reality, semen can remain in the reproductive tract for several days (Patterson and Campbell, 2012). In this study, the victim's belief that she had been drugged or was unconscious during the attack was not related to sending the evidence for analysis, although that analysis could confirm the use of drugs and identify the offender if the victim was not aware of his identity (Patterson and Campbell, 2012).

In a study of adolescent victims, Shaw and Campbell (2013) also found victim and assault-related characteristics to be associated with the likelihood of a rape kit being submitted for analysis. They found that 40.7 percent of rape kits were not submitted for analysis, and that the kits of younger victims (ages 13 to 15) were more likely to be submitted than older victims (ages 16 to 17). This could be due to the perception that younger teens are less likely to willingly engage in sexual intercourse, so these cases may have been perceived as more likely to be genuine. Shaw and Campbell (2013) also found that non-White victims were more likely to have their rape kits submitted for analysis than White victims, which is not what would be expected if the cases that are taken most seriously are more likely to have evidence submitted for analysis. Single offender cases were more likely to have evidence submitted for analysis than multiple offender cases; cases with multiple types of sexual assault were more likely to have evidence submitted than cases where there was only one assault (Shaw and Campbell, 2013).

In addition to the investigative reasons for analyzing rape kits, there may be legal reasons that these kits should be analyzed. At least six police departments have been sued by women who completed a forensic medical exam that did not result in analyzing the rape kit (Jones, 2021). The basis for the lawsuits is the allegation that police departments have violated the Equal Protection Clause of the Fourteenth Amendment in that they discriminated based on gender in their failure to test the rape kits. The women would have to show that, although there is no policy explicitly discriminating against women, women have been disadvantaged and that bias was a factor that contributed to that outcome (Jones, 2021). Indeed, while police denied it, Campbell and Felher-Cabral (2018) found that other stakeholders believed gender, race, and class-related bias were significant factors in why rape kits were not tested in Detroit.

As Detroit's situation demonstrates, testing all rape kits for DNA can help solve rapes and identify serial rapists; however, there are arguments against testing and legitimate reasons to not test particular rape kits. The DNA evidence in a rape kit can identify a person who left semen or other biological evidence on the body of the victim. Unfortunately, there is no difference between DNA left during a sexual offense and DNA left during a consensual encounter, so the evidence obtained cannot prove a sexual offense occurred. With most victims of sexual offenses knowing their offender, it is not so much a matter of identifying the perpetrator (Sallomi, 2013) as it is proving that the sexual encounter was not consensual. Other aspects of a rape kit, such as photographs of injuries, may help with this, but there may not be a need for DNA testing in these cases. However, even in cases of a known perpetrator, testing the DNA can assist in linking two or more assaults committed by the same individual, as some offenders repeatedly victimize people known to them (Campbell et al., 2018).

TYPES OF EVIDENCE

Many types of forensic evidence can be collected in any crime, including a sexual offense. Despite limitations and untested rape kits discussed above, one of the most commonly used forms of forensic evidence used in identifying the perpetrator of a sexual offense is DNA. Other forms of forensic evidence may be used to corroborate a victim's description of the use of force by the perpetrator or may help tie a particular individual to the crime scene.

DNA

Since the mid-1980s **deoxyribonucleic acid (DNA)** has proved to be one of the most useful forensic tools in the investigator's arsenal. DNA is the genetic code that is unique to every single individual on earth, with the exception of identical (monozygotic) twins. DNA is found in the nuclei and mitochondria of cells. Nuclear DNA can provide a match to a specific individual; however, mitochondrial DNA (mtDNA) contains DNA from the mother only (Lee, 2010a; Saferstein, 2013). DNA is present in all human cells and as such is commonly found at crime scenes in the form of blood, sweat, saliva, semen, hair where the follicle is attached, and tissue. As discussed above, when a forensic medical exam is performed on a victim of a sexual offense, the body is examined for the presence of all of these forms of evidence that might be left by the perpetrator.

Three main methods are used to obtain a DNA profile from a sample at a crime scene. First is polymerase chain reaction (PCR), which involves unwinding DNA from its double helix structure and adding it to a solution of unattached nucleotides. This method allows the forensic scientist to copy strands of DNA. The benefit of the replications of DNA strands is that it allows DNA profiles to be obtained from very small amounts of evidentiary DNA (Saferstein, 2013).

The second method is restriction fragment length polymorphism (RFLP), which involves cutting sections of DNA and multiplying them to create a profile (Lee, 2010a). The previous two methods are not generally considered as reliable as the third method, which is short tandem repeats (STR). In each chromosome, small areas exist known as loci. According to Saferstein (2013), these loci are only five base pairs long. As a result, the STR DNA analysis requires much shorter base pair samples than those obtained from RFLP. The advantage of a shorter strand of base pairs is that the DNA evidence is more resistant to degeneration over time (Saferstein, 2013). Short tandem repeats are replicated using the PCR method. Less than one-hundredth of the evidentiary source is needed for an STR-created profile as opposed to the amount of evidence required for an RFLP (Lee, 2010a).

Once the DNA profile is developed, it is entered into the **Combined DNA Index System (CODIS)**, where it can be matched to DNA profiles obtained from other crime scenes, known offenders, and/or a suspect in the sex offense from which evidence was obtained. One of the main advantages of DNA evidence is that when a match is obtained, the chance of the DNA sample coming from another individual is lower than in many other forms of evidence. For example, some DNA profiles have allowed expert witnesses to state chances in the range of one to hundreds of millions that the sample came from another individual (Lee, 2010a).

Semen

While DNA can be obtained from the many forms of biological evidence discussed above, semen is a particularly important type of evidence often found in sexual offenses. It is important to be able to determine, when examining items such as bedclothes where a sexual offense may have occurred or the undergarments of the victim, if semen is present. These items are generally first examined using an alternative light source, commonly known as a blacklight or a Wood's lamp; however, there are many types of material, including semen, that will fluoresce when exposed to a Wood's lamp (Saferstein, 2013). These materials include common products such as body lotion and contraceptive creams, as well as vaginal secretions. To determine if a particular fluorescing stain is semen, it can be tested for the enzyme acid phosphatase (AP), which is present in high concentrations in seminal fluid. When chemically treated, the stain will turn purple if AP is present, indicating that the material is likely to be semen (Saferstein, 2013).

The definitive test as to whether or not a stain is indeed seminal fluid is a microscopic examination of the stain itself. In most cases, if a stain is seminal fluid, it will contain spermatozoa, which will be visible using a microscope. This is due to the fact that males release 250 million to 600 million spermatozoa per ejaculation; however, this must be treated with caution as not all males have spermatozoa in their ejaculate. For example, those individuals who have undergone vasectomies will exhibit aspermia (no spermatozoa present). This problem has been compounded in recent years due to the increasing popularity of vasectomies (Safterstein, 2013).

Bite Marks

7

In some cases, a perpetrator of a sexual offense will bite the victim, and these bites can leave visible marks on the skin. A forensic odontologist can attempt to match the impression made on the skin to a suspect's teeth. The effort to link a suspect to a particular mark on the skin is done by superimposing an outline of the suspect's teeth over a photograph of the **bite mark**, at the same scale as the outline (Metcalf et al., 2010). The evidence of a link between the suspect and the bite mark can then be considered inconclusive, can exclude the suspect, suggest that the suspect probably left the impression, or give reasonable scientific certainty that the suspect left the bite mark (Metcalf et al., 2010).

Bite mark evidence has come under some scrutiny recently as there are a number of issues that may make such identifications inaccurate (Metcalf et al., 2010; Beecher-Monas, 2009). For instance, during a violent assault where the perpetrator might bite the victim, the victim is most likely squirming and trying to escape, so the bite mark impression is not left on stationary skin, but rather can be distorted by movement (Metcalf et al., 2010). Additionally, there is no evidence that all individuals' teeth are distinct to the extent that a bite mark could conclusively identify the perpetrator. It is possible that two people with similar, although not identical, teeth could leave bite marks that could not be distinguished (Metcalf et al., 2010).

Despite these limitations, bite marks can actually be used to obtain DNA evidence, rather than to try to match a suspect to the shape of the mark left on the skin. If the mark is swabbed before the victim washes, the teeth marks and the area inside them, where the offender's tongue would have contacted the victim's skin, can contain saliva, which can be used to develop a DNA profile (U.S. Department of Justice, 2013b). Bite marks can also indicate a degree of force, corroborating that the sexual encounter was not consensual. Biting is often present in sexual offenses where the offender displays brutality and physical violence (McCabe and Wauchope, 2005) or in the power assertive rapist and the anger excitation rapist as discussed in Chapter 4 (Holmes and Holmes, 2009b).

Fingerprints

Fingerprints, the ridge patterns located at the tips of the fingers in all humans, are thought to be unique to individuals, and thus a way of identifying them. Fingerprints can be left by individuals when they touch surfaces, even including human skin, and leave behind oil from their fingertips (Lee, 2010b). Fingerprints left in this manner are called latent fingerprints, and can be identified and preserved by crime scene technicians using a variety of techniques. Some prints are visible to the naked eye, while others can be detected after gently applying powder to the area where prints are suspected. There are also chemicals that can cause fingerprints to become visible (Saferstein, 2013). After prints are made visible, they must be preserved, first by photographing them, and then by "lifting" them. This can be done using an adhesive film, similar to tape, which is pressed onto the latent fingerprint, and then removing it. The film is then pressed onto a background such as cardboard so that the fingerprint is visible. Fingerprints can then be converted to digital images, using a very advanced scanner (Saferstein, 2013).

In order to use the digital image of the latent fingerprint to help identify or match to a suspect, computer technology is utilized. There are **automated fingerprint identification systems (AFIS)** which can store millions of fingerprints (Saferstein, 2013) and, similar to the process for DNA, can identify similar fingerprints from other crime scenes, known offenders, or a particular suspect. While the computer system can identify fingerprints that are likely identical to the fingerprint that was submitted, the final decision regarding a match is left to a trained fingerprint examiner (Saferstein, 2013). Similar to DNA profiling, fingerprinting can be useful in a sexual offense when the offender is not known to the victim. This type of forensic evidence may help identify suspects if they leave latent fingerprints at the scene of the crime.

Other Types of Forensic Evidence

Many types of evidence can be collected by crime scene technicians and analyzed by forensic scientists to help identify suspects or corroborate a victim's statement that the sexual encounter was not consensual. In cases where it is suspected that the victim may have been exposed to an intoxicating substance that may have been administered by the perpetrator, it is possible to test the victim's blood and urine for specific commonly used "date rape drugs" (U.S. Department of Justice, 2013b). Computer forensics can be useful in cases where the suspect may have recordings or photographs of the assault, or possess pornography that depicts acts similar to those that occurred during the assault. Information provided by the victim about the assault may help in developing a psychological profile of the offender. There are numerous types of physical evidence that can link a suspect or victim to a particular scene, help identify the suspect, or help describe the event. These include tool marks, ballistic analysis, foot prints, tire marks, fiber, soil, and many others.

All of the evidence that is collected by crime scene technicians can then be analyzed and the results sent to police detectives to help them identify a suspect or understand what happened during the offense. Once enough evidence has been collected, the police may want to interview, arrest, and/or interrogate a suspect.

INTERROGATING THE SUSPECT

Little research has been conducted regarding how to best interview people suspected of sex offenses, and most of these studies use police departments outside the United States. Regardless, there are general interview techniques suggested to police, and the research on their effectiveness that has been completed in other countries is still instructive to discuss. The main goal of an **interrogation** is to get a confession from the suspect, as this is generally viewed as one of the strongest types of evidence of guilt (Lyman, 2014). There are a number of techniques investigators use to try to elicit confessions from suspects, and these may vary based on the type of sex offender profile (Holmes and Holmes, 2009a).

While there are rules investigators must follow to protect the constitutional rights of the suspects, they tend to believe that these unfairly restrict what they can do and that the rules are more in favor of the suspect (Leo, 2008). Within the law, one technique an investigator may use is that of role playing. He or she may assume an attitude that would suggest to the suspect that he or she is more interested in helping them than in obtaining information to help convict them later. This is often done using a "good cop/bad cop" technique or by having an investigator take on the role of someone in a position of trust (Braswell, McCarthy, and McCarthy, 2012).

Investigators can also use fabricated evidence to try to convince the suspect to confess. They may tell the suspect that their demeanor suggest that they are guilty. They can tell the suspect that there are other suspects or witnesses who have talked to police and told them that the suspect is guilty, suggesting to the suspect that it would be better if he or she confessed. Finally, they may also fabricate the existence of forensic evidence. They may tell a suspect that they have DNA, fingerprints, or other evidence linking the suspect to the crime; however, the courts have ruled that actually creating false evidence is unconstitutional. These techniques all lead the suspect to believe that they have been caught and would be better off confessing (Braswell, McCarthy, and McCarthy, 2012).

Police investigators may also use one of two opposite techniques regarding the way they present the crime. First, they may exaggerate the severity of the offense for which the suspect is under investigation. By doing so, the suspect may feel that the consequences of hiding their involvement in the more minor offense are too great, as they may be convicted of a more serious one (Braswell, McCarthy, and McCarthy, 2012). In contrast, they may also normalize or minimize the crime of which the suspect is accused. They may give suspects the opportunity to see their behavior as justifiable or provide justifications as to why the behavior is not their fault. This would encourage the suspect to confess, as they may perceive that the consequences would not be great (Braswell, McCarthy, and McCarthy, 2012).

Under some conditions police can misrepresent their identity to suspects such that they might be more likely to confess. While police cannot pretend to be a suspect's lawyer or priest, or anyone else to whom the suspect would feel compelled to confess, they can pretend to be someone such as a fellow jail inmate and use information obtained in that conversation (Braswell, McCarthy, and McCarthy, 2012). Similarly, there are also certain conditions under which investigators are able to make promises to suspects. While they cannot make specific offers of leniency, they are able to suggest that outcomes would be better for the suspect if he or she confessed (Braswell, McCarthy, and McCarthy, 2012).

For a power reassurance rapist, where the rapist does not intend to do harm but rather seeks to reassure himself of his masculinity, investigators may have the most success if they take on the role of a trusted individual to whom the suspect can confess, and also if they minimize the crime, indicating that the victim did not suffer (Holmes and Holmes, 2009a). For the anger retaliation rapist, who has a hatred of women, a possible interviewing strategy is similar to "good cop/bad cop" but involves a female interviewer and a male interviewer, where the male expresses dominance over the female, perhaps making disrespectful comments about her when she has left the room, in order to develop a rapport with the suspect and increase his cooperation with the male interviewer (Holmes and Holmes, 2009a). For the power assertive rapist, who may have poor impulse control, it is essential the police present a professional case detailing how they intend to prove this suspect is guilty. They should not be incorrect about details or the suspect may view them as incompetent and not wish to cooperate (Holmes and Holmes, 2009a). Finally, for the sadistic rapist, who rapes to express sexually aggressive desires, there does not appear to be a most successful interviewing strategy; however, the interviewer should be professional and competent in order to maximize cooperation (Holmes and Holmes, 2009a). Because the techniques may vary for different types of rapists, it is important that investigators thoroughly interview the victim, as discussed above, to help determine what type of rapist the suspect may be.

FALSE REPORTS

Given the difficulties that victims of sexual offenses face when reporting their victimization to the police, it is difficult to discuss false reports of sexual offenses, as doing so may create the perception that false reports occur often. Studies of the percentage of false reports show they occur quite rarely. Studies have generally reported rates of false rape allegations of less than 10 percent, with recent studies indicating 4.5 percent of rapes reported to the Los Angeles Police Department in 2008 were false reports (Spohn, White, and Tellis, 2014) and 5.9 percent of rapes reported to a university police department between 1998 and 2007 were false reports (Lisak et al., 2010). Despite low rates of false reporting, police officers estimate the percentage of rape reports that are false to be quite high. One study demonstrated that, on average, police officers believe approximately one-third of rape reports to be false (Venema, 2018). Police also believe teenagers are particularly likely to make false reports (O'Neil and Hayes, 2020).

One of the problems in discussing false allegations of sexual offense is defining what, exactly, constitutes a false allegation. If the police "unfound" a sexual offense complaint, it does not necessarily mean that the assault did not happen. Unfounding must occur after investigation where the police determine that the claim is false or baseless (Spohn, White, and Tellis, 2014). A baseless claim is one in which the event reported does not meet the legal definition for a sexual assault but is still a true account of what happened. A false report is a report of a sexual offense that investigation indicates did not happen (Lisak et al., 2010). It is also possible that law enforcement agencies do not follow these guidelines and will classify a case as unfounded based on the victim's character or other factors not related to actual investigation determining that the event did not occur (Spohn, White, and Tellis, 2014).

The rape myth culture suggests that women have multiple motivations for lying about sexual assault, including to cover up an unwanted pregnancy, being caught in an affair, or to explain whereabouts to parents or partners when they are late (Burt, 1980); however, the true reasons for making false complaints are related to internal processes. For instance, people with very strict and deeply held value systems who engage in an act of casual sex that does not fit within their value system may be disturbed and unable to take responsibility for their actions. They may react in one of several ways in order to protect their self-esteem and one rare possibility is that they make a false allegation of rape (McDowell and Hibler, 1993). There is a continuum of false rape reports from "a slightly distorted report of an actual event to the completely false report of an assault or rape" (McDowell and Hibler, 1993, p. 280). While rare, some false reports of sexual offenses include the victim self-inflicting injuries and using props to support her claim (McDowell and Hibler, 1993).

While the characteristics of a false allegation can also apply to a legitimate allegation of a sexual offense, there are some factors more strongly associated with false reports. For instance, false allegations are more likely than genuine allegations to have the perpetrator be a stranger, or a very vague acquaintance whose name the victim cannot remember. This reduces confrontation with another version of the story, and also avoids getting a specific person in trouble (McDowell and Hibler, 1993). False complainants more often provide police with "face-saving" reasons that they were not able to resist their attacker, and they are less likely to report multiple sexual acts during the attack than victims of genuine sex offenses. False complainants do not often present with serious injuries, although self-inflicting serious injuries does sometimes occur. When injuries are self-inflicted they often avoid sensitive areas of the body and are not in locations that would cause long-term damage. They are also more indifferent to their wounds than victims who sustain similar injuries during a real sexual offense (McDowell and Hibler, 1993).

Of course, all of these characteristics can occur in a true complaint of a sexual offense, which makes the investigator's job very difficult, as he or she may be dealing with someone who is extremely traumatized and needs to carefully determine if the events described are genuine. Aggressively confronting someone who is telling the truth will both upset the victim and reduce the quality of any further information provided to the investigator (McDowell and Hibler, 1993).

LAW ENFORCEMENT ONLINE

While most of Chapter 7 has focused on the law enforcement response to and investigation of sex crimes that are reported to them by a victim, the use of the Internet by sexual predators has led to a new avenue for investigation, and perhaps prevention, of sex crimes. In the last several years, there has been increasing concern over sexual offenders using the Internet as a means of communicating with children and luring them to meet the offender (Seto et al., 2012). In response, law enforcement officers have utilized the Internet for undercover operations. They can pose as minors online and wait for adults to solicit them in a **proactive investigation**; they can take over the online account of a real minor who has been targeted and make contact with that suspect in a reactive investigation; or they can pose as someone dealing in child pornography (Mitchell, Wolak, and Finkelhor, 2005). Arrests as a result of proactive investigations increased dramatically between 2000 and 2006, with an estimated 644 arrests in 2000 and 3,100 in 2006. That is an increase of 381 percent. In contrast, arrests for soliciting an actual minor online are not as common and did not increase at nearly the same rate. In 2000 there were approximately 508 arrests for soliciting a minor online and 615 arrests in 2006. That was an increase of 21 percent (Wolak, Finkelhor, and Mitchell, 2009). Note that this does not mean that there are more undercover investigations of potential sex offenders than there are solicitations of real minors, simply that the number of arrests for such is greater. Remember that many crimes against children, including Internet solicitations, are not reported to the police.

While a proactive investigation would seem like a good strategy for removing child predators, it is important to note that not all of the people arrested in proactive investigations had a history of sexually victimizing children. Indeed, only 2 percent of those arrested in proactive investigations were registered sex offenders (Wolak, Finkelhor, and Mitchell, 2009). Of the sample of arrests examined from data from 2000, 13 percent were found to have also committed a sex offense against a child. Ninety-four percent of those arrested were charged with a felony such as an attempted crime, an Internet specific crime, or inducement. Sixty-eight percent received a sentence involving incarceration. Eighty-five percent were required to register as a sex offender (Mitchell, Wolak, and Finkelhor, 2005). A relatively small portion of the cases (23 percent) included aspects that were problematic for prosecution, such as raising the issue of entrapment (12 percent). All of the individuals arrested in proactive investigations were arrested when they showed up to a meeting they had set online, many with "sex-related items," suggesting they did, in fact, intend to sexually victimize a child, whether they had done so previously or not (Mitchell, Wolak, and Finkelhor, 2005).

Proactive investigation may have some challenges associated with it, but policing the use of the Internet for engaging in activities such as sex trafficking can be difficult due to issues associated with jurisdiction and identifying offenders. In a study consisting of interviews of police personnel who were members of units addressing sex trafficking and Internet crimes, participants described several difficulties with their investigations (Nhan and Bowen, 2020). Jurisdictional issues can arise because social media and online advertisement websites can be used to "market" sex trafficking victims to clients, and the trafficker and victim often travel around the United States to meet with clients. Indeed, the offenders often use social media to recruit victims into prostitution. Due to the nature of the relationship with the trafficker, the victims may not see themselves as victims, and may also be reluctant to provide information about traffickers to investigators (Nhan and Bowen, 2020). The use of the Internet can lead to jurisdictional issues as well as problems with identifying offenders. Administrators of some of the websites used by offenders may be helpful to investigators, but others may be less willing to provide information. Investigators working in this area have had to adjust to the way technology is being used by offenders and have had to develop technical skills in computer forensics as well (Nhan and Bowen, 2020).

CONCLUSION

Chapter 7 covered many aspects of law enforcement's response to a report of a sexual offense. Much of the information that police use in investigating a sex offense comes from interviewing the victim, both immediately after the report is made and later in more detail with detectives present, and from the forensic medical examination. Chapter 7 discussed interviewing strategies and suggested topics, as well as the way police often view and treat victims of sexual violence. The forensic medical examination was discussed in detail, as were several main forms of forensic evidence used in sexual assault investigations. Finally, law enforcement's contact with the suspect was discussed, as were the special issues of false sexual assault allegations and online investigation. Chapter 8 shifts focus from law enforcement to the next phase of criminal justice processing: the courts.

KEY TERMS

automated fingerprint identification systems (AFIS)
bite mark
Combined DNA Index System (CODIS)
detective
DNA
fingerprints
forensic medical examination
interrogation
patrol officer
proactive investigation
rape kit
sexual assault nurse examiner (SANE)

EXERCISES

1. Describe the types of evidence that may be collected during a forensic medical examination of a sexual assault victim. How might this evidence be used?
2. What types of detailed information about a sexual offense must a detective ask of a victim? Why is this information important?
3. Find a recent news story about an investigation of a sexual offense. How does this story seem similar to and different from the procedures discussed here?

ESSAY QUESTIONS

1. Using information from Chapter 7, discuss the issues associated with interviewing a victim of a sexual offense. How might law enforcement's need to obtain information conflict with a victim's emotional needs? How can police get detailed information and determine if the complaint is genuine in the most tactful manner possible?
2. What are the characteristics of a false report of sexual assault? How are these different from truthful reports of sexual assault? Is it possible to determine, based on these characteristics, if a report is false or genuine? What should the police do to determine this?
3. What types of forensic evidence can be analyzed in a sexual offense? In what ways are these types of forensic evidence useful and in what ways are they not?
4. Why is a police officer's attitude about rape important in his or her investigation of a reported rape? Be sure to discuss the impact on the victim as well as the type of information reported.

8

PROSECUTING SEX OFFENDERS IN THE COURTS

Chapter Objectives

After reading this chapter, students will be able to:

- Explore the nature of the judiciary in the United States.
- Identify the differences between determining guilt and sentencing criminals.
- Demonstrate the problems with empirical evaluations of sex offender processing through the courts.
- Explore the forces that drive sentencing decisions.
- Explain the differences between disparity and discrimination.
- Explain the genesis of rape shield laws.
- Understand the nature of false rape allegations.
- Explain the use of CCTV for child victims of sex offenders.

INTRODUCTION

Once the investigation of sex crimes is complete, the next step in the criminal justice system is to prosecute these offenders. As seen thus far, bringing sex offenders to justice is a time consuming and complicated process; this does not get any easier once the case has been referred to the judiciary. All criminal defendants must be proven guilty beyond a reasonable doubt. In the case of sex offenders, this can be a real struggle for prosecutors. From the decision to indict, through the trial to the sentencing of the offender, the prosecution of sex offenders can be difficult, particularly when the issue is regarding whether the victim consented to sexual activity. Take the following examples.

In many cases, the investigation completed by law enforcement may adversely affect the ability of prosecuting attorneys to indict criminals in general, and sex offenders particularly. In 2013, Jameis Winston, the freshman quarterback for the Florida State University (FSU) Seminoles football team, was accused of rape. Erica Kinsman claimed she was drinking with friends on December 6, 2012, at Potbelly's restaurant in Tallahassee, Florida. She said that she had at least five drinks and someone gave her an unidentified shot. At that point, Kinsman was largely unaware of what occurred next.

The alleged victim claimed she was raped early in the morning on December 7, 2012. When Kinsman was next aware, she found herself in a taxi with an unknown man. She was taken to an apartment, she did not know where it was, her clothes were removed, and the male had sex with her. Kinsman claimed she told him to stop; another male in the apartment came in the room and told the offender to stop. Kinsman was then taken to a bathroom, the door was locked, and she was mostly unaware of what happened after that point. Later, Kinsman was dressed by her attacker, driven on his scooter, and dropped off about a block from her home.

While Kinsman stated that she did not know who the suspect was, she called the police and submitted to a rape kit test within hours of the incident; DNA evidence from shorts and underwear suggested two different men had sex with Kinsman on December 7. She claimed to have had sex with her boyfriend earlier in the day. Blood work indicated that she had no drugs in her system, but had likely been inebriated when the rape had occurred; when taken later, her blood alcohol level was 0.048. On January 10, 2013, Kinsman left a voicemail for the lead investigator identifying Jameis Winston as the accused rapist; she identified him based on having a class with him at FSU during the new semester. Once Kinsman identified Winston, the subsequent course of the investigation has been disputed.

Officials discouraged Kinsman from filing charges against Winston. Winston's attorney would not allow him to be interviewed. The case became inactive for a time. Law enforcement officials in Tallahassee claimed that Kinsman stopped cooperating and decided not to press charges; Kinsman, her family, and lawyer all deny this claim. When Kinsman asked about the status of the investigation in November of 2013, the media picked up the story. Winston's attorney claimed the sex was consensual and Winston did nothing wrong. Winston's teammates, Chris Casher and Ronald Darby, both supported Winston's claims, although they submitted their affidavits to the police almost 11 months later through Winston's attorney. Their stories and Kinsman's are very similar but for a few important points. Darby stated that Kinsman approached Winston at Potbelly's; in her pursuit of Winston, Kinsman tried to get her friend to go home with Casher. Kinsman followed Winston and his friends out of the bar and did not appear to be intoxicated. When they got to the apartment, Kinsman followed Winston into the bedroom. Because the door didn't lock, Casher looked in on the sexual act. While Casher was looking in on the two, he also was "playing jokes" on Winston; Winston and Kinsman then went to the bathroom and locked the door. According to Casher, at no point did Kinsman appear to be an unwilling participant. Casher's affidavit was similar. He said the victim was willing, that he witnessed Kinsman performing oral sex on Winston, and that he even attempted to have sex with Kinsman later.

Based on the nature of the investigation and disparities in witness statements, the state did not indict Winston because it would be a difficult case to prosecute. Due to the issues with the investigation (the 11-month gap in particular) and conflicting stories about the sexual interaction, Florida State District Attorney Willie Meggs was cited as saying "these kinds of sexual assault cases are the most difficult cases . . . without a question."

FSU conducted its own investigation of Kinsman's allegations in 2014. Kinsman was not interviewed until January of 2014; the school hearing did not occur until the fall of 2014—two years after the alleged rape. A retired Florida Supreme Court Justice, Major Harding, was tasked with presiding over the hearing. While the victim answered all questions, Winston only read a statement and refused to answer any questions. At the end of the FSU hearing process, the judge found that he could not determine the true story of what had occurred from the testimony of Winston and Kinsman. Winston was found "not responsible" for violating FSU's conduct code. Only Winston's teammate, Chris Casher, was found responsible for breaching FSU's code of conduct: recording images without consent. Casher had filmed the sexual activity between Winston and Kinsman.

In the end, it was the shoddy investigative work by law enforcement, the credibility of the alleged victim due to intoxication, and the sworn statements of two friends of Winston that resulted in no prosecution. Winston would go on to win the Heisman Trophy, the most coveted award in college football, and be drafted as the first pick in the National Football League in 2015 by the Tampa Bay Buccaneers. While Kinsman has largely faded into obscurity, she did file a civil lawsuit against both FSU and Jameis Winston in his individual capacity. The suit against FSU was for allowing Kinsman to be harassed on and off campus; this harassment led her to drop out of FSU in November of 2013 during Winston's Heisman Trophy campaign. The suit against Winston is for sexual battery, assault, false imprisonment, and distress. The civil cases against FSU and Winston were settled in 2016; while the agreement with Winston was confidential, FSU paid Kinsman almost one million dollars.

Even if the sex offender is indicted, the rights afforded accused offenders can make for contentious court proceedings.

Take the example of Luis Munuzuri-Harris, who was indicted for impersonating a police official, kidnapping, aggravated assault, and sexual battery. In July of 2010, Harris drove along Bayshore Boulevard in Tampa, a very scenic road next to Tampa Bay, impersonating a narcotics agent. Harris pulled over a woman with a flickering blue light. Harris forced the woman to an ATM and coerced her to withdraw money from her bank account. Once the money was obtained, Harris turned the victim toward the car and proceeded to rape her. While the case itself is straightforward, the trial proceedings were anything but.

Harris decided early on that he would defend himself. On the first day of the trial, Harris fired his court appointed lawyer and proceeded with his defense, despite the judge, Chet Tharpe, trying to get him to accept a public defender throughout the trial. As such, Harris was allowed to cross-examine the prosecution's key witness: the victim. In this case, the alleged offender was able to question the victim of a sexual offense. Harris questioned the witness over two hours about the night of the offense. The judge became increasingly irritated by Harris' line of questioning, which he referred to as "badgering," that simply restated the victim's deposition. It was a very slow pace that Harris set on the questioning. In her defense, the victim stood up to every one of Harris' questions; she noted repeatedly that "I was raped by you" and "You forced sex upon me."

The day after Harris questioned his victim, he finally accepted the judge's plea to use a public defender. In defending his questioning of the victim, Harris noted that, "For the record, I'm making a good faith effort to defend myself the best that I can. Maybe I should have prepared better for the questions. I understand that now, but I'm making a good-faith effort, judge." The trial normalized to some extent after a public defender was appointed to Harris, at least until the end of the trial. Harris was found guilty after a jury deliberated for ten hours. Harris had an outburst at the reading of the verdict; he pointed at the jury and babbled on about the victim's arrest record and not waiving something he referred to as "speedy trial." Harris had to be forcibly removed from the court by bailiffs.

A victim being questioned in a sexual assault trial can be upsetting, and while it is uncommon for the offender to do the questioning, this example shows the burden that can be placed on victims of sex offenses when testifying before a court. Most victims would not want to have to be questioned after having being sexually assaulted by the same person earlier. This is tantamount to **double victimization** and can be a deterrent for other victims coming forward.

While the preceding case is an anomaly, there are instances when the case outcome can also be a slap in the face of the victims of sex offenses.

In Dallas, Texas, in 2014, Sir Young, 18 years old, was tried for raping a 14-year-old female in 2011 in a deserted classroom at Booker T. Washington High School. During the trial, both Young and the victim testified that the victim had said "no" and "stop" repeatedly before and during the sexual encounter. Young described the incident in a police report as: "She and I started kissing, so I put my hands in her pants. She said no twice before I stopped. Then we started to kiss again and this time I took her pants off and mine as well. She kept saying no and stop, but I just didn't stop." Young continued, "she said [after the assault] oh my God why did you do this? I couldn't even answer. I just said sorry numerous times because I couldn't believe I had did that." Thus, both individuals involved in the crime testified that the sexual relations between the two was in fact a rape. This case was not vague as the facts were very clear. The judge did not see it that way.

Young was found guilty and sentenced to 45 days in jail and five years' probation. In addition, Young was required to complete 250 hours of community service at a rape crisis center in Dallas; the sentence did not mandate that Young stay away from children or receive treatment. There were two problems with this sentence. First, Young faced up to 20 years of incarceration. Second, a convicted sex offender working at a rape crisis center is counterintuitive as victims of a sex offense would not like to be around a convicted sex offender. The shelter later declined Young's presence.

In her decision, Judge Jeanine Howard openly disputed the victim's story. Howard would later recuse herself from the case so that she might publicly comment on her decision. Howard suggested that the victim "wasn't the victim she claimed to be." Howard indicated that the victim had previously agreed to have sex with Young, but not on school grounds. Howard also noted an exchange of racy text messages between the victim and Young. In addition, the judge indicated that the victim's medical records illustrated that she had sexual relations with no less than three partners previously; the victim had given birth to a child. Judge Howard argued there "are rape cases that deserve life. There are rape cases that deserve 20 years. Every now and then you have one of those that deserve probation. This is one of those and I stand by it." Finally, Howard argued that she wanted Young to work in the rape crisis shelter by mopping, mowing, cooking, or cleaning, not interacting with the victims.

The victim argued that this case "sends a message that, basically, you can come forward as you're supposed to and tell the truth and say what happened to you and nothing's going to happen." She also added that she was a virgin before the offense. The victim's mother indicated that her daughter had not given birth to a baby. The virginity or sexual history of a potential victim is irrelevant before the law. All that matters is that a crime occurred in a particular instance. Columbia Broadcasting System (CBS) news reported on an executive at a rape crisis center who likened this conflation to driving while intoxicated (DWI). "If you've driven a car before, you can't be the victim of a DWI? That's just stupid."

District Attorney Craig Watkins publicly criticized Judge Howard and asked the new judge to review Howard's handling of the case. Watkins was most concerned that the judgment could push rape victims away from reporting sex offenses. As Watkins noted, "The judge basically blamed the victim for what happened to her. In this case, when a victim comes forward and the person they put their trust in — the judge — calls into question their credibility, it does a disservice to our abilities as prosecutors." Watkins was pushing the new judge to extend the incarceration period to five years.

What is clear from the above examples is that it is difficult to obtain convictions for sex offenders and that a myriad of issues must be dealt with in relation to the prosecution of sex offenders. Chapter 8 examines the prosecution and **sentencing** of sex offenders. In particular, Chapter 8 first provides an overview of the judicial branch in the United States. Once this overview is complete, the next section explores the official statistics associated with sex offenders in the United States. Chapter 8 then explores some of the special issues that are associated with the prosecution of sex offenders, including the predictors of sentences for sex offenders, disparities in sentencing across different sex offender characteristics, rape shield laws, false allegations of sexual offenses, and the use of closed-circuit television (CCTV) in witness testimony. Each of these topics elicit specialized handling by the judicial system. Before we get to these though, we begin with an overview of the courts in the United States.

THE NATURE OF CRIMINAL COURTS

Most individuals are somewhat cognizant of the trial process. This awareness of the judicial system largely stems from the mass media: many have seen a judicial proceeding in movies or on television. Indeed, most movies and television shows are based on crime and criminal justice; in some cases these depictions even focus on sex offenders. This section outlines the judicial component of the criminal justice system before we address sex offenders in the courts.

All criminals who have either been accused or indicted are ensured due process rights. In particular, the Constitution affords due process rights in relation to judicial proceedings. The Fifth Amendment indicates that no individual shall be tried for a crime without a presentment or grand jury indictment, no individual shall be subject to double jeopardy (being tried twice for the same crime), or have to testify against one's self. The Sixth Amendment indicates that individuals have the right to a speedy and public trial, to be informed of the charges, to confront accusers and witnesses, to present his/her own witnesses/evidence, and to have the assistance of counsel. While abhorred more than most other types of criminals, sex offenders enjoy the same due process rights as any other indicted criminal.

Court processing can be characterized in multiple ways. We can discuss court processing in terms of federal and state courts. Federal courts deal with the breach of federal laws, federal agency policy, the Constitution, or any crimes that cross state lines (Internet crimes, for instance). State courts deal with the violation of state laws. The Constitution indicates that most criminal justice power is relegated to the states. Thus, states deal with more crime than the federal level. This is especially true when it comes to sex crimes: most sex offenses are handled through state criminal courts.

The next major distinction for court processing has to do with if the offender elects to go to trial. This may seem counterintuitive, especially since all indicted offenders have the right to a trial, but the vast majority of offenders will elect not to go to trial. Rather, these defendants will elect to plea. A plea means that the defendant formally admits guilt and in return the court will, generally, select a more lenient sentence since the offender is appearing to show some modicum of responsibility/remorse for his/her actions. Roughly 95 percent of all criminal cases are handled through plea bargains. Another way of saying that is around 5 percent of defendants choose to utilize their constitutional right to a trial.

Provided the defendant elects to go to trial rather than plead out of a case, another way that we can differentiate court processing is whether the trial is characterized as a jury trial or a bench trial. A jury trial, again afforded to individuals under the Constitution, allows a group of ordinary citizens, generally a group of 12, to determine the guilt or innocence of a defendant. In a bench trial, the judge (from the bench) will determine if the defendant is guilty or not. The sentence is generally given by the judge. One major exception to this occurs in murder cases where the prosecutor is seeking execution as the punishment; in these cases juries determine guilt and then determine the sentence in a separate hearing.

Three primary actors are imperative to criminal court processing and the make-up of the courtroom workgroup: the judge, the prosecutor, and the defense attorney. Most would assume that the judge is the most important actor in any courtroom.

There is no doubt that the judge has a great deal of power in the courtroom. The judge approves plea deals, decides what evidence is admitted in a trial, decides on jury instructions, potentially determines guilt in bench trials, and determines sentences for most convicted offenders. While this is a great deal of power, there are many who suggest that the prosecutor is the most important individual when it comes to criminal court processing. Spohn (2009) noted the importance of the prosecutor in judicial actions. She argued that the prosecutor may have more importance in judicial processing than even the judge; the prosecutor makes the decision to indict offenders, negotiates any pleas, and is involved in a host of other important decisions, an example being to seek the death penalty for certain crimes revolving around murder.

The defense attorney is the final key actor in criminal court processing. All felony indicted defendants have the right to counsel. The defense attorney attempts to defend the accused from the criminal charges. There are primarily two types of defense counsel: public and private. Public defenders are provided by the state. Private attorneys are procured by defendants. There is some debate as to which type of defense attorney is better. The private attorney will have more time to give to the defense than a public defender; however, the private attorney is sometimes viewed negatively by the courtroom workgroup as a "hired gun." Alternatively, public defenders have an inordinate case load, but these attorneys are well known to judges and prosecutors in a court and can possibly get better plea deals via these closer relationships. The research is inconclusive on which attorney type is better in terms of the determination of guilt or the sentence given to defendants. Of course, a defendant has the right to defend him- or herself (pro se). This is generally a bad move. As the old saying goes, a person who chooses to defend him/herself has a fool for a client. Just look at the example of Luis Munuzuri-Harris provided at the beginning of this chapter.

The final element of criminal court processing is sentencing. **Sentencing** occurs after the determination of guilt and is intimately linked to criminal statutes (see Chapter 2). There are many forms of sentencing that exist across various statutory schemes. **Determinate sentences** are fixed sentences; a person is convicted of a crime and they receive a flat time period of incarceration. An **indeterminate sentence** is not fixed; there is generally a time frame within the law that includes a maximum and minimum time period (10 to 20 years in prison, for example). Indeterminate sentences are thought to be individualized justice as everyone does not rehabilitate/reform at the same rate. **Mandatory sentences** associate a certain penalty in relation to certain crimes or criteria of crimes. An example of mandatory sentence is a mandatory minimum sentence for those convicted of drug possession or distribution. **Sentencing enhancements** seek to increase criminal sanctions by adding extra time for specific offenders or class of offenses. For instance, a criminal with a more extensive **criminal history** might receive a career criminal enhancement in addition to the sanction for the crime he/she was convicted of. **Sentencing guidelines** (presumptive sentences) attempt to make sentences across judges and courts more uniform. Sentencing guidelines are a response to sentencing disparities and perceived discrimination in the judicial system. We will discuss disparities in sentencing more fully below in relation to sex offenders. **Truth-in-sentencing** policies make sure that criminals serve the majority of a sentence they receive. In most jurisdictions, truth-in-sentencing policies will make sure that a convicted felon will serve at least 75 percent of their sentence;

for example, a criminal will have to serve at least seven and a half years on a ten-year prison sentence. Before the advent of truth-in-sentencing policies, it was common for criminals to serve less than 25 percent of their sentence.

This section has provided a brief outline of the judicial process for criminals in the United States. This review is only cursory; if you are interested in the courts and the sentencing of criminal defendants, there are many books that can provide a more expansive discourse on the judicial processing of criminals (see Spohn, 2009; Hartley, Rabe, and Champion, 2017). Now we turn to the conviction of sex offenders in American courts.

CRIMINAL CONVICTIONS OF SEX OFFENDERS

While our knowledge of sex offenders in the courts is a bit dated, it is the best comprehensive information available for our discussion here about sex offenders in the state courts; federal court data is much more current in collection. Two issues must be addressed before we discuss sex offender processing through the courts. First, the statistics provided here are differentiated across federal courts and state courts. This is an important distinction because the vast majority of sex offenses occur within state criminal justice systems. This is due to some of the observations listed above on how crimes are distinguished by federal and state courts. Thus, most sex offenses are formally handled at the state level; the one exception to this is child pornography. Because child pornography largely occurs on the Internet (which goes across state lines), the federal government is mostly responsible for the prosecution of this crime type.

The second issue here is one we encountered earlier in the book: the dark figure of crime. As was discussed in Chapter 1, the majority of our information about sex offenders is based on official records of sex offending. These official numbers always miss information. This occurs when victims do not report crimes they were subjected to. In relation to sex offenders, and as we have illustrated throughout this book, this issue is compounded by victims who are embarrassed or fear having to relive the experience by reporting the victimization to the authorities. All crime that is not reported to the police is known as the **dark figure of crime**. As criminal cases progress from the investigation phase to the courts, this problem is exacerbated. A criminal report does not necessarily produce an arrest; an arrest does not necessarily mean that a case will be prosecuted. Once a criminal is indicted, however, it is very likely that the offender will be found guilty via a trial or plea. Keep this in mind as we discuss the court processing of sex offenders in the United States.

State courts account for the majority of all felony sentences in the United States (Rosenmerkel, Durose, and Farole, 2009). Rosenmerkel et al. (2009) provide the statistics on state courts from 1990 to 2006. From 1990 to 1998, the number of persons sentenced for a felony in state courts rose from 829,340 to 927,720; this was a change in rate from 447 to 489 per 100,000 residents above the age of 18. In 2006, this rate increased again to 503 per 100,000 residents above the age of 18, representing a total of 1,132,290 individuals sentenced for a felony in state courts. This indicates that court processing of criminals has been increasing over the last 26 years, despite the fact that crime rates have been falling dramatically.

In 2006, convicted felons received sentences of incarceration in 69 percent of all state felony cases—41 percent to state prisons and 28 percent to jails (Rosenmerkel et al., 2009). Prison sentences for convicted felons averaged almost five years (four years and 11 months); jail sentences averaged six months. Less than 1 percent of convicted felons received a life sentence. It was estimated that around 27 percent of convicted felons received probation. Men accounted for the largest percentage of convicted felons (83 percent) while only accounting for 49 percent of the overall population. Most felony defendants chose to plea rather than go to trial (94 percent).

In relation to sex offenders, sentencing statistics are aggregated to account for two primary groups of sexual assault offenders: (1) rape and (2) other sexual assaults. According to Rosenmerkel et al. (2009), "Rape is forcible intercourse (vaginal, anal, or oral) with a female or male" (p. 33). Rape includes forcible sodomy, penetration with a foreign object, and attempts, but excludes statutory rape and non-forcible sexual acts. Other sexual assaults include "(1) forcible or violent sexual acts not involving intercourse with an adult or minor, (2) non-forcible sexual acts with minors (statutory rape), and (3) non-forcible sexual acts with someone unable to give consent (mental or physical defect or intoxication)" (Rosenmerkel et al., 2009, p. 33). In many instances, court statistics will combine the category of other sexual assaults into the other violent crimes category; when this occurs, sex offenses cannot be distinguished from other lesser violent crimes like negligent manslaughter, kidnapping, and extortion. Offenses like child pornography, pimping, and prostitution, as well as any other sexual offenses not listed above, are incorporated into an aggregate typology called other specified offenses. This category does not separate the sex crimes from other crimes within this category (child neglect, contributing to the delinquency of a minor, etc.).

In 2006, 33,200 felons were convicted of sexual assault (both rape and other sexual assault) in state courts. This accounted for 2.9 percent of all felons sentenced. For these convictions, 81 percent of sexual assault defendants were incarcerated, while the remainder (5,230) received a community sentence (probation). Of the percentage of sex offenders incarcerated, 64 percent (21,210) were sentenced to a prison term and 18 percent (5,810) were sentenced to a jail term. Sex offenders tended to receive lengthier prison sentences than other offenders (with the exception of murderers); the average length of prison sentences was 106 months (almost nine years). The average incarceration time for all convicted felons was 38 months (just over three years).

At the state level, 89 percent of sex offenders were convicted for completed offenses. Among all sex offenders convicted at the state level, 65 percent were convicted on a single felony, 20 percent were convicted of two felonies, and 15 percent were convicted of three or more felonies; these other felonies could be violent, property, or other sex offenses. The average age of sex offenders convicted of a felony was 34 years. This age is higher than most other convicted criminal types; only fraud/forgery convicts and those convicted of drug possession had a similar average age. The overall average of all convicted felons in 2006 was 33 years.

Eighty-eight percent of sex offenders chose to plea out; this is greatly out of line with the 94 percent of all offenders who chose to plea rather than go to trial. For those sex offenders who chose to go to trial, 89 percent were incarcerated; the average incarceration period for these offenders was 158 months. For those sex offenders who made a plea, 82 percent were incarcerated; the average sentence length for these offenders was 80 months. Thus, there is clearly a trial tax associated with convicted sex offenders in relation to conviction and sentence length. In 2006, the time between arrest and sentencing was a median of 348 days. Other than for the crime of murder, which is a median of 505 days, no other crime takes that long for the courts to process.

Reaves' (2013) research on the 75 largest counties in the United States indicated similarities in state sentencing practices for the year 2009. Reaves suggested very few sex offenders (focus was on rape offenses only) were on probation or parole at the time of their current arrest; likewise, 34 percent of sex offenders did not have a criminal history (prior arrest for any crime). It took almost one year for most sex offenders to be adjudicated after being arrested. Of those incarcerated, 84 percent of convicted rapists received a prison sentence and 5 percent received a jail sentence. The average sentence for rapists in the 75 largest counties was 142 months; again, only murderers received more time (373 months) and the average sentence length for all offenses was 52 months. Reaves' (2013) report suggested similarities with age and gender to the Rosenmerkel (2009) study; race differed as more Blacks were present in the total number of sex offenders prosecuted.

As noted above, sex crimes are rarely handled at the federal level. At the federal level, the federal courts sentenced 73,000 convicted felons in 2006 (Rosenmerkel et al., 2009). Of these criminals, Rosenmerkel et al. (2009) reported only 366 defendants were convicted of rape or other sexual assaults in 2006. While Rosenmerkel et al. (2009) reported these statistics for comparison purposes, newer data exists on federal level court processing.

Federal sentencing statistics are much more uniform in collection than state level statistics, so the numbers reported here for the federal level are much more recent (United States Sentencing Commission, 2021a; 2021b). In 2021, the federal courts reported on the sentencing of two types of aggregate sex offenses: sexual abuse and child pornography. In 2013, there were 881 convicted offenders sentenced for sexual abuse and 1,023 convicted offenders sentenced for child pornography; since 2016, sexual abuse offenses decreased by 19.2 percent and child pornography offenses decreased by 36 percent (United States Sentencing Commission, 2021a; 2021b). As at the state level, the majority of these sex offenders were male (92.3 percent for sexual abuse and 99.7 percent for child pornography), White (57.4 percent for sexual abuse and 81.3 percent for child pornography), and the average ages were 38 (sexual abuse) and 42 (child pornography). While 96.9 percent of all federally convicted offenders made a plea rather than go to trial, only 89.9 percent of those convicted of sexual abuse elected to plea. Those convicted of sexual abuse received an average of 192 months in prison whereas those convicted of child pornography received 74 months in prison. The total average of prison sentence length was only 353 months and 74 months for sexual abusers and child pornographers respectively; sex offenders are punished harshly at the federal level just as they are at the state level.

While these statistics provide a picture of a court system that is harsh on sex offenders, it is only a partial snapshot of what is occurring. The first reason for this is the lack of initial reporting by victims of sex offenses. The second reason is an aggregation issue. While reported serious rapes are always presented in official data, lesser sex offenses may be hidden under groups of lesser offenses. These are often referred to as other sex offenses or other violent offenses; in some cases, sex crimes can appear in a glut of crimes referred to as "other crimes." Third, the statistics provided here are somewhat dated. The most comprehensive data on state felony court processing is from 2006 and 2009. As this edition goes to press, there is an effort to collect data on state felony courts. Thus, our picture of the court processing of sex offenders is an incomplete one, serving as an underestimate of the number of sentences for sex offenders.

Now that you have an idea about the level of sex offender court processing, we now turn to miscellaneous issues that are somewhat unique to the processing of sex offenders. The next section explores various characteristics and issues associated with the prosecution and sentencing of sex offenders.

GENERAL ISSUES IN OBTAINING SEX OFFENSE CONVICTIONS

While the court processing of criminals is relatively easy to follow, there are special issues and concerns for both those accused and those victimized by sex offenses in the criminal courts. This section examines several issues associated with sex offender sentencing: the predictors of sex offender sentencing outcomes, disparities across sex offender sentencing, the implementation and use of rape shield laws, false accusations of sex offenses, and the use of CCTV for vulnerable victims/witnesses. Each of these topics are either unique to the prosecution and sentencing of sex offenders or have unique properties that differ from other criminal court processing.

Predictors of Court Outcomes for Sex Offenders

In the vast majority of research on sentencing, the key determinants of sentences are related to the seriousness of the offense and the criminal history of the offender (Spohn, 2009). **Offense seriousness** is characterized by how significant a crime is; the more serious the offense, the greater the sentence an offender is likely to receive. Criminal history is concerned with how extensive the criminality of an offender is in the past; an offender who has been convicted of prior crimes will generally receive a harsher sentence than someone who is a first-time offender. Criminal history is largely focused on official criminal convictions; past criminality that has gone unpunished is more difficult to use in the sentencing process. Knowledge about offense seriousness and criminal history does not fully predict sentences meted out by courts, there are also external (extra-legal) factors to the crime that can impact **sentencing outcomes**. External offender sentencing factors can include the relationship of the offender and victim, education, income, employment, race, ethnicity, gender, and age (just to name a few); each of these has been shown to impact sentencing outcomes with minimal to moderate effect sizes. So, are sentencing outcomes for sex offenders driven by the same factors that drive other criminal sentences?

Holleran, Beichner, and Spohn (2010) intimated that while research on sex offenders and criminal court processing is relatively small, the area of study has been increasing over the last couple of decades. There is some suggestion that court processing outcomes (charging decisions, determination of guilt, and sentencing) for sex offenders is based on "stereotypes about rape and rape victims" (Spohn and Holleran,

2001, p. 655). Offense seriousness, offender characteristics (criminal history, education, income, employment), and victim characteristics (Black offender/White victim in the death penalty literature) have all been shown to effect sex offender sentencing outcomes. For instance, Levesque (2000) found that a sex offender's criminal history and the victim characteristics mediated the number of months in prison sex offenders received.

Early arguments suggested there should be a difference between the court processing of sex offenders in simple rape and aggravated rape cases. It was originally hypothesized that aggravated rape would be more likely to result in criminal charges and a criminal sentence. Estrich (1987) argued that aggravated assault fits into the idea of "real rape" (see Chapter 4); in aggravated cases there is no reason to doubt the victim's credibility. Victim characteristics are more important for simple assault cases. If the alleged offender claims the rape was consensual (implies the offender and victim knew each other), then a jury will inevitably have to deal with both the victim's and offender's character and behavior at the time of the sexual assault. The jury will determine if the victim is fabricating/exaggerating the story or if the victim has some reason for lying about the case. In stranger sexual offenses, there is less of an issue with a consent defense. Horney and Spohn's (1996) research in Detroit, Michigan, largely refutes the idea that simple and aggravated assault are predicted by different factors (legally relevant and extralegal). In this study, quick reporting of the sexual assault made prosecution more likely in simple rape cases.

Other research has evaluated the link between the offender and the victim. Kingsworth, MacIntosh, and Wentworth's (1999) research indicated that stranger and non-stranger sex offenses were equally likely to be prosecuted, but different factors contributed to each decision. In stranger sex offense cases, prosecution was likely if the offender had a criminal record, if the victim cooperated with law enforcement officials, and if witness accounts supported the victim's story. When the sex offense included non-strangers, prosecution was more likely if the victim had visible injuries, the suspect made incriminating statements and was arrested for multiple offenses, if the victim reported the crime quickly, if the victim cooperated with law enforcement officials, and if witness accounts supported the victim's story. Quick reporting mattered the most for non-stranger sex offenses.

Some research has examined the link between the victim and the offender in relation to the court processing of sex offenders. Studies have shown that the relationship between the victim and the offender (acquaintance, intimate, or stranger) can affect court outcomes. Stranger rapes are more likely to result in more stringent investigations, indictments, convictions, and prison sentences (McCahill, Meyer, and Fischman, 1979). Spohn and Holleran's (2001) research in Kansas City, Missouri, and Philadelphia, Pennsylvania, showed that the relationship between the victim and the offender did not moderate the effect of prosecutors' decisions to charge offenders. In this research, the victim's characteristics were more important (credibility and blameless in the incident). While the decision to prosecute was not mediated by offender/victim relationship, Spohn (2009) later noted that sexual assault case outcomes (punishments) are mediated by the relationship of the offender to the victim; strangers are sentenced more severely than offenders who had a previous relationship with the victim.

Spohn and Holleran (2001) found that only half of sexual assault arrests resulted in prosecution. Their findings suggested that the charging decision is not based on victim, suspect, or case characteristics. In this research, prosecutors were more likely to file charges if there was physical evidence, the suspect had a prior history, and there were no questions about the offender's characteristics/behavior at the time of the sexual assault. The relationship of the victim and offender did not impact charging decisions; all relationship types were associated with charging decisions, but the effect is larger for stranger-related cases. Charging decisions in this research were mediated by legal and extralegal indicators; further evidence of this was found by Spohn and Tellis (2020) in Los Angeles, California.

Some research in this area has examined whether specialized prosecution units geared toward sex offenses had any impact on the court processing of sex offenders. There are two methods district attorneys use in prosecuting criminal offenders through the courts: horizontal and vertical prosecution. Horizontal prosecution occurs when different prosecuting attorneys handle cases at different phases on the judicial process. Vertical prosecution occurs when a single prosecutor shepherds a case from start to finish. It is hypothesized that sex offenders, in particular, are more likely to be prosecuted, found guilty, and sentenced more harshly when vertical prosecution is utilized.

Beichner and Spohn (2005) examined the effect of vertical prosecution, in the guise of specialized prosecutorial units, on rape case outcomes. Data for this study came from Kansas City, Missouri, which has a specialized prosecutorial unit for sex crimes, and Miami, Florida, which used horizontal case processing. Beichner and Spohn (2005) found that decisions to charge in both jurisdictions were nearly identical (57 to 58 percent of cases were prosecuted). Both jurisdictions based their decisions to charge on evidence of proof beyond a reasonable doubt. Prosecutors in Kansas City were more likely to take their cases to trial while Miami prosecutors were more likely to plea bargain. When evidence was weak, questions about the victim's moral character had strong effects in both jurisdictions.

Holleran et al. (2010) examined agreement between the law enforcement decision to refer a sex crime to the prosecutor (founding decision) and the prosecutor's decision to charge the sex offender. Data from Kansas City, Missouri, and Philadelphia, Pennsylvania, examined police and prosecutor agreement on sex offense charges. Their findings indicated that the nature of the sexual assault (aggravated sex assaults with strangers and use of weapons) and the effect of victim characteristics (believability) on the decision to prosecute varied based on jurisdiction.

Amirault and Beauregard's (2014) research largely focused on differences between sentencing outcomes for child victims and adult victims of sex crimes. Amirault and Beauregard (2014) examined sex offense cases in Quebec, Canada, from 1994 to 2000. There were 519 offenders in the study. Amirault and Beauregard (2014) found that sex offenders with child victims received slightly longer prison sentences than sex offenders with adult victims. They also found that sex offenders who were family members of the victim received shorter sentences; strangers received longer sentences. Physical injury and victim age (younger victims) also led to longer prison sentences. These latter results echoed a study by Patrick and Marsh (2011) who found that sex offenders with child victims received more time in prison when the sex offender was older, there were more total charges, and the victim was younger. When the relationship of the victim and offender was closer, the sex offender received less time.

Research on key judicial decision points (charging, determination of guilt, and sentencing) in sexual assault cases suggests that legally relevant factors (the seriousness of the offense, the strength of evidence, and the culpability of the defendant) are the best predictors of judicial outcomes (Spohn and Holleran, 2001). In more serious cases, the prosecutor necessarily has less discretion. For minor forms of sex offenses, the prosecutor may have more leeway to use extra-legal factors in key judicial decision points. Because prosecutors like to win cases, they have to have a great deal of certainty that they can win a case before filing charges. Spohn (2009) indicated that a great deal of research has shown "that sexual assault case processing decisions, including decisions about sentence severity, are affected by the victim's age, occupation, and education, 'risk-taking' behavior, and reputation of the victim" (p. 96). Quick reporting and victim characteristics influence charging decisions in at least some types of sexual assault cases (Spohn and Holleran, 2001). The most interesting thing coming from this line of research is that sex offender court outcomes (sentence lengths) appear to have little to no impact on recidivism (Budd and Desmond, 2014).

The research clearly indicates that the sentencing of sex offenders is becoming more punitive in nature over the last couple of decades. Cochrane et al.'s (2021) study of the sentencing of sex offenders in Florida indicated that punitiveness towards all defendants increased between 1995 and 2011, but this increased punishment severity was more pronounced for sex offenders. Rydberg et al. (2018) found similar results in Pennsylvania. Differences were seen between all violent offenders and sex offenders; quantile regression indicated that the severity of sex offender sentences were linked to judicial stereotypes about specific crimes. In this, sex offender sentences are more severe than general violent offender sentences.

Disparities in Sex Offender Sentencing

Disparities in sentencing occur when two offenders commit the same crime but receive different sentences/punishments. **Disparities** in sentencing occur all the time. The question becomes if those disparities are due to legitimate, mitigating reasons or if the disparities are related to something more nefarious, such as discrimination. **Discrimination** occurs when one group of individuals is sentenced more harshly based on a singular characteristic. There is a fine line between a **disparity** and discrimination. For instance, for the same crime, males tend to receive more time in prison than females. Does this mean that males are discriminated against by the courts? The answer is not necessarily. In most cases, males tend to commit the most serious crimes or that the circumstances of the case were much more serious.

In the sentencing literature, there are largely two rationales for difference in sentencing patterns: differential treatment and differential offending. **Differential treatment** implies that the criminal justice system is somehow handling different criminals through unsystematic approaches. **Differential offending** suggests that some groups are more likely to commit crimes based on some characteristic. Disparities and discrimination in sentencing practices largely revolve around race, ethnicity, and gender; race is one of the most frequently studied offender characteristics in the sentencing literature (Spohn, 2009). Sentencing research has consistently shown that males and minorities are the most likely groups to indicate disparities across sentences, especially in relation to the length of the sentence.

Are sex offenders with different characteristics treated differently? The answer to that is yes. Predominantly, the disparities revolve around male and female sex offenders. Think back to Chapter 1. One of the examples provided at the beginning of the chapter revolved around two female teachers who had sex with a male student; these teachers received much more lenient treatment by the criminal justice system. Another example of similar behavior is that of Debra LaFave. LaFave was a teacher who had sex with one of her underage students. LaFave was also treated very leniently by the criminal court, effectively earning a slap on the wrist. What angered many is that LaFave even argued at the time that a pretty teacher like herself would never be sent to prison; she received three years of house arrest. Imagine if LaFave had been a male teacher. It is unlikely that a court would allow a male teacher to only receive three years of house arrest; likely this crime would have been punished with incarceration.

According to Rosenmerkel et al. (2009), males accounted for 97 percent of all sex offenders convicted in 2006. For all felony convictions, males comprised 83 percent of the population and females comprised 17 percent of the population. Breaking it up by sex, 82 percent of convicted male sex offenders were incarcerated whereas only 69 percent of females were incarcerated. Convicted female sex offenders were more likely to receive probation. Males tended to average 109 months of incarceration as opposed to only 63 months for females, a difference of almost four years. Some would argue that this is a form of institutional discrimination based on societal norms and beliefs about gender. While there are clearly disparities between males and females, what of other group characteristics among sex offenders?

8

Race accounts for the majority of sentencing disparity research. According to Rosenmerkel et al. (2009), the overall felony convictions for race were 60 percent White, 38 percent Black, and 2 percent other. For sex offenders, this was 74 percent White and 24 percent Black. While still off, this number much more closely approximates the percentage of Whites and Blacks in the general U.S. population. Black and White sex offenders were treated very similarly in relation to incarceration and probation decisions, both getting very similar sentences. This was also true for the length of the sentence. In relation to race, sex offenders are treated very similarly by the courts.

Based on the data reported by Rosenmerkel et al. (2009), the most visible disparity in sex offender sentencing revolves around gender. Gendered disparities in sentencing for sex offenders are emphasized by the media in reports of teachers having sexual relations with underage students. These media depictions would suggest that teacher-student sex offending is more prevalent than in the past and that females are treated more leniently by the criminal justice system, especially the courts. It should be noted in relation to the latter, and with greater awareness by prosecutors, judges, and the public, female educators who sexually assault students are beginning to be treated more like their male counterparts when they enter the criminal justice system. Gendered stereotypes are beginning to be discarded and female teacher on student sexual encounters are not always being treated as "some male student who got lucky."

Whether it be a male student or female student who has become sexually involved with a teacher, the relations can result in trauma for the student that can have lifelong consequences that include depression, low self-esteem, and difficulty in future relationships. There is often confusion for the victim in relation to guilt about whether they are actually victims. All of this psychological trauma can produce falling grades in classes and issues with social interactions. While the prosecution for such crimes has always been severe for male teacher sex offenses, the prosecution of female teachers who sexually assault students is beginning to increase as well.

Rape Shield Laws

Does a victim's sexual history have anything to do with a victim being raped? The answer to this question is an obvious no; however, before the 1970s, it was common for defense counsel in sexual assault and rape cases to vigorously cross-examine victims/ witnesses about their prior experiences with sexual intercourse. This testimony was thought to be relevant for two reasons: "(1) because consent on a prior occasion was indicative that the victim gave consent on the occasion in question and (2) because promiscuity reflected negatively on the victim's credibility" (Applegate, 2013, p. 911). The implication of jurisprudence at this time was that a woman who had a lengthy history of sexual partners would always consent to sex and therefore could not be raped. As such, many victims did not come forward out of shame or embarrassment. This led to many sexual assaults going unreported and unprosecuted.

These ideas remained critical obstacles for successful prosecutions of sex offenders due to gendered stereotypes. In the 1970s, the women's and victims' rights movements both fought this notion in relation to the victims of sex crimes. One of the results of these competing movements were rape shield laws. **Rape shield laws** were developed to protect the victim from intrusive personal questions about sexual history that have no bearing on the particular case. There are three underlying purposes of rape shield laws: "(1) to protect the victim's privacy, (2) to encourage reporting and prosecution of sexual assaults, and (3) to focus the trial on the conduct of the defendant rather than that of the victim" (Applegate, 2013, p. 911). Rape shield laws limit the questions that can be posed by defense counsel.

All 50 states have adopted rape shield laws, but these laws are different across states (Applegate, 2013). The primary focus of these laws revolves around keeping information about a victim's sexual history out of a trial. This means anytime a defense attorney wants to insert information about the prior sexual history of a victim, a pre-trial, in camera hearing determines if the information is admissible. According to Applegate (2013), this "hearing provides the benefit of a private pre-trial procedure infused with the victim-protective policy and history underlying rape shields" (p. 912). Based on the state or federal statute, evidence of sexual history can be included at trial if there is an exception in the law, a constitution requires it, or the court finds it admissible within its own discretion.

Currently, the area of rape shield laws that is most often tested has to the do with the admissibility of evidence of prior false accusations of rape by the victim. As has been seen throughout this book, in sex offense cases, individual credibility is imperative. The inclusion of a victim's prior accusations of a sexual assault is legally relevant in that the defense can show the accusation is false or the accusation impugns the victim's credibility (Applegate, 2013). Rape shield statutes in most states do not address prior false rape accusations (Applegate, 2013). As will be seen below, determining if a victim has falsified a prior rape accusation is a difficult prospect. The next section explores the incidence of false rape allegations by alleged victims of sex offenses.

False Rape Allegations

Some members of society actually believe that a woman can never be raped. While this segment of society is relatively small, its beliefs seem to have traction within the criminal justice system in the form of false rape allegations. Applegate (2013) argued that "the perception that false accusations of sexual assault are common is longstanding" (p. 902). This misperception stems from two sources. The first is anecdotal. Every so often, high-profile cases emerge that solidify the notion that women regularly falsify rape charges against men. The second has to do with early empirical studies on false rape accusations that suggest the incidence of **false allegations** lies anywhere between 1 and 100 percent of all rape reports. Most readers of these studies err toward the upper limit of false allegations rather than the lower limit. If the incidence of false rape allegations is indeed high, this is a serious problem. "One of the most troubling aspects of false rape allegations is the miscarriage of justice . . . Merely to be a rape suspect, even for a day or two, translates into psychological and social trauma" (Kanin, 1994, p. 88).

Gross (2008) argued there is a fine line between supporting victims and the due process rights of accused sex offenders. In most states, the accuser must admit an allegation is false before the charges against a suspect can be dropped. The falsely accused individual in this case has had his/her life turned upside down, if not destroyed (Gross, 2008). Issues a falsely accused person may experience, regardless if the case goes to trial, are legal costs, possible jail/prison time, employer conflicts, issues with family and friends, and civil lawsuits (Gross, 2008). The falsely accused individual's reputation is likely ruined forever, especially in this digital age. Thus, it is important to understand the etiology of false accusations of sex offenses.

Gross (2008) noted false accusers will experience few consequences for their allegations. The accuser, unless they inform the authorities that the allegation was false, will likely never have to admit the claim was false and it is a rarity if civil action is ever pursued against them (Gross, 2008). When they do go to trial, false accusers are largely protected by rape shield laws (see the previous section).

Gross (2008) indicated that there are several reasons for false rape allegations: cover story/alibi, revenge/rage/retribution, attention, and extortion. The alibi is needed when some problem arises for the victim in what she sees as a desperate dilemma (feelings of shame or guilt that arose from pregnancy or a sexually transmitted disease). In most of these situations, the victim is not trying to harm the suspect, but to protect him/herself (Gross, 2008). Revenge/rage/retribution is thought to occur when the alleged victim is spurned by the person they had sexual relations with. The false allegation is a way to get back at the person who has spurned the alleged victim's advances. False allegations may revolve around extortion when the alleged victim thinks that the alleged offender has deep pockets (i.e., wealthy) and can pay for the allegation to "go away."

When a victim of a sex crime reports it to the police, the police must determine if they think a crime has occurred; if they determine a crime has occurred, the police must then determine who is responsible for the crime. If law enforcement believes a crime has occurred, the case will be submitted to the prosecuting attorney's office; if law enforcement does not believe a crime occurred, it is not submitted to prosecutors. This is known as the founding decision. Unfounding by law enforcement agencies is much higher for sex offenses than other crimes. According to Applegate (2013), there are three primary reasons why law enforcement will unfound a sexual assault case: the officer does not like the victim, the officer thinks the victim "asked for it," or the officer thinks the case will not hold up in court (p. 919). Kanin (1994) indicated that unfounded rape cases "can and does mean many things, with false allegations being only one of them, and sometimes the least of them" (p. 81). Once the case has been transmitted to the prosecuting attorney, the prosecutor has wide latitude in discretion moving forward with the case.

Lisak et al. (2010) argued that within "the domain of rape, the most highly charged area of debate concerns the issue of false rape allegations. For centuries, it has been asserted and assumed that women cry rape, that a large proportion of rape allegations are maliciously concocted for purposes of revenge or other motives" (p. 1,318). These beliefs are rarely based on empirical findings. Of the research that exists in this area, only a handful can be considered credible.

Kanin conducted some of the earliest studies in this area. Kanin's (1985) oldest research suggested the incidence of false rape allegations ranges anywhere from 1 to 90 percent of all cases. In a later study of false rape accusations, Kanin (1994) examined the rape case files from a Midwestern city (population of 70,000) over a nine-year period. The total number of cases evaluated in this study was 109; 45 (41 percent) of these cases were declared to be false allegations. Kanin argued that there were three rationales for false allegations: "providing an alibi, a means of gaining revenge, and a platform for seeking attention/sympathy" (p. 85); he found no instances of extortion. Kanin (1994) also found that false accusation reports tended to describe penile-vaginal intercourse only; none of these cases included any information about other forms of sex (oral or anal). Kanin (1994) concluded that false rape allegations "can be viewed as the impulsive and desperate gestures of women simply attempting to alleviate understandable conditions of personal and social distress" (p. 88).

Kanin's work has been widely criticized for wrongly equating false accusations with false recantations. Applegate (2013) noted that this conflation was a problem. Recantations are when victims stop cooperating with officials, which is based on a myriad of reasons, not just false allegations; recantations are generally not false allegations. Equating recantations with false accusations makes it seem like false accusations are more prevalent than they actually are; in addition, when the courts allow this form of evidence, the recantation can have a profound impact on a case despite the fact that it may not be indicative of a false accusation. Applegate (2013) also argued "many rape victims are vulnerable individuals who suffer multiple rapes, and for this reason, it is likely that a victim will have made prior accusations that lack traditional indicia of credibility" (p. 906).

Rumney (2006) indicated the difficulties in researching false rape accusations due to definitional constraints and a lack of generalizability. Rumney denoted the difference between law enforcement definitions and academic definitions of false allegations. Law enforcement often abandons its own definitions for more subjective criteria and academics do such a poor job with conceptualization that research designs and definitions vary greatly across false rape allegation research. Rumney (2006) discounts much of the past research in attempting to understand the nature of false rape allegations. Additionally, Rumney (2006) argued against criminal justice policy being based on current research as it likely would be either unnecessary or misguided.

Kelly (2010) argued that institutional cultures and practices create a risk of law enforcement over-identifying false allegations. Kelly (2010) suggested that false complaints are not higher for rape than for any other crime type. Not only do researchers in this area wrongly conflate unfounded cases and false allegations, but also criminal justice personnel, the media, and politicians regularly do so as well. In addition, part of this conflation in law enforcement and politics was attributable to closing cases and keeping an image of falling crime rates.

Lisak et al. (2010) argued that to classify a case as a false rape allegation, "a thorough investigation must yield evidence that a crime did not occur" (p. 1,319). Law enforcement policies do not have guidelines for what constitutes a false allegation; rather they have guidelines on what actions do not mean a case is a false allegation (Lisak et al., 2010). These guidelines include cases where the victim does not cooperate with investigators, when law enforcement determines there is not enough evidence to move the case forward, cases where the victim is making inconsistent statements or lying about aspects of the crime, and cases where the victim delayed in reporting the crime (Lisak et al., 2010). Some unfounded cases are based on biases and stereotypes (rape myths that include victim intoxication, non-stranger assaults, delayed reporting, and assaults by intimates). Lisak et al. (2010) examined law enforcement records from a university police department in a large northeastern school from 1998 to 2007. Of the 136 cases filed, only 5.9 percent were deemed to be false reports. Lisak et al. (2010) concluded that "the greater the scrutiny applied to police classifications, the lower the rate of false reporting detected" (p. 1,331). False rape allegations in this university were uncommon.

Hunt and Bull (2012) argued that defining the concept of "false allegation" is important when it comes to understanding the nature of false rape allegations. Currently, there is no universally accepted definition of false allegations, and this has hindered research that attempts to evaluate the nature of false rape allegations. Hunt and Bull (2012) echoed the argument that research in this area has suffered from poor conceptualization and a host of methodological issues that range from small sample sizes to lack of statistical analyses.

Hunt and Bull (2012) compared a sample of "genuine" rape allegations to confirmed false rape allegations (N=240); this was a larger sample size than most studies in this area. Hunt and Bull (2012) found that false rape allegations were associated with unemployment, no alcohol use at the time of the alleged incident, and race (White complainants were more likely to file false reports). The most important finding of this research was those who reported a theft in addition to the sex offense were more likely to be genuine cases. False allegations were more likely to place the alleged rape outdoors, to have been a "surprise" attack, reported the crime to the police themselves, and took longer than 24 hours for the victim to report the crime. Genuine allegations included reports of extra violence and injuries, more sexual acts (median of three different types of sexual act), more likely to include an offender who took precautions (gagging, blindfolding, etc.), the offender spoke more, and someone other than the victim reported the crime to the police. Both genuine and false reports were likely to include physical resistance by the victim and for the victim to tell someone other than the police at first.

What is clear from this discussion is that false rape allegations do exist. What we do not know is what the true incidence of false rape allegations are. With current law enforcement reporting policies, it is almost impossible to determine how many reports of sex offenses are false allegations. Based on the limited research, it is likely that false allegations account for between 5 and 25 percent of all sex offense reports. All crimes must be investigated fully to determine if a claim of rape is genuine or false. "While it may not be politically correct to question the veracity of a woman's complaint of rape, failing to consider the accuser may be intentionally lying effectively eradicates the presumption of innocence" (Gross, 2008, p. 49).

Testimony via CCTV

As indicated above, one of the rights an accused defendant retains is the right to confront witnesses against him/her. In the case of sex offenders, the confrontation between the accused and the victim can be difficult, especially for the victim. The example provided at the beginning of this chapter illustrated an accused sex offender, representing himself, getting to cross-examine the victim of his crime. Testifying in court can be a traumatic experience for child and adult victims of violent crimes, especially sex offenses. Reliving the victimization before the offender and strangers (members of the jury and various individuals in the courtroom gallery) can be exceptionally difficult. Due to this tension between offender rights and victim wariness, the criminal justice system has introduced alternative modes of providing evidence from witnesses.

Several primary strategies have been employed: screens, videotaping, CCTV (one-way or two-way), or closing the courtroom. Screens separate the victim from the accused offender within the courtroom during the victim's testimony, but the testimony is still heard by both parties. Videotaping testimony occurs before trial (deposition); this strategy allows for no cross-examination of the witness, save that which has been recorded in advance. One-way **CCTV testimony** allows the witness to be seen by the courtroom, but the witness cannot see what is occurring in the courtroom; the witness is either in a different part of the courthouse or anywhere else outside of the courtroom. Two-way CCTV allows the individuals in the courtroom to view the witness/victim and the witness/victim can also view what is going on within the courtroom; again, the witness/victim is in another location away from the courtroom where the trial is occurring. CCTV is used in both federal and state trials. The federal government has even provided funding to states to obtain CCTV technology for use in state courts. Finally, judges can choose to close the court to those except counsel, the jury, and any other necessary court officers (stenographer for instance). It should be noted that CCTV and virtual meetings were used heavily for all cases during the Covid-19 pandemic.

CCTV is considered appropriate for children only; older children and adults are required to give testimony before the court. "Every day children are victims or witnesses of violent crime" (Bennett, 2003, p. 234). Many crimes against children go unreported. Those that are reported do not necessarily result in a conviction. Most victims, adult and child, report feeling victimized again (secondary victimization) by the criminal justice system's processing of their cases. The legislation generally permits the use of CCTV for child victims/witnesses for four reasons: victim fear, potential for victim to suffer emotional trauma from testifying, if the victim suffers from a mental issue or some other infirmity, or conduct by either the defendant or defense counsel that causes the child to be unable to continue his/her testimony (Bennett, 2003, p. 243). Children are more likely to refuse to testify in open court than testifying via CCTV (Bennett, 2003).

The use of CCTV varies across states; some embrace the practice while others reject it. In general, the public strongly supports the use of CCTV for child victims/ witnesses (Bennett, 2003). Constitutional challenges to the use of CCTV have been unsuccessful. Key legal issues relate to CCTV and the alleged crime (some crimes warrant CCTV, others do not), age of victim/witness (age limit to those who can testify via CCTV), the admissibility of CCTV testimony (how much trauma does the victim/ witness have before CCTV is merited), and persons allowed in the room during the CCTV (usually prosecutor, defense counsel, and CCTV operators).

8

How effective is CCTV when it comes to the court processing of sex offenders? Bennett (2003) suggested that there were several issues that were key to the use of CCTV in trials. These included how it affects child testimony, jury perceptions, and juror ability to "detect deception" (Bennett, 2003, p. 262). Research has indicated that observers are more likely to concentrate on what the witness is saying rather than non-verbal cues when testimony is videotaped (Davies, 1999; Bennett, 2003)

Some research indicates that in-person testimony is more effective than CCTV testimony. Landstrom, Granhag, and Hartwig (2007) found that the manner of presentation can impact jurors watching child witnesses; jurors responded more favorably and were more likely to remember in-person testimony. Research by Hanna et al. (2012) indicated that juries could be more suspicious of CCTV testimony since witnesses may be more composed than if they were in the courtroom itself; likewise, the distance between the victim/witness and the judge and jury could lessen the impact of the testimony.

While there is evidence that in-person testimony has more impact on jurors than CCTV testimony, other research suggests that victim/witness testimony could be hampered even more by not using CCTV. Goodman et al. (1992) argued that if "children's testimony is compromised by confrontation or courtroom stress, then jurors' duty as fact finders may be impeded. Indeed, confronting the accused is a major stress for child witnesses . . . the completeness and accuracy of children's testimony can be seriously hampered by intimidation and/or heightened emotion" (p. 167). Most importantly, Hanna et al. (2012) suggested there is no evidence that testifying by CCTV reduces the accuracy of child testimony, nor does it impact the ability of jurors to detect lies. As such, CCTV will continue to be used for some child victims of sex offenses.

CONCLUSION

Chapter 8 evaluated the court processing of sex offenders. After providing an overview of the judicial system in the United States, Chapter 8 examined sex offenders who were prosecuted and sentenced through the criminal courts. The key correlates of sex offenders were evaluated to understand what offense and offender characteristics are most likely to result in a guilty verdict and a more severe sentence. Disparities in sentencing were also reviewed in relation to sex offenders with different characteristics. Chapter 8 also explored several specialty topics in this area: rape shield laws, false rape allegations, and the use of CCTV for child victims of sex offenses.

In the end, many victims of sex offenses do not see their case make it to the legal system; some who do may not want to be involved with it. Some victims have concerns including not wanting the perpetrator to be charged, not wanting to describe their attack to jurors during a trial, or not wanting their lifestyle scrutinized during a trial (Spohn, Beichner, and Davis-Frenzel, 2001). These concerns may be realistic, as at least half of victims involved in the legal system reported that their experience was harmful (Campbell et al., 2001; Herman, 2003). This rating was also correlated with negative physical health outcomes. Victims reported that confronting the offender in court and being cross-examined by the defense attorney were the most stressful aspects of their involvement, and often severely disrupted their lives; however, positive mental health outcomes were reported when the victim had a feeling of empowerment and inclusion in the legal process (Herman, 2003).

Chapter 9 shifts focus from the sentencing of sex offenders to the actual punishment of sex offenders. Chapter 9 examines the nexus of corrections and sex offenders. In particular, the focus is on the imprisonment of sex offenders. There is also a discussion of the use of castration as a punitive measure for sex offenders. Finally, Chapter 9 examines the United States' abandonment of the death penalty when dealing with sex offenders.

KEY TERMS

CCTV testimony
criminal history
dark figure of crime
determinate sentences
differential offending
differential treatment
discrimination
disparity
double victimization
false allegations
indeterminate sentences
mandatory sentence
offense seriousness
rape shield laws
sentencing
sentencing enhancements
sentencing guidelines
sentencing outcomes
truth in sentencing

EXERCISES

1. Examine the rights afforded to indicted sex offenders under the Fifth and Sixth Amendments. Do you think sex offenders should be afforded the same rights as other types of criminals? Why?
2. Based on the statistics provided in Chapter 8, are sex offenders treated differently than other types of criminals? Support your answer.
3. Explain the problem of determining the incidence of false rape allegations. Be sure to discuss the unfounding of cases by law enforcement agencies and victim credibility.
4. What are the primary challenges to the use of CCTV in criminal court proceedings?
5. Discuss the differences between disparity and discrimination in sentencing decisions. Are different types of sex offenders treated differently by the criminal courts? Support your answer with information from Chapter 8.
6. Find the rape shield law of the state in which you reside or are attending school. Describe the legal mandates contained within the law. If there are exceptions to the rape shield, please explain them.

ESSAY QUESTIONS

1. Find an article from a local news source that deals with a sex offender who is being tried through the criminal court system. Describe the nature of the offense and the media depiction of the trial. How does it compare to the various facets of the trial process discussed in this chapter?
2. Discuss the use of CCTV in sex offense cases where the victim is a vulnerable child. Should the use of CCTV be expanded to include adult victims of sex offenses? Support your answer.

9

SEX OFFENDERS AND CORRECTIONS

Chapter Objectives

After reading this chapter, students will be able to:

- Explain the nature of corrections.
- Understand the various goals/philosophies of punishment.
- Explain the history of correctional sanctions.
- Identify the ways in which the United States punishes sex offenders.
- Evaluate the problems associated with punishing sex offenders.
- Discuss the abandonment of the death penalty in punishing sex offenders.
- Identify how castration is a punishment for sex offenders.

INTRODUCTION

Once a criminal offender has been found guilty and sentenced by a criminal court in the United States, the next phase of the criminal justice system is to implement the punishment upon the convicted criminal. This component of the criminal justice system is commonly referred to as corrections. The term corrections is a bit of a misnomer. Corrections is a politically correct word that would suggest the goal of punishment is to rehabilitate criminals. In reality, corrections is the punitive arm of the criminal justice system. Chapter 9 examines how the correctional system in the United States deals with sex offenders.

Most convicted sex offenders will be punished through some form of **incarceration**. *An example of a sex offender's punishment can be found in the case of Ariel Castro.*

To say that Ariel Castro was a monster would be an understatement. In Ohio, Castro lured teenaged girls into his car by offering them rides. In three cases, he kidnapped the victims and kept them imprisoned in his home for over ten years. Castro abducted Michelle Knight in 2002, Amanda Berry in 2003, and Georgina DeJesus in 2004. We largely know what happened in Castro's house of horrors due to personal accounts of these victims and their diaries, which all three kept with Castro's permission; the accounts provided extensive details of the abuse each experienced.

After he kidnapped the victims, Castro reconfigured his house's interior to help keep the victims' whereabouts a secret. He installed alarms, obscured the interior of the house, boarded-up windows, removed doorknobs, and even barricaded parts of the house. He would also chain the victims to objects throughout the house (e.g., a support pole in the basement). Over the time of their confinement, Castro raped and beat the victims on a regular basis. He even fathered a daughter with Amanda Berry.

In May of 2013, Amanda Berry managed to escape Castro's house. As she was clawing through a boarded up window, a neighborhood resident heard her breaking out of the house. The individual lent Berry a cell phone, where she called 911. When they were found, the victims were described as pale, malnourished, scared, and dehydrated.

Castro was soon arrested, and a neighborhood was perplexed that such a criminal lurked in their midst. The arrest led to an indictment of Castro on a myriad of offenses. Before any trial proceedings, Castro pleaded guilty to 937 criminal counts including murder, kidnapping, assault, and rape. The sole reason that he pleaded guilty was to avoid a death penalty sentence.

At the sentencing hearing, Castro suggested he was addicted to porn and masturbation; he also accused Knight, DeJesus, and Berry of lying, suggested that none of the women were virgins, and that he had been sexually molested as a child. Despite these meager defenses to his actions, Castro was sentenced to life in prison plus 1,000 additional years.

After his sentencing, Castro was placed into administrative segregation due to the thought that another inmate might take revenge on Castro for his crimes. This meant that Castro was not a part of the general prison population. In administrative segregation, Castro resided in a cell of his own and rounds were made every 30 minutes to check on his safety. Even with these precautions, Castro was found dead in his cell on September 4, 2013. He had committed suicide by hanging himself with a bed sheet. He had served less than a month on his life plus 1,000-year sentence. While his victims did not immediately make statements, some family members suggested that Castro was depressed, while his mother claimed his spirits were high based on a letter she had recently received.

Chapter 9 examines sex offenders in the correctional system. We begin by providing a brief history of the punishment and corrections of criminals. In addition, Chapter 9 evaluates the various philosophies and goals of punishment. We then address the punishment of sex offenders in the United States historically and in the present. In particular, we evaluate America's use of prisons, castration, and the death penalty to deal with sex offenders. Chapter 9 begins with the history of correctional practices and thought.

THE HISTORY OF PUNISHMENT AND CORRECTIONS IN THE UNITED STATES

There are four goals, or philosophies, that form the basis of all punishments: retribution, deterrence, incapacitation, and rehabilitation (Cullen and Jonson, 2012). **Retribution** is the idea that a punishment must have some balance to the crime. In biblical nomenclature, retribution concerns the philosophy of an "eye for an eye." To some extent, punishment associated with a retributive philosophy is punishment for the sake of punishment (Cullen and Jonson, 2012). The second philosophy of punishment is deterrence. **Deterrence** is the concept of a punishment being sufficient to curb future criminal behavior. To some extent most punishments denoted in criminal statutes are supposed to serve as deterrents. There are two forms of deterrence: specific and general. Specific deterrence pertains to a punishment's effect on a particular offender. If the punishment for a crime keeps the offender from recidivating, then the punishment is said to be a specific deterrent. General deterrence pertains to the effect of a punishment on everyone else in a society. If the punishment of a criminal will prevent other society members from engaging in crime, then the punishment is said to be a general deterrent.

The third goal of punishment is incapacitation. **Incapacitation** is the most simplistic punitive philosophy. It basically suggests that if a person commits a crime, that person must be locked up. If the criminal is in a correctional facility, **prison** or jail, they cannot be engaging in crime within the community. While simplistic in its nature, it is also one of the costlier punitive strategies as convicted offenders must be segregated from the rest of society in some form of correctional institution. The fourth philosophy of punishment is rehabilitation. Under the idea of **rehabilitation**, punishment is not actually the goal; rather, rehabilitation seeks to "fix" a criminal to keep them from engaging in future criminality. Much more on rehabilitation and sex offenders will be discussed in Chapter 13.

Currently, there is an emerging goal/philosophy of punishment found in the idea of restorative justice. Restorative justice attempts to repair damage to the victim and the community. In essence, this goal seeks to restore the offender, victim, friends of each, and the community to their previous state before the crime occurred; this is essentially a reset. Of all the goals discussed, this goal would be very difficult for sex offenders and victims of sex offenders. Due to its relative newness, little research has occurred on the impact of restorative justice, so our discussion in Chapter 9 revolves around retribution, deterrence, incapacitation, and rehabilitation.

The goal of the punishment is intimately linked to the time period in which particular punishments have occurred. For instance, punishments and sanctions for the better part of human existence have followed the retributive philosophy. From the earliest times, people have punished others for misbehavior. For most of human history these punishments have been termed blood punishments. The reason for this is that most punishments were either death or corporal. Corporal punishment is any punishment that is physical. **Blood punishments** typically resulted in the spilling of blood from the execution or the beating/torture of the offender. Before the 1700s, alternative, non-blood punishments were used sparingly and generally only for those with social position. There was limited use of shaming, the deprivation of property, being thrown into dungeons (usually included physical beating and/or torture), and banishment. There was nothing corrective about punishments before the 1800s; this era was highlighted by a retributive spirit.

The 1700s gave us the Age of Enlightenment. At its roots, the Enlightenment was a new way for humans to look at the world. This period was marked by great advances in science and a new, secular way of examining people and society. Prior to this era, religious views dominated the discourse on the etiology of human behavior and misbehaviors. Indeed, prior to the Enlightenment, the predominant theory of human criminality was referred to as the demonic school of criminology. Individuals were not responsible for engaging in behaviors detrimental to others and society by choice, but because the devil, a demon, or some other supernatural entity made them do it. This notion is highlighted by the Salem witch trials. Many individuals were hanged for allegedly being witches; at this time, witchcraft was intimately linked to service to Satan.

At its core, the Enlightenment examined the human aspiration to attain perfection. With this quest to perfection, there were going to be both failures and successes built into the human condition. Overall, it was a rather optimistic view of humanity that had been lacking during the demonic era. Under these ideals, individuals who misbehaved or engaged in crime did not have to be "destroyed" through blood punishments. Society could attempt to "correct" and "reform" offenders. This new ideal would allow the use of new philosophical goals associated with punishments: deterrence, incapacitation, and rehabilitation. All of these would be largely associated with a new invention: the **penitentiary** (prison).

Clear, Reisig, and Cole (2012) suggest there are seven eras of corrections in America. The first era was termed the Colonial era, when America was still largely under the control of the British Empire; most of the ideas of corrections at this time were transplanted from England and tended to be brutal, blood punishments. The Enlightenment brought about the second period of corrections in the United States: the Penitentiary era. In the waning years of the eighteenth century and beginning of the nineteenth century, the ideals associated with the Enlightenment gave birth to the modern-day prison. Originally known as penitentiaries, the idea behind the first prisons was the reclamation of an offender's soul through reflection and repentance. Hard labor, solitude, and silence measures prevented further deterioration of the soul and corruption from other criminals. The solitude and silence were thought to lessen the time needed for reforming prisoners. The strict order of life and hard work were also believed to help offenders reform.

Two versions of the prison emerged at this time: the **Pennsylvania system** and the **Auburn system**. Pennsylvania was founded by Quakers, a religious sect that brought a great deal of religion into their new prisons. The Pennsylvania system was also known as the separate system because offenders had their own cells and had no contact with other inmates or guards. The Auburn system, also known as the congregate system, kept offenders segregated at night in their own cells; during the day, the offenders would work together in silence in a large room. The Auburn system would be utilized in all prisons by the turn of the twentieth century, when the last Pennsylvania system prison was closed in the early 1900s.

According to Clear et al. (2012) there were problems with the original prisons, under both systems. Corporal punishments were still used frequently. While there was supposed to be solitude and silence, oftentimes there was little silence. Inmates still found ways to communicate with each other, especially in the congregate system. Most importantly, the solitude, especially in the Pennsylvania system, resulted in making some prisoners have mental breakdowns. People are inherently social beings and the solitude/silence got to many inmates.

Due to these problems, new ways of thinking about the function of **prisons** were needed. The Reformatory era (1850s–1900) provided some new ways of addressing criminal offenders in prison. Reformatory era philosophers recognized that different offenders reformed at different paces; in addition, not every offender was in need of prison. During this time, **parole** and **probation** were introduced as mechanisms to help offenders successfully reform. Within the prison (**reformatory**), inmates were classified, adhered to a schedule of work/vocation/education, and released upon reform.

After the 1700s and the 1800s, advances in correctional thought became more standardized. The Progressive era (1900–1930s) saw the widespread use of probation/parole and the introduction of the juvenile justice system. The Medical Model (1930s–1960s; Clear et al., 2012) focused on rehabilitation and individual treatment of individual offenders; it was at this time that punishment started to be known as corrections, but the name would not be universally applied to criminal justice sanctions until the 1980s. The cost associated with rehabilitation and a spike in crime in the 1960s led to the Community era. The reality is that the vast majority of prison inmates were inevitably released back into society. Unfortunately, around 70 percent of released offenders (even to the present) invariably return to prison for the commission of a subsequent criminal offense. The Community era focused on the reintegration of offenders back into society. When positive results did not emerge quickly enough, the 1970s gave way to the Crime Control era. This era focused on the goal of incapacitation. Thus, prisons came to serve as warehouses for criminals, with largely no rehabilitative function whatsoever. Based on the economic downturn in 2008, the United States may be headed into a new era of corrections. Since funding is so great for corrections and money is very tight across federal and state governments, many state governments began to pull funding from criminal justice organizations to fund other areas in need of resources. Despite the changes in economic conditions across the last decade, the emergence of a new era has not been fully realized to date.

Today, the various forms of punishment extend from the **death penalty** to fines. We differentiate the types of punishment by institutional and community corrections. **Institutional corrections** pertain to any punishment that occurs within a formal correctional institution, like a prison or a jail. **Community corrections** are any punishments that are meted out without the offender having to serve time in a correctional institution. This latter is designed to divert offenders from the correctional institution setting. These punishments are listed in Table 9.1.

Prisons and jails are obviously examples of institutional corrections. As a general rule, an offender sentenced to less than one year of incarceration will serve their time in jail (misdemeanor); an offender sentenced to more than one year of incarceration

TABLE 9.1 FORMS OF CRIMINAL SANCTIONS

Institutional Corrections	Community Corrections
Death Penalty	Probation
Prison	Intensive supervised probation
Jail	Parole
Day reporting	Restitution
Boot camp	Fines
	Community service
	Substance abuse treatment
	House arrest
	Electronic monitoring
	Halfway house

will go to prison (felony). The death penalty is administered inside of prisons; usually one prison in a state will contain the death row and death house for offenders sentenced to die for their crimes. Day reporting (and an alternative version called weekend reporting) is a mix of institutional and community corrections where the offender goes to jail during the day (or on the weekend) but is in the community the rest of the time. This allows for most of the sentence to be carried out in the community. **Boot camps** are examples of shock incarceration; the convicted offender experiences a great deal of punishment in a truncated time period.

Community corrections focus on the offender serving the time for their punishment within the community so as not to displace the offender who is either a first-time offender or a non-serious offender. Probation is the punishment whereby convicted offenders serve their punishments under supervision in the community. They are free to live their lives, but generally, probation will incorporate multiple forms of correction in addition to stipulations (terms) that the offender must abide by (curfew, no drinking, maintain a job, etc.). As well, an offender on probation who was convicted of drug possession might be mandated to attend drug therapy or counseling. Intensive supervised probation (equated with shock probation) is a form of probation that adds further stipulations to an offender's probation. For example, a convicted offender might be subject to more meetings with the probation officer or more random home or work inspections by the probation officer. Parole is exactly like probation with one exception: parole only occurs for an offender after that offender has served time in prison or jail. The remainder of community corrections listed in Table 9.1 (restitution, fines, community service, substance abuse treatment, house arrest, electronic monitoring, and halfway houses) often occur simultaneously to either probation or parole.

This section has examined the philosophical bases for the use of punitive sanctions. We have also provided a brief history of the evolution of corrections and punishments currently used in the United States. The next section examines how we apply these punishments to sex offenders.

THE PUNISHMENT OF SEX OFFENDERS

Sex offenders are a unique class among criminal offenders. These offenders are driven by biological urges for sexual gratification or psychological urges for power or dominance over victims. In either case, there are limits to any criminal sanction's ability to deter offenders from future similar behaviors. Packer (1968) indicated that the effectiveness of any punishment can be limited. In the case of sex offenders, it is arguable that punishments are largely incapable of meeting the correctional goal of deterrence. Effective sanctions for sex offenders should be a balance of punishment (retribution/incapacitation) and treatment (rehabilitation).

Due to the fact that sex offender crimes are not a choice but contingent upon biological urges (desires that cannot be satisfied in other ways) or paraphilias (see Chapter 3), Lippke (2011) argued the long-term "control of such desires is difficult, perhaps exceedingly so" (p. 163). Lippke (2011) suggested that corrections are left with only four possible policy choices: psychological treatment, chemical or surgical castration, monitoring, or quarantine. Psychological treatment deals with trying to help the offender; this is closely tied to the correctional goal of rehabilitation. **Castration** (chemical or surgical) is an attempt to "reduce the strength or intensity of illicit sexual desires" (Lippke, 2011, p. 163). This policy is linked primarily to rehabilitation but also has strong links to retribution as well. Closer monitoring of sex offenders would revolve around limiting the movement of offenders via intensive parole/probation, registries, or residence restrictions (deterrence). Quarantine would focus on the long-term imprisonment of sex offenders, which would align with the goal of incapacitation.

While the policies outlined by Lippke (2011) are linked to criminal sanctions, it is debatable that all of these policies are in fact punitive with respect to the goals of punishment enumerated above. We will discuss sex offender registration and notification laws, residence restrictions, civil commitments, and rehabilitation for sex offenders in later chapters. Chapter 9 focuses on three primary sanctions that the United States has applied to sex offenders historically and in the present: incarceration, castration, and the death penalty.

Incarceration

The punishment that the most mid-level to serious sex offenders (rapists) will receive upon their conviction of a sex crime is incarceration in either a prison or a jail. As noted above, the key goal of punishment associated with institutional corrections is both deterrence and incapacitation. Overall, Maruschak and Minton (2020) noted that 6,410,000 offenders were under the supervision of the adult correctional system in 2018, this was a 19-year low in the number of individuals under supervision. In 2007, the total correctional population was 7,339,600. According to Maruschak and Minton (2020), 1 in 35 adults (2.8 percent) in the United States were under some form of correctional supervision (institutional and community corrections). The total number of offenders in federal and state prisons in 2019 was 1,430,800 (Carson, 2020). Inmates sentenced for violent crimes (sex offenses included) made up 55 percent of the states' prison populations; those sentenced for violent crimes made up 8 percent of the federal prison population. Prison decreases were largely attributable to state prison systems.

In relation to sex offenders specifically, Greenfield (1997) noted that 240,000 sex offenders were under the control of the correctional system on any given day. Just under half of these sex offenders were incarcerated; the remaining sex offenders were under community correctional control (Greenfield, 1997). In 2012, 160,900 sex offenders were serving time in prisons for rape or sexual assault; this accounts for 12.2 percent of all inmates under state jurisdictions (Carson, 2014). The federal level rarely prosecutes the crime of rape in addition to most sex crimes, so the total number of prisoners in federal prisons is not reported (Carson, 2014). In 2016, 164,928 sex offenders (12.8 percent) were prisoners in the state correctional systems (Bronson and Carson, 2019). This number does not account for less serious sex offender classes. As with the Uniform Crime Report and other official data sources (see Chapter 1), lesser sex offenses are only counted within an overall glut of "other offenses." As such, the sex offenders we know are in custody and are the most serious of these offenders. Of course, this group is the one criminologists are most interested in.

According to Greenberg (1997), the serious sex offender inmates were predominantly male (98.7 percent) and White (48.8 percent); Hispanics accounted for 22.3 percent of all sex offender inmates. In 2012, the median time served for inmates convicted of sexual assault was 48 months (four years). This was an increase of ten months served since 2002 for those convicted of sexual assault or rape. Other than murderers, sex offenders tend to serve the longest sentences in prison. No replication of Greenfield's study has been completed or published as of 2021. Thus, our most recent statistics are almost 25 years old at the publication of this edition.

Castration

Castration is one of the most interesting punishments for sex offenders as it falls in the nexus of punitive and rehabilitative sanctions. For the most part, castration falls under a rehabilitative philosophy. The belief is that if the sexual drive is muted by castration, this will also result in the decrease of sexual **recidivism**. This is supposed to suppress a sex offender's urges from sex offending. Letourneau and Caldwell (2013) outlined the evolution of sex offender policies across the twentieth century. In this discussion, they examined the role of castration as punishment of sex crimes.

Meyer and Cole (1997) indicated the oldest form of castration was the physical castration (removal) of the testes; this had been done for centuries. The removal of the testes decreases the production of testosterone, which affects "the libido and reduces sexual behavior in the male of the species" (Meyer and Cole, 1997, p. 2). In animals, this creates docile creatures. In the earliest times, slaves were castrated by monarchs to guard the king's harem; it was believed that castrated males would not desire their charges or impregnate them even if they did (Meyer and Cole, 1997). Meyer and Cole (1997) indicated the first use of castration as a therapeutic technique was done in Switzerland to treat an "imbecile for hypersexuality" (p. 2).

Castration to deal with sexual misbehaviors began in Europe in the early 1900s. Lemaire (1956) indicated that Dr. Sharp, in 1899, was one of the first to castrate prisoners in Indiana. Meyer and Cole (1997) noted that castration was used in the south when authorities suspected that Black offenders had raped White women. During the first wave of U.S. sex crime legislation (late 1800s to World War II), sterilization became a mechanism to deal with sex offenders, other types of offenders, the mentally ill, and the mentally incapacitated.

Letourneau and Caldwell (2013) attributed the use of castration to the emerging fields of sexology and eugenics; both of these views greatly, if wrongly, still have a profound impact on how sex offenders are seen today. Sexologists suggested that even minor forms of sexual misbehavior could result in later sexual violence and, possibly, sexual homicide (Letourneau and Caldwell, 2013). Eugenicists suggested crime was a function of genetic determination (Letourneau and Caldwell, 2013); eugenics was effectively selective breeding with the sterilization of "defective" individuals (criminals, insane, handicapped, etc.). Between these two views, sex offenders are deviant criminals who are incapable of change and highly likely to escalate in their criminal behaviors. Sterilization programs were designed to address this ideal of the sex offender; these tended to focus on children in prison and reform schools. Only anecdotal evidence suggested the programs were effective. Castration was largely eschewed once it became synonymous with Nazi Germany's holocaust.

A general discussion of castration revolves around male subjects. Castration is also available for the female of the species. This procedure is referred to as an oophorectomy. According to Meyer and Cole (1997), this technique removes the ovaries from a female; the procedure often occurs in league with a hysterectomy out of a medical need (cancer for instance). "There is no medical literature on performing such a procedure in the female to decrease sexual arousal or behavior" (Meyer and Cole, 2007). To date, the practice of castration has not been used on female sex offenders.

The courts have largely permitted the use of castration for sex offenders. The underlying basis for the various court conclusions focused on the rehabilitative nature of castration; if castration was used punitively, courts did not support the practice. In *Buck v. Bell* (1927), the Supreme Court upheld the use of sterilization in cases where proper Eugenics, not punishment, was the goal. This decision would be reversed in 1942 (*Skinner v. Oklahoma*), when castration was differentially used for similar crimes (white-collar crimes versus street level crimes). The courts today support castration provided there is a rehabilitative intent to the laws and practices.

Physical castration today is used primarily for stemming the advance of cancer, especially prostate cancer; however, it is still a sentencing option for sex offenders in a few states. The modern-day form of castration is actually referred to as chemical castration. In 1944, chemical castration was argued to control the sexual drive of sex offenders. Chemical castration requires the use of pharmaceutical drugs to either reduce or entirely eliminate the sexual drives of offenders. Chemical castration requires the injection of Depo-Provera, a testosterone-reducing drug, into subjects. Under this policy, the drugs must be continually administered to achieve the desired end; if not continually administered, the effect of the drug can and likely will diminish. Other than the permanence of the procedure, physical castration is argued to be more effective than chemical castration at reducing sexual desire and recidivism (Chisum, 2013).

Chemical castration is used in several states for both repeat and first-time rapists. Wilson (2004) indicated that California adopted the first modern castration policy in 1996; it was soon adopted in Florida, Michigan, Massachusetts, Missouri, Texas, Washington, and New York. As of 2019, eight states still used some form of chemical castration (Alabama, California, Florida, Iowa, Louisiana, Montana, Texas, and Wisconsin); Georgia and Oregon repealed their castration policies in 2006 and 2011, respectively (Chisum, 2013).

Use of castration both has general support and meets opposition. Proponents of chemical castration suggest that the practice is both justified and proper; the continued used of pharmaceutical drugs allows the sex offender to be released back into the public without endangering people. According to Wilson (2004), opponents to chemical castration invoke two primary rationales. First, legislatures do not have the expertise to enact such legislation. Second, chemical castration violates the Eighth Amendment's ban on cruel and unusual punishment. Physical castration causes an irreversible loss to the offender (Meyer and Cole, 1997). Meyer and Cole (1997) indicated that it was questionable if an offender could give consent to castration if the alternative was imprisonment. In addition, if a sex offender has a "medical problem," this inherently means they cannot take responsibility for their so-called medical disorder (Meyer and Cole, 1997). Wilson (2004) argued that "such laws demonstrate the difficulty in combining rigid and formalistic laws with complex medical treatments" (p. 383).

Wilson (2004) argued that chemical castration was a very physically intrusive technique. Even so, society is largely okay with the practice of castration on sex offenders. The sex offender committed a crime and deserved to lose all their rights, including procreation. Comartin, Kernsmith, and Kernsmith (2009) argued that support for severe policies against sex offenders, like castration, was associated with lower income, less education, being a parent of children under the age of five, and general fear of sex offenders. General fear of sex offenders was the most important variable in determining support for severe sex offender policies.

Thus, the practice of castration inherently contains a retributive goal. The retributive philosophy argues an "eye for an eye" approach to punishment. Castration, even if it is done to treat a sex offender, still echoes the retributive spirit. If an individual commits a serious sex offense, that individuals is stripped of their ability to procreate as well as their sexual drive. With the exception of the death penalty (death for a death), no other correctional practice is inherently so retributive (loss of sexuality for a rape). Unfortunately, it is not known what the incidence of castration for sex offenders actually is. This is due to the fact that it is rarely imposed, but criminal justice data collection efforts should attempt to account for the total number of sex offender castrations imposed every year. Much more on the practice of castration will be discussed in Chapter 13 in relation to rehabilitation.

Death Penalty

In 1906, Ed Johnson was convicted of raping Nevada Taylor in Chattanooga, Tennessee. Johnson was a Black man who had only made it through the fourth grade. Taylor was 21 and White. On January 23, 1906, Taylor was traveling home from her bookkeeping job when an attacker came up behind her and choked her (Curriden and Phillips, 1999). The suspect hissed for Taylor not to scream. When she had passed out from the strangulation, the offender raped her. The next day's newspaper suggested the suspect was Black. Based on witness accounts and a sheriff who was running for reelection, Ed Johnson was identified as the rapist a few days later. While the story is a stunning portrait of the interaction between race and criminal justice in the early twentieth century (for a full accounting of the case read Curriden and Phillips, 1999), Johnson was convicted of the rape. His sentence was death.

Three points about this story are important. First, Johnson was innocent of the crime. When the Supreme Court became involved with the case, Justice John Marshall Harlan, the Great Dissenter, issued a stay of execution. A mob formed when the stay was issued; Johnson was dragged from his cell, beaten, and lynched from a nearby bridge. The police did not hinder the mob's actions in the least. Second, the Supreme Court was so outraged by the lynching perpetrated by the mob, it conducted its first, and only, criminal trial; the case was against the sheriff, his deputies, and the mob for contempt of court. Third, and most important for our discussion here, the death penalty has been used to punish sex offenders in the not-too-distant past.

As recently as 1925, the death penalty was authorized as a punishment for the crime of rape in the majority of states. Court actions across the twentieth century have evaluated whether juveniles, the mentally handicapped, and sex offenders should be potentially subjected to the death penalty as a viable punitive measure. In a 1963 dissent (*Rudolph v. Alabama*, 375 U.S. 889, 1963), Justice Arthur Goldberg, joined by Justices William J. Brennan and William O. Douglas, argued that the Supreme Court should determine whether or not the death penalty was warranted when a rape occurred without the taking of life. Goldberg argued that to execute an offender who raped a victim, but did not kill that victim, was a violation of the Eighth Amendment's prohibition on cruel and unusual punishments. Rudolph's attorneys had not challenged the constitutionality of the punishment, so it was beyond the Court's ability to rule on whether or not executing sex offenders was cruel and unusual. That case would come over a decade after Justice Goldberg's suggestions.

In 1977, the Supreme Court officially took up the Eighth Amendment's prohibition on cruel and unusual punishment with regard to rape and the death penalty (*Coker v. Georgia*, 433 U.S. 584, 1977). In 1974, Ehrlich Anthony Coker escaped from the Ware Correctional Institution near Waycross, Georgia. Coker had been serving time for convictions of murder, rape, kidnapping, and aggravated assault. Upon his escape, Coker invaded the home of Allen and Elnita Carver. After threatening the Carvers, Coker tied up Allen Coker in the bathroom, took a knife from the kitchen, the Carvers' money, and the keys to a car. Coker then raped Elnita Carver, kidnapped her, and stole the Carver's car. When Mr. Carver managed to escape, he contacted the police who quickly captured Coker; Mrs. Carver had suffered no further harm.

Based on his escape and criminal rampage, Coker was charged with new counts of escape, armed robbery, motor vehicle theft, kidnapping, and rape. The jury at the subsequent trial found Coker guilty and sentenced him to death. The Supreme Court heard the case to determine if the sentence was a violation of the Eighth Amendment.

Under *Gregg v. Georgia* (1976), the Court determined that a punishment is excessive if it "(1) makes no measurable contribution to acceptable goals of punishment and hence is nothing more than the purposeless and needless imposition of pain and suffering; or (2) is grossly out of proportion to the severity of the crime." In the *Gregg* case, the Court found that the act of murder could be punished by the death penalty because murder fit both of these criteria. Does the same apply for rape, even if it is related to another felony or a sex offender with a prior criminal history that includes murder?

The Court concluded that a "sentence of death is grossly disproportionate and excessive punishment for the crime of rape and is therefore forbidden by the Eighth Amendment as cruel and unusual" (*Coker v. Georgia*, 1977). As justification for this argument, the Court noted that the number of states imposing the death penalty for rape had been decreasing across the twentieth century; indeed, at the time of the ruling, only a minority of states (16) authorized the death penalty for the crime of rape and that had been consistent across the preceding 50 years. After *Furman v. Georgia* (1972), which nullified the death penalty for the better part of the 1970s, only three states changed their policies to include the death penalty as possible sanctions for the crime of rape (Georgia, North Carolina, and Louisiana); three other states (Florida, Mississippi, and Tennessee) kept the death penalty as a possibility for rape cases where the victim was a child.

In its rejection of the death penalty for rape, the Court also noted the serious nature of rape. "It is highly reprehensible, both in a moral sense and in its almost total contempt for the personal integrity and autonomy of the female victim . . . short of murder, it is the ultimate violation of self" (*Coker v. Georgia*, 1977). The Court did not think that rape compared to murder, in either injury to the victim or the public. "Life is over for the victim of murder; for the rape victim, life may not be nearly so happy as it was, but it is not over and normally is not beyond repair" (*Coker v. Georgia*, 1977).

The Court's final decision was that "a sentence for death for the rape of an adult woman is grossly disproportionate and excessive punishment forbidden by the Eighth Amendment" (*Coker v. Georgia*, 1977). This was a seven-to-two decision. Two dissents highlighted the premeditated manner of rape and the extreme variation/brutality that can occur within different rape events. Justice Lewis Powell argued that, in essence, some victims' lives are in fact beyond repair. Chief Justice Warren Burger and Justice William Rehnquist suggested that the death penalty could serve as a deterrent to the crime of rape based on its premeditated nature. *Coker* only applied to rape cases where victims were adults. Based on the nature of Coker's crime, the Court was not compelled in 1977 to deal with rape offenses where the victim was a child. A case in Louisiana over 30 years later would determine the constitutionality of the use of the death penalty in sex offenses where the victim was a child.

On March 2, 1998, Patrick Kennedy was allegedly getting his son ready for school when his eight-year-old stepdaughter was taken from the house's garage, dragged to the side of the house, and raped. Kennedy found his stepdaughter bleeding profusely from the vaginal area; the stepdaughter claimed two neighborhood boys had raped her. Kennedy called 911 and reported the crime. The victim's injuries were so bad, immediate surgery was required to repair the damage; a pediatric forensic expert claimed the injuries were some of the most severe he had ever seen.

Initially, the story Kennedy and his stepdaughter gave seemed genuine. Upon subsequent investigation, it became clear to authorities that Kennedy had raped his stepdaughter and forced her to make up the story about the neighborhood kids raping her. Eight days after the crime was reported, Kennedy was arrested, despite the fact that his stepdaughter refused to identify him as the offender. The arrest was based on inconsistencies Kennedy had given when describing the boys' bikes, the lack of evidence at the alleged rape scene, a great deal of blood found on the underside of the stepdaughter's bed, and several phone calls Kennedy made before the 911 call in which he asked for instructions on how to clean blood out of carpet. Based on this evidence, the State of Louisiana charged Kennedy with aggravated rape of a child; due to the nature of the offense, prosecutors sought the death penalty. Louisiana had legalized the use of the death penalty for rape against minors in 1995; this law suggested that "children are a class in need of special protection . . . short of first-degree murder, there is no crime more deserving of death" (*Kennedy v. Louisiana,* 2008). Georgia, Montana, Oklahoma, South Carolina, and Texas followed Louisiana's lead in this area by creating their own child rape death penalty statutes. Kennedy was the first rapist to be charged and successfully convicted under Louisiana's new death penalty law; the jury found him guilty and sentenced him to death. Kennedy appealed to the Supreme Court, making the argument that the punishment was inconsistent with the crime.

The Supreme Court took up Kennedy's appeal in *Kennedy v. Louisiana* (2008). The Supreme Court held that the death penalty cannot be applied to rape cases where there was no murder, even in cases pertaining to child victims. As with the rape of adult females, the rape of children was a violation of the Eighth Amendment's ban on cruel and unusual punishment. The Court suggested there was a great deal of consensus in relation to views on the death penalty. To establish this, the opinion noted that legislatures were not rushing to create laws providing the death penalty as a sanction for sexual offenses against children; 44 states have not made child rape a capital offense. Likewise, statistics indicated that the death penalty has not been used to punish a sex offender since 1964 (Ronald Wolfe). Of the 37 jurisdictions (federal and states) with the death penalty, only 6 states offered the death penalty for child rape; in 45 states, a child rapist could not be executed. Louisiana is the only state that has attempted to execute an individual for child rape since this time.

The Supreme Court also held that there were moral reasons for not executing individuals who have not killed victims. While the victims of sexual assault will experience fright, betrayal, physical injuries, and mental suffering, especially in the current case, "the death penalty should not be expanded to instances where the victim's life is not taken" (*Kennedy v. Louisiana*, 2008). Child rape occurs much more frequently than first-degree/capital murder. This would necessarily increase the number of executions every year in the United States. This, despite the fact that there is likely no deterrent value of the death penalty in these cases. In addition, the juxtaposition of the death penalty and rape of child victims could be seen as over-punishment. The deterrent effect is likely linked to the possibility of underreporting, especially if the victim and offender are related. Lastly, if the punishment is death for raping a child victim, offenders may have license to murder the victims as they are going to be executed anyway.

As the Court noted, capital cases require a great investment of time by those who are going to testify. This places a burden especially on a child, who is immature, having to deal with the ramifications of a sexual assault, and could be the key to getting a death sentence; both of these occur during the formative years in a public trial. Additionally, there are problems with child witnesses. Witnesses are often wrong; child witnesses/victims can be even more wrong. It would be a problem if wrongful executions occurred over unreliable, induced, or imagined child testimony. Finally, the Court also noted that it was not commenting on the use of the death penalty for the offenses of treason, espionage, terrorism, and drug kingpin activity (narcoterrorism).

While there was largely agreement between the Justices in *Coker*, the decision in *Kennedy* was much more contentious. The decision was split five to four. In a dissent written by Justice Samuel Alito, and joined by Chief Justice John Roberts and Justices Antonin Scalia and Clarence Thomas, great umbrage was taken with the majority decision. The majority's notation that only 6 of 50 states have allowed the death penalty for the crime of rape where the victim was a child was erroneous according to Justice Alito. Legislative action on the death penalty for sex offenses involving child victims was necessarily "stunted" because most state legislative bodies believed the question was answered in the *Coker* case. If the legislative belief is that a law would not survive judicial scrutiny, a legislative body is likely not to take up such legislative bills. Justice Alito argued that this was the rationale for so few states offering the death penalty for child rape.

In relation to the differential harm caused by the crimes of rape and murder, Justice Alito indicated that the majority did not address why the harm associated with murder is greater that the harm associated with rape. The Court takes the position that "no harm other than loss of life is sufficient" (*Kennedy v. Louisiana*, 2008). Justice Alito noted the apparent contradiction of the Court that rape "has a permanent psychological, emotional, and sometimes physical impact on a child" (*Kennedy v. Louisiana*, 2008). In addition to individual victimization, child victims of sex crimes are often problems for the rest of society as well. Child victims of sex crimes and rape are "considered seriously disturbed" in almost 40 percent of such cases and often times result in issues with substance abuse, dangerous sexual behaviors, and an inability to relate to others. For the dissenters, the rape of children should merit the death penalty, especially when the characteristics of the offense are particularly heinous. The majority discounted these views, and the death penalty is now reserved only for murderers.

Two other cases are tangentially linked to the execution of sex offenders. First, individuals who commit sex crimes who have been diagnosed as mentally ill or handicapped may not be executed. In *Atkins v. Virginia* (2002), the Supreme Court ruled that the criminal justice system cannot execute mentally retarded offenders. Daryl Atkins was convicted of abduction, armed robbery, and capital murder. During two different sentencing hearings (due to appeals), Atkins was twice sentenced to death. In both hearings, Atkins was noted to be "mildly mentally retarded." The Court (*Atkins v. Virginia,* 2002) held that "the deficiencies of mentally retarded criminals do not warrant exemption from criminal sanctions, but they do diminish their personal culpability." Thus, executing mentally handicapped/ill offenders is cruel and unusual punishment under the Eighth Amendment. This is an important case as most state statutes conflate sex offenders and mental handicaps/illness (see Chapter 12).

Second, juvenile offenders who perpetrate crimes before their 18th birthday are also exempt from the death penalty. In *Roper v. Simmons* (2005), Christopher Simmons was convicted of a murder at the age of 17 and was sentenced to death. Using arguments from the *Atkins* (2002) case as a basis, the Court noted that many states had already veered away from execution as a sanction for juvenile offenders; this would suggest American society was viewing juveniles as less culpable for their actions. In addition, the Court concluded that juveniles lacked maturity (with an underdeveloped sense of responsibility), were more susceptible to peer influence (peer pressure), and the "character of a juvenile was not as well formed as that of an adult" (*Roper v. Simmons,* 2005). Due to these facts, the Court ruled that the execution of juveniles was a violation of the Eighth Amendment's ban on cruel and unusual punishment.

Today, the use of the death penalty for sex offenders is a historical artifact. Unless the sex offense results in the death of a victim, sex offenders will not be put to death. Convicted sex offenders will likely receive some term of incarceration as punishment for their crimes.

CONCLUSION

Chapter 9 has evaluated the formalized punishment of sex offenders. In particular, Chapter 9 has examined the underlying goals/philosophies of punishment and the evolution of correctional punishments across human history. Turning these goals and punishments toward sex offenders indicated the limits of the criminal sanction in dealing with sex offenders, who are driven by sexual urges or the need to exert power over others. While incarceration is the primary punishment of serious sex offenses today, we also evaluated the use of castration and the death penalty on sex offenders.

There are two issues that need to be addressed when it comes to sex offender sanctions. The first is the impact of punishment on sex offenders' propensity to recommit sex offenses. There is a great deal of controversy about the extent of sex offender recidivism in the United States. Sex offender recidivism is the focus of Chapter 10. The second issue that must be addressed is alternatives to punishing sex offenders. These alternatives include sex offender registration and notification policies, the civil commitment of sex offenders, residence restrictions, and rehabilitation. While all of these polices have punitive qualities, they are not considered punitive sanctions by the courts. Chapters 11 to 13 will discuss these alternative methods of dealing with sex offenders.

KEY TERMS

Auburn system
blood punishment
boot camp
castration
community corrections
death penalty
deterrence
incapacitation
incarceration
institutional corrections
parole
penitentiary
Pennsylvania system
prison
probation
recidivism
reformatory
rehabilitation
retribution

EXERCISES

1. Discuss the differences between the four philosophies/goals of punishment.
2. What is the difference between community and institutional corrections? List examples of each.
3. Examine the change in the number of sex offenders in prisons over the last decade. How does this relate to the other inmates in prisons? Be sure to evaluate the length of time sex offenders remain in prisons.
4. What is the key problem with examining correctional statistics on sex offenders?
5. Discuss the conflicting views on castration (support and opposition). How do you feel about the use of castration as a means of dealing with sex offenders?

ESSAY QUESTIONS

1. Evaluate the evolution of the use of the death penalty for sex offenders. Be sure to discuss the relevant case law to support your answer.
2. Evaluate the evolution of the use of castration as a retributive punishment. From your point of view, is castration about retribution or rehabilitation?
3. After reading the section on sex offenders and the death penalty, what is your opinion on the use of the death penalty for sex crimes where the victim is a minor?

10

SEX OFFENDER RECIDIVISM

Chapter Objectives

After reading this chapter, students will be able to:

- Define the concept of recidivism.
- Identify the differences between specific and general recidivism.
- Demonstrate the empirical problems associated with determining recidivism rates.
- Evaluate the recidivism of sex offenders in the United States.
- Evaluate the findings of research on sex offender recidivism.

INTRODUCTION

In 1972, Christopher Hubbart began sexually assaulting women in the Los Angeles area of California. During 1972 alone, he sexually assaulted between 25 and 29 victims. Hubbart sought out victims by driving around residential neighborhoods in the early morning hours and looking for open garage doors, as evidence that the "man-of-the-house" had gone to work, or children's toys in the yard, an indication that the mother would be more cooperative if the children were to be threatened. In most of his crimes during 1972, Hubbart would bind the women's hands, cover their faces with a pillowcase, and then proceed to sexually assault them. Due to the use of the pillowcase he used to muffle screaming victims, Hubbart was nicknamed the "Pillowcase Rapist."[1]

1. Another Pillowcase Rapist operated in South Florida in the 1980s. Like Hubbart, this sex offender had around 40 victims.

After many victims and much investigation, Hubbart was finally apprehended by the authorities. Due to the nature of his offenses and his diagnosed mental issues, Hubbart was not sent to prison, but to a medical facility for the mentally ill. In 1979, Hubbart was released from the medical facility when the doctors indicated that he posed no threat to the public. Hubbart immediately moved north to the San Francisco area of California, where he began sexually assaulting women in both San Francisco and Sunnyvale. After attacking several victims, authorities again arrested Hubbart. Hubbart was sent back to a mental hospital where he remained until 1990.

When Hubbart was paroled in 1990, he almost immediately attacked a female jogger. This time, Hubbart was sent to a state prison where he resided until 1993. Upon this release, Hubbart relocated to Claremont. Within two months of his release, Hubbart felt he was losing control and about to go on another sexual offending spree. A petition by San Bernardino County recommitted Hubbart to a mental facility where he, then 63 years old, resided until 2014. Over three decades, Hubbart attacked 38 women and is an admitted serial rapist.

The Pillowcase Rapist is a prime example of the general public's beliefs about sex offenders. It is believed by most that sex offenders are perpetually sexually violating victims. All sex offenders are thought to be serial recidivists. This belief about sex offenders is so widespread that it is accepted as truth (Radford, 2008). While the media is the primary culprit for this misinformation and the hysteria it fuels, Radford (2008) noted that very "few sex offenders commit further sex crimes" (p. 57). When looking at **recidivism** rates across various kinds of criminals, the bulk of research illustrates that sex offenders are no more likely than other types of criminals to recidivate.

Chapter 10 examines the commonly accepted truth that sex offenders will inevitably recidivate. To better understand the issues associated with sex offender recidivism, Chapter 10 first examines the nature of recidivism and associated measurement issues. With an understanding of the concept of recidivism, an overview of recidivism rates among sex offenders is compared to the recidivism rates of other criminals in the United States to evaluate the claim that sex offenders are more likely to recidivate than any other criminal category utilizing official statistics. Chapter 10 concludes by providing an overview of the findings from the research on sex offender recidivism.

THE NATURE OF RECIDIVISM

Before delving deeper into the research on the recidivism of sex offenders in particular, there is a need to briefly outline some of the major issues related to recidivism research. Although the research on the recidivism of sex offenders is faced with some special challenges, it is also faced with the requirements and issues related to recidivism studies in general. There is a huge volume of research on recidivism (Holland et al., 1978; Gottfredson et al., 1978; Barton and Turnbull, 1979; Gottfredson et al., 1982; Klein and Caggiano, 1986; Rhodes, 1986; Zamble and Quinsey, 1997; Schlesinger, 2000; Sherman et al., 2000; Langan and Levin, 2002 are but only a few examples through the decades). The idea of and the measurement of recidivism and recidivism rates has been greatly debated in criminological circles. Questions arise over what acts should be considered recidivism, how recidivism is to be measured, and over what length of follow-up time should be used to determine reoffending.

One can classify this body of research in terms of both the dependent and independent variables utilized, as well as in terms of the methodology and theoretical framework employed. The dependent (or outcome) variable is "recidivism," which may be conceptualized and operationalized in different ways. With regard to the dependent variable, recidivism, there have been many studies and publications discussing both the conceptual and the operational definition of this key term.

Recidivism as Dependent Variable

A good example of the operationalization of recidivism is provided by Klein and Caggiano (1986). In their self-report study of inmates in three state prison systems who were being paroled, Klein and Caggiano had to determine what recidivism meant. They had to do so in terms of what acts constituted recidivism and over what time frame. Klein and Caggiano used three official indexes of recidivism: rearrest, reconviction, and reincarceration (this measure is sometimes broken up to view new offending versus technical violations [see Langan and Levin, 2002]). While these omit offenses that go unreported to police (more on this below), this type of official data are commonplace in the recidivism literature (Zamble and Quinsey, 1997).

Klein and Caggiano's operationalization also had to address how much time was required after parole in which to measure recidivism. A very commonly used **follow-up period** is five years. This five-year ceiling, which may be analyzed in terms of days, weeks, months, and years, is, in essence, a matter of practicality and feasibility. Indeed, unless a researcher is utilizing retrospective data, not many researchers are going to spend more than five years collecting data before the project can even come close to being completed.

While five years is seen as the average time in which an offender will potentially reoffend (Zamble and Quinsey, 1997), Klein and Caggiano defined their follow-up time frame as 12-, 24-, and 36-month periods. For purposes of their research, the one-, two-, and three-year follow-up periods were more appropriate than the more typical five-year follow-up time period. Thus, it depends upon the purpose of the research which follow-up time period is most appropriate. The researcher's decision to use a particular follow-up period (be it one year, three years, five years, ten years, or more) invariably introduces a certain level of bias in the findings. That is, there will always be some offenders who reoffend outside the (artificially determined) follow-up period. Such offenders will be counted as "false negatives" (i.e., as those who do not reoffend), simply because they delay their reoffending until after the follow-up period ends. This offender simply slips through the researcher's net as do offenders who are not counted in official data (i.e., those who are never caught).

Another issue associated with the study of recidivism revolves around general and specific recidivism. **General recidivism** refers to offenders who engage in any further criminality after their initial criminal act. The initial act could be any crime and the follow-up crime could be any crime. The two types of crime committed can be mutually exclusive of one another, for example, a convicted burglar who recidivates by committing arson. These two crimes are not linked in terms of style or content of the crime commissioned. In studies of sex offender recidivism, there are up to three measures of general recidivism: (1) whether or not a sex offender in this sample was rearrested for a general, non-sex offense; (2) if the offender was reconvicted of a general, non-sex offense; and (3) if the offender was reincarcerated for a general, non-sex offense.

Alternatively, **specific recidivism** measures whether an offender who formerly committed a crime later engages in the same type of criminal offending. Specific recidivism implies that there is some kind of link between the two offenses (Sample and Bray, 2003). If someone were to shoplift for their first offense and then later commit theft, or even embezzlement, this would be more in line with specific recidivism. If a person convicted of a sex offense commits another sex offense at a later time, this would be an example of specific recidivism. Studies of sex offender recidivism can utilize up to three measures of specific recidivism: (1) whether a sex offender in this sample was rearrested for a sex offense, (2) if the offender was reconvicted of a sex offense, and (3) if the offender was reincarcerated for a sex offense.

Another issue that must be addressed in recidivism studies pertains to what actions will be considered recidivism. All continued criminal acts will be considered recidivism (specific or general). Unfortunately, some offenders who are on parole or probation can be rearrested for behaviors that are not necessarily criminal in and of themselves. Parolees, especially, are limited in what they can or cannot do pursuant to parole terms and guidelines. Under these types of guidelines, it is common that parolees must look for work, not associate with other criminals, not consume alcoholic beverages, must attend rehabilitative meetings, and/or have a curfew. None of these are criminal behaviors for most citizens. If a parolee violates one of the terms of their parole, they can be rearrested and, potentially, reincarcerated for violating these terms. This is known as a technical violation. Recidivism studies that use rearrest and reincarceration as dependent variables must determine if they will include technical violations as acts of recidivism or not. While most studies do not include technical violations as recidivism, this decision is up to the researcher who must provide a rationale for their incorporation of technical violations into their study.

The final issue associated with sex offender recidivism research's dependent variables focuses on the nature of sex offenses and victimization. As discussed earlier in Chapters 1 and 6, victims do not always report sex crimes. While this can be due to a myriad of reasons, the impact on evaluating the findings of recidivism studies is readily apparent. If a sex offense is not reported, it is difficult to ascertain a correct baseline for when the offender began committing sex offenses; likewise, it is difficult to determine subsequent offending (recidivism) if victims choose not to report the crime. Thus, the dark figure of crime can prominently be featured as a limitation in studies of sex offender recidivism that rely on official counts of crime.

These are the key issues of treating recidivism as a dependent variable. To further evaluate recidivism studies, information about the factors that influence recidivism must also be accounted for. These factors are commonly known as independent variables.

Recidivism and Independent Variables

A variety of independent variables are used in recidivism research. For present purposes, it suffices to focus on two main types of independent variables: "program" or "treatment" variables (including the effect of a prison sentence, rehabilitative programs such as substance abuse treatment programs, or criminal justice system programs such as current drug courts) and offender/offense characteristics.

A large number of recidivism studies are in effect evaluation studies of the impact of treatment programs (see, for example, Martinson,1974 "nothing works"; another study evaluating the effect of treatment includes the research of Sherman et al. [2000] on reintegrative shaming). In addition, and more specifically, a number of studies assess the deterrent effect of a prison sentence (length, certainty, and so on), using recidivism as the outcome variable (Holland et al., 1978; Gottfredson et al., 1978; Barton and Turnbull, 1979; Gottfredson et al., 1982; Klein and Caggiano, 1986; Rhodes, 1986; Langan and Levin, 2002).

The second set of independent variables are those related to the nature of the offender/offense: Are drug users more or less likely to recidivate? Are violent offenders more or less likely to recidivate? And so on. These types of variables are indicative of more conventional sociological variables used in research. Zamble and Quinsey (1997) argued that a variety of measures are related to the probability of criminal recidivism in general. According to these authors though, the best predictors are youthfulness and previous arrests, while age at first arrest, criminal versatility, alcohol abuse, education, and social class all play roles in the process of recidivism.

The theoretical and methodological bases of recidivism studies are important as well. The theoretical underpinnings of these studies vary a great deal. A majority of the time, a **deterrence** framework is utilized. In the past, sometimes labeling theory also has been used to evaluate research findings on recidivism. There are a wide variety of methodological approaches used to study the determinants of recidivism. The strongest design is that of a time series approach (a quasi-experimental design outlined in Campbell and Stanley, 1966); due to the nature of recidivism, longitudinal data are preferable. It is beyond the limits of Chapter 10 to try to evaluate the substantive conclusions of current recidivism research, except to state that the evidence "does not look good" (Walker, 2001). According to Walker (2001, p. 231), we have not developed any planned intervention program that has worked any better at curbing recidivism than the traditional correctional practices of imprisonment, probation, and parole. Similarly, the methodological issues related to assessing recidivism remain, to a large degree, unresolved.

This section has explored the empirical and theoretical issues associated with studies of recidivism. While there are a great many problems with this area of research, social scientists still continue to evaluate the recidivism of various types of criminals. The next section examines sex offender recidivism in the United States.

SEX OFFENDER AND GENERAL OFFENDER RECIDIVISM IN THE UNITED STATES

Only a handful of studies have been completed by the U.S. Department of Justice when evaluating the recidivism patterns of criminals. The first set of studies focused on prisoners released in 1994 and the most recent study focused on sex offenders released from state custody in 2005. This section examines the nature of official recidivism for criminals in the United States.

Langan and Levin (2002) tracked 272,111 (N) inmates who were released in 1994; these inmates represented two-thirds of all prisoners released in 1994 and came from prisons in 15 states: Arizona, California, Delaware, Florida, Illinois, Maryland, Michigan, Minnesota, New Jersey, New York, North Carolina, Ohio, Oregon, Texas, and Virginia. These offenders were in prison for a multitude of offenses; 22.5 percent were incarcerated for violent offenses, 33.5 percent for property offenses, 32.6 percent for drug offenses, and 9.7 percent for public-order offenses; in particular, 1.2 percent of those prisoners released were convicted of rape. Langan and Levin (2002) had access to criminal history information from the states and from the Federal Bureau of Investigation (FBI). Their key dependent variables were rearrest, reconviction, and reincarceration; technical violations were included in this research.

Langan and Levin (2002) found that the first year was the period when the most recidivism occurred; two-thirds of all recidivism among the offenders occurred during this time period. Within the first six months, 29.9 percent of the offenders were rearrested for a felony or serious misdemeanor. Within the first year, 44.1 percent of the offenders recidivated. Within the first two years, 59.2 percent of the offenders were rearrested.

Langan and Levin (2002) discovered that 67.5 percent of all criminals were rearrested within three years of release from prison. Further, 46.9 percent of released offenders were reconvicted of a new crime, 25.4 percent were resentenced, and 51.8 percent were reincarcerated for a new crime or technical violation. Particular offenders were more likely to recidivate; robbers, burglars, larcenists, motor vehicle thieves, and those who possessed/sold stolen property or illegal weapons has rearrest rates well over 70 percent. Other offenders were much less likely to recidivate; offenders who perpetrated homicide, rape, other sexual assault, and driving under the influence had recidivated 40.7 percent, 46 percent, 41.4 percent, and 51.5 percent, respectively. Overall, and within three years, 61.7 percent of violent offenders were rearrested, 73.8 percent of property offenders were rearrested, 66.7 percent of drug offenders were rearrested, and 62.2 percent of public-order offenders were rearrested.

Langan and Levin (2002) evaluated recidivism across several characteristics. Men were more likely to be rearrested (68.4 percent) than women (57.6 percent). Blacks (72.9 percent) were more likely to be arrested than Whites (62.7 percent). Non-Hispanics (71.4 percent) were more likely to recidivate than Hispanics (64.6 percent). Younger prisoners were more likely to recidivate than older offenders. Most importantly, those offenders with longer criminal histories were more likely to be subsequently rearrested. No evidence was found to suggest that extended prison terms had an impact on recidivism rates.

In relation to sex offenders, Langan and Levin (2002) found that sex offenders were among the least likely type of offenders to recidivate. In relation to specific recidivism, only 2.5 percent of those convicted of rape (3,138 released offenders) were likely to be rearrested for rape within three years. Only those criminals convicted of homicide had a lower specific recidivism rate (1.2 percent). Of the other sex offenders (rapists) who were rearrested, 18.6 percent were rearrested for a new violent offense, 8.7 percent were rearrested for a new non-sex assault, and 11.2 percent were rearrested for a drug offense. Thus, sex offenders (rapists) cannot be considered to be specialists when it comes to sex offending.

While percentages suggest that sex offenders are not likely to specialize in sex offending behaviors, Langan and Levin (2002) also calculated the odds-ratio for each type of offender to determine their likelihood of specific recidivism. The odds-ratios indicated that rapists and perpetrators of other sexual assaults were more likely to specifically recidivate. Rapists were 4.2 times more likely to be rearrested for another rape; those who perpetrated other sexual assaults were 5.9 times more likely to be rearrested for perpetrating another sexual assault. No other group was as likely to be rearrested for a sex offense. This lends some support to the notion that sex offenders will recidivate. It should be noted that those who commit fraud are 5.3 times more likely to be rearrested for another fraud, burglars are 3.7 times more likely to be rearrested for a burglary, those who commit theft are 3 times as likely to be rearrested for a theft, and robbers are 2.7 times as likely to be rearrested for a robbery. Across all offense categories there is a certain level of specialization that occurs. So, it should not be surprising that sex offenders (rapists) are more likely to recidivate for a crime with which they are familiar.

Utilizing a survey instrument, Langan, Schmitt, and Durose (2003) further studied the almost 10,000 sex offenders and 262,420 non-sex offenders from the same 15 states for three years after their release. Of the sex offenders evaluated, Langan et al. (2003) outlined the four overlapping categories of sex offenders (overlap occurred due to multiple charges). Offenders who could be considered rapists accounted for 3,115 individuals in the study; 6,576 individuals could be considered sexual assaulters, 4,295 were child molesters, and 443 individuals were statutory rapists. Across all sex offenders, the average time spent in prison for their crime was three and a half years of an eight-year sentence.

As noted above, compared with other types of criminals, sex offenders were almost four times as likely to be rearrested for a sex offense; this is in line with common sense and supports research that suggests that other crimes do not act as gateway offenses for sexual offending (Sample and Bray, 2003). Compared to other types of offenders, sex offenders actually had the lower rearrest rate. For rearrest of any crime, 43 percent of sex offenders were rearrested, while 68 percent of non-sex offenders were rearrested. The first 12 months were the most likely time for specific recidivism to occur. Most interestingly, while older offenders tend to be less likely to recidivate, when it comes to sex offenders, there is little difference across older and younger offenders. Langan et al. (2003) reported that more prior arrests were associated with a higher likelihood of recidivism.

The most interesting findings from this study are in relation to the released child molesters. Sixty percent of this group of sex offenders violated victims who were 13 years old or younger. Half of the child molesters were at least 20 years older than their victims. Most importantly, child molesters were more likely to recidivate than the other sex offender types studied. Within three years of release, 3.3 percent of child molesters were rearrested for another sex crime against a child; this is opposed to 2.2 percent of other types of sex offenders being rearrested for any sex offense. Thus, child molesters are viewed as being more likely to recidivate than other types of sex offenders.

In terms of reconviction associated with rearrest, only 3.5 percent of sex offenders were reconvicted of a sex offense; 24 percent were reconvicted of any type of offense (Langan et al., 2003). These numbers are similar to sex offenders' general offender counterparts. Of the 38.6 percent of sex offenders returned to prison, the majority of these were for technical violations of their parole, not the commission of another offense or sex offense (Langan et al., 2003).

In 2014, Durose, Cooper, and Snyder replicated the original study on recidivism conducted by Langan and Levin (2002). Due to advancements in technology, 30 states were evaluated based on inmates released in 2005; these states included Alaska, Arkansas, California, Colorado, Florida, Georgia, Hawaii, Iowa, Louisiana, Maryland, Michigan, Minnesota, Missouri, Nebraska, Nevada, New Jersey, New York, North Carolina, North Dakota, Ohio, Oklahoma, Oregon, Pennsylvania, South Carolina, South Dakota, Texas, Utah, Virginia, Washington, and West Virginia. For each of these states, criminal history data from the state and the FBI were collected to determine recidivism (rearrest, reconviction, and reincarceration). Overall, 404,638 offenders were analyzed for recidivism using both a three-year follow-up and five-year follow-up period. The offenses for which the released inmates were convicted of were violent (25.7 percent), property (29.8 percent), drugs (31.8 percent), and public order offenses (12.7 percent).

The findings in the Durose et al. (2014) study are similar to the findings from the original 2002 study by Langan and Levin. Across the states, 67.8 percent of released inmates were rearrested within three years of release; 76.6 percent were rearrested within five years of release. Property offenders were the most likely group to be rearrested (82.1 percent of all property offenders). Across the other offenders, 76.9 percent of drug offenders were rearrested, 73.6 percent of public order offenders were rearrested, and 71.3 percent of violent offenders were rearrested. As with the preceding study, most recidivism occurred within the first year. Only two in five released offenders were not subsequently arrested or only arrested once in the five-year follow-up period. In relation to reconviction, 45.2 percent of offenders were reconvicted within three years of release and 55.4 percent were reconvicted within five years. For reincarceration, 49.7 percent of offenders were sent back to prison after three years and 55.1 percent of offenders were sent back to prison at the five-year follow-up. A sixth of all released prisoners (16.1 percent) were responsible for almost half of the recidivism by the five-year follow-up period.

In particular, sex offenders were again one of the least likely groups to recidivate generally. Only murderers and drunk drivers were less likely to generally recidivate. In relation to specific recidivism, only 1.7 percent of those convicted of rape were likely to be rearrested for rape within the five-year follow-up period. This is actually a decrease from those offenders released in 1994 (Langan and Levin, 2002). Thus, there is great consistency between the 2002 study and the 2014 study on recidivism.

In 2019, Alper and Durose examined the recidivism of sex offenders released from custody over a nine-year follow-up period (2005–2014). Within nine years, rape and sexual assault offenders were less likely to be rearrested than other offender groups, but they were more likely to be rearrested for rape or sexual assault (three times as likely: 7.5 percent versus 2.3 percent). Sixty-seven percent of sex offenders were rearrested for general offenses as compared to 84 percent of other non-sex offenders. Over half of the rearrested sex offenders were subsequently convicted. This line of research indicates the importance of follow-up periods. Recidivism for sex offenders increased from three-year to nine-year follow-up time frames.

While these government reports provide a great deal of information about recidivism among sex offenders and other criminals, the results should be examined with caution. As noted in the preceding section, victims of sex offenses do not always report their victimization. As such, the reports must be looked at with skepticism due to the official data that their analyses are built on. In addition, when evaluating official reports, we must be careful in conflating sex offenders with rapists as official data largely collects information on rapists; all delineations of sex offenders are seldom fully examined. Despite this fact, these official studies indicate that sex offenders are one of the least likely groups of offenders to recidivate. To further evaluate this conclusion, we must examine peer-reviewed research in the area. The next section looks at academic research on the topic of sex offender recidivism.

RESEARCH ON SEX OFFENDER RECIDIVISM

Sex offenders have been argued to be greater risks for recidivating than other types of criminal offenders. This is, however, one of the biggest myths about sex offenders according to Center for Sex Offender Management (2001). While the Center for Sex Offender Management makes this bold assertion, the fact is that criminologists do not know which offender type is more likely to recidivate. Hanson (2000) argued that it is difficult to know if a sex offender will reoffend because some do and some do not. "Every case has its own set of unique features, along with a bewildering array of potentially relevant characteristics" (Hanson, 2000, p. 1). Peer-reviewed research evidence can be found to support an argument that sex offenders pose a greater threat of recidivism or that sex offenders are less likely to recidivate than other types of offenders (Furby et al. 1989; Hanson and Bussiere 1998; Sample 2001). While only future research and time will be able to disentangle the mixed findings related to sex offenders, this section explores research conducted on sex offender recidivism.

One quick note before we begin this discussion. Most of the research that will be reviewed here is prior to 2000. The reason for this is that the study of sex offender recidivism has largely been conflated with current policies that attempt to socially control sex offenders. These policies include sex offender registration and notification (SORN), civil commitments, and residence restrictions. Most of the recidivism research in relation to sex offenders today looks at the effectiveness of these policies. While these are inherently recidivism studies, we will leave this recidivism research for Chapters 11 and 12, where we address the impact of these policies individually. Likewise, studies that focus on the impact of treatment on sex offender recidivism (which looks promising in curbing recidivism according to Kim, Benekos, and Merlo, 2016) will be explored in Chapter 13, which deals with the topic of treatment of sex offenders.

In terms of sex offender recidivism research, many studies have examined the perception that sex offenders are more likely to reoffend than other types of offenders utilizing official sex offender recidivism rates; these studies have come to many different conclusions. Like other research on recidivism noted above, Bynum (2001) argued that the special case of sex offender recidivism has been defined and measured in three primary ways: subsequent arrest, subsequent conviction, and subsequent incarceration. Because of this, reliance on "measures of recidivism as reflected through official criminal justice system data obviously omit offenses that are not cleared through an arrest or that are never reported to the police" (Bynum, 2001, p. 2). From his examination of the literature, Bynum (2001) concluded that studies on "sex offender recidivism vary widely in the quality and rigor of the research design, the sample of sex offenders and behaviors included in the study, the length of follow-up, and the criteria for success or failure" (p. 8). Further, due to these methodological and conceptual differences, there is often a perceived lack of consistency across studies of sex offender recidivism.

Lisak and Miller's (2002) research on repeat rape and multiple offending among sex offenders is not a recidivism study per se, but it does speak to the subject. Lisak and Miller (2002) argue that most rapists are never punished by the criminal justice system, whether through lack of reporting or lack of evidence. Their study of 120 subjects' self-reported acts that met the legal definition of rape or attempted rape illustrated that a small number of offenders are responsible for the majority of rape offenses. Through questionnaire research, Lisak and Miller found that 63.3 percent of the subjects reported committing repeat rapes against multiple victims. As well, repeat offenders perpetrated just under six sexual offenses. This is consistent with Marvin Wolfgang's conception of the career criminal. With this study in mind, we turn to the research on recidivism.

What Constitutes Sex Offender Recidivism?

The conceptual dilemma surrounding recidivism also depends on what offenses are accepted as reflecting recidivism. Furby, Weinrott, and Blackshaw (1989) wrote that to "recidivate is to relapse into former patterns of behavior" (p. 7). Some criminologists will argue that the recommission of any criminal offense qualifies as recidivism. According to Furby et al., however, there is "no single best definition of what constitutes recidivism for sex offenders . . . in the majority of cases it will be advisable to define recidivism as the recommission of any *sex* offense." In Furby and colleagues' view, then, the best way to determine sex offender recidivism is to explore only the recommission of sex offenses.

Studies have examined sex offender recidivism as well as general recidivism (or the recommission of *any* offense). From a review of sex offender recidivism studies, Sample (2001) argued that despite "methodological difficulties, differences in sample size, and variability in follow-up lengths, most studies report inconsistent levels of reoffending among sexual offenders" (p. 106). Fortunately, most recent studies tend to evaluate both general and specific recidivism as well as delineating technical violations that offenders may have committed.

Meta-Analyses of Sex Offender Recidivism

Two studies are viewed as essential in understanding sex offender recidivism: Furby, Weinrott, and Blackshaw (1989) and Hanson and Bussiere (1998). These two studies rely on **meta-analysis** as their underlying analytic strategy. A study that incorporates meta-analysis collects the data used in previous empirical research and combines that data to analyze findings across multiple studies. The strengths of meta-analysis are that it can be replicated by others and creates large sample sizes predicated on the work of other social scientists. There are also weaknesses of the meta-analysis as an empirical strategy. Meta-analyses lose detail across the different studies utilized since studies included different variables and different measurements of similar variables. Meta-analyses also rely on the subjectivity of the researcher as coding decisions about variables must be made at every stage of the analysis. The problem with this is that two different researchers could code similar variables in much different fashions. Despite these limitations, meta-analyses are useful techniques to gauge findings across multiple studies in an area. This is especially helpful with sex offender recidivism.

Furby et al. (1989) reviewed the evidence provided by prior sex offender recidivism studies. Overall, Furby et al. (1989) evaluated 42 studies (N) that examined the recidivism of sex offenders. These studies were conducted from 1961 through 1988. The studies examined included follow-up data on male sex offenders with sample sizes greater than ten cases. The information gained from past studies included a description of the sample, the time frame of follow-up, the measure of recidivism, and the recidivism rate. "The most common definition of recidivism [was] conviction of another sex offense" (Furby et al. 1998, p. 21). The key limitation of this study was that the majority of studies evaluated relied on official statistics and were subject to victim underreporting. Due to the fact that the samples used in the studies were so heterogeneous in terms of sample size and treatment, the meta-analysis was not performed on the data (Furby et al., 1989). Despite the limitations of the study and the abandonment of meta-analysis, the qualitative findings from the study are still instructive.

10

Furby et al. (1989) concluded that despite "the relatively large number of studies on sex offender recidivism, we know very little about it . . . methodological shortcomings are present in virtually all studies, making the results from any single study . . . hard to interpret" (p. 27). Furby et al. (1989) tried to evaluate the incidence of sex offender recidivism in the 42 studies. This effort was stifled due to differential follow-up periods or the inclusion of all offenses within the study. It was impossible to determine the extent of recidivism among the various studies of sex offenders. The only conclusion they could make from the studies was the qualitative suggestion that the longer sex offenders were followed, the more likely they were to recidivate, albeit across all offense categories rather than sex offenses specifically.

The other key finding from the Furby et al. (1989) research concerned differentiation between various types of sex offenders. Again, the studies evaluated were not well suited to address recidivism across sex offender typologies. A qualitative review of the research indicated mixed results when it came to pedophiles. Some of the studies indicated similarity between pedophiles and other types of sex offenders. Other studies suggested pedophiles were less likely to recidivate than other sex offenders. Overall, the Furby et al. (1989) study's conclusions are discounted by criminologists. The study failed in its empirical designs and the ex post facto qualitative nature of the research renders the conclusions irrelevant. The study should get a great deal of credit for being a call to research action in this area, which other academics would take up.

A decade later, Hanson and Bussiere (1998) succeeded in completing a meta-analysis of studies on sex offender recidivism where Furby et al. (1989) failed. From studies gathered by examining the PsychLIT and National Criminal Justice Reference Service, an international sample of 87 studies (representing 28,972 sex offenders) was generated. Due to various methodological issues, the final N of articles analyzed was 61 studies.

The average recidivism rate for sex offenses was only 13.4 percent, while the average recidivism rate for any offense was 36.3 percent. Of the demographic variables, only age and marital status predicted sex offense recidivism; the impact of these variables was further exacerbated if an offender had committed prior sexual offenses, had victimized strangers, had an extra-familial victim, began offending at an early age, had a male victim, or had engaged in diverse sexual crimes. General recidivists were those most likely to have used force against their victims and less likely to have selected child victims. Hanson and Bussiere (1998) argued that their findings "contradict the popular view that sexual offenders inevitably reoffend . . . even in studies with thorough searches and long follow-up periods the recidivism rate almost never exceeded 40 percent" (p. 357).

The importance of the Hanson and Bussiere (1998) study is that it outlined the factors that should and should not be evaluated in the study of sex offender recidivism. The best predictive factors included interest in child victims, age, and marital status (Hanson and Bussiere, 1998). Other factors like criminal lifestyle (antisocial disorders and lengthier criminal histories), sexual criminal history, and failure to complete treatment only indicated moderate to small effect sizes on sex offender recidivism (specific and general). The factors identified by Hanson and Bussiere (1998) form the primary variables seen in sex offender recidivism studies.

Correlates of Sex Offender Recidivism

Hanson (2000) outlined all of the variables that are linked to the likelihood of sex offender recidivism. These include negative childhood environment, social/demographic factors, psychological maladjustment, general criminality, sexual deviancy, offense characteristics, and clinical presentation. Negative childhood environment includes whether or not the subject was sexually abused as a child, the presence of general family problems, and negative relationships with either the father and/or the mother. Social and demographic factors include age, low socioeconomic status, lack of education, deficient social skills, and race. Psychological maladjustment refers to low intelligence, issues with depression, anxiety, general psychological problems, and alcohol abuse. General criminality refers to criminal history (as adult or child; if the crimes were violent or non-violent; if the crimes were sexual or non-sexual), and psychopathy and antisocial disorder. Deviant sexuality includes deviant sexual preferences, phallometry or penile plethysmography (PPG) of the blood flow to the penis when shown sexually suggestive imagery of rape of children, prior sex offenses, early onset of sex offending, and deviant sexual attitudes. Offense characteristics include violence in addition to the sex offense, if the offense was a rape, if the offense included child victims, sex of the child victims, if the child victims were related, victims who were strangers, victim empathy, denial, and low motivation for treatment. The field of criminology tends to focus primarily on criminal history variables, offense characteristic variables, and socio-demographic variables.

Criminal history, sexual and non-sexual offenses, stands as one of the key concepts that are evaluated in sex offender recidivism studies. The problem with this is that it is common that sex offenders do not have criminal histories. Take for instance research that occurred in Arkansas. Walker and McLarty (2000) examined the characteristics of sex offenders in the Arkansas sex offender registry from September 1, 1997, to February 1, 1999. They found that the majority of the offenders (97 percent) were male, White (75.4 percent), between the ages of 30 and 69 (61 percent), and the majority of the offenders were from Arkansas (54.9 percent). The average offender committed 1.55 sex offenses and the majority of the offenders (53.3 percent) were charged with first degree sexual abuse. Most importantly, in relation to recidivism, sex offenders were predominantly first-time offenders (73 percent of sample). This could indicate that this was the sex offender's first time offending or that this was the offender's first offense that resulted in arrest. This finding was also found in a sample of Finnish child sex offenders (less than 25 percent of the sample had a previous sex offense; Laajasalo et al., 2020).

Sample (2001) examined official data sources in Illinois to analyze sex offender recidivism. She found that from 1990 to 1997 sex offenders represented only 1.2 percent of the total criminal charges in Illinois, and the number of sex offenses remained stable over this time period as well. The typical offender was male, did not differ racially, and was similar in age to other types of offenders. Most importantly, sex offenders did not reoffend at a higher rate than other types of offenders.

When examining sex offenders who committed only sex offenses in their criminal history, Sample (2001) found that the majority of crimes included adult victims, not adolescent victims as popularly portrayed in the media. More importantly, sex offenders, of any type, had a little over a 6 percent rearrest rate within five years of the same offense and most sex offenders were not rearrested for sex offenses. Finally, sex offenders "with child victims had lower rates of rearrest for any sex crime than those who victimize adults, the one exception being child pornographers" (Sample 2001, p. 162).

Hanson and Bussiere (1998) also identified age as a key predictor of sex offender recidivism. Doren (2006) examined the effect of aging on sex offender recidivism through an expanded review of the literature. Based on his review, Doren (2006) argued that the risk of recidivism for sex offenders decreased with age. Unfortunately most studies reviewed had sample size issues; samples were too small to make generalizable and valid conclusions. Likewise, most studies suffered from multiple empirical shortcomings. Even almost 20 years later, studies were suffering the same fate as the Furby et al. (1989) research.

Other studies indicate that juvenile sex offenders are not more likely to reoffend than their adult counterparts. McCann and Lussier (2008) indicated that juvenile sex offenders were unlikely to commit another sex offense (12 percent) but were much more likely to generally recidivate (53 percent). Chu and Thomas (2010) concluded that juvenile sex and non-sex offenders were similar in relation to sexual re-offending; 14.3 percent of non-sex offenders and 9.9 percent of juvenile sex offenders sexually recidivated. Calleja (2015) compared a sample of juvenile sex and non-sex offenders. Of the 166 subjects, only 3 percent of sex offenders recidivated compared to 23.4 percent of non-sex offenders who generally recidivated. While only using a two-year follow-up, there was not a single instance of a sex offense for those who recidivated. Laajasalo and colleagues (2020) found that only 1 percent of child sex offenders recommitted a sexual crime over a seven-year follow-up period. This cumulative body of research indicates that juvenile sex offenders are not very likely to recidivate like their adult counterparts.

An alternative approach to exploring the impact of age on sex offender recidivism came from Zimring and colleagues (2007; 2009). Zimring, Piquero, and Jennings (2007) examined the continuity of sex offending across juvenile and adult sex offending. To date, little research has examined sex offenders in this manner. Zimring et al. (2007) used data from three birth cohorts in Racine, Wisconsin, to evaluate the continuity of sex offending as one moves from teenager to adult. The juvenile sex offenders in the cohort that subsequently committed a sex offense as an adult was very small; this suggested that there was not continuity between youthful and adult sex offending. In addition, sex offenders seldom recidivated. The biggest predictor of adult sex offending was the number of general offenses committed as a juvenile. Finally, concentrating on juvenile sex offenders to reduce recidivism will miss over 90 percent of those offenders who were sexual offenders as adults.

Zimring, Jennings, Piquero, and Hays (2009) further explored the persistence of sex offending as juveniles grew into adulthood. Using the second Philadelphia, Pennsylvania, birth cohort, Zimring et al. (2009) found that 92 percent of prior sex offenders had no previous official contact with police for a sex offense. As with their previous efforts, Zimring and colleagues (2009) found that general offending as a juvenile was the best predictor of sex offending as an adult. Overall, sex offenders in this study had low recidivism rates. Being a juvenile sex offender did not increase the likelihood of sex offending as an adult.

Reingle (2012) noted that there were very few longitudinal research designs used in the study of sex offender recidivism that linked juvenile and adult offending. For the most part, sex offenders are not specialists when engaging in crime. Rather, sex offenders tend to be generalist offenders who commit a variety of crimes. Reingle's (2012) overall assessment of the link between sex offending as a juvenile and as an adult is that sex offenders tend to be habitual offenders who offend sexually only occasionally. Thus, research indicates that sex offenders are not perpetual sex offending machines that will only sexually recidivate.

Sample and Bray (2003) examined the underlying proposition of sex offender recidivism. The proposition is that sex offenders were more likely to recommit their crimes (i.e., sex crimes) than other types of criminals. The second assumption is that some types of crime (drug use, burglary, etc.) serve as gateway offenses that lead to sexual offending. From an analysis of official criminal data in Illinois from 1990 to 1997, Sample and Bray (2003) found that of the sex offenders in Illinois, 93 percent were not rearrested for another sex offense. Only 3 percent of offenders who were convicted of a non-sex offense were rearrested for a sex offense. Sample and Bray's research supported the work of Zimring and colleagues (2007; 2009) and Reingle (2012).

In addition to criminal history and age, Hanson (2000) also identified several other concepts associated with sex offender recidivism. Marital status was linked to sex offender recidivism; those who are single are more likely to recidivate (Hanson,

2000). Those who are unemployed are more prone to recidivism. Edwards (2008) argued that treatment reduces recidivism. Schultz (2008) noted that sex offenders with no treatment had a recidivism rate of 18.5 percent, whereas the recidivism rates for violent and drug offenses were 30 percent and 25 percent, respectively. According to Schultz (2008), intense "psychological counseling has been shown to lower sex offender recidivism rates" (p. 87). More on this line of research will be discussed later in Chapter 13.

The Link Between Sex Offense Type and Recidivism

The casual use of the term "sex offender" leads to a definitional and measurement problem and one that necessarily obscures any differences among offenders and offenses. Beyond scientific investigation, policy makers as well as the community in general may benefit from knowing whether different types of sex offenders will recidivate differentially. Current sex offender legislation implies similarity across all types of sex offenders and offenses regardless of type of offense, age of victim, or age of offender in relation to age of victim.

Sample and Bray (2003) conclude that sex offenders are not the homogenous group of offenders the laws seem to assume. In terms of general recidivism, where general recidivism is measured with a felony arrest within five years of the qualifying sex offense, offenders in the child molestation category (i.e., the touching or fondling of victims younger than 18 years old) had the highest rate of recidivism at 51.9 percent (Sample and Bray, 2003). Offenders in the pedophilia category, which includes offenses involving sexual penetration of victims 12 and younger, had a much lower recidivism rate at 31.4 percent (Sample and Bray, 2003). Among offenses involving penetration, those who victimized adults 18 and older (rape) had higher recidivism rates than offenders who victimized children (pedophilia) and teenagers (hebophilia). In short, Sample and Bray report statistically significant differences in recidivism rates across different types of sex offenders.

Hanson (2000) linked sex offenders and child victims to higher levels of recidivism. According to Hanson (2000), multiple studies report that a sexual interest in children is associated with a greater risk of recidivism. The Association for the Treatment of Sexual Abusers (2008) noted that the recidivism rates for all sex offenders tended to range from 14 to 20 percent over a five-year follow-up period. In particular, pedophiles who molested boys and rapists who victimized adult women were the most likely types of sex offenders to recidivate, 52 percent and 39 percent, respectively (Association for the Treatment of Sexual Abusers, 2008). Research on the link between SVP laws and recidivism is new. As of 2008, Levenson found no existing research evaluating the impact of **civil commitments** on sex offender recidivism. This could be linked to the fact that so few sex offenders are actually released from civil commitment. As Levenson (2008) noted:

> Inquiry into the effectiveness of civil commitment is especially problematic due to the extremely small number of individuals released from commitment programs and the long follow-up periods necessary to efficiently evaluate recidivism rates after involuntary treatment. Confounding this issue is the difficulty in determining whether any

> observed reduction in recidivism is due to treatment effects, maturation, concurrent implementation of other legislative initiatives, the decreasing trend in violent crime rates, or other factors (p. 46).

Another area of research on civil commitments evaluates the length of time that sex offenders are committed to treatment facilities. Levenson (2008) argued that despite the increasing number of those sex offenders committed, release from such programs is exceedingly rare.

Studies aggregately analyzing a variety of sex offenders while assuming heterogeneity are likely to produce misleading conclusions. Some studies indicate that sex offenders with adult victims are more likely to recidivate. Other studies indicate that sex offenders with victims that are 18 and younger are more likely to recidivate. As with the entire study of sex offender recidivism, the exact answer to which group is more likely to recidivate is unclear. What is clear is that all sex offenders should not be treated the same when it comes to recidivism.

Drawing Conclusions from Sex Offender Recidivism Research

Hanson and colleagues concluded that the recidivism rate for the majority of sex offenders is around 10 to 15 percent over a five-year follow-up period. For a ten-year follow-up period, the recidivism rate jumps to 20 percent. Across any follow-up period in any given year, the recidivism rate for sex offenders seldom reaches over 40 percent. The recidivism patterns for rapists and child molesters are similar (Hanson, 2000). While Hanson's conclusion serves as the overall conclusion of sex offender recidivism, these numbers should be considered tentative. Sex offender recidivism research results from the overreliance on official crime statistics. In addition, these studies largely ignore all sex crimes to focus on the most serious iterations of sex crimes, rape. These results could change if better data were available and the focus was not on primarily rape crimes. Even with this overuse of official data, the findings of sex offender recidivism studies, the research conclusions that sex offenders do not reoffend at high levels is amazingly consistent, even with the development of more stringent public policies (SORN, residence restrictions, and civil commitments). The next section explores the conclusions we can draw in relation to sex offender recidivism.

CONCLUSION

It is commonly believed that sex offenders are more likely to recidivate than any other type of criminal offender. While this belief is linked to conservative values and negative attitudes towards sex offenders and crime in general (DeLuca et al., 2018), evidence to support the arguments that when compared to other types of offenders, sex offenders pose either a greater or lesser threat of recidivism exists throughout the literature (e.g., Furby et al., 1989; Hanson and Bussiere, 1998; Langan et al., 2003; Maddan, 2008; Sample, 2001). The general evidence-based conclusion is that there is no overall conclusion regarding reoffending habits among sex offenders. Recent research utilizing official data indicates that sex offenders have relatively low recidivism rates; this finding is robust across studies. However, official data cannot account for the dark figure of crime.

In their review of 49 articles, Furby et al. (1989) noted the "truly remarkable" difference in reported recidivism across studies. Some studies report recidivism rates above 50 percent whereas other findings suggest a marginal reoffending rate. In a prior literature review of sex offender recidivism, Quinsey's (1984) conclusion still resonates today. Quinsey (1984) stated that the "difference in recidivism across studies is truly remarkable; clearly by selectively contemplating the various studies, one can conclude anything one wants" (p. 101). Criminologists simply do not know whether sex offenders are more or less likely to recidivate than other classifications of offenders. This can be attributed to the differences across sex offenders (child molesters versus rapists), methodological issues, or the reliance on official data.

What is most troublesome from the mixed findings on sex offender recidivism is that the notion that sex offenders are more likely to recidivate forms the basis of most contemporary criminal justice policies that attempt to control sex offenders. SORN, civil commitments, and sex offender residence restriction policies were all based on beliefs about sex offender recidivism. If the underlying basis of such policies is faulty, do these policies have any chance of success in curbing sex offender behavior? This question is addressed in the next two chapters.

KEY TERMS

civil commitment
deterrence
follow-up period
general recidivism
meta-analysis
recidivism
specific recidivism

EXERCISES

1. Discuss the differences between general recidivism and specific recidivism.
2. What are the variables linked to sex offender recidivism? Explain.
3. According to Chapter 10, which type of criminal offender is most likely to recidivate?
4. Explain recidivism in terms of rearrest, reconviction, and reincarceration.
5. Discuss the concept of technical violations. Should technical violations be considered recidivism? Explain.

ESSAY QUESTIONS

1. Find a recent news story on sex offenders. Was the sex offender a first-time offender or did he/she have a history of sex offending? What type of sex offender was the story about? Discuss the characteristics of the victim.
2. Before reading Chapter 10, what did you believe about the link between sex offenders and recidivism? Did reading Chapter 10 change your mind?
3. Find a research article that addresses sex offender recidivism. Summarize the article. Be sure to focus on what kind of data was used (official or survey) and the factors that led to recidivism.

11

SEX OFFENDER REGISTRATION AND NOTIFICATION LAWS

Chapter Objectives

After reading this chapter, students will be able to:

- Trace the evolution of sex offender registries in the United States.
- Identify the key laws that govern sex offender registration and notification policies.
- Explain how each law enhances sex offender registration and notification.
- Outline the legal challenges and criticisms of these laws.
- Examine the impact of sex offender registration and notification policies on sex offending and sex offender recidivism.

INTRODUCTION

In Chapter 10, we examined the hypothesis that sex offenders were more likely to recidivate than any other category of criminal offender. As was illustrated through empirical research, the veracity of this belief is highly dubious. What is unfortunate about the myth of sex offender **recidivism** is that this notion serves as the underpinning of most sex offender policies today. These policies include **sex offender registration and notification (SORN)**, residence restrictions, and civil commitments. Chapter 11 focuses on SORN; Chapter 12 examines residence restrictions and civil commitment policies in the United States. The key piece of SORN legislation policy in use today is named after the victim of a convicted sex offender who recidivated multiple times: Megan Kanka.

On July 29, 1994, seven-year-old Megan Kanka was playing outside of her house in Hamilton Township, New Jersey, when her neighbor from across the street, Jesse Timmendequas, offered to show her his new puppy if she followed him to his house (Simon, 1998). Megan, like most children, found the lure of a puppy irresistible and followed Timmendequas into his residence. There he proceeded to rape and murder her. Upon arrest, it was discovered that Timmendequas had two previous convictions for crimes against little girls; in 1979 he was convicted of attempted aggravated assault on a five-year-old girl, and in 1981 he was convicted of sexually assaulting a seven-year-old girl. He served time for both convictions.

Megan's parents argued in court that they would never have allowed their daughter to play outside alone if they knew that a twice-convicted sex offender lived next door (Bureau of Justice Statistics, 1998, p. vii). The murder of Megan Kanka would garner massive national media attention and serve to enhance the evolution of ***sex offender registration*** *policies. Sex offender registration had been around since the 1980s, but notification was not a feature of earlier versions of the laws. Megan's Law would change that.* ***Megan's Law*** *and a host of other legislation sought to refine the sex offender registration policy. Based on these laws, community notification became the central feature of all contemporary sex offender registries.*

Chapter 11 explores the implementation of recent SORN laws in the United States. In particular, Chapter 11 describes the legal evolution of these laws, the inner workings of registry systems, the rationale for notification, criticisms of the policy, and the research surrounding the effectiveness of SORN. As will be seen, the effect of SORN policies is just as dubious as the notion of sex offender recidivism that these laws are based on.

SORN POLICIES

Specialized sex offender laws have been in existence since the 1930s; early laws came in the form of sexual psychopath laws. These sexual psychopath laws attempted to confine sex offenders for longer periods of time with the intent of forcing treatment on sex offenders (Farkas and Stichman, 2002; Levenson and D'Amora, 2007). Sex offender registration laws themselves date back to the 1950s in California. The sex offender registry in California gained little traction due primarily to information sharing across law enforcement agencies and the courts; especially in this time period where there was no widespread use of computers, keeping records of all offenders across the criminal justice system, the records of sex offenders in particular, was largely impossible. As such, these laws dissolved into history very quickly. The 1980s saw a revival of the registration of offenders. These registries were not focused on sex offenders per se, but all offenders who had recidivated multiple times. These habitual offender registries were in effect for the late 1980s; but these registries were once again hampered by information sharing across law enforcement agencies and courts both within and across states.

To this point it is important to recognize that while there were registration policies for sex offenders, there was no semblance of community notification with the exception of law enforcement agencies and courts. Registration is merely the collection of names and information in a database. Notification is the process of disseminating information contained within a registry. While registration had been a failure going into the 1990s, notification would have been a disaster; keeping up with sex offender registration information would have taken much time and effort while notification would always have occurred late due to the data collection abilities of the time. Technology in the form of more advanced computers would make the process of registration and notification more attainable.

In 1994, the United States began a movement to better protect its citizens from the threat of sex offenders. This movement stemmed from a series of highly publicized incidents where the sex offender had a prior record of committing sexual offenses; Megan Kanka is one example of the cases over this period. This and the common misperception that sex offenders pose a higher risk of reoffending than other types of criminals led to a host of legislation being passed in the United States in the 1990s and the 2000s at both the federal and state levels.

Federal SORN Legislation

Several federal statutes have governed the states in developing, implementing, and maintaining a sex offender registry and guidelines on how to release the information contained in the registry to other agencies and the public. These codes are the Jacob Wetterling Crimes Against Children Act of 1994, Megan's Law of 1996, the Pam Lychner Sexual Offender Tracking and Identification Act of 1996, and the Adam Walsh Child and Safety Protection Act of 2006. These laws "focus principally on sex offenders due to their perceived high rate of reoffending" (Hebenton and Thomas 1997, p. 22). While other laws have been enacted to modify the registration process (The Departments of Commerce, Justice, and State, the Judiciary, and Related Agencies Appropriations Act of 1998 and the Campus Sex Crimes Prevention Act of 2000), the above laws form the basis of modern sex offender management.

> *In October of 1989, 11-year-old Jacob Wetterling, his brother, and a friend were sent to the video store to pick up a couple of movies. They rode their bicycles to the convenience store in their St. Joseph, Minnesota, neighborhood. On the way back home, Jacob, his brother, and his friend were stopped by a masked man holding a gun standing in the middle of the road. The masked man forced them off the road and into the woods. He told them to lie down in a ditch and not to move or he would shoot them. The man told Jacob's brother to run off into the woods and then did the same to Jacob's friend. As the last boy ran off into the woods, he turned around and saw the man grab Jacob. A minute later, the boy, thinking it was now safe, went back to where he had seen the man grab Jacob. Both Jacob and the man were gone. While it was long unknown what kind of offender abducted Jacob, many jumped to the conclusion that it was a sex offender based on the fact that a nearby halfway house dealt primarily with sex offenders (Levenson and D'Amora, 2007). Patty Wetterling (1998) and her husband were outraged that the investigation could have been helped with the pool of potential suspects that may have resided at the halfway house. The Wetterlings became victim's rights advocates for advancing laws to recover missing children.*

For nearly 27 years, Jacob Wetterling's whereabouts were unknown. In 2015, 53-year-old Danny Heinrich confessed to the sexual assault and murder of Jacob; the confession stemmed from Heinrich's arrest for child pornography. When Jacob originally went missing, Heinrich had been interrogated several times in 1990. At this time, Heinrich was also linked to the sexual assault of another boy, Jared Scheierl. While considered a bit of an "oddball," Heinrich did not have any previous convictions for sex crimes. Heinrich's confession stemmed from a plea deal, where he would plead guilty to a single, federal count of child pornography, but he would not be held accountable for the Wetterling or Scheierl crimes. This plea was approved by Jacob's parents for the sake of closure. The unusual plea was contingent on admission of guilt and giving the location of Jacob's remains. Heinrich admitted to sexually assaulting Jacob and then shooting him twice in the back of the head; Jacob's body was located in a field some 30 miles from where the abduction had occurred. While the plea deal will only provide Heinrich with a 20-year prison term, it is believed that he will be committed to a mental facility upon release, where he will likely spend the rest of his life.

Following the abduction of Jacob Wetterling in 1992, the Jacob Wetterling Crimes Against Children Act of 1994 established that a state's Attorney General shall create a registry that will contain information, primarily the address, of convicted sex offenders that have been released into the public. Either the court, the prison, or law enforcement officials were required to inform the offender of their duty to register, to register the offender, and to transfer the information to the agency in the state that is in charge of the registry. States also had to maintain accurate, current registries so that information could be disseminated to law enforcement agencies in the state (Sorkin, 1998, p. 16). To obtain this end, the offender must verify his or her address at least once a year. This act did not specifically outline the development of registration requirements for several types of individuals: out-of-state offenders, juvenile offenders, federal offenders, and military offenders. States were, however, encouraged to establish guidelines to deal with these kinds of offenders.

A procession of court cases dealing with the constitutionality of the registration and notification requirements of the Jacob Wetterling Act illustrated the need for change in the SORN laws. These legal criticisms are presented on page 234. In addition to legal challenges, the community itself was pushing for more knowledge when it came to the transmission of information contained on sex offender registries. This fact and the rape and murder of Megan Kanka gave the United States its next sex offender registration law.

Megan's Law, in 1996, amended the notification guidelines of the Jacob Wetterling Act. Megan's Law stated that information about registered sex offenders could be released under purposes that are allowed by a state's laws. This duty is entrusted to the agency in the state that maintains the registry; any enforcement agency could then release information that is necessary to protect the public. Basically, Megan's Law eliminated confidentiality of the registration data collected by the states and mandated the release of sex offender information (Semel, 1997, p. 21). The public would now be provided information about the presence of more dangerous sex offenders within their neighborhoods. Thus, a state-sanctioned label would be added to any labels that an individual already had received in the past (i.e., through his/her trial, conviction, or prison experience). The goal of Megan's Law was to give the public the ability to protect itself from convicted sex offenders residing in an area.

> *Later in 1996, another law would be passed bearing the name of yet another victim of a sexual offender: Pam Lychner. Lychner, a Houston real estate agent, and her husband were supposed to show a house to a potential buyer; when they arrived, they met William David Kelley, who claimed to be from the cleaning company hired to clean the house. Kelley suggested they had missed some areas of the house and needed to complete the cleaning. What the Lychners did not know was that Kelley had a history of sexual violence. The offender attempted to sexually assault Lychner, who narrowly escaped when her husband happened on the offense in progress; both the Lychners fought off and detained Kelley in the closet until the police arrived. Ironically, Lychner was sued by her assailant for the mental anguish of being detained in the closet after he received parole for the incident. Lychner died in a plane crash before the end of that lawsuit, but the next piece of legislation in the evolution of SORN laws in the United States would have her name.*

The Pam Lychner Sexual Offender Tracking and Identification Act, in late 1996, directed the Federal Bureau of Investigation (FBI) to establish a national database to track the whereabouts and movement of sex offenders across state borders. This national registry would do two basic things: (1) obtain all information on sex offenders from the states on a continuing basis and (2) act as sex offender registries in those states that had not yet established a minimally sufficient sex offender registration program and to act as such until those states had implemented their own registries that were up to the guideline standards. The Lychner Act also prescribed more stringent registration requirements such as a ten-year mandatory registration period for convicted sex offenders and lifetime registration for sexually violent predators (Sorkin, 1998, p. 17). This act made the ability of the government to provide information to the public much easier, especially when sex offenders and their acts crossed state lines.

In the late 1990s, other legislation helped further the evolution of sex offender registration laws in the United States. The Departments of Commerce, Justice, and State, The Judiciary, and Related Agencies Appropriations Act of 1998 (U.S. Attorney General, 1999) was passed without a specific preceding incident or victimization; this law gave the states more flexibility in achieving compliance with the aforementioned laws. It extended the date of compliance and gave the states more discretionary power to implement procedures and policy required by the Jacob Wetterling Act. Most importantly, this act also provided suggestions and encouragement to the states when dealing with juvenile sex offenders, federal sex offenders, and sex offenders adjudicated in the military.

Another change in sex offender statutes occurred in October of 2000. The Campus Sex Crimes Prevention Act was passed to further amend the Jacob Wetterling Act of 1994. It required sex offenders, who were already required to register, to provide notice to any institution of higher education in which the offender is employed, carries on a vocation, or is a student. This information was to be added to the offender's file with all of the offender's other registration information. This act also required "institutions of higher education to issue a statement advising the campus community where law enforcement agency information is provided by a state concerning registered sex offenders may be obtained" (Campus Sex Crimes Prevention Act, 2000). Finally, this act noted that nothing contained in its wording could be "construed to prohibit an educational institution from disclosing information provided to the institution concerning registered sex offenders," making it legal for the institutions of higher learning to notify the campus community of the presence of sex offenders on campus.

> *The most recent advance in sex offender registry law stems from a crime against a child in the 1980s. Adam Walsh was abducted on July 27, 1981, outside a mall in Hollywood, Florida. Later, his body was found decapitated. Otis Toole, a convicted serial killer, later claimed responsibility for the atrocity, but was never prosecuted due to a lack of evidence. He later retracted his confession, causing confusion for Walsh's family. In either case, Toole died in 1996 of liver failure. The truth in this case was never known. John Walsh, host of America's Most Wanted, began his victims' rights advocacy with the death of his son Adam.*

The Adam Walsh Child Protection and Safety Act of 2006 sought to increase the impact of all sex offender policies. Under this law, SORN and other sex offender laws across the states were both standardized and intensified in their impact on sex offenders. In fact, this law is the most comprehensive piece of sex offender legislation to date. In general, this act expanded the definition of sex offenders; provided a blueprint for the civil commitment of sex offenders; created sentencing enhancements and mandatory minimum sentences at the federal level; placed no statute of limitations on all federal sex crimes; indicated when a sex offender was to be registered (before the completion of sanctions), what information was to be included in the registry, the inclusion of DNA, fingerprints, photographs, and valid identification information on the registry; and mandated regular in-person verification in addition to the mail-in verification. As well, access to registry information through state Internet websites was ensured for all registered sex offenders; a state could opt to omit information on Tier 1 offenders, their employment information, and any attendance at any school. A national sex offender websites registry was created and compiled by the FBI. An emphasis was placed on child sex offenders through Project Safe Childhood, which integrated federal, state, and local criminal justice agencies against child sex offenses and exploitation.

The Sex Offender Registration and Notification Act (SORNA) (Title I) portion of the Adam Walsh Act also identified special sex offender populations that had been omitted from most previous laws. Juveniles, Native Americans, and international sex offenders entering the United States would all be subject to registration and notification if they had been convicted of sex offenses previously. Across all sex offenders, this law created a three-tiered system to help the community identify the risk of recidivism of sex offenders residing in the community. The assessment of sex offenders (discussed more on page 233) into Levels 1, 2, and 3 was linked to mandatory registration periods of 15 years, 25 years, and life for the respective levels of risk. The law also allowed for a reduction in registration period for acknowledged good behavior by the offender; Tier 1 offenders who had a good record or received treatment could reduce their sentence by 5 years and Tier 3 juvenile offenders could decrease their registration period to a minimum of 25 years.

The other important feature of the Adam Walsh Act is the increase in duration of registration. Instead of 10 years, the Sex Offender Registration and Notification Act increased registration to a minimum of 15 years; this was up from the 10 years proscribed by the Pam Lychner Act. Additionally, the most serious sex offenders were required to verify their residence every three months instead of the old six-month or annual verification. Essentially, the Adam Walsh Act replaced the Jacob Wetterling Act.

Finally, the Adam Walsh Act also identified and defined child exploitation enterprises, which are punishable by 20 years to life, and increased federal sentencing enhancements for sex offenders. The sex offender sentencing enhancement was ten years in addition to the rest of the sanctions the offender received from conviction. The overall law also provided a great deal of funding to the states and various nonprofit organizations for research and procurement of data repositories. The Sex Offender Management Assistance (SOMA) program provided money to the states to upgrade and/or implement a state registry.

The Adam Walsh Act is so specific that many states have not adopted its guidelines. This failure to comply stems from registration requirements linked to the treatment of juveniles on the registries. Many states do not follow some provisions of the Adam Walsh Act because juveniles are treated too generously. The ideas that color the view of sex offenders are very strong. More on state registries will be discussed in the next section.

Changes to SORN laws continue into the present, albeit, not at such a breakneck pace. In 2015, the Military Sex Offender Reporting Act required the Department of Defense to register sex offenders convicted through court martial in the national database. In 2016, the International Megan's Law required sex offenders traveling internationally to provide advance notice of their plans; jurisdictions were also required to transmit these international travel disclosures. Additionally, the Attorney General continues to modify guidance to assist jurisdictions in implementing and enforcing SORNA.

This section has outlined the evolution of sex offender laws at the federal level in the United States. The passage of the Adam Walsh Child Protection and Safety Act in 2006 indicates that sex offender laws in the United States still have room for change and growth. The next section examines the implementation of SORN in the states and how the states have dealt with assessing sex offender risk.

SORN at the State Level

The different SORN laws throughout the states are relatively similar since the guidelines provided by the federal government must be followed if states want to qualify for government funding for help with data repositories and training. The major differences in states' sex offender registration laws pertain to how often an offender must verify his or her address, how offenders can verify their residence, if juveniles are required to register, if the laws apply to out-of-state offenders, when offenders can petition the court for relief of registration, and how community notification is to occur. The Adam Walsh Act sought to standardize these criteria. Offenders who are required to register generally are those who have been found guilty of a sexually violent offense, a sex offense, or certain offenses where the victim was a minor (this includes those on probation or parole or anyone else serving any other form of community punishment); any person who was acquitted on the grounds of mental disease or defect; out-of-state sex offenders who were required to register in their own state; and convicted sex offenders from other countries.

Pinpointing enactment of the federal law is easy as compared to state laws, where various factors led to the enactment of SORN at various times. Table 11.1 shows the implementation year of SORN in the states.

Many of the states in Table 11.1 already had a habitual offender registry, if not a sex offender registry, in the 1980s. The real advance of registration in the 1990s was the advent of community notification. The years in Table 11.1 correspond to the year

TABLE 11.1 SORN IMPLEMENTATION DATES BY STATE OR DISTRICT

State	Year	State	Year
Alabama	1998	Nebraska	1997
Alaska	1994	Nevada	1998
Arizona	1996	New Hampshire	1996
Arkansas	1997	New Jersey	1993
California	1996	New Mexico	1995
Colorado	1998	New York	1995
Connecticut	1998	North Carolina	1996
Delaware	1994	North Dakota	1995
Florida	1997	Ohio	1997
Georgia	1996	Oklahoma	1998
Hawaii	1998	Oregon	1993
Idaho	1993	Pennsylvania	1996
Illinois	1996	Rhode Island	1996
Indiana	1998	South Carolina	1999
Iowa	1995	South Dakota	1995
Kansas	1994	Tennessee	1997
Kentucky	1994	Texas	1999
Louisiana	1992	Utah	1996
Maine	1995	Vermont	1996
Maryland	1995	Virginia	1997
Massachusetts	1999	Washington	1990
Michigan	1995	Washington, DC	1999
Minnesota	1998	West Virginia	1993
Mississippi	1995	Wisconsin	1997
Missouri	1995	Wyoming	1999
Montana	1995		

Source: Vasquez, Maddan, and Walker (2008).

that notification was added to the state's registry. You will note that many states were creating registries with notification before the passage of Megan's Law in 1996. In fact, Washington State was the first state to implement a notification component to their habitual offender registry in 1990, six years before the advent of Megan's Law.

Two processes are triggered by community notification: The assessment of the offender's risk of reoffense and the level of community notification. "Disclosure has become a key public policy concern, and the police, as the key agency in undertaking notification to the wider public, are at the forefront of managing this sensitive area of police work" (Hebenton and Thomas, 1997, p. vi). The SORN laws are intended to help law enforcement agencies be more proactive in combatting sex crimes. "Police have . . . been entrusted to release highly sensitive information which will have an impact on both the offender and the community" (Wilson, 1999, p. 59).

The goals of sex offender registration laws are to deter offenders, "provide law enforcement with additional investigative tools, and increase public protection" (Matson and Lieb, 1996, p. 2). The information law enforcement agencies receive about sex offenders can potentially help in identifying suspects with similar crime patterns (Matson and Lieb, 1996). The public protection goal is the one that is most observed in the courts when deciding the constitutionality of registration and notification laws.

The groups to whom information is disclosed are generally related to the assessment level of the sex offender (Hebenton and Thomas, 1997, p. 30). Levels of assessment are based on the seriousness of the offense, the offender's criminal history, offender characteristics, and community support (Hebenton and Thomas, 1997, p. 29). Hebenton and Thomas (1997) wrote, "Risk assessment . . . forms the basis of any strategy for monitoring sex offenders in the community" (p. 17).

According to the recently enacted Adam Walsh Act, sex offenders in many states are required to register as one of three levels of risk: Level 1, Level 2, and Level 3. A Level 1 offender is an offender who is considered to pose a low risk of reoffending, warranting minimal notice for protection of the community. Only state agencies such as the police have to be notified of this type of offender; oftentimes these offenders will still appear on Internet registries. A Level 2 offender is any offender who is considered to pose a moderate risk of recidivism to the community, warranting limited notice for the protection of the community. State licensing boards and schools at all levels are notified about a Level 2 offender, plus state agencies such as the police; Level 2 offenders will always be present on Internet sex offender registries. A Level 3 offender is an offender who is considered to pose the highest risk of reoffense to the community. For Level 3 offenders, all of the entities for Level 1 and Level 2 are notified as well as the rest of the community. This level usually also contains sexually violent predators. Some states have even added a fourth level that deals exclusively with sexually violent predators, but, on the whole, there are generally only three offender risk levels.

Levenson and D'Amora (2007) noted that just under half of the states utilize risk levels in relation to which groups in the public are notified to the presence of sex offenders. The other states do not make any distinctions as to the potential threat of sex offenders. The states without assessment notify the public as to the presence of all sex offenders, no matter how little or great their threat of recidivism. It has been argued that not distinguishing between sex offenders who pose a high risk of recidivism and those who pose a low risk of recidivism further dilutes the impact of SORN policies.

The reason that many states do not utilize **sex offender assessment** is that it is both costly and time consuming. It is estimated that the average cost per offender is between $800 and $1,000; the average time to complete an assessment is roughly one month. When there are thousands of sex offenders on a state's registry, it is not difficult to see how the costs accrue and the time to assess offenders becomes unmanageable. This is why many states select to simply notify on all sex offenders.

The justification for public notification is public safety. "Notifications are a proactive procedure that attempt to prevent/deter crime before it occurs. By receiving information about an offender's presence, the public is better able to use precautions which they may otherwise not practice" (Wilson, 1999, p. 59). Notification can also "inhibit the offender's ability to select and contact the next victim because the public will be aware of the offender's preferences and practices" (Wilson, 1999, p. 59). This is the dilemma in community notification laws: "Balancing the public's right to know with the need to successfully reintegrate offenders into the community" (Zevitz and Farkas, 2000, p. 1).

Currently, three types of notification laws exist (Zevitz and Farkas, 2000). The first type is notification by law enforcement to the community. In this type of notification strategy, the police either go door-to-door informing members of communities or holding town hall meetings where those who attend are informed of the presence of sex offenders. In the second type it is incumbent on the public to come to the police station or go to Internet sites to learn of the presence of registered sex offenders; the police agency's responsibility is limited to only providing information concerning a given sex offender. The third type is where the sex offender is required to personally inform the community in which he or she lives; this is completed in a door-to-door fashion (this occurred in Louisiana, but has since been replaced by an Internet registry). Today, the most utilized form of notification is the second type. Citizens learn of sex offenders in their neighborhood primarily by going to the Internet and searching for registered sex offenders.

Simon (1998) wrote that the very essence of SORN laws supports the idea of the new penology, or the management of different types of offenders. Simon (1998, p. 453) argued that the risk of recidivism has long preoccupied decision makers in designing criminal justice policy; Megan's Law names a "subpopulation or category of persons as its target." Defenders of the laws argue that they are not "punitive," in that their primary purpose is not to punish offenders, but to protect potential victims from dangerous offenders; any punitiveness is only an unavoidable side-effect. This idea of community protection derives from the idea that sex offenders are more likely to recidivate than other types of offenders (see Chapter 10). The next section focuses on how the courts have handled some of the legal challenges to the sex offender laws of the United States.

Legal Challenges to SORN

Several legal issues were raised by sex offender laws in the U.S. judicial system; these constitutional issues concerned due process rights, the double jeopardy and the ex post facto clauses of the Constitution, and, in a few cases, the right against cruel and unusual punishment in respect to the registration and notification provisions of all the SORN laws. Most of these legal challenges have been resolved in the courts at various levels and are discussed here (SMART, 2013).

Due process issues in SORN revolve around a sex offender's ability to participate in their registration and assessment. When SORN first went into effect, sex offenders who had recently been convicted of a sex offense or were on probation/parole for a sex offense were automatically placed on the registry. Technically, these offenders were not sentenced under an existing registry law. As such, early sex offenders who were convicted before the law was enacted argued that they had not received adequate due process of law. The courts at all levels rejected this claim. SORN was applied to all convicted sex offenders regardless of when their conviction occurred as long as they were currently under some form of correctional supervision (prison, jail, probation, or parole).

The other primary due process issue revolved strictly around notification. As noted above, many states do not follow a tier assessment in deciding which sex offenders pose the most serious threat of recidivism; these states just notify the community about all sex offenders. Likewise, this is often completed through the Internet. In *Connecticut Department of Public Safety v. Doe* (2003), the Supreme Court examined blanket notification of all sex offenders via the Internet. The Court held that a state's failure to assess a sex offender's risk of recidivism was not a due process violation. This is why many states' citizens have access to registered sex offenders' information online.

Double jeopardy in the legal system suggests that an offender is punished twice for committing the same offense. Many sex offenders convicted prior to the implementation of SORN argued that a prison term followed by parole and probation was their sentence. To add registration and notification on top of those punishments was a violation of double jeopardy; SORN was an added punishment in essence. The courts have rejected this claim outright. Across cases, courts at all levels have held that SORN is not a punishment; rather, SORN is a mechanism by which the public can protect itself. As such, the legal concept of double jeopardy does not apply.

The legal argument that had the greatest chance of success was the potential violation of the ex post facto clause. The ex post facto clause suggests that a person cannot be held liable for behavior that a law once considered legitimate, but subsequently finds illegitimate. For example, when prohibition was initiated, all people who had consumed/possessed alcohol up to that point could not be tried for that behavior unless they engaged in the same behavior after the new law was implemented. A person cannot be held responsible for behavior that had been previously deemed legal by statute. Early sex offenders in SORN were convicted, but not under a law that required registration/notification. This would seem to suggest a clear violation of ex post facto laws. Yet, the courts have not ruled in favor of these sex offenders. Again, because SORN was considered to be a non-punitive measure designed to promote public safety, the ex post facto claim was dismissed across the courts as non-punitive.

Finally, some cases have used the Eighth Amendment's prohibition on cruel and unusual punishment as a basis for appeal. Sex offenders suggested that the law placed a heavy burden on them, costing them social ties, jobs, and resulting in potential altercations with the public. While these arguments, and more, will be discussed in the next section, the principle that SORN is not a punishment helped the courts easily dismiss all Eighth Amendment claims.

The federal and state court case law indicate one key fact: SORN laws are here to stay and are becoming more uniform across the nation with each new piece of legislation passed and each new case heard by the courts. The registration of sex offenders has effectively been upheld as constitutional by the different courts. This has been true in every type of case (ex post facto, double jeopardy, cruel and unusual punishment, or due process rights) that has been heard by the judiciary. The notification provisions of most sex offender registration laws were originally found to be unconstitutional in the mid-1990s. Since the passing of Megan's Law, states have followed the new standards of notification to change their laws and have gained constitutional acceptance. While the Adam Walsh Act of 2006 has opened the door to retrying some of these legal challenges, the precedent in *Connecticut Department of Public Safety v. Doe* (2003) will most likely hold as state and federal laws become more standardized (SMART, 2013). The next section evaluates general criticisms of SORN policies.

Criticisms of SORN

In addition to the legal challenges to SORN, multiple criticisms have met the policy from sex offenders and critics of the law. The criticisms include net widening, potential vigilantism, the negative impact of SORN on sex offenders, consensual sex between teenagers, a false sense of public safety, and the unintended effects of state-sanctioned labels of sex offender behavior. This section evaluates these claims.

Critics of SORN claim that this policy serves to widen the net of criminal offending. Net widening occurs when additional behavior by a criminal group becomes considered criminal. For instance, SORN has created two new behaviors that are criminal for sex offenders: failure to register and failure to verify an address. Sex offenders are subject to new criminal laws that other criminals are not subject to. A corollary to the principle of net widening is the extra supervision that sex offenders receive from the community. As will be shown on page 240 sex offenders are more likely to be rearrested for non-sex offense related crimes than sex crimes. SORN makes it likely that the public and law enforcement will closely monitor sex offenders; this could, and often does, result in these offenders being caught engaging in some illicit behaviors.

In 2012, Patrick Drum, a vigilante, was convicted of killing two sex offenders who had been on the sex-offender registry in the state of Washington. During the investigation, he suggested that he was going to kill registered sex offenders until he was captured. The fear of vigilantism is pervasive for some sex offenders; they believe that because their address is open to the public, vigilantes can find them and either kill them or force them to suffer in some other way. Despite this criticism, vigilantes pursuing revenge against registered sex offenders are an extremely rare phenomenon.

Other critics of SORN argue that these policies have a profound negative impact on the lives of sex offenders. When a sex offender's information is posted for everyone to see, this could result in a loss of family, friends, and employment. This is a massive social sanction that is placed on sex offenders through SORN. The research on these assertions indicates conflicting results; these studies will be discussed more on page 239. Community reintegration of convicted offenders is a major focus of corrections today; this correctional goal is greatly impeded when the offender is publicly stigmatized by the SORN policy.

An early issue with SORN was in relation to teenagers having sex. In most states the age of consent is 18. What happens if two teenagers have sex when one is 18 and the other is 17? Statutory rape occurs when an individual who is not old enough to consent has sex with an individual who is old enough to give consent. Many individuals were convicted as sex offenders and then forced to register even though there was no actual sex offense involved. The sexual activity was consensual, but the age was restricted. In many of these types of cases, it was a boyfriend and a girlfriend engaging in consensual sex. In these instances, upset parents reported the sexual activity to the police. Since these early days of SORN, many states have placed a three-to-five-year age gap in the ages of consent to get around this issue. As such, an 18-year-old could have sex with a 17- or 16-year-old without being placed on a sex offender registry. While many states have implemented this stopgap, this still remains a problem in a handful of states.

Another issue with SORN is that it creates a false sense of security for members of society. It is believed by many that the existence of sex offender registries acts as a deterrent for sex offenders. While this claim will be evaluated below, the fact is that SORN does little to protect the community in and of itself. Members of the community must utilize information on a registry to protect themselves and loved ones. Whether or not people do regularly review the information on a registry is questionable. The only group that regularly checks registries are parents; the majority of other citizens seldom, if ever, review information on a registry. Likewise, due to the nature of victim reporting of sex offenses, there exists a portion of sex offenders who are not present in registries.

Finally, one criminological theory, the labeling perspective, suggests that SORN may have undesirable effects on sex offenders. The labeling perspective argues that individuals who are labeled, usually through convictions, are likely to internalize that label and begin to act in ways that are consistent with that label. In the case of sex offenders, the label of "sex offender" as brought about by both the conviction and the subsequent registration/notification could spur sex offenders to recidivate. While the theory is interesting in its claims, the bulk of the research (see the next section) has indicated that there is no labeling effect of SORN policies.

THE EFFICACY OF SORN POLICIES

Research that seeks to determine how effective SORN is at curbing sex offending has raised serious questions about the ability of SORN to reduce sex offending and recidivism. Numerous studies have evaluated the success of SORN policies. Studies in this area take on several different approaches to the problem of sex offenders. Research has evaluated how the public and law enforcement feel about SORN. Studies have evaluated the impact of SORN on the sex offenders themselves (i.e., how being a registered sex offender effects their day-to-day lives). Research has taken a time-series approach to evaluating the incidence of sex offenses before and after the implementation of SORN. Finally, empirical work has examined individual recidivism patterns among sex offenders. These various lines of inquiry are addressed in the following sections.

Public and Law Enforcement Opinions of SORN

Generally, sex offenders, across all forms of sex crimes, elicit fear from the public (Kernsmith, Craun, and Foster, 2009); members of society tend to think SORN policies are necessary to prevent the predatory threat of sex offenders and their inevitable recidivism (Quinn, Forsyth, and Mullen-Quinn, 2009). Proponents of SORN argue that such laws are effective because they inform the public of the presence of sex offenders in the community, thereby enabling them to take action to protect themselves. These laws are also thought to reduce sex crimes because the public is able, and more likely, to report suspicious behavior by sex offenders. This was supported by the research of Phillips (1998), who found that over 60 percent of the respondents to a survey felt that sex offender laws made sex offenders act better than if their criminal history was not known; the majority also felt safer with the laws in place. These results were later confirmed by Levenson et al.'s (2007) work and multiple opinion polls on public perceptions of sex offenders and treatment.

Matson and Lieb (1996) conducted a survey of law enforcement officials in the state of Washington. Law enforcement agencies noted several advantages of SORN: They felt the laws provided better community surveillance, created better public awareness, deterred future crimes by the offender, and promoted child safety. Although law enforcement officers found several advantages to the registration and notification laws, they also noted several disadvantages. Law enforcement agents felt the laws created more work to their already large work load. Adding to this were the problems inherent in collecting information from courts and other agencies dealing with sex offender registration. Overall, law enforcement officers held a very harsh general view of sex offenders (Matson and Lieb, 1996; Tewksbury and Mustaine, 2013).

Salerno et al. (2010) evaluated public perceptions of juvenile sex offenders. Family law attorneys in the sample supported registration for juveniles, but less so than for adults. In addition, attorneys who were prosecutors and the general public supported registration for adult and juvenile sex offenders equally. This was the case in spite of the fact that people tend to view juvenile sex offenders as less dangerous. It was suggested that the threat of juvenile sex offenders was mediated by how old the offender was (age) and the severity of the offense; the younger the offender and the less serious the offense, the less likely the public was to view juvenile sex offenders as dangerous. Additional research by Stevenson et al. (2013) suggested that support for juvenile registration decreases with higher levels of education.

A growing body of research suggests that the public is not utilizing sex offender registries for protection. Indeed, Anderson and Sample (2008) reported that the vast majority of Nebraska residents had not ever accessed the state's sex offender registry. The research does indicate that the public is aware of the existence of the registry, but people tend not to check the information on registries. What is more problematic for the policy is that for those who do have or regularly check the registry, very few of these individuals will take protective measures as a result of the information they received off the registry (Anderson and Sample, 2008). These results were later supported by the work of Sample, Evans, and Anderson (2011). Even with a widespread lack of usage of the registries, people still favor harsh punishments for sex offenders (Comartin, Kernsmith, and Kernsmith, 2009) and support SORN policies even though there is a doubt that sex offender registration is an effective method of deterrence (Schiavone and Jeglic, 2009).

SORN's Impact on Sex Offenders' Lives

One of the criticisms of SORN is it has negative consequences for the sex offenders in their personal lives. Matson and Lieb (1996) found that sometimes there could be an overreaction to sex offenders upon community notification in neighborhoods. This could lead to harassment and embarrassment of sex offenders or their families. While there is plenty of anecdotal evidence to suggest that sex offenders could be targeted by a vengeful community, no research has yet confirmed that sex offenders will suffer reprisals due to the fact that their personal and residential information is easily attainable via the Internet or through other means.

The adverse consequences of registration and notification policies on sex offenders' daily lives are debatable. Levenson, D'Amora, and Hern (2007) indicated that less that 25 percent of sex offenders in Indiana and Connecticut suffered adverse effects from current sex offender policies; this has been supported by work in Florida (Levenson and Cotter, 2005b). Levenson and Cotter's work has been refuted by sex offender samples in Kentucky (Tewksbury, 2005; Tewskbury and Lees, 2006), Texas (Worley and Worley, 2013), and Wisconsin (Zevitz et al., 2000), where sex offenders suffered moderate to severe forms of harassment in addition to legal issues, feelings of despair, and collateral consequences (lack of employment opportunities) of registration (Ackerman, Sacks, and Osier, 2013). The majority of these studies rely on qualitative analyses of small, non-probability samples of sex offenders.

Lasher and McGrath (2012) qualitatively reviewed eight studies to evaluate the social and psychological impact of SORN on adult sex offenders. Of the 1,503 subjects evaluated, Lasher and McGrath (2012) noted that the research designs and analyses were very similar across the eight studies. In their review, it was noted that sex offenders were seldom the targets of vigilante attacks. Very few individuals in this study reported exclusion from housing and jobs as a result of notification in their communities. Finally, while the sex offenders generally reported negative psychological consequences, most sex offenders also acknowledged the benefits of the public monitoring their behavior. For now, the impact of SORN on sex offenders seems to suggest a moderate effect at best.

SORN and General Sex Offending

A large amount of research on SORN has evaluated the impact of SORN on general sex offending patterns. The hypothesis being tested is if SORN has a general deterrent effect on individuals engaging in rape and other sex offenses every year. Time-series analysis is the best way to gauge if the incidence of sex offending increases, decreases, or remains the same before and after a law goes into effect.

Vasquez, Maddan, and Walker (2008) conducted the first time-series study to evaluate whether SORN laws impact the incidence of rape as counted in the Uniform Crime Report (see Chapter 1 for a full discussion). While they set out to evaluate all 50 states, data constraints limited their study to only ten states: Arkansas, California, Connecticut, Hawaii, Idaho, Nebraska, Nevada, Ohio, Oklahoma, and West Virginia. Pre- and follow-up periods of data ranged from three to five years. Vasquez et al.'s results indicated that only three states (Idaho, Ohio, and Hawaii) had statistically significant decreases in the incidence of rape after the implementation of SORN; one state, California, actually had a statistically significant increase in the incidence of rape. For the remaining six states, there was no difference before and after the implementation of SORN. Since this first time-series analysis, there has been little support illustrating that SORN impacts general sex offending patterns.

Sandler, Freeman, and Socia (2008) conducted a more intensive time-series analyses of New York's SORN law. Unlike the Vasquez et al. (2008) study, Sandler et al. examined various types of sex offending; these disaggregated offenders included rapists, child molesters, sexual recidivists, and first-time offenders. Their analyses before and after the implementation of SORN in New York indicated that the laws had no impact on the incidence of sex offending in New York. Additionally, 95 percent of sex offenses were completed by first-time offenders. SORN had little impact on the incidence of rape, but probably had no impact on recidivism as well. Freeman et al. (2009) also found that SORN did not affect the rate of plea agreements for sex offenders in New York.

Ackerman et al.'s (2012) research used state data from 1970 to 2002 to examine the impact of SORN on the incidence of rape in the United States. Like earlier time-series analyses, this study indicated that SORN was not effective in curbing rape across the United States. This research also supported the findings of the initial Vasquez et al. study from 2008.

In the most supportive time-series analysis of the impact of SORN on the incidence of rape, Maurelli and Ronan (2013) studied data from 1960 to 2008 across each state. In their findings, 17 states showed statistically significant decreases in the incidence of rape. While this is one of the best results to indicate success for SORN, 32 of the states studied showed no changes before and after implementation of the registration and notification. This was true even controlling for differential notification strategies and registration practices.

The results of time-series analyses on SORN indicate a consistency in findings. SORN has no general deterrent effect on sex offending. Even the most supportive of results show that only 17 of the 50 states had any kind of statistically significant decrease associated with the implementation of SORN. The next section presents the research that has examined whether SORN has any impact on sex offender recidivism; this is also known as specific deterrence.

SORN and Recidivism

Empirical research on the effect of SORN laws on recidivism has been limited (Zevitz and Farkas 2000, p. 1), but has grown over the past decades. In one of the earliest evaluations, Schram and Milloy (1995) compared 139 Level 3 sex offenders to 90 sex offenders who were not subject to notification in an effort to gain basic demographic characteristics of Level 3 sex offenders and compare recidivism between the two groups of offenders in Washington. Schram and Milloy (1995) focused on the demographic characteristics of both juvenile (N=14) and adult (N=125) Level 3 sex offenders. A high percentage (79 percent) of juvenile offenders recommitted any kind of offense while on the registry, but only 43 percent of the juveniles committed a new sex offense. Of the adult sample, less than half (43 percent) recidivated, but not for a sex offense. Only 14 percent of the adult sample committed a new sex offense. When the entire Level 3 sample was compared to a control group of sex offenders who were not notification eligible, Schram and Milloy (1995) found that community notification had little effect on sex offender recidivism. Further, "the estimated rates for sex offenses are remarkably similar for each group throughout the follow-up period" (p. 17). Since this early study, research has been persistent in its refutation of SORN as a mechanism for inhibiting recidivism.

An extensive study of the potential influence of registration and notification on sex offenders was presented by Petrosino and Petrosino (1999). Petrosino and Petrosino evaluated the efficacy of sex offender laws on a sample of 136 offenders in Massachusetts. Petrosino and Petrosino (1999) examined criminal history records of each offender to "determine how many of the serious sex offenders would have been in the registry before the instant offense . . . how many of the offenders committed stranger-predatory instant offenses . . . and if the Massachusetts Registry Law might have prevented them" (p. 148). Cumulatively, the sample contained 291 prior arrests (0 to 19 per offender), which included property, sexual, and violent offenses. Only 74 of the 291 prior arrests were for sexual offenses; thus only 27 percent of the offenders would have been eligible for registration. "Prevention by notification or police investigation could not have occurred for most cases" (Petrosino and Petrosino 1999, p. 148). Petrosino and Petrosino (1999, p. 154) concluded that "the public safety potential of the Massachusetts Registry Law to prevent stranger-predatory crimes . . . is limited." Further, of the "instant offenses committed by 136 serious sex offenders, we rated the potential of notification reaching the eventual victim as good in only four stranger-predatory cases and as poor to moderate in two others."

One of the best evaluations of SORN laws occurred in Washington State in 2005. Recall, Washington was the birthplace of notification in the country in 1990. The Washington State Institute for Public Policy examined recidivism rates of Washington sex offenders (N=8,359) during three periods, before the 1990 initial notification act, after the 1990 act, and after the 1997 amendments of **sex offender notification**. This report indicated that general, non-sex offense felony recidivism remained the same, while both sex and violent felony recidivism decreased substantially. To date, this is the best evidence supporting the utility of SORN laws.

Research on sex offender recidivism has largely followed the design utilized in Washington State and come to similar conclusions. In Minnesota, the Minnesota Department of Correction (2008; Duwe and Donnay, 2008) released a report that compared Level 3 offenders from 1997 to 2002 to a control group from 1990 to 1996 and a control group consisting of Level 1 offenders (N=405). Their results suggested that sex offender notification policies were having a deterrent effect, but that sex offenses were the least likely offenses perpetrated by those who did recidivate. This suggests that the policies were better at net widening than preventing sex crimes. Research from New Jersey (Zgoba et al., 2008) utilizing a similar design (N=550) concluded that SORN policies had no impact on sexual reoffending and argued that the "growing costs may not be justifiable" (p. 2). These results were further validated by the work of Tewksbury, Jennings, and Zgoba (2012) and Jennings, Zgoba, and Tewksbury (2012). Similar results were found in Wisconsin (Zevitz, 2006) and Iowa (Tewksbury and Jennings, 2010); these results also hold internationally in England (Piquero et al., 2012).

Maddan, Miller, Walker, and Marshall (2011) examined the effectiveness of SORN in Arkansas. Using a quasi-experimental design, this research evaluated the recidivism of the first three waves of sex offenders registered in Arkansas (1997 to 1999) in relation to a comparison group of sex offenders from a decade earlier (1987 to 1989). The research found that the vast majority of offenders were, at least officially, first-time offenders; these individuals would not have been subject to SORN for their most recent convictions. Most importantly, the results indicated that very few sex offenders in either group recidivated; the recidivism rate for sex offenses in the treatment group (N=2,165) was 9.5 percent and in the comparison group (N=755) was 10.8 percent. The SORN policy was not statistically significant in predicting if offenders would recidivate. These results are consistent with Letourneau et al.'s (2010) results that found only 8 percent of sex offenders subjected to SORN had new sex crime charges.

Further research by Levensen et al. (2010) found that only around 10 percent of sex offenders were convicted of failure to register. In relation to this subset, only 11 percent were rearrested for a sexual offense. Thus, even those who fail to register were not considerably more likely to be dangerous.

Research has found almost identical results when focusing on juvenile sex offenders. Letourneau et al. (2009) studied juvenile sex offenders in South Carolina who had been registered (N=1,275). The follow-up time average was nine years. Their survival analysis indicated that registered juvenile sex offenders were unlikely to be recharged with a sex offense. Rather, they found that juveniles who were on the registry were more likely to receive a new non-sex-offense-oriented charge. While these findings may be consistent with youth impulsivity, the results are similar to findings in adult sex offender studies. Letourneau et al.'s research was supported by the work of Caldwell and Dickinson (2009).

The studies on the efficacy of SORN policies are limited, but the results seem to indicate that the public and law enforcement officials like the policy, but the policy itself seems to have no meaningful influence on sex offender recidivism (general or specific deterrence). There is little empirical evidence that supports the utility of SORN; the empirical studies that have been conducted found no significant influence of these policies on sex offenders' reoffending patterns.

The conclusions here are further cemented by a trio of studies. In a 20-year, systematic follow-up study of Megan's Law, Call (2018) argued conclusively that Megan's Law has not had a significant impact on rates of sex offending or sex offender recidivism. This conclusion was also repeated by the 20-year follow-up study of SORN completed by Zgoba and colleagues (2018). In a 25-year follow-up of SORN policies, Zgoba et al. (2021) completed a meta-analysis of 18 key studies, spanning 25 years of research, exploring the impact of SORN on recidivism. Their analysis indicated that "the implementation of SORN over the last 25 years has demonstrated no effect on the deterrence of adult offenders" in relation to general or specific recidivism (p. 19).

CONCLUSION

As can be seen from Chapter 11, the impact of SORN is highly questionable. As Levenson and D'Amora (2007) noted, "Law makers designed registration as a tool to assist law enforcement agents to track sexual criminals and apprehend potential suspects" (p. 172). Notification served to increase public awareness, thereby strengthening community members' ability to protect themselves from potential victimization. What is clear from this review of SORN is that sex offenders are not recidivating to the degree imagined by the public, or the public is not utilizing sex offender registries to their fullest benefit. Terry (2011) suggested that SORN is ineffective at curbing sex offenses and sex offender recidivism because it is not rooted in the crime prevention theoretical framework.

Two more anecdotes serve to complete our discussion of the ineffectiveness of SORN policies. At the beginning of Chapter 11 we discussed the case of Megan Kanka and how she was brutally raped and murdered by a twice-convicted sex offender living next door. Indeed, this incident brought about notification components to sex offender registration across the United States. What is seldom mentioned in this story is that Jesse Timmendequas did not live alone. Timmendequas shared the house across the street from Megan Kanka with two other previously convicted sex offenders, Joseph Cifelli and Brian Jenin. Timmendequas' defense team tried to even insert reasonable doubt in the jury at trial by suggesting one of these two convicted sex offenders had raped and killed Megan. Both had alibis at the time of the crime and were not considered legitimate suspects in the case by law enforcement officials. To this day, neither Cifelli nor Jenin have been subsequently convicted of a sex offense.

■■■

The second anecdote we present indicates a logistical issue for SORN; it is the case of Jaycee Dugard. On June 10, 1991, 11-year-old Jaycee was kidnapped while walking on her way home from school. She was missing for 18 years. In late August of 2009, Phillip Garrido and two little girls were protesting on the University of California, Berkeley campus. Their somewhat erratic behavior spurred an investigation that led to the discovery of Jaycee Dugard having been kidnapped by Garrido and his wife, Nancy. The two little girls were Jaycee's children who had been fathered by Garrido.

Phillip Garrido had been previously convicted of kidnapping and raping a girl in Reno, Nevada, in 1976; when he was released from his 50-year federal sentence in the early 1990s, he was placed on a sex offender registry. The registry did not stop Garrido from kidnapping and sexually assaulting Jaycee Dugard over the 18 years she was missing. The Garridos had forced Jaycee to live in a tent in the back yard of their house. Despite this, when community corrections officials visited the house on multiple occasions, Jaycee was never discovered in the back yard and the children were passed off as the Garridos' grandchildren. It was later found that Garrido had been incorrectly assessed in the assessment phase of his registration. This suggests the failure of the registry since probation/parole officers are oftentimes bogged down with exceptionally large caseloads, giving them little time to fully supervise their clients. Phillip Garrido was eventually sentenced to 431 years for his actions against Jaycee Dugard; his wife, Nancy, received 36 years to life.

Taken together with the evidence presented in Chapter 11, SORN policies appear to have little impact in fulfilling their goal of decreasing sex offenses or lessening recidivism rates. Many sex offenders tend to be either first-time offenders or their activities have not been reported (e.g., Danny Heinrich in relation to the Jacob Wetterling case); these sex offenders are not included on sex offender registries. All sex offenders are not going to recidivate (e.g., Joseph Cifelli and Brian Jenin). Additionally, even if a sex offender is on a registry, there is no guarantee that the offender will not recidivate (e.g., Phillip Garrido). Problems with SORN stem from knee-jerk legislation that failed to get all the facts surrounding the etiology of sex offenses. Alternatives to SORN must then be evaluated to determine if they are any better at curbing sex crimes in the United States. Chapter 12 explores two other relatively radical approaches to dealing with convicted sex offenders: residence restrictions and civil commitments.

KEY TERMS

Megan's Law
recidivism
sex offender assessment
sex offender notification
sex offender registration
SORN

EXERCISES

1. Go to your state's online sex offender registry. Locate sex offenders that live close to your residence and your university. How many sex offenders are listed in these two areas? What kind of information is available on the website? Discuss what you think about the information you found.
2. Find a recent news story on sex offenders. Was SORN a part of the story? If not, why was it not discussed? Be sure to discuss the sex offender's criminal history if it is provided in the story.
3. Find an appellate case that deals with SORN. Discuss the legal implications of the case in relation to the legal criticisms of SORN discussed in Chapter 11.

ESSAY QUESTIONS

1. Should juvenile sex offenders be subject to registration and notification? Explain your response.
2. Discuss the evolution of federal laws in relation to SORN policies in the United States.
3. What is the general consensus of research on the utility of SORN policies in the United States?

12

RESIDENTIAL RESTRICTIONS AND CIVIL COMMITMENTS OF SEX OFFENDERS

Chapter Objectives

After reading this chapter, students will be able to:

- Explain the policy of sex offender residence restrictions.
- Evaluate the underlying basis of residence restriction policies.
- Examine the effectiveness of sex offender residence restrictions.
- Explain the policy of sex offender civil commitments.
- Evaluate the underlying basis of sex offender civil commitments.
- Examine the effectiveness of sex offender civil commitment policies.

INTRODUCTION

From 2007 to 2010, the area underneath Miami's Julia Tuttle Causeway became the home for over 100 convicted sex offenders. Most of the sex offenders living under the bridge resided in tents, giving the colony of sex offenders the unofficial name of tent city; offenders also lived in shanties and campers. The reason these sex offenders lived underneath this bridge was due to a local law that prohibited sex offenders who had sexually abused minors from living within 2,500 feet of any place where children congregate (schools, parks, libraries, daycare centers, etc.); this was more than the 1,000-foot buffer mandated by state law. This law in Miami meant that there was almost no place within the Miami city limits where a sex offender convicted of sexually abusing a minor could legally reside. The Florida Department of Correction began to release these sex offenders, who had completed their prison sentences, underneath the causeway. Some of the sex offenders were even issued driver's licenses with the bridge as their home address for registration and notification purposes.

Two groups of opponents of the sex offender shantytown emerged. Some decried the squalid conditions (mounting trash, the smell of urine and feces, and the sound of vehicles perpetually overhead which led to sleep deprivation in many cases) in which were placed individuals with mental and physical illnesses. In addition, residents lacked electricity, running water, and sewage services. Dr. Pedro Greer stated in a news interview, "This is the stupidest damn law I have ever seen and it's purely mandated by revenge without any consideration for the well-being of these people—who deserve better despite the severity of their crimes." These sex offenders who have served their time cannot live with their wives, families, or lead any kind of normal life.

The other group of opponents to the shantytown recognized that these offenders committed heinous crimes and felt no sympathy or remorse for their predicament. This group opposed the shantytown due to the threat posed by a congregation of sex offenders whose ranks swelled to as many as 140 sex offenders at one point. These opponents noted two issues with the shantytown. First, there was a nearby island that served as a weekend getaway for boaters and their children; politicians attempted to get this island recognized as a park. This would have made the area under the bridge an invalid area for sex offenders to reside if the island was considered a park. Second, these opponents believed that sex offenders would not continue to live in such squalor. Theoretically, these offenders would then ignore the law, move farther into Miami, and become the threat that the law had attempted to diminish.

Regardless of the standpoint one takes, the tent city under the Miami causeway indicated a glaring problem with the reintegration of sex offenders back into the community. The sex offender colony was eventually dismantled in the winter of 2010. The sex offenders were moved to motels, apartments, and trailer parks with free rent paid for six months. As the sex offenders were moved out of the area under the causeway, they were quickly replaced by the homeless.

In addition to sex offender registration and notification policies outlined in Chapter 11, two other extracurricular criminal justice system mechanisms to deal with the sex offender threat have been implemented across the United States. The first of these policies are **residence restrictions**. These policies attempt to keep sex offenders from residing anywhere near the most vulnerable targets: children. Thus, sex offenders cannot live in dwelling places near schools, parks, and other public or private places where children may congregate en masse. The second policy is the **civil commitment** of sex offenders. This policy places sex offenders into mental facilities after they have served their time in prison or jail. In states with civil commitments, sex offenders are essentially placed in mental institutions until the doctors believe that the sex offender has been cured of their illicit sexual proclivities.

Just like sex offender registration and notification laws, residence restrictions and civil commitments are not seen to be punitive. Residence restrictions act to help society, especially children, to better protect itself from sex offenders; civil commitments help the sex offenders to rehabilitate through forced mental treatment. Are these claims true? Chapter 12 explores these two alternatives to the punishment of sex offenders and their effectiveness. We begin by exploring sex offender residence restrictions.

RESIDENCE RESTRICTIONS

Residence restrictions, sometimes referred to as **spatial restriction zones (SRZ)**, are geographic strategies focused on limiting the interaction between convicted sex offenders and children (Grubesic et al., 2008). Such geographic areas include schools, parks, preschools, bus stops, and any place where children might congregate. Burchfield (2011) noted that residence restrictions are implemented because of political motivation, public outcry, and misinformation about sex offender likelihood to recidivate.

Under residence restrictions, sex offenders are precluded from residing near SRZs, based on the belief that sex offenders are more likely to recidivate (see Chapter 10). The nearness of residence restrictions is measured in feet; various policies can range from 500- to 2,500-foot **buffer zones**, or halos, around the child congregation areas (National Conference of State Legislatures, 2006; Socia, 2011). Some of the states have included grandfather clauses for sex offenders who were living in areas prior to implementation of the policy (Levenson et al., 2007b); this is the exception rather than the rule.

Residence restrictions necessarily create two types of areas: unrestricted and restricted/partially restricted. Unrestricted areas are any places where sex offenders can lawfully reside. Restricted areas are those areas where a sex offender cannot lawfully reside; even if the residence is only partially in a restricted area, the backyard but not the front yard or house for example, the sex offender cannot lawfully reside in this location.

The origins of residence restriction policies are rooted in the drug-free zone policies of the 1970s (Walker, 2007). In 1970, the United States passed a "school zone" law which increased criminal penalties for anyone engaging in drug crimes (distribution or possession) near schools and other public places, spaces, and areas. States began to pass similar legislation throughout the 1980s. In the 1990s, legislation began to expand penalties on other types of crime in the same areas. Schools and certain public areas became "gun-free zones." According to Walker (2007), by 2000, "all 50 states had passed laws creating drug-free and gun-free zones surrounding schools" (p. 864). Expanding such policies to sex offenders was a logical next step.

The first residence restriction policy that prohibited where sex offenders were capable of living was passed in Florida in 1995. The original sex offender residence restriction law in Florida only applied to sex offenders whose victims were minors. The law focused on places where children congregated, such as schools, day care centers, and parks. Around each of these locations, the Florida law placed a 1,000-foot halo zone in which sex offenders on probation or parole could not enter without fear of prosecution. In 1996, Alabama passed the second residency restriction (Walker, 2007). By 2005, 14 states had residence restrictions for sex offenders; by 2013, 33 states had such policies (Walker, 2007).

Logue (2012a) has likened residency restrictions to modern-day banishment in which sex offenders are cast aside to fend for themselves. It is assumed that this will decrease **recidivism** among sex offenders. Unfortunately, residency restrictions may provide society with a false sense of security. This section examines residency restrictions. In particular, it evaluates the legal challenges to residence restrictions, research on the efficacy of sex offender residency restrictions, and criminal justice practitioner responses to the policy.

Legal Challenges to Residence Restrictions

Legal challenges to residency restrictions have followed similar arguments to the challenges of sex offender registration and notification policies (sex offender registration and notification [SORN]; see Chapter 11). Legal issues like due process, double jeopardy, and ex post facto claims have all been used in attempts to invalidate the law. Just as with SORN, the courts have mostly found these claims to have no merit. This is due to the fact that the goal of residence restrictions is to further the goals of community protection efforts. Because residence restrictions are meant to protect society, the policy is not viewed as punitive in nature.

In various legal challenges to residence restrictions, the findings have been inconsistent as to the constitutionality of the policies. According to the U.S. Department of Justice (2013a), some of the challenges to residence restrictions have been more nuanced than challenges to SORN. In addition to laws at the state level, many residence restrictions policies are passed at the municipal or local level. When this happens, there can be a contradiction between local ordinances and state, potentially federal, laws. In some cases, residency restrictions have been declared illegal due to conflicts with state law (*G.H. v. Township of Galloway*, 2008; *People v. Oberlander*, 2009; *People v. Blair*, 2009). In at least one case, residency restrictions for sex offenders were found to be punitive, and therefore illegal (*Commonwealth v. Baker*, 2009). In most cases, though, residency restrictions tend to be upheld due to their public safety function (*State v. Stark*, 2011).

The Supreme Court has refused to hear any cases on residence restrictions. The highest court challenge of sex offender residency restrictions to date occurred in the Eighth Circuit. In *Doe v. Miller* (2005), the court determined that "the Constitution of the United States does not prevent the state of Iowa from regulating the residency of sex offenders in this manner in order to protect the health and safety of the citizens of Iowa." Further, these laws do not violate the ex post facto clause of the Constitution in that the punitive effect of the statute does not override the legislature's intent "to enact a non-punitive, civil regulatory measure that protects health and safety." Just as with other sex offender policies, residency restrictions are not punitive, but public safety.

Research on Residence Restrictions

Most current sex offender policies are predicated on the dubious assumption that sex offenders pose a greater dangerous threat to the public than other offender groups. Greenfield (1997) found that the majority of sex offenses occur within the home, the offender has legitimate access to the victim, and/or the offender is known to the victim. Residency restrictions would have little to no effect on these sex offenses.

One of the first empirical efforts to evaluate the geographic link between sex offenders, key areas, and potential victims was conducted by Walker, Golden, and VanHouten (2001). The research evaluated sex offender housing in Pulaski County (Little Rock), Arkansas. The total N was 170 sex offenders. Walker et al. (2001) found that almost half (48 percent) of sex offenders who had been convicted of victimizing child victims lived within 1,000 feet of schools, day cares, and parks; only 26 percent of sex offenders with adult victims lived within the 1,000-foot buffer. Based on the routine activities theory, Walker and colleagues suggested that sex offenders might be "placing themselves in a position to have access to potential targets" (2001; Walker, 2007, p. 864).

This congregation of sex offenders around schools, day cares, and parks was also seen in the research of Maghelal and Olivares (2005), who found that 55 percent of all sex offenders in one Texas county lived within 1,000 feet of a school. Similar to Walker et al.'s research in Arkansas, Grubesic, Mack, and Murray (2007) found that sex offenders in Hamilton County, Ohio, resided close (within 304.8 meters) to schools. While this earlier research indicated that sex offenders tended to cluster around child congregation areas, it did not indicate how sex offenders in these areas were comporting their behavior and did not evaluate the effectiveness of residence restriction policies.

12

Very little research examines the nexus of residence restriction policies and recidivism (Levenson et al., 2007b). In 2003, the Minnesota Department of Correction examined sex offender residential patterns. Unlike the earlier studies, this study indicated that there was no statistical relationship between sex offender residences and proximity to schools, day cares, and parks. Most importantly, there was no link between residential location and recidivism of the sex offenders evaluated. Qualitative interviews with the sex offender subjects indicated that sex offenders were more likely to travel farther from their neighborhoods to find victims; the reason for this was that they would be less likely to be recognized (Minnesota Department of Correction, 2003). None of the new sex offenses was committed on school grounds or in the buffer zone nor was the crime in any way linked to the sex offender's residence.

A follow-up study further examined the link between residence restrictions and recidivism in Minnesota (Minnesota Department of Corrections, 2007). This study found that proximity to social support networks was more important in predicting recidivism than the creation of areas in which sex offenders could not reside. What is key is that sex offenders did not select victims in close proximity to their residence but traveled farther to find victims.

Research conducted by the Colorado Department of Public Safety in 2004 evaluated 130 sex offenders for up to 15 months to assess recidivism. This study did not find any congregation of sex offenders who had victimized children around schools, day cares, and parks. Rather, these sex offenders tended to be dispersed randomly throughout the study area. In addition, the Colorado Department of Public Safety (2004) found that those sex offenders who did live close to restriction areas were no more likely to recidivate than sex offenders residing in other areas; these sex offenders clustered about restricted areas were significantly less likely to reoffend. This research also indicated that sex offenders with positive social support networks were less likely to recidivate, something that is made difficult to maintain by the presence of geographic spatial zones.

One of the first peer-reviewed studies examining the link between residence restrictions and recidivism was conducted by Levenson, Zgoba, and Tewksbury in 2007. Levenson et al. (2007b) found no evidence that sex offenders who live near child congregation areas were more likely to recidivate. They do note that the instability associated with unstable housing can lead to recidivism indirectly.

Socia (2012) examined the effectiveness of residence restriction policies in New York. In particular, Socia (2012) evaluated whether such policies would curb the total number of sex crimes in New York at the county level before and after implementation of sex offender residence restriction policies. The data was able to evaluate sex offenders who had been registered and not registered through the New York sex offender registry. Across a 12-year period, Socia's (2012) results indicated that residence restriction had no impact on the incidence of sex offense recidivism.

Huebner et al. (2014) evaluated the impact of residence restrictions in Michigan and Missouri. Overall, this study found that residency restrictions did not lessen the number of sex offenders living near schools, parks, and other child congregation areas. Most importantly, the policy only minimally effected recidivism rates if at all. In Michigan, sex offenders were a little more likely to recidivate than non-sex offenders; In Missouri, sex offenders were a little less likely to recidivate. Most interesting about this study, the level of sex offense recidivism was so low that it could not be calculated by the research team.

Socia (2011) noted that no published research supports the efficacy of sex offender residence restrictions in curbing recidivism. Research in this area does indicate unintended consequences associated with the implementation of residential restrictions. Socia (2014) indicated that another line of research on residence restrictions tended to focus on housing options/availability, perceptions of the consequence of the policy on sex offender lives, and the effect of the policy on subsequent sex offending. The bulk of the research in this area has been focused on the unintended side effects of the policy.

Burchfield (2011) noted that sex offenders had a difficult time securing housing before residency restrictions went into effect in concert with SORN. Before residence restrictions, most criminals released, including sex offenders, had difficulty with affordable housing that would be located close to family, friends, and employment (Burchfield, 2011; Burchfield and Mingus, 2008; Levenson and Cotter, 2005a; Tewksbury and Lees, 2006; Zevitz and Farkas, 2000). After implementation of these policies, it became more difficult for sex offenders. There have been many studies that linked the social disorganization of neighborhoods to primary residences of sex offenders (Hughes and Burchfield, 2008; Mustaine and Tewksbury, 2008; Mustaine,

Tewksbury, and Stengel, 2006; Tewksbury and Mustaine, 2008). Sex offenders tend to have a great deal of residential mobility, moving more than other types of criminal offenders who have been released into the community (Burchfield, 2011). Generally, this mobility is a downward one into more socially disorganized neighborhoods (Mustaine, Tewksbury, and Stengel, 2006; Turley and Hutzel, 2001).

Burchfield (2011) argued that residence restrictions can push sex offenders into "sparsely populated rural areas away from social supports, cluster them together into small spaces like apartment complexes or trailer parks, or force them 'off the map' because they will not or cannot comply with the policy" (p. 414). All these outcomes make supervision by the community more difficult. This "not-in-my-backyard" (NIMBY) mentality "fails to consider the potential negative consequences of residence restriction policies and often leaves sex offenders with nowhere to go" (Burchfield, 2011, p. 413). Other research shows similar results in that sex offenders are forced out of dense, urban neighborhoods (Zandbergen and Hart, 2006; Zgoba et al., 2009). Socia (2011) noted this can lead to long-distance commutes to treatment, employment, and ability to use public transportation.

Residence restrictions research has consistently found that residence restriction policies reduced the levels of affordable housing; this has been seen in Chicago, Illinois (Hughes and Burchfield, 2008) and Franklin County, Ohio (Red-Bird, 2009). Residence restrictions research in Hamilton County, Ohio, also found that residence restriction policies reduced the total number of rental properties (Grubesic et al., 2007). Two other side effects to residency restrictions also emerged in research. First, Linden and Rockoff (2006) found that the policies led to a decrease in housing value/prices in the immediate area next to where sex offenders resided. Second, Edwards and Hensley (2001) found the residence restrictions lead to vigilante attacks against some sex offenders.

Levenson and Hern (2007) found that residence restrictions made re-entry difficult for sex offenders as it impacted housing stability, employment opportunities, and social support. This impact was intensified for sex offenders who were young adults; these offenders were prevented from living with their families in most cases. For these offenders, affordable housing was an issue when they could not live at home.

In some areas, residence restrictions leave almost no place for sex offenders to reside. Residence restrictions research in Minneapolis and St. Paul, Minnesota, found that residence restriction policies eradicated the availability of most housing (Minnesota Department of Correction, 2003). Zandbergen and Hart (2006) had similar findings; 64 percent of Orange County, Florida, was in range of schools, day cares, and parks. Once bus stops were taken into consideration, sex offenders could only legally reside in 5 percent of the surface area of the county.

Barnes et al. (2009) found that residence restrictions limited housing options for sex offenders across multiple jurisdictions; most importantly, many sex offenders actually lived in a buffer zone or in a proposed buffer zone (Barnes et al., 2009; Zgoba et al., 2009). When there is no housing in legal areas for sex offenders, research indicates that some sex offenders will select to live in illegal areas. Levenson and Cotter (2005a) suggested that residence restrictions increased homelessness among sex offenders they evaluated in Florida; this simple fact makes it more difficult for SORN and other sex offender policies to effectively supervise sex offenders. This may also push convicted sex offenders outside of metropolitan areas (suburbs or rural areas), places with fewer restrictions on sex offender residences.

Grubesic, Murray, and Mack (2008) evaluated sex offender "spatial restriction zones" in relation to demographic and socioeconomic characteristics in Hamilton County, Ohio. These findings contradict the prevailing wisdom found in other studies. In Hamilton County, unrestricted block groups had more favorable demographic and socioeconomic conditions (i.e., more educated individuals, older populace, and less unemployment) than SRZs. These unrestricted areas tended to have higher sex offender population density. Unrestricted zones did have some association to higher poverty rates. Thus, unrestricted residences were actually less socially disorganized than SRZs. Unfortunately, there was no guarantee of available housing in the unrestricted zones though.

The final area of research on residence restrictions focuses on the size of the buffer zone incorporated within cities and counties. As noted above, residence restriction policies prohibit sex offenders residing on property fully or partially within a buffer zone (Socia, 2011). Some studies have explored the relationship between the size of the buffer zones and sex offender behavior.

Socia's (2011) study on the difference in buffer zone size is one of the most important studies in this area. Socia's research was conducted in New York on 47 counties; Socia (2011) evaluated the differential sex offender residence restriction policies within each jurisdiction; the buffer zones ranged from 500 to 2,500 feet depending on the jurisdiction. Indeed, Socia's (2011) research identified 15 unique residence restriction policies. The study utilized spatial analysis to evaluate coverage area of the housing residence restrictions, neighborhood social disorganization, housing affordability, housing availability, and spatial density of housing. The results of the study indicated that the least restricted areas were also less dense and less disorganized, but were both less available and affordable. Within residence restrictions of larger sizes, "the least restricted neighborhoods ceased to be significantly less available and affordable than other neighborhoods" (Socia, 2011, p. 375).

Socia (2011) concluded that residency restrictions have many unintended consequences. The densest neighborhoods were always the most restricted. Residence restrictions increased the likelihood of emotional and financial stress, homelessness, and non-compliance with various sex offender policies. Socia (2011) surmised that residence restrictions "could force sex offenders to cluster into a handful of neighborhoods, where there may not be enough unrestricted housing left to meet the needs of these relocating sex offenders" (p. 379). The only benefit to residence restriction policies noted by Socia (2011) is that it limited sex offender housing in the most socially disorganized areas. Unlike most research in this area, Socia (2011) found that the size of the restriction buffer area did not have an effect on the social disorganization or the neighborhood density of the areas where sex offenders could reside.

Nobles, Levenson, and Youstin (2012) evaluated the impact of increasing the residency restriction buffer zone from 1,000 to 2,500 feet. They found no statistically significant relationship between larger buffer zones on the number of sex crime arrests. An interrupted time-series design also indicated no statistically significant change before and after the increase in the buffer zone area. No matter the size of the residence restriction, the policy was a failure.

Newer research tends to support earlier studies of residence restrictions. Empirical findings illustrate the ineffectiveness of these policies on sex offender behaviors like recidivism. Savage and Windsor's (2018) research did expand this line of inquiry to the impact of residence restrictions on sex offenders with child victims; they concluded that residence restrictions did not "even have the potential to substantially reduce sex crimes against children" (p. 23). Terry (2015) concluded that "moving sex offenders to socially and disadvantaged areas, away from family and other forms of support, may enhance the likelihood of reoffending" (p. 124). All-in-all, there is not much in the way of support for residence restrictions.

Practitioner Reaction to Sex Offender Residence Restrictions

Burchfield (2011) argued that there has been a backlash against sex offender residence restrictions. This backlash can be attributed to a large body of research that indicates the policy's ineffectiveness and the reality of sex offenders becoming transients. Other than academics, one of the first criminal justice practitioner groups to publicly decry residence restriction laws was the Iowa County Attorneys Association (ICAA). In 2005, Iowa implemented a 2,000-foot residency restriction for sex offenders who victimized minors surrounding places where children congregated; at the time, this was one of the most restrictive policies in the United States. According to Logue (2012a), rural motels and trailer parks began to fill up with sex offenders who had nowhere else to live; other sex offenders became homeless, living primarily in their vehicles. The Iowa residence restriction increased the number of failure to register offenses by sex offenders and law enforcement reported being unable to locate many registered sex offenders due to the new laws. Many registered sex offenders in Iowa chose to leave the state.

The ICAA (2008), in a particularly strong statement, argued that the residency restrictions did not protect the public, cost too much, and negatively impacted sex offenders' families. They based this statement on research on the lack of relationship between residence restrictions and sex offense reduction and the lack of relationship between child sex victimizations and offenders who were strangers. The ICAA also cited the net widening inherent in current sex offender policies, the number of sex offenders and their victims who had subsequently been reunited (statutory rape), and the burden placed on family members of sex offenders.

Law enforcement in Iowa had also observed the unintended consequence of sex offenders being displaced from their homes or ending up homeless. This latter consequence of displacement is a problem; finding affordable housing becomes difficult for sex offenders and negatively impacts physically or mentally ill sex offenders who can no longer live with family members who were primary caregivers. In addition, the ICAA (2008) noted the lack of a time limit for residence restrictions; once the requirement kicked in for an offender, it seemed to be for the remainder of the offender's life.

The ICAA made multiple policy suggestions. First, the ICAA (2008) suggested getting rid of the buffer zones; sex offenders would only be precluded from entering specific areas ("child safe zones") with very few exceptions and under safe circumstances. These special circumstances would only apply to sex offenders with children and with the approval of those in charge of the facilities/areas. The impetus should be on sex offenders who victimized children (less than 14) not minors (under 18). Second, the ICAA (2008) argued that local municipalities must be precluded from enacting their own buffer zones. Third, treatment must be a part of any sex offender policy (ICAA, 2008). The ICAA (2008) concluded, "These observations are not motivated by sympathy for those committing sex offenses against children, but our concern that legislative proposals designed to protect children must be both effective and enforceable" (p. 125).

The Colorado Sex Offender Management Board (Walker, 2007) also spoke out against residency restrictions. In 2007, the Kansas Sex Offender Policy Board, in league with academics and practitioners, decided to advise the Kansas legislature to "forego implementing residency restrictions and to consider other means to protect the community from sexual predators" (Walker, 2007, p. 865). Based on similar sentiments some states have changed their residence restriction policies. Iowa and Oklahoma were some of the first states to reform or repeal residence restrictions. Iowa scaled back the policy for most sex offenders in 2009. While many other states have begun to modify or repeal residence restriction laws, other states have elected to stay the course with residence restriction policies. Florida still has not reformed or repealed its residence restrictions in spite of the negative attention associated with the tent city in Miami described on page 247.

Discussion

Burchfield (2011) noted that current sex offender polices are not a panacea to the threat of victimization by sex offenders (p. 415). Sex offenders are precluded from living in locations adjacent to child congregation areas. Oftentimes residence restrictions place an increased burden on the sex offender's ability to reintegrate back into society. As Walker (2007) concluded, "the totality of the evidence at this point indicates that residency restrictions are not effective residency restrictions should be eliminated and replaced with more effective means of reducing recidivism" (p. 866). A sex offender under this policy could not live in a residence close to a school due to the nearness of children; however, under the policy, that sex offender could live in an apartment complex that contains many children. This is a major contradiction in the policy. Socia (2014) also argued that residence restrictions should be repealed and prohibited; if kept, these laws should be more targeted and tailored to particular sex offenders. Unfortunately, Casady (2009) noted that policy makers, law enforcement personnel, and the public are largely unconcerned with the struggles of sex offenders.

Other alternatives to residence restrictions may prove more effective in dealing with sex offenders. First, sex offender residence restrictions could be completely abolished. Even though research indicates the complete failure of the policies, the public is still supportive of the residence restrictions. Second, Socia (2014) suggested that the criminal justice system target the most dangerous sex offenders and apply residence restrictions only to that group of offenders using actuarial risk assessment metrics (see Chapter 13 for more details on the risk assessment of sex offenders). Third, Walker (2007) argued for child congregation locations themselves to be off-limits to sex offenders, but eliminate the halo or buffer zones. With this approach, sex offenders will have more residential choices when finding a place to live. This is also supported by research that indicates sex offenders do not offend close to their homes (Minnesota Department of Corrections, 2007).

While residence restrictions may be popular, they are not effective. Like sex offender registration and notification laws, residence restrictions do not curb sex offending behavior and tend to have negative unintended consequences that can have a detrimental impact on convicted sex offenders' future behavior. We now turn to another alternative method of dealing with sex offenders: civil commitment.

SEX OFFENDER CIVIL COMMITMENTS

In Texas, if an offender has at least two prior sex offense convictions for violent sex offenses and is deemed to be dangerous to the community, that offender is termed a **sexually violent predator (SVP)** and is eligible for civil commitment in a mental institution. That offender is sent to a treatment facility, where he/she is required to stay (inpatient) and abide by treatment requirements.

Bradton Dewayne Carter is a twice-convicted violent sex offender who was civilly committed under Texas law. During the commitment, Carter failed to follow the conditions of his commitment and treatment by the institution; Carter had assaulted employees, failed to attend meetings, and left the facility grounds. Carter was subsequently criminally charged with violating the terms of his civil commitment. In January of 2014, Carter was convicted of the felony of violation of a civil commitment. For this crime, he was sentenced to 30 years in a maximum-security prison facility. Carter could have been sentenced up to 99 years.

12

The involuntary hospitalization of individuals with mental problems has traditionally occurred for individuals who pose a danger to themselves or to others. The state takes custody of these individuals and segregates them from the public. For a state to take custody, a recent action indicating dangerous behavior on the part of the individual must be present as this is the primary indicator of "imminent risk" (Fanniff et al., 2010). When the individual is committed, it is generally limited in time. For instance, someone who has attempted suicide will be held for 72 hours to make sure that the individual is no longer a danger to him/herself. In other cases of mental illness, the review period is generally required at least every six months to one year. Traditional civil commitment is designed to release the individual as quickly and safely as possible (Fanniff et al., 2010).

The use of civil commitments has largely been reserved for civil legal procedures. The use of civil commitments to deal with criminals is largely unheard of. Between 1930 and 1960, this changed. During this time period, the United States began to implement sexual psychopath laws. These laws attempted to lessen the threat of sex offenders to the public. Since sex offenders were viewed at this time as "mentally disordered," the belief was that sex offenders were "ill and could be cured" (Fitch, 1998). Instead of incarceration, sex offenders who had perpetrated multiple sex offenses would be placed in indefinite hospitalization for the sake of treatment. By the 1950s, over half of the states had a sexual psychopath law that placed sex offenders in mental institutions rather than in prisons. The new laws were lauded as successful. In 1939, the Columbia Law Review Association thought the sexual psychopath laws could lead to great innovation in corrections. As the association suggested, "Although the manifest purpose of the act is to incapacitate sex offenders who are dangerous when at liberty, none the less it makes several contributions in the realm of individualization of treatment" (1939, p. 543).

As discussed in Chapter 9, the philosophy of punishment began to change in the 1980s to a more punitive ideal. Rehabilitation efforts and treatment were deemed to be too "soft" on crime and a focus on incapacitation and truth-in-sentencing made the old sexual psychopath laws seem to lack punitive effect. It was imperative under the incapacitation model that all criminals serve their time in prison. Schlank (2008) noted that during the sexual psychopath legislation of the mid-twentieth century, it was common for sex offenders to make themselves look more dangerous than they were so that they would qualify for treatment rather than imprisonment. As such, the earlier sexual psychopath laws were repealed in most states in the 1980s. The very era that marked the end of the old sexual psychopath laws formed the basis of the SVP statutes of the 1990s.

In the early 1990s, states began to reimagine the old sexual psychopath laws with an incapacitation spin. In Washington in 1990, the state legislature passed the first modern "sexual predator" statute (Zonana, 1997). This law would mandate that sex offenders complete their criminal sentences in prison. At the end of this sentence, sex offenders who were considered to be sexual predators, under civil statute, could then be committed to a mental institution for treatment until they were no longer considered to be a danger to society. SVPs were considered to have a "mental abnormality" that would lead to recidivism; these abnormalities can be defined so broad as to include many forms of behavior (antisocial personality traits, for instance; Zonana, 1997).

The term "SVP" is a legal term, not a clinical one. Fanniff et al. (2010) noted the wide range in terminology used for dangerous sex offenders (sexually violent predators, sexually violent persons, and sexually dangerous persons). Definitions across jurisdictions are similar: "any person who has been convicted of or charged with a sexually violent offense and who suffers from a mental abnormality or personality disorder which makes the person likely to engage in repeat acts of sexual violence" (Fanniff et al., 2010, p. 649). Criteria for determining commitment include sexual offense history, current mental disorder, impaired **volitional control**, and risk of sexual recidivism requiring further confinement and treatment (Fanniff et al., 2010).

Many states began to incorporate the Washington model throughout the 1990s. As of 2013, 20 states have SVP laws (Janus, 2013). The promulgation of SVP laws has been facilitated by the Adam Walsh Act. The Adam Walsh Act (see Chapter 11) attempted to expand the use of civil commitments across the states. Under Title III of the act, also known as the Jimmy Ryce State Civil Commitment Programs for Sexually Dangerous Persons, the federal government will provide funding to existing state sex offender civil commitment programs and to states that wanted to create new programs. Jimmy Ryce was a victim of rape and murder at the hands of an SVP in Florida in 1995. The act also delineated which sex offenders would be considered for civil commitment. To be considered for civil commitment, the sex offender must have been convicted of a sexually violent offense and be deemed by a state to be a high risk for recidivism.

To be committed, the sex offender with the above criteria must suffer from a "serious mental issue, abnormality, or disorder" that would leave them incapable of desisting from sexual violence or child molestation.

The Adam Walsh Act also gave guidelines on the nature of the civil commitment process to be utilized to commit SVPs. Levenson (2004) outlined the commitment process for sex offenders. The process begins before the sex offender is released from prison when he/she is screened for an initial risk of dangerousness. A preliminary decision is made at this stage on dangerousness; those who are considered to be dangerous during this preliminary assessment will be selected for a face-to-face risk assessment by a mental health professional.

Levenson (2004) noted that actuarial instruments like the Static-99, the Rapid Risk Assessment for Sex Offense Recidivism, the Minnesota Sex Offender Screening Tool-Revised, and Psychopathy Checklist Revised are often used in assessing sex offender risk of dangerousness to the community. If the sex offender is determined to be dangerous, a prosecutor will determine if there is enough evidence to "file a probable cause petition" (Levenson, 2004, p. 639); probable cause being found results in a judicial hearing where evidence of dangerousness is presented before a judge or jury who will determine if the sex offender is to be committed. If the sex offender is civilly committed, the offender will be remanded into the custody of the state until they pose no risk to the community; this often equates to indefinite detention in mental institutions as there is no limit on civil custody.

The sex offender can be discharged unconditionally or conditionally. To be released unconditionally, a sex offender must be found to be no longer sexually dangerous to others; to be released conditionally, a sex offender must be found to be no longer sexually dangerous to others provided they meet certain criteria or conditions. Under this latter release strategy, there must be an explicit condition of release, usually additional outpatient treatment of some kind. If the sex offender fails to meet any conditions, he or she will be remanded back into the custody of the state and possibly charged with the crime of violation of a civil commitment as discussed on page 257.

SVP legislation has received much criticism. Practitioner, philosophical, and economic criticisms are discussed here; legal criticisms are addressed in the next section. La Fond (2000) noted that the criminal justice system is a reactive process that emphasizes deterrence and incapacitation whereas the mental health care system is a preemptive approach to preventing harm to individuals with mental disorders and to the community. La Fond (2000) listed several differences between the old sexual psychopath laws and the newer SVP laws of the 1990s. The newer SVP laws do not require a serious mental disorder, proof of recent criminal wrongdoing, or treatment. The newer SVP laws do require sex offenders to serve their sentence before commitment. SVP laws naturally erode the line between criminal and civil law and sanctions. Fitch (1998) noted that "the medical model of long-term civil commitment is used as a pretext for extended confinement" (preventative detention; p. 238).

Zonana (1997) outlined the concerns of medical professionals about the current sexual predator laws. First, the laws redefine sexual behavior as a mental illness for allowing continued prevention. Second, the primary goal of the laws is preventive detention, not treatment. Third, mental disorders do not always impact volition (ability to make choices). Fourth, the policy will place an additional burden on the health care system. Fifth, criminal law could make sentences longer rather than misuse psychiatry, medicine, and treatment. Fitch (1998) and La Fond (2000) argued that the current sex offender predator laws are not therapeutic in nature. Since treatment occurs after incarceration, which can be many years or decades, it is unreasonable to view the laws as rehabilitation.

The civil commitment of SVPs can be very expensive. Matson and Lieb (1996) and La Fond (2000) calculated that civil commitments per sex offender client ranged anywhere from $60,000 to over $100,000 per year; this is compared to the cost of $20,000 per year per inmate in prison. These costs are exacerbated by a policy that potentially has no end, since SVPs are committed for long time periods. This policy is most likely cost prohibitive for society in the long term.

Legal Challenges to Civil Commitments

As with the old sexual psychopath laws (Schlank, 2008), there have been many legal challenges to the newer SVP statutes that result in the civil commitment of sex offenders. As with SORN and residence restrictions, claims of due process, cruel and unusual punishment, ex post facto, and double jeopardy were leveled at SVP laws. Across the different legal issues, these cases have resulted in both support and refutation of the law. Overall, it was a Supreme Court decision on Kansas's SVP law that would legitimize the civil commitment of sex offenders. The legitimizing issue was once again public safety.

In 1994, Kansas enacted the Sexually Violent Predator Act, which established procedures for the commitment of persons who, due to a "mental abnormality" or a "personality disorder," are likely to engage in "predatory acts of sexual violence." Leroy Hendricks was the first person civilly committed under this statute; he was also the first to challenge the law (Koehle, 2016). Hendricks had a long history of sexually molesting children and was committed after his prison term, to which he had been sentenced prior to the enactment of the Kansas law (*Kansas v. Hendricks*, 1997). Hendricks claimed that this act violated the double jeopardy and ex post facto clauses of the Constitution. The Supreme Court found that the Kansas SVP law did not violate the Constitution's ban on double jeopardy and ex post facto lawmaking. The Court reasoned "As commitment under the Act is not tantamount to 'punishment,' Hendricks' involuntary detention does not violate the double jeopardy clause, even though that confinement may follow a prison term; the ex post facto clause, which 'forbids the application of any new punitive measure to a crime already consummated,' has been interpreted to pertain exclusively to penal statutes." A sexual offender can be held past their prison term in a mental institution, if need be, following a civil commitment hearing without violating the double jeopardy or ex post facto clauses of the Constitution.

In a strong dissent, Justice Kennedy cautioned against the dangers associated with using civil confinement laws in conjunction with the criminal justice process. If civil confinement becomes a vehicle for retribution or deterrence, it would not be constitutional. Kennedy noted at the time of his appeal, Hendricks had received no treatment of any kind, which is counter to the statutory requirements. In addition, Kennedy noted that the treatment of SVPs did not occur until after the imprisonment and supporters of the bill saw the law as a mechanism to permanently confine SVPs. For Kennedy, all of these facts suggested the law was more criminal than civil.

After 22 years, only 3 out of 287 sex offenders committed under the Kansas law have been released (Koehle, 2016). Hendricks was one of those released (in 2005). This release rate speaks to the concerns Justice Kennedy raised in his dissent. Similar statutory schemes to Kansas in Minnesota and Missouri have been declared unconstitutional under the *Kansas v. Hendricks* decision. In Kansas, capacities are being surpassed and expenditures are increasing, making the law unsustainable in its current version (Koehle, 2016). Koehle (2016) argued that the law in Kansas was likely unconstitutional and that those who conducted risk assessments of sexually violent predators should use the correct legal standard.

Kansas v. Hendricks (1997) would not be the end of Constitutional challenges to the Kansas SVP law. In 2002, the Supreme Court heard *Kansas v. Crane.* Crane had a history of sexual offending. In his most recent conviction, Crane had exposed himself and threatened to rape a clerk of a video store. This case dealt with an SVP, Crane, who challenged his assessment. Crane's evaluation suggested that he suffered from exhibitionism and social personality disorder, but that neither of these impacted his volitional control. Crane was classified as an SVP and was committed for treatment. The Kansas Supreme Court overturned this finding, interpreting the law to mean a lack of total volitional control was necessary to commit a sex offense.

12

The Crane case dealt with the Kansas Supreme Court's narrow interpretation of Hendricks (i.e., that a dangerous offender must be completely unable to control his/her behavior). The Court said the lower court's interpretation of their decision was too rigid; the Court merely indicated that the offender must have some inability to control their behavior. The Supreme Court noted a contradiction in the lower court's interpretation of the law as someone who is diagnosed with a mental abnormality or personality disorder cannot inherently control his/her dangerous behavior. The Supreme Court remanded the case back to the Kansas court.

Research on Sex Offender Civil Commitments

Doren and Epperson (2001) found half to three-quarters of committed sex offenders are child molesters with the remainder being rapists. Other than this general description of which sex offenders have been committed, there are relatively few lines of inquiry that evaluate the civil commitment of sex offenders. Duwe (2014) noted that most of the research on the civil commitment of sex offenders focuses on describing the sex offenders who have been committed or the process of civil commitment itself. Very few studies address the impact of civil commitments on sex offender behavior.

To date, few peer-reviewed studies have evaluated the effect of civil commitment policies on sex offender recidivism. In one study of the link between civil commitment and recidivism, Wilson et al.'s (2012b) research compared 120 sex offenders who had been civilly committed in Florida to 459 sex offenders who had not been committed but had undergone intensive treatment akin to commitment at a facility in Canada. Wilson et al. (2012b) found that over a 30-month follow-up period (two and a half years), those sex offenders in Florida who had been committed had a recidivism rate of 3.2 percent. Those sex offenders in the extensive treatment in Canada had a recidivism rate of 5.5 percent. This outcome suggested that committed sex offenders were slightly less likely to recidivate than sex offenders who were not committed. This research should be viewed cautiously. Due to cultural differences and views on criminal justice between Florida and Canada, it may be erroneous to compare these two groups of sex offenders.

Duwe's (2014) research attempted to evaluate actual and estimated rates of recidivism for those sex offenders committed to mental facilities in Minnesota. Duwe (2014) measured recidivism as rearrest or reconviction of a new sex crime. This recidivism data was collected through 2010 for all sex offenders who were not currently committed. Duwe's (2014) research focused on all sex offenders released from Minnesota in the 1990s (N=220) and sex offenders released between 2004 and 2007 (N=1,653). For the sex offenders released in the 1990s, 12.3 percent had been reconvicted of a new sex offense within four years; by the end of 2010, 18.6 percent had been reconvicted of a new sex offense.

For the group of sex offenders released from 2004 to 2007, only 2.8 percent had been reconvicted of a new sex offense. Duwe's (2014) research indicated recidivism for the group of sex offenders released in the 2000s was low. Duwe concluded that only 10 of the 105 civilly committed sex offenders would likely have been reconvicted of a new sex offense over a four-year follow-up period. Civilly committing sex offenders would decrease recidivism from 3.2 percent to 2.8 percent, which is a relatively modest reduction.

Research on the link between SVP laws and recidivism is new. As of 2008, Levenson found no existing research evaluating the impact of civil commitments on sex offender recidivism. This could be linked to the fact that so few sex offenders are actually released from civil commitment. As Levenson (2008) noted:

> Inquiry into the effectiveness of civil commitment is especially problematic due to the extremely small number of individuals released from commitment programs and the long follow-up periods necessary to efficiently evaluate recidivism rates after involuntary treatment. Confounding this issue is the difficulty in determining whether any observed reduction in recidivism is due to treatment effects, maturation, concurrent implementation of other legislative initiatives, the decreasing trend in violent crime rates, or other factors (p. 46).

Another area of research on civil commitments evaluates the length of time that sex offenders are committed to treatment facilities. Levenson (2008) argued that despite the increasing number of those sex offenders committed, release from such programs is exceedingly rare.

Research indicates that civil commitments are long term. Janus and Walbeck (2000) reported no sex offenders had received a full release over the preceding 16 years and no sex offenders had received a conditional release in the previous 11 years. Fitch (2003) found that only 3.3 percent of 2,478 sex offenders who had been committed in 16 states had been release from confinement. Gookin's (2007) analysis of 4,534 sex offenders in 20 states indicated that only 11 percent of civilly committed sex offenders had been released. Fanniff et al. (2010) reported that the highest reported national release of sex offenders who have been civilly committed was only 11 percent.

Research has also been conducted to evaluate how sex offenders are assessed for civil commitment. For instance, Mercado et al. (2001) examined if sex offenders were assessed the same as non-sex offenders in the civil commitment process. The subjects in the study were 35 mental health professionals. Their findings indicated similarities and differences between the assessment of sex offenders and non-sex offenders. The clinicians listed many of the same factors in assessing both groups: social support, aggressiveness, a history of violence, substance abuse, insight, social skills, lack of remorse, and anger. In terms of differences, for non-sex offenders, the mental health professionals emphasized medication compliance and the patient understanding the underlying processes (delusional thinking and guardedness). For sex offenders, the subjects focused on contextual factors like social support, employment opportunities, and relationship to the victim.

Levenson (2004) examined sex offenders in Florida to evaluate the factors used to commit sex offenders. Focusing on two groups of sex offenders (229 recommended for commitment and 221 recommended for release), Levenson (2004) hypothesized that sex offenders recommended for civil commitment would display a higher risk of dangerousness/recidivism. Levenson (2004) found that sex offenders selected for commitment had higher frequencies of paraphilia and antisocial personality. Levenson concluded that evaluators were correctly selecting sex offenders for commitment under the Florida statute. This research was largely confirmed by Levenson and Morin's (2006) study that indicated recommendations of civil commitment for sex offenders were based on diagnoses of pedophilia and paraphilia not otherwise specified, psychopathy, actuarial risk assessment scores, younger victims, and non-minority race.

Jackson and Hess (2007) evaluated 41 experts who conduct civil commitment evaluations of sex offenders to examine common practices of assessment. There was great agreement in the assessment of sex offenders when determining whether the offender should be committed. The vast majority of the subjects reported the assessment of paraphilia, substance abuse, and psychopathy as essential to evaluating sex offenders. In addition, evaluators relied on actuarial risk assessment tools like the Static-99 (see more on the assessment of sex offenders in Chapter 13) to ascertain future risk of recidivism. Jackson and Hess (2007) concluded that a personality disorder or paraphilia in conjunction with a history of sex offending was the key information necessary to establish mental abnormality and risk of future sexual violence; this link led to commitment.

While not peer-reviewed, Hoppe, Meyer, De Orio, Vogler, and Armstrong's (2020) research indicated some possible unintended consequences of sex offender civil commitments. First, there appears to be racial disparity in the application of this policy. Black offenders were more than twice as likely to be committed than White offenders (rate of 7.72 per 100,000 and 3.11 per 100,000, respectively). Second, in New York and Texas, men who had victims that were male were two to three times more likely to be committed than sex offenders with only female victims. More research is necessary to further explore these troubling findings from Hoppe et al.'s (2020) study.

Discussion

Currently, 20 states, the District of Columbia, and the federal government have enacted laws allowing the civil commitment of sex offenders (Association for the Treatment of

Sexual Abusers, 2020). These states include Arizona, California, Florida, Illinois, Iowa, Kansas, Massachusetts, Minnesota, Missouri, Nebraska, New Hampshire, New Jersey, New York, North Dakota, Pennsylvania, South Carolina, Texas, Virginia, Washington, and Wisconsin. According to D'Orazio et al. (2019), very few sex offenders meet the criteria for civil commitment. Despite this, and as of 2018, an estimated 5,400 sex offenders are civilly committed in state and federal programs (Tolman, 2018; Herbert et al., 2020); Hoppe et al. (2020) puts this number closer to 6,300 civil commitments. The commitment of SVPs is a fine line between criminal and civil sanctions (Wilson, 2004). The punishment of sex offenders followed by indefinite detention in a treatment facility suggests a policy focused on punishment rather than rehabilitation. Some have suggested that current SVP laws even violate international human rights norms (Janus, 2013). While the legality of SVP laws seems to be well established, Janus (2013) believed that SVP laws will come under continued legal scrutiny in the coming years based on a review of Minnesota's SVP legislation.

The early evidence suggests that SVP laws have relatively little impact on sex offending behavior (Wilson et al., 2012b; Duwe, 2014; Deck, 2016). As with SORN and residence restrictions, civil commitments appear to be ineffective in reducing sex offending behaviors and recidivism levels. Unlike the other policies, SVP laws do not have the overwhelming empirical evidence to suggest failure. This is due to the fact that very few sex offenders are released from civil commitments. This is explained by the sex offender's inability to rehabilitate or a medical treatment provider being afraid to release the sex offender. Release means that the sex offender is no longer a dangerous threat to society. In a couple of cases, medical treatment providers have been held responsible when they have cleared a sex offender, and that offender has gone on to recidivate. This indicates a serious problem with the final stage of SVP policies.

Many SVPs are being detained for long periods of time in prison followed by civil commitment. Unlike prison, civil commitment does not have a definite endpoint. If preventative detention is the goal of SVP laws, Levenson (2008) suggested that rather than commit dangerous sex offenders to mental facilities, criminal laws should be changed to create longer criminal sentences for sex offenders. Under this scenario, the criminal and civil processes do not overlap, giving the appearance of potential impropriety.

CONCLUSION

Chapter 12 examined the effectiveness of residence restrictions and civil commitments on sex offenders. As was noted, both of these policies are just as ineffective as SORN laws. Empirical evidence shows that neither policy, whether it be residence restrictions or civil commitments, have any impact on sex offending or sex offender recidivism. Despite their empirically demonstrated ineffectiveness, these policies still persist. SORN, residence restrictions, and civil commitments continue to drain money from public coffers, but the public continues to be largely supportive of these efforts it believes to curb sex offending. Burchfield (2011) argued that policy makers "must find a way to negotiate public emotion with scientific empiricism" (p. 414).

After the last two chapters, you might be wondering if there is anything that can be done to curb sex offending behavior. Fortunately, one area that has shown some indication of success in curbing sex offending behavior and recidivism is treatment. Research indicates that treating sex offenders is the most effective manner of dealing with the threat of sex offenders and associated recidivism. The assessment and treatment of sex offender is the topic of Chapter 13.

KEY TERMS

buffer zone
civil commitment
recidivism
residence restrictions
sexually violent predator (SVP)
spatial restriction zones (SRZ)
volitional control

EXERCISES

1. Explain the legal challenges to residence restriction laws.
2. If you are in a state or city that has a residence restriction policy, has there been any case law that has evaluated the legality of the policy? If yes, explain the legal arguments and the outcome of the case(s).
3. Explain the legal challenges to civil commitment policies.
4. Does your state utilize civil commitments for dealing with sex offenders who have been released from prison? If so, describe the policy.
5. After reading Chapter 12, where do you stand on the use of residence restrictions and civil commitment policies? Support your answer.

ESSAY QUESTIONS

1. Whether you agree or disagree, explain why residence restrictions and civil commitments are inherently punitive rather than designed for public safety.
2. Find out if the state, city, and/or both in which you currently reside has a residence restriction. If yes, describe the policy (i.e., buffer zone size and locations covered). If no, research if your state/city has ever contemplated a residence restriction policy. Why did they choose to accept or reject the policy?
3. Find a newspaper article on a sex offender who has been subject to civil commitment. Discuss the story and how the sex offender in the story is dealing with the commitment process.

13

TREATMENT FOR SEX OFFENDERS

Chapter Objectives

After reading this chapter, students will be able to:

- Describe the historical developments in sex offender treatment.
- Understand the common modern treatments for sex offenders.
- Discuss the research outcomes associated with common modern treatments for sex offenders.
- Describe various applications of sex offender treatment.
- Explain how the efficacy of sex offender treatment is tested.
- Understand ethical issues associated with sex offender treatment.

INTRODUCTION

Douglas Alsteen was convicted of sexually assaulting a ten-year-old girl in 1986 and pled guilty to several attempted rape charges in 1990. He served sentences after each conviction (LaBoe, 2007a). After his release from prison, Alsteen was not sent home on parole as would have occurred if he were a non-sexual offender. Instead, the state of Washington determined that he was a sexually violent predator (SVP)—he had a mental illness and was likely to reoffend—and he was sent to the Special Commitment Center (SCC) on McNeil Island for an indeterminate period of time until he could be safely released (LaBoe, 2007b). Alsteen has challenged his confinement since he was sent to the SCC in 2007 (LaBoe, 2014).

Washington state's McNeil Island provides an example of an attempt to treat sex offenders who have been civilly committed as SVPs under the Community Protection Act of 1990. McNeil Island houses the SCC Program, which has facilities for total confinement, as well as a transitional community for those sex offenders who have been conditionally released from total confinement. The facilities house over 250 sex offenders undergoing treatment (Washington State Department of Social and Health Services, n.d.).

Although the SCC is not a prison, it is a high-security facility. The sex offenders housed there are permitted to wear street clothes rather than uniforms, and some are given a bit more freedom of movement around the facility than in a prison, although the more high-risk residents live in cells like those found in a prison (Doll, 2012). The facility does take serious security precautions, such has having a very low number of residents per staff member, and constantly monitoring activities through an electronic security system (Washington State Department of Social and Health Services, n.d.). Although the facility resembles a prison, the primary goal is treatment and protecting the community by preventing the sex offenders from having access to new victims. While treatment is offered, it is not mandatory and less than half of the offenders participate (Doll, 2012).

These sex offenders are given intensive treatment, with the ultimate goal being to prevent relapses of sexual offending should they be released into the community. Treatment for residents consists of seven stages: (1) orientation and evaluation, in which residents are told what to expect in treatment and their needs are evaluated; (2) treatment readiness, in which residents learn to understand their behavior; (3) skills acquisition, in which residents examine their cycle of sexual offending and learn what might stop their offending; (4) skill application, in which residents accept responsibility for their actions and learn how to avoid situations that might trigger offender; (5) skill generalization, in which residents help each other, and understand the effects of sexual abuse; (6) discharge readiness, in which residents disclose their offending to support persons and work on preparing themselves for living without offending. Residents must agree to continue with treatment to move past this stage. (7) Aftercare, in which residents who have been released into a less restrictive alternative placement continue meetings with treatment staff (Washington State Department of Social and Health Services, n.d.).

Each resident is reviewed annually to determine if they still meet the criteria for civil commitment or if less restrictive alternatives would be appropriate. In 1994, the SCC itself was issued an injunction requiring the SCC to provide "constitutionally adequate mental health treatment" (Washington State Department of Social and Health Services, n.d.). In 1998, the center was held in contempt of court due to a failure to take actions to improve the mental health care for residents. The center was reviewed in 2000; the judge found that the center had made great progress in providing treatment, but that it was not providing less restrictive alternatives for residents (McKinney, 2002). As part of the less restrictive alternatives provision, the center opened a transitional housing facility on the mainland, and in 2004 the court found that the center was no longer in contempt. The injunction was dismissed in 2007 (Washington State Department of Social and Health Services, n.d.).

While the SCC is providing constitutionally adequate treatment, is it providing effective treatment? Chapter 13 examines the types of treatment that have been shown to be useful in reducing reoffending in sex offenders. We will review the history of sex offender treatment, risk assessment methods, and studies of effectiveness.

HISTORY

Attempts to treat or cure sex offenders have been going on for hundreds of years, although Chapter 13 focuses on the history beginning in the 1930s. In the 1930s to 1950s, also known as the **sexual psychopath era** (Leon, 2011), sex offenders were considered to be mentally and/or physically different from non-offenders; treatment in this era focused on psychiatric and medical treatment (London and Caprio, 1950). Indeed, Sheldon Glueck considered that

> the aggressive sex offender is more a problem for psychopathology than for criminal justice. Sometimes he is feeble-minded; sometimes he suffers from some epileptic condition; frequently he is a chronic alcoholic; often his uninhibited impulses are related to premature senility (1937, p. 319).

Of course we often involve both psychology and the criminal justice system in responding to sex offenders and in treating them. To step away from criminal justice, we will discuss the practices of castration, drug therapy, lobotomy, and electroshock as they were used in this era. While some of these practices are still in use today, they have been significantly modified, and will be discussed as current practices later in Chapter 13.

Sexual Psychopath Laws

Starting in 1937 states began enacting **sexual psychopath laws**, which allowed for someone who was diagnosed as a sexual psychopath to be confined in a state hospital for an indefinite period of time (Sutherland, 1950). These laws were based on the belief that committing a sex crime was the actual evidence of a mental disorder, and thus, the offender required treatment rather than imprisonment (Hacker and Frym, 1955). Sutherland pointed out the problems with these laws, stating:

> Implicit in these laws is a series of propositions which have been made explicit in popular literatures, namely, that the present danger to women and children from serious sex crimes is very great, for the number of sex crimes is large and is increasing more rapidly than any other crime; that most sex crimes are committed by "sexual degenerates," "sex fiends," or "sexual psychopaths" and that these persons persist in their sexual crimes throughout life; that they always give warning that they are dangerous by first committing minor offenses; that any psychiatrist can diagnose them with a high degree of precision at an early age, before they have committed serious sex crimes; and that sexual psychopaths who are diagnosed and identified should be confined as irresponsible persons until they are pronounced by psychiatrists to be completely and permanently cured of their malady (1950, p. 142).

As Sutherland (1950) noted, most of these propositions can be demonstrated to be false and the others questionable.

Hacker and Frym (1955) also point out that the sexual psychopath laws appear not to have lived up to expectations, despite the very finest of care received by the sex offenders in the state hospitals where they conducted observations. Reinhardt and Fisher (1949) discussed the failings of sexual psychopath laws, suggesting that the people confined under these laws were not even psychopaths as any other person with a mental illness would be classified; these sex offenders knew right from wrong and expressed remorse for their actions. Regardless of the problems pointed out by social scientists, support for these types of laws was high among the public, as they tended to be enacted as a result of a wave of fear associated with sex crimes produced by the media (Sutherland, 1950). Some of the treatments discussed below were carried out on offenders who were confined under the sexual psychopath laws, although there was no agreed upon treatment that should be applied in the case of all sex offenders (Cole, 2000).

Electroshock

Electroshock treatment was initially conducted on patients who suffered from serious mental illnesses to attempt to change the functioning of their brains (Shutts, 1982). Sex offenders who were committed to hospitals under sexual psychopath laws were sometimes subjected to electric shock as a form of therapy. Electroshock can be used as a negative stimulus to discourage deviant sexual arousal, known as **aversion therapy** (discussed on page 275) or as a way of changing brain activity by causing grand mal convulsions (Murphy, 1992), known as **electroconvulsive therapy (ECT).** Even at the time, clinical results suggested that this treatment was ineffective (Freedman, 1987; Karpman, 1954). Karpman (1954) reported six cases where electroshock therapy was tried across several types of sex offenders; none of these offenders desisted in their sexually abusive behaviors.

Currently, ECT is mainly indicated for the treatment of psychiatric conditions that are resistant to medications (Schoeyen et al., 2015). To the extent that sex offenders have psychiatric disorders, and the disorders are associated with their offending, ECT may be helpful in the treatment of sex offenders. Schoeyen et al. (2015) did find that ECT was more effective in treating bipolar disorder than medication. Booth and Gulati (2014) state that for offenders with severe mental disorders, treatment of the disorder may allow them to participate in therapeutic activities to allow for rehabilitation. ECT got a bad reputation in the past as it was done with high doses of electricity, and/or without anesthesia, which resulted in serious side effects such as memory loss and broken bones. Today ECT is done with medication and monitoring, which have increased safety for patients (Mayo Clinic, n.d.).

Lobotomy

While the manner in which a **lobotomy** is performed has changed over time, the basic outcome of the procedure is that nerves in the frontal lobe of the brain are cut so as not to connect with other areas of the brain (Shutts, 1982). This procedure was originally used to treat patients suffering from serious mental disorders, such as major depressive disorders and schizophrenia. The doctors who performed this procedure noted drastic changes in the patient's personality; these changes were not necessarily positive changes. These doctors suggested that sometimes lobotomy resulted in an increase in sexual desire that would last for several months (Shutts, 1982).

Rigorous scientific data on the success of lobotomy specifically for sex offenders is not available, but there have been multiple case studies. Friedlander and Banay (1948) report on a male sex offender who suffered from tension and obsessive compulsive symptoms who underwent a lobotomy at the age of 54 in 1941. This patient had a history in which his mother applied ointment to his anus, he had several surgeries of the rectum, and a circumcision at age 14. His mother often spanked him on his bare buttocks, in response to which he would often ejaculate. As a teenager, he was often caught engaging in homosexual acts with other boys. As an adult, he was a pedophile who offended against young boys. After the lobotomy he initially seemed healthy; he claimed not to have the sexual fantasies associated with sexual offending that he had had in the past. He was released from prison a year after undergoing a lobotomy and after his release he spent a few years living in the shelters of charitable organizations. He was also placed in mental hospitals on several occasions. He wrote copious obscene notes, had very poor memory, and was unable to take care of himself properly. When not in a hospital he visited parks in order to interact with young boys; this suggests that the lobotomy did not eliminate his sexual urges or offending, rather it may have left him requiring more medical care than before the procedure was performed (Friedlander and Banay, 1948). Indeed, more modern researchers suggest that lobotomies may result in inappropriate sexual behavior as a result of behavioral disinhibition (Mendez and Shapira, 2011).

Castration

While we often refer to **castration** as a punitive measure for sex offenders (see Chapter 9), there has been a long history of the use of surgical castration as a mechanism for treatment of sex offenders. Both physical and **chemical castration** are used today. This is a measure that has historically found strong support from the public (Leon, 2011). Surgical castration involves the removal of the testes and has been practiced as both a legal measure and a treatment measure in the United States and in other countries (van der Meer, 2014). The testes produce approximately 95 percent of the androgen/**testosterone** in the male (Chism, 2013) so if these hormones are associated with sex offending, the removal of the testes seems like a potentially successful treatment for sex offending. There are a number of potential positive and negative outcomes associated with castration, as well as the consideration of its effectiveness.

The first manner of castration is known as sterilization. Sterilization involves the castration of individuals by disrupting the chemical processes within the body. A good example of sterilization is the vasectomy in which the mechanism of delivering sperm to the penis is detached. Sterilization does not provide any benefit in reducing sex offending and it does not influence sexual arousal or functioning; however, it does prevent procreation as a result of sexual intercourse, both legitimate and illicit (Karpman, 1954). Sterilization was supported as part of the earlier eugenics movement due to the belief that sex offenders would have offspring who were also sex offenders (Leon, 2011).

The second form of castration is the outright removal of the penis, the testicles, or both. Removal of both the testicles and penis is also regarded as a poor option for reducing sexual offending, as it may result in extreme maladjustment. This could actually lead to an increase in sexual offending. There are many kinds of sex offenses and deviant sexual behavior that do not require the male sex organ. Sadists for instance, use sex acts as a means of inflicting pain and can continue to do so even after castrated (Karpman, 1954). Even castration that involves the removal of the testicles only can result in maladjustment and does not necessarily affect the ability to commit sexual offenses or the deviant drives associated with them (Karpman, 1954). While there is potential for increased offending, the studies described by Karpman (1954) indicate that castration did reduce both "potency and libido" (p. 245) and that the offenders who underwent this procedure had very low recidivism rates. Most sex offenders were able to be released into the community without harm.

A more recent and detailed study of castration practices in the Netherlands between 1938 and 1968 points out that it is unclear whether the original aim of the castration of sex offenders was eugenics, to prevent them from producing inferior offspring, or treatment to prevent them from committing further sexual offenses (van der Meer, 2014). Determining whether castration is successful was sometimes based on whether the offender had lost sexual functioning; at other times, success was a function of sex offender recidivism. There were reports that some castrated offenders were still able to both have erections and to ejaculate. Recidivism was reported to be very low among the castrated offenders. In three studies the recidivism rates were all under 4 percent, compared to 60 to 70 percent recidivism among sex offenders who had not been castrated (van der Meer, 2014).

While castration may seem to be effective, there are possible negative physical and legal side effects. Castration, and thus a loss of male hormones, can result in "hot flashes, hair loss, osteoporosis, softening of the skin, lethargy, and decrease in muscle mass" (Chism, 2013, p. 199). It is also irreversible, meaning that should better options become available, there would not be a potential to switch to that treatment. In addition to physical side effects, there is a concern that castration as a treatment may be coercive, particularly when castration is a condition for being released back into society (McMillan, 2013).

CONTEMPORARY TREATMENT

The period from the 1950s to the 1980s has been labeled the era of rehabilitative debate (Leon, 2011). During this period, research on sexual offenses and sex offenders increased, and while some of the medical treatment, most notably castration, was not abandoned, perspectives about the cause of sex offending switched toward viewing offenders as monstrous psychopaths to individuals who were sick, which meant they were amenable to treatment (Leon, 2011). Psychiatrists and psychotherapists were involved in rehabilitative treatment; this form of treatment involved less medical intervention and more attempts to change behavior through different types of therapy (Leon, 2011). This involved applying different types of therapy used for a variety of mental and behavioral problems to sex offender treatment specifically. Types of therapy included psychotherapy aimed at understanding what went wrong during sexual development, **behavioral therapy**, which discouraged inappropriate arousal, and cognitive-behavioral treatment, which taught offenders the skills necessary to control their own sexual behavior (MacKenzie, 2006). Treatment from the 1980s onward was based on refining these therapies as a result of studies regarding what was successful, and on risk assessment (Beech, Craig, and Browne, 2009). One manner of using these treatments in a prison environment is the therapeutic community.

Therapeutic Communities

A **therapeutic community** (TC) in a prison environment is a treatment program that involves a small community of inmates. These inmates live together and go through treatment together (Baker and Prete, 2011). These communities were initially developed for individuals with substance abuse problems, both in and out of prison, and showed some promising results related to recovery and reduced recidivism. TCs have been modified now to treat a variety of populations, including sex offenders (Baker and Prete, 2011). The goal of TCs is rehabilitation for those who have had positive community interactions in the past and habilitation for those who have not. This is done by socializing the inmates in a small community of other inmates, where inmates who have completed more treatment influence the newer members and help them develop appropriate social skills (Jensen and Kane, 2012). These communities must be places where the inmates can develop relationships and hold each other accountable for individual actions. While TCs vary somewhat from prison to prison, important factors in their success include the degree of support from correctional staff and administration, the effectiveness of treatment staff, and the design of the prison facility itself (Baker and Prete, 2011).

A TC must have a clear philosophy, which is generally "no more victims" (Baker and Prete, 2011, p. 307), a strong treatment model grounded in theory, an appropriate facility, and excellent staff. There are three types of staff associated with a TC. The first is the treatment team, for which it is important that staff have appropriate degrees and training associated with their occupation, but they must also have personalities such that they are able to take criticism and avoid personalizing issues. Their motivations for being involved in this type of treatment should be considered, taking care that treatment providers are not attempting to address their own issues. Both men and women are appropriate service providers (Baker and Prete, 2011). The second type of staff is the correctional staff. All of the correctional officers having contact with the sex offender TC should be trained in the treatment of sex offenders. They have the advantage of observing inmates in situations that the treatment staff may not see and, thus, can report valuable information to the treatment staff (Baker and Prete, 2011). Finally, there are the supervisory staff, who are experts in sex offender treatment and who consult with the treatment staff regularly to improve their treatment approach and assess their emotional ability to continue the work (Baker and Prete, 2011).

A number of TC components are standard, despite variation by prison. TCs will have primary therapy groups, where inmates meet in smaller groups and are guided by one or more therapists (Baker and Prete, 2011). They will also have psychoeducational classes, where inmates learn coping skills appropriate to their needs, and specialty groups where inmates with particular conditions or situations, such as the need for remedial education, their own victimization, or substance abuse treatment needs, can meet in small groups to address these issues that will be associated with their individual treatment success (Baker and Prete, 2011). Finally, TCs have community meetings where all members of the TC and the staff group together to address any problems within the community. Community meetings are initially held by staff but the inmates may elect officers and later take control of the meetings themselves, which shows community development (Baker and Prete, 2011).

Finally, a number of tools used in a TC that are part of daily procedures are not discussed above, but are necessary to ensure the smooth operation of the TC should problems arise. Community interventions are a confrontational technique used whenever a problem arises in the community that does not support treatment, such as the discovery of pornography within the community. These interventions may occur several times per year and may last an entire day (Baker and Prete, 2011). A committee of inmates also intervenes in conflicts among themselves, such as struggles with roommates or inappropriate behavior. These committees may also assign contracts when an inmate has a behavioral problem that needs to be addressed. This contract will outline behavioral expectations, and men within the community can help the inmate conform to the terms of the contract (Baker and Prete, 2011). If an inmate engages in negative behavior not serious enough for a contract, he may be asked to write out an explanation for his behavior and how it is related to his offending. If an inmate has a serious infraction of the TC or Department of Corrections rules or fails to uphold a contract, he may be terminated from the TC program. This would only be done as a last resort (Baker and Prete, 2011).

Rice, Harris, and Cormier (1992) studied the recidivism rates of both psychopathic and non-psychopathic violent offenders who were treated in a TC and those who were not treated but were imprisoned. These offenders were not necessarily sexual offenders. Their results suggested that offenders who were psychopaths actually had a higher rate of recidivism if they were treated in a TC compared to if they did not receive treatment; however, for those offenders who were not psychopaths, treatment in a TC was associated with a lower recidivism rate. These results suggested that all patients learned social skills, but that psychopaths used those skills to increase their offending, whereas other offenders developed more prosocial habits (Rice, Harris, and Cormier, 1992). As some sex offenders are psychopaths, this is useful information relative to the treatment of sexual offenders in TCs. It is possible that psychopathic sexual offenders may use their new-found social skills to attract victims.

In 2003, Colorado published a report related to an evaluation of a TC for sex offenders that had been running since 1993. This report evaluated both the adherence of the program to best practices in running a TC and the success of the program for inmates who participated in treatment. The researchers found there were deficits in funding, facilities, staff, and in providing treatment plans for the inmates. Non-therapeutic staff were not adequately trained in sex offender treatment, there were not enough therapists, and there was not enough meeting space for therapy. Indeed, these spaces were not private from the rest of the prison, which would lead to very limited open sharing between the TC residents. Because of the funding deficit, the TC beds were not always filled with TC residents; rather, the open beds were filled with inmates from the general population, which had a negative influence on the TC program itself (Lowden et al., 2003). Despite these serious implementation issues, the Colorado Department of Corrections still found success with the program. They found lower rates of parole revocation for those sex offenders in the TC compared to those not treated in the TC and lower rates of rearrest for violent crimes (Lowden et al., 2003). It should be noted that these data do not relate specifically to committing sexual offenses after having been released, but rather to all parole revocations and arrests for all violent crimes.

Ware, Frost, and Hoy (2010) argued that empirical evidence showing TCs are successful in the treatment of sexual offenders is limited, although some studies do find lower rearrest rates for TC-treated sexual offenders than non-treated sexual offenders. Ware et al. (2010) suggest the real benefit of TCs is creating a treatment friendly environment in areas such as prisons, which would ordinarily not be conducive to receiving treatment. The potential for openness regarding discussions of inappropriate sexual desires encouraged in a TC may help enhance the content of specific types of treatment, as opposed to a typical prison environment where disrespect and secretiveness are more common reactions to this topic (Ware et al., 2010). The types of treatment discussed below could be conducted as part of a TC, or in a different environment.

Behavioral Treatment

Behavioral treatment can be applied to a number of problematic behaviors and patterns. If sexual offending is associated with deviant sexual arousal, changing the offender's pattern of arousal could stop his offending. Using behavioral therapy to change deviant sexual arousal as a treatment for sexual offending relies upon sexual offenders having deviant sexual interests and relies upon sexual interests being malleable (Marshall, O'Brien, and Marshall, 2009). While not all sex offenders display arousal to deviant sexual interests, for those that do there is no definitive evidence that behavioral treatment methods are successful. Regardless, these methods are used in a majority of programs that treat sexual offenders, both adult and juvenile (Marshall, O'Brien, and Marshall, 2009).

A number of forms of aversion therapy can be used to change sexual arousal patterns, including shame aversion, ammonia aversion, faradic (electrical) aversion, and olfactory (smell) aversion. The basic idea behind each of these techniques is that the offender should come to associate his deviant arousal with something unpleasant and will therefore reduce deviant sexual fantasies (Marshall, O'Brien, and Marshall, 2009). **Shame aversion** is the most ethically questionable and least researched of these treatments. In this technique treatment staff watch an offender in treatment act out deviant behavior and stare at him, causing him to experience shame. There is evidence that offenders going through this treatment experience nightmares and anxiety; however, there is only anecdotal evidence that this form of treatment is successful. Despite the potential problems with this treatment, it is still practiced in approximately 20 percent of treatment facilities, including those for adolescents and children (Marshall, O'Brien, and Marshall, 2009).

Ammonia aversion and **olfactory aversion** are often conflated, although inhaling ammonia really triggers the pain system of the body, rather than the olfactory system (Marshall, O'Brien, and Marshall, 2009). Both forms of aversion therapy require the offender in treatment to inhale either ammonia or some other foul-smelling substance, such as rotten meat, in response to deviant fantasies or being exposed to simulations of their deviant interest (Marshall, O'Brien, and Marshall, 2009). Ammonia can be particularly unpleasant, causing not just a reaction to the smell, but watering of the eyes and coughing (Laws, 2001). Over the course of a few weeks, an offender in treatment will watch films or see pictures with their deviant interest featured and will then inhale the unpleasant substance. The offender's erectile response to the deviant sexual stimuli can be tracked over time to determine if the treatment is causing a reduction in arousal to deviant sexual interests. The offender is also given "homework," where he will self-administer the unpleasant substance should he have deviant fantasies. This procedure is meant to work not just through a conditioning mechanism, but because unpleasant smell is specifically a sexual turn-off, reducing arousal (Laws, 2001). A case study indicated that this method reduced the amount of time an offender spent in masturbation to deviant fantasies (Craig and Campbell-Fuller, 2009).

Faradic (electrical) aversion therapy has been used to treat a number of different problem behaviors, most notably alcoholism. While it appears that for alcoholism specifically, inducing vomiting as the negative stimulus is more successful than giving an electrical shock in reducing alcohol consumption (Cannon and Baker, 1981). Electric shock aversion therapy has been applied with some success to people with negative sexual behaviors (Kilmann et al., 1982). For electric shock to be most effective at reducing deviant sexual arousal, it should be applied only when evidence shows such arousal is occurring. This can be done by monitoring erectile response and only applying electric shock when the offender undergoing treatment has an erection in response to deviant sexual stimuli. Electric shock is applied to the fingers of the offender undergoing treatment. When an erection is present in response to appropriate sexual stimuli, no shock is applied (Callahan and Leitenberg, 1973). In Callahan and Leitenberg's (1973) study of electrical shock therapy, they found that subjects did reduce erectile response to deviant sexual stimuli, but also noted that this does not necessarily mean that they reduced their arousal; they could have just learned to inhibit their erection.

Callahan and Leitenberg (1973) tested electric shock therapy against another behavioral treatment, covert sensitization. In covert sensitization treatment, the offender undergoing treatment is told to imagine acting out their deviant sexual behavior and then to imagine an unpleasant consequence that would be associated with their activity (Marshall, O'Brien, and Marshall, 2009). It is called covert because neither the behavior which is to be avoided nor the negative stimuli is presented in real life; rather they are in the mind of the person undergoing treatment (Cautela, 1967). Imagining unpleasant consequences can also be supplemented with other negative stimuli, such as unpleasant smells, as discussed above (Marshall, O'Brien, and Marshall, 2009). Barlow, Leitenberg, and Agras (1969) report using covert sensitization to manipulate the deviant sexual behavior in two subjects. They had subjects imagine being ill after a deviant fantasy and noted that deviant sexual urges declined quickly; however, when they stopped having the subject imagine the unpleasant scene the deviant urges returned. They were able to lower the urges again by reapplying the condition where the subject imagines being ill (Barlow, Leitenberg, and Agras, 1969), but it is unclear how long the effect would last if the treatment was not consistently applied or if subjects would become desensitized to the treatment.

In addition to negative responses to deviant sexual fantasies, sex offenders can be treated to increase their appropriate sexual urges and decrease their deviant interests through **directed masturbation**. To increase appropriate arousal, people in treatment are shown images of adult females, or asked to imagine appropriate sexual situations, and are told to masturbate to orgasm (Marshall, O'Brien, and Marshall, 2009). In this way, sexually appropriate thoughts are associated with sexual arousal. This is sometimes used after deviant sexual interests have been extinguished using aversion therapies (Marshall, O'Brien, and Marshall, 2009). Masturbation can also be used to reduce deviant interests in a process called satiation therapy. This process relies upon the "refractory state," a period of up to 20 minutes after orgasm where normally sexually arousing stimuli do not cause arousal (Marshall, O'Brien, and Marshall, 2009). During the refractory period, sometimes the treated offender is requested to continue masturbating while fantasizing about deviant sexual interests (Marshall, 1979) and sometimes requested to stop masturbating after ejaculation, but to verbalize deviant sexual fantasies, in a process called verbal satiation (Laws, 1995). When directed masturbation is done prior to the satiation or verbal satiation therapy, arousal to adult females has been seen to increase, while arousal to children decreases. This was found in a two-case study (Marshall, 1979). This was not a large, controlled experiment, so it is unclear how robust these finding are.

Cognitive Behavioral Therapy

Behavioral therapies set the stage for the development of **cognitive behavioral therapy** (CBT) (Marshall and Laws, 2003) and it has become the most popular and dominant type of treatment for sex offenders (Schaffer et al., 2010). Indeed, it is one of the most common and successful treatments for things ranging from mental illness to deviant and criminal behavior of all kinds (Hofmann et al., 2012). O'Donohue and Fisher (2012) have identified 13 core principles of CBT as a general practice, each of which will be discussed briefly, and then CBT will be applied specifically to the case of treatment of sexual offenders.

The first core principle of CBT is functional analysis and contingency management. In this stage of treatment, the therapist and client work to discover the function of a particular behavior for that specific client. This then leads to individual interventions. In this stage the therapist and client also work to understand the antecedents to the specific behavior and the consequences of the behavior (Rummel et al., 2012).

The second core principle of CBT is skills training, during which the client is taught how to perform specific behaviors, such as those that might help respond to high levels of emotional arousal (Twohig and Dehlin, 2012). The third core principle is exposure therapy, which is used in CBT "to reduce pathological fear and related emotions" (Zalta and Foa, 2012, p. 75). The fourth core principle is relaxation, which is a specific skill clients can apply in the face of anxiety-provoking situations (Hazlett-Stevens and Bernstein, 2012). The fifth core principle is cognitive restructuring, which involves identifying negative automatic thoughts and confronting them with questions about the credibility of these thoughts and changing the content of these thoughts. These thoughts may be supported by confirmation bias, the tendency to only notice information that supports the thought (Leahy and Rego, 2012), thus making the conscious identification of negative automatic thoughts and the challenging of that information a very important step in CBT.

The sixth core principle of CBT is problem solving. The problem-solving process is a step in which the client finds positive ways of dealing with everyday problems by finding ways to alter the situation, their reaction, or both (Nezu and Nezu, 2012). The seventh core principle is self-regulation, in which the client is taught to practice the skills they have learned so that they become automatic (Karoly, 2012). The eighth core principle of CBT is behavioral activation, which "may be defined as the therapeutic scheduling of specific activities for the client to complete in his or her daily life that function to increase contact with diverse, stable, and personally meaningful sources of positive reinforcement" (Kanter and Puspitasari, 2012, p. 217). The ninth core principle is social skills, which are comprised of three functions:

> *social perception*: the ability to perceive social cues accurately, (2) *social problem solving*: the ability to analyze the social situation correctly and identify an effective response, and (3) *behavioral competence*: the ability to implement the appropriate response effectively. (Kinnaman and Bellack, 2012, p. 252).

Social skills training will help individuals learn to overcome deficits in these three areas (Kinnaman and Bellack, 2012).

The tenth core principle of CBT is emotion regulation. This includes teaching the client to select the situations in which they become involved in order to control emotions, to change the situations, and to change the way situations evoke emotions (Papa, Boland, and Sewell, 2012). The eleventh core principle is communication, during which clients are taught strategies to maximize positive communication and minimize negative communication (Lavner and Bradbury, 2012). The twelfth core principle is positive psychology, which focuses on building on strengths and positive emotions rather than focusing on weaknesses and negative emotions (Magyar-Moe, 2012). The thirteenth core principle of CBT is acceptance, which encourages the client to be open to their experiences (Wilson et al., 2012a). These principles can be used in the treatment of a variety of different disorders, and have been applied successfully to the treatment of sex offenders.

This type of therapy takes a cognitive behavioral approach to changing problems that are associated with sexual offending. For instance, **cognitive distortions**, or false thought processes and beliefs, have been shown to be associated with sexual offending. These include "beliefs that children are sexual beings, that individuals are entitled to sex, that sexual activity does not harm children, that society's rules and norms may be disregarded, and that women are game-playing, deceitful, and/or hurtful individuals. . ." (Schaffer et al., 2010, p. 95). Another problem associated with sexual offending is emotional dysregulation, "which may be defined as a propensity to experience negative affect, a slow return to baseline after emotional arousal, and/or non-normative emotional reactions to stimuli. . ." (Schaffer et al., 2010, p. 96). Additionally, deficits in interpersonal skills, preoccupations with deviant sexual behavior, and a lack of empathy are also associated with sexual offending. Each of these issues can be addressed using CBT. In CBT, a therapist will address cognitive distortions by discussing the incorrect belief in a group setting and coming up with alternative interpretations.

A therapist may also use role playing where the offender plays the role of a victim in order to address some of this cognitive distortion regarding victims (Schaffer et al., 2010). Emotional dysregulation can be addressed by labeling emotions and learning about the functions of emotions, and then working to find the underlying cause of emotions that precede sexual offending. CBT for interpersonal skills deficits can include training and role-playing in social situations and discussions regarding age-appropriate friends and relationships (Schaffer et al., 2010). Deviant sexual behaviors are usually treated using the behavioral techniques described above, while a lack of empathy can be treated in a CBT context by examining victim reactions in videos or letters to help the offender understand the victim's perspective (Schaffer et al., 2010).

Most studies of cognitive behavior treatment for sex offenders have been done by treating incarcerated offenders and tracking them after their release. For instance, participants in a Vermont sexual offender treatment program during a 12-year period were followed for an average of just over 5 years to determine if they committed sexual, violent but non-sexual, non-violent offenses, and parole violations. The specialized treatment group, which was a cognitive behavioral group program, focused on accepting responsibility, modifying cognitive distortions, developing victim empathy, controlling sexual arousal, improving social competence, and developing relapse prevention skills (discussed in detail on page 280) (McGrath, Hoke, and Vojtisek, 1998). One control group consisted of offenders who received peer group therapy and individual therapy, but they were not part of the specialized group discussed above. There was also a control group that received no treatment. Although the number of sexual reoffenders was quite small, it was still determined that the specialized treatment group had the lowest rate of sexual reoffending (McGrath, Hoke, and Vojtisek, 1998), indicating that CBT was effective in treating sexual offenders. A similar study was conducted using a group of sex offenders in a CBT treatment program in California, with the finding that sex offenders in the CBT treatment were less likely to commit new sex offenses than offenders who did not wish to (and did not) receive treatment (Marques et al., 1994).

Some widely used programs utilize CBT components, one of which is the Good Lives Model (GLM). The GLM focuses on the capabilities or strengths of offenders and uses these to teach other skills that will help offenders interact in society in acceptable ways. The correct choices and type of life depend on the context of the individual, but there are certain characteristics that will help the individual obtain positively valued human goods (Ward and Stewart, 2003). This model has been applied to sexual offenders with mental disorders, as these are offenders who are especially likely to have difficulty achieving certain goods due to their condition. Although this was evaluated with a group of case studies rather than a controlled experiment, the researchers were positive about the potential for the GLM to be successful with sex offenders (Gannon et al., 2011).

Risk-Need-Responsivity

Another common use of cognitive behavioral treatment for the treatment of offenders is with the **Risk-Need-Responsivity (RNR)** model. As the name suggests, the three principles of the RNR model are 1) risk, where the individuals at highest risk of offending are identified, 2) need, where the needs of an offender that are associated with why they commit crime and that require treatment are identified, and 3) responsivity, where effective treatments are tailored to specific individuals (Bonta & Andrews, 2007). Using this model, the highest risk offenders are given the most treatment, and offenders are assessed to determine what needs are associated with their criminal behavior, and then treated using CBT that is adjusted to account for characteristics of the individual offender so that treatment is most effective for them (Bonta and Andrews, 2007).

When this model is applied specifically to treating sex offenders, sex offenders should first be assessed using a validated assessment tool. Those with higher risk should be assigned to a treatment program that is higher in intensity, including a greater number of treatment hours over a longer period of time, compared to those with lower risk factors (Olver, 2017). Based on assessment, the needs of an offender that should be treated would be identified. There are a number of factors associated with increased sexual reoffending, including "sexual preoccupation, any deviant sexual interest, offense-supportive attitudes, emotional congruence with children, intimacy deficits, lifestyle impulsivity, poor problem-solving ability, poor cooperation with rules/supervision, hostility, and negative social influences" (Olver, 2017, p. 1316). Treatment should address the needs the offender displays most seriously. For the responsivity principle, treatment should respond to specifics of the offender, such as their "strengths, motivation level, cognitive ability, learning style, cultural ancestry, readiness to change, [and] personality characteristics" (Olver, 2017, p. 1322).

Research shows that the RNR model can be effective in reducing recidivism. A study comparing sex offenders treated in an in-prison RNR program in Canada with those in other in-prison sex offender treatment programs, and to those who received no treatment, found that those in the RNR program generally had a lower rate of sexual recidivism and a lower rate of violent recidivism. This is particularly true for offenders who were classified as medium or high risk; there were no significant differences for low risk offenders in most recidivism categories (Olver et al., 2020). The degree to which a program adheres to the principles of the RNR model is an important consideration in predicting whether it will be effective. Programs that show effectiveness in studies run by researchers often do not show these positive results when run by correctional staff (Bonta and Andrews, 2007). In a study of probation officers, Viglione (2019) found that these officers often did not adhere to RNR principles. The probation officers often did not trust risk assessment, did not make case plans that took client needs into consideration, and used treatment as a punishment rather than to address mental health concerns (Viglione, 2019). These findings suggest concerns with the effectiveness of such programs in practice compared to in research settings.

Relapse Prevention

Relapse prevention is a strategy used after other treatment has already been applied; this strategy teaches the offender methods of preventing himself from reoffending. It is based on treatment used in the case of "indulgent" behaviors, such as alcoholism, gambling addiction, and drug addiction (Pithers et al., 1983). While similar to cognitive-behavioral therapy, it has a different structure and different terminology that make it distinct (Laws, 1999). In relapse prevention, the therapist takes the perspective that while relapse (committing another sexual offense) is not to be expected, it should be planned for. Even after undergoing treatment, an offender should not expect to never have urges or fantasies associated with their offending again. Learning how to control such urges from turning into offending will reduce the incidence of relapse (Pithers et al., 1983).

In the relapse prevention model, high-risk situations, which generally involve negative emotional states or interpersonal conflict, are identified. High-risk situations can lead to fantasizing about the inappropriate behavior, which can lead to developing a plan and engaging in the inappropriate behavior (Pithers et al., 1983). Reoffending, or relapse, can occur due to an "apparently irrelevant decision" (AID) that results in the offender being exposed to a high-risk situation. Using a coping strategy during high-risk situations can reduce the likelihood of relapse. If a treated offender successfully avoids committing an offense in such a situation, his confidence about the next high-risk situation increases; whereas, if an offender does not avoid committing an offense, he believes he cannot control his urges, and the likelihood of continuing to offend increases (Pithers et al., 1983). An offender's belief that he cannot control his offending and that he will always be a sex offender is known as the "abstinence violation effect." The offender who has failed and attributed it to his always being a sex offender will continue to fulfill that role (Pithers et al., 1983).

The first stage in relapse prevention treatment is to help the offender develop reasonable expectations regarding continuing to experience sexually inappropriate fantasies. The offender must be made aware that these may continue to occur, but that there are still ways of avoiding offending (Pithers et al., 1983). During the first stage, the therapist should assess the offender's suitability for treatment using the relapse prevention model. Those who are generally well socialized, other than their sexual offending, do best in this treatment. The offender must commit to the treatment and have a limited number of high-risk situations to be addressed. Those who are experiencing psychosis or who do not have a grasp of reality will not be successful in this program (Pithers et al., 1983).

High-risk situations are identified in treatment through having the offender self-monitor, using direct observation, and structured interviews. Offenders must record when they have negative moods that may lead to offending, when they have inappropriate fantasies, and if they begin to plan committing an offense (Pithers et al., 1983). Offenders are also observed to determine their level of arousal to appropriate and inappropriate sexual situations. Their erectile response is measured while watching or listening to tapes that depict different degrees of force, and different ages and genders of victim/partner. When aggressive sexual acts or sexual acts with children result in arousal, those situations are considered a risk for reoffending (Pithers et al., 1983). In the structured interview, the therapist helps identify the AIDs that resulted in committing an offense. For example, these would be things that seemed innocent, but put the offender in contact with potential victims or resulted in him being alone with a potential victim (Pithers et al., 1983).

Because avoiding all risk is not practical, the offender is taught coping strategies for when he does find himself in such situations. He outlines a "problem-solving procedure" (Pithers et al., 1983, p. 231) by fully describing a risky situation and how he can best react. He describes these situations to a therapist as practice for encountering them and to receive feedback to modify coping strategies if necessary. He is taught to cope with urges by imagining himself as something disgusting if they consider acting out an urge. He is also taught to avoid situations and behaviors, to the extent possible, which put him at risk of feeling deviant sexual urges (Pithers et al., 1983).

Relapse prevention has been evaluated in a number of sex offender treatment programs, including a program in Vermont and a program in California. The Vermont Treatment Program for Sexual Aggressors (VTPSA) followed those who received relapse prevention treatment long term and compared their outcomes to data gathered from the program for Mentally Disordered Sex Offenders at Atascadero State Hospital in California, which was a similar program with the exception of not offering relapse prevention (Pithers and Cumming, 1989). Offenders in the VTPSA were followed for six years, with a high degree of community supervision, making it unlikely that they would relapse without being detected. An interesting element of this follow-up study is that rapists and pedophiles[1] were analyzed separately and yielded different results. Over the follow-up period, 15 percent of rapists relapsed, compared to 3 percent of pedophiles who committed a new sexual offense, and this difference was statistically significant (Pithers and Cumming, 1989). In the Atascadero sample, a greater, but not statistically significantly greater, percentage of rapists reoffended than in the VTPSA sample, but there was a statistically significant difference in the rate of pedophile reoffending. In the VTPSA sample, 3 percent of pedophiles reoffended, whereas 18 percent of the Atascadero sample of pedophiles recidivated. It seems that relapse prevention was not more effective than other treatment with rapists, but it may be successful at reducing sexual reoffending among pedophiles (Pithers and Cumming, 1989). A possible reason for this difference is that anger, which may be difficult to control with relapse prevention, is a precursor to rapists sexually offending (Pithers and Cummings, 1989).

Although at the time the Atascadero data were collected California did not offer a relapse prevention sex offender program, it did begin one in 1984. The study of relapse prevention in California's Sex Offender Treatment and Evaluation Project (SOTEP) is somewhat different from the Vermont study in that those who were convicted of sexually offending against their biological children were not eligible for the program, excluding one group of pedophiles that would have been included in the Vermont study. The SOTEP study included a relapse prevention treatment group, a control group in prison, and a matched control group who met the eligibility criteria for the treatment program but did not participate (Miner et al., 1990). Evaluating just those in the treatment group, the data showed that between intake into the program and release into the community, sexual offenders reduced their score on the Cognitive Distortions and Immaturity scale, measuring perceptions that others caused their sexual offending, and the Justification Scale, which measures perceptions that the victim was not harmed or that his offending was justified. When comparing the treatment group to the non-treated control group, those convicted of child molesting (not rape of adult women), treated inmates took more responsibility for their offending

1. While the terms "pedophile" and "child molester" are not interchangeable, the authors here are switching between the terms according to the term used by the author or authors of the research being discussed.

than did the control group (Miner et al., 1990). Comparing these groups on reincarceration (not specific to sexual offending), the relapse prevention treatment group had lower rates of reoffending than did the control groups (Miner et al., 1990), but as this is not broken down into sexual and non-sexual offending, it is unclear whether the treatment is effective at reducing the behavior it targeted specifically.

A later analysis of the SOTEP found that there were positive steps taken for treated offenders in terms of learning relapse prevention skills and achieving program goals; however, some offenders leave the program after being released and immediately go back to their high-risk behaviors, ignoring the relapse prevention skills they have learned. Additionally, there is no statistically significant difference between the reoffense rates of those who were treated and those who were not (Marques et al., 2000). This leads to questions regarding who was successfully treated, how those who were invested in the program can be differentiated from those who were not, and what type of community follow-up would be needed to sustain any improvements.

The relapse prevention program has been revised in response to evaluations of the results. In the first revision, the number of relapse prevention sessions was increased and an activity called "the decision chain" was added to replace the offense cycle method. The decision chain activity has offenders link the situations they face, their feelings, and behaviors, as well as devise a list of things they should do differently (Mann and Thornton, 2000). In the second revision, the program developers attempted to deal with a new issue. Previously it had been assumed that all offenders in the treatment program desired to stop their offending. The second revision accounted for the fact that there were offenders who were still motivated to offend, so relapse is an active process rather than the result of poor decision making (Mann and Thornton, 2000). This revision included an "Old Me, New Me" method in which offenders record their achievements and articulate the emotional changes they experience. It also includes a game where offenders progress around a board and encounter high-risk situations and provide their strategies for dealing with such situations (Mann and Thornton, 2000).

Multisystemic Therapy for Juveniles

Like several of the therapeutic methods discussed above, **multisystemic therapy (MST)** was developed and has been used to address antisocial behavior of many kinds. Unlike these other therapies, MST is used specifically with juveniles. MST is designed to address needs in several different "systems," including the individual and the family, peer groups, school or work settings, and community settings in which they are involved (Henggeler, 1999). Treatment using MST is quite intensive, involving the youth and their family members, and is delivered at least weekly, with the family's involvement taking from 2 to 15 hours per week. Therapeutic sessions are delivered by highly qualified practitioners who have low caseloads and who are widely available to the families they are treating (Henggeler, 1999). MST is based on identifying the strengths in the individual, family, and other contexts, and using those to promote change. MST has been extensively evaluated (Henggeler, 1999), including evaluations of its effectiveness specifically with juvenile sex offenders.

In a study comparing youth with a history of sex offenses randomly selected to receive MST with a comparison group who received the standard treatment in the community, Borduin and colleagues (2009) found that MST offered substantial improvement over the standard treatment. The group receiving MST had fewer arrests overall and fewer arrests for sexual crimes, as well as spending less time in a detention center during the follow-up period. The participants in this study were reassessed an average of approximately 25 years later to determine if the effects of MST were long lasting. During the follow-up period, the participants in MST were less likely to have an arrest than those with the standard treatment, and they had fewer arrests overall, fewer arrests for sexual offenses, and spent fewer days incarcerated (Borduin et al., 2021). The authors found that some of the positive results associated with the original MST treatment, such as having more peers who followed societal norms, fewer delinquent peers, and a better family life, may have been the driving factor behind the success of MST in relation to reduced arrests (Borduin et al., 2021).

Drug Therapies

As discussed in the section on castration, "chemical castration" is the more modern attempt to reduce deviant sexual activity in sexual offenders by removing or reducing hormonal causes of this behavior. There are several types of drug therapies that have been used to attempt to cause this outcome, including anti-androgen drugs and drugs used as anti-depressants. The most studied of these drugs is Medroxyprogesterone acetate, also known as **Depo-Provera**. Medroxyprogesterone acetate, or Depo-Provera, is most commonly used as a contraceptive injection for women. It is administered for this purpose in a dose of 150 mg every 13 weeks as an intramuscular injection. At this dose, the manufacturer warns that Depo-Provera has been shown to reduce bone density in users and should not be used for more than two years (Pharmacia and Upjohn, 2015). Depo-Provera has also been used to attempt to reduce reoffending in sexual offenders. In studies of sex offenders, the dose given is as high as 400 mg every week (Meyer, Cole, and Emory, 1992).

The mechanism by which Depo-Provera should work to reduce sexual offending is that it will reduce testosterone levels, which is the source of sexual arousal; Depo-Provera also has a tranquilizing effect on individuals (Kiersch, 1990). The effect of the Depo-Provera injection was tested in a study at Atascadero State Hospital in California using eight volunteer sex offenders, four of whom completed the entire study. Each subject was given 16 weeks of the Depo-Provera injection and 16 weeks of a saline injection in four rotations, so each subject served as his own control. With this small sample size, the researchers did not find a consistent difference in arousal to deviant sexual stimuli during the saline injection phases and the Depo-Provera injection phases. They do suggest that this is possibly because it took several weeks for subjects to return to their pre-treatment testosterone levels after the last Depo-Provera injection, thus weakening any impact that might have been seen (Kiersch, 1990).

A larger study of 40 sex offenders who received Depo-Provera and 21 control group sex offenders who refused treatment followed subjects for up to 12 years to determine both their reoffending rates and any side effects subjects may have experienced as a result of receiving Depo-Provera (Meyer, Cole, and Emory, 1992). These researchers found that 58 percent of the untreated group reoffended, while only 18 percent of the treated group did; however, these reoffense rates are not specific to sexual reoffending and include all arrests (Meyer, Cole, and Emory, 1992). It is unclear from this study what effect Depo-Provera has specifically on sexual offending. The researchers did find that one-third of the treated subjects experienced weight gain greater than ten pounds, 10 percent experienced gallstones, and 8 percent experienced diabetes (Meyer, Cole and Emory, 1992); however, the control group did not list their physical symptoms, so it is unclear if these effects are a result of receiving the drug.

An evaluation of the use of Depo-Provera in Oregon from 2000 to 2004 compared sex offenders who received the treatment, sex offenders who were recommended to receive the treatment but did not receive it, and sex offenders who were not recommended to receive Depo-Provera treatment (Maletzky, Tolan, and McFarland, 2006). During the evaluation period, only 5.1 percent of the 79 offenders receiving Depo-Provera committed an offense of any kind, and none of them committed a sexual offense. In contrast, of those who were recommended to receive the drug but did not receive it, 30.9 percent committed an offense, with nearly 60 percent of those offenses being sexual in nature, and 26.9 percent of those not recommended for Depo-Provera committed a new offense, with 55.3 percent of those being sexual (Maletzky, Tolan, and McFarland, 2006). With this larger sample and more rigorous scientific methodology, it seems that using Depo-Provera to treat sex offenders can be successful, at least for those that are recommended to receive the treatment.

ASSESSING TREATMENT EFFECTIVENESS

Assessing the effectiveness of any type of sex offender treatment with rigorous scientific methodology is difficult because such studies require control groups and accurate measures of whether the offender continues to commit sex offenses after treatment (Marques et al., 1994). In addition to determining whether an offender has committed another sexual offense since being treated, which can be done using self-report or arrest/conviction for a sex offense (often inaccurate), there are other methods for determining the offender's likelihood of committing a sexual offense based on his response to stimuli or deviant fantasies.

Penile plethysmography (also known as phallometry) is a procedure used to gauge male arousal to varying types of stimuli by measuring tumescence, or erectile response. This is most commonly done using a band placed around the penis that acts as a strain gauge and measures the circumference of the penis (Fernandez, 2009). The subject undergoing plethysmography is presented with stimuli as either slides, videotapes, or audiotapes; subject erectile response is measured as various categories of stimuli are shown or heard. Slides and videotapes present ethical challenges, as some of the stimuli would need to be images of nude children in order to gauge responses in pedophiles and some would need to depict forced sex to gauge responses in rapists (Fernandez, 2009).

Other than ethical concerns, there are measurement validity concerns with plethysmography as there are some sex offenders who show no erectile response, or very low response, to any type of sexual stimuli. This means that this method of measuring sexual interest would be invalid for these subjects. The less explicit, and therefore potentially more ethical, the stimuli, the larger the problem of non-responders becomes (Fernandez, 2009). Despite these concerns, and problems with a lack of standardization in stimuli and instructions, this method is still widely used and is considered a valuable tool in determining levels of arousal to deviant and non-deviant sexual stimuli (Fernandez, 2009).

The **Abel Assessment for Sexual Interest (AASI)** uses similar stimuli to those described above. The subject views slides of clothed adult, adolescent, and young males and females and uses a computer to rate from one to seven his view of the slides as highly sexually disgusting to highly sexually arousing. The subject then advances to the next slide. Without the subject's knowledge, the computer measures the amount of time that the subject spends looking at each slide (Abel et al., 1998). This type of measurement has been tested while subjects were measured using plethysmography, and researchers found that there was consistency with the type of slides the subjects found arousing using both methods (Abel et al., 1998). This instrument has also been validated using adolescent male subjects in distinguishing between those who were sexually interested in young children and those who were not (Abel et al., 2004). As a result, measuring the amount of time subjects look at slides may be a better method of evaluating sexual interest than plethysmography, as it does not involve procedures that subjects might find offensive, and subjects who are able to control their erectile responses may still be evaluated with the AASI (Krueger, Bradford, and Glancy, 1998).

Olver and Wong (2011) stated that in the search for effective treatment to reduce the risk of recidivism, we must believe that this risk of recidivism is changeable. Thus, of the numerous instruments designed to measure recidivism risk in sex offenders, those that measure dynamic factors are likely to be more valid. Offenders with higher static risk factors have a greater responsiveness to treatment than those with low static risk factors, as their likelihood of recidivism was greater to begin with. For high-risk individuals, changes in dynamic factors can significantly reduce their likelihood of recidivism (Olver and Wong, 2011). Indeed, for a group of moderate to high-risk sex offenders, a treatment program reduced their risk of sexual recidivism over ten years compared to a group of untreated sexual offenders (Olver, Wong, and Nicholiachuk, 2009). Offenders were tracked for ten years, and while the percent who sexually offended over that time period continued to increase, after ten years 21.8 percent of the treatment group had reoffended and 32.3 percent of the control group had reoffended (Olver, Wong, and Nicholiachuk, 2009).

As noted earlier, results for sex offender treatment programs are mixed and may depend on factors specific to the way a particular program is run rather than the treatment philosophy or design. Another theoretically sound treatment program did not show a difference between those who completed treatment, those who started but did not complete treatment, and those who were not treated in terms of general reoffending, sexual reoffending, or violent reoffending (Schweitzer and Dwyer, 2003). This study did not follow participants for the long time period mentioned in the previous study, so it is possible that differences between these groups would develop over a greater time period.

CONCLUSION

Many types of treatment for sex offenders are discussed in Chapter 13. Modern treatments include therapeutic communities, behavioral therapy, CBT, relapse prevention, and drug therapies. Each method has shown some degree of success in reducing reoffending, sexual reoffending, or deviant sexual interests, although there is no clear choice in terms of what is the most effective treatment. The common myth that sex offenders cannot be treated seems to be not entirely true, but perhaps the type of treatment that is effective for one may not be the best treatment for another. More research is needed into the characteristics of sex offenders as they relate to the success of different methods of treatment. Also to be considered are ethical issues associated with treatment, particularly drug therapies that can have both medical and behavioral side effects, and behavioral therapies that have the potential to seriously disturb an offender. Alternatively, how do these potential negative outcomes compare with the negative outcome of the offender committing another sex offense?

This discussion of sex offender treatment also concludes our discussion of sex offenders and the American criminal justice system. Chapter 14, which concludes this book, will specifically address future challenges associated with sex offenders and identify the best practices that the criminal justice system can use when dealing with sex offenders.

KEY TERMS

- Abel Assessment for Sexual Interest (AASI)
- ammonia aversion
- aversion therapy
- behavioral therapy
- castration
- chemical castration
- cognitive behavioral therapy
- cognitive distortions
- Depo-Provera
- directed masturbation
- electroconvulsive therapy (ECT)
- faradic (electrical) aversion
- lobotomy
- multisystemic therapy (MST)
- olfactory aversion
- penile plethysmography
- relapse prevention
- Risk-Need-Responsivity (RNR)
- sexual psychopath era
- sexual psychopath laws
- shame aversion
- testosterone
- therapeutic communities

EXERCISES

1. Describe each of the modern sex offender treatments. Does past research indicate that these treatments are effective? Provide examples of successes and failures.
2. Describe the historical methods of sex offender treatment. Have these been shown to be effective? Are there ethical problems associated with older methods of treatment? Explain your response with examples.
3. Find a recent news story about sex offender treatment. What type of treatment is being used? Would the information in Chapter 13 suggest that this treatment will be effective? Why or why not?

ESSAY QUESTIONS

1. Based on the information in Chapter 13, how would you design an effective sex offender treatment program? For what types of offenders would this treatment be most effective? What research would suggest the treatment's effectiveness? Are there any ethical issues associated with your proposed treatment?
2. Thinking of castration and chemical castration as responses to sex offenders, do you think these responses are more punitive or rehabilitative? What makes you think so? What benefits do you see to this response? Are there any drawbacks or ethical concerns with the response?
3. What makes it so difficult to determine if a sex offender treatment program is effective? What are some ways you can measure effectiveness? What are the strengths and weaknesses of each?

14

CONCLUSION

Chapter Objectives

After reading this chapter, students will be able to:

- Explore the future issues associated with sex offender policies in the United States.
- Identify the problems associated with evaluating sex offenders as an aggregate group.
- Examine future directions of sex offender research.
- Evaluate the future directions of sex offender laws.
- Explore the future of sex offender treatment practices.
- Evaluate target hardening practices to avoid sexual victimization.

INTRODUCTION

Sex offenders are every bit the modern-day boogeyman (Tewskbury, 2014). Sex offenses inflict physical violence on the victim while also exacting a psychological toll. Former U.S. Attorney General Alberto Gonzalez (2008) argued, "As a society, we already share a revulsion for what these criminals do to our children. The crimes are so terrible, that people are uncomfortable thinking about them" (p. 29). For Gonzalez, the criminal justice system's fight against the threat of sex offenders is tantamount to a "war against evil."

Stinson, Sales, and Becker (2008) argued that to understand how to prevent a problem behavior, one must know what causes the behavior and its correlates. In addition to preventing problem behaviors, understanding the genesis of problem behaviors also allows professionals to assess future risk and create treatment programs to curb the problem behaviors. Stinson et al. (2008) argued that understanding the etiology of sex offending specifically can better inform public policies that pertain to sex offenders.

This textbook outlines the etiology of sex offenders. From evaluating the nature of sex offending to the policies that seek to protect U.S. citizens from the threat of sex offenders, we identify the historical and contemporary problems associated with sex offenders. While Chapters 1 through 13 focus on the current picture of sex offending and sex offender legislation, Chapter 14 examines where we should go next when it comes to effectively curbing sex offending. Chapter 14 explores the research in the area of sex offending and what academics can do to further the study of sex offenders. Next, we examine the failures of sex offender policies and what can be done to increase the chances of success when punishing sex offenders. Finally, Chapter 14 concludes by evaluating what individuals can do to decrease their chances of becoming the victims of sex offenders and discussing how victims of sex offenses can be supported.

THE CONCEPTUALIZATION OF SEX OFFENDERS

Sex offenders are treated as a single, monolithic group complete with similar behaviors, motivation, and most importantly, punishment. Sex offenders are considered to be "incurable, insatiable, and psychologically similar" (Dokoupil, 2014). The term sex offender is then applied to a "broad cross section of juveniles and adults, flashers, and rapists" (Dokoupil, 2014, p. 4). As a society, law makers, criminal justice practitioners, and even as academics, we tend to lump all sex offenders together in one giant group. Even the title of this textbook and our treatment of sex offenders has fed into this same principle.

Walker (2007) argued that sex offenders are not a homogenous group; some sex offenders are more likely to recidivate, for instance. Sex offenders must be disaggregated by different offenses and behaviors if we are to truly understand the etiology of sex offending. Research indicates differences across different types of sex offenders. For instance, research tends to show that sex offenders whose victims are adults and sex offenders whose victims are children display similar behaviors but are motivated by different factors; likewise, these offenders differ in their response to punishment and treatment. Under our current monolithic conception of sex offenders, an 18-year-old individual who has "consensual sex" at a party with an underage victim (statutory rape) is equated with an individual who rapes and violently beats a victim in a park in the middle of the night.

This does not even include the net-widening that has occurred through current sex offender policies where states further add offense types that have nothing to do with sex offending. In most states, kidnapping is linked to sex offending via sex offender registration and notification (SORN) policies. In other states, all violent crimes may be included on the state's sex offender registry. In still other states, prostitution is included as a registerable sex offense. To lump these offense types with actual sex offenses convolutes our efforts to better understand and contain the threat of sex offenders. Kidnapping, due primarily to the Jacob Wetterling incident (see Chapter 11), has been associated with sex offending. In fact, most kidnappings are the result of family members embroiled in a custody dispute; still another type of kidnapping revolves around ransoms. Neither of these types of kidnappers should be confused for a sex offender. Likewise, other types of violent crime are not related to sex offending. Not every sex offender violently physically assaults their victim and/or murders their victim. Similarly, a sex offender will not necessarily become an armed robber or vice versa. Finally, prostitution is a crime that is predicated by a capitalistic exchange. While sex occurs, it is generally a consensual sex act revolving around the exchange of money. Sex offenders must no longer be treated as an aggregate group.

Conclusion #1: Disaggregate the conceptualization of sex offenders by offense and victim types to gain a better understanding of the etiology of sex offending.

Conclusion #2: All offenses that are not sex offenses should be excluded from the study of sex offenders and the creation of sex offender policies.

FUTURE RESEARCH ON SEX OFFENDERS

Current research on sex offenders indicates the lack of effectiveness of current sex offender policies. Unfortunately, there is an overreliance on official statistics when making these conclusions; this is linked to the issues seen in the previous section. More important, this overreliance on official data means that most studies are plagued by a singular limitation: only those sex offenders who have been caught and/or convicted through the criminal justice system can be evaluated. This is also known as problems with sampling effects.

Stinson et al. (2008) outlined several issues surrounding sampling effects that must be addressed in future research of sex offender psychological characteristics and behavior. First, even in psychological studies, only sex offenders who have been identified via conviction are part of the samples or population evaluated. This excludes those who have not been arrested and those who have not acted on sexually deviant urges. Second, scientific research involves voluntary participation. For sex offenders, this can be problematic. Many sex offenders deny or minimize their sexually inappropriate behaviors; these individuals will be less likely to participate in research exploring the genesis and continuity of sex offending behaviors (Stinson et al., 2008).

Third, sex offender research is predominated by male subjects. There are very few studies that explore female sex offenders. Are male and female sex offenders equivalent in their offending behaviors? There is some indication that male and female sex offenders are treated differentially by the criminal justice system. Think about the news stories of teachers who have had sexual relations with students in high school or junior high school. If the teacher is a male and the student is a female, the teacher is going to be viewed negatively and punished to the fullest extent of the law. Take the alternative to this situation. If the teacher is a female and the student is a male, the reaction becomes more nuanced. Due to cultural beliefs, males and females in society can have differing views of the incident. In many cases this will result in a different criminal justice system response than for a male offender. Remember, both male and female teachers perpetrated the exact same criminal offense, but they are not always treated similarly. Recently, reported incidents of sex offences on student victims by female teachers have been treated more similarly to those by their male counterparts in public opinion and in the courts.

Quantitative studies on sex offenders are abundant in the academic record. Unfortunately, most of this research is based on official data sources. More qualitative data is necessary in the study of sex offenders and sex offender policy. Tewksbury and colleagues have led the way in this avenue of research. While this data is desirable in sex offender research, it should be noted that it suffers from methodological limitations as well. Researchers should be careful of self-report studies due to the fact that many sex offenders deny the victim or minimize their sexually deviant behavior (Stinson et al., 2008). This can stem from deliberate deception or can be a function of the offender's fear of prosecution or risk of additional sanctions. As well, it is important for sex offenders to present minimal future risk of offending to avoid more stringent sentences, sanctions, and application of the various public safety policies (SORN, residence restrictions, and civil commitments).

Two final issues with the qualitative study of sex offenders include subject beliefs and recall. Qualitative studies of sex offenders may have to contend with the fact that sex offenders may have "beliefs that represent significant distortions of reality" (Stinson et al., 2008, p. 18). For instance, the sex offender may well believe that the victim "wanted or desired" the sexual act. A sex offender with this belief system does not think that he/she committed a crime. Subject recall of events can lead to faulty research results as well. The memory or recall issues can be due to substance abuse, childhood experiences (sexual, emotional, and physical abuse) that caused memory problems and/or lowered intellectual functioning, increased denial, and the impact of institutionalization on memories before the incarceration/hospitalization began.

Finally, in the area of research, academics must make their research more accessible to those who create sex offender legislation. It is clear from the research that current sex offender policies are having little impact on sex offending behavior or recidivism. Unfortunately, there is a disconnect between this line of inquiry and the laws that are passed at the federal, state, and local levels. The way to make research more accessible to policymakers is to decrease the "academic jargon" and limit the amount of statistical tables (or place them in appendices) that inevitably cause people to zone out when reading an academic report or peer-reviewed article.

Conclusion #3: Future research in the area of sex offenders must strive to incorporate better data and effective research designs. This could be the use of qualitative research designs and the collection of qualitative data.

Conclusion #4: More research is needed on the etiology of female sex offenders.

Conclusion #5: More funding is necessary for research that evaluates the effectiveness of current sex offender policies.

Conclusion #6: Make research more accessible to politicians and the public.

FUTURE SEX OFFENDER POLICY

As noted in the previous section, it is clear that politicians do not keep up with current research in the area of sex offenders. For instance, George Allen (2008), former governor and senator from Virginia who was instrumental in passing sex offender legislation at the federal and state levels, is on record as saying, "it is the way it is across this country—the highest recidivism rate, or the highest repeat offender rate of any crime—even higher than murderers, even higher than armed robbers—is [among] sex offenders" (p. 24). Every portion of this statement is factually incorrect. Murderers are the least likely group of offenders to recidivate. Sex offenders are typically the second least likely group of offenders to recidivate. Allen's "facts" are indicative of politicians' and the public's general beliefs about sex offenders.

As Alberto Gonzales (2008), former U.S. Attorney General, argued, the greatest threat to children "is the one posed by sexual pedophiles and predators" (p. 28). Many other threats to children are much more prevalent than that of predatory sex offenders. Recent legislation has focused on community re-entry as the focal point for dealing with sex offenders. Rice (2008) considers these policies both simplistic and venomous. Rice (2008) stated that "60 percent of boys and 80 percent of girls who are sexually victimized are abused by someone known to the child or the child's family" (p. 195).

Meloy, Boatright, and Curtis (2013) acknowledged that "there are more laws aimed at apprehending, convicting, punishing, and managing sex offenders than there are laws directed towards any other type of offender" (p. 617). This has resulted in more behavior denoted as sex crimes, net-widening, longer sentences, and specialized community supervision requirements (Meloy et al., 2013). Their research on legislator and practitioner perceptions of current sex offender policies was conducted over 12 months and utilized a non-probability sampling procedure (purposive); the total number of subjects interviewed was 61 policy makers and 25 practitioners who have been heavily involved with SORN (the response rate was around 35 percent). Meloy et al. (2013) found that the media's impact on sex offender policies is profound. Most of the respondents in the study suggested that current sex offender policies were predicated on incidents that occurred outside of the respondent's state. In addition, most respondents noted the "overextension of the law, anti-therapeutic characteristics, and the effects of stigmatization and labeling" (Meloy et al., 2013, p. 633). These results are not surprising. Sample's (2001) research from around the turn of the century indicated the knee-jerk nature of sex offender legislation and policy makers' desires to appease an incensed public outcry against sex offenders.

Across the criminal justice system, politicians who create and maintain public policies tend to ignore criminological research. This is even truer in the area of current sex offender policies. The greatest declines in reported sex crimes occurred in the early 1990s, before the spread of registries. The drop has continued when more sex offenses should be reported due to intensive community supervision by the public (Dokoupil, 2014). This would suggest the utter failure of SORN, residence restrictions, and civil commitments in protecting society from the sex offender threat. This failure is further

14

exacerbated by the fact that most in the public do not even utilize the information that is collected across these policies (Anderson and Sample, 2008). The disregard for research in this area costs taxpayers' money with little to no benefit for those public funds. While current sex offender policies seem to make the public happy, which in turn makes politicians happy, this is not the hallmark of effective public policy.

Policy makers should also be concerned about the ramifications of old and new sex offender laws. For instance, in South Carolina, a neo-Nazi couple (Jeremy and Christine Moody) murdered Charles Parker and his wife, Gretchen. The Moodys pretended to have car trouble, asked for assistance from the Parkers, and then proceeded to stab and shoot them. The reason for the murder stemmed from Charles Parker's conviction for a sex crime and his registration under SORN. Jeremy Moody is on record as stating, "Child molesters do not deserve to live. [If I] had to do it over again, I'd kill more." Christine Moody said, "I have no regrets. Killing that pedophile was the best day of my life." While Charles Parker was a sex offender, his wife was not. Charles Parker's sister, Brenda Franklin, did not appreciate being taunted by the Moodys, who plead guilty to her brother's murder. Franklin stated, "It made me mad. They was [sic] laughing about what they did, took somebody's life the way they did. Nobody should die like that. Nobody." While the incidence of such reprisals against sex offenders are rare (see Chapter 11), they could not occur without the presence of current sex offender policies.

■■■

In another example, Sharie Keil is not a sex offender, but her child is (Dokoupil, 2014). In 1998, her 17-year-old son was convicted of having sex with a pre-teen at a party (aggravated sexual assault). This resulted in a six-month jail sentence and lifetime mandatory registration as a sex offender. Later after Keil's conviction, a new law was passed that banned sex offenders from participating in Halloween. Punishable by a year in jail, the Keils had to stay inside their home and post a sign saying they had no candy. In this instance, the special blend of punishment and societal protection resulted in harm/stigma to the offender's family members. Family members must then choose to "serve time" with the sex offender or throw them out. Either instance will result in household instability. Lotke and Hoelter (2008) argued that "Web-based notification, community leafleting, burdensome regulations, public stigma, and possible harassment and flight make it difficult to stabilize one's life" (p. 72). Current sex offender policies have a destabilizing effect on convicted offenders.

Talman (2008) wrote that current sex offender policies are not a "cure-all." Radford (2008) noted that current sex offender policies that separate sex offenders from the public are "of little value because they are based on faulty assumptions" (p. 62). He further noted,

> Simply knowing where a released sex offender lives — or is at any given moment — does not ensure that he or she won't be near potential victims. Since relatively few sexual assaults are committed by released sex offenders, the concern over the danger is

> wildly disproportionate to the real threat . . . legislation should be based on facts and reasoned argument instead of fear in the midst of a national moral panic (p. 62).

This is one of the primary reasons current sex offender policies are failing; they are predicated on beliefs rather than on facts. For the future of sex offender policy, it is essential that hyperbole and political hysteria be excluded from the public discourse on what should be done about sex offenders. The law should be realigned with the notion of a criminal paying his or her debt to society (punishment for the crime) and then being allowed to go on with their lives (reintegration). This is not happening for sex offenders today who are oftentimes registered for the duration of their lives. Under this scenario, it is "harder to stay out of trouble than is even possible" (Dokoupil, 2014, p. 6). Many sex offenders are forced to jump from location to location, state to state, when it is discovered they are registered sex offenders; it is also difficult to get a job and maintain housing. Some suggest repealing current sex offender laws outright. It would be better to keep these laws for the most serious sex offenders; in this scenario, the criminal justice system would target those sex offenders at the highest risk of recidivism. Through this targeted approach, current sex offender policies like SORN, residence restrictions, and civil commitments might have a better chance of success.

One of Meloy et al.'s (2013) key findings was that academic researchers need to do a better job marketing their research by making it more accessible to lay people. Even if policy makers do pay attention to the research, it is still difficult for a politician to be opposed to sex offender policies. If the politician votes for repeal or a lowering of sex offender post-release restrictions, political enemies will necessarily attack the approach. The only glimmer of hope is found in periods of economic downturns. Many "get-tough" approaches to crime have been questioned over the last couple of decades. While many commonly held political beliefs about stringent crime policies have been reworked in recent years, this has not extended to sex offender policies to date. The impact of the Covid-19 pandemic will likely have an impact on criminal justice policies across the board as there is some indication that crime is on the rise.

Conclusion #7: Sex offender policies should not be based on beliefs.

Conclusion #8: Sex offender policies should not be based on knee-jerk legislation responding to a particularly heinous, yet rare, victimization.

Conclusion #9: Sex offender policies should be grounded in empirical research.

Conclusion #10: SORN, residence restrictions, and civil commitments should be reserved for only the most dangerous sex offenders.

Conclusion #11: Sex offender policies should target specific types of sex offenders in order to be more effective.

Conclusion #12: Sex offender policies should universally include some form of treatment for sex offenders.

TREATMENT FOR SEX OFFENDERS

Before beginning our discussion of the treatment of sex offenders, recall that sex offenders are almost the least likely criminal group to recommit any crimes according to official statistics. The vast majority of studies indicate that sex offenders do not recidivate to the scale that most in society believe. Treatment for offenders who are not likely to recidivate could misdirect public funds from other areas that are in more need and could be more effective. Despite this fact, many still want sex offenders to be treated for their compulsions.

According to the Association for the Treatment of Sexual Abusers (ATSA) (2008), sex offenders cannot be cured. The ATSA (2008) likens the desire to perpetrate sex crimes to the desire to use drugs. Through treatment, drug users can change their behavior because they are committed to a productive and healthy lifestyle. As with drug offenders, the ATSA argued that the use of cognitive behavioral treatment can help sex offenders to better control their behavior. Cognitive behavioral therapy for offenders focuses on victim awareness, patterns of behavior (people, places, and things that put the offender at-risk), situational avoidance, viewing their own behavior differently, and the acquisition of new coping skills. The ATSA (2008) wrote, "Although sex offenders may continue to be attracted to children, they can learn to avoid acting on their impulses" (p. 43). Just as with drug offenders, the ATSA (2008) noted that treatment does not work for all sex offenders. Treatment duration, treatment dosage, and offender amenability to the treatment all impact the outcome for the sex offender.

Early studies from the 1970s and 1980s indicated that treatment had little impact in rehabilitating sex offenders. These early studies have led to the general belief that treatment is not a viable solution to sex offending. More recent research tends to show that those sex offenders who have been treated have lower rates of recidivism than sex offenders who have had no treatment. In some studies, the recidivism rate for treated sex offenders is 40 percent lower than for those sex offenders who did not have treatment (Hanson, 2000).

Several meta-analyses indicate the efficacy of treatment for sex offenders (Alexander, 1999; Aos et al., 2001; Hall, 1995; Hanson et al., 2002; Losel and Schumaker, 2005; Mandeville-Norden and Beech, 2004). Hall (1995) found that treatment reduced sex offender recidivism by 30 percent, Alexander (1999) found that treatment reduced sex offender recidivism by 59 percent (sex offenders who completed treatment had a rearrest rate of 7.2 percent and those who were untreated had a rearrest rate of 17.6 percent), and Lipsey et al. (2007) found that treatment reduced sex offender recidivism by 37 percent. It is clear, sex offenders who complete treatment programs are less likely to recidivate than those who did not participate in such a program.

The ATSA (2008) wrote, "Because treated offenders reoffend at lower rates than untreated offenders, providing therapeutic intervention saves money on investigation, prosecution, incarceration, and victim services" (p. 46). The ATSA (2008) suggested that the cost of treatment is cheaper than incarceration; treatment for sex offenders costs about $5,000 per year and incarceration costs over $20,000 per year. The combination of the two is what makes it difficult for correctional organizations perpetually facing funding dilemmas. Thus, more money is needed for sex offender treatment across the United States. There is also a need for the training of correctional staff and the inclusion of clinical staff in sex offender treatment; maintaining the integrity of a sex offender treatment program designed by researchers is an important factor in its success.

It should be noted that some sex offenders are more dangerous (sexual predators for instance); these offenders need more intensive treatment. Risk assessment instruments are used to gauge the dangerousness of sex offenders. Qualified professionals use risk assessment tools to screen sex offenders into risk categories. "Progress has been made in the science of risk assessment, which allows us to determine the likelihood that a sex offender will commit a new sex crime in the future" (ATSA, 2008, p. 45). Estimates for the risk of danger are relatively accurate in the area of sex offenders. Hanson and Morton-Bourgon's (2005) work on predicting sex offenders' risk of recidivism has shown great reliability. Hanson and Morton-Bourgon's (2005) assessment efforts show that demographic information, criminal history, troubled childhood environment (sexual or physical abuse), deviant sexual interest, antisocial behavior, impulsivity, and lifestyle instability all guide and improve predictions of sex offenders' risk of recidivism.

In Meloy et al.'s (2013) study of policy makers' beliefs about current sex offender treatment, there was a divide in beliefs in the effectiveness of treatment. Respondents indicated that therapy was necessary for sex offenders to maintain law-abiding lives; however, most subjects also believed that sex offender treatment was not an effective public policy strategy. Many subjects suggested "you can't change these people" (Meloy et al., 2013, p. 633). Again, research disputes the prevailing wisdom among policy makers and the public.

Due to the lack of effectiveness of current sex offender policies, treatment for sex offenders is the most promising approach to reducing offending and recidivism. Talman (2008) went so far as to argue for treatment of all sex offenders, whether it works or not. Fortunately, the majority of states integrate treatment with the convicted sex offender's punishment (probation or prison). Talman (2008) suggested that combining treatment and community reintegration serve the purpose of extending an offender's responsibility for their actions. Current policies do not help sex offenders take responsibility for their prior and current actions. Sex offender treatment should be given more attention and funding by policy makers.

Conclusion #13: Academics and practitioners should continue to hone assessment procedures and instruments to better predict sex offender threat and potential recidivism.

Conclusion #14: More funding should be allocated for sex offender treatment at the federal and state levels.

Conclusion #15: Academics and practitioners should continue to hone treatment programs to more effectively curb sex offender recidivism.

SEX OFFENDERS AND POTENTIAL VICTIMS

Victims of sex offenses are never inherently responsible for their victimization. The sex offender is the one that is responsible for the sex crime. Despite this, victims do have a role in any criminal event. The routine activities theory, developed by Cohen and Felson (1979), examines daily activity patterns to assess when crimes will occur. The routine activities perspective is stated most simply as "the probability that a violation will occur at any specific time and place might be taken as a function of the convergence of likely offenders and suitable targets in the absence of capable guardians" (1979, p. 590). Cohen and Felson argued that "routine activity patterns" affected the convergence in space and time of three key elements of direct-contact predatory crime: a motivated offender, a suitable target, and the absence of a capable guardian. The lack of any one of these three elements would be sufficient for deterring a criminal act; all three of these elements were necessary for a predatory criminal act to occur.

While the routine activities theory does not evaluate the motivation of either criminals or victims, it does illustrate that how individuals go about their lives may put them in a criminal situation at some point. A person who goes out at night, imbibes too much alcohol, does drugs, and does not have a support system of friends watching out for him/her can make an individual a suitable target for sex offenders or many other types of criminals. Individuals may not be able to avoid sexual victimization, but they can take steps to decrease the likelihood of victimization. These steps are known as target hardening.

Many things can be done to help protect against potential sexual victimization, and other forms of victimization as well. Most of these target hardening actions are posted on university websites that students mostly ignore, especially in the heat of the moment of being out on the town on a weekend night. Things people should remember when out at night to decrease the chances of victimization include:

- Don't travel alone.
- Call campus safety for escorts if you do not feel safe on campus.
- Avoid contact with strangers.
- Avoid dark or secluded places.
- Keep vehicle doors locked at all times.
- Keep room/apartment doors locked at all times.
- Trust your instincts.

While these actions can help decrease the chances of victimization, they do not completely protect an individual. These actions are also more likely to reduce the chances of stranger victimization than the more common acquaintance or intimate partner rape. These crimes are very difficult to prevent at the victim level because there is generally a degree of trust between the victim and the offender, meaning that the victim voluntarily associates with the offender. In these cases, prevention methods targeted at the offender, such as sexual assault prevention and awareness programs on college campuses, may be more successful.

In addition to the above target hardening strategies, technology has been created that can also help a person decrease their chances of victimization. There are a myriad of smartphone apps that can help to prevent victimization. *Guardly* sends emergency alerts to friends and family and links the user to 911. *Circle of 6* links six friends' or family members' phone numbers in case of rape/sexual assault or domestic violence. *OnWatch* alerts friends and family members in case of emergency and can alert police and/or campus security. *MyForce* triggers calls and pinpoints location if a person feels they are in danger; this a monitored subscription service. Organizations, such as colleges and universities, can also employ apps such as *LiveSafe*, which allows users to contact campus emergency services, request a safety escort, or contact friends. All these apps can technologically help individuals with target hardening, which can be more effective at preventing sexual assault committed by strangers. In addition to target hardening apps, apps that record consent, and thus would be more relevant to acquaintances and people in relationships, have been developed. These are of questionable value, as "consent" can be digitally recorded under duress, and that consent could be used to discredit a victim if a sexual assault is committed.

While target hardening has value for adults who have more control over their routine activities, children's routine activities are controlled much more by their parents or guardians. Parents and guardians can attempt to reduce their children's risk by keeping them away from situations where they will encounter an offender; however, many people are unaware of the risk posed by trusted individuals in their children's lives. Additionally, parents and guardians may be offenders themselves. Individuals should be more educated about the nature of sex offending in the United States. As anyone can be the victim of a sex crime, education can help with target hardening practices for adults, but it can also help individuals to assess if children have been the victims of sex offenses.

Many who are sexually victimized do not report the incident. This can be due to a sense of embarrassment, not wanting to get the offender in trouble, and not wanting to deal with the criminal justice system. It is important that anyone unfortunate enough to suffer a sexual victimization report the victimization. This is for their safety as well as other individuals who could fall prey to that same sex offender. A side effect of better reporting is that academics will be better able to explain the nature of sex offending; likewise, policy makers may be able to create more effective laws to combat the threat of sex offenders. This is important as most studies rely on official data to some extent. Regardless of whether a victim of a sex offense chooses to report the offense, supportive counselors with knowledge about the impact of sexual assault should be available to them. Technology can assist with access to support. For instance, the Rape, Abuse & Incest National Network (RAINN) has developed an app that will connect victims of sexual offenses to a hotline, by phone or chat, with access to trained crisis counselors and resources for additional support. The app also provides information about sexual assault and about self-care for those who have been victimized.

Unfortunately, many victims of sex offenses report negative experiences with law enforcement and medical personnel, which can deter reporting. Law enforcement officers have a tendency to ask questions in a way that can imply victim blaming, or can directly blame the victim, especially in the common situation where alcohol or drugs are involved in the assault. They may also disbelieve the victim, or ascribe motives to her reporting the crime, such as revenge against an unfaithful boyfriend, or explaining away being caught in an affair. Police officers are trained to question suspects and may not act empathetically when questioning a victim who has just undergone a traumatic experience.

In addition to problems with law enforcement, victims also have experienced long waits at emergency rooms to obtain a forensic medical exam, and they may be examined by a physician who does not have experience collecting forensic evidence. They also may not be able to choose to have a female physician complete the exam, and they may find a male performing such an invasive exam after being violated by a male to be further traumatizing. Additionally, the emergency room setting does not provide a great deal of privacy for victims, and the presence of law enforcement, along with the talk of medical staff in the hallways, may make it clear to others present that the individual is a victim of a sex crime, which they may wish to keep private.

In response to issues with law enforcement and medical staff, many jurisdictions have developed Sexual Assault Response Teams (SARTs), which consist of a law enforcement officer, a specially trained Sexual Assault Nurse Examiner, and a victim advocate. In counties with SARTs, when a sexual assault is reported, all three of these professionals are contacted to meet the victim, often in a specialized, private section of a medical facility, where they may be more comfortable than in a typical emergency room setting. The victim advocate is responsible for ensuring that the victim's rights are protected, that the victim is as comfortable as possible, and may provide emergency counseling services. This member of the SART team is not responsible for investigation or evidence collection and helps the victim feel more in control. Rape crisis centers, which provide the victim advocate, may also provide training to law enforcement in their area to help them respond to sexual assault reports more sensitively. SART teams may improve the victim's experience in reporting sexual assaults and encourage reporting in communities where there is awareness of this support system.

Conclusion #16: Individuals should practice target hardening techniques to decrease their chances of sexual victimization.

Conclusion #17: Individuals should be educated on the nature of sex crimes to better decrease their chances of sexual victimization.

Conclusion #18: Funding should be provided for the creation of SART teams, and law enforcement should be trained to respond to sexual assault victims in a sensitive manner.

Conclusion #19: Victims of sex crimes should be encouraged to report the offense to authorities.

CONCLUSION

While sex offenders are the current boogeyman facing society today, they are a threat that can be managed effectively and efficiently. It is emotion and fear that undermine our best efforts to deal with sex offenders. The ATSA (2008) argued that emotionally "charged reactions to sex crimes often lead to legislation that is not driven by data or science but rather by outrage and fear" (p. 53).

Zott (2008) indicated that the primary underlying assumption of current sex offender policies is that ensuring that sex offenders "live and work as far away from children as possible will significantly reduce the sexual victimization of children" (p. 20). This assumption has only been heightened by the role the mass media plays in perpetuating high profiles of sex offender cases that are intrinsically abnormal to most sex crimes. For Zott (2008), these "tragic stories compel an outraged and frightened public to urge their elected officials to pass laws to protect children from such dangers, and lawmakers respond enthusiastically" (p. 20).

Zott (2008) noted that the assumption that children are in the most danger of sexual victimization from strangers is patently false and unsupported in the research. Most children are sexually abused by family members and/or friends of the family (Lotke and Hoelter, 2008). Radford (2008) argued that hundreds of thousands of "children are abused/neglected each year by parents and caregivers and 1,500 American children died from that abuse in 2003—most of the victims under the age of four. That is more than *four children per day*—not by convicted sex offenders or internet predators" (p. 62).

We will never be able to fully eliminate sex crimes from occurring. We can create laws that will keep the current level of sex offending at historic lows. As the ATSA (2008) argued, "Lawmakers and citizens should advocate for research-based social policies that protect women and children as well as rehabilitate perpetrators" (p. 53). This can only occur through ignoring the myths underlying sex offending and understanding the nature of sex crimes, planning, the development of goals/objectives, and ongoing research.

GLOSSARY

Abel Assessment for Sexual Interest Uses images of clothed adult and adolescent males and females for sex offenders to rate their sexual interest. Also measures the time spent looking at each image and uses this as the measure of sexual interest.

Actus Reus An element of defining an action as criminal, which refers to committing the criminal act.

Ammonia Aversion An aversion therapy where a sex offender inhales ammonia, triggering the pain system of the body, while viewing deviant sexual material or having deviant sexual fantasies, thus reducing their arousal to deviant stimuli.

Auburn System Also known as the congregate system, a plan to deal with prison inmates by segregating offenders at night into their own cells; during the day, the offenders work together in silence in a large room.

Autoerotic Asphyxiation The constriction of oxygen during masturbation or sexual intercourse where a strangulation device of some sort is used (belt, bag, chemicals, choking, etc.).

Automated Fingerprint Identification System (AFIS) Used by law enforcement to store and match fingerprints from crime scenes, offenders, and suspects.

Aversion Therapy A type of therapy in which an offender will come to associate deviant arousal with something unpleasant.

Behavioral Therapy A type of therapy for sex offenders which discourages inappropriate arousal.

Bestiality The act of having sexual intercourse with an animal

Bite Mark A mark left on the skin of an individual who is bitten by an offender; useful for identification of the offender as it often contains DNA.

Blood Punishments Punishments that result in the spilling of blood from the execution or the beating/torture of the offender.

Boot Camp Shock Incarceration The convicted offender experiences a great deal of punishment in a truncated time period.

Buffer Zone Also known as halos, these are areas that prohibit the presence of sex offenders. These prohibited zones are generally outlined in terms of feet or meters.

Carnal Abuse Another term for sexual abuse.

Castration An attempt to reduce the intensity of sexual desires through surgical removal of the testes.

CCTV Testimony Closed-Circuit Television Testimony, allows the witness to be seen by the courtroom, but the witness is not actually present. The testimony is provided through a closed-circuit television system installed in the courthouse.

Chemical Castration Removing or reducing male hormones in the body, often done using a drug called medroxyprogesterone acetate (Depo-Provera).

Child Abuse The act or series of acts of physically or emotionally injuring a child.

Child Cruelty Child abuse, including the sexual abuse of a child.

Child Molestation Any indecent or sexual activity on, involving, or surrounding a child, usually under the age of 14.

Child Molester An individual who commits a contact sex offense with a minor, ranging from fondling to forcible rape.

Child Porn Another term for child pornography.

Child Pornography The use of underage children in various media for the purposes of sexual arousal for the viewer.

Child Sexual Abuse Occurs when a child experiences sexual contact, ranging from fondling to forcible rape.

Civil Commitment Based on the linking of some sex crimes, violence, and mental disorders, a policy where sex offenders are placed in mental health facilities for an indeterminate time after completion of a prison sentence.

CODIS Combined DNA Index System, used by law enforcement to store and match DNA profiles obtained from crime scenes, offenders, and suspects.

Cognitive Behavioral Therapy Therapy based on three principles: thinking can affect behavior, thought process can be altered, and behavioral change may be achieved through changes in the thought process.

Cognitive Distortion Thought processes in which there are conflicts between external reinforcements and internal self-condemnation; for child sexual abusers, this type of thought process is suggested to allow the abuser to have beliefs that normalize the sexual abuse of children.

Community Corrections Any punishments that are meted out without the offender having to serve time in a correctional facility.

Crime Control A purpose of criminal law, which serves to protect society.

Criminal History How extensive the criminality of an offender is in the past.

Criminal Law Involves public wrongs where the state is the plaintiff, the potential punishments are loss of liberty or life, a unanimous verdict is required, and proof must be beyond a reasonable doubt.

CSEM Child Sexual Exploitation Material, depictions of child exploitation, including those commonly known as child pornography, but it also includes additional material such as audio or written descriptions of child exploitation

Dark Figure of Crime Crime that goes unreported to criminal justice agencies.

Date Rape A rape committed by a person who is escorting the victim on a social occasion. Also sometimes used in reference to what is more accurately called acquaintance rape or relationship rape.

Death Penalty Imposed sanction that results in death for the convicted offender.

Depo-Provera Medroxyprogesterone acetate, marketed as a contraceptive injection for women. The drug is also used in chemical castration of sex offenders as it reduces testosterone.

Detective An investigator within law enforcement who takes over an investigation after the initial information is gathered.

Determinate Sentences Fixed sentences for criminal convictions. All offenders receive identical sentences for identical crimes.

Deterrence When either offenders or members of society do not engage in criminal behavior due to the possible consequences or formal sanctions associated with that criminal behavior.

Deviance Violations of societal norms and group informal rules. In relation to sex offenders, deviance revolves around paraphilias.

Differential Offending Some groups are more likely to commit crimes based on some singular characteristic.

Differential Treatment Implies that the criminal justice system is somehow handling different criminals through unsystematic approaches.

Directed Masturbation A part of some sex offender treatments in which the offender is directed to masturbate to appropriate sexual stimuli in order to increase arousal to appropriate targets.

Disclosure When someone who has been the victim of a sex crime tells another person about their victimization. Studies often measure disclosure rates to the police, as well as disclosure to other service providers or friends.

Discrimination In sentencing, when one group of individuals is sentenced more harshly based on a singular characteristic (race, for example).

Disparity In sentencing, differences in sentences across individuals with similar characteristics; disparities are not necessarily indicative of discrimination.

DNA Deoxyribonucleic acid, which is a genetic code that is unique to every individual with the exception of monozygotic twins. Useful in identifying the offender in a sexual offense, as DNA is contained in every cell, and is left in semen, sweat, blood, tissue, and hair follicles.

Double Victimization The criminal justice system response to sex offenses where the victim is subject to vigorous and repeated questioning about the crime and is subject to medical examinations for evidence collection, which may result in additional trauma.

Due Process A purpose of criminal law, which serves to protect the rights of the accused and ensure the fairness of the case.

Electroconvulsive Therapy A therapy during which electricity is passed through the brain, triggering a seizure. Today this is used in the treatment of severe psychiatric disorders, and has also been part of sex offender treatment.

Empirical Studies Research The collection of evidence or data conducted by researchers, including studies to determine the prevalence of rape.

Ephebophilia Sexual attraction to minors older than the age of 13.

Evolutionary Theory Suggests that rape is the result of biological drives men have to reproduce, in contrast with the drives women have to limit sexual access.

Exhibitionism Exposure of the genitals to another person, generally a stranger.

False Allegations When a person reports a sex offense that did not actually happen.

Faradic (Electrical) Aversion An aversion therapy during which an electrical current is applied (usually to the fingertips) during arousal to inappropriate stimuli, thought to reduce the sexual arousal to that stimuli.

Felonies Crimes that are more serious than misdemeanors, which are punishable by more than one year of imprisonment, which is generally served in a prison facility.

Female Juvenile Sex Offenders A female under the age of 18 who commits a sex offense.

Female Sex Offenders A female who commits a sex offense; this is more prevalent than typically believed.

Feminist Theory As it relates to sex offenses, suggests that rape is the result of a patriarchal society.

Fetishism Sexual fantasies about either inanimate objects or specific body parts; both of these are symbolic of another person.

Fingerprints The ridge patterns located at the tips of the fingers in all humans, thought to be unique to individuals, and used as a way of identifying them.

Follow-Up Period In recidivism research, the time between when an offender is convicted of a crime and when or if they are convicted of another crime. For sex offenders, the general follow-up period is five years.

Forensic Medical Examination Often called a rape kit or sexual assault kit, but refers to the process of examining the body of a victim of a sexual offense for evidence of injury and evidence of the identity of the perpetrator.

Frotteurism Sexual arousal stemming from the touching of or rubbing against a non-consenting person.

General Recidivism Refers to offenders who engage in any further criminality after their initial criminal act. Generally studied after a conviction.

Grooming Child molesters inserting themselves into a new environment around a new target before sexually molesting victims. This is done to gain access to a child, gain compliance, and maintain secrecy.

Groth's Typology Divides rape into anger rape, power rape, and sadistic rape.

Hebephile Someone who has a sexual attraction to pubescent children.

Hierarchy Rule The rule in the UCR that dictates that only the most serious crime is recorded in the data source, so if an offender raped and murdered a victim, only the murder would be recorded.

Holmes and Holmes' Typology Divides rapists into power reassurance rapists, anger retaliation rapists, power assertive rapists, and sadistic rapists.

Human Trafficking The illegal movement of individuals for the purposes of either commercial sexual exploitation or forced labor.

Hypoxia The result of the deprivation of oxygen.

Incapacitation Goal/philosophy of punishment that emphasizes imprisonment of offenders under the aegis that if the criminal is in prison, they cannot be in the community perpetrating further crimes.

Incarceration Sanction where the convicted criminal serves his/her time in a prison or jail facility.

Incest A type of child sexual abuse in which the perpetrator has a familial relationship with the victim.

Incidence Study A study that attempts to estimate the rate of child sexual abuse, in which the number of cases reported within a one-year period is recorded and an annual rate is produced.

Indecent Exposure An offensive display of one's body in public, especially the genitals.

Indeterminate Sentences Criminal sentences that provide a range of sentences with a maximum and minimum limit (10 to 20 years, for example); the judge selects the time based on the specifics of the case.

Index Crimes The eight most serious crimes recorded by the UCR: arson, murder and non-negligent manslaughter, forcible rape, robbery, burglary, larceny, and motor vehicle theft.

Initial Effects The effects of childhood sexual abuse that affect the victim during the time period that the abuse is ongoing and up to two years after.

Institutional Corrections Penological practices that focus on convicted offenders who serve time in a prison or jail facility.

Interrogation An interview with a suspect to a crime, the main goal of which is to get the suspect to confess to the crime.

Johns Patrons of prostitutes.

Juvenile Sex Offenders Sex offenders who commit a sex offense when they are below the age of 18.

Kiddie Porn Another term for child pornography.

Law A set of formalized rules that delineate acceptable and unacceptable behaviors for a population.

Lifestyle Theory A theory of victimization, specifying lifestyle characteristics or behaviors that place a person at risk for criminal victimization.

Lobotomy A procedure in which the nerves in the frontal lobe of the brain are cut so as not to connect with other areas of the brain. Historically used as a treatment for sex offenders.

Long-Term Impacts Effects of childhood sexual abuse that affect the victim long after the abuse has stopped, and which may not be resolved without treatment.

Mala En Se A category of crime, which includes behaviors that are considered wrong in and of themselves.

Mala Prohibita A category of crime, which includes behaviors that are only considered bad because of the existence of a law against such behaviors.

Male Peer Support Theory Suggests that rape supportive attitudes are maintained in all-male peer groups.

Mandatory Sentence Removes the selection of a punishment from the judge's hands if a defendant is convicted of particular crimes; an example is a mandatory minimum for crack cocaine possession.

Megan's Law Federal statute that legalized the release of information contained on sex offender registries in the United States.

Mens Rea Refers to the criminal mindset or intent of an individual who commits a crime.

Meta-Analysis Research that collects the data used in previous empirical studies and combines that data to analyze findings across multiple studies.

#MeToo Movement A social movement in response to sexual assault and sexual harassment; A hashtag used on social media for the user to indicate they had experienced sexual harassment or assault, which was used to demonstrate the prevalence of these experiences.

Misdemeanors Crimes that are less serious than felonies, which are punishable by less than one year of imprisonment in a jail.

MST Multisystemic therapy, a therapeutic method that has been applied to sex offenders, which addresses needs within the individual and family, peer groups, school or work setting, and community setting

MTC: CM3 Massachusetts Treatment Center: Child Molester, version 3 A typology of child molesters based on level of fixation with children and level of contact with children

NAMBLA North American Man/Boy Love Association, supports adult sexual interest in children with the goal to "end the extreme oppression of men and boys in mutually consensual relationships" and to "support the rights of youth as well as adults to choose the partners with whom they wish to share and enjoy their bodies."

NatSCEV National Survey on Children's Exposure to Violence, a nationally representative telephone survey of children to measure different types of victimization, including sexual victimization.

NCANDS The National Child Abuse and Neglect Data System, a national collection of data about child abuse and neglect collected by each of the states.

NCVS National Crime Victimization Survey, a method of crime measurement that relies upon victim self-reports to a nationally representative survey.

Necrophilia Attraction to dead bodies that may result in sexual intercourse with a dead body.

NIBRS National Incident-Based Reporting System, a UCR program that attempts to overcome the problems with the hierarchy rule. NIBRS is a data set that utilizes police report data and provides more detailed information about each criminal incident.

NIS National Incidence Study, measures the incidence of child maltreatment, including child sexual abuse, using official sources and reports from professionals. Measures using both the harm standard and the endangerment standard.

NISVS National Intimate Partner and Sexual Violence Survey, a nationally representative telephone survey of adult men and women, measuring lifetime prevalence and 12-month rates of several types of violence, including rape and other unwanted sexual activity.

Non-Contact Sexual Offense A sexual offense in which the offender does not have physical contact with the victim, including exhibitionism and the consumption of child pornography.

Norms Informal societal or group rules that regulate individual behavior.

NVAWS National Violence Against Women Survey, nationally representative survey conducted to establish, among other things, the lifetime prevalence of rape.

Offense Seriousness How significant a crime is. This has great ramification for sentences imposed on convicted offenders.

Official Data Sources Records collected by organizations, usually governmental, in the course of day-to-day operations.

Olfactory Aversion An aversion therapy in which a sex offender is exposed to a noxious smell during arousal to inappropriate sexual stimuli, thought to reduce the arousal to those stimuli.

Omission Failing to act (in this context, in a way that would be considered criminal).

Paraphilias Sexual disorders that can result in sexual fantasies and urges in relation to behaviors, individuals, and/or objects.

Paraphilias Not Otherwise Specified (NOS) Thirty-eight uncommon paraphilias that are aggregated into a single category in the *DSM-5*.

Parole Period of community corrections served by a criminal offender after serving time in either a prison or jail.

Partialism Intense eroticism associated with bodily actions or body parts.

Patrol Officer A police officer, often the first to respond to the report of a sexual offense, who conducts a basic investigation before the offense is more fully investigated by a detective.

Pederasty Anal intercourse between a man and a boy.

Pedophile Someone who has a sexual interest in prepubescent children.

Pedophilia Paraphilia involving individuals who are sexually attracted to children aged 13 and under.

Penile Plethysmography A procedure used to gauge male arousal to varying types of stimuli by measuring erectile response, using a band placed around the penis that acts as a strain gauge and measures the circumference of the penis.

Penitentiary The original name for modern-day prisons; early penitentiaries had a very religious orientation devoted to helping the offender repent.

Pennsylvania System Also known as the separate system, inmates had their own cells and had no contact with other inmates or guards.

Primary Deviance The first deviant act that violates norms in which the individual does not consider him/herself to be a deviant.

Prison Correctional facility for offenders convicted of a felony and generally incarcerated for a period of over one year.

Prison Rape Rape that occurs in a prison or jail. There are three kinds: inmate on inmate rape, correctional officer on inmate rape, and inmate on correctional officer rape.

Proactive Investigation When law enforcement officers pose as minors online and wait for adults to solicit them for sex, in an attempt to arrest such individuals.

Probation Community correction that diverts convicted offenders from a correctional institution; probation is characterized by a series of conditions the offender must follow for successful completion.

Prostitution The act or practice of engaging in sexual activity for money or its equivalent.

PTSD Post-Traumatic Stress Disorder, a mental health condition in which someone who has been exposed to a traumatic event suffers from intrusion symptoms, avoidance symptoms, negative changes in thought process or moods, and changes in arousal and reactivity which last 30 days or more.

Rape Penetration, no matter how slight, of the vagina or anus with any body part or object, or oral penetration by a sex organ of another person, without the consent of the victim.

Rape Crisis Counseling Short-term counseling for victims of rape that may address the immediate aftermath of an assault, and may also include accompaniment to police stations or hospitals to assist the victim.

Rape Kit Also called a sexual assault kit, which refers to a standardized set of evidence collection tools and receptacles that are generally packaged together and used for the forensic medical examination of victims of sexual offenses.

Rape Myths Widely held negative beliefs about rape and rape victims. Rape myths include the belief that victims lie, that rape is not harmful, and that victims want or deserve rape.

Rape Shield Laws During a trial, these laws were developed to protect the victim from intrusive personal questions about sexual history that have no bearing on a particular case.

"Real Rape" Stereotype that rapes occur between strangers, include violence and weapons, and an appropriately upset and virtuous victim.

Recidivism The recommission of a crime after engaging in crime previously. Generally, this means that the offender has been previously convicted of a crime.

Reformatory Type of prison created during the mid-1800s; the focus of these correctional institutions was to reform inmates into law-abiding citizens.

Rehabilitation Goal/philosophy of punishment that seeks to "fix" offenders through a variety of institutional and community corrections programs.

Relapse Prevention An offender treatment strategy used after other treatment has been applied. Teaches the offender that relapse is not to be expected but should be planned for, and teaches the offender strategies for preventing relapse.

Residence Restrictions Geographic laws and policies that limit the interaction between convicted sex offenders and children by creating zones where sex offender presence is prohibited.

Retribution Goal/philosophy of punishment that seeks to match punishment and crime; biblically speaking, this is an "eye-for-an-eye" doctrine.

Retrospective Incidence Study A study of childhood sexual abuse in which youths are asked to recall sexual abuse incidents that occurred within the last year, producing an annual rate of childhood sexual abuse.

Retrospective Prevalence Study A study of childhood sexual abuse in which an adult sample is asked to recall sexual abuse that took place at any point during their childhood, producing a lifetime prevalence rate.

Revenge Porn The distribution of sexually explicit images of an individual where at least one of the individuals depicted did not consent to the dissemination.

Revictimization When someone who experiences childhood sexual abuse or an adult sexual assault is sexually victimized again.

RNR Risk-Need-Responsivity, a use of cognitive behavioral therapy that has been applied to sex offenders, where high-risk individuals are targeted, the needs associated with offending are identified, and treatment is tailored to those individuals and needs.

Routine Activities Theories of crime that focus on the conditions under which crime occurs, or the factors that put someone at risk for victimization.

RTS Rape Trauma Syndrome, describes the impact of rape upon the survivor. RTS is broken into the acute or disruptive phase, and the long-term process of reorganization.

Sadomasochism A disorder that contains a combination of factors associated with sexual sadism and sexual masochism.

SANE Sexual Assault Nurse Examiner, a medical provider who is specially trained in the collection of evidence from sexual assault victims.

Secondary Deviance Any deviance that occurs after primary deviance has been discovered; it is argued that secondary deviance stems from labels applied by group members.

Self-Blame A victim of a rape or sexual assault attributes the blame for the assault to their character or activities preceding the assault.

Sentencing Phase of a trial that occurs after the determination of guilt. Refers to the sanction an offender will receive for criminal behavior.

Sentencing Enhancements Increasing criminal sanctions by adding extra time for specific offenders or class of offenses.

Sentencing Guidelines Attempt to make sentences across judges and courts more uniform; guidelines are designed to decrease disparities in sentencing.

Sentencing Outcomes The results of the sentencing decision; the type of sanction imposed by the judge.

SES Sexual Experiences Survey, a survey used to measure lifetime prevalence of rape victimization

Sex Offender Any individual who commits a sex offense.

Sex Offender Notification Federal and state laws that determine what information on a sex offender registry can be released and who it can be released to.

Sex Offender Registration Federal and state collection of data related to convicted sex offenders, with primary emphasis on the sex offender's current residence.

Sex Offense An offense that involves unlawful sexual behavior; these crimes include contact and non-contact sexual behaviors.

Sexual Abuse A term that is often used interchangeably with rape; often refers specifically to sexual abuse committed against a child.

Sexual Assault A term that is often used interchangeably with rape, but also refers to offensive sexual contact with another person, exclusive of rape.

Sexual Battery A term that is often used interchangeably with rape, and also refers to forced penetration of a victim.

Sexual Deviance Paraphilias; these sexual acts are considered to be violations of social norms or socially approved. These forms of sexual behavior are generally considered to be less serious than sex crimes.

Sexual Masochism Sexual arousal from being humiliated, beaten, bound, or otherwise made to suffer, as manifested by fantasies, urges, or behaviors.

Sexual Misconduct A term for sexual abuse or sexual assault of a child.

Sexual Offense Any offense involving unlawful sexual conduct, such as prostitution, indecent exposure, incest, pederasty, and bestiality.

Sexual Psychopath Era The 1930s to 1950s when sex offenders were considered mentally and/or physically different from non-offenders.

Sexual Psychopath Laws Allowed for someone who was diagnosed as a sexual psychopath to be confined in a state hospital for an indefinite period of time. Committing a sex offense was often considered evidence that someone was a sexual psychopath.

Sexual Sadism A psychological disorder that revolved around the infliction of humiliation, pain, and/or suffering on others.

Shame Aversion An aversion therapy in which the offender acts out a deviant fantasy and treatment staff stare and make the offender feel shame, thus reducing his arousal to the deviant fantasy.

Shotland's Typology Divides courtship rape into beginning date rape, early date rape, relational date rape, and rape within sexually active couples (further divided into those including battery and those not including battery).

SORN Sex offender registration and notification policies.

Specific Recidivism Measures whether an offender who formerly committed a crime later engages in the same type of criminal offending. Specific recidivism implies that there is some kind of link between the two criminal offenses

SRZ Spatial Restriction Zone, another term for a residence restriction. See residence restrictions.

Statutory Rape The crime of engaging in sexual activity with a minor (as defined by state law) when the perpetrator has reached the age of majority, regardless of that individual's "consent" to the activity.

Substance-Related Sexual Assault A sexual assault that occurs when the victim or offender is under the influence of alcohol or drugs.

SVP Sexually Violent Predator, a convicted sex offender who jointly engaged in sex crimes and violent crimes in the same criminal event.

Testosterone A male hormone which is responsible for sexual arousal.

Therapeutic Communities A prison environment treatment program that can be used to treat sex offenders.

Transvestic Fetishism Recurrent and intense sexual arousal from cross-dressing, as manifested by fantasies, urges, or behaviors.

Truth-in-Sentencing Policies that make sure criminals serve the majority of a sentence they receive.

Type I Offenses The most serious type of crime recorded by the UCR, also known as index crimes. For this type of offense, all reports of the crime are recorded.

Type II Offenses Crimes recorded by the UCR that are not Type I offenses. For this type of offense, only arrests for the crime are recorded.

UCR Uniform Crime Report, a method of crime measurement that records crimes reported to the police.

Unacknowledged Rape A situation where a person has an experience that meets the legal definition of rape, but they do not personally label the experience rape.

Victim Precipitation Acts of commission or omission that an offender perceives to be signals that encourage sexual activity.

Volitional Control Under civil commitment policies, the ability of the sex offender to control his/her behavior, especially in relation to sex offending.

Voyeurism By stealth, a desire to see another person in some state of undress or involved in a sexual act.

REFERENCES

2014 Crime in the United States. (2014). Retrieved from https://www.fbi.gov/about-us/cjis/ucr/crime-in-the-u.s/2014/crime-in-the-u.s.-2014/tables/table-1

Abel, G., Gore, D., Holland, C., Camp, N., Becker, J., and Rathner, J. (1989). The measurement of the cognitive distortions of child molesters. *Annals of Sex Research, 2,* 135-153.

Abel, G., Huffman, J., Warberg, B., and Holland, C. (1998). Visual reaction time and plethysmography as measures of sexual interest in child molesters. *Sexual Abuse: A Journal of Research and Treatment, 10*(2), 81-95.

Abel, G., Jordan, A., Rouleau, J., Emerick, R., Barboza-Whitehead, S., and Osborn, C. (2004). Use of visual reaction time to assess male adolescents who molest children. *Sexual Abuse: A Journal of Research and Treatment, 16*(3), 255-265.

Abrams, D., Tendayi, V., Masser, B., and Bohner, G. (2003). Perceptions of stranger and acquaintance rape: The role of benevolent and hostile sexism in victim blame and rape proclivity. *Journal of Personality and Social Psychology, 84*(1), 111-125.

Acierno, R., Kilpatrick, D., Resnick, H., Saunders, B., DeArellano, M., and Best, C. (2000). Assault, PTSD, family substance use, and depression as risk factors for cigarette use in youth: Findings from the National Survey of Adolescents. *Journal of Traumatic Stress, 13*(3), 381-396.

Ackerman, A.R., Sacks, M., and Greenberg, D.F. (2012). Legislation targeting sex offenders: Are recent policies effective in reducing rape? *Justice Quarterly, 29,* 858-887.

Ackerman, A.R., Sacks, M., and Osier, L.N. (2013). The experiences of registered sex offenders with Internet offender registries in three states. *Journal of Offender Rehabilitation, 52,* 29-45.

Adam Walsh Child Protection and Safety Act. (2006). *United States Code.* Vol. 42, Section 16911.

Addington, L., and Rennison, C. (2008). Rape co-occurrence: Do additional crimes affect victim reporting and police clearance of rape? *Journal of Quantitative Criminology, 24,* 205-226.

Akel, M.A. (2018). The good, the bad, and the evils of the #MeToo movement's sexual harassment allegations in today's society: A cautionary tale regarding the cost of these claims to the victims, the accused, and beyond. *California Western International Law Journal, 49*(1), 103-136.

Alaggia, R. (2005). Disclosing the trauma of child sexual abuse: A gender analysis. *Journal of Loss and Trauma, 10,* 453-470.

Alaggia, R., Collin-Vezina, D., and Lateef, R. (2019). Facilitators and barriers to child sexual abuse (CSA) disclosures: A research update (2000-2016). *Trauma, Violence, & Abuse, 20*(2), 260-283.

Alexander, M.A. (1999). Sexual offender treatment efficacy revisited. *Sexual Abuse, 11,* 101-116.

Allen, G.F. (2008). Tougher laws on sex offenders increase public safety. In L.M. Zott (Ed.), *Sex Offenders and Public Policy* (pp. 22-27). Farmington Hills, MI: Greenhaven Press.

Alper, M., and Durose, M.R. (2019). *Recidivism of sex offenders released from state prison: A 9-year follow-up (2005-2014).* Washington, DC: Bureau of Justice Statistics.

Alter, C. (2014). No more cold cases. *Time, 184*(4), 28-31.

American Psychiatric Association. (2013). *Diagnostic and statistical manual of mental disorders: DSM-5.* Retrieved from http://dsm.psychiatryonline.org

Amir, M. (1967). Victim precipitated forcible rape. *Journal of Criminal Law, Criminology & Police Science, 58*(4), 493-502.

Amir, M. (1971). *Patterns in forcible rape.* Chicago, IL: The University of Chicago Press.

Amirault. J., and Beauregard, E. (2014). The impact of aggravating and mitigating factors on the sentence severity of sex offenders: An exploration and comparison of differences between groups. *Criminal Justice Policy Review, 25,* 78-104.

Amstadter, A., McCauley, J., Ruggiero, K., Resnick, H., and Kilpatrick, D. (2011). Self-rated health in relation to rape and mental health disorders in a national sample of women. *American Journal of Orthopsychiatry, 81*(2), 202-210.

Anderson, A.L., and Sample, L.L. (2008). Public awareness and action resulting from sex offender community notification laws. *Criminal Justice Policy Review, 19.* 371-396.

Anderson, I., and Lyons, A. (2005). The effects of victim's social support on attributions of blame in female and male rape. *Journal of Applied Social Psychology, 35*(7), 1,400-1,417.

Angelone, D., Mitchell, D., and Grossi, L. (2014). Men's perceptions of an acquaintance rape: The role of relationship length, victim resistance, and gender role attitudes. *Journal of Interpersonal Violence, 30*(13), 2,278-2,303.

Aos, S., Phipps, O., Barnoski, R., and Lieb, R. (2001). *The comparative costs and benefits of programs to reduce crime.* Olympia, WA: Washington State Institute for Public Policy.

Aosved, A., and Long, P. (2006). Co-occurrence of rape myth acceptance, sexism, racism, homophobia, ageism, classism, and religious intolerance. *Sex Roles, 55,* 481-492.

Applegate, B.E. (2013). Prior (false?) accusations: Reforming rape shield laws to reflect the dynamics of sexual assault. *Lewis and Clark Law Review, 17,* 899-930.

Arata, C. (2002). Child sexual abuse and sexual revictimization. *Clinical psychology: Science and Practice, 9*(2), 135-164.

Association of the Treatment of Sexual Abusers. (2008). Research and statistics debunk common misconceptions. In L.M. Zott (Ed.), *Sex Offenders and Public Policy* (pp. 43-53). Farmington Hills, MI: Greenhaven Press.

Association of the Treatment of Sexual Abusers. (2020). *Civil Commitment: One approach for the management of individuals who have sexually abused, 2020.* Beaverton, OR: Association of the Treatment of Sexual Abusers.

Bach, M.H., and Demuth, C. (2018). Therapists' experiences in their work with sex offenders and people with pedophilia: A literature review. *Europe's Journal of Psychology, 14,* 498-514.

Bachman, R. (1998). The factors related to rape reporting behavior and arrest: New evidence from the National Crime Victimization Survey. *Criminal Justice and Behavior, 25*(1), 8-29.

Bachman, R., and Saltzman, L. (1995). Violence against women: Estimates from the redesigned survey. Washington, D.C.: Bureau of Justice Statistics.

Bacon, J. (2013, September 6). Judge apologizes for teen rape remarks, not sentence. *USA Today.* Retrieved from www.usatoday.com.

Baker, D., and Prete, M. (2011). Developing therapeutic communities for sex offenders. In B. Schwartz (Ed.), *Handbook of Sex Offender Treatment* (pp. 30.1-30.10). Kingston, NJ: Civic Research Institute, Inc.

Balsamo, M., and Tucker, E. (2020, November 14). That 2008 Jeffry Epstein plea deal? It was just "poor judgement," Justice Department report concludes. *Chicago Tribune.* https://www.chicagotribune.com/nation-world/ct-nw-jeffrey-epstein-report-plea-deal-20201114-yaax2wvumfcijlonedn64us3hq-story.html

Barlow, D., Leitenberg, H., and Agras, W. (1969). Experimental control of sexual deviation through manipulation of the noxious scene in covert sensitization. *Journal of Abnormal Psychology, 74*(5), 596-601.

Barnes, J.C., Dukes, T., Tewksbury, R., and De Troye, T.M. (2009). Analyzing the impact of a statewide residence restriction law on South Carolina sex offenders. *Criminal Justice Policy Review, 20,* 21-43.

Barr, J. (2020, March 11). Harvey Weinstein sentenced to 23 years in prison. *The Hollywood Reporter.* https://www.hollywoodreporter.com/business/business-news/harvey-weinstein-sentenced-23-years-prison-1283818/

Barton, R.R., and Turnbull, B.W. (1979). Evaluation of recidivism data: Use of failure rate regression models. *Evaluation Quarterly, 3,* 629-641.

Baumer, E., and Lauritsen, J. (2010). Reporting crime to the police, 1973-2005: A multivariate analysis of long-term trends in the National Crime Survey (NCS) and National Crime Victimization Survey (NCVS). *Criminology, 48*(1), 131-185.

Beck, A.J., Rantala, R.R., and Rexroat, J. (2014). *Sexual victimization reported by adult correctional authorities, 2009-11.* Washington, DC: Bureau of Justice Statistics.

Beech, A., Craig, L., and Browne, K. (2009). Overview. In A. Beech, L. Craig, and Browne, K. (Eds.), *Assessment and Treatment of Sex Offenders: A Handbook* (pp. 1-12). West Sussex, UK: Wiley-Blackwell.

Beech, A.R., and Harkins, L. (2012). DSM-IV paraphilia: Descriptions, demographics, and treatment. *Aggression and Violent Behavior, 17,* 527-539.

Beecher-Monas, E. (2009). Paradoxical validity determinations: A decade of antithetical approaches to admissibility of expert witness. *International Commentary on Evidence, 6,* DOI: 10.2202/1554-4567.1081.

Beichner, D., and Spohn, C. (2005). Prosecutorial charging decisions in sexual assault cases: Examining the impact of a specialized prosecution unit. *Criminal Justice Policy Review, 16,* 461-498.

Belknap, J. (1987). Routine activity theory and the risk of rape: Analyzing ten years of National Crime Survey data. *Criminal Justice Policy Review, 2*(4), 337-356.

Bell, R. (n.d.). Green River Killer: River of Death. Retrieved from http://www.crimelibrary.com

Bennett, K.J. (2003). Legal and social issues surrounding closed-circuit television testimony of child victims and witnesses. *Journal of Aggression, Maltreatment and Trauma, 8,* 233-271.

Bergen, R., and Maier, S. (2011). Sexual assault services. In C. Renzetti, J. Edleson, and R. Bergen (Eds.), *Sourcebook on Violence Against Women* (2nd ed., pp. 227-243). Los Angeles, CA: Sage Publications, Inc.

Berger, R., and Searles, P. (1985). Victim-offender interaction in rape: Victimological, situational, and feminist perspectives. *Women's Studies Quarterly, 13*(3/4), 9-15.

Best, J. (2004). *Deviance: Career of a concept.* Belmont, CA: Thomson-Wadsworth.

Bickly, J., and Beech, A. (2001). Classifying child abusers: Its relevance to theory and clinical practice. *International Journal of Offender Therapy and Comparative Criminology, 45*(1), 51-69.

Biderman, A.D., and Reiss, A.J. (1967). On exploring the "dark figure" of crime. *Annals of the Academy of Political and Social Sciences, 374,* 1-15.

Black, M.C., and Merrick, M.T. (2013). *Prevalence of intimate partner violence, stalking, and sexual violence among active duty women and wives of active duty men—Comparisons with women in the U.S. general population, 2010.* Atlanta, GA: Centers for Disease Control and Prevention.

Blanchard, R. (2010). The DSM diagnostic criteria for transvestic fetishism. *Archives of Sexual Behavior, 39*, 363-372.

Bloom, S. (2014). No vengeance for "revenge porn" victims: Unraveling why this latest female-centric, intimate-partner offense is still legal, and why we should criminalize it. *Fordham Urban Law Journal, 42*(1), 233-289.

Bloomberg Law. (2022, March 22). Practical guidance - Sexual harassment. Retrieved from https://www.bloomberglaw.com/product/health/page/le_pg_sexual_harassment.

Blumstein, A. (2006). Disaggregating the violence trends. In Blumstein, A., and Wallman, J. (Eds.), *The Crime Drop in America, Revised Edition.* Cambridge: Cambridge University Press.

Bonta, J., and Andrews, D.A. (2007). Risk-need-responsivity model for offender assessment and rehabilitation. *Rehabilitation, 6*(1), 1-22.

Booth, B., and Gulati, S. (2014). Mental illness and sexual offending. *Psychiatric Clinics of North America, 37*(2), 183-194.

Borduin, C.M., Quetsch, L.B., Johnides, B.D., and Dopp, A.R. (2021). Long-term effects of multisystemic therapy for problem sexual behaviors: A 24.9-year follow-up to a randomized clinical trial. *Journal of Consulting and Clinical Psychology, 89*(5), 393-405.

Borduin, C.M., Schaeffer, C. M., & Heiblum N. (2009). A randomized clinical trial of multisystem therapy with juvenile sexual offenders: Effects on youth social ecology and criminal activity. *Journal of Consulting and Clinical Psychology, 77*(1), 26-37.

Bouffard, J. (2000). Predicting type of sexual assault case closure from victim, suspect, and case characteristics. *Journal of Criminal Justice, 28*, 527-542.

Bouffard, L.A., and Bouffard, J.A. (2011). Understanding men's perceptions of risks and rewards in a date rape scenario. *International Journal of Offender Therapy and Comparative Criminology, 55*, 626-645.

Bourke, M., and Hernandez, A. (2009). The 'Butner study' redux: A report of the incidence of hands-on child victimization by child pornography offenders. *Journal of Family Violence, 24*, 183-191.

Braswell, M., McCarthy, B., and McCarthy, B. (2012). *Justice, crime, and ethics, 7th Edition.* Boston, MA: Elsevier.

Briere, J., Evans, D., Runtz, M., and Wall, T. (1988). Symptomatology in men who were molested as children: A comparison study. *American Journal of Orthopsychiatry, 58*(3), 457-461.

Briggs, P., Simon, W., and Simonsen, S. (2011). An exploratory study of internet-initiated sexual offenses and the chat room sex offender: Has the internet enabled a new typology of sex offender? *Sexual Abuse: A Journal of Research and Treatment, 23*(1), 72-91.

Bronson, J., and Carson, E.A. (2019). *Prisoners in 2017.* Washington, DC: Bureau of Justice Statistics.

Brown, M. (2014, May 30). Ex-teacher Stacey Rambold, who got just 1 month for rape of teen, to be re-sentenced. *The Huffington Post.* from www.huffingtonpost.com

Browne, A., and Finkelhor, D. (1986). Impact of child sexual abuse: A review of the research. *Psychological Bulletin, 99*(1), 66-77.

Brownmiller, S. (1975). *Against our will: Men, women and rape.* New York: Fawcett Books.

Budd, K., and Desmond, S.A. (2014). Sex offenders and sex crime recidivism: Investigating the role of sentence length and time served. *International Journal of Offender Therapy and Comparative Criminology, 58*, 1481-1499.

Burchfield, K.B. (2011). Residence restrictions. *Criminology and Public Policy, 10*, 411-419.

Burchfield, K.B., and Mingus, W. (2008). Not in my neighborhood: Assessing registered sex offenders' experiences with local social capital and social control. *Criminal Justice and Behavior, 35*, 356-374.

Bureau of Justice Statistics. (1998). *National conference on sex offender registries.* Washington D.C.: Department of Justice.

Burgess, A., and Hazelwood, R. (1993). The victim's perspective. In R. Hazelwood and A. Burgess (Eds.), *Practical Aspects of Rape Investigation: A Multidisciplinary Approach* (pp.19-41). Boca Raton, FL: CRC Press, Inc.

Burgess, A., and Holmstrom, L. (1974). Rape trauma syndrome. *American Journal of Psychiatry, 131*(9), 981-986.

Burt, M. (1980). Cultural myths and supports for rape. *Journal of Personality and Social Psychology 38*(2), 217-230.

Burt, M. (1991). Rape myths and acquaintance rape. In Parrot, A., and Bechhofer, L. (Eds.), *Acquaintance Rape: The Hidden Crime.* New York: John Wiley & Sons, Inc.

Burt, M., and Albin, R. (1981). Rape myths, rape definitions, and probability of conviction. *Journal of Applied Social Psychology, 11*(3), 212-230.

Burt, M., and Katz, B. (1987). Dimensions of recovery from rape: Focus on growth outcomes. *Journal of Interpersonal Violence, 2*(1), 57-81.

Bynum, T. (2001). *Recidivism of sex offenders.* Silver Spring, Maryland: Center for Sex Offender Management.

Cairnes, F.J., and Ranier, S.P. (1981). Death from the electrocution during auto-erotic procedures. *New Zealand Medical Journal, 94*, 258-260.

Caldwell, M.F., and Dickinson, C. (2009). Sex offender registration and recidivism risk in juvenile sexual offenders. *Behavioral Sciences and the Law, 27*, 941-956.

Call, C. (2018). Megan's Law 20 years later: A systematic review of the literature on the effectiveness of sex offender registration and notification. *Journal of Behavioral and Social Sciences, 5*, 205-217.

Callahan, E., and Leitenberg, H. (1973). Aversion therapy for sexual deviation: Contingent shock and covert sensitization. *Journal of Abnormal Psychology, 81*(1), 60-73.

Calleja, N.G. (2015). Juvenile sex and non-sex offenders: A comparison of recidivism and risk. *Journal of Addictions and Offender Counseling, 36*, 2-12.

Campbell, D.T., and Stanley, J.C. (1966). *Experimental and quasi-experimental designs for research.* Chicago: Rand McNally.

Campbell, R. (1998). The community response to rape: Victims' experiences with the legal, medical, and mental health systems. *American Journal of Community Psychology, 26*(3), 355-379.

Campbell, R., and Fehler-Cabral, G. (2018). Why police "couldn't or wouldn't" submit sexual assault kits for forensic DNA testing: Focal concerns theory analysis of untested rape kits. *Law & Society Review, 52*(1), 73-105.

Campbell, R., Feeney, H., Pierce, S.J., Sharma, D.B., and Fehler-Cabral, G. (2018). Tested at last: How DNA evidence in untested rape kits can identify offenders and serial sexual assaults. *Journal of Interpersonal Violence, 33*(24), 3792-3814.

Campbell, R., and Johnson, C. (1997). Police officers' perceptions of rape: Is there consistency between state law and individual beliefs? *Journal of Interpersonal Violence, 12*(2), 255-274.

Campbell, R., Wasco, S., Ahrens, C., Sefl, T., and Barnes, H. (2001). Preventing the "second rape:" Rape survivors' experiences with community service providers. *Journal of Interpersonal Violence, 12*(2), 1,239-1,259.

Campus Sex Crimes Prevention Act. *United States Code.* Vol. 42, Section 1601 (2000).

Cannon, D., and Baker, T. (1981). Emetic and electric shock alcohol aversion therapy: Assessment of conditioning. *Journal of Consulting and Clinical Psychology, 49*(1), 20-33.

Cantor, D., and Lynch, J.P. (2000). Self-report surveys as measures of crime and criminal victimization. In *Measurement and analysis of crime and justice*, pp.85-138. Washington D.C.: National Institute of Justice.

Carey, K., Durney, S., Shepardson, R., and Carey, M. (2015). Incapacitated and forcible rape of college women: Prevalence across the first year. *Journal of Adolescent Health, 56* (6), 678-680.

Carson, E.A. (2020). *Prisoners in 2019.* Washington, D.C.: Bureau of Justice Statistics.

Casady, T. (2009). A Police chief's viewpoint: Geographic aspects of sex offender residency restrictions. *Criminal Justice Policy Review, 20.* 16-20.

Cautela, J. (1967). Covert sensitization. *Psychological Reports, 20*, 459-468.

Center for Sex Offender Management. (2001). Sex offender myths. Retrieved from http://www.csom.org/

Chaffin, M., Chenoweth, S., and Letourneau, E. (2016). Same-sex and race-based disparities in statutory rape arrests. *Journal of Interpersonal Violence, 31*(1), 26-48.

Chaitin, D. (2019, July 7). Jeffrey Epstein arrested for sex trafficking of minors in Florida and New York. *Washington Examiner.* https://www.washingtonexaminer.com/news/jeffrey-epstein-arrested-for-sex-trafficking-of-minors-in-florida-and-new-york-report.

Chism, L.S. (2013). The case for castration: A "shot" towards rehabilitation for sex offenders. *Law and Psychology Review, 37*, 193-209.

Chu, M.C., and Thomas, S.D.M. (2010). Adolescent sexual offenders: The relationship between typology and recidivism. *Sexual Abuse, 22*, 218-233.

Citizen's guide to U.S. federal law on child pornography. (2020, May 28). The United States Department of Justice. Retrieved August 14, 2021, from https://www.justice.gov/criminal-ceos/citizens-guide-us-federal-law-child-pornography.

Clear, T.R., Reisig, M.D., and Cole, G.F. (2012). *American corrections*, Tenth Edition. Independence, KY: Cengage Publishing.

Clinard, M.B. (1968). *Sociology of deviant behavior.* New York, NY: Holt, Rinehart and Winston.

Cochran, J.C., Toman, E.L., Shields, R.T., and Mears, D.P. (2021). A uniquely punitive turn? Sex offenders and the persistence of punitive sanctioning. *Journal of Research in Crime and Delinquency, 57*, 74-118.

Cohen, L.E., and Felson, M. (1979). Social change and crime rate trends: A routine activity approach. *American Sociological Review, 44*, 588-608.

Cohen, M., Seghorn, T., and Calmas, W. (1969). Sociometric study of the sex offender. *Journal of Abnormal Behavior, 74*(2), 249-255.

Cole. S. (2000). From the sexual psychopath statute to "Megan's Law": Psychiatric knowledge in the diagnosis, treatment, and adjudication of sex criminals in New Jersey, 1949-1999. *Journal of the History of Medicine and Allied Sciences, 55*(3), 292-314.

Collins, L. (2013, August 28). Exclusive: Cherry was raped by her teacher at 14 and shunned for reporting it. Then she shot herself dead in her mother's bed. Now her mom reveals her "living hell" and furry that attacker got just 30 days jail. *The Daily Mail.* Retrieved from www.dailymail.co.uk

Colorado Department of Public Safety. (2004). *Report on safety issues raised by living arrangements for and location of sex offenders in the community.* Denver, CO: Colorado Sex Offender Management Board.

Columbia Law Review Association. (1939). Criminal law, sex offenders, civil commitment for psychiatric treatment. *Columbia Law Review, 39*, 534-544.

Comartin, E.B., Kernsmith, P.D., and Kernsmith, R.M. (2009). Sanctions for sex offenders: Fear and public policy. *Journal of Offender Rehabilitation, 48*, 605-619.

Corbett, R. (2019, July 9). Jeffrey Epstein's latest accuser is an artist who claims the billionaire sex offender lured her in with promises to help her career. *Artnet.* https://news.artnet.com/art-world/artist-accuses-jeffrey-epstein-1595977.

Corrigan, R. (2013). The new trial by ordeal: Rape kits, police practices, and the unintended effects of policy innovation. *Law and Social Inquiry, 38,* 920-945.

Cortoni, F., Hanson, R.K., and Coache, M.E. (2009). The recidivism rates of adult sexual offenders are low: A meta-analysis. *Sexual Abuse, 22*(4), 387-401.

Coskun, M., and Ozturk, M. (2013). Sexual fetishism in adolescence: Report of two cases. *Journal of Psychiatry & Neurological Sciences, 26,* 199-205.

Cossins, A. (2020). Feminist criminology in a time of "digital feminism": Can the #MeToo movement create fundamental cultural change? In S. Walklate, K. Fitz-Gibbon, J. McCulloch, and J. Maher (Eds.) *The Emerald handbook of feminism, criminology and social change* (pp. 69-94). Emerald Publishing.

Cowan, G. (2000). Beliefs about the causes of four types of rape. *Sex Roles, 42*(9/10), 807-823.

Craig, L., and Campbell-Fuller, N. (2009). The use of olfactory aversion and directed masturbation in modifying deviant sexual interest: A case study. *Journal of Sexual Aggression, 15*(2), 179-191.

Craven, S., Brown, S., and Gilchrist, E. (2006). Sexual grooming of children: Review of literature and theoretical considerations. *Journal of Sexual Aggression, 12*(3), 287-299.

Cullen, F.T., and Jonson, C.L. (2012). *Correctional theory: Context and consequences.* Thousand Oaks, CA: Sage.

Curriden, M., and Phillips, Jr., L. (1999). *Contempt of court: The turn-of-the-century lynching that launched a hundred years of federalism.* New York, NY: Faber and Faber, Inc.

Curtis, L. (1974). Victim precipitation and violent crime. *Social Problems, 21*(4), 594-605.

Davies, G. (1999). The impact of television on the presentation and reception of children's testimony. *International Journal of Law and Psychiatry, 22,* 242-256.

Davis, J. (2002). Voyeurism: A criminal precursor and diagnostic indicator to a much larger sexual predatory problem in our community. In R.M. Holmes and S.T. Holmes (Eds.), *Current Perspectives on Sex Crimes* (pp. 73-84). Thousand Oaks, CA: Sage Publications.

De Block, A., and Adriaens, P.R. (2013). Pathologizing sexual deviance: A history. *Journal of Sex Research, 50,* 276-298.

de Leon, K., and Jackson, H. (2015, October 13). Why we made 'yes means yes' California law. *The Washington Post.* Retrieved from https://www.washingtonpost.com/news/in-theory/wp/2015/10/13/why-we-made-yes-means-yes-california-law/

Deck, R. (2016). Grown-up justice isn't child's play: The case for data driven reassessment of civil commitment for juvenile sex offenders. *The University of the Pacific Law Review, 48,* 371-393.

DeHart, D., Dwyer, G., Seto, M.C., Moran, R., Letourneau, E., and Schwarz-Watts, D. (2017). Internet sexual solicitation of children: A proposed typology of offenders based on their chats, e-mails, and social network posts. *Journal of Sexual Aggression, 23*(1), 77-89.

DeKeseredy, W., Hall-Sanchez, A., Nolan, J., and Schwartz, M. (2017). A campus LGBTQ community's sexual violence and stalking experiences: the contribution of pro-abus peer support. *Journal of Gender-Based Violence, 1*(2), 169-185.

DeKeseredy, W., and Schwartz, M. (2013). *Male peer support and violence against women: The history & verification of a theory.* Boston, MA: Northeastern University Press.

DeLuca, J.S., Vaccaro, J., Rudnik, A., Graham, N., Giannicchi, A., and Yanos, P.T. (2018). Sociodemographic predictors of sex offender stigma: How politics impact attitudes, social distance, and perceptions of sex offender recidivism. *International Journal of Offender Therapy and Comparative Criminology, 62,* 2879-2896.

Department of Defense. (2014). *Report to the President of the United States on sexual assault prevention and response.* Washington, D.C.: U.S. Department of Defense.

Department of Defense. (2020). *Annual report on sexual assault in the military.* Washington, D.C.: U.S. Department of Defense.

Depo-Provera-medroxyprogesterone acetate injection, suspension. (n.d.). Retrieved from labeling.pfizer.com/ShowLabeling.aspx?id=522

DeYoung, M. (1989). The world according to NAMBLA: Accounting for deviance. *A Journal of Sociology and Social Welfare, 16*(1), 111-126.

Dinitz, S., Dynes, R.R., and Clark, A.C. (1969). *Deviance: Studies in the process of stigmatization and societal reaction.* New York, NY: Oxford University Press.

Dobson, K., and Dozois, D. (2010). Historical and philosophical bases of the cognitive behavioral therapies. In K. Dobson (Ed.) *Handbook of Cognitive Behavioral Therapies,* Third Edition. New York, NY: The Guilford Press.

Dokoupil, T. (2014). My son, the sex offender: One mother's mission to fight the law. Retrieved May 8, 2014, from http://www.nbcnews.com/news/us-news

Doll, N. (2012, March 13). Pacific Northwest island houses violent sex predators. *Fox 12 Oregon.* Retrieved from www.kptv.com

D'Orazio, D., Azizian, A., and Olver, M. (2019). Recidivism and other outcomes of sexual offenders committed as "Sexually Violent Predators" in California. Paper presented at the Annual Meeting of the ATSA Research and Treatment Conference; Atlanta, GA, November 2019.

Doren, D.M. (2006). What do we know about the effect of aging on recidivism risk for sexual offenders. *Sexual Abuse: A Journal of Research and Treatment, 18,* 137-157.

Doren, D.M., and Epperson, D.L. (2001). Great analysis, but problematic assumptions: A critique of Janus and Meehl (1997). *Sexual Abuse, 13,* 45-52.

Downes, D., and Rock, P. (1998). *Understanding deviance: A guide to the sociology of crime and rule breaking,* Third Edition. New York, NY: Oxford University Press.

Drezett, J., de Vasconcellos, R., Pedroso, D., Blake, M., and de Abreu, L. (2012). Transmission of anogenital warts in children and association with sexual abuse. *Journal of Growth and Development, 22*(1), 34-41.

DuMont, J., Miller, K., and Myhr, T. (2003). The role of "real rape" and "real victim" stereotypes in police reporting practices of sexually assaulted women. *Violence Against Women, 9*(4), 466-486.

Durkin, F. (1997). Misuse of the internet by pedophiles: Implications for law enforcement and probation practice. *Federal Probation, 61*(3), 14-19.

Durkin, K.F. (2002). Misuse of the internet by pedophiles: Implications for law enforcement and probation practice. In R.M. Holmes and S.T. Holmes (Eds.), *Current Perspectives on Sex Crimes* (pp. 162-169). Thousand Oaks, CA: Sage Publications.

Durose, M.R., Cooper, A.D., Snyder, H.N. (2014). *Recidivism of prisoners released in 30 states in 2005: Patterns from 2005-2010.* Washington D.C.: Bureau of Justice Statistics.

Duwe, G. (2014). To what extent does civil commitment reduce sexual recidivism? Estimating the selective incapacitation effects in Minnesota. *Journal of Criminal Justice, 42*, 193-202.

Duwe, G., and Donnay, W. (2008). The impact of Megan's Law on sex offender recidivism: The Minnesota experience. *Criminology, 46*, 411-446.

Duwe, G., Donnay, W., and Tewksbury, R. (2008). Does residential proximity matter? A geographic analysis of sex offense recidivism. *Criminal Justice and Behavior, 35*, 484-504.

Edwards, D.J. (2008). Treatment for pedophiles reduces victimization. In L.M. Zott (Ed.), *Sex Offenders and Public Policy* (pp. 90-98). Farmington Hills, MI: Greenhaven Press.

Edwards, W., and Hensley, C. (2001). Contextualizing sex offender management legislation and policy: Evaluating the problem of latent consequences in community notification laws. *International Journal of Offender Therapy and Comparative Criminology, 45*, 83-101.

Eigenberg, H. (1990). The National Crime Survey and rape: The case of the missing question. *Justice Quarterly, 7*(4), 655-671.

Eigenberg, H., and Baro, A. (2003). If you drop the soap in the shower you are on your own: Images of male rape in selected prison movies. *Sexuality and Culture, 7*, 56-89.

Ellis, L. (1989). *Theories of rape: Inquiries into the causes of sexual aggression.* New York: Hemisphere Publishing Corporation.

Erikson, K.T. (1986). *Wayward puritans: A study in the sociology of deviance.* New York, NY: Macmillan Publishing Company.

Estrich, S. (1987). *Real rape: How the legal system victimizes women who say no.* Cambridge, MA: Harvard University Press.

Ewing, C.P., and McCann, J.T. (2006). *Minds on trial: Great cases in law and psychology.* New York: Oxford University Press.

Fanniff, A.M., Otto, R.K., and Petrila, J. (2010). Competence to proceed in SVP commitment hearings: Irrelevant or fundamental due process right? *Behavioral Sciences and the Law, 28*, 647-670.

Farkas, M.A., and Stichman, A. (2002). Sex offender laws: Can treatment, punishment, incapacitation, and public safety be reconciled? *Criminal Justice Review, 27*(2), 256-283.

Fater, K., and Mullaney, J. (2000). The lived experience of adult male survivors who allege childhood sexual abuse by clergy. *Issues in Mental Health Nursing, 21*, 281-295.

Fazlollah, M., Matza, M., and McCoy, C. (1999, October 18). Crimes uncounted: How Philadelphia police hid rape complaints. *Philadelphia Inquirer.* Retrieved from http://www.inquirer.philly.com

FBI. (2015). *Crime in the United States, 2014.* Washington, D.C.: U.S. Department of Justice.FBI. (2015a). *Human trafficking, 2014.* Washington, D.C.: U.S. Department of Justice.

FBI. (2020). *Crime in the United States, 2019.* Washington, D.C.: U.S. Department of Justice.

FBI. (2020). *Human trafficking, 2019.* Washington, D.C.: U.S. Department of Justice.Federoff, J.P. (2008). Sadism, sadomasochism, sex, and violence. *The Canadian Journal of Psychiatry, 53*, 637-646.

Feelgood, S., Cortoni, F., and Thompson, A. (2005). Sexual coping, general coping and cognitive distortions in incarcerated rapists and child molesters. *Journal of Sexual Aggression, 11*(2), 157-170.

Feelgood, S., and Hoyer, J. (2008). Child Molester or pedophile? Sociolegal versus psychopathological classification of sexual offenders against children. *Journal of Sexual Aggression, 14*(1), 33-43.

Felson, R.B., and Palmore, C. (2018). Biases in blaming victims of rape and other crime. *Psychology of Violence, 8*(3), 390-399.

Fenichel, O. (1945). *The psychoanalytic theory of neurosis.* New York, NY: Norton.

Fenton, J. (2010, August 4). Lack of police reports stalls review of city rape allegations. *Baltimore Sun.* Retrieved from www.baltimoresun.com

Fenton, J. (2011, July 8). A year later, progress in Baltimore sex offense investigations. *Baltimore Sun.* Retrieved from www.baltimoresun.com

Fernandez, Y. (2009). The standardization of phallometry. In A. Beech, L. Craig, and Browne, K. (Eds.), *Assessment and Treatment of Sex Offenders: A Handbook* (129-143). West Sussex, UK: Wiley-Blackwell.

Feuerherd, B. (2021, August 27). "Firm trial date" set for Ghislaine Maxwell's sex crimes case. *New York Post.* https://nypost.com/2021/08/27/firm-trial-date-set-for-november-in-ghislaine-maxwell-case/.

Field, H. (1978). Attitudes toward rape: A comparative analysis of police, rapists, crisis counselors, and citizens. *Journal of Personality and Social Psychology, 36*(2), 156-179.

Finch, E., and Munro, V.E. (2007). The demon drink and the demonized woman: Socio-sexual stereotypes and responsibility attribution in rape trials involving intoxicants. *Social & Legal Studies, 16*(4), 591-614.

Finkelhor, D. (1987). The trauma of child sexual abuse: Two models. *Journal of Interpersonal Violence, 2*(4), 348-366.

Finkelhor, D. (1994). Current information on the scope and nature of child sexual abuse. *The Future of Children, 4*(2), 31-53.

Finkelhor, D., and Araji, S. (1986). Explanations of pedophilia: A four factor model. *The Journal of Sex Research, 22*(2), 145-161.

Finkelhor, D., and Jones, L. (2012). *Have sexual abuse and physical abuse declined since the 1990s?* Durham, NH: Crimes against Children Research Center.

Finkelhor, D., Jones, L., Shattuck, A., and Saito, K. (2013). *Updated trends in child maltreatment, 2012.* Durham, NH: Crimes against Children Research Center.

Finkelhor, D., Turner, H.A., Shattuck, A., and Hamby, S.L. (2015). Prevalence of childhood exposure to violence, crime, and abuse: Results from the National Survey of Children's Exposure to Violence. *JAMA Pediatrics, 169*(8), 746-754.

Fisher, B. (2009). The effects of survey question wording on rape estimates: Evidence from a quasi-experimental design. *Violence Against Women, 15*(2), 133-147.

Fitch, W.L. (1998). Sex offender commitment in the United States. *The Journal of Forensic Psychiatry, 9*, 237-240.

Fitch, W.L. (2003). Sexual offender commitment in the United States: Legislative and policy concerns. *Annals of the New York Academy of Sciences, 989*, 489-501.

Forgac, G.E., Cassel, C.A., Michaels, E.J. (1984). Chronicity of criminal behavior and psychopathology in male exhibitionists. *Journal of Clinical Psychiatry, 40*, 827-832.

Frangež, D., Klančnik, A.T., Karer, M Ž., Ludvigsen, B.E., Kończyk, J., Perez, F.R., Veijalainen, M., and Lewin, M. (2015). The Importance of Terminology Related to Child Sexual Exploitation. *Revija za kriminalistiko in kriminologijo/Ljubljana, 66*(4), 291-299.

Franklin, C., Franklin, T., Nobles, M., and Kercher, G. (2012). Assessing the effect of routine activity theory and self-control on property, personal, and sexual assault victimization. *Criminal Justice and Behavior, 39*(10), 1,296-1,315.

Franklin, K. (2010). Hebophilia: Quintessence of diagnostic pretextuality. *Behavioral Sciences and the Law, 28*, 751-768.

Frazier, P., and Haney, B. (1996). Sexual assault cases in the legal system: Police, prosecutor and victim perspectives. *Law and Human Behavior, 20*(6), 607-628.

Freedman, E. (1987). "Uncontrolled desires": The response to the sexual psychopath, 1920-1960. *The Journal of American History, 74*(1). 83-106.

Freeh, Sporkin, and Sullivan, LLP. (2012). *Report of the Special Investigative Counsel Regarding the Actions of the Pennsylvania State University Related to the Child Sexual Abuse Committed by Gerald A. Sandusky.* Happy Valley, PA: Pennsylvania State University.

Freeman, N.J., Sandler, J.C., and Socia, K.M. (2009). A time-series analysis on the impact of sex offender registration and community notification laws on plea bargaining rates. *Criminal Justice Studies, 22*, 153-165.

Freund, K., Seto, M.C., and Kuban, M. (1995). Masochism: A multiple case study. *Sexology, 4*, 313-324.

Frey, L.L. (2010). The juvenile female sexual offender: Characteristics, treatments, and research. In T.A. Gannon and F. Cortoni (Eds.), *Female Sexual Offenders: Theory, Assessment, and Treatment* (pp. 54-71). Hoboken, NJ: John Wiley and Sons, Ltd.

Friedlander, J., and Banay, R. (1948). Psychosis following lobotomy in a case of sexual psychopathy. *Archives of Neurology and Psychiatry, 59*(3), 302-321.

Fromuth, M., and Holt, A. (2008). Perception of teacher sexual misconduct by age of student. *Journal of Child Sexual Abuse, 17*(2), 163-179.

Fulkerson, A., and Bruns, D. (2014). Defenses, excuses and rationalizations of perpetrators of sex offenses against children. *Journal of International Criminal Justice Research, 1*, 1-23.

Furby, L., Weinrott, M.R., and Blackshaw, L. (1989). Sex offender recidivism: A review. *Psychological Bulletin,* 105(1), 3-30.

Gagnier, C., and Collin-Vezina, D. (2016). The disclosure experiences of male child sexual abuse survivors. *Journal of Child Sexual Abuse, 25*(2), 221-241.

Gajanan, M. (2019, July 17). Here's what to know about the sex trafficking case against Jeffrey Epstein. *Time.* https://time.com/5621911/jeffrey-epstein-sex-trafficking-what-to-know/.

Gannon, T.A., and Cortoni, F. (2010). *Female sex offenders: Theory, assessment, and treatment.* Malden, MA: Wiley-Blackwell.

Gannon, T., King, T., Miles, H., Lockerbie, L., and Willis, G. (2011). Good Lives sexual offender treatment for mentally disordered offenders. *The British Journal of Forensic Practice, 13*(3), 153-168.

Garner, B.A. (2000). *Black's law dictionary*, Seventh Edition. St. Paul, MN: West Group.

Garrison, E., and Kobor, P. (2001). Weathering a political storm: A contextual perspective on a psychological research controversy. *American Psychologist, 53*(3), 165-175.

Gidycz, C., Coble, C., Latham, L., and Layman, M. (1993). Sexual assault experience in adulthood and prior victimization experiences: A prospective analysis. *Psychology of Women Quarterly, 17*(2), 151-168.

Glosser, A., Gardiner, K., and Fishman, M. (2004). *Statutory rape: A guide to state laws and reporting requirements.* Washington, DC: U.S. Department of Health and Human Services.

Glueck, S. (1937). Sex crimes and the law. *The Nation, 145*(13), 319-320.

Gonzalez, A.R. (2008). Tough laws and vigilant prosecution are the best defense against sexual predators. In L.M. Zott (Ed.), *Sex Offenders and Public Policy* (pp. 28-38). Farmington Hills, MI: Greenhaven Press.

Goodman, G.S., Tobey, A.E., Batterman-France, J.M., Orcutt, H., Thomas, S., Shapiro, S., et al. (1992). Face-to-face confrontation: Effects of closed-circuit technology on children's eyewitness testimony and jurors' decisions. *Law and Human Behavior, 22,* 165-203.

Goodman-Brown, T., Edelstein, R., Goodman, G., Jones, D., and Gordon, D. (2003). Why children tell: A model of children's disclosure of sexual abuse. *Child Abuse and Neglect, 27,* 525-540.

Gookin, K. (2007). *Comparison of state laws authorizing involuntary commitment of sexually violent predators: 2006 update, revised.* Olympia, WA: Washington State Institute for Public Policy.

Gornick, J., Burt, M., and Pittman, K. (1985). Structure and activities of rape crisis centers in the early 1980s. *Crime & Delinquency, 31*(2), 247-268.

Gottfredson, D.M., Wilkins, L.T., and Hoffman, P.B. (1978). *Guidelines for parole and sentencing.* Toronto: Lexington.

Gottfredson, M.R., Mitchell-Herzfeld, S.D., and Flanagan, T.J. (1982). Another look at the effectiveness of parole supervision. *Journal of Research in Crime and Delinquency, 19,* 277-298.

Goudriann, H., Lynch, J., and Nieuwbeerta, P. (2004). Reporting to the police in Western nations: A theoretical analysis of the effects of social context. *Justice Quarterly, 21*(4), 933-969.

Greenfield, L.A. (1997). *Sex offenses and offenders: An analysis of data on rape and sexual assault.* Washington, D.C.: Bureau of Justice Statistics.

Gross, B. (2008). False rape allegations: An assault on justice. *Annals of the American Psychotherapy Association, Winter,* 45-49.

Groth, A.N., and Burgess, A. W. (1977). Motivational intent in the sexual assault of children. *Criminal Justice and Behavior, 4*(3), 253-264.

Groth, N. (1979). *Men who rape: The psychology of the offender.* New York: Plenum Press.

Grubesic, T.H., and Mack, E.A. (2008). Spatio-temporal interaction of urban crime. *Journal of Quantitative Criminology, 24,* 285-306.

Grubesic, T.H., Mack, E.A, and Murray, A.T. (2007). Geographic exclusion: Spatial analysis for evaluating the implications of Megan's Law. *Social Science Computer Review, 25,* 143-162.

Grubesic, T.H., Murray, A.T., and Mack, E.A. (2008). Sex offenders, housing and spatial restriction zones. *GeoJournal, 73,* 255-269.

Guterman, J.T., Martin, C.V., and Rudes, J. (2011). A solution-focused approach to frotteurism. *Journal of Systemic Therapies, 30,* 59-72.

Hacker, F., and Frym, M. (1955). The sexual psychopath act in practice: A critical discussion. *California Law Review, 43*(5), 766-780.

Hall, G. (1995). Sex offender recidivism revisited: A meta-analysis of recent treatment studies. *Journal of Consulting and Clinical Psychology, 63,* 802-809.

Hall, R.C., and Hall, R.C. (2007). A profile of pedophilia: Definition, characteristics of offenders, recidivism, treatment outcomes, and forensic issues. *Mayo Clinic Proceedings, 82,* 457-471.

Hamby, S., Finkelhor, D., and Turner, H. (2013). Perpetrator and victim gender patters for 21 forms of youth victimization in the National Survey of Children's Exposure to Violence. *Violence and Victims, 28*(6), 915-939.

Hanna, K., Davies, E., Crothers, C., and Henderson, E. (2012). Child witnesses' access to alternative modes of testifying in New Zealand. *Psychiatry, Psychology and Law, 19,* 184-197.

Hanson, R.K. (2000). *Predicting sex offender recidivism.* Thousand Oaks, CA: Sage Publications, Inc.

Hanson, R.K., and Bussiere, M.T. (1998). Predicting relapse: A meta-analysis of sexual offender recidivism studies. *Journal of Consulting Psychology, 66,* 348-362.

Hanson, R.K., Gordon, A., Harris, A.J.R., Marques, J.K., Murphy, W., and Quinsey, V.L. (2002). First report of the collaborative outcome data project on the effectiveness of psychological treatments for sex offenders. *Sexual Abuse, 14,* 169-194.

Hanson, R.K., and Morton-Bourgon, K.E. (2005). The characteristics of persistent sexual offenders: A meta-analysis of recidivism studies. *Journal of Consulting and Clinical Psychology, 73,* 1,154-1,163.

Harlow, A.F., Willis, S.K., Smith, M.L., and Rothman, E.F. (2021). Bystander prevention for sexual violence: #HowIWillChange and gaps in Twitter discourse. *Journal of Interpersonal Violence, 36*(11-12), NP5753-NP5771.

Harris, D.A. (2010). Theories of female sexual offending. In T.A. Gannon and F. Cortoni (Eds.), *Female Sex Offenders: Theory, Assessment, and Treatment* (pp. 31-51). Malden, MA: Wiley-Blackwell.

Hartley, R.D., Rabe, G.A., and Champion, D.J. (2017). *Criminal courts: Structure, process, and issues,* 4th ed. Upper Saddle River, NJ: Prentice Hall.

Hayashino, D., Wurtele, S., and Klebe, K. (1995). Child molesters: An examination of cognitive factors. *Journal of Interpersonal Violence, 10*(1), 106-116.

Hazelwood, R., and Burgess, A. (1993). The behavioral-oriented interview of rape victims. In R. Hazelwood and A. Burgess (Eds.), *Practical Aspects of Rape Investigation: A Multidisciplinary Approach* (pp.151-168). Boca Raton, FL: CRC Press, Inc.

Hazelwood, R.R., and Warren, J.I. (1995). The relevance of fantasy in serial sexual crime investigation. In R.R. Hazelwood and A.W. Burgess (Eds.), *Practical Aspects of Rape Investigation: A multidisciplinary Approach*. Boca Raton, FL: CRC Press.

Hazlett-Stevens, H., and Bernstein, D. (2012). Relaxation. In W. O'Donohue and J. Fisher (Eds.), *Cognitive Behavior Therapy: Core Principles for Practice* (pp. 105-132). Hoboken, NJ: John Wiley & Sons.

Hebenton, B., and Thomas, T. (1997). Keeping track? Observations on sex offender registers in the U.S. *Crime Detection and Prevention Series* 83.

Henggeler, S.W. (1999). Multisystemic therapy: An overview of clinical procedures, outcomes, and policy implications. *Child Psychology & Psychiatry Review, 4*(1), 2-10.

Herbert, L., D'Orazio, D., and Lobanov-Rostovsky. (2019). Civil commitment: One element of a comprehensive approach for the management of individuals who have sexually abused. Paper presented at the Annual Meeting of the ATSA Research and Treatment Conference; Atlanta, GA, October 2020.

Herman, J. (2003). The mental health of crime victims: Impact of legal intervention. *Journal of Traumatic Stress, 16*(2), 159-166.

Higgins, P.C., and Butler, R.R. (1982). *Understanding deviance*. New York, NY: McGraw-Hill Book Company.

Higginson, J. (1999). Defining, excusing, and justifying deviance: Teen mothers' accounts for statutory rape. *Symbolic Interactionism, 22*(1), 25-44.

Hindelang, M., Gottfredson, M., and Garofalo, J. (1978). *Victims of Personal Crime: An Empirical Foundation for a Theory of Personal Victimization*. Cambridge, MA: Ballinger Publishing Company.

Hine, B., and Murphy, A. (2019). The influence of "high" vs. "low" rape myth acceptance on police officers' judgements of victim and perpetrator responsibility, and rape authenticity. *Journal of Criminal Justice, 60*, 100-107.

Hockett, J., Smith, S., Klausing, C., and Saucier, D. (2015). Rape myth consistency and gender differences in perceiving rape victims: A meta-analysis. *Violence Against Women, 22*(2), 139-167.

Hofmann, S.G., Asnaani, A., Vonk, I.J.J., Sawyer, A.T., and Fang, A. (2012). The efficacy of cognitive behavioral therapy: A review of meta-analyses. *Cognitive Therapy and Research, 36*, 427-440.

Holland, T.R., Holt, N., and Brewer, D.L. (1978). Social roles and information utilization in parole decision-making. *Journal of Social Psychology, 106*, 111-120.

Holleran, D., Beichner, D., and Spohn, C. (2010). Examining charging agreement between police and prosecutors in rape cases. *Crime and Delinquency, 56*, 385-413.

Holmes, R.M., and Holmes, S.T. (2002a). *Current perspectives on sex crimes*. Thousand Oaks, CA: Sage Publications.

Holmes, S., and Holmes, R. (2002b). *Sex Crimes: Patterns and behavior, 2nd Ed.* Thousand Oaks: Sage Publications.

Holmes, R., and Holmes, S. (2009a). *Profiling Violent Crimes: An Investigative Tool,* 4th ed. Thousand Oaks, CA: Sage Publications, Inc.

Holmes, S., and Holmes, R. (2009b). *Sex Crimes: Patterns and Behavior, 3rd Ed.* Thousand Oaks: Sage Publications.

Holzman, C. (1996). Counseling adult women rape survivors: Issues of race, ethnicity, and class. *Women & Therapy, 19*(2), 47-62.

Hoppe, T., Meyer, I.H, De Orio, S., Vogler, S., and Armstrong, M. (2020). *Civil Commitment of people convicted of sex offenses in the United States*. Los Angeles, CA: William Institute.

Horne, C.F. (1915). *The Code of Hammurabi*. Accessed at http://avalon.law.yale.edu/ancient/hamframe.asp

Horney, J., and Spohn, C. (1996). The influence of blame and believability factors on the processing of simple versus aggravated rape cases. *Criminology, 34*, 135-162.

Hucker, S.J. (2011). Hypoxyphilia. *Archives of Sexual Behavior, 40*, 1,323-1,326.

Huebner, B.M., Kras, K.R., Rydberg, J., Bynum, T.S., Grommon, E., and Pleggenkuhie, B. (2014). The effect and implications of sex offender residence restrictions: Evidence from a two-state evaluation. *Criminology and Public Policy, 13*, 139-168.

Hughes, L.A., and Burchfield, K.B. (2008). Sex offender residence restrictions in Chicago: An environmental injustice? *Justice Quarterly, 25*, 647-673.

Hunt, L., and Bull, R. (2012). Differentiating genuine and false rape allegations: A model to aid rape investigations. *Psychiatry, Psychology and the Law, 19*, 682-691.

Hunter, S. (2011). Disclosure of child sexual abuse as a life-long process: Implications for health professionals. *The Australian and New Zealand Journal of Family Therapy, 32*(2), 159-172.

Iowa County Attorneys Association. (2008). Iowa's residency restrictions have proven unsuccessful. In L.M. Zott (Ed.), *Sex Offenders and Public Policy* (pp. 120-125). Farmington Hills, MI: Greenhaven Press.

Irish, L., Kobayashi, I., and Delahanty, D. (2010). Long-term physical health consequences of childhood sexual abuse: A meta-analytic review. *Journal of Pediatric Psychology, 35*(5), 450-461.

Jackson, R.L., and Hess, D.T. (2007). Evaluation for civil commitment of sex offenders: A survey of experts. *Sex Abuse, 19*, 425-448.

Jacob Wetterling Crimes Against Children and Sexually Violent Offender Registration Program Act. (1994). *United States Code*. Vol. 42, Section 14071.

Jaffe, S. (2018). The collective power of #MeToo. *Dissent, 65*(2), 80-87.

Janoff-Bulman, R. (1979). Characterological versus behavioral self-blame: Inquiries into depression and rape. *Journal of Personality and Social Psychology, 37*(10), 1,798-1,809.

Janus, E.S. (2013). Preventive detention of sex offenders: The American experience versus international human rights norms. *Behavioral Sciences and the Law, 31*, 328-343.

Janus, E.S., and Walbek, N.H. (2000). Sex offender commitments in Minnesota: A descriptive study of second generation commitments. *Behavioral Sciences and the Law, 18*, 343-374.

Jenkins, P. (2004). *Moral panics: Changing concepts of the child molester in modern America.* New Haven, CT: Yale University Press.

Jennings, W.G., Zgoba, K.M., and Tewskbury, R. (2012). A comparative longitudinal analysis of recidivism trajectories and collateral consequences for sex and non-sex offenders released since the implementation of sex offender registration and community notification. *Journal of Crime and Justice, 35.* 356-364.

Jensen, E., and Kane, S. (2012). The effects of therapeutic community on recidivism up to four years after release from prison: A multisite study. *Criminal Justice and Behavior, 39*(8), 1,075-1,087.

Johnson, K. (1995). Attributions about date rape: Impact of clothing, sex, money spent, date type, and perceived similarity. *Family and Consumer Sciences Research Journal, 23*(3), 292-310.

Johnston, E.R. (2017). Dick, K. (director), and Ziering, A. (producer). The Hunting Ground. *Women's Studies in Communication, 40*(3), 312-314.

Jones, E. (2021). Untested and neglected: Clarifying the comparator requirement in equal protection claims based on untested rape kits. *Northwestern University Law Review, 115*(6), 1781-1828.

Jones, R. (2003). Research and practice with adolescent sexual offenders. In T. Ward, D.R. Laws, and S.M. Hudson (Eds.), *Sexual Deviance: Issues and Controversies* (pp. 190-206). Thousand Oaks, CA: Sage Publications.

Jordan, J. (2002). Will any woman do? Police, gender, and rape victims. *Policing: An International Journal of Police Strategies & Management, 25*(2), 319-344.

Jordan, J. (2004). *The word of a woman? Police, rape, and belief.* New York, NY: Palgrave MacMillan.

Kafka, M.P. (2010). Hypersexual disorder: A proposed diagnosis for DSM-V. *Archives of Sexual Behavior, 39*, 377-400.

Kafka, M.P. (2010a). The DSM diagnostic criteria for fetishism. *Archives of Sexual Behavior, 39*, 357-362.

Kahlor, L., and Morrision, D. (2007). Television viewing and rape myth acceptance among college women. *Sex Roles, 56*, 729-739.

Kanin, E.J. (1994). False rape allegations. *Archives of Sexual Behavior, 23*, 81-84.

Kanin, E.J. (1985). Unfounded rape. Paper presented at the Annual Academy of Criminal Justice Sciences Conference: Las Vegas, NV.

Kanter, J., and Puspitasari, A. (2012). Behavioral activation. In W. O'Donohue and J. Fisher (Eds.), *Cognitive Behavior Therapy: Core Principles for Practice* (pp. 215-250). Hoboken, NJ: John Wiley & Sons.

Kantor, J., and Twohey, M. (2017, October 5). Harvey Weinstein paid off sexual harassment accusers for decades. *The New York Times.* https://www.nytimes.com/2017/10/05/us/harvey-weinstein-harassment-allegations.html

Karoly, P. (2012). Self-regulation. In W. O'Donohue and J. Fisher (Eds.), *Cognitive Behavior Therapy: Core Principles for Practice* (pp. 183-213). Hoboken, NJ: John Wiley & Sons.

Karpman, B. (1954). *The Sexual Offender and His Offenses: Etiology, Pathology, Psychodynamics and Treatment.* New York, NY: The Julian Press, Inc.

Katz, B. (1991). The psychological impact of stranger versus nonstranger rape on victims' recovery. In A. Parrot and L. Bechhofer (Eds.), *Acquaintance Rape: The Hidden Crime.* New York: John Wiley & Sons, Inc.

Kelly, L. (2010). The (in)credible words of women: False allegations in European rape research. *Violence Against Women, 16*, 1,345-1,355.

Kernsmith, P.D., Craun, S.W., and Foster, J. (2009). Public attitudes toward sexual offenders and sex offender registration. *Journal of Child Sexual Abuse, 18*, 290-301.

Kiersch, T. (1990). Treatment of sex offenders with Depo-Provera. *Bulletin of the American Academy of Psychiatry and the Law, 18*(2), 179-187.

Kilmann, P., Sabalis, R., Gearing, M., Bukstel, L., and Scovern, A. (1982). The treatment of sexual paraphilias: A Review of the outcome research. *The Journal of Sex Research, 18*(3), 193-252.

Kim, B., Benekos, P.J., and Merlo, A.V. (2016). Sex offender recidivism revisited: Review of recent meta-analyses on the effects of sex offender treatment. *Trauma, Violence, and Abuse, 17*, 105-117.

Kingsworth, R.F., MacIntosh, R.C., and Wentworth, J. (1999). "Sexual assault" The role of prior relationship and victim characteristics in case processing. *Justice Quarterly, 16*, 275-302.

Kinnaman, J., and Bellack, A. (2012). Social skills. In W. O'Donohue and J. Fisher (Eds.), *Cognitive Behavior Therapy: Core Principles for Practice* (pp. 251-272). Hoboken, NJ: John Wiley & Sons.

Klein, S.P., and Caggiano, M.N. (1986). *The prevalence, predictability, and policy implications of recidivism.* Washington D.C.: Bureau of Justice Statistics.

Knight, R., Carter, D., and Prentky, R. (1989). A system for the classification of child molesters: Reliability and application. *Journal of Interpersonal Violence, 4*(1), 3-23.

Knight, R., and Prentky, R. (1990). Classifying sexual offenders: The development and corroboration of taxonomic models. In W.L. Marshall, D.R. Laws, and H.E. Barbaree (Eds.), *Handbook of Sexual Assault: Issues, Theories, and Treatment of the Offender* (pp 23-160). New York: Plenum Press.

Knoll, J. (2010). Teacher sexual misconduct: Grooming patterns and female offenders. *Journal of Child Sexual Abuse, 19*(4), 371-386.

Knott, T. (2014). Maternal response to the disclosure of child sexual abuse: Systematic review and critical analysis of the literature. *Issues in Child Abuse Accusations, 20,* 1-1.

Koehle, J.T. (2016). Twenty years after *Kansas v. Hendricks*: Reforming the Kansas Sexual Predator Treatment Program is crucial to the future of the Kansas Sexually Violent Predator Act. *Kansas Journal of Law and Public Policy, 26,* 1-23.

Koon-Magnin, S., and Ruback, B. (2013). The perceived legitimacy of statutory rape laws: The effects of victim age, perpetrator age, and age span. *Journal of Applied Social Psychology, 43,* 1,918-1,930.

Koss, M. (1985). The hidden rape victim: Personality, attitudinal, and structural characteristics. *Psychology of Women Quarterly, 9*(2), 193-212.

Koss, M. (1993). Detecting the scope of rape: A review of prevalence research methods. *Journal of Interpersonal Violence, 8*(2), 198-222.

Koss, M. (2011). Hidden, unacknowledged, acquaintance, and date rape: Looking back, looking forward. *Psychology of Women Quarterly, 35*(2), 348-354.

Koss, M., Gidycz, C., and Wisniewski, N. (1987). The scope of rape: incidence and prevalence of sexual aggression and victimization in a national sample of higher education students. *Journal of Consulting and Clinical Psychology, 55*(2), 162-170.

Koss, M., Goodman, L., Browne, A., Fitzgerald, L., Keita, G., and Russo, N. (1994). *No safe haven: Male violence against women at home, at work, and in the community.* Washington, DC: American Psychological Association.

Koss, M., and Oros, C. (1982). Sexual Experiences Survey: A research instrument investigating sexual aggression and victimization. *Journal of Consulting and Clinical Psychology, 50*(3), 455-457.

Kreinert, J.L., and Fleisher, M.S. (2005). "It ain't happening here": Working to understand prison rape. *The Criminologist, 30*(6), 1-6.

Krieger, M.A. (2017). Unpacking "sexting": A systematic review of nonconsensual sexting in legal, educational, and psychological literatures. *Trauma, Violence, & Abuse, 18*(5), 593-601.

Krueger, R.B. (2010a). The DSM diagnostic criteria for sexual masochism. *Archives of Sexual Behavior, 39,* 346-356.

Krueger, R.B. (2010b). The DSM diagnostic criteria for sexual sadism. *Archives of Sexual Behavior, 39,* 325-345.

Krueger, R., Bradford, J., and Glancy, G. (1998). Report from the committed on sex offenders: The Abel Assessment for Sexual Interest—A brief description. *Journal of the American Academy for Psychiatry and the Law, 26*(2), 277-280.

Krueger, R.B., and Kaplan, M.S. (2008). Frotteurism: Assessment and treatment. In D.R. Laws and W.T. O'Donohue (Eds.), *Sexual Deviance: Theory, Assessment, and Treatment,* Second Edition (pp. 150-163). New York, NY: Guilford.

Kubrin, C.E., Stucky, T.D., and Krohn, M.D. (2009). *Researching theories of crime and deviance.* New York, NY: Oxford University Press.

LaBoe, B. (2007a, November 8). Civil commitment sought for sex offender. *The Daily News Online.* Retrieved from www.tdn.com

LaBoe, B. (2007b, November 15). Alsteen not fit for release, jury finds. *The Daily News Online.* Retrieved from www.tdn.com

LaBoe, B. (2014, May 4). Sex offender's hearing delayed until May 12. *The Daily News Online.* Retrieved from www.tdn.com

La Fond, J.Q. (2000). The future of involuntary civil commitment in the USA after *Kansas v. Hendricks. Behavioral Sciences and the Law, 18,* 153-167.

La Fond, J.Q. (2005). *Preventing sexual violence: How society should cope with sex offenders.* Washington, D.C.: American Psychological Association.

Laajasalo, T., Ellonen, N., Pakkanen, T., and Aaltonen, O.P. (2020). Low recidivism rates of child sex offenders in Finnish 7-year follow-up. *Nordic Journal of Criminology, 21,* 103-111.

Landstrom, S., Granhag, P.A., and Hartwig, M. (2007). Children's live and videotaped testimonies: How presentation mode affects observers' perception, assessment and memory. *Legal and Criminological Psychology, 12,* 333-347.

Langan, P.A., and Levin. D.J. (2002). *Recidivism of prisoners released in 1994.* Washington D.C.: Bureau of Justice Statistics.

Langan, P.A., Schmitt, E.L., and Durose, M.R. (2003). *Recidivism of sex offenders released from prison in 1994.* Washington D.C.: Bureau of Justice Statistics.

Langone, A. (2018, March 22). #MeToo and Time's Up founders explain the difference between the 2 movements — and how they're alike. *Time.* Retrieved from https://time.com/5189945/whats-the-difference-between-the-metoo-and-times-up-movements/

Langstrom, N. (2010). The DSM diagnostic criteria for exhibitionism, voyeurism, and frotteurism. *Archives of Sexual Behavior, 39,* 317-324.

Langstrom, N., and Seto, M.C. (2006). Exhibitionistic and voyeuristic behavior in a Swedish national population survey. *Archives of Sexual Behavior, 35,* 427-435.

Langstrom, N., and Zucker, K.J. (2005). Transvestic fetishism in the general population: Prevalence and correlates. *Journal of Sex and Marital Therapy, 31,* 87-95.

Lasher, M.P., and McGrath, R.J. (2012). The impact of community notification on sex offender reintegration: A qualitative review of the research literature. *International Journal of Offender Therapy and Comparative Criminology, 56,* 6-28.

Lavin, M. (2008). Voyeurism: Psychopathology and theory. In D.R. Laws and W.T. O'Donohue (Eds.), *Sexual Deviance: Theory, Assessment, and Treatment,* Second Edition (pp. 61-75). New York, NY: Guilford.

Lavner, J., and Bradbury, T. (2012). Communication. In W. O'Donohue and J. Fisher (Eds.), *Cognitive Behavior Therapy: Core Principles for Practice* (pp. 325-351). Hoboken, NJ: John Wiley & Sons.

Laws, D. (1995). Verbal satiation: Notes on procedure, with speculation on its mechanism of effect. *Sex Abuse: A Journal of Research and Treatment, 7*(2), 155-166.

Laws, D. (1999). Relapse prevention: The state of the art. *Journal of Interpersonal Violence, 14*(3), 285-302.

Laws, D. (2001). Olfactory aversions: Notes on procedure, with speculations on its mechanism of effect. *Sexual Abuse: A Journal of Research and Treatment, 13*(4), 275-287.

Lawyer, S., Resnick, H., Bakanic, V., Burkett, T., and Kilpatrick, D. (2010). Forcible, drug-facilitated, and incapacitated rape and sexual assault among undergraduate women. *Journal of America College Health, 58*(5), 453-460.

Leahy, R., and Rego, S. (2012). Cognitive restructuring. In W. O'Donohue and J. Fisher (Eds.), *Cognitive Behavior Therapy: Core Principles for Practice* (pp. 133-158). Hoboken, NJ: John Wiley & Sons.

Lee, G. (2010a). DNA Evidence. In D. Schultz (Ed.), *Encyclopedia of American Law and Criminal Justice* (pp. 247-248). New York, NY: Facts on File.

Lee, G. (2010b). Fingerprints. In D. Schultz (Ed.), *Encyclopedia of American Law and Criminal Justice* (pp. 331-332). New York, NY: Facts on File.

Leitenberg, H., and Saltzman, H. (2003). College women who had sexual intercourse when they were underage minors (13-15): Age of their male partner, relation to current adjustment, and statutory rape implications. *Sexual Abuse: A Journal of Research and Treatment, 15*(2), 135-147.

Lemaire, L. (1956). Danish experience regarding treatment of sex offenders. *Journal of Criminal Law and Criminology, 473,* 274-310.

Lemert, E.M. (1967). *Human deviance, social problems, and social control.* Englewood Cliffs, NJ: Prentice-Hall, Inc.

Leo, R. (2008). *Police Interrogation and American Justice.* Cambridge, MA: Harvard University Press.

Leon, C. (2011). *Sex fiends, perverts, and pedophiles: Understanding sex crime policy in America.* New York, NY: New York University Press.

Leopold, S.S. (2019). Editorial: Fears about #MeToo are no excuse to deny women mentorship in orthopaedic surgery. *Clinical Orthopaedics and Related Research, 477*(3), 473-476.

Letourneau, E.J., Bandyopadhyay, D., Sinha, D., and Armstrong, K.S. (2009). The influence of sex offender registration on juvenile sexual recidivism. *Criminal Justice Policy Review, 25,* 189-207.

Letourneau, E.J., and Caldwell, M.F. (2013). Expensive, harmful policies that don't work or how juvenile sexual offending is addressed in the U.S. *International Journal of Behavioral Consultation and Therapy, 8,* 23-29.

Letourneau, E.J., Levenson, J.S., Bandyopadhyay, D., Sinha, D., and Armstrong, K.S. (2010). Effects of South Carolina's sex offender registration and notification policy on adult recidivism. *Criminal Justice Policy Review, 21,* 435-458.

Levenson, J.S. (2004). Sexual predator civil commitment: A comparison of selected and released offenders. *International Journal of Offender Therapy and Comparative Criminology, 48,* 638-648.

Levenson, J.S. (2008). Policy interventions designed to combat sexual violence: Community notification and civil commitment. *Journal of Child Sexual Abuse, 12,* 17-52.

Levenson, J., Becker, J., and Morin, J. (2008). The relationship between victim age and gender crossover among sex offenders. *Sexual Abuse: A Journal of Research and Treatment, 20*(1), 43-60.

Levenson, J.S., and Cotter, L.P. (2005a). The impact of sex offender residence restrictions: 1,000 feet from danger or one stop from absurd? *International Journal of Offender Therapy and Comparative Criminology, 49,* 168-178.

Levenson, J.S., and Cotter, L.P. (2005b). The effect of Megan's Law on sex offender reintegration. *Journal of Contemporary Criminal Justice* 21, 49-66.

Levenson, J.S., and D'Amora, D.A. (2007). Social policies designed to prevent sexual violence: The emperor's new clothes? *Criminal Justice Policy Review, 18,* 168-199.

Levenson, J.S., D'Amora, D.A., and Hern, A.L. (2007a). Megan's Law and its impact on community re-entry for sex offenders. *Behavioral Sciences and the Law* 25, 287-602.

Levenson, J.S., and Hern, A.L. (2007). Sex offender residence restrictions: Unintended consequences and community reentry. *Justice Research and Policy, 9,* 59-74

Levenson, J.S., Letourneau, E., Armstrong, K., and Zgoba, K.M. (2010). Failure to register as a sex offender: Is it associated with recidivism? *Justice Quarterly, 27,* 305-311.

Levenson, J.S., and Morin, J.W. (2006). Factors predicting selection of sexually violent predators for civil commitment. *International Journal of Offender Therapy and Comparative Criminology, 50,* 609-629.

Levenson, J.S., Zgoba, K., and Tewksbury, R. (2007b). Sex offender residence restrictions: Sensible crime policy or flawed logic? *Federal Probation, 71,* 2-9.

Levesque, R.J.R. (2000). Sentencing sex crimes against children: An empirical and policy analysis. *Behavioral Sciences and the Law, 18,* 331-341.

Lewis, P., and Swaine, J. (2015, January 10). Jeffrey Epstein: Inside the decades of scandal entangling Prince Andrew.

The Guardian. https://www.theguardian.com/world/2015/jan/10/jeffrey-epstein-decade-scandal-prince-andrew

Linden, L.L., and Rockoff, J.E. (2006). There goes the neighborhood? Estimates of the impact of crime risk on property values from Megan's Law. Social Science Research Network. Retrieved from http://ssrn.com

Linderman, J. (2018, December 13). Congress passes overhaul of sexual harassment policies. *Associated Press.* https://apnews.com/article/1926df9804214b19991eec24ac1ddb5b.

Lippke, R.L. (2011). Why sex (offending) is different. *Criminal Justice Ethics, 30,* 151-172.

Lipsey, M.W., Landenberger, N.A., and Wilson, S.J. (2007). *Effects of cognitive-behavioral programs for criminal offenders.* Nashville, TN: The Campbell Collaboration.

Lisak, D., and Miller, P.M. (2002). Repeat and multiple offending among undetected rapists. *Violence and Victims, 17,* 73-84.

Lisak, D., Gardinier, L., Nicksa, S.C., and Cote, A.M. (2010). False allegations of sexual assault: An analysis of ten years of reported cases. *Violence Against Women, 16,* 1,318-1,334.

Liska, A.E. (1987). *Perspective on deviance,* Second Edition. Englewood Cliffs, NJ: Prentice-Hall, Inc.

Litton, S. (2006). Pedophilia. In E.W. Hickey (Ed.), *Sex Crimes and Paraphilia* (pp. 309-314). Upper Saddle River, NJ: Pearson.

Logue, D.W. (2012a). *Banishment by attrition: The truth about residency restrictions.* Retrieved from http://www.oncefallen.com

Logue, D.W. (2012b). Timeline of sex offender history. Retrieved from http://www.oncefallen.com/timeline.html

London, K., Bruck, M., Ceci, S., and Shuman, D. (2005). Disclosure of child sexual abuse: What does the research tell us about the ways that children tell? *Psychology, Public Policy, and Law, 11*(1), 194-226.

London, L., and Caprio, F. (1950). *Sexual Deviations.* Washington: Linarce Press.

Lonsway, K., and Fitzgerald, L. (1995). Attitudinal antecedents of rape myth acceptance: A theoretical and empirical reexamination. *Journal of Personality and Social Psychology, 68*(4), 704-711.

Lonsway, K., Welch, S., and Fitzgerald, L. (2001). Police training in sexual assault response: Process, outcomes, and elements of change. *Criminal Justice and Behavior, 28*(6), 695-730.

Losel, F., and Schumaker, M. (2005). The effectiveness of treatment for sexual offenders: A comprehensive meta-analysis. *Journal of Experimental Criminology, 1,* 117-146.

Lotke, E., and Hoelter, H.J. (2008). Clarifying the facts can strengthen public policy. In L.M. Zott (Ed.), *Sex Offenders and Public Policy* (pp. 64-73). Farmington Hills, MI: Greenhaven Press.

Loughnan, S., Pina, A., Vasquez, E., and Puvia, E. (2013). Sexual objectification increases rape victim blame and decreases perceived suffering. *Psychology of Women Quarterly, 37*(4), 455-461.

Lowden, K., Hetz, N., Harrison, L., Patrick, D., English, K., and Pasini-Hill, D. (2003). Evaluation of Colorado's Prison Therapeutic Community for Sex Offenders: A report of findings. Denver, CO: Office of Research and Statistics, Division of Criminal Justice.

Lown, E., Nayak, M., Korcha, R., and Greenfield, T. (2011). Child physical and sexual abuse: A comprehensive look at alcohol consumption patterns, consequences, and dependence from the National Alcohol Survey. *Alcoholism: Clinical and Experimental Research, 35*(2), 317-325.

Lyman, M. (2014). *Criminal investigation: The Art and the science, 7th Edition.* Boston, MA: Pearson.

MacKenzie, D. (2006). *What works in corrections: Reducing the criminal activities of offenders and delinquents.* New York, NY: Cambridge University Press.

Maddan, S. (2008). *The labeling of sex offenders: The unintended consequences of the bets intentioned public policies.* Lanham, MD: University Press of America.

Maddan, S., Miller, J.M., Walker, J.T., and Marshall, I.H. (2011). The efficacy of sex offender registration and notification laws in Arkansas: Utilizing criminal history information to explore sex offender recidivism. *Justice Quarterly, 28*(2), 303-324.

Maghelal, P., and Olivares, M. (2005). Critical risk zones: Violators of Megan's Law. ESRI User Conference Proceedings, Technical Papers. Unpublished manuscript.

Magyar-Moe, J. (2012). Principles of positive psychology. In W. O'Donohue and J. Fisher (Eds.), *Cognitive Behavior Therapy: Core Principles for Practice* (pp. 353-375). Hoboken, NJ: John Wiley & Sons.

Maleng, N. (2003). Prosecutor's summary of the evidence. *State of Washington vs. Gary Leon Ridgway.* No. 01-1-10270-9 SEA.

Maletzky, B., Tolan, A., and McFarland, B. (2006). The Oregon Depo-Provera program: A five-year follow-up. *Sex Abuse, 18,* 303-316.

Mandeville-Norden, R., and Beech, A.R. (2004). Communit-based treatment of sex offenders. *Journal of Sexual Aggression, 10,* 193-214.

Mandeville-Norden R., and Beech, A.R. (2009). Development of a psychometric typology of child molesters: Implications for treatment. *Journal of Interpersonal Violence, 24*(2), 307-325.

Mangan, D., and Breuninger, K. (2019, July 18). Jeffrey Epstein's lust for young girls appears "uncontrollable," judge says in denying bail to accused sex trafficker. *CNBC.* https://www.cnbc.com/2019/07/18/jeffrey-epstein-bail-hearing-in-child-sex-traffic-case.html.

Mann, C. (2011, Mar 25). Brian David Mitchell sentenced to life in prison of Elizabeth Smart kidnapping. *CBS News.* Retrieved from www.cbsnews.com

Mann, R., and Thornton, D. (2000). An evidence-based relapse prevention program. In R. Laws, S. Hudson, and T. Ward (Eds.), *Remaking Relapse Prevention with Sex Offenders: A Sourcebook* (pp. 341-350). Thousand Oaks, CA: Sage Publications.

Marques, J., Day, D., Nelson, C., and West, M. (1994). Effects of cognitive-behavioral treatment on sex offender recidivism: Preliminary results of a longitudinal study. *Criminal Justice and Behavior, 21*(1), 28-54.

Marques, J., Nelson, C., Alarcon, J., Day, D. (2000). Preventing relapse in sex offenders: What we learned from SOTEP's experimental treatment program. In R. Laws, S. Hudson, and T. Ward (Eds.), *Remaking Relapse Prevention with Sex Offenders: A Sourcebook* (pp. 321-340). Thousand Oaks, CA: Sage Publications.

Marsh, P.J., Odlaug, B.L., Thomarios, N., Davis, A.A., Buchanan, S.N., Meyer, C.S., and Grant, J.E. (2010). Paraphilias in adult psychiatric inpatients. *Annals of Clinical Psychiatry, 22*, 129-134.

Marshall, W. (1979). Satiation therapy: A procedure for reducing deviant sexual arousal. *Journal of Applied Behavioral Analysis, 12*(3), 377-389.

Marshall, W.L. (1997). Pedophilia: Psychopathology and theory. In D.R. Laws and W.T. O'Donohue (Eds.), *Sexual Deviance: Theory, Assessment, and Treatment* (pp. 152-174). New York, NY: Guilford.

Marshall, W., and Laws, D. (2003). A brief history of behavioral and cognitive behavioral approaches to sexual offender treatment: Part 2. The modern era. *Sexual Abuse: A Journal of Research and Treatment, 15*(2), 93-120.

Marshall, W., O'Brien, M., and Marshall, L. (2009). Modifying sexual preferences. In A. Beech, L. Craig, and Browne, K. (Eds.), *Assessment and Treatment of Sex Offenders: A Handbook* (pp. 311-327). West Sussex, UK: Wiley-Blackwell.

Marsil, D. F., and McNamara, C. (2016). An examination of the disparity between self-identified versus legally identified rape victimization: A pilot study. *Journal of American College Health, 64*(5), 416-420.

Martin, E., and Silverstone, P. (2013). How much child sexual abuse is "below the surface," and can we help adults identify it early? *Frontiers in Psychiatry, 4*(58), 1-10.

Martin, P., and Hummer, R. (1989). Fraternities and rape on campus. *Gender and Society, 3*(4), 457-473.

Martinson, R. (1974). What works? Questions and answers about prison reform. *Public interest, 35*, 22-54.

Maruschak, L.M., and Minton, T.D. (2020). *Correctional populations in the United States, 2017-2018.* Washington, DC: Bureau of Justice Statistics.

Maruschak, L.M., and Buehler, E.D. (2021). *Survey of sexual victimization in adult correctional facilities, 2012-2018 - Statistical tables.* Washington, DC: Bureau of Justice Statistics.

Mason, I.G. (2004, October 11). When Harvey met Mickey. *New Statesman.* http://www3.sympatico.ca/ian.g.mason/Harvey_Weinstein.htm

Matson, S., and Lieb, R. (1996). *Community notification in Washington state: A 1996 survey of law enforcement.* Olympia, WA: Washington State Institute for Public Policy.

Matza, D. (1969). *Becoming deviant.* Englewood Cliffs, NJ: Prentice-Hall, Inc.

Maurelli, K., and Ronan, G. (2013). A time-series analysis of the effectiveness of sex offender notification in the USA. *Journal of Forensic Psychiatry and Psychology, 24*, 128-143.

Mayo Clinic. (n.d.). Tests and procedures: Electroconvulsive therapy (ECT). Retrieved from http://www.mayoclinic.org/tests-procedures/electroconvulsive-therapy/basics/definition/prc-20014161

McCabe, M., and Wauchope, M. (2005). Behavioural characteristics of rapists. *Journal of Sexual Aggression, 11*(3), 235-247.

McCahill, T., Meyer, L., and Fischman, A. (1979). *The aftermath of rape.* Lexington, MA: Lexington Books.

McCann, K., and Lussier, P. (2008). Antisociality, sexual deviance, and sexual reoffending in juvenile sex offenders: A meta-analytical investigation. *Youth Violence and Juvenile Justice, 6*, 363-385.

McDowell, C.Y, and Hibler, N. (1993). False allegations. In R. Hazelwood and A. Burgess (Eds.), *Practical Aspects of Rape Investigation: A Multidisciplinary Approach* (pp.275-299). Boca Raton, FL: CRC Press, Inc.

McElvaney, R., Greene, S., and Hogan, D. (2014). To tell or not to tell? Factors influencing young people's informal disclosure of child sexual abuse. *Journal of Interpersonal Violence, 29*(5), 928-947.

McGrath, R., Hoke, S., and Vojtisek, K. (1998). Cognitive-behavioral treatment of sex offenders: A treatment comparison and long-term follow-up study. *Criminal Justice and Behavior, 25*(2), 203-225.

McKinley, J.C. (2018, July 2). Harvey Weinstein faces new sex assault charges in Manhattan. *The New York Times.* https://www.nytimes.com/2018/07/02/nyregion/harvey-weinstein-sex.html

McKinney, J. (2002). Washington state's return to indeterminate sentencing for sex offenses: Correcting past sentencing mistakes and preventing future harm. *Seattle University Law Review, 26*, 309-336.

McLaughlin, E.C. (2013, August 30). Montana teen loved bit bulls, poetry before rape and suicide. *CNN.* Retrieved from www.cnn.com

McMillan, J. (2013). The kindest cut? Surgical castration, sex offenders and coercive offers. *Journal of Medical Ethics.* Published online [May 11, 2013] doi:10.1136/medethics-2012-101030 1

McMullin, D., and White, J. (2006). Long-term effects of labeling a rape experience. *Psychology of Women Quarterly, 30*, 96-105.

Meloy, M., Boatright, J., and Curtis, K. (2013). Views from the top and bottom: Lawmakers and practitioners discuss sex offender laws. *American Journal of Criminal Justice, 38*, 616-638.

Mendes, K., Ringrose, J., and Keller, J. (2018). #MeToo and the promise and pitfalls of challenging rape culture through digital feminist activism. *European Journal of Women's Studies, 25*(2), 236-246.

Mendez, M., and Shapira, J. (2011). Pedophilic behavior from brain disease. *Journal of Sexual Medicine, 8*(4), 1,092-1,100.

Mercado, C.C., Elbogen, E.B., Scalora, M., and Tomkins, A. (2001). Judgments of dangerousness: Are sex offenders assessed differently than civil psychiatric patients? *Psychiatry, Psychology, and Law, 8*, 146-153.

Merdian, H.L., Perkins, D.E., Dustagheer, E., and Glorney, E. (2020). Development of a case formulation module for individuals who have viewed, distributed and/or shared child sexual exploitation material. *International Journal of Offender Therapy and Comparative Criminology, 64*(10-11), 1055-1073.

Messman-Moore, T., Ward, R., and Zerubavel, N. (2013). The role of substance use and emotional dysregulation in predicting risk for incapacitated sexual revictimization in women: Results of a prospective investigation. *Psychology of Addictive Behaviors, 27*(1), 125-132.

Metcalf, R., Lee, G., Gould, L., and Stickels, J. (2010). Bite this! The role of bite mark analysis in wrongful convictions. *Southwest Journal of Criminal Justice, 7*(1), 47-64.

Meyer, W., Cole, C., and Emory, E. (1992). Depo Provera treatment for sex offending behavior. An evaluation of outcome. *Bulletin of the American Academy of Psychiatry and the Law, 20*(3), 249-259.

Meyer, W.J., and Cole, C.M. (1997). Physical and chemical castration of sex offenders: A review. *Journal of Offender Rehabilitation, 25*, 1-16.

Milano, A. [@Alyssa_Milano]. (2017, October 15). *If you've been sexually harassed or assaulted write "me too" as a reply to this tweet* [Tweet]. Twitter. https://twitter.com/Alyssa_Milano/status/919659438700670976

Miller, A., Markman, K., and Handley, I. (2007). Self-blame among sexual assault victims prospectively predicts revictimization: A received sociolegal context model of risk. *Basic and Applied Social Psychology, 29*(2), 129-136.

Milner, J.S., and Dopke, C.A. (1997). Paraphilia not otherwise specified: Psychopathy and theory. In D.R. Laws and W.T. O'Donohue (Eds.), *Sexual Deviance: Theory, Assessment, and Treatment* (pp. 394-423). New York, NY: Guilford.

Miner, M., Marquez, J., Day, D., and Nelson, C. (1990). Impact of relapse prevention in treating sex offenders: Preliminary findings. *Annals of Sex Research, 3*(2), 165-185.

Minnesota Department of Correction. (2003). *Level three sex offenders residential placement issues*. St. Paul, MN: Minnesota Department of Correction.

Minnesota Department of Correction. (2007). *Residential proximity and sex offense recidivism in Minnesota*. St. Paul, MN: Minnesota Department of Correction.

Minnesota Department of Corrections. (2008). *Megan's Law in Minnesota: The impact of community notification on sex offender recidivism*. St. Paul, MN: Minnesota Department of Corrections.

Mitchell, K., Finkelhor, D., Jones, L., and Wolak, J. (2012). Prevalence and characteristics of youth sexting: A national study. *Pediatrics, 129*(1), 13-20.

Mitchell, K., Wolak, J., and Finkelhor, D. (2005). Police posing as juveniles online to catch sex offenders: Is it working? *Sexual Abuse: A Journal of Research and Treatment, 17*(3), 241-267.

Moak, S., Walker, J., and Lee, G. (2011). Does the shoe fit? Using child pornography laws to respond to sexing. *International Journal of Crime, Criminal Justice, and Law, 5*(1).

Monroe, L., Kinney, L., Weist, M., Spriggs, D., Mekpor, D., Dantzler, J., and Reynolds, M. (2005). The experience of sexual assault. *Journal of Interpersonal Violence, 20*(7), 767-776.

Moreau, D. (1993). Concepts of physical evidence in sexual assault investigations. In R. Hazelwood and A. Burgess (Eds.), *Practical Aspects of Rape Investigation: A Multidisciplinary Approach* (pp. 61–93). Boca Raton, FL: CRC Press, Inc.

Morgan, R.E., and Truman, J.L. (2020). *Criminal victimization, 2019*. Washington, D.C.: U.S. Department of Justice.

Morin, J.W., and Levenson, J.S. (2008). Exhibitionism: Assessment and treatment. In D.R. Laws and W.T. O'Donohue (Eds.), *Sexual Deviance: Theory, Assessment, and Treatment*, Second Edition (pp. 76-107). New York, NY: Guilford.

Morral, S., and Gore, K. (2014). *Sexual assault and sexual harassment in the military*. Santa Monica, CA: Rand Corporation.

Muehlenhard, C., and Linton, M. (1987). Date rape and sexual aggression in dating situations: Incidence and risk factors. *Journal of Counseling Psychology, 34*(2), 186-196.

Murphy, T. (1992). Redirecting sexual orientation: Techniques and justifications. *The Journal of Sex Research, 29*(4), 501-523.

Murphy, W., and Page, I. (2008). Exhibitionism: Psychopathology and theory. In D.R. Laws and W.T. O'Donohue (Eds.), *Sexual Deviance: Theory, Assessment, and Treatment*, Second Edition (pp. 61-75). New York, NY: Guilford.

Murray, J.B. (2000). Psychological profile of pedophiles and child molesters. *Journal of Psychology, 134*, 211-224.

Mustaine, E., and Tewksbury, R. (2002). Sexual assault of college women: A feminist interpretation of a routine activities analysis. *Criminal Justice Review, 27*(1), 89-123.

Mustaine, E.E. (2014). Sex offender residency restrictions: Successful integration or exclusion? *Criminology and Public Policy, 13,* 169-178.

Mustaine, E.E., and Tewksbury, R. (2008). Registered sex offenders, residence, and the influence of race. *Journal of Ethnicity in Criminal Justice, 6,* 65-82.

Mustaine, E.E., Tewksbury, R., and Stengel, K.M. (2006). Residential location and mobility of registered sex offenders. *American Journal of Criminal Justice, 30,* 177-192.

NAMBLA (n.d.). http://www.nambla.org

National Conference of State Legislatures. (2006). *States with sex offender residency restriction laws.* Denver, CO: National Conference of State Legislatures.

Nezu, A., and Nezu C. (2012). Problem solving. In W. O'Donohue and J. Fisher (Eds.), *Cognitive Behavior Therapy: Core Principles for Practice* (pp. 159-182). Hoboken, NJ: John Wiley & Sons.

Nhan, J., and Bowen, K.N. (2020). Policing Internet sex trafficking. *Journal of Qualitative Criminal Justice & Criminology, 9*(1), 1-25.

Nitschke, J., Mokros, A., Osterheider, M., and Marshall, W.L. (2012). Sexual sadism: current diagnostic vagueness and the benefit of behavioral definitions. *International Journal of Offender Therapy and Comparative Criminology, 57,* 1441-1453.

Nobles, M.R., Levenson, J.S., and Youstin, T.J. (2012). Effectiveness of residence restrictions in preventing sex offense recidivism. *Crime and Delinquency, 58,* 491-513.

Oberman, M. (1994). Turning girls into women: Re-evaluating modern statutory rape law. *The Journal of Criminal Law and Criminology, 85*(1), 15-79.

O'Donohue, W., and Fisher, J. (2012). The core principles of cognitive behavior therapy. In W. O'Donohue and J. Fisher (Eds.), *Cognitive Behavior Therapy: Core Principles for Practice* (pp. 1-12). Hoboken, NJ: John Wiley & Sons.

Olver, M.E. (2017). The risk-need-responsivity model: Applications to sex offender treatment. In D.P. Boer, A.R. Beech, T. Ward, L.A. Craig, M. Rettenberger, L E. Marshall, and W.L. Marshall (Eds), *The Wiley handbook on the theories, assessment and treatment of sexual offending* (pp. 1313-1329). Wiley Blackwell.

Olver, M.E., Marshall, L.E., Marshall, W.L., and Nicholaichuk, T.P. (2020). A long-term outcome assessment of the effects on subsequent reoffense rates of a prison-based CBT/RNR sex offender treatment program with strength-based elements. *Sexual Abuse, 32*(2), 127-153.

Olver, M., and Wong, S. (2011). A comparison of static and dynamic assessment of sexual offender risk and need in a treatment context. *Criminal Justice and Behavior, 38*(2), 113-126.

Olver, M., Wong, S., and Nicholaichuk, T. (2009). Outcome evaluation of a high-intensity inpatient sex offender treatment program. *Journal of Interpersonal Violence, 24*(3), 522-536.

O'Neil, E.N., and Hayes, B.E. (2020). "Most [false reports] involve teens": Officer attitudes toward teenage sexual assault complainants—A qualitative analysis. *Violence Against Women, 26*(1), 24-45.

O'Sullivan, C. (1991). Acquaintance gang rape on campus. In A. Parrot and C. Bechhofer (Eds.), *Acquaintance Rape: The Hidden Crime* (pp. 140-156). New York: Wiley.

Oudekerk, B., Farr, R., and Reppucci, N. (2013). Is it love of sexual abuse? Young adults' perceptions of statutory rape. *Journal of Child Sexual Abuse, 22,* 858-877.

Packer, H. (1968). *The limits of the criminal sanction.* Stanford, CA: Stanford University Press.

Page, A. (2007). Behind the blue line: Investigating police officers' attitudes toward rape. *Journal of Police and Criminal Psychology, 22*(1), 22-32.

Page, A. (2008). Gateway to reform? Policy implications of police officers' attitudes toward rape. *American Journal of Criminal Justice, 33*(1), 44-58.

Page, A. (2010). True colors: Police officers and rape myth acceptance. *Feminist Criminology, 5*(4), 315-334.

Pak, E. (2020). Jeffrey Epstein Biography. Retrieved August 28, 2021 from https://www.biography.com/crime-figure/jeffrey-epstein.

Pam Lychner Sexual Offender Tracking and Identification Act. (1996) *United States Code.* Vol. 42, Section 13701.

Papa, A., Boland, M., and Sewell, M. (2012). Emotion regulation and CBT. In W. O'Donohue and J. Fisher (Eds.), *Cognitive Behavior Therapy: Core Principles for Practice* (pp. 273-323). Hoboken, NJ: John Wiley & Sons.

Patrick, S., and Marsh, R. (2011). Sentencing outcomes of convicted child sex offenders. *Journal of Child Sexual Abuse, 20,* 94-108.

Patterson, D. (2011). The impact of detectives' manner of questioning on rape victims' disclosure. *Violence Against Women, 17*(11), 1,349-1,373.

Patterson, D., and Campbell, R. (2012). The problem of untested sexual assault kits: Why are some kits never submitted to a crime laboratory? *Journal of Interpersonal Violence, 27*(11), 2,259-2,275.

Pazzani, L. (2003). *The social construction of rape.* (Unpublished undergraduate thesis). Reed College, Portland, OR.

Peter, T. (2009). Exploring taboos: Comparing male- and female-perpetrated sexual abuse. *Journal of Interpersonal Violence, 24,* 1,111-1,128.

Peters, M.A., and Besley, T. (2019). Weinstein, sexual predation and "rape culture": Public pedagogies and hashtag internet activism. *Educational Philosophy and Theory, 51*(5), 458-464.

Peterson, Z., and Muehlenhard, C. (2004). Was it rape? The function of women's rape myth acceptance and definitions of sex in labeling their own experiences. *Sex Roles, 51*(3/4), 129-144.

Petrosino, A.J., and C. Petrosino. (1999). The public safety potential of Megan's Law in Massachusetts: An assessment from a sample of criminal sexual psychopaths. *Crime and Delinquency, 45*(1), 140-158.

Pflugradt, D., and Allen, B. (2012). A grounded theory analysis of sexual sadism in females. *Journal of Sexual Aggression, 18*, 325-337.

Pharmacia and Upjohn Company, LLC. (2015). Depo-Provera- medroxyprogesterone acetate injection, suspension. Retrieved from labeling.pfizer.com/ShowLabeling.aspx?id=522

Phillips, D.M. (1998). *Community notification as viewed by Washington's citizens.* Olympia: Washington State Institute for Public Policy.

Piemont, L. (2007). Fear of the empty self: The motivations for genital exhibitionism. *Modern Psychoanalysis, 32*, 79-93.

Piquero, A.R., Farrington, D.P., Jennings, W.P., Diamond, B., and Craig, J. (2012). Sex offenders and sex offending in the Cambridge study in delinquent development: Prevalence, frequency, specialization, recidivism, and (dis)continuity over the life-course. *Journal of Crime and Justice, 35*, 412-426.

Pithers, W., and Cumming, G. (1989). Can relapses be prevented? Initial outcome data from the Vermont Treatment Program for Sexual Aggressors. In D. R. Laws (Ed.) *Relapse Prevention with Sex Offenders* (pp. 313-325). New York, NY: The Guilford Press.

Pithers, W., Marques, J., Gibat, C., and Marlatt, A. (1983). Relapse prevention with sexual aggressives: A self-control model of treatment and maintenance of change. In J. Greer and I. Stuart (Eds.) *The Sexual Aggressor: Current Perspectives on Treatment* (pp. 214-239). New York, NY: Van Nostrand Reinhold Company.

Pitts, V., and Schwartz, M. (1993). Promoting self-blame in hidden rape cases. *Humanity and Society, 17*(4), 383-397.

Planty, M., Langton, L., Krebs, C., Berzofsky, M., and Smiley-McDonald, H. (2013). *Female victims of sexual violence, 1994-2010.* Washington, DC: Bureau of Justice Statistics Special Report.

Posner, R.A. (1992). *Sex and reason.* Cambridge, MA: Harvard University Press.

Quinn, J.F., Frosyth, C.J., and Mullen-Quinn, C. (2004). Societal reaction to sex offenders: A review of the origins and results of the myths surrounding their crimes and treatment amenability. *Deviant Behavior, 25*, 215-232.

Quinsey, V.L. (1984). Sexual aggression: Studies of offenses against women. In D.N. Weisstub (Ed.), *Law and Mental Health: International Perspectives* (pp. 140-172). New York, NY: Pergamon.

Radford, B. (2008). Americans exaggerate threats posed by sexual predators. In L.M. Zott (Ed.), *Sex Offenders and Public Policy* (pp. 54-63). Farmington Hills, MI: Greenhaven Press.

Ransom, J. (2020, March 11). Harvey Weinstein's stunning downfall: 23 years in prison. *The New York Times.* https://www.nytimes.com/2020/03/11/nyregion/harvey-weinstein-sentencing.html

Reaves, B.A. (2013). *Felony defendants in large urban counties, 2009—Statistical tables.* Washington, D.C.: Bureau of Justice Statistics.

Reaves, B.A. (2015). *Campus law enforcement, 2011-2012.* Washington, D.C.: Bureau of Justice Statistics.

Reavy, P. (2010, May 22). Wanda Barzee sentenced to 15 years in federal prison, gets scolding from Elizabeth Smart's mother. *Desert News.* Retrieved from www.desertnews.com

Red-Bird, B. (2009). *Assessing housing availability under Ohio's sex offender residency restrictions.* Columbus, OH: Ohio State University.

Reingle, J.M. (2012). Evaluating the continuity between juvenile and adult sex offending: A review of the literature. *Journal of Crime and Justice, 35*, 427-434.

Reinhardt, J., and Fisher, E. (1949). The sexual psychopath and the law. *Journal of Criminal Law and Criminology, 36*(6), 734-742.

Rhodes, W. (1986). A survival model with dependent competing events and right-hand censoring: Probation and parole as an illustration. *Journal of Quantitative Criminology, 2*, 113-137.

Rice, D.D. (2008). Targeting offenders' re-entry into society and community education are key. In L.M. Zott (Ed.), *Sex Offenders and Public Policy* (pp. 194-203). Farmington Hills, MI: Greenhaven Press.

Rice, M., Harris, G., and Cormier, C. (1992). An evaluation of a maximum security therapeutic community for psychopaths and other mentally disordered offenders. *Law and Human Behavior, 16*(4), 399-412.

Richards, K. (2018). Born this way? A qualitative examination of public perceptions of the causes of pedophilia and sexual offending against children. *Deviant Behavior, 39*, 835-851.

Richardson, D., and Campbell, J. (1982). Alcohol and rape: The effects of alcohol on attributions of blame for rape. *Personality and Social Psychology Bulletin, 8*(3), 468-476.

Richardson, D., and Hammock, G. (1991). Alcohol and acquaintance rape. In Parrot, A., and Bechhofer, L. (Eds.), *Acquaintance Rape: The Hidden Crime.* New York: John Wiley & Sons, Inc.

Robertson, C.A., and Knight, R.A. (2014). Relating sexual sadism and psychopathy to one another, non-sexual violence, and sexual crime behaviors. *Aggressive Behavior, 40*, 12-23.

Rosenmerkel, S., Durose, M., and Farole, D. (2009). *Felony sentences in state courts, 2006—Statistical tables.* Washington, D.C.: Bureau of Justice Statistics.

Rummel, C., Garrison-Diehn, C., Catlin, C., and Fisher, J. (2012). Clinical functional analysis: Understanding the contingencies of reinforcement. In W. O'Donohue and J. Fisher (Eds.), *Cognitive Behavior Therapy: Core Principles for Practice* (pp. 13-36). Hoboken, NJ: John Wiley & Sons.

Rumney, P.N.S. (2006). False allegations of rape. *Cambridge Law Journal, 65*, 128-158.

Rydberg, J., Cassidy, M., and Socia, K.M. (2018). Punishing the Wicked: Examining the correlates of sentence severity for convicted sex offenders. *Journal of Quantitative Criminology, 34*, 943-970.

Rye, B., Greatrix, S., and Enright, C. (2006). The case of the guilty victim: The effects of gender of victim and gender of perpetrator on attributions of blame and responsibility. *Sex Roles, 54*, 639-649.

Rye, B.J., and Meaney, G.J. (2007). Voyeurism: It is good as long as we do not get caught. *International Journal of Sexual Behavior, 19*, 47-56.

Saad, N. (2018, May 25). Harvey Weinstein's accusers: List includes fledgling actresses and Hollywood royalty. *Los Angeles Times. https://www.latimes.com/entertainment/la-et-weinstein-accusers-list-20171011-htmlstory.html*

Saferstein, R. (2013). *Forensic Science: From Crime Scene to the Crime Lab.* Boston, MA: Pearson.

Salerno, J.M., Najdowski, C.J., Stevenson, M.C., Wiley, T.R.A., Bottoms, B.L., Vaca, B.L., and Pimental, P.S. (2010). Psychological mechanisms underlying support for juvenile sex offender registry laws: Prototypes, moral outrage, and perceived threat. *Behavioral Sciences and the Law, 28*, 58-83.

Sallomi, M. (2013). Coopting the antiviolence movement: Why expanding DNA surveillance won't make us safer. *Social Justice, 39*(4), 97-114.

Sample, L.L. (2001). The social construction of the sex offender. Unpublished doctoral dissertation, University of Missouri, St. Louis.

Sample, L.L., and Bray, T.M. (2003). Are sex offenders dangerous? *Criminology and Public Policy, 3*(1), 59-82.

Sample, L.L., Evans, M.K., and Anderson, A.L. (2011). Sex offender community notification laws: Are their effects symbolic or instrumental in nature? *Criminal Justice Policy Review, 22*, 27-49.

Sanday, P.R. (1981). The socio-cultural context of rape: A cross-cultural study. *Journal of Social Issues, 37*(4), 5-26.

Sandler, J.C., Freeman, N.J., and Socia, K.M. (2008). Does a watched pot boil? A time-series analysis of New York State's sex offender registration and notification law. *Psychology, Public Policy, and Law, 14*, 284-302.

Saradjian, J. (2010). Understanding the prevalence of female-perpetrated sexual abuse and the impact of that abuse on victims. In T.A. Gannon and F. Cortoni (Eds.), *Female Sexual Offenders: Theory, Assessment, and Treatment* (pp. 9-30). Hoboken, NJ: John Wiley and Sons, Ltd.

Savage, J., and Windsor, C. (2018). Sex offender residence restrictions and sex crimes against children: A comprehensive review. *Aggression and Violent Behavior, 43*, 13-25.

Schaaf, S., Jeglic, E.L., Calkins, C., Raymaekers, L., and Leguizama, A. (2019). Examining ethno-racial related differences in child molester typology: An MTC:CM3 approach. *Journal of Interpersonal Violence, 34*(8), 1683-1702.

Schaffer, M., Jeglic, E., Moster, A., and Wnuk, D. (2010). Cognitive-behavioral therapy in the treatment and management of sex offenders. *Journal of Cognitive Psychotherapy: An International Quarterly, 24*(2), 92-103.

Schiavone, S.K., and Jeglic, E.L. (2009). Public perception of sex offender social policies and the impact of sex offenders. *International Journal of Offender Therapy and Comparative Criminology, 53*, 679-695.

Schlank, A. (2008). The civil commitment of sexual offenders: Lessons learned. In G.A. Serran (Ed.), *Sexual Offender Treatment: Controversial Issues.* West Sussex, England: John Wiley & Sons, Ltd.

Schlesinger, L.B. (2000). *Serial offenders: Current thought, recent findings.* London: CRC Press.

Schmitt, F.E., and Martin, P.Y. (1999). Unobtrusive mobilization by an institutionalize rape crisis center: "All we do comes from victims." *Gender and Society, 13*(3), 364-384.

Schoeyen, H., Kessler, U., Andreassen, O., Auestad, B., Bergsholm, P., Malt, U., Morken, G., Oedegaard, K., and Vaaler, A. (2015) Treatment-resistant bipolar depression: A randomized controlled trial of electroconvulsive therapy versus algorithm-based pharmacological treatment. *American Journal of Psychiatry, 172*(1), 41-51.

Schram, D.D., and Milloy, C.D. (1995). *Community notification: A study of offender characteristics and recidivism.* Washington: Washington State Institute for Public Policy.

Schuknecht, C. (2019, June 19). A young Jeffrey Epstein made an impression on his high school students. *NPR.* https://www.npr.org/2019/07/19/742725946/a-young-jeffrey-epstein-made-an-impression-on-his-high-school-students.

Schuller, R., and Stewart, A. (2000). Police responses to sexual assault complaints: The role of perpetrator/complainant intoxication. *Law and Human Behavior, 24*(5), 535-551.

Schultz, P.D. (2008). Treating sex offenders makes sense. In L.M. Zott (Ed.), *Sex Offenders and Public Policy* (pp. 85-89). Farmington Hills, MI: Greenhaven Press.

Schwartz, M.D. (2021). Masculinities, sport, and violence against women: The contribution of male peer support theory. *Violence Against Women, 27*(5), 688-707.

Schwartz, M. (2010). National Institute of Justice Visiting Fellowship: Police Investigation of Rape — Roadblocks and Solutions. Washington, D.C.: U.S. Department of Justice.

Schwartz, M., and DeKeseredy, W. (1997). *Sexual assault on the college campus: The role of male peer support.* Thousand Oaks, CA: Sage Publications.

Schwartz, M., and Pitts, V. (1995). Exploring a feminist routine activities approach to explaining sexual assault. *Justice Quarterly, 12*(1), 9-31.

Schweitzer, R., and Dwyer, J. (2003). Sex crime recidivism: Evaluation of a sexual offender treatment program. *Journal of Interpersonal Violence, 18*(11), 1,292-1,310.

Scully, D., and Marolla, J. (1984). Convicted rapists' vocabulary of motive: Excuses and justifications. *Social Problems, 31*, 530-544.

Sedlak, A., Mettenburg, J., Basena, M., Petta, I., McPherson, K., Green, A., and Li, S. (2010). *Fourth National Incidence Study of Child Abuse and Neglect (NIS-4) Report to Congress.* Washington, DC: U.S. Department of Health and Human Services, Administration for Children and Families.

Semel, E. (1997). Megan's Law is a knee-jerk reaction to a senseless personal tragedy. *Corrections Today*, October, 21.

Serjeant, J. (2021, July 21). Harvey Weinstein extradited to Los Angeles to face second rape trial. *Reuters*. https://www.reuters.com/world/us/harvey-weinstein-extradited-california-face-second-rape-trial-2021-07-20/

Serna, J. (2014, Sept. 26). Rapist first sentenced to 31 days gets 10 years in prison. *The Los Angeles Times.* Retrieved from http://www.latimes.com

Seto, M.C. (2018). *Pedophilia and sexual offending against children: Theory, assessment, and intervention*, Third Edition. Washington, DC: American Psychological Association.

Seto, M.C., and Eke, A. (2005). The criminal histories and later offending of child pornography offenders. *Sexual Abuse: A Journal of Research and Treatment, 17*(2), 201-210.

Seto, M.C., Federoff, J.P., Bradford, J.M., Knack, N., Rodrigues, N.C., Curry, S., Booth, B., Gray, J., Cameron, C., Bourget, D., Messina, S., James, E., Watson, D., Balmaceda, R., Ahmed, A.G. (2016). Reliability and validity of the DSM-IV-TR and proposed DSM-5 criteria for pedophilia: Implications for the ICD-11 and the next DSM. *International Journal of Law and Psyciatry, 49*, 98-106.

Seto, M.C., Wood, J., Babchishin, K., and Flynn, S. (2012). Online solicitation offenders are different from child pornography offenders and lower risk contact sexual offenders. *Law and Human Behavior, 36*(4), 320-330. Shakeshaft, C. (2004). Educator Sexual Misconduct: A Synthesis of Existing Literature PPSS 2004-09. *US Department of Education.*

Shaw, J., and Campbell, R. (2013). Predicted sexual assault kit submission among adolescent rape cases treated in forensic nurse examiners programs. *Journal of Interpersonal Violence, 28*(18), 3,400-3,417.

Shechory, M., and Idisis, Y. (2006). Rape myths and social distance toward sex offenders and victims among therapists and students. *Sex Roles, 54*, 651-658.

Sherman, L.W., Strang, H., and Woods, D.J. (2000). *Recidivism patterns in the Canberra reintegrative shaming experiments (RISE).* Australia: Australian National University.

Shindel, A.W., and Moser, C.A. (2011). Why are the paraphilias mental disorders? *Journal of Sexual Medicine, 8*, 928-929.

Shipp, E.R. (1992, March 27). Tyson gets 6-year prison term for rape conviction in Indiana. *The New York Times.* Retrieved from www.nytimes.com

Shotland, R.L. (1992). A theory of the causes of courtship rape: Part 2. *Journal of Social Issues, 48*(2), 127-143.

Shutts, D. (1982). *Lobotomy: Resort to the Knife.* New York, NY: Van Nostrand Reinhold Company.

Simon, J. (1998). Managing the monstrous: Sex offenders and the new penology. *Psychology, Public Policy, and Law, 4*, 452-467.

Sims, C.M., Noel, N.E., and Maisto, S.A. (2007). Rape blame as a function of alcohol presence and resistance type. *Addictive Behavior, 32*, 2766-2,775.

Sinozich, S., and Langton, L. (2014). *Rape and sexual assault victimization among college-age females, 1995-2013.* Washington, D.C.: Bureau of Justice Statistics.

Sisak, M., Balsamo, M., and Neumeister, L. (2019, August 16). Medical examiner rules Epstein death a suicide by hanging. *Associated Press.* https://apnews.com/article/suicides-us-news-ap-top-news-bernard-madoff-new-york-city-a947e0d85d31496eb5bd9ff4994c9718.

Sleath, E., and Bull, R. (2012). Comparing rape victim and perpetrator blaming in a police officer sample: Differences between police officers with and without special training. *Criminal Justice and Behavior, 35*(5), 646-665.

Smart, E. (2013). *My story.* New York: St. Martin's Griffin.

SMART (Office of Sex Offender Sentencing, Monitoring, Apprehending, Registering, and Tracking). (2013). *Sex offender registration and notification in the United States: Current case law and issues.* Washington, D.C.: U.S. Department of Justice.

Smith, H. (2013). Common enemy and political opportunity leave archaically modern sentencing unchecked: The unconstitutionality of Louisiana's chemical castration statute. *Loyola Law Review, 59*, 212-266.

Smith, S.G., Chen, J., Basile, K.C., Gilbert, L.K., Merrick, M.T., Patel, N., Walling, M., and Jain, A. (2017). The National Intimate Partner and Sexual Violence Survey (NISVS)L 2010-2012 state report. Retrieved from: https://www.cdc.gov/violenceprevention/datasources/nisvs/summaryreports.html

Smith, S.G., Zhang, X., Basile, K.C., Merrick, M.T., Wang, J., Kresnow, M., & Chen, J. (2018). The National Intimate Partner and Sexual Violence Survey: 2015 data brief—updated release. Retrieved from: https://www.cdc.gov/violenceprevention/ datasources/nisvs/summaryreports.html

Snyder, H. (2000). *Sexual assault of young children as reported to law enforcement: Victim, incident, and offender characteristics.* Washington, DC: Bureau of Justice Statistics.

Socia, K.M. (2011). The policy implications of residence restrictions on sex offender housing in Upstate NY. *Criminology and Public Policy, 10,* 351-389.

Socia, K.M. (2012). The efficacy of county-level sex offender residence restrictions in New York. *Crime and Delinquency, 58,* 612-642.

Socia, K.M. (2014). Residence restrictions are ineffective, inefficient, and inadequate: So now what? *Criminology and Public Policy, 13,* 179-188.

Sorkin, L.G. (1998). The trilogy of federal statutes. In *National Conference on Sex Offender Registries.* Washington D.C.: Department of Justice.

Spohn, C. (2009). *How do judges decide? The search for fairness and justice in punishment.* Thousand Oaks, CA: Sage.

Spohn, C., and Holleran, D. (2001). Prosecuting sexual assault: A comparison of decisions in sexual assault cases involving strangers, acquaintances, and intimate partners. *Justice Quarterly, 18,* 651-689.

Spohn, C., Beichner, D., and Davis-Frenzel, E. (2001). Prosecutorial justifications for sexual assault case rejection: Guarding the "gateway to justice." *Social Problems, 48*(2), 206-235.

Spohn, R., Bjornsen, A., Wright, E. M. (2017). Factors associated with reporting of sexual assault among college and non-college women. *Journal of Aggression, Conflict, and Peace Research, 9*(4), 279-289.

Spohn, C., White, C., and Tellis, K. (2014). Unfounding sexual assault: Examining the decision to unfound and identifying false reports. *Law and Society Review, 48*(1), 161-192.

Spohn, C., and Tellis, K. (2019). Sexual assault case outcomes: Disentangling the overlapping decisions of police and prosecutors. *Justice Quarterly, 36,* 383-411.

Steel, C.M., Newman, E., O'Rourke, S., and Quayle, E. (2020). An integrative review of historical technology and countermeasure usage trends in online child sexual exploitation material offenders. *Forensic Science International: Digital Investigation, 33,* 300971.

Stein, M., Lang, A., Laffaye, C., Satz, L., Lenox, R., and Dresselhaus, T. (2004). Relationship of sexual assault history to somatic symptoms and health anxiety in women. *General Hospital Psychiatry, 26,* 178-183.

Stekel, W. (1924). *Sexual aberrations: The phenomenon of fetishism in relation to sex.* New York, NY: Liveright.

Stern, M. (2013, November 6) Mike Tyson opens up about his rape conviction, Brad Pitt, and love of Pinkberry. *The Daily Beast.* Retrieved from www.thedailybeast.com

Stevenson, M.C., Smith, A.C., Sekely, A., and Farnum, K.S. (2013). Predictors of support for juvenile sex offender registration: Educated individuals recognize the flaws of juvenile registration. *Journal of Child Sexual Abuse, 22,* 231-254.

Stinson, J.D., Sales, B.D., and Becker, J.V. (2008). *Sex offending: Causal theories to inform research, prevention, and treatment.* Washington, DC: American Psychological Association.

Strom, K., and Hickman, M. (2010). Unanalyzed evidence in law-enforcement practices: A national examination of forensic processing in police departments. *Criminology and Public Policy, 9*(2), 381-404.

Summit, R. (1983). The child sexual abuse accommodation syndrome. *Child Abuse and Neglect, 7,* 177-193.

Sutherland, E. (1950). The diffusion of sexual psychopath laws. *American Journal of Sociology, 56*(2), 142-148.

Swaine, J. (2015). Jeffrey Epstein's donations to young pupils prompts US Virgin Islands review. *The Guardian.* https://www.theguardian.com/us-news/2015/jan/13/jeffrey-epstein-donations-us-virgin-islands-review.

Swindell, S., Stroebel, S.S., O'Keefe, S.L., Beard, K.W., Robinett, S.R., and Kommor, M.J. (2011). Correlates of exhibition-like experiences: A model for development of exhibitionism in heterosexual males. *Sexual Addiction and Compulsivity, 18,* 135-156.

Talman, K. (2008). Containment and surveillance plus registries equals real protection. In L.M. Zott (Ed.), *Sex Offenders and Public Policy* (pp. 184-193). Farmington Hills, MI: Greenhaven Press.

Tambe, A. (2018). Reckoning with the silences of #MeToo. *Feminist Studies, 44*(1), 197-202.

Tark, J., and Kleck, G. (2014). Resisting rape: The effects of victim self-protection on rape completion and injury. *Violence Against Women, 20*(3), 270-292.

Tenzer, L.Y.G. (2019). #MeToo, statutory rape laws, and the persistence of gender stereotypes. *Utah Law Review, 2019*(1), 117-158.

Terry, K.J. (2011). What is smart sex offender policy? *Criminology and Public Policy, 10*(2), 275-281.

Terry, K.J. (2013). *Sexual offenses and offenders: Theory, practice, and policy,* Second Edition. Belmont, CA: Wadsworth.

Terry, K.J. (2015). Sex offender laws in the United States: Smart policy or disproportionate sanctions? *International Journal of Comparative and Applied Criminal Justice, 39,* 113-127.

Terry, K.J., and Ackerman, A. (2008). Child sexual abuse in the Catholic Church: How situational crime prevention strategies can help create safe environments. *Criminal Justice and Behavior, 35*(5), 643-657.

Testa, M., VanZile-Tamsen, C., Livingston, J., and Koss M. (2004). Assessing women's experiences of sexual aggression using the sexual experiences survey: Evidence for validity and implications for research. *Psychology of Women Quarterly, 28,* 256-265.

Tewksbury, R. (2005). Collateral consequences of sex offender registration. *Journal of Contemporary Criminal Justice* 21, 67-82.

Tewksbury, R. (2014). Evidence of ineffectiveness: Advancing the argument against sex offender residence restrictions. *Criminology and Public Policy, 13,* 135-138.

Tewksbury, R., and Jennings, W.G. (2010). Assessing the impact of sex offender registration and community notification on sex-offending trajectories. *Criminal Justice and Behavior Policy Review, 37*, 570-582.

Tewskbury, R., and Lees, R. (2006). Perceptions of sex offender registration: Collateral consequences and community experiences. *Sociological Spectrum, 26*, 309-334.

Tewksbury, R., and Mustaine, E.E. (2008). Where to find sex offenders: An examination of residential locations and neighborhood conditions. *Criminal Justice Studies, 19*, 61-75.

Tewksbury, R., and Mustaine, E.E. (2013). Law-enforcement officials' views of sex offender registration and community notification. *International Journal of Police Science and Management, 15*, 95-113.

Tewksbury, R., Jennings, W.G., and Zgoba, K.M. (2012). A longitudinal examination of sex offender recidivism prior to and following the implementation of SORN sex offenders and recidivism. *Behavioral Sciences and the Law, 30*, 308-328.

Thomas, L. (2002, October 28). Jeffrey Epstein: International moneyman of mystery. *New York*. https://nymag.com/nymetro/news/people/n_7912/.

Thornhill, R., and Palmer, C.T. (2000). *A natural history of rape: Biological bases of sexual coercion*. MIT Press.

Tippett, E.C. (2018). The legal implications of the metoo movement. *Minnesota Law Review, 103*(1), 229-302.

Titcomb, C., Goodman-Delahunty, J., and De Puiseau, B. (2012). Pretrial diversion for intrafamilial child sexual offending: Does biological paternity matter? *Criminal Justice and Behavior, 39*(4), 552-570.

Title VII of the Civil Rights Act. (1964). *United States Code*. Vol. 42, Section 2000.

Tittle, C.R., and Paternoster, R. (2000). *Social deviance and crime: An organizational and theoretical approach*. Los Angeles, CA: Roxbury Publishing Company.

Tjaden, P., and Thoennes, N. (2000). *Full report of the prevalence, incidence, and consequences of violence against women: Findings from the National Violence Against Women Survey* (NCJ Publication No. 183718).

Tjaden, P., and Thoennes, N. (2006). *Extent, nature, and consequences of rape victimization: Findings from the National Violence Against Women Survey*. Washington, D.C.: National Institute of Justice.

Tolman, A.W. (2018). Sex offenders civil commitment to prison post-*Kingsley*. *Northwestern University Law Review, 113*, 157-193.

Troup-Leasure, K., and Snyder, H. (2005). *Statutory rape known to law enforcement*. Washington, DC: Office of Juvenile Justice and Delinquency Prevention.

Truman, J.L., and Langton, L. (2015). *Criminal victimization, 2014*. Washington, D.C.: Bureau of Justice Statistics.

Turley, E., and Hutzel, L. (2001). *West Virginia sex offender study*. Charleston, SC: Criminal Justice Statistical Analysis Center.

Tuttle, G. (2012, July 14). Parents settle lawsuit against Billings teacher who raped daughter. *Missoulian*. Retrieved from www.missoulian.com

Twohig, M., and Dehlin, J. (2012). Skills training. In W. O'Donohue and J. Fisher (Eds.), *Cognitive Behavior Therapy: Core Principles for Practice* (pp. 37-73). Hoboken, NJ: John Wiley & Sons.

UCR Offense Definitions. (2014). *Uniform Crime Reporting Statistics*. Retrieved from http://www.ucrdatatool.gov/offenses.cfm

Ullman, S. (1999). A comparison of gang and individual rape incidents. *Violence and Victims, 14*(2), 123-133.

Ullman, S. (2007). Comparing gang and individual rapes in a community sample of urban woman. *Violence and Victims, 22*(1), 43-51.

Ullman, S., and Filipas, H. (2001). Predictors of PTSD symptom severity and social reactions in sexual assault victims. *Journal of Traumatic Stress, 14*(2), 369-389.

Ullman, S., Starzynski, L., Long, S., Mason, G., and Long, L. (2008). Exploring the relationship of women's sexual assault disclosure, social reactions, and problem drinking. *Journal of Interpersonal Violence, 23*(9), 1235-1257.

U.S. Attorney General. (1999). Final guidelines for the Jacob Wetterling Crimes Against Children and Sexually Violent Offender Registration Act, as amended. *Federal Register, 64*(2), 1-30.

U.S. Department of Health and Human Services, Administration for Children and Families, Administration on Children, Youth and Families, Children's Bureau. (2016). *Child maltreatment 2014*. Retrieved from http://www.acf.hhs.gov/programs/cb/research-data-technology/statistics-research/child-maltreatment

U.S. Department of Health and Human Services, Administration for Children and Families, Administration on Children, Youth and Families, Children's Bureau. (2021). *Child maltreatment 2019*. Retrieved from http://www.acf.hhs.gov/sites/default/files/documents/cb/cm2019U.S. Department of Justice. (2012). *Equal access to education: 40 years of Title IX*. https://www.justice.gov/crt/about/edu/documents/titleixreport.pdf.

U.S. Department of Justice. (2013a). *Sex offender registration and notification in the United States: Current case law and issues*. Washington, DC: U.S. Department of Justice.

U.S. Department of Justice. (2013b). *A National Protocol for Sexual Assault Medical Forensic Examinations: Adults/Adolescents, 2nd Edition*. (NCJ 228119). Washington, D.C.: U.S. Department of Justice.U.S. Department of Justice. (2020). *PREA data-collection activities, 2020*. Washington, D.C.: U.S. Department of Justice.

United States Sentencing Commission. (2014). *2013 annual report and 2013 sourcebook of federal sentencing statistics*. Washington, D.C.: U.S. Sentencing Commission.

United States Sentencing Commission. (2021a). *Quick facts: Child pornography offenders*. Washington, D.C.: U.S. Sentencing Commission.

United States Sentencing Commission. (2021b). *Quick facts: Sexual abuse offenders*. Washington, D.C.: U.S. Sentencing Commission.

van der Meer, T. (2014). Voluntary and therapeutic castration of sex offenders in the Netherlands (1938-1968). *International Journal of Law and Psychiatry, 37*, 50-62.

van der Voo, L. (2014). Ten percent of female University of Oregon students raped: Survey. Retrieved from www.msn.com/en-us/news/us

Vasquez, B.E., Maddan, S., and Walker, J.T. (2008). The influence of sex offender registration and notification laws in the United States: A time series analysis. *Crime and Delinquency 54*(2), 175-192.

Vercammen, P., and Lah, K. (2013, August 30). Prosecutors weigh appeal of 30-day rape sentence in Montana. *CNN*. Retrieved from www.cnn.com

Venema, R.M. (2018). Acceptance: Examining the role of officer characteristics, estimates of false reporting, and social desirability bias. *Violence and Victims, 33*(1), 176-200.

Viglione, J. (2019). The risk-need-responsivity model: How do probation officers implement the principles of effective intervention? *Criminal Justice and Behavior, 46*(5), 655-673.

Vold, G.B., Bernard, T.J., and Snipes, J.B. (2002). *Theoretical criminology*, 5th ed. New York, NY: Oxford University Press.

von Krafft-Ebing, R. (1965). *Psychopathia sexualis*. New York, NY: Scarborough.

Walker, J.T. (2007). Eliminate residency restrictions for sex offenders. *Criminology and Public Policy, 6*, 863-870.

Walker, J.T., and McLarty, G.E. (2000). *Sex offenders in Arkansas*. Little Rock: Arkansas Crime Information Center.

Walker, J.T., Golden, J.W., and VanHouten, A.C. (2001). The geographic link between sex offenders and potential victims: A routine activities approach. *Justice Research and Policy, 3*, 15-33.

Walker, S. (2001). *Sense and nonsense about crime and drugs: A policy guide*. Belmont, CA: Wadsworth-Thompson Learning.

Walsh, K., Zinzow, H., Badour, C., Ruggiero, K., Kilpatrick, D., and Resnick, H. (2015). Understanding disparities in service seeking following forcible versus drug- or alcohol-facilitated/incapacitated rape. *Journal of Interpersonal Violence*, 0886260515576968.

Ward, T., and Keenan, T. (1999). Child molesters' implicit theories. *Journal of Interpersonal Violence, 14*(8), 821-838.

Ward, T., and Siegert, R. (2002). Rape and evolutionary psychology: A critique of Thornhill and Palmer's theory. *Aggression and Violence Behavior, 7*, 145-168.

Ward, T., and Stewart, C. (2003). The treatment of sex offenders: Risk management and good lives. *Professional Psychology: Research and Practice, 34*(4), 353-360.

Ware, J., Frost, A., and Hoy, A. (2010). A review of the use of therapeutic communities with sexual offenders. *International Journal of Offender Therapy and Comparative Criminology, 54*(5), 721-742.

Warren, J.I., and Hazelwood, R.R. (2002). Relational patterns associated with sexual sadism: A study of 20 wives and girlfriends. *Journal of Family Violence, 17*, 75-89.

Warshaw, R., and Parrot, A. (1991). The contribution of sex-role socialization to acquaintance rape. In A. Parrot and L. Bechhofer (Eds.), *Acquaintance Rape: The Hidden Crime*. New York: John Wiley & Sons, Inc.

Wasco, S. (2003). Conceptualizing the harm done by rape: Applications of trauma theory to experiences of sexual assault. *Trauma, Violence, & Abuse, 4*, 309-322.

Washington State Department of Social and Health Services (n.d.). The Special Commitment Center Program. Retrieved from http://dshs.wa.gov/SCC/default.shtml

Washington State Institute for Public Policy. (2005). *Sex offender sentencing in Washington State: Has community notification reduced recidivism?* Olympia, WA: Washington State Institute for Public Policy.

Weinberg, T.S. (2006). Sadomasochism and the social sciences. *Journal of Homosexuality, 50*, 17-40

Weinrott, M.R. (1996). *Juvenile sexual aggression*. Boulder, CO: University of Colorado.

Weiss, C., and Friar, D. (1974). *Terror in the prisons*. New York, NY: Bobbs-Merrill Company, Inc.

Wentland, J., and Reissing, E. (2011). Taking casual sex not to casually: Exploring definitions of casual sexual relationships. *The Canadian Journal of Human Sexuality 20*(3), 75-91.

Westmarland, N., and Alderson, S. (2013). The health, mental health, and well-being benefits of rape crisis counseling. *Journal of Interpersonal Violence, 28*(17), 3,265-3,282.

Wetterling, P. (1998). The Jacob Wetterling story. In *National Conference on Sex Offender Registries*. Washington D.C.: Department of Justice.

Wexler, L., Robbennolt, J.K., and Murphy, C. (2019). #MeToo, time's up, and theories of justice. *University of Illinois Law Review, 2019*(1), 45-110.

White House Task Force to Protect Students from Sexual Assault. (2014). *Not alone: First report*. Washington, D.C.: The White House.

Wiederman, M.W. (2003). Paraphilia and fetishism. *The Family Journal, 11*, 315-321

Wilkins, L.T. (1965). *Social deviance: Social policy, action, and research*. Englewood Cliffs, NJ: Prentice-Hall, Inc.

Williams, J. (2017, October 30). Harvey Weinstein accusers: Over 80 women now claim producer sexually assaulted or harassed them. *Newsweek*. https://www.newsweek.com/harvey-weinstein-accusers-sexual-assault-harassment-696485

Wilson, C.R. (1999). Megan's Law: Public notification of sex offender information. *Law and Order, 47*(4), 59-62.

Wilson, F.T. (2004). Out of sight, out of mind: An analysis of *Kansas v. Crane* and the fine line between civil and criminal sanctions. *The Prison Journal, 84*, 379-394.

Wilson, K., Flynn, M., Bordieri, M., Nassar, S., Lucas, N., and Whiteman, K. (2012a). Acceptance and cognitive behavior therapy. In W. O'Donohue and J. Fisher (Eds.), *Cognitive Behavior Therapy: Core Principles for Practice* (pp. 377-398). Hoboken, NJ: John Wiley & Sons.

Wilson, R.J., Looman, J., Abracen, J., and Pake, D.R. (2012b). Comparing sexual offenders at the Regional Treatment Centre (Ontario) and the Florida Civil Commitment Center. *International Journal of Offender Therapy and Comparative Criminology, 57,* 377-395.

Wingood, G., and DiClemente, R. (1998). Rape among African American women: Sexual, psychological, and social correlates predisposing survivors to risk of STD/HIV. *Journal of Women's Health, 7*(1), 77-84.

Wolak, J., Finkelhor, D., and Mitchell, K. (2005). *Child pornography possessors arrested in internet-related crimes: Findings from the National Juvenile Online Victimization Study.* Alexandria, VA: National Center for Missing and Exploited Children.

Wolak, J., Finkelhor, D., and Mitchell, K. (2009). *Trends in Arrests of Online Predators.* Durham, NH: Crimes against Children Research Center.

Wolak, J., Finkelhor, D., Mitchell, K., and Jones, L. (2011) Arrests for child pornography production: Data at two time points from a national sample of U.S. law enforcement agencies. *Child Maltreatment, 16*(3), 184-195.

Wolfgang, M. (1958). *Patterns in criminal homicide.* Philadelphia: University of Pennsylvania Press.

Wooden, J. M. (2000). *Sexual assault in our society: women (and men) take back the night.* (7101). [Master's thesis, University of Iowa]. Retrospective Theses and Dissertations.

Woody, J., and Beldin, K. (2012). The mental health focus in rape crisis services: Tensions and recommendations. *Violence and Victims, 27*(1), 95-108.

Worley, R.M., and Worley, V.B. (2013). The sex offender next door: Deconstructing the United States' obsession with sex offender registries in an age of neoliberalism. *International Review of Law, Computers, and Technology, 27,* 335-344.

Yalom, I.D. (1960). Aggression and forbiddenness in voyeurism. *Archives in General Psychiatry, 3,* 305-319.

Yamawaki, N. (2007). Rape perceptions and the function of ambivalent sexism and gender-role traditionality. *Journal of Interpersonal Violence, 22*(4), 406-423.

Yung, C. (2014). How to lie with rape statistics: America's hidden rape crisis. *Iowa Law Review, 99,* 1,197-1,256.

Zalta, A., and Foa, E. (2012). Exposure therapy: Promoting emotional processing of pathological anxiety. In W. O'Donohue and J. Fisher (Eds.), *Cognitive Behavior Therapy: Core Principles for Practice* (pp. 75-104). Hoboken, NJ: John Wiley & Sons.

Zamble, E., and Quinsey, V.L. (1997). *The criminal recidivism process.* New York: Cambridge University Press.

Zandbergen, P.A., and Hart, T.C. (2006). Reducing housing options for convicted sex offenders: Investigating the impact of residency restriction laws using GIS. *Justice Research and Policy, 8,* 1-24.

Zeccardi, J., and Dickerman, D. (1993). Medical exam in the live sexual assault victim. In R. Hazelwood and A. Burgess (Eds.), *Practical Aspects of Rape Investigation: A Multidisciplinary Approach* (pp. 315-325). Boca Raton, FL: CRC Press, Inc.

Zevitz, R.G. (2006). Sex offender community notification: Its role in recidivism and offender reintegration. *Criminal Justice Studies, 19,* 193-208.

Zevitz, R.G., and Farkas, M.A. (2000). Sex offender community notification: Assessing the impact in Wisconsin. *National Institute of Justice Research in Brief,* December:1-11.

Zgoba, K.M., Jennings, W.G., and Salerno, L.M. (2018). Megan's Law 20 years later: An empirical analysis and policy review. *Criminal Justice and Behavior, 45,* 1028-1046.

Zgoba, K.M., Levenson, J.S., and McKee, T. (2009). Examining the impact of sex offender residence restrictions on housing availability. *Criminal Justice Policy Review, 20,* 91-110.

Zgoba, K.M., and Mitchell, M.M. (2021). The effectiveness of sex offender registration and notification: A meta-analysis of 25 years of findings. *Journal of Experimental Criminology, 18,* https://doi.org/10.1007/s11292-021-09480-z.

Zgoba, K., Witt, P., Dalessandro, M., and Veysey, B. (2008). *Megan's Law: Assessing the practical and monetary efficacy.* Washington, D.C.: U.S. Department of Justice.

Zimring, F.E., Jennings, W.G., Piquero, A.R., and Hays, S. (2009). Investigating the continuity of sex offending: Evidence from the second Philadelphia Birth Cohort. *Justice Quarterly, 26,* 58-76.

Zimring, F.E., Piquero, A.R., and Jennings, W.G. (2007). Sexual delinquency in Racine: Does early sex offending predict later sex offending in youth and young adulthood? *Criminology and Public Policy, 6,* 507-534.

Zinzow, H., Amstadter, A., McCauley, J., Ruggiero, K., Resnick, H., Kilpatrick, D. (2011). Self-rated health in relation to rape and mental health disorders in a national sample of college women. *Journal of American College Health, 59*(7), 588-594.

Zolondek, S.C., Abel, G.G., Northey, Jr., W.F., and Jordan, A.D. (2002). The self-reported behaviors of juvenile sex offenders. In R.M. Holmes and S.T. Holmes (Eds.), *Current Perspectives on Sex Crimes* (pp. 153-161). Thousand Oaks, CA: Sage Publications.

Zonana, H. (1997). The civil commitment of sex offenders. *Science, 278,* 1,248-1,249.

Zott, L.M. (2008). *Sex offenders and public policy.* Farmington Hills, MI: Greenhaven Press.

Zucker, K.J., Bradley, S.J., Owen-Anderson, A., Kibblewhite, S.J., Wood, H., Singh, D., and Choi, K. (2012). Demographics, behavior problems, and psychosexual characteristics of adolescents with gender identity disorder or transvestic fetishism. *Journal of Sex and Marital Therapy, 38,* 151-189.

Zuckerman, L. (2014, May 1). Stacey Rambold: Why Montana teacher will be re-sentenced. *The Christian Science Monitor.* Retrieved from www.csmonitor.com

Cases and Other Legal Sources

Atkins v. Virginia, 536 U.S. 304, (2002).
Buck v. Bell, 240 U.S. 200, (1927).
Coker v. Georgia, 433 U.S. 584, (1977).
Commonwealth v. Baker, 295 S.W.3d 437 (2009).
Connecticut Department of Public Safety v. Doe, 538 U.S. 1 (2003).
Doe v. Miller, 405 F.3d 900, (2005).
Furman v. Georgia, 408 U.S. 232, (1972).
G.H. v. Township of Galloway, 951 A.2d 221 (2008).
Gregg v. Georgia, 428 U.S. 153, (1976).
Kansas v. Crane, 534 U.S. 407, (2002)
Kansas v. Hendricks, 521 U.S. 346, (1997).
Kennedy v. Louisiana, 554 U.S. 407, (2008).
People v. Blair, 873 N.Y.S.2d 890 (2009).
People v. Oberlander, 880 N.Y.S.2d 875 (2009).
Roper v. Simmons, 543 U.S. 551, (2005).
Rudolph v. Alabama, 375 U.S. 889, (1963).
Skinner v. Oklahoma, 316 U.S. 535, (1942).
State of Alabama. *Alabama Criminal Code*. §13A-1, (1975).
State of Arkansas. *Arkansas Criminal Code*. §5-1-101, (2010).
State of Florida. *Florida Criminal Code*. §46-775, (2014).
State of Idaho. *Idaho Code Annotated*. §18-41-4116, (2006).
State of Louisiana. *Louisiana Code Annotated*. §283.1, (2004).
State of Nebraska. *Nebraska Criminal Code*. §28-101, (2014).
State of Nevada. *Nevada Code Annotated*. §201.450, (2005).
State of Ohio. *Ohio Criminal Code*. §2901.1, (2014).
State of South Dakota. *South Dakota Criminal Code*. §22-22-42, (2012).
State of Vermont. *Vermont Criminal Code*. §13-1, (2014).
State of Wisconsin. *Wisconsin Criminal Code*. §939, (2014).
State of Washington. *Washington Criminal Code*. §9A.RCW, (2014).
State v. Stark, 802 N.W.2d 165, (2011).
United States. *United States Code Annotated*. §18, (2014).

INDEX